Praise for THE SECRET LIFE OF

Marilyn Monroe

"As Taraborrelli brushes away cobwebs of myth and rumor, his remarkable research and fluid writing capture Marilyn's élan, sensitivity, desperation, and despair with a haunting intimacy."
—*Publishers Weekly* (starred review and Pick of the Week)

"A revelatory and insightful book . . . Taraborrelli conducted interviews over decades and utilized FBI files. He digs especially deep into Monroe's (fractured) family ties . . . Read it and weep."
—*BookPage*

"An unflinching look at the private life of one of America's most fascinating and elusive icons of the twentieth century. It is balanced, sympathetic, surprisingly moving—and yes, even haunting . . . we get as close to the real Marilyn Monroe as we are likely to get."
—King Features Weekly Service

"J. Randy Taraborrelli's new bio of Marilyn Monroe is already on the bestseller lists. No surprise. Every book this guy has written since *Call Her Miss Ross* in 1989 has achieved bestseller-dom. He has put an undeniable stamp on the celeb-bio biz."   —Liz Smith

"The truth is that Taraborrelli has researched his socks off . . . the reader is hooked."   —*Toronto Globe and Mail*

"You'd think there was nothing left to discover about Marilyn Monroe, but Mr. Taraborrelli has found it . . . he's dug around in newly released FBI files [and] interviewed previously untapped sources."
—*Wall Street Journal*

"Sheds light on the starlet's family life and delves into her struggle with mental illness." —*Atlanta Journal-Constitution*

"Taraborrelli promises never-before-told facts about Marilyn Monroe's family dynamic, the identity of her father, and her relationship with the Kennedys. And he delivers . . . He had access to newly released documents that were not scrutinized for other biographies, and he researched family and medical files and personal correspondence and interviewed countless family members, friends, costars, Secret Service agents, and others. He also provides previously unseen photographs. Highly recommended."

—*Library Journal* (starred review)

"Reveals new details of the actress's life . . . and reminds us why, forty-seven years after her death, we're still captivated." —*Elle*

"An intimate portrait . . . It may be difficult to imagine that there are any secrets about Marilyn Monroe left to discover, but Taraborrelli's dogged research style helps him sort fact from fiction in the many conflicting accounts of Monroe's life . . . Readers will find this a surprisingly sensitive portrait, not easy to put down."

—Booklist

"Excellent . . . a bang-up book, a book about what it is to be a human being . . . Add THE SECRET LIFE OF MARILYN MONROE to your list of must-be-read books. It will touch your heart." —BasilandSpice.com

"The book made me, for the first time, understand just a little bit what life must have been like for a beautiful face behind a beautiful mask and a brain on quicksand—Taraborrelli comes amazingly close to comprehending the utter unease beauty bestows along with its glory." —*Lincoln County News*

THE SECRET LIFE OF

Marilyn Monroe

J. RANDY TARABORRELLI

GRAND CENTRAL
PUBLISHING

New York   Boston

For My Family

———————————

Grand Central Publishing
Hachette Book Group
237 Park Avenue
New York, NY 10017

www.HachetteBookGroup.com

Printed in the United States of America

Originally published in hardcover by Grand Central Publishing.

First Trade Edition: September 2010
10 9 8 7 6 5

Grand Central Publishing is a division of Hachette Book Group, Inc.
The Grand Central Publishing name and logo is a trademark of Hachette Book Group, Inc.

The Hachette Speakers Bureau provides a wide range of authors for speaking events. To find out more, go to www.hachettespeakersbureau.com or call (866) 376-6591.

The publisher is not responsible for websites (or their content) that are not owned by the publisher.

The Library of Congress has cataloged the hardcover edition as follows:

Taraborrelli, J. Randy
　　The secret life of Marilyn Monroe / J. Randy Taraborrelli.—1st ed.
　　　　p. cm.
　　Includes index.
　　ISBN 978-0-446-58082-3 (regular edition)—ISBN 978-0-446-50541-3 (large print edition)
1. Monroe, Marilyn, 1926-1962. 2. Motion picture actors and actresses—United States—Biography. I. Title.
　　PN2287.M69T37 2009
　　791.4302'8092—dc22   2008044704

ISBN 978-0-446-19818-9 (pbk.)

Book design by Giorgetta Bell McRee

CONTENTS

PART EIGHT / The Kennedys   391

PART NINE / Sad Endings   441

PREFACE

*M*arilyn Monroe.

The mere name alone represents different images for different people. For some, it suggests the absolute standard of female sensuality. Beauty. Grace. Sophistication. For others, insecurity comes to mind. Misery. Tragedy. However, in order to appreciate the complex and fascinating life of this enigmatic star, one must attempt to put aside any preconceived notions about her—certainly no easy feat, considering her iconic status.

Perhaps the first step toward truly understanding Marilyn is to accept that all of the vivid images conjured by her name are true—from the good to the bad, the glorious to the tragic. Indeed, she was a woman who enjoyed and suffered a wide spectrum of experiences, many that are well known and quite a few—as you will read on these pages—that have remained private and undisclosed until now. Still, her devoted fans have always felt that they've known her well. Some who admire her without reservation can be moved to tears by the memory of a certain, maybe haunting, performance she gave on film. They fall into a group of devotees who would sacrifice almost anything to have their idol back among the living—only this time healthy and happy. To them, she is someone to be adored and placed high on a pedestal—preferably in a pose befitting her cinematic royalty. Others who are more circumspect view her as a spoiled Hollywood celebrity. They see her life as a cautionary tale of the dangers of excessive superstardom. To them, she is someone to be pitied as much as loved. Again, though all judgments and musings about her have an element of truth, there is a group I'd like to invite you to join with the reading of this biography—the select group of people who simply want one thing: the truth.

To say that much has been written about Marilyn Monroe is an understatement if ever there was one. Yet during the time I spent researching this book, I was surprised by just how muddled and conflicting the previous accounts of her life have been over the years. I also learned that there are some intriguing reasons why many of the stories about Marilyn have felt at arm's length from her, as if her time on this earth had been viewed through a diffusion filter. For one thing, many fantastic legends about her have been accepted as fact. Therefore, separating truth from fiction is not an easy task—especially since a good deal of the fanciful tales about her were created by the lady herself! Then there's the residue of old Hollywood's public relations tactics. Some of those who were personally involved in Marilyn's life were products of a vastly different era. Once upon a time, there was a hands-off policy when it came to the images of celebrities, and there is to this day, among surviving members of that community, a feeling of reverence—a respect for the way the studios wanted us to view movie stars . . . from a distance.

However, Marilyn's presence, both onscreen and off, promised something quite different. She often appeared open and available, as if the answer to anything you wanted to know about her was just a question away. That, though, was an illusion. You see, Marilyn Monroe had a love-hate relationship with the truth, and at times with reality itself. It's no great mystery why she so desperately tried to avoid the truth. Often it was agonizing, unbearable, and, she hoped, escapable. Why? Because, Marilyn—the picture of glamour and confidence to the outside world—was a woman far more troubled than most people knew. Though she would try to hide it from the world with her seamless portrayal of style and wit, those closest to her were privy to her deepest, darkest secret: She feared for her own sanity. Because her grandmother and mother were committed to insane asylums, Marilyn lived with the constant threat of impending madness. The often heartwrenching war she fought with her own mind has never, until now, been properly examined and presented. Thankfully for this biography, many of Marilyn's contemporaries were convinced to come forward and discuss the specifics of her secret battle. These interviewees, many in the twilight of their lives, were vital to the completion of this book. In part, I believe their cooperation came with the realization that certain details of Marilyn's life had not yet been accurately revealed, and that the truth of her struggles would die with them.

Much of what can be taken from Marilyn Monroe's story is inspirational. After all, she is a woman who overcame seemingly insurmountable odds to become not only adored and respected but also, arguably, the biggest movie star in all the world. While a large part of her life was spent building and maintaining her career, in private Marilyn was passionate in her quest for *family*. She sought the permanency that the notion of a family promised. Sadly, it rarely delivered. Undaunted, she maintained close relationships with a mother who was constantly being institutionalized and a half sister the world didn't know existed. On these pages, you will read about those fascinating relationships for the first time, and numerous others that have been previously misunderstood. Marilyn also went to great lengths to identify and then meet her father. Indeed, her quest for genuine and meaningful bonding would continue throughout her life.

Perhaps the real story of this woman revolves around something she—at her best—possessed in great abundance: hope. She believed throughout her entire time on this earth that anything was possible, and she often proved just that. Those who find it difficult to read the unsettling details of her life outlined in this book should remember that, even toward the very end, Marilyn had moments when she believed ultimate happiness to be just within her grasp.

In fact, if there is one thing that set her apart from most people, it was her ability to maintain an urgency to the present moment. She believed that her "now" was more important than her past and future. Sadly, while she attempted to remain in the present, her past haunted her almost as much as her future frightened her.

Marilyn Monroe was so much more than just a famous movie star. She was a vulnerable soul, a generous spirit, and a brave soldier in a devastating battle with her own mind. Attempting to explain her difficult journey is the challenge I set for myself with this book. At the heart of the story, I discovered a very different kind of Marilyn, a woman far more complex and serious—and maybe even tragic—than the one I thought I knew.

PROLOGUE

The cavernous arena is electric, its walls vibrating with applause one moment, laughter the next. Yet at the end of one of its long hallways and sitting behind a closed door is a woman having an experience all her own. Just minutes earlier, she had breezed through a crowd of onlookers and backstage technicians with a confident smile and a glamorous way. At this moment, however, while waiting for a drink she'd requested of a stagehand, she seems to shiver with apprehension. "They're making fun of me," she tells the young man as he offers her a glass of New York City tap water. "Listen." But he can't follow her direction, for he is too taken aback by how her eyes are locked on his . . . how *she* is talking to *him* . . . and how she is . . . *Marilyn Monroe*. Indeed, even though he shook hands with the president of the United States less than an hour ago, *this* is the moment he will always treasure.

Moments earlier, the woman was an emotional wreck, confused and panicked when she popped her head out of her dressing room to ask him for the favor of a drink. But now she is looking to him for something altogether different. Perspective. Reassurance. Maybe even wisdom. After it's clear that he is nearly immobilized by her presence, she drops her look of concern and smiles knowingly. After all, he's just another one, and she knows it—another one of the millions of men who love her. One thing he *doesn't* know, however, is something that might surprise him: She loves him back.

By May 19, 1962, Marilyn Monroe had whittled down her circle of close friends to a precious few—or perhaps the circumstances of her life had done it for her. Along the way, there had been many who tried to talk her through her bouts of anxiety or paranoia. However, their efforts were almost always in vain. Marilyn was convinced that she knew better. In a heartbreaking catch-22, those dearest to her would throw up their hands and surrender to her need to be right—even if what she was correct about was her own misery. Without anyone left in her world able to lift her from her darkest periods, she would spend the majority of her time alone . . . thinking—which was, of course, exactly what kept her in such despair. Therefore, it would often be in small moments like this one—time spent with a starstruck stranger rendered speechless in her presence—that she would be reminded of who she was, and of what was expected of her.

She pushes away from the wall she's been leaning against and approaches the young man. Once standing before him, she bends forward, holds his ears between her palms, and kisses the top of his head. "Thank you," she says in a soft voice. "Now I need to get ready."

As he slips out of the room, he notices her moving to a large mirror, sighing loudly. She begins laughing as he pulls the knob—and then, when the door clicks shut: silence, again. This strange behavior leaves him thinking what everyone else backstage that night has been: What is going on in there? Not just in that dressing room, but inside that beautiful head of hers.

"Marilyn had practiced so hard for that performance," explained her friend Susan Strasberg, "far too much if you ask me. It was too important to her. All she had to do was sing 'Happy Birthday.' Most performers could have done that with their eyes closed."

Marilyn, of course, was not "most performers." In fact, she wasn't even most "people." Rather, she was a woman waging a specific battle fought by many in the world on a daily basis: mental illness. Her mood swings and unpredictable behavior were usually viewed by her public as mere eccentricities incidental to who Marilyn Monroe was as a woman. Yet the difficult emotional tug-of-war she endured for much of her life, ignored by almost everyone, may have been her most defining characteristic.

On this night, however, why would Marilyn, globally recognized as a major celebrity, think that she was being made fun of? While she had often wrongly believed in the past that the worst was being thought and said about her, on this evening she happened to be right. They *were* making fun of her.

By this time in her history, gallons of newspaper ink had been used to describe to the world just who Marilyn Monroe was—that was nothing new. However, in the weeks leading up to this performance at Madison Square Garden in New York City, much of that ink was used to explain that she was, above all, irresponsible. She had been chronically late or completely absent for the making of her most recent film—a production from which she would ultimately be fired. The world knew about it and didn't care. After all, she was Marilyn Monroe. In the public's collective reasoning, she had carte blanche. Those who had been fans for at least the last decade viewed her mounting unpredictability as a necessary evil—just one of the things that made Marilyn . . . Marilyn. However, the truth was that her increasingly troubling behavior was much more than just a star's idiosyncrasy, to be joked about over cocktails. It was a sign that something was terribly wrong with her.

Onstage that night, many renowned performers were assembled to celebrate the birthday of President John F. Kennedy. Frank Sinatra was present, as were Diahann Carroll, Jack Benny, Henry Fonda, Leontyne Price, and many other luminaries. Each of them took to the stage to perform after being introduced in a dignified manner. Marilyn, however, received a very different introduction.

"Mr. President, Marilyn Monroe," the distinguished British actor Peter Lawford intoned numerous times throughout the evening. However, the "gag" of these many introductions was that when her arrival was announced, the spotlight would swing to the side of the stage and then—nothing. She wouldn't appear. Everyone would laugh, of course. After all, it had become a not-so-inside joke that Marilyn Monroe was a woman upon whom nobody could depend. Funny? Not particularly, especially if one took the time to examine just *why* she had become so unreliable.

She had been in on the joke that night, of course, and had even seemed tickled that her eventual appearance would be teased throughout the four-hour-long event. Indeed, as had often been the case in Marilyn's life, she knew that the public's expectations of her revolved around what they thought she lacked, not what she possessed. "Most people didn't think of talent when they thought of Marilyn," Dean Martin once observed. "They saw this creature who happened to be blessed with the beauty of a goddess and the brain of a peacock." However, Marilyn was no dumb blonde; she was much more intelligent than most people realized. For years she had used her intellectual abilities to conceal her most private struggles.

Once again, every ounce of willpower would be brought to bear this evening in order that the mere mortal could transform herself into the goddess the world had come to know and love. When Marilyn finally took the stage, the theater erupted into thunderous applause. She was charismatic, empowered, and, of course, spectacularly beautiful. Peter Lawford watched her wriggle toward him, her steps restricted to tiny strides due to her sheer gown's tightly tailored hem. After delivering a final punch line to the running joke of the evening—"Mr. President, the *late* . . . Marilyn Monroe"—he reached toward the star's ample bosom and took from her an ermine fur. There she stood, looking almost naked, wrapped only in her ethereal beauty, shimmering in sequins, beads, and sparkling light.

Alone now, she waited for the crowd's reaction to wane before she could start to sing. It didn't for quite some time. The applause became less apparent, though, as a low-pitched throng of gasps and cheers came forth, mostly from the men in attendance. In fact, there was a full thirty seconds between the moment her outfit was revealed and the time she was able to begin singing. During that time, the audience's reaction changed from hoots and hollers to audible mumbles and, finally, to smatterings of laughter. She held her hands at her brow in order to shield her eyes from the spotlight, maybe hoping to see more clearly the man of honor—a man she had hoped might one day be more to her than just her commander in chief. Then, after a particularly loud guffaw from a man in one of the first few rows, Marilyn's shoulders dropped and she sighed audibly. Eventually, deciding not to wait for silence, she started to sing while the masses continued expressing their reaction.

"Happy birthday . . . to you," she cooed, her voice a sexy—and maybe just a tad off-key—whisper. "Happy birthday to you. Happy birthday . . . Mr. *Pre-si-dent*. Happy birthday to you." The room continued its rowdy response as she did her best to give her public what it wanted—an unmistakable and very specific memory of Marilyn Monroe. Finishing the first chorus, she motioned for the audience to join in—"Everybody! Happy birthday . . ." The crowd responded to her invitation by taking up the song and trying to follow her somewhat erratic, arm-waving conducting.

After she finished her performance, a man approached Marilyn from behind. While the cameras cut to a birthday cake being wheeled in, she was escorted from the stage and away from a moment in which she had wanted to participate: President John F. Kennedy climbing the stairs to the stage to say a few words of appreciation. Marilyn had wanted to simply give him a quick peck and then shuffle back offstage. Yet there were many who felt that she was too unpredictable that night, too erratic. "Yes, there was some anxiety surrounding her appearance," recalled Diahann Carroll. "I can't say that I knew why, or what was going on. But I do remember a certain level of . . . tension. Some people were quite . . . edgy."

Once backstage, Marilyn heard the president express his gratitude for her performance. "Now I can retire from politics," he said, "after having 'Happy Birthday' sung to me in such a sweet and wholesome way." A couple of months prior, she had told JFK how her ex-husband, Joe DiMaggio, wanted her to retire from show business to be his wife. Now, hearing his words, a look of astonishment crossed her face. Later, she would ask his sister, Pat Kennedy Lawford, if he had made the statement for her benefit. The reasonable response to her question was most certainly no. However, at that point, Marilyn's supply of reason had been dwindling for quite some time. She had begun living her life in clearly defined segments of clarity and confusion. For years Marilyn Monroe had been able to use her craft to perpetuate an illusion. Indeed, the star that people saw toward the end of her life was but a shell game—a well-crafted presentation of someone who had disappeared years ago . . . that is, if she ever really existed.

PART ONE

The Beginning

Norma Jeane's Foster Mother, Ida

$\mathcal{H}$ow to describe Ida Bolender? With dark brown eyes behind large, round spectacles on an elongated and severe face, she looked like the classic schoolmarm. She could have been attractive, had she been interested. However, she didn't have time to worry about superficialities. Her hairstyle spoke volumes. Cut bluntly just below her ears and unevenly around her head, her hair looked as if she'd taken scissors and chopped away without any forethought. The total effect was a haphazard, inky black coif around her head. Her clothing also said much about her. She wore the same type of dress every day—a short-sleeved frock that hung loosely on her frame like a gunnysack. She called this garment, functional and practical, her "house dress." Though still a young woman of just thirty-seven, she was such a model of efficiency and diligence she seemed much older—maybe in her fifties. She was always busy, whether with a full schedule of housework or with the day's errands of devotion to the Hawthorne Community Church in Hawthorne, California, of which she was a parishioner.[*]

To some, Ida seemed a somewhat cold and unfeeling woman who, despite being a foster mother, didn't really take to children. Sometimes she appeared distant and remote, which is why there was some question as to whether she sincerely had the desire to raise children or simply had an interest in the money she received to take care of them—roughly twenty-five dollars a week per child from either the child's family or the State of California.[†] It wasn't

---

[*] The Hawthorne Community Church was nondenominational but more Baptist than not in doctrine.

[†] It should be noted that this wasn't foster care in the strictest sense of the word. What Ida was offering would today be considered "full-time child care." However, she and her husband were licensed to care for children through the County of Los Angeles.

a fair characterization. In fact, Ida had opened her home to under-privileged children during the challenging 1920s. This was a time when scores of young people were being put up for adoption, due in part to a floundering economy, and also to the needs of a growing number of young women who felt a calling to enter the workforce. Though she certainly had no interest in business, Ida did want a better life, one her husband's meager salary as a mailman could not provide. The extra income she received from foster parenting may not have been plentiful, but it was enough for her to feel some worth and also a certain degree of independence. Moreover, as her foster daughter Nancy Jeffrey explains, "One of the reasons Ida may have appeared disconnected was because she was hearing impaired and without the benefit of a hearing aid. She often had to read lips, especially as she got older." A proud woman, Ida Bolender would just as soon people think she was hearing what they were telling her when she really wasn't. Thus her seeming aloofness.

The daughter of devout Baptists, Ida was taught that an abundance of pride was the devil's work. Therefore, she rarely acknowledged her own achievements, such as good grades in school or being popular with other students. Her parents were strict and uncompromising. Every day was a test from God. Pass or fail (and she usually failed, according to them anyway, especially her mother), it was sure to be a long and difficult exam. Her parents had instilled in her so urgent a sense of responsibility and duty, she'd allowed her youth on a small farm near Buffalo, New York, to pass her by without ever having much fun.

In 1918, after living a chaste early adulthood, Ida married a quiet, gentle man named Albert Wayne—known primarily by his middle name. He'd also been raised on a farm, this one in Brown County, Ohio. Since he had been brought up with essentially the same beliefs as Ida, he had simple, attainable goals for the future. In fact, the couple had no plans when they married, other than to work hard, pray hard, and try to live what they both viewed as decent lives based on scripture. They moved to California in 1919.

Besides foster caring, Ida had few passions in life—and, truthfully, being a foster mother wasn't as much a passion for her as it was a duty. However, as a fervent member of her church, she was quite enthusiastic about fund-raising. The church held bake sales and raffles, but its most lucrative venture by far was its widely praised rummage sale. Women would travel great distances to pick through the discarded belongings of the church's many parishioners while searching for just the right hat, dress, or other clothing at a price that could be considered a "steal." However, not only would the possessions of churchgoers go up for sale, but other items as well. According to the family's history, in order to enhance her own sales table, Ida formed a secret alliance with a woman named Anna Raymond, a seamstress in Hollywood who would bring boxes chock-full of items to the Bolender residence on a monthly basis. These pieces were mostly garments that Ida would never think to wear, such as colorful flapper dresses, ornate costume jewelry with enormous imitation stones, or high-heeled shoes that made Ida shudder. It's a safe assumption that these items were leftovers from various film productions, but just how Miss Raymond happened to come into possession of them is, all these years later, impossible to ascertain.

Over the years, Ida often spoke to other members of her congregation about certain women in her community she felt were "too boastful." Inevitably, these were ladies who flaunted their femininity to get what they wanted, conduct Ida viewed as tantamount to a mortal sin. As it would happen, a woman whose behavior fit just that description came into Ida's life in a place that might seem ironic: the Hawthorne Community Church. Indeed, whenever Ida Bolender stood watch at her rummage-sale table, she looked forward to selling as much of her tacky merchandise as possible to one eager customer in particular—her neighbor across the street, Della Monroe.

Norma Jeane's Grandmother, Della

By 1925 standards, forty-nine-year-old Della Monroe was certainly not a wealthy woman, but she still had a craving for extravagance. Without the ability to purchase particularly lavish items at retail prices, she hunted down bargains wherever she could—even in places where she didn't feel particularly welcome. Descending the steps into the basement of the Hawthorne Community Church, she had to have heard the judgmental whispers of those who wouldn't have used the word "elegant" to describe her secondhand fur and costume jewelry.

In her prime, Della had been a spectacularly attractive woman. Back then, a mane of full, thick brunette tresses had framed an almost constantly smiling face set with stunning blue-green eyes. She was eye-catching and full of life. However, time had not been kind. Her skin, once so porcelain and smooth, had loosened and lost its glow. Now she appeared unkempt, her hair thinning to wiry locks that seemed to lie lifeless atop her head. It hadn't simply been the expected signs of aging that altered Della, either. She had once been gregarious with a quick wit and exuberant personality. There had always been a dazzling smile under her bright red lipstick. However, over time, the light behind her eyes began to flicker. As she got older, she became remote. It was as if a great distance had come between the world and Della Monroe's experience of it. Everyone she knew noticed this gradual change in her, but no one knew what to do about it. Actually, it had started with the birth of her children.

"The way I heard it, she would fall into deep depressions after having the babies," recalled Louise Adams, whose mother was the secretary to Reverend Charles Lewis, pastor of the Hawthorne Community Church. "My mother said [Della] would cry uncontrollably at the drop of a dime [sic], and she had never been one to cry. Then she would be fine. But a few days later, she would start crying again, for no apparent reason, and she would cry for days, or at least it seemed like it. Then, fine. She wouldn't eat and got painfully thin. She couldn't sleep. No one knew what was wrong with her, but there wasn't much anyone could do back then but just worry about it and hope for the best."

It's possible, of course, that Della Monroe was suffering from postpartum depression. However, with modern obstetrics procedures just starting to be developed in the early 1900s, grave symptoms such as hers were often ignored or just attributed to "baby blues" and not taken seriously. In her case, though, whatever was happening to her as a result of her pregnancies would be a harbinger of things to come. Of course no one knows for sure, but the family's belief is that Della's pregnancies triggered a mental illness in her that was never reversed.

Time, however, could not steal from Della the memories of her untamed youth. She had often welcomed the wandering eyes of the opposite sex, which threatened her peers and made the possibility of having many close girlfriends remote. Therefore, when she sought companionship, it was usually in the company of men. Indeed, earlier in her life, Della would happily share a stiff drink with a fellow, often with no desire at all for any sort of romantic relationship. She was "one of the guys" during many happy hours at the local watering hole, which led to a good number of groggy late-night encounters of the intimate variety, and of course the inevitable tongue-wagging of women familiar with her behavior.

Now past her prime, Della was living with a man named Charles Grainger at her home on East Rhode Island Street in Hawthorne. She insisted they were man and wife, but no one ever saw a marriage certificate—nor did anyone believe they'd ever been wed. Though her desire for male attention had weakened, Della's instinct to package herself in what she considered stylish attire remained—thus her visit to church on this day in October 1925, where she would meet her neighbor across the street, thirty-seven-year-old Ida Bolender.

Obviously, Della's life had been very different from Ida's. Whereas Della had always been a free spirit who enjoyed what would most certainly have been considered in the early 1900s a loose morality, Ida's personality was constricted by a rigid religious code. Had Ida been aware of some of Della's past experiences, she wouldn't have allowed herself to even share the same oxygen with her. As it was, the two women formed an unusual bond. In fact, for her wardrobe, Della had come to depend upon the constant stream of garish garments and baubles found only at Ida's booth at the rummage sale. Over time, Ida would even leave a smattering of the gaudiest of merchandise on display—clothing and other items that no one else would ever think to purchase—knowing full well that even these most offensive pieces would be eagerly snapped up by Della.

As Della's style "dealer," Ida made a decent amount of money for the church—and possibly even a bit for herself. Eventually, she even opened up her home to Della in order that she might purchase items without waiting for the next sale. On one such occasion in October 1925, Della noted how well-behaved two foster children being raised by Ida were, and then mentioned that her own daughter, twenty-five-year-old Gladys Baker, was pregnant with her third child. The pregnancy posed quite a problem, she explained, since Gladys was not married. Gladys had been pursuing a career in Hollywood, Della said, working for Consolidated Studios as a film cutter. In fact, as she went on, Della had actually given her some of the clothing she had purchased from Ida. She wanted to brighten her daughter's days, she said, because she'd never been the same since giving up the first two children she bore. Both were now being raised by her ex-husband and his new wife. After losing them, Della admitted, Gladys became a heavy drinker.

As it happened, Della was getting ready to join her husband, Charles, in India, where he'd been transferred by the oil company for which he worked. She was going to leave in December. He didn't seem anxious to see her, though. In a postcard to her, he wrote that he felt the trip would be "too much" for her and that perhaps she should "stay where you are for an indefinite period of time." Della's mind was made up, though. However, she told Ida that she was worried about what might happen to Gladys and the new baby. "I'm not going to be around to see to it that things are okay," she explained. Ida said, "Well, maybe you should stay behind until you know they are okay." Della thought it over a moment and decided, "No, I don't think so."

During that conversation, Ida became very concerned not so much about what might happen to Gladys, but over the future of the child she was carrying. It was clear to Ida that not only were Gladys's work schedule and social life going to be an issue in raising the new baby, but there was also another undeniable truth, one to do with morality. There was a question about the paternity of Gladys's pregnancy. Della said that she didn't quite know who the father of her daughter's baby was—and any number of men could have been candidates. This unfortunate situation was more than just distasteful to Ida, it was unseemly. In her view, neither Gladys—given what she had heard—nor Della—given what she had seen—was, as she put it, "following the Lord's path."

Ida quizzed Della about just how Gladys planned to raise the child, especially if Della was to be out of the country. Would it be in accordance with God's plan? Had they considered what school the young one would attend? Was she going to be able to set a good example for him or her? As Ida saw it, it was an untenable situation, so much that she could barely believe they were even discussing it. In her mind, all questions were moot since Gladys wasn't even married, "and in this situation, she most certainly should not be allowed to keep that child," she said.

"And what about you, Della?" Ida asked with a faint smile. "You know, you're not the most stable woman, either."

Della—according to a later recollection—seemed to not be able to connect to what Ida was talking about. On some level, though, she must have known that Ida was referring to her unpredictable mood swings, and especially her insistence of late that she was the subject of some sort of surveillance. "When I leave the house, I *know* I'm being followed," she had often told Ida. "As long as they know that I know, I feel I'm fine. However, I never let my guard down. I'm not a stupid woman." Paranoia had become such a recurring theme in Della's life that her friends had begun to disregard it, even if they did find it upsetting.

"If Gladys can't raise that child," Ida told her candidly, "I certainly don't think you can, either."

"It doesn't make any difference," Della told her, "because I'm going to India, and I'm not coming back."

None of this made sense to Ida. She was twelve years younger than Della, but it was Della who must have seemed like the immature one to her. At the very least, she couldn't imagine how this woman could leave the country when her child was in trouble. Moreover, she couldn't fathom how any mother could ever have allowed her daughter to find herself in such a predicament. "You need to think about this," Ida told Della. "You and I should discuss this further. We're both mothers. We know what's right."

In the days to come, Ida's continuing attempts to alert Della to the seriousness of the task at hand would lead to an unexpected set of circumstances that would alter the lives of everyone involved. No doubt directly related to Ida's finger-wagging, the day soon came when Della was able to convince Gladys that she should not be the primary caretaker of the baby she was carrying. First of all, it couldn't be denied that she was a woman to whom the night called—and when it did, she answered with a resounding yes. Also, she too had certain other . . . problems. Indeed, someone was following Gladys as well. Maybe the same person who had been following Della? Mother and daughter understood each other's fears because they shared them.

Eventually, Della Monroe successfully convinced her daughter, Gladys Baker, that when she had her baby, she should "temporarily" place it in the care of the very religious and righteous woman who lived nearby—Ida Bolender.

Marilyn's Mother, Gladys

From all outward appearances, Gladys Pearl Monroe had always seemed like such a happy youngster, surprising considering her tumultuous youth. She was born on May 27, 1900, to Otis and Della Monroe in Piedras Negras, Mexico—at the time called Porfirio Diaz, after Mexico's president José de la Cruz Porfirio Díaz Mori. It was here that her father had found employment with the Pacific Electric Railway. Soon after her birth, the family moved to Los Angeles.

Gladys's mother, Della, always caused heads to turn as she sashayed down the street. However, she was apparently as tough as she was eye-catching. Early photographs taken of Gladys's parents show a handsome, somewhat robust woman with a severe countenance—that would be Della—standing next to a gentleman who looks rather scared to death—Otis. If he ever thought he would be able to tell Della what to do, Otis soon found out it was not the case. Della was never one to acquiesce to anyone's will. Therefore, the arguments between them started on their honeymoon and never ceased. In one of the family's photographs Otis has a deep scar on his cheek, and there's no telling how he got it. However, one thing is clear: He doesn't have it in pictures taken before he married Della.

Soon, Gladys and her brother, Marion Otis—born in 1905—became accustomed to a transient lifestyle as the Monroes moved in and out of nearly a dozen different rented apartments and houses in California between 1903 and 1909. Otis, who couldn't keep a job, began to live a reckless and cavalier life. Not only was his drinking a growing problem, but he also started having sudden blackouts and frightening memory lapses.

By 1908, when Otis was just forty-one, his health and emotional state had declined so rapidly it became clear that something was very wrong with him. He was temperamental and unpredictable, and his body seemed to always be in a tremulous state. His headaches would become so numbing and severe, he could barely stand. When not physically debilitated, he was filled with blind rage. On occasions when he would fly into fits of fury, Della would have no choice but to take their frightened children to a neighbor's home and wait for the storm to pass. Doctors were at a complete loss to explain Otis's mystifying behavior. "Otis has lost his mind, and I'm just going to have to come to terms with it," Della wrote in a letter at this time.

In 1909, Otis Monroe died of syphilis of the brain. He was just forty-three. "How will I explain this to my children?" Della asked the doctors at the hospital. Because the professionals were of no help to her, Della simply told Gladys, nine, and Marion, four, that their father had gone mad and died. In years to come, some family members would argue that he actually hadn't died an insane man but rather had contracted syphilis, which then led to his death. Others would say that it was precisely because of the syphilis that he had gone insane. Back in the early 1900s, though, such distinctions were generally not made outside of the medical community. "He went nuts and then went to God," is how Della described it, and she hoped that would be the end of it. However, this would most certainly not be the end of it. In fact, a fear of genetic madness would hold the Monroe descendants in its suffocating grip for decades to come—and it all started with Della's declaration that Otis Monroe's death was the direct result of insanity.

After Otis passed away, Della—just thirty-three years old—was on her own with two small children. She was attractive and usually fun to be around, but she could also be unpredictably volatile and, if in one of her moods of despair, even morose. In March 1912, when she was thirty-five, she married a railway switchman supervisor named Lyle Arthur Graves, six years her junior. That union was over quickly. After the divorce, Della began to date an assortment of characters, some respectable but most unsavory, who came and went from her life swiftly, most not before spending at least one amorous night with her. In fact, it was at this time, after the end of her second marriage, that Della developed a looser sense of morality and didn't seem particularly concerned as to how it might adversely affect or otherwise influence her two children, Gladys, who was now twelve, and Marion, seven.

By the time she was a teenager, Gladys Monroe wore her chestnut brown hair—though it sometimes appeared more reddish—in soft waves and long curls that cascaded luxuriously down her back. She was a real looker, with Wedgwood blue eyes, a full mouth, a dazzling set of white teeth, and skin that glowed with vitality. Enviably thin and petite, as an adult she would grow to only five feet tall. However, an oversized personality and captivating quality made her well-liked at school and the life of any party.

When Gladys was about sixteen, her mother banished Marion, eleven, from the household. Because he was constantly in trouble at school and obstreperous at home, Della didn't know what to do with him. Disciplining him didn't seem to work. Stubborn and willful, he tried her patience. Therefore, one morning she collected all of his toys and tossed them into a pillowcase. Then, as Marion cried softly in the backseat and Gladys sat quietly staring straight ahead in the front passenger seat, Della drove to San Diego. There she left the boy in the care of a cousin, and that was the last anyone ever heard of Marion.

At about this same time, in 1916, Gladys met a young businessman named John Newton Baker, known primarily as Jasper. He'd just moved to Los Angeles from Kentucky after serving in the military. Jasper was tall and lanky with a lean, angular face and straight dark hair that he parted with great purpose to one side. Seeming genuinely interested in Gladys from the start, he not only wanted to hear about her many problems at home but also assist her in coming up with reasonable solutions. Twelve years her senior, he had more experience than her and seemed eager to insulate her from her troubled life and maybe even protect her from future heartache. Therefore, when he asked for her hand in marriage, she eagerly agreed. Della not only accepted the coupling of her young daughter with Jasper, she wholeheartedly encouraged it.

Sixteen-year-old Gladys Monroe took John Newton Baker as her husband on May 17, 1917. They had two children, Robert

Kermit—nicknamed Jack—and Berniece, before their marriage began to crumble. It turned out that Jasper was an alcoholic with a violent temper. He beat Gladys, making her young life a misery, often striking her about the head and twice giving her concussions. When she finally divorced him, Jasper took both of their children and moved to Kentucky because he'd decided she'd been an unfit mother. Gladys didn't have any say in the matter, and she certainly didn't have the money for an attorney.

In 1924 Gladys, who was twenty-four, took a second husband, Martin Edward Mortenson—known as Edward. The twenty-seven-year-old son of Norwegian immigrants, Mortenson was not classically handsome in the strictest sense of the word, but he was nonetheless a good-looking man with a broad brow, high cheekbones, and a full, wide smile. Tall and solid, he seemed like a stable and amiable fellow who only wanted to please and take care of his new wife. It was impossible for him to do so, though, because by the time she was in her mid-twenties it was clear that something was terribly wrong with Gladys. Like her mother, she began experiencing mood swings and crying jags. With the marriage all but over after just four months, Edward Mortenson filed for divorce.

Once she felt free of her matrimonial bonds, though she was not yet divorced, Gladys Baker mirrored her mother's behavior and became notoriously promiscuous. Taking many lovers, she developed a terrible reputation at her job at Consolidated Studios, where she worked as a film editor or "cutter." Soon she began an affair with a man named Charles Stanley Gifford, a sales manager at the company.

Stanley Gifford was born in Newport, Rhode Island, in 1898. When he was twenty-seven, he moved to Los Angeles after an unsuccessful marriage during which he had fathered two children. He found employment at Consolidated, as foreman of the day shift. When Gladys met him, she fell hard. A good-looking man with a thin mustache, dark eyes, and wavy jet black hair, he was both elegant and distinctive. Debonair and personable, he was a real lady-killer. He had a quick wit, a wonderful sense of humor, and, as someone who came from a family with a little money, he also enjoyed the occasional game of polo. His family had made a fortune in the shipbuilding business and Gifford was well-off enough to be able to afford two houses in Los Angeles during the Depression, a bleak period when most people were fortunate to even have one.

"He had a decent job," says his son, Charles Stanley Gifford, who today is eighty-six years old. "He had a good life. Along with polo, he enjoyed hunting and fishing. I was born in 1922, and he and my mother divorced in 1926. Still, he was a wonderful father to both me and my sister. I knew the only three women that he seriously dated over the years. He married two of them, my mother and then his second wife, Mary. Gladys was not one of the three women. The other one was a Catholic woman, a very nice lady he decided not to marry for his own personal reasons—not Gladys. I don't believe he was ever serious about Gladys, or he would have told me about it at one time or another over the years. He said he knew her, they dated casually, but that was it. The truth is that Gladys was a very attractive woman and she dated many people back then."

In late 1925, Gladys learned that she was pregnant. But who was the father? It's been published repeatedly over the years that Gladys didn't have a clue, that she wasn't keeping score of her lovers, she was just enjoying them. That's not the case, though. In fact, she always insisted that Stanley Gifford was the father of her child, and she never wavered from that belief. Biographers and other historians over the years have simply not wanted to believe her, citing her mental instability and promiscuity as reasons for doubt. However, it seems unfair to conclude that just because Gladys had serious problems, her identification of her daughter's paternity should be completely dismissed, especially since she was so consistent about it over the years.

In 1925, when Gladys told Stanley Gifford he was the father of her child, he refused to accept responsibility, claiming that he knew she'd been with other men. The more she insisted, the angrier he got, until finally he stormed off. She would see him a few more times, but he simply never believed her. She knew she would have to raise the child on her own, and was prepared to do so—or at least that's what she thought at the time.

In the 1940s, as we will later see, Gladys would continue to insist that Gifford was the baby's father. Then, in the 1960s, she would again confirm what she had been saying all along about him. In fact, in 1962, right after the death of Marilyn Monroe, Gladys discussed the actress's paternity with Rose Anne Cooper, a young nurse's aide at the Rock Haven Sanitarium in La Crescenta. Cooper was just twenty at the time she worked there. Gladys was sixty-two. "She was very clear," recalls Cooper. "She said that she'd been intimate with a number of men, and she talked about her past, openly saying that when she was young she was, as she put it, 'very wild.' However, she said that the only kind of intimacy that could have resulted in a pregnancy was what she had shared with the man she called 'Stan Gifford.' She said she had always been bothered by the fact that no one seemed to want to believe her, but that it was the truth. She said that even her own mother didn't believe her. 'Everyone thought I was lying,' she said, 'or that I just didn't know. I knew. I *always* knew.'"

Norma Jeane Is Born

On the morning of June 1, 1926, Della Monroe's daughter, Gladys Baker, gave birth to a child in the charity ward of the Los Angeles General Hospital (known today as the Los Angeles County USC Medical Center at 1200 North State Street). A collection had been taken up from concerned coworkers at Consolidated in order to tide Gladys over until she could return to work, and also for any medical expenses that would not be covered by charity. As she lay in the recovery room, bone tired from hours of labor, there was of course no expectant father pacing in a waiting room hoping for news about his child's arrival. Even her own mother was nowhere in sight since she'd taken off for India the previous December.

It should be remembered that during this period, there was a tremendous judgment on single mothers. No doubt Gladys could feel the condemnation directed toward her from the nurses at General Hospital. The paperwork she was required to fill out upon admittance did little to quiet any uneasiness she felt because of her situation. For instance, one of the first questions asked on the form was the father's name. Gladys wrote that a man named Edward Mortenson was the baby's father, even though she had been separated from him for some time. She also misspelled his name as "Mortensen." That she and the father didn't share a last name was controversial enough, but it was the response to the next question that was sure to start tongues wagging: father's residence. Examining the paperwork from that day as filled out by Gladys, the word "unknown" appears to be scrawled in a bolder, more deliberate handwriting. Indeed, filling out this paperwork had to have been difficult for her. She provided her address, which was no problem. Then, in answering the question of how many children she'd previously given birth to, her reply was "three"—odd, since she hadn't yet had the third. The next question—"Number of children of this mother now living"— was either answered incorrectly or dishonestly, depending on her understanding of it. She said that only "one" of those three was still living. Of course, she had borne two other children, who were presently being raised by her ex-husband, Jasper. Yes, Gladys did have a colorful past. Maybe she'd been deliberately dishonest in order to garner sympathy from an attending nurse. Perhaps she thought that if her first two children had passed away, she could be forgiven for having this third child out of wedlock. Whatever her reasoning, the questions put to her and the way she responded certainly suggest that the day was difficult her. Years later she told a friend, "I keep dreaming of that [hospital]. Everything seemed bright, too bright, and the nurses all seemed like nuns to me, mean awful nuns."

As is the case with many women, Gladys had a major emotional spiral immediately after the birth. Postpartum depression may have been a factor. It certainly appeared to many people in the family that her mother, Della, suffered from it as well—and maybe never got past it. Whatever the case, Gladys seemed disoriented and troubled for many days after giving birth. When the nurse brought the baby into the recovery room, the tiny child was placed on her mother's chest. "She just held her, with her eyes closed," Della later wrote to a family member when speaking of that moment, even though she wasn't present for it. "I feel awful. I know she can't keep [the baby]. She is not well. She needs to get her mind right first."

Gladys would have two weeks with her baby girl before she would have to do what she had agreed to do: Before her mother had left town, Gladys had agreed to hand over the infant to a stranger, Ida Bolender. During those two weeks, something dreadful occurred, making it clear that the arrangement made between Della and Ida was necessary. A friend and coworker of Gladys's at Consolidated Studios named Grace McKee came by the house to take care of the baby for an afternoon while Gladys went grocery shopping. (Grace would play a very important role in the lives of Gladys and Norma Jeane in years to come.) When Gladys returned, she went into a manic state for reasons unknown and began to accuse Grace of poisoning the child. One thing led to another, and somehow Grace ended up on the receiving end of a kitchen knife, stabbed by Gladys. Though Grace's wound was superficial, it was clear that Gladys could be a danger to her baby. After that violent episode, which panicked and bewildered everyone, it was an easy decision to turn Norma Jeane over to Ida.

The emotionally charged transfer happened on June 13, 1926— that was the sad day Gladys Baker showed up on Ida Bolender's doorstep with a two-week-old infant. After a long and difficult farewell, she walked out the front door of Ida's house without the child named Norma Jeane Mortensen.* Norma Jeane was a help-

---

* Note to reader: From this point on, when referring to Edward, it's Mortenson. When referring to Norma Jeane, it's Mortensen.

less infant who had entered this world without any form of welcome. There was no freshly furnished nursery awaiting her, no tiny wardrobe, and in fact no one on earth whose future plans included her. She spent the first few days of her life simply being sustained, not nurtured. She was a burden, one that needed to be unloaded. No one can know for certain, but it very well may have been at a tender age that she began to sense that something wasn't quite right in her world—that there wasn't sufficient attention being paid her. Indeed, she would spend much of the rest of her life trying to change those circumstances—but to do so, she would need to one day become . . . Marilyn Monroe.

Della's Terrible Fate

Within just days of surrendering Norma Jeane to Ida and Albert Wayne Bolender, Gladys Baker began to feel remorse over the decision. "It occurred to her, I think, that maybe she could have done for this child what her mother had not done for her—love her, be there for her," said one of her family members. The deal was that she would pay the Bolenders twenty-five dollars per week to raise Norma Jeane, which she did the entire time Norma Jeane was in their care. In the beginning, though, she gave them a few extra dollars a week so that she could stay with them on occasional weekends and at least be with her baby. That didn't last long, though. "The truth was that Gladys had a problem watching Ida raise her child," said Mary Thomas-Strong, whose mother was a close friend of Ida's. "Ida could be strict and controlling. She felt she knew what was right. She was a professional mother, in a sense. She wanted to have her way with Norma Jeane and it was hard for Gladys to be on the sidelines. Therefore, she moved back to Hollywood determined to visit the baby every weekend. She was back and forth a lot." In a 1930 census the Bolenders and Gladys were reported to live all in the same household.

Adding to Gladys's bewilderment at this time was the arrival of her mother, Della, who returned from India with malaria. Her "husband" Charles Grainger decided not to come back to the States with her, leaving most people to believe that their relationship was over. Della was delusional and sick with a fever for many weeks. It took a terrible toll on her.

In summer of 1927, Della walked across the street from her home to the Bolenders' with the intention of seeing Norma Jeane. She banged on the front door, but Ida didn't want to let her into the house. It's unknown why Ida took this position, but she may have felt that Della was out of control and a danger to the baby. Indeed, Della broke the door's glass with her elbow and let herself in. The family history has it that she confronted Ida and said she believed that Norma Jeane was dead and that no one had told her or Gladys. Alarmed and not knowing how to handle the situation, Ida let Della see Norma Jeane sleeping in her crib. She went to get Della a glass of water and when she returned she found Della smothering the baby with a pillow. "Ida became almost hysterical," said one friend of Gladys's in the telling of the story. "She grabbed the child. Della said that the baby's pillow had slipped and she was simply readjusting it. But Ida was very upset and demanded that Della leave the house." Marilyn Monroe—and even the Bolenders—would tell variations of this story many times over the years.

"Ida and Wayne called the police," said Mary Thomas-Strong. "When they came, they found a very mixed-up Della babbling incoherently. With Norma Jeane crying in her bedroom, and Ida shouting accusations at Della, it was such a chaotic scene the police didn't know what to do about it. So they escorted Della back to her house and left her there. What they should have done was taken her to a hospital."

For a long time, Della had been filled with an aching sadness. Now it was not only more acute but had also turned into abject anger directed at whoever happened to be in the room with her—and unfortunately, that was usually Gladys, who had recently moved in with her mother to care for her. After a battery of tests, it was determined that Della was suffering from a weakened heart, and probably heart disease as well. Of course, that diagnosis certainly did not account for her many years of unpredictable behavior, which had started back when she gave birth to her children. Once she began taking the prescribed medication, things went from bad to worse. Her swift decline reminded some family members of the sudden descent into madness that had been suffered by Della's late husband, Otis. Gladys couldn't help but fear the worst. The horrifying likelihood was that the same thing that had happened to her father was now afflicting her mother.

A few nights after Gladys moved into the house with her, Della came rushing into her bedroom screaming that Charles Grainger had broken into the house and raped her. Gladys didn't even have to check the property to verify that Grainger wasn't on it—she just knew he wasn't. However, there was no calming Della that night. A couple of days later, she started to complain that the local butcher had put shards of glass in her ground beef. Then, a week later, on August 1, Della took a turn for the worse, so much so that Gladys and Grace had to rush her back to the doctor. "He said there was no doubt about it, Della needed to be institutionalized," said Mary Thomas-Strong. "Gladys couldn't believe it. She wasn't going to allow it. But then the strangest thing happened."

According to the family's history, handed down a generation, on August 3 mother and daughter were having a silent and contemplative meal at the kitchen table. Perhaps Gladys was trying to sort through her emotions, maybe attempting to divine how she might proceed with her mother. Over the years, Della had become Gladys's most loyal confidante. After all, mother and daughter shared the same kinds of mental problems, and often one would have to convince the other that the voices being "heard" were not real, that the people "watching" were imaginary. How could Gladys say goodbye to Della now? In her absence, who would be there for her? She had already lost her three children, and now her mother, this woman sitting across from her with an empty look in her eyes? Gladys couldn't accept it, especially with the knowledge that when her father had been sent to a similar place, he never returned. His fate had rarely left her thoughts, especially during the last couple of weeks.

Suddenly, in a moment of surprising lucidity, Della looked up from her plate and stared at her daughter with sad eyes. "You must let me go, Gladys," she said earnestly. "It's time for me to go. I *want* to go." Mother and daughter looked intently at each other for a long, infinitely heartbreaking moment. Then, as the tears began to roll down Gladys's face, Della went back to her meal.

On August 4, 1927, Della Monroe was taken to the Norwalk State Hospital. Nineteen days later, on August 23, she died. She was buried in the Rose Hill Cemetery in Whittier, California, next to her first husband, Otis. She was just fifty-one.

Living with the Bolenders

$\mathcal{B}$y the time she was three, in 1929, Norma Jeane Mortensen was an extraordinarily pretty girl with honey blonde curls and baby blue eyes. Hers was a face that somehow seemed perfect, as if carved from pale, polished marble. It was difficult for anyone to just pass her by without taking notice. Interestingly, despite all of the confusion around her during these early years, she seemed remarkably well-adjusted to her life at the Bolenders'. She was not unhappy. "We treated her like our own child," Ida Bolender said in 1966, "because we loved her." However, in years to come, writers would paint a very bleak picture of this time in Marilyn's life.

"I guess there was an effort to sensationalize things," says Nancy Jeffrey, the only surviving member of the foster Bolender siblings. "Because of the way things turned out for Norma Jeane, every one of her biographers over the years has wanted to make it sound like it was awful at our home, but I'm the only one of us still alive and I can tell you that it wasn't. Norma Jeane was happy in our home. It was a loving family, just a happy home full of children. Mother was very industrious, too. She made all of our clothes for us. She loved us beyond words and she hung on to us. She didn't want anything to happen to us. Whenever we left the house, I don't care where we were going, she would say, 'Stop just for a second,' and she would then say a quick prayer for our safety."

Of course, a big part of the problem was that Marilyn constantly referred to her impoverished background when she became famous, and very often made the circumstances of her first seven years seem much worse than they were. Jeffrey says that when Ida was alive, she was "very upset" by the mischaracterizations of Norma Jeane's time in the Bolender household.

On Ida and Wayne Bolender's two-acre agricultural property in Hawthorne, they raised chickens and goats and grew vegetables. "We grew up on fresh tomatoes, corn on the cob, watermelon, green beans, and squash," recalls Nancy Jeffrey. "We also had trees that were full of plums, apples, and lemons. There was one huge fig tree that Norma Jeane and Lester—our foster brother who was the only one Mother and Daddy actually adopted—loved to climb. They would drag blankets up there and make a fort for themselves. We also had chickens and rabbits, and Daddy even bought a goat because a couple of us were allergic to cow's milk as little children. It wasn't necessary to go to the store often, but on those occasions when we did go Daddy would drive us in his Model T Ford and we would wait in the car while Mother shopped. We played guessing games of the surrounding sights, sang favorite songs, or Daddy would tell us stories. Another childhood memory was that on rainy days we had to stay in the house, so we would make a fort under the dining room table, leaning the top of the chairs around it for rooms. Then we would cover it all with blankets. Mother even let us eat lunch under there at times. Norma Jeane loved that."

The house itself, at 459 East Rhode Island Street,* was small and cramped, a ramshackle-looking structure in the middle of what must have seemed to little children to be . . . nowhere. During the seven years Norma Jeane would live there, quite a few children came and went, but there were five foster children who were there most, if not all, of the time: the aforementioned Lester, plus Mumsy, Alvina, Noel, and Nancy. "Around the time of the Depression, a lot of parents simply didn't have the resources to care for their own children," recalls Nancy Jeffrey, "so they would drop them off in foster homes until they were ready to take proper care of them. It was a common thing." From all accounts, Norma Jeane got along well with all of her foster siblings, especially with Lester, who was two months younger.

Wayne Bolender was an amiable and openhearted fellow who was pleasant to everyone and had always eagerly embraced the idea of raising foster children. He was wiry, with light gray eyes behind thick tortoiseshell glasses, and the most prominent feature on his face was his very large nose. He had a jolly air about him. Sturdy and dependable, as a mail carrier for the United States Postal Service he would work the same route for thirty-five years (48th Street and Vermont Avenue in Los Angeles). "He loved being with the kids," says one source who knew the Bolenders, "and the kids loved him. He was devoutly Baptist, like Ida. He had a little printing press in the house and he would make prayer cards for the church with it."

Though they shared many of the same ideals, Wayne and Ida didn't have much of a relationship. He and Ida rarely spoke and when they did it was usually Ida chastising him for some perceived transgression or insisting he do something he obviously did not want to do. He was clearly intimidated by her and, some thought, maybe even afraid of her. Indeed, she ran her household with the stringent rules and regulations of an Old World orphanage, taking her responsibility to the foster children quite seriously.

---

* Redistricting took place in Hawthorne in the 1940s, and at that time the address was changed to 4201 West 134th Street. The original home is still standing.

Much has been made over the years of Ida and Wayne's fanatical religious leanings. It's been written that they were zealots about their Protestant faith. "First of all, we were Baptists," says Nancy Jeffrey. "Though I think along the way Mother did belong to a United Pentecostal Church. We went to Sunday school on Sunday mornings and then Wednesday night services. I don't think that was too much. Mother sometimes did the cooking for big church dinners—there would be a big dinner at the church for the congregation—or sometimes many of them would come to our home. I'm not sure how it evolved that my parents were religious fanatics. Maybe it was just part of the myth that was created around Norma Jeane when she became Marilyn Monroe. Mother taught us to love the Lord and, by extension, to love each other. It was really the only foundation Norma Jeane ever had, and I think it did her a lot of good in her life. I know that was Mother's intention."

Supposedly, at least according to the stories written about the adult Marilyn Monroe, she was forced to memorize the following prayer when she was about four—and she would be quizzed often to make sure she remembered it: "I promise, God helping me, not to buy, drink or sell or give alcoholic liquor while I live; from all tobaccos I'll abstain and never take God's name in vain." Her foster sister Nancy Jeffrey scoffs at the notion. "I never heard that prayer in my entire life. I'm not sure that there's anything wrong with it, anyway, even if Mother had made us say it. But she never did."

Another story has it that going to the movies was out of the question because there was no telling what Norma Jeane would be exposed to in the theater. In fact, Marilyn once recalled Ida having told her, "If the world came to an end with you sitting in the movies, do you know what would happen? You'd burn along with all the bad people. We are churchgoers, not moviegoers." Years later, Marilyn would say, "I don't think it's right to use God to frighten a child like that. I just think that was an awful thing for her to do to a child."

Again, Nancy Jeffrey disagrees with that piece of history. "The truth is that we were only not allowed to go to the movies on Sundays. However, we really didn't go to movies that much anyway. We were little kids. How many movies were we going to see between the ages of one and seven? I just don't think Mother would have frightened Norma Jeane like that. She may have said something like, 'We are churchgoers not moviegoers.' That sounds like her. But the rest of it, burning with bad people? That doesn't sound like Mother to me."

Whether or not she went to the movies—and of course she wasn't going without an adult anyway—it sometimes seemed that there wasn't much Norma Jeane could ever do to please Ida. No matter how hard she tried, she could never measure up to the Bolender matriarch's standards of cleanliness or behavior. "Poor Norma Jeane always seemed to be in some kind of trouble," said Mary Thomas-Strong. "She loved to play in dirt, like a lot of kids. Ida would be unhappy about that. Ida would dress her in pretty clothes and Norma Jeane would go and play and come back thirty minutes later, dirty again. It drove Ida crazy. She wanted Norma Jeane to toe the line. She was strict, at times."

Yes, Ida Bolender could be difficult—there seems to be no argument there from any quarter. She was tough and resilient, an indomitable woman. "But I believe to this day that she was one of the major stabilizing influences in Norma Jeane's young life, and truly the first powerful woman she'd been exposed to," says her foster daughter Nancy Jeffrey. Maybe Ida sensed there might be a shortage of stable and decisive adults in Norma Jeane's world, and she was determined to be one of them—no matter what her foster daughter or anyone else thought of her. "I was hard on her for her own good," she once explained to Jeffrey. Then, with great positiveness, she added, "But I know I raised her the right way. I know it in my heart."

Many of Ida Bolender's best character traits were impressed upon Norma Jeane Mortensen during her seven years at the Bolender home. Because she was born to a mother who was in emotional disarray, perhaps it served the young girl well to be molded by a foster mother who was firm and controlled. Indeed, it was Ida's strength and determination that Norma Jeane would one day need to draw upon in order to make it in show business. However, Gladys's traits of extreme vulnerability and emotional instability were also an undeniable part of Norma Jeane's biology. For instance, she would be well equipped to handle rejection in her professional life, just as Ida would have in her place. However, to handle it in her personal life would prove to be very difficult—just as it would have been for Gladys.

"All she ever wanted for Norma Jeane was for her to be strong, like she was," said Nancy Jeffrey of her foster mother. "She always knew that [Norma Jeane] would have a very difficult life. She could see that her family background was not going to be helpful to her and, in fact, could possibly be the downfall of her. So she wasn't going to coddle her. She would say, 'The girl will face stronger foes than me, I can tell you that much. She has to be able to stand on her own. For all I know, she may hate me now, but she will be strong. She *will* have a good life.'"

A Frightening Encounter with Gladys

*B*y the fall of 1929, with Della Monroe dead for two years, Gladys had become accustomed to not having anyone in her life upon whom she could totally depend. She hadn't been able to make any of her romantic relationships last, and her children had either been taken from her or given away *by* her. Her job at Consolidated Studios offered her little opportunity to build friendships. In fact, as a film cutter, her role was menial. She was told where and how to cut and splice together pieces of film so they could be viewed as a whole. The irony of that vocation most likely never occurred to Gladys, but it could be considered an interesting metaphor representing the major challenge of her mental state: putting the pieces of her life together. It's true, she had made a good friend in Grace McKee. However, since Della's death, Grace hadn't been able to reach Gladys. It was as if something in Gladys had been switched off and she simply didn't care that much about connecting with other people. Perhaps it was because Gladys was simply not able to quiet the increasingly loud voices in her head. After all, only her mother had possessed the key to settling her back into a more reasonable thought process. On her own, she lacked the ability to view her circumstances from a distance. Without that perspective, each moment became about exactly what was happening right then and there. Goals were impossible to set, consequences impossible to calculate. She was in a mental tailspin, and everyone in her life knew it but didn't know what to do about it.

While her moment-to-moment experiences may have been torturous, Gladys was still able to complete tasks. For instance, she could show up for work on time, go grocery shopping, and remember to water the plants. Therefore, if someone's life could be judged solely by her daily agenda, Gladys Baker would have appeared quite unspectacular. Yet it was *how* she experienced and reacted to the string of events that made her different.

Even toward the end of Della's life, she had been a somewhat stabilizing factor for her daughter. In part, it may have been because Gladys was responsible for managing her mother's health and state of mind. This duty helped keep her focus off her own paranoid delusions. That paranoia, however, was now building— and during Gladys's time alone she began to find it more difficult to remain rational. Naturally, her first plan of action was to find a man, which she would do often at one of the nearby speakeasies. Of course, these unions rarely lasted more than an evening or two. Also, it was getting harder for her to lure the opposite sex, not so much because of her reputation as a woman of loose morals, but because something just seemed a little "off" about her. Through it all, though, Gladys felt she had a reasonable expectation of having at least one person with her all the time: Norma

Jeane. She *was* her daughter, after all. When she gave her to Ida, it was in the hope that she would one day be capable of caring for the baby herself.

One afternoon, in the middle of what must have been a full-force episode of paranoia, Gladys pounded on the front door of the Bolender home. The daughters of a friend of Ida's from church—both interviewed for this book—explained for the first time the exchange that occurred, as described to them by their mother:

"Where's Norma Jeane?" Gladys demanded, pushing past Ida.

"What is it, Gladys?" Ida replied, regarding her carefully. "What's happened?"

Gladys said that Norma Jeane could no longer stay at the Bolenders'. She had come to take her, she insisted, as her eyes darted about the small home. It was impossible to reason with her. Ida told her that she wasn't making any sense and suggested that she sit down and talk to her. However, Gladys was adamant. With her eyes flashing, she cried out again that Norma Jeane was *her* daughter and that she was taking her home. Ida grabbed Gladys's arm, delaying her momentarily. "This *is* her home," she told her. "We just haven't made it official yet . . . but once we get the adoption papers together . . ." Gladys then insisted that there would never be an adoption. Norma Jeane was hers, she said, not Ida's. With that, she yanked herself free and ran to the backyard, where the three-year-old was playing with a dog that had followed Wayne home one day and whom Norma Jeane had named Tippy. Ida followed Gladys into the backyard, begging her to come to her senses. However, Gladys insisted that she was only taking what was rightfully hers. Then she scooped up a now crying Norma Jeane and said, "You're coming with Mommy, sweetheart."

According to the story passed down a generation, there was mayhem—a barking dog, a weeping child, and Ida pulling at Gladys in an effort to save a little girl from a confused, possibly dangerous woman. Still tussling as they got to the kitchen, Gladys managed to push Ida outside, slamming the back door and quickly locking it.

Frantic, Ida pounded on the door. Then she tried to force it open with all her weight. After a few moments of futile effort, she ran down the driveway, around the house, and entered her home through the front door. By this time, she was out of breath, panting. She listened for a moment. Nothing.

Ida then ran back out the door again to see if Gladys had somehow made it out to the sidewalk in front of the house. Once outside, she looked both ways down the street—no one was in sight. At a loss, she was about to burst into tears when suddenly the front door flew open. It was Gladys, her face now flushed and red.

Then Ida heard the muffled screams of Norma Jeane. To Ida's horror, Gladys had managed to stuff the child into a large military duffel bag that Wayne Bolender had used to store his tools. The bag hung on her shoulder, completely zipped shut. Gladys, now moving clumsily with her awkward baggage, attempted to cross the lawn. Ida grabbed one of the handles of the canvas sack and tried to free it from Gladys's grip. This bizarre tug-of-war would last only moments, ending with the bag splitting open and the helpless Norma Jeane tumbling onto the ground. Norma Jeane's weeping ceased for a moment before she finally screamed out, "Mommy!" Both women turned and looked down at the child, whose arms were now outstretched—in Ida's direction. Ida whipped the child quickly up into her arms and ran inside the house, locking the door behind her.

Now inside, an extremely shaken Ida Bolender stood in a doorway to the kitchen. Clinging to little Norma Jeane with everything she had, she kept her eyes on the front door, all the while ready to run out the back if Gladys tried to get into the house. All she could hear was the child's whimpering as she watched the front doorknob turn slightly back and forth. Gladys could not get into the house. Ida spent the next few minutes peeking out various windows as Gladys circled the house, muttering to herself and occasionally trying to open a window or a door. Finally, Ida screwed up enough courage to shout through a closed window, "I've called the police! They'll be here shortly!"

With the now quiet Norma Jeane still in her arms, Ida Bolender listened. There was silence. Gladys Baker had disappeared just as abruptly as she had arrived.

Ida Wants to Adopt Norma Jeane

Within three years' time, Ida Bolender had taken to little Norma Jeane and begun to love her as if she were her own. Norma Jeane had bonded with her as well, and now called her "Aunt Ida." Ida's intention had always been to see to it that this child be raised with a sense of independence, even at such an early age. She knew that her life would be a difficult one and she'd already decided that she wanted to prepare her for it. She thought of it as a mission, a part of God's plan not only for Norma Jeane but for herself as well. She was serious about it, too—as she was about most things. However, that said, Ida often worked against her own intentions, because whenever her charge displayed any degree of determination—when she was willful or stubborn—Ida reprimanded her as if trying to reel her back in, lest she become too noncompliant. In Ida's mind, there was a fine line between independence and disobedience, and with Norma Jeane she seemed to have trouble defining it. Still, she loved the child with all her heart and decided that she wanted to legally adopt her.

According to memories of family members—Monroes and Bolenders—Ida invited Gladys over to see Norma Jeane, have supper, and discuss adoption possibilities. Grace McKee had explained to Ida that Gladys's behavior the day she tried to take Norma Jeane was the unfortunate consequence of her not having taken her medication. Therefore, Ida tried to put the dreadful episode out of her mind. It wasn't easy, though. It's probably a testament to Ida that she was ever able to strike a conciliatory tone with Gladys, so traumatized was she by the events of that day. Still, she was the type of woman who always found a way to stay focused on the business at hand. She needed to meet with Gladys—there was no way around it—and she knew that Wayne was home and in the next room in case anything went wrong.

Once they finished their meal, Gladys began playing with her daughter. Ida walked over and lifted the child into her arms. When she did so, Norma Jeane clung to her. Ida went to the couch and took her seat next to Gladys. With the baby in her lap, Ida reminded Gladys that it had been three years since she'd left her child in the care of her and her husband. She explained that they both loved Norma Jeane very much and now thought it would be best if Gladys allowed them to adopt her. As she spoke, the child fell asleep, cradled in Ida's arms and seeming blissfully content.

After hearing Ida out, Gladys began to cry softly. She told Ida that she couldn't bear to lose another child. She had already lost two, after all. Certainly, Ida understood. However, as she patted Norma Jeane on the back, it was easy to see that the little girl was very happy with her. Surely, she told Gladys, "you want her to be this happy for the rest of her life, don't you?"

"Of course."

"Then, please. Make the proper decision," Ida said, according to a later recollection. "Give this little girl the life she deserves. It's the best thing for her. She'll always live deep in your heart, dear."

Gladys rose from the couch. "Never," she said firmly. Then she reached over to take her child from Ida. However, as soon as she touched her, Norma Jeane began to cry. Her tears came without relief for at least a minute. Even though Ida was still holding the little girl, she sat motionless, maybe waiting for Gladys to reach out to her. The moment hung awkwardly, mingled emotions running together as both women just stared at the child. Then, finally, Ida swung into action and began to comfort the girl. When she could take no more, a tearful Gladys ran from the room and out of the house.

"Now It's Time to Know Your Mother"

The years passed quickly . . .

By the time Norma Jeane turned seven in June 1933, she was having a difficult time relating to other people. She also didn't get along with children her own age at the Washington Street School she attended in Hawthorne. Certainly, Lester, the child who'd been adopted by the Bolenders, was an ally. But as for everyone else, she seemed afraid to know them or didn't want to play with them. There was an understandably deep sadness about her. She was shy, withdrawn. However, that said, she had only become more uncommonly pretty with the passing of the years. With her face so clear and luminous and her blonde hair seeming somehow aglow—Ida actually washed it in lemon juice for just such an effect, which suggests that even she was taken by the child's beauty—little Norma Jeane really was stunning.

In recent years, Norma Jeane had grown to think of Ida Bolender as her mother. However, Ida would always disabuse her of that notion. Once it had been clarified that no official adoption would take place, whenever Norma Jeane referred to Ida as her mother, she was quickly reprimanded. "I'm not your real mother," Ida would say very abruptly, "and I don't want you having people believe otherwise." In Marilyn Monroe's autobiography, she quotes Ida as having told her, "You're old enough to know better. I'm not related to you. Your mama's coming to see you tomorrow. You can call *her* mama." The truth was the truth, as far as Ida was concerned, and she wasn't the girl's mother, plain and simple. The sooner Norma Jeane reconciled herself to that fact of life, the better. Ida was a pragmatic woman, not usually sentimental. True, she could have been more sensitive, but she was who she was and she never apologized for it.

It's been said (by Marilyn, actually) that Norma Jeane was also not allowed to refer to Wayne Bolender as her father. That's not true at all. In fact, she called him "Daddy" and did so all of her life. His face weather-beaten from being outdoors, Wayne had a wide, engaging smile and kind, humor-filled eyes. It was as if Norma Jeane sensed his empathy for her, because she quickly became very attached to him. Since he truly believed her circumstances were sad, he went out of his way to be nice. Nancy Jeffrey recalled, "My mother was definitely the disciplinarian in our family, whereas my father was very quiet and comforting. I'm sure that's why Norma Jeane gravitated to him. She was very inquisitive. There was a stool by the bathtub and I remember that she would sit there and, as he shaved, she would ask him all sorts of questions." Marilyn also once recalled, "Which way was east or south? How many people are there in the world? Why do flowers grow? I had so many questions and Daddy always seemed to know the answers."

Unfortunately, Wayne could not offer much assistance to Norma Jeane if Ida was angry at her. Cowed by his wife, he kept the peace by keeping his mouth shut. If he felt the girl was being treated unfairly, he wouldn't like it but neither would he do anything about it. Moreover, if he paid too much attention to Norma Jeane or any of the other children who passed through the Bolender home, Ida would become annoyed. With her dark eyes blazing, she would lash out at him and accuse him of coddling them, thereby making them that much more difficult to raise. Then, of course, she would feel badly about losing her temper and apologize to him hours later.

By June 1933, shortly after her seventh birthday, Norma Jeane's life was settled—such as it was. Yes, there were problems at the Bolender home, but it was all that she knew and she was fine there. She got along with her foster siblings and also had one faithful friend who was always there for her and never once brought her anything but joy: her pet dog, Tippy.

Sadly, however, a tragedy involving Tippy would be the catalyst to Norma Jeane's departure from the Bolender home. As the story goes—and it's been told countless times over the years in different variations—a neighbor of the Bolenders became annoyed by the dog's constant barking. In Marilyn's memoir, she writes that the neighbor, finally fed up and in a moment of fury, attacked the dog with a hoe, savagely cutting Tippy in half.

A Bolender family member explained that what really happened was that Tippy was hit by a car and killed. Ida, having witnessed the event, didn't want the dead animal continually run over in the street. Therefore, using a garden hoe, she lifted the carcass and dropped it on the driveway. She wanted nothing more to do with it, and decided that the gruesome task of disposing of the pet should wait for Wayne's return. However, before Wayne got home, Norma Jeane showed up after playing with some friends down the street. Obviously, she was devastated by the sight of her best friend's dead body, mangled and lying in the driveway with a nearby garden tool seemingly part of the macabre scene. She let out a shriek, burst into tears, and ran into the house. For the next few hours, it was impossible for Ida to calm her down.

Ida, in an attempt to make the pain of the dog's death seem more bearable to Norma Jeane, explained that some unknown party had shot Tippy in the head and that his death was immediate. She thought that if the girl believed that not much suffering had been involved, she would feel better. However, Norma Jeane refused to believe Ida and had invented her own story. "Tippy was cut up with a hoe," Norma Jeane insisted through her tears. "The neighbors finally killed him!"

Ida tried everything she could think of to shake that scenario from Norma Jeane's mind, even telling her the truth at one point. It didn't work. The girl was absolutely convinced that the neighbors had been plotting her dog's death for some time and had finally succeeded at it. Ida found this very disturbing—maybe even paranoid. "Ida wondered if Norma Jeane was starting to have delusions like her mother, Gladys," explains a relative, "because she wouldn't let go of this crazy idea that the neighbors had hacked up her dog. On some level, I think Ida had always been afraid of Gladys . . . and now she was wondering about her daughter. She had become very uneasy about it."

Norma Jeane's paroxysm lasted into the next day, with the family enjoying silence only during her slumber. Ida had a real problem with this kind of expression of emotion. Actually, she'd recently begun to wonder if she had even been put on this earth to raise such a sensitive child. This certainly hadn't been the first time Norma Jeane became upset when something in her little world went awry. Ida started to wonder if perhaps her influence was backfiring. While her goal had always been to strengthen Norma Jeane, maybe her firm hand and distant affection was actually having a negative effect on the girl. Had it created a child who would spin out of control when faced with any emotional trauma?

It seems clear now that Ida was confused and felt she was at a crossroads with her foster daughter. She had once believed she and Wayne would adopt the girl. However, Gladys had again made it clear that this would not be the case. In fact, in recent months, Gladys had started saying that she wanted Norma Jeane back. Stalling, Ida always had an excuse as to why the girl could not be returned—she was in school, she had made friends, she was not feeling well. Finally, Ida decided that perhaps the time had come. Norma Jeane was already distraught, Ida told Wayne, so why not let her traumatizing memory of her dog's death blend with the difficulty she would suffer during a transfer of custody? The next afternoon, she telephoned Gladys. "I think it would be best now if you came and took Norma Jeane," she told her. "She's very upset. I think she needs her mother."

This was not an easy decision for Ida. "She loved her," said one of her relatives, "but I think she began to feel as if she was failing where Norma Jeane was concerned. She took the child's fragility as an indication that she had not done what she set out to do with her, which was to make her stronger. But Norma Jeane *was* strong. She was just a girl. She was very sensitive, very vulnerable . . . and that's what threw Ida off, I think."

The next day, Norma Jeane was told that her mother was on her way and that she would be taking her home with her. This was confusing. "But I *am* home," Norma Jeane said. "Yes you are," Ida told her, "and you can come back anytime you want to."

Still quietly sniffling through tearful moments for the rest of the day, the little girl kept her eyes fixed on the street outside the front window waiting for the mysterious—and sometimes even scary—woman who had come from time to time to visit and promise her a good life "someday."

Silent and focused only on getting the job done in an efficient manner, Ida packed a little suitcase for Norma Jeane, just a few things. Then she called her into the kitchen and sat her down at the table for a talk. "I want you to know that we'll always be here for you," she told her, according to a later recollection. She spoke very slowly as if to give more weight to her words. "We'll always love you," she added reassuringly. "But we just think that it's time for you to know your mother. Your *real* mother. Do you understand?" As Ida spoke to Norma Jeane, all of the other foster children were grouped in the living room, crying. The noise must have driven Ida crazy. Clearly, no one wanted to see Norma Jeane go, even though the time had come for her departure. Ida began to rethink things. Was this really the right decision? Perhaps she was being hasty? Should she call Gladys back and say she had changed her mind? No. She had always been decisive and now was not the time to change.

Finally, Gladys pulled up in front of the Bolender home and tooted her vehicle's horn. She didn't get out of the car.

Inside the house, Ida put Norma Jeane's coat on her and buttoned it. Bending down to her eye level, she put strong hands on narrow shoulders. Her eyes filled with sudden warmth as she gazed at her sad foster child, this girl she'd known and loved since infancy. She hugged her tightly. "I'll miss you, Norma Jeane," she said. Then, handing her the small suitcase, she sent her on her way.

With a very troubled look on her little face, Norma Jeane walked down the sidewalk and got into the car with a woman she thought of as a stranger. She didn't sit in the front seat next to her, though. Rather, she opened a rear door and got into the back of the vehicle. Then, peering out the window as the car drove off, she watched the only mother she'd ever known fade into the distance. Norma Jeane

Mortensen had no idea where she was going. She only hoped that wherever it was, it would be . . . home.

A New—and Temporary—Life

*W*hen Gladys Baker picked up her daughter from the Bolenders, she did not arrive alone. With her was her close friend who had once babysat Norma Jeane, the woman who, as it would turn out, would become a key figure in the young girl's life, Grace Atchinson McKee. She was Gladys's roommate for some time and worked with her at Consolidated Studios, also as a splicer, or "cutter," of film negatives.

Consolidated was a film laboratory and processing company, the leader in its industry for many decades in Los Angeles. Finally, Gladys was making a good wage there and was able to settle into a more stable life. It was tedious work, though. Basically, she spent six days a week reviewing endless rolls of film negatives in order to cut the sections that had been previously marked by studio editors. She then handed the material over to another department for the final splicing. The walls of the building in which she worked were thick cement with not many windows. There was no air conditioning, and at times it was absolutely stifling inside. However, it was a steady job, and that was all that mattered. She'd also made a good friend there, Grace.

Born Clara Grace Atchinson in Montana, she was thirty-seven in 1933. Grace—a two-time divorcee by then—was a petite woman like Gladys, barely five feet tall.* In fact, they were able to wear the same clothes, and they often did. She was known for her personal

---

* It's been previously reported that she was married three times by 1933. Not true. She had two husbands by this time: Reginald Evans and John Wallace McKee.

magnetism. When Grace was in a room, it was difficult not to focus on her, so powerful was her presence. Although not beautiful in the accepted sense of the word, she was so vital and charismatic she gave the impression of beauty. Her wavy hair was usually dyed a peroxide blonde but sometimes left to its original brown color. She also had deep-set brown eyes and a thin mouth usually curled into a smile. Grace aspired to become an actress, but though she had plenty of ambition and maybe even some talent, she would never apply herself to that goal. She once wrote to a cousin, "If I could only have Jean Harlow's life, what a good time I would have. To be an actress is my dream, I guess. I don't know that it could happen. But, still, I can dream, can't I?"

Grace and Gladys got along famously, even though they obviously did have their problems from time to time. It's a testament to Grace's loyalty to Gladys that they were able to get past that troubling stabbing incident, shortly after Norma Jeane was born. Both were good-time gals in the Roaring Twenties and as such had no problem finding bootleg liquor and men. To say that they merely enjoyed their flapper-girl lifestyles would be to understate their fun times. "We have FUN," Grace wrote to her cousin, making sure to capitalize each letter in the word.

Moreover, Gladys began to depend on Grace for direction and advice in almost all areas of her life. With Della gone, she needed someone to lean on, and for now that would be Grace. They started acting as a team, making joint decisions about their lives. Grace was smart and self-sufficient, and she always felt she knew the solution to every problem—not just her own, but everyone else's as well. She felt compelled to give people advice, even those who didn't ask for it. It was one of the reasons her marriages had not worked out. For instance, she'd often start a conversation with the statement, "You know what your problem is?" Then she would proceed to explain the "problem" whether a solution was asked for or not. Gladys, who never had a guiding maternal influence, gravitated to Grace and appreciated that her best friend cared enough about her to offer advice.

"In many ways, Grace lived her life through others," Bea Thomas, who knew Grace, observed in 1976. "Some felt she wasn't particularly attractive and that she tried to do for others what she couldn't do for herself in terms of beauty. She had an inner beauty, though, and you can see it from her photos. However, she gave Gladys a complete makeover. When she told her that her brunette hair made her look 'mousy' and suggested bright red as a more suitable color, Gladys promptly dyed her hair. When she told Gladys that her clothing style was too conservative and suggested she be more provocative, Gladys agreed. The two went shopping for new dresses and it was Grace—not Gladys—who selected each one of them. Grace also felt that Gladys's vocabulary should be expanded, and often corrected her grammar when the two were with friends. Grace couldn't have children, so she encouraged Gladys to take more responsibility for Norma Jeane."

At this time, Gladys and Grace were living in a very small apartment in Hollywood. Norma Jeane had been there before. Occasionally, Gladys would pick her up at the Bolenders' and bring her to her home for an awkward visit or sleepover. Marilyn would later say that she spent most of this time with her mother "in the closet of her bedroom hiding among her clothes. She seldom spoke to me except to say, 'Don't make so much noise, Norma.' She would say this even when I was lying in bed at night and turning the pages of a book. Even the sound of a page turning made her nervous."

Now, suddenly, mother and daughter were expected to forge a happy relationship. It wouldn't be easy. After all, they didn't even really know each other. Once Norma Jeane began living with her, Gladys became convinced that the girl was unhappy. "She spent seven years living on a spacious farm, and now this?" she asked Grace. "I'm sure she's miserable here." In fact, Gladys was not wrong. Norma Jeane missed her Aunt Ida terribly, as well as her foster siblings. She was just a little girl who had been uprooted from the only life she'd known, the only people she'd ever loved. It must have seemed so unfair. She certainly couldn't hide her emotions about it, even if they did upset her mother. "Are we going to visit Aunt Ida soon?" she kept asking. However, Gladys and Grace had made the decision that it would be best if they not allow Norma Jeane to spend any more time at the Bolenders'. They felt it would just make her adjustment to her new life all the more difficult.

"Meanwhile, Gladys's depression was deepening during this time and she seemed more confused than ever," said Esther Thompson, whose mother, Ruth, worked with Grace at Consolidated. The two were very close friends. "She said she needed more time to make some changes. She wanted to be more settled and possibly even be living in a house when she finally had her daughter in her care. Then Grace, who believed that anything was possible, encouraged her that such a thing could happen if they just put their heads together."

It's interesting that Grace McKee felt so certain she and Gladys would be able to buy a home, given that the economy in America was in such desperate shape in 1933. Almost fifteen million Americans were unemployed. Of these, about two million were wandering aimlessly about the country in search of work. Hundreds of thousands of people were homeless, living in tents or abandoned ramshackle dwellings. Banks in thirty-eight states were forced to close as anxious investors began withdrawing all of their deposits. It's almost impossible to imagine the country in such turmoil, but indeed the Great Depression was a devastating time in our history. From the beginning, America's new president, fifty-one-year-old Franklin Delano Roosevelt, tried to restore popular confidence. "The only thing we have to fear," he said in his inaugural address in March 1933, "is fear itself—nameless, unreasoning, unjustified terror." One thing was certain about Grace McKee, and that was that she was fearless. Her confidence that she would find a way inspired Gladys to believe that maybe their future would be a bright one, despite what was going on all around them.

Therefore, it was the two women's decision to give Norma Jeane to yet another foster family—the Atkinsons—but just temporarily.

George and Maud Atkinson, both English, were in the periphery of show business as bit players in films. George had also worked as a stand-in for George Arliss, the distinguished British actor and the first Brit to win an Academy Award as Best Actor. He and Maud had a young daughter named Nellie who was around Norma's age. It was decided that Norma Jeane could be happy with them while Gladys and Grace strategized their next move.

Roosevelt had promised that he would not stand by and watch the Depression deepen. He wanted to restore the public's confidence in the government, and to that end he established a number of programs between 1933 and 1938 in his so-called New Deal for the country, a way to give relief and reform to Americans during such incredibly difficult times. Indeed, in order to make it possible for Americans with small incomes to purchase homes with low-cost mortgages, he established the Home Owners' Loan Corporation. In July 1933, Grace did her research and figured out a way for Gladys to take advantage of Roosevelt's plan. She took care of all of the paperwork and navigated her way through all of the red tape in order to help make a real estate purchase. However, at the last minute, Grace had second thoughts about the timing of such a financial commitment after hearing the studio they worked for was going on strike and knowing that would mean trouble for them.

In August, Gladys purchased a two-story home with three bedrooms on Arbol Drive near the Hollywood Bowl. Gladys made the down payment of $5,000 by obtaining a loan from the Mortgage Guarantee Company of California. Interestingly, on the application she falsely stated that she was "Gladys Baker, a married woman."

Once in the home, Gladys was unsure about raising Norma Jeane there. She simply could not get past the notion—or the excuse—that Norma Jeane would be unhappy, no matter how much Grace tried to convince her that this was not the case. In the end, Gladys was just nervous having Norma Jeane and assuming responsibility for her. It's understandable. After all, she knew in her heart that she was unstable and was never sure how she would react to everyday situations. From time to time, she still heard those voices in her head, scaring her, taunting her, warning her of some imminent—and in truth, nonexistent—reality.

It was Grace's idea to have the Atkinsons move in with Gladys and Norma Jeane so that Gladys wouldn't feel the weight of too much responsibility. As it happened, the Atkinsons were having a difficult time financially and decided it would be a good idea. Though this was a strange turn of events, it did make Gladys more comfortable.

Whereas the Bolenders were religious and, where Ida was concerned, quite strict, the Atkinsons were more easygoing in nature. "They liked to drink a little, smoke, dance and sing and play cards, all the things that I had been taught were sinful," Marilyn Monroe would recall many years later. "And they still seemed like very nice people to me."

One day, George Atkinson showed Norma Jeane a magazine with the actress Joan Bennett on the cover and said that she looked like a younger version of Bennett. Norma Jeane didn't think she resembled Bennett at all, she later said, "but it was an interesting moment for me. It made me think . . ." Indeed, it was during the months that she knew the Atkinsons that Norma Jeane began to appreciate films and start to wonder what it might be like to be on the screen herself.

The early 1930s were an interesting time in show business history. The strains of FDR's rousing campaign song, "Happy Days Are Here Again," were still ringing in the ears of Americans in 1933, but Hollywood's output did not reflect the same euphoria and upbeat mood. At least not yet. Dominating the film capital's output in 1932 had been crime dramas from Warner Bros. (*Scarface, I Am a Fugitive from a Chain Gang*, both starring Paul Muni); horror pictures (*Freaks, Murders in the Rue Morgue, White Zombie, The Old Dark House, The Mummy*); the star-heavy *Grand Hotel* and the back-to-nature jungle movie *Tarzan the Ape Man*, both from MGM; and Marlene Dietrich's vampy eastern, *Shanghai Express*. Quigley's Almanac's first annual Top Ten list of movie stars for 1932–33 was headed by sixty-four-year-old character actress Marie Dressler. She would be dead within two years from cancer, but her place would shortly be taken by the world's soon-to-be most popular child star of all time, Shirley Temple. The following year, 1933, was a different picture, with a mix of Top Ten film fare that included three musicals from Warner Bros.—*42nd Street*, *Footlight Parade*, and *Gold Diggers of 1933*. Grace knew just about all there was to know about all of these films—who was in them, who directed them, who produced them. She delighted in bringing Norma Jeane to see these kinds of films with the Atkinsons and encouraged the little girl that, one day, it might be her up on that screen.

Though Gladys didn't know what to make of her daughter's sudden interest in being an entertainer, she did sometimes take Norma Jeane to Grauman's Chinese Theatre to see the latest film. Like many generations of movie buffs to come, Norma Jeane Mortensen would put her hands and feet into the cement imprints of famous stars of the day, thrilled at the opportunity to be so "close" to the actors and actresses she'd grown to love by their work in her favorite movies. It's worth noting, though, that during this time Norma Jeane would also feel the influence of the Bolenders in her life. She would remember feeling somewhat guilty about enjoying the more carefree lifestyles of Gladys, the Atkinsons, and even Grace. Therefore, she would get down on her knees at night and pray for all of them—as Ida Bolender might have insisted—in the hope that they be forgiven their sins.

The Voices Return

For just a few months—August until October—life was relatively tranquil for young Norma Jeane Mortenson. She was adjusting well to living with Gladys and the Atkinsons. In September

1933, Norma Jeane enrolled in the second grade at the Selma Avenue elementary school, and she seemed to be settling in with her fellow classmates and teachers. As far as she was concerned, it felt like Gladys was really trying to make it work with her, which no doubt gave her a sense of security. Would it have been too much to ask for it to last more than two months?

Unfortunately, in October, everything was ruined by a letter Gladys received from her former brother-in-law, Audrey. She hadn't heard from him in years. Now he was writing to give her the horrible news that her thirteen-year-old son, Jackie, had died back in August of tuberculosis of the kidneys. Gladys always hoped that her children were happy in the care of their father and his wife. She didn't know that Jasper had done a questionable job of raising Jackie. For instance, he'd taken him out of the rehabilitation center against the advice of doctors. Then, there was an incident with a firecracker, which cost the boy an eye. Shortly after, his kidneys began to fail him. "Daddy should have taken him to the hospital," Gladys's daughter Berniece once recalled. "Finally, Jackie's kidneys failed completely."

Remember that Jackie and Berniece had been born into a relatively stable home. In their first few years, Gladys had every intention of raising them herself. After they were taken from her by Jasper, Gladys reconciled the loss and began to wait for the unfolding of a different period in her life, one where she would be emotionally equipped to be a mother to her two children. She believed that day would come when the children were adults.

In contrast, Norma Jeane was born under vastly different circumstances: illegitimately to a single mother fighting a losing battle with her own psyche. Gladys knew she was giving up this baby—there was no question about it. In her reasoning, Norma Jeane was the child who mattered the least to her. Of course, Norma Jeane always sensed as much. However, on this day, she was reminded of her place in the cruelest of ways. In her anguish, Gladys lashed out at her, "Why wasn't it you? *Why wasn't it you?*" Gladys felt she could have dealt with Norma Jeane's death—but not Jackie's.

After that awful day, Norma Jeane had no choice but to watch as her mother went from bad to worse.

Shortly after the news of Jackie's death, Gladys received a telephone call from a family member: Her grandfather had passed away. During the call, her cousin went on for some time about how Tilford Marion Hogan had apparently gone mad before his death. Also, it wasn't a death from natural causes—he had hanged himself. Gladys believed that both her parents had gone mad, and now her grandfather too? Worse yet, she had always wondered about her own sanity. With that phone call, the question grew louder: Was she next?

Gladys had tried to disregard the voices in her head for many years. But with tragedy all around her, they became more insistent, impossible to ignore. In trying to cope with her two recent losses, she became delusional, saying that she had heard her son calling out to her, beckoning her to come outside and play with him. She also said she saw her grandfather sitting in different rooms in the house. Both of the Atkinsons were alarmed enough to not even want to be near her. For her part, Grace was also frightened and at a loss as to how to handle the desperate situation—unusual for her in that she was a formidable woman capable of solving almost every problem. However, this one seemed to have no solution. Gladys was slipping away. "It was as if a light went out in her," Grace would later say. "From that time on, she was in total darkness."

As if fate hadn't dealt Gladys enough disappointment and misery, more was on its way. Within weeks of her learning of the suicide of her grandfather, the studio where she and Grace worked was struck by the union. "It seemed like a lot of things happened all at once to put pressure on her," Grace later told Berniece in what was arguably an understatement.

The first few months of 1934 were dreadful. Norma Jeane spent most of this time watching her mother go further out of her mind. "The poor child witnessed so many hair-raising experiences in the first six months of that year, it's hard to imagine the way it may have shaped her life," said Mary Thomas-Strong. "When family members talk about this time, they tend to gloss over it. I think it's because everyone knows that Norma Jeane suffered through it in many ways, and that there was nothing anyone could do about it. She was living in the house with a mother who was going crazy. Who knows what day-to-day horrors she witnessed? I can tell you, though, that Grace was concerned enough to ask Ida to talk to the girl."

Indeed, during this time, Ida did telephone Norma Jeane. "Do you want to come back here and live with us, dear?" she asked, unable to keep the concern from her voice. "Because if that's what you want, Daddy will come and get you. In fact, I think that would be best." Norma Jeane said that she would have to ask her Aunt Grace for permission. (Norma Jeane knew that Grace wasn't really her aunt, but she liked to call her so.) When she did, however, Grace became extremely upset and phoned Ida back immediately. "I asked you to speak to the girl just to tell her you still loved her," Grace said angrily, according to the family's history. "I certainly didn't think you were going to try to take her from us again." Again? Ida's feelings were immediately hurt. "All I have ever wanted is for that child to feel that she was loved," she told Grace. "How dare you speak to me like this! I love her too. I raised her for seven years! Have you forgotten?" Grace hung up on her. It would seem that, by this time, raw nerves were barely being controlled.

By the middle of 1934, it was clear that *something* needed to be done for Gladys. Grace finally decided to take her to a neurologist, where Gladys spent a day undergoing a battery of tests. However, no doubt because mental care in the 1930s was so unsophisticated, there was no clear-cut diagnosis. It was simply decided that she was going insane and there was nothing anyone could do about it.

Then one day Grace came home and found Gladys lying on the couch, having what appeared to be some sort of seizure. "She started kicking and yelling," Grace later recalled. "She was lying on her back, staring up at the staircase and yelling, 'Somebody's coming down those steps to kill me.'"

There are many conflicting accounts of what happened in the following minutes, some claiming that Gladys had brandished a knife in order to fight off her imagined "attackers." Marilyn remembered the fallout of the event in her memoir. She and "the English couple" (the Atkinsons) were having breakfast when she heard someone fall down the stairs. It was her mother. Though she was told to stay in the kitchen, the little girl peeped out and managed to catch a glimpse of Gladys screaming, laughing, and acting in a completely irrational manner. With eyes alert and knowing— not even fearful—Norma Jeane seemed to realize that this moment would be a defining one where her mother was concerned. Indeed, Gladys Baker had suffered a severe psychotic break. Because it appeared that she was now a danger to herself and others, the police were called and it was quickly determined that she would be sent for psychiatric evaluation.

Once she was at a hospital, a number of doctors came to the same conclusion. Gladys was diagnosed as being paranoid schizophrenic and would now have to be committed to the state mental institution, Norwalk Hospital, indefinitely. It seemed to have happened so fast—or had it? Truly, it had been coming for years. Schizophrenia is an often misunderstood brain disorder that affects over 1 percent of the country's adult population. Each year more than one hundred thousand people are diagnosed with schizophrenia in the United States alone. One in four of them will attempt suicide at least once in their lifetime, and one in ten will succeed. Paranoid schizophrenia— a severe and disabling form of the condition—has frightening symptoms, which most commonly include sufferers hearing voices, thinking others can read their minds, and believing that plots are being developed to harm them. Often, schizophrenics have no signs of the disease until a certain period after adolescence, when a mental shift takes place. While this change in behavior occurs earlier in men (their late teens and early twenties), women sufferers can experience this dramatic shift later, usually in their twenties and thirties.

It's worth noting that this terrible diagnosis came with some sense of relief for Gladys, as well as for those who loved her. After years of worrying about a total mental collapse in the future, that fear was now relegated to the past. At thirty-two, Gladys Baker had spent much of her life battling the voices—and now, undoubtedly, the voices had won.

Grace Is Norma Jeane's Legal Guardian

With Gladys in the sanitarium for an indeterminate period of time, the question, as always, remained: What to do about Norma Jeane?

As an adult, Marilyn Monroe would recall having overheard a conversation between Grace McKee and friends as they tried to convince her not to take on the responsibility of raising the child. They said she was a "mental case." Marilyn said that she lay in bed "shivering" because even though she didn't know what a mental case was, she was sure it wasn't good. Indeed, Grace's friends talked about all of the people in Norma Jeane's family who had mental problems and said they were sure the same fate would befall the little girl. Still, Grace decided that she would take care of her friend's daughter, somehow. She soon filed the necessary papers and became her legal guardian.

It was decided, though, that Norma Jeane would continue to live, at least for the time being, with the Atkinsons. Therefore, for the rest of 1934, she stayed with them in the Arbol Drive home. After just becoming accustomed to having her mother around, now she had to readjust to living without her. For weeks, she would ask where Gladys was and when she was going to return. Even though she'd had that terrible exchange with her mother where her mother wished her dead, Norma Jeane felt that they'd gotten closer in recent months. She was finally happy. Now it seemed as if it were all over, and she wanted to know why. As always, Grace was very patient with her. "Your mommy is gone, sweetheart," she told her, "and she's not going to be back for a long time. But I'm here for you now."

Following the union strike at Consolidated Studios, Grace was working at Columbia Pictures in the movie company's film library. Because she worked on the periphery of show business, she knew a great many people in the movie business and often discussed with them the current crop of movie stars and their careers at Columbia. Columbia Pictures, though, was considered a "poverty row" operation, not the huge film company it would become in later years.

In the early 1930s, Columbia was a fledgling company that laid claim to the most popular comedy trio of the day, the Three Stooges, who would display their screwball slapstick comedy in 190 short films between 1934 and 1957. The studio's primary focus was low-budget comedies, westerns, Saturday afternoon serials, and any story that could be shot in a week and in theaters in another week. Speed and economy were its strong suits, and Columbia was the best studio in Hollywood for that kind of fare. Grace was inspired by her surroundings and began to wonder if perhaps she could become involved in the movie business in some way other than as a film cutter.

As Grace came to know Norma Jeane better, she began to believe that the young girl had some potential in show business, maybe as an actress. Not only was she very pretty, but there was something more complex about her. Her eyes were large and intelligent. She was interesting to look at, to watch. She had unusual charisma for such a young child. Of course, it is easy to make such a retrospective judgment about the girl who would one day become Marilyn Monroe, but it was really true just the same. Grace told everyone she knew that she had a strong feeling about the child and that, as she put it, "there might be something there." Today it would be said that what Grace perceived in Norma Jeane was the "X" factor—a quality that can't be described but that somehow conveys stardom.

"My mother told me that Grace would dress her up in the prettiest little outfits and bring her to work," recalls Dia Nanouris, whose mom was an assistant film editor at Columbia. "She doted on her and seemed to love her very much, as if she was her own daughter. In fact, most people did think they were mother and daughter.

"Grace was a big fan of Jean Harlow's and my mom thought it

was Jean Harlow's career that Grace had in mind for Norma Jeane. One thing was sure, Grace had made up her mind that Norma Jeane would be in show business, and from what was known about Grace, once she had her mind made up about something, it usually happened. She took Norma Jeane to see several Jean Harlow films back then and talked a lot about Harlow to the little girl."

Arriving in Hollywood during the declining years of the silent era, Jean Harlow (née Harlean Carpenter) traveled the usual starlet route, appearing in Hal Roach shorts and bit parts in forgettable films, before her career took off like a rocket thanks to the legendary Howard Hughes, who cast her in the principal female role in his 1930 World War I aviation epic, *Hell's Angels*, an international blockbuster. She would appear in five films the following year for five different studios, including *The Public Enemy*, a groundbreaking gangster film that established James Cagney as a superstar and Warner Bros. as the premier studio for the gangster genre. This was also the year—1931—that Columbia Pictures' top director, Frank Capra, cast her in a film, *Platinum Blonde*, whose title provided her with a lifelong identification.

Grace McKee's prediction about Norma Jeane's film future was perhaps more prescient than even she could have imagined. *Saratoga*, Jean Harlow's last film, though incomplete, costarred Clark Gable, and with an irony that's hard to ignore, Marilyn's last film *completed* was *The Misfits*, also starring Gable. (Some Monroe biographers list as her final film *Something's Got to Give*, but the picture was never finished and never released to theaters.)*

---

* Besides appearing as Clark Gable's leading ladies in their cinematic swan songs, Harlow and Monroe share a couple of other coincidental parallels in their lives. Like Marilyn would do years later, seventeen-year-old Jean Harlow was photographed nude (in Griffith Park in 1928 by Edward Bower). Harlow would also be the first movie star to appear on the cover of *Life* magazine, in the edition of May 3, 1937. Similarly, Marilyn appeared on the cover of the first issue of *Playboy*, in August 1954.

Marilyn was once shown the script of a proposed biopic on Harlow, but turned it down after reading it, reportedly telling her agent, "I hope they don't do that to me after I'm gone." Of course, they did do that to her after she was gone—many times, in fact. And among the first to do it was her ex-husband Arthur Miller, who based his main character in *After the Fall* on an unflattering portrait of Marilyn.

"There was something a little unusual about Grace's intense interest in Jean Harlow," recalled Dia Nanouris. "My mom said that every time she brought the girl to work it was like an audition. She would have her prance about and pose or pout. 'Show them how pretty you are, Norma,' she would say. 'Just like Jean Harlow! Or show them how you smile. Just like Jean Harlow. Show them.' My mom thought it was strange. After all, Norma Jeane was just eight. The girl was wearing a little bit of makeup, she had her hair curled, and Grace was talking about having her nose 'fixed'! Grace gave her an enormous wide-brimmed hat to shield her little face from the sun. 'Doesn't it look stylish?' she would ask. But Grace was always a little eccentric. If you look at pictures of her back then, she had peroxided blonde hair, wore a lot of makeup—but wore it well. She wasn't trashy. She was very theatrical. When I see those pictures today in family scrapbooks, I can't help but think, yes, this is where Marilyn Monroe got it from."

Marilyn Monroe summed it up best herself: "Aunt Grace would say things to me like no one else would ever talk to me. . . . She would sit me down and tell me things and hold my hands. I felt as whole as a loaf of bread nobody's eaten."

Norma Jeane's Troubling Visit with Gladys

Late in 1934, it was decided that Gladys Baker would be able to obtain leave from the sanitarium on occasional weekends. Because her medication seemed to be working, her doctors thought it might be beneficial if she were able to travel in the outside world, just as long as her time away from the facility was supervised by a responsible person. Grace, of course, was eager for her friend to regain some sense of normalcy in her life and said she would be more than happy to be accountable for her during these intermittent sojourns.

However, as it would happen, these weekends with Gladys—once every month or so—which began in September, were to be quite difficult. Gladys, though better than she was when first institutionalized, was still not well.

On one such weekend in late November 1934, Grace took Gladys and Norma Jeane to the Ambassador Hotel for what she hoped would be a lovely lunch in elegant surroundings. The Ambassador, a grand, sprawling hotel on Wilshire Boulevard in Los Angeles, was quite the "in" place at this time, its Coconut Grove nightclub a destination point for an evening on the town for some of Hollywood's biggest stars. In fact, because the sixth annual Academy Awards presentation had taken place in its Fiesta Room eight months earlier, Grace was certain that a luncheon at such an auspicious place would be a special treat for all of them. Moreover, Grace was proud of the physical transformation that had taken place in her little charge over the last year, and she wanted Gladys to see it for herself.

Norma Jeane now wore her long blonde hair in dangling curls. Of course, she had those cornflower blue eyes, and now even a touch of red brushed across her pouting lips. Somehow, she seemed much more precocious than the last time Gladys saw her. Actually, some in Grace's circle found the makeover a tad disconcerting. It was as if Norma Jeane were far more mature than her eight years, perhaps even being forced into adulthood—not that her childhood had been, thus far, one to cherish. However, Grace had a specific image of how she wanted the youngster to appear and comport herself in public, and she'd spent many hours tutoring her in order that she would rise to those standards. For instance, she'd taught her to curtsy, to be polite, to look people in the eyes when speaking to them, and also to speak clearly and enunciate every syllable. It was as if Grace were running a charm school with only one pupil.

According to a later recollection, when Gladys laid eyes on this new version of her daughter, she didn't seem interested one way or the other. "I think we could have eaten in the coffee shop downstairs and that would have been a lot better than this," she told

Grace, ignoring Norma Jeane from the outset. She seemed angry. In fact, the severity of her expression did not change during the entire meal. "I shouldn't be in that place," she kept insisting, speaking of the sanitarium, "and I want out."

Obedient and very quiet, Norma Jeane just picked at her food while Grace struggled to engage Gladys in conversation.

In truth, Gladys was too self-involved at this point in her sickness to care about Norma Jeane or anyone else. So immersed was she in her mental illness and in her desire to obtain her freedom, it didn't matter to her that her daughter was sitting before her. This kind of scene would be repeated for many years to come, whenever Norma Jeane would have an occasional weekend with her mother. "I just don't think she even liked me very much, let alone loved me," is how the adult Marilyn would recall it. Of course, there were myriad reasons for Gladys's emotional disconnect from her daughter, so many that it had become impossible for others—like Grace—to even begin to understand the complex machinations of Gladys's mind.

At one point during the troubling meal, Grace said to Norma Jeane, "Tell your mother what you want to be when you grow up." Norma Jeane, perhaps hoping to impress her mother with her exciting goal, turned to Gladys with eager brightness and said, "I want to be a movie star." In response, Gladys just looked at her daughter with eyes cold as steel. Then she went back to her meal without saying a word.

Norma Jeane in an Orphanage

The next chapter in young Norma Jeane's life has always been confusing to Marilyn Monroe historians. In the fall of 1935, Grace McKee decided to take nine-year-old Norma Jeane to the

Los Angeles Orphans' Home Society at 815 North El Centro Avenue in Hollywood.* The question has always been why Grace, who not only had strong maternal instincts toward Norma Jeane but also a goal of stardom in mind for her, would suddenly put her in an orphanage. Some Marilyn Monroe historians have theorized that the Atkinsons had become abusive to Marilyn, though she never suggested as much in any of her interviews. However, Grace McKee did tell Berniece many years later that she learned they had not been treating Norma Jeane well and dismissed them. That may have been true, but the Atkinsons also felt they had film opportunities in London and decided to return to their homeland.

At this same time, Grace became the legal custodian of all of Gladys's affairs and, as such, took on the complicated responsibility of caring for all the loose ends her friend had left behind before being institutionalized. One of her first decisions was to sell Gladys's home in order to pay off her debts, mostly medical expenses. Next on her agenda was the possibility of adopting Norma Jeane. It was just a seed of an idea, but it was something she would discuss openly with her friends (most of whom seemed to be against it). Grace already thought of the girl as her own and she knew that Gladys would not oppose the idea. For her part, there was no one else Norma Jeane would have wanted to be with at this time, other than perhaps her Aunt Ida. She loved her "Aunt Grace" and felt that she could do no wrong.

By this time, Grace had married and divorced a third husband and was on her fourth. That she was barren had become an issue in all three of her earlier marriages. In fact, it was specifically responsible for the demise of at least one of them and caused tension in the other two. In her fourth marriage, she found a man who came with a ready-made family. Her new husband was Ervin Silliman Goddard—known as Doc. Ten years her junior, he was divorced and had custody of his three children, aged nine, seven,

---

* This orphanage was rebuilt in 1956 and a year later renamed Hollygrove Orphanage.

and five. An amateur inventor by trade—thus the nickname—his profession wasn't exactly a lucrative one. Grace felt that she had to make this marriage work. In her forties, she viewed it as her last hope for true happiness. As strong-minded and self-sufficient as she was, she still wanted to have a romantic partner in life. "I just don't want to end up old and alone," she had said. She also felt that little Norma Jeane would be a perfect addition to her new family. However, there was to be a big stumbling block in her way.

Because Norma Jeane had grown so attached to Grace, it became difficult for her to watch her guardian alter her focus and direct some of it not only to a man but, more troubling, to his daughter, Nona, the only one of his three children who was living with him at this time. There's little doubt that it called to mind Norma Jeane's growing abandonment issues. She had lost so much in her nine years, and now it must have felt like she might lose Grace as well. Doubtless in reaction to these disconcerting feelings, Norma Jeane suddenly became obstreperous. She started having surprising temper tantrums and alarming emotional outbursts. She also began making impossible demands of Grace, crying whenever she couldn't be with her. Sometimes she and Nona got along beautifully, but often they did not. Grace found herself being harsh and exacting where Norma Jeane was concerned, and that wasn't like her at all.

Norma Jeane's fear of losing Grace quickly became a self-fulfilling prophecy. Doc felt that they didn't have enough money to support the one child living with them, and he wanted to bring his other two children into the household at some point soon. "I think she has to go," he said of Norma Jeane. Grace feared that if something didn't change very quickly, she would end up alone again. She definitely didn't want to lose her new husband. What she really wanted was to adopt Norma Jeane, bring her into the domestic fold, and have all of them live happily together. At a loss as to how to handle this complicated situation, she made a difficult decision. Taking Norma Jeane for a short, private walk, she explained to her that she would have to put her into an orphanage, "but just for a little while, I promise." Of course, Norma Jeane didn't understand. "I can be a good girl," she said, crying. "Please don't send me away." Grace tried to calm her, but it was useless.

Somehow, it's not known how, Ida Bolender heard that Norma Jeane was going to be sent to an orphanage. " 'Over my dead body' was her reaction," said a relative of hers. "She said that she simply wouldn't allow it. She called Grace and said, 'Please, I am begging you to now allow us to adopt that child. Or, at the very least, let us take care of her again. Don't put her in an orphanage. Think of what's best for her. Her brother and sisters miss her. We love her. She has a home here. Don't do this!' "

It was clear that, by this time, Grace Goddard did not like Ida. In fact, she felt that Ida had been much too territorial where Norma Jeane was concerned. Besides, she had made a promise to Gladys that she would never allow Ida to have the girl again. Gladys had apparently told Grace that she was afraid that if they allowed Ida to ever take in Norma Jeane, they would never see her again. Of course, this was Gladys's sickness talking, yet Grace allowed it to influence her. Thus the two women had it in their heads that Ida Bolender was the enemy, and there was nothing Ida could do to change that perception.

Ida Bolender wrote Grace Goddard a long letter at this time, reminding her of all she had done for Norma Jeane. "We loved her, we cared for her . . . when she was sick, we were there for her. My husband and I feel that we were the only family she had ever known and we would happily take her back rather than see her be sent to a frightening place like an orphanage."

"Thank you for your kind offer," Grace wrote back to Ida. "But we have already made suitable arrangements for Norma Jeane."

On September 13, 1935, Grace packed up Norma Jeane's things in one suitcase and one shopping bag and drove the little girl to her new home.

"I thought I was going to a prison," Marilyn would remember many years later. "What had I done that they were getting rid of me? I was afraid of everything and afraid to show how scared I was. All I could do was cry."

Norma Jeane was nine years old when she found herself in the Los Angeles Orphans' Home. The adult Marilyn Monroe would always paint her time there—roughly a year and a half, from 1935 to mid-1937—as one of the darkest periods of her life. "Do you know what it's like to be forced into uncertainty?" she once asked. She would also recall that she did not feel like an orphan since her mother was still alive and she also had her Aunt Grace. She didn't want to go to the orphanage, and she stood on the steps of the building crying out, "But I'm not an orphan. I'm not an orphan." It was just another cruel twist of fate in a life already filled with this kind of despair.

Magda Bernard's stepbrother, Tony, was at the Los Angeles Orphans' Home at the same time as Norma Jeane. She recalls, "My family's circumstances were such that Tony had to stay at the orphanage until we could take him in, but we went to visit him every week. I clearly remember Norma Jeane as being this pretty blue-eyed girl with a big heart who seemed to just want to be loved. She was a beautiful but somehow sad-seeming child.

"The orphanage wasn't as bad as you might think it was if you judge it only on what Norma [as an adult] would say about it. Personally, I think they did a pretty good job with the kids. There were about sixty children there, twenty-five of them being girls. There were twelve beds to a room. The age range was from about six to fourteen.

"There were holiday parties, day trips to the beach. The orphanage actually had a beach house, so the kids got to go there quite often and play in the sand and ocean. There were presents for everyone at Christmastime. They had a bit of pocket money for sweets. They went to the circus, had many kinds of day trips like that . . . the Griffith Park Observatory, for instance. They went to the RKO film lot for tours, got to meet celebrities. During the week, they attended the Vine Street School in their gingham uniforms. On Sundays they would get dressed properly so that they could attend the Vine Street Methodist Church. It actually was quite nice for the kids, I think.

"I know in later years Marilyn complained about all of the chores she had to do at the orphanage. I remember reading that she said she had to wash hundreds of dishes and was stuck doing laundry for hours and hours at a time. She said she had to clean toilets and wash floors. She was exaggerating!"

After Marilyn was famous, an orphanage official named Mrs. Ingraham was quoted as saying, "I really don't know why Miss Monroe tells these awful stories about it. And people print them, whatever she says. This story of Marilyn washing dishes is just silly. She never washed any dishes. She never scrubbed toilets. She dried dishes an hour a week. That's all. She had to make her own bed and keep her section of the girls' cottage tidy, and that was all."

"I used to wake up and sometimes I'd think I was dead," Marilyn once told her friend Ralph Roberts of this time, "like I had died in my sleep, and I wasn't part of my body anymore. I couldn't feel myself and I thought that the world had ended. Everything seemed so far away and like nothing else could bother me."

Perhaps what's most interesting about these terrible days in her childhood is the way Marilyn described how she would pass the time. She would fall back into her fantasy world, and now her dreams were about being picked from the lot of other children as something special. "I dreamed of myself becoming so beautiful that people would turn to look at me when I passed," she would recall. "I dreamed of walking very proudly in beautiful clothes and being admired by everyone—men and women—and overhearing words of praise. I made up the praises and repeated them aloud as if someone else were saying them."*

---

* Of course, she would get her wish—men *and* women. An interesting story from Marilyn Monroe historian James Haspiel: "She had a 'Man Friday' named Peter Leonardi who drove her around the city. His sister, Marie, went shopping with Marilyn one day to Saks Fifth Avenue. When they got back to Marilyn's apartment at the Waldorf Towers, they were going to try on the clothing. But Marilyn felt she should take a bath before she put on the new clothes. So she went into the bathroom and got into the bathtub and the two women continued talking, Marie from the living room. Finally, Marilyn said, 'Come in here, so I can hear you.' Marie, this 100 percent heterosexual female, went to the bathroom door and, later, she said to me, 'Jimmy, I looked into the tub and she was so breathtakingly beautiful, I couldn't believe it. Even her *toes* were beautiful. And I felt myself being drawn into the bathtub with her, and I said, "Marilyn, I have to leave. Right now!" I was going to go over there and make a fool of myself, if I didn't leave at once!'"

Grace v. Ida

*G*race Goddard felt that she had no choice but to place Norma Jeane Mortensen in an orphanage, but she was still devoted to her. Life just hadn't worked out the way she had hoped, but she remained determined to one day find a way to bring Norma Jeane back to the Goddard home. Meanwhile, she visited Norma Jeane every week, bringing her presents and new clothing. Often she would take the little girl off the property and to the movies. "She felt terrible about it," said Bea Thomas. "Every time she went, she'd leave crying. But while she was with her they would talk about movies and Grace used to tell Norma Jeane, 'One day you'll be just like Shirley Temple. Just wait and see.' She still had this idea that Norma Jeane was going to be in films, but she had switched her ideal from Jean Harlow to Shirley Temple."

An interesting twist occurred in Norma Jeane's daily activities at the orphanage when Ida and Wayne Bolender began visiting her. It was no surprise that they wanted to see her, given their strong feelings for her. Norma Jeane was overjoyed to see them. She still thought of them as her parents, and if it had been up to her, she no doubt would have very much preferred living with them and her foster siblings rather than with strangers in an orphanage. As it happened, each time Ida came to the orphanage with warm chocolate chip cookies and hand-me-down clothing from one of Norma Jeane's siblings, the girl would parrot back to her the notion that she was one day going to be the next Shirley Temple. Soon, even Ida began encouraging her in her Shirley Temple fantasies. When Norma Jeane mentioned as much to Grace, she became suspicious. She felt it strange that the religious and often sanctimonious Ida Bolender had suddenly begun endorsing Norma Jeane's show business aspirations. The more Grace thought about it, according to her relatives, the unhappier she became about it. After all, times were tough. Wayne Bolender was a mailman and government jobs were in jeopardy during the Depression. Did Ida think that she might have an opportunity to one day exploit Norma Jeane for profit? The girl was uncommonly pretty and maybe even talented. Grace speculated that if she was so convinced that it could happen— that the girl could one day become famous—who was to say that Ida didn't think so as well?

"When Grace would ask Norma Jeane what she and Ida talked about, it was always 'Shirley Temple, Shirley Temple, Shirley Temple,'" said Bea Thomas. "Grace didn't like it. She disliked Ida already, and for Ida to now take an interest in Norma Jeane's movie star aspirations was just a little too strange. I wouldn't go so far as to say that Grace herself wanted to exploit her in films, but . . . well, all I can say is that she didn't want Ida visiting Norma Jeane, that's for sure."

Indeed, on December 5, 1935, Grace wrote a stern letter to the orphanage's headmistress, Sula Dewey—a kindly older woman who looked like a prototype grandmother—to tell her in no uncertain terms that no one was allowed "to see or talk to little Norma Jeane Baker unless you have my written permission to do so." (Sometimes Norma Jeane was called Baker; no one was ever consistent with her last name, not even Grace.) Moreover, Grace was very specific in her letter that one person who was definitely barred from visiting the girl was Ida Bolender. She wrote that Norma Jeane was very upset every time Ida came to call. It might have been true. Mrs. Dewey wrote back to Grace and confirmed, "Norma is not the same since Mrs. B. visited with her. She doesn't look as happy." In the end, the headmistress concluded, "I'll do as you have requested." However, in a follow-up letter, Mrs. Dewey seemed to have a change of heart: "I think that it's probably not in her best interest to evaluate Norma Jeane's moods based on her visitors. We have noticed that this is a child who can sometimes be very unhappy for no apparent reason. In thinking about it, maybe it is not best to keep her from Mrs. B. I had a long conversation with Mrs. B yesterday when she telephoned me. I am convinced that she is not the problem. I would like to have a meeting with you to discuss Mr. and Mrs. B's future visitations." Grace responded immediately with a very terse note: "Please do as I say. I have good reason for my wishes. Thank you for honoring them."

"I think all of this business said much more about Grace, than it did Ida," Bea Thomas posited. "Please. Ida had no thought of trying to get Norma Jeane into the movies in order to exploit her. How would she have gone about it? She had no connections. It was Grace who had all the connections. In my mind, this just spoke to Grace's own very strange paranoia.

"It got extremely contentious between the two ladies, especially when Ida found out she was barred from visiting Norma Jeane. You can imagine her reaction when she got to the orphanage one day and was told in no uncertain terms by Mrs. Dewey that she could not visit the little girl. Let's just say she did not go quietly into the night."

Finally, on June 26, 1937, Norma Jeane left the Los Angeles Orphans' Home to live once again with Grace and Doc Goddard. A month earlier, the young actress whom Grace had hoped to fashion Norma Jeane after—Jean Harlow—had died at just twenty-six. With typical flair for the dramatic, Marilyn Monroe recalled many years later that she had a "strange feeling I was being set free into a world in which Jean Harlow no longer lived."*

Grace had hoped that when Norma Jeane moved back into her home, she would be able to convince Doc that she belonged there. However, it was not meant to be. The second time Norma Jeane was with the Goddards, there was enough domestic turmoil to convince Grace that, again, her marriage could be in jeopardy. It's difficult to believe that one little girl could cause so much havoc, and in retrospect it sounds like Grace experienced problems with Doc that probably had nothing to do with Norma Jeane. He was drinking heavily at this time, and Marilyn would recall many years later that he made her feel extremely uncomfortable. "A couple of

---

* In October 1947, ten years after Norma Jeane left the orphanage, Mrs. Dewey wrote to Grace Goddard to ask how the girl was faring. Grace wrote back, "Norma Jean [sic] Baker has great success in pictures and promises to be a star. She is a very beautiful woman and is now acting as Marilyn Monroe."

times he said, 'Aren't you going to give me a kiss?' I would sneak out of the room. He scared me." However, six months after she got to the Goddards', her bags were being packed and she was on the move once again. "But I really want to stay here," she told Grace. "I know," Grace responded. "But it's time for you to go." Indeed, it was always time for Norma Jeane to go, wasn't it? Perhaps Grace should have just left her in the orphanage. However, every time she went to visit her, the girl was so clearly miserable.

In December 1937—around the time eleven-year-old Norma Jeane was enrolled in the Lankershim Elementary School—Grace asked the girl's aunt, Olive Monroe, to take her into her home in North Hollywood. Olive Monroe had her own problems. Ten years earlier, her husband, Marion Otis—Gladys's brother, the one who had been banished from the family by Della—had deserted her and her three children. Her mother, Ida Martin, a strict disciplinarian, had moved in with her and the two did not get along well. The broken family had little money and was barely scraping by. It's a wonder that Olive agreed to take in Norma Jeane, and that Grace asked her to do so suggests that Grace must have been quite desperate to find a home for her little charge. Once she got there, Norma Jeane didn't like living with the Monroes at all. "The other kids knew I was related to them," she recalled, "but I felt on a desert island with natives or primitive people out of the hills of Appalachia. I was more alone and separated from anything than I had ever been. I was feeling the predicament of my life, and that frightened and depressed me so much I would get sick and couldn't eat. When I did I would often throw up." As an adult, Marilyn would later recall that she was last in line after her cousins for "everything from breakfast to play time to bath time and then bed."

Norma Jeane Learns She Has a Half Sister

By the winter of 1938, Gladys Baker was more desperate than ever as she continued her unhappy life, now as a patient in the Agnews State Hospital in San Jose, California. In fact, she almost managed to escape. Precipitating her attempt was a series of telephone calls from Edward Mortenson, her former husband and the man she'd listed on Norma Jeane's birth certificate as the child's father. Gladys actually thought Mortenson was dead by this time, but he was alive and well and telling her he was interested in resuming their relationship. How could that occur, though, if she was locked up? Gladys—who would prove with the passing of the years to have the greatest determination when it came to trying to gain her freedom—somehow got her hands on a nurse's uniform, put it on, and then slipped out of the sanitarium. It was hours before she was found, walking down the street with no apparent destination. She later explained that Mortenson had promised to meet her at a specific location if she managed to escape, but that he didn't show up. She was returned to the facility with no trouble, though she was heartbroken. Later that same week, when Grace Goddard arrived for a visit, Gladys begged her to "get me out of here." However, Grace knew better. Gladys was obviously mentally incompetent and was exactly where she needed to be at that time in her life. Grace had no choice but to turn down her friend's pleas. However, Gladys then decided to try another route. She wrote to her long-lost daughter, Berniece. Of course, she didn't know exactly how to locate her, so she sent the letter to the address of one of her ex-husband's relatives in Flat Lick, Kentucky. Somehow, the correspondence ended up in Jasper's hands. He wasn't sure how to proceed, but after discussing the matter with his wife he reluctantly decided to give it to Berniece. By this time, Berniece was nineteen. She'd just been married, was living in Pineville, and was pregnant with her first child—Gladys's grandchild.

Berniece was stunned to receive a letter from her mother, a woman she had long ago decided was probably dead. Though she didn't know much about Gladys, what she did know was not favorable. For years, her stepmother, Maggie, had criticized Gladys for leaving her children behind, as if Gladys had had a choice in the matter. Berniece's daughter, Mona Rae Miracle, says that anything her mother learned about Gladys had to be "squeezed like water from a stone from Jasper and Maggie." Berniece, however, was still always curious about her mother and kept a small framed photograph of her on her dresser. Often she would remark to Jasper about Gladys's beauty. Jasper agreed that, indeed, Gladys was a gorgeous woman, but, he said, she was also an irresponsible woman. It seemed clear to Berniece that she would never have much of a relationship with her mother, and so after many years of wondering, she had made up her mind that Gladys was dead. Then, out of the blue, she received a letter from her. Most of Gladys's missive was a long rant begging her daughter to help her get out of the mental hospital. She asked Berniece to get in touch with an aunt of Gladys's, Dora, in Oregon and ask her to also try to get a release for her. Then she gave Berniece some stunning news. She told her that she had a twelve-year-old half sister named Norma Jeane. Gladys also sent Norma Jeane's and Grace Goddard's addresses to Berniece and suggested that she contact both of them.

Berniece was surprised: She was amazed that her mother was alive, stunned to learn that Gladys was in a mental hospital, and shocked to learn that she had a half sister. There was no question about it: She wanted a relationship with her. She decided to first write to Grace. A week later, she received a return letter from Grace, who was elated to hear from her. She suggested that Berniece write to Norma Jeane. Then Grace told Norma Jeane that she had a half sister. "Grace decided that it might do Norma Jeane some good to know that she wasn't really alone in the world," recalled a relative of Grace's, "that she had a family member who wanted to know her. It all seemed to come together at the same time, Gladys's letter to Berniece, Grace's decision that it was the right thing to do to have Berniece contact Norma Jeane, and then telling Norma Jeane about Berniece."

Norma Jeane was astonished to learn that she had a half sister in Kentucky. "It was like the answer to a prayer," said a Monroe family member. "It changed everything for Norma Jeane. She wanted to know Berniece, everything about her. She wrote her a letter and sent a picture of herself. Berniece wrote back immediately with her own photograph. It was an amazing connection from the start. From the very beginning, Norma Jeane signed all of her letters 'Your Sister.' She and Berniece then began a new friendship, one that would last throughout Norma Jeane's life."

"We grew up feeling abandoned," Berniece would explain many years later, "and, though both of us were told we were pretty and talented, we still needed courage and strength. We got that from each other."

Norma Jeane Marries

$\mathcal{I}$n the fall of 1938, it was decided that Norma Jeane Mortensen would go to live with Edith Ana Lower, sister to Grace's father. Lower seemed a better candidate for foster motherhood than most of the adults who took Norma Jeane in over the years. At fifty-eight, she was a kindly, gray-haired woman with a soft face and warm hug who just seemed to want the best for everybody in her life. Divorced but financially secure, she owned a two-story apartment building at 11348 Nebraska Avenue, renting out one unit while she lived in the other. To supplement her income, she also worked as a Christian Science practitioner, meaning she sat and prayed with clients and also instructed them in the teachings of Mary Baker Eddy, the founder of the Christian Science movement. A positive-thinking and extremely spiritual woman, Ana would prove to be an enormous asset in young Norma Jeane's life. Norma Jeane soon referred to her as "Aunt Ana," and the two hit it off immediately.

When Norma Jeane moved in, Ana made it a priority to have inspirational conversations with her in an effort to build her self-esteem. "She would tell her that she should not care what others thought of her," said Marybeth Miller–Donovan, whose aunt, Ethel, was Ana's best friend. "She reminded her that she was a beautiful young girl not only outside but inside as well, and she had no reason to feel like anything less."

About a year and a half after moving in with Ana, Norma Jeane began attending Emerson Junior High School in Westwood at the age of thirteen. Mabel Ella Campbell, her science teacher, once recalled, "She looked as though she wasn't that cared for. Her clothes separated her a little bit from the rest of the girls." Once there, though, she did begin to exhibit more self-confidence, dressing in sweaters that would show off her young figure and even wearing a little more makeup. She began to see herself in a different light, and as she did so, the other students soon followed and she became more popular. It was at this time that she began to recognize the value of her beauty and how she might be able to make it work for her. She also began to see her stunning appearance as its own entity, quite apart from anything sexual. Indeed, it was a magnet that could draw people in. When she realized as much, she started looking for ways to make them love her even more and think she was even more beautiful. She kept adding to the presentation. Makeup. Lipstick. Tighter clothing. Whatever it took to enhance the package, that's what she wanted to do. She began to create a character that people would not only love, but also adore—a process that started at the age of thirteen and would continue all the way up to her death at thirty-six. "I just felt like I was on the outside of the world," she later recalled, "but then, suddenly, everything opened up. Even the girls paid a little attention to me just because they thought, 'Hmmm, she's to be dealt with.' And I had this long walk to school—two and a half miles to school, two and a half miles back—it was just sheer pleasure. Every fellow honked his horn . . . the world became friendly."

True to form in the youngster's life, Norma Jeane's time with Ana would not last long. Now sixty, Ana had a number of health problems, including a serious heart ailment. Reluctantly, in February 1940 she decided to turn the girl back over to Grace and Doc Goddard. At this same time Ana moved to West Los Angeles, and the Goddards moved into her former home in Van Nuys. But before Ana parted ways with Norma Jeane, she was sure to talk to her about being self-sufficient. "You mustn't spend your entire life dependent on others," she told her, according to the recollection of a friend of her family's. "When you grow up, you have to be your own person. I'm not always going to be there for you. In fact, no one will always be there for you."

Hopefully, this time Norma Jeane would be able to blend in with the Goddard family. It looked promising. When Norma Jeane moved back in with Grace and Doc, she became friendly with Doc's daughter, BeBe, and even the extended Goddard relatives. Now that Norma Jeane had more self-confidence, there seemed to be less conflict with the Goddard family.

In September 1941, Norma Jeane and BeBe both enrolled in Van Nuys High School. A problem did arise in getting the two girls back and forth to school, though. Grace's previous residence had been in close proximity to Van Nuys High. Ana's home—where she and Norma Jeane now lived—was quite far from the school. Because Norma Jeane was finally so happy and popular, Grace didn't want to uproot her and enroll her in a different school. As it happened, Grace was still close to her former neighbor, Ethel Dougherty. Grace knew that Ethel's son, Jim, had an automobile. If the girls walked to the Doughertys' home after school, would it be possible for Jim to then drive them back to their own neighborhood? Ethel asked Jim, who was reluctant because he said the girls were young and giggly—he was five years their senior—and he knew he wouldn't have anything in common with them. But he agreed.

Born in Los Angeles on April 12, 1921, James Dougherty was a good-looking young man with tousled brownish blond hair and blue eyes so deep they were almost violet. He wore a small mustache over his massive, toothy grin. Lanky and sturdy, this young man was a real so-called "jock." He was the youngest of five children raised in difficult circumstances, the family always in financial trouble. Popular in school, he was on the football team and was also president of the student body in his senior year. Grace liked him a great deal and thought he would be a good match for Norma Jeane. She even arranged the first date between Jim and Norma Jeane, at a party in 1941. After a few more dates, it became clear that the two were at least mildly interested in one another. Grace's decision to encourage Norma Jeane into a relationship with the older Jim does seem strange, that is until one considers what happened next. At this same time, Doc Goddard got a job as head of East Coast sales at Adel Precision and the Goddards decided to move to Virginia. It was also decided that Norma Jeane would not be going with them. Doc simply didn't want the responsibility of another child at the same time as his big move. So what to do about Norma Jeane now?

Understandably, Norma Jeane was very disillusioned. She trusted Grace implicitly, and now that she was being left behind, she could not help but feel that she'd been betrayed. "Of course she was absolutely right," Jim Dougherty observed. "When Grace had taken her out of the orphanage to her last foster home, she'd told Norma Jeane that she would never have that kind of life again. Norma Jeane felt that Grace had gone back on her word."

With all possibilities exhausted, it looked as if Norma Jeane was going to have to go back to the orphanage until someone adopted her or until she was eighteen, whichever came first. Knowing how unhappy this would make her, Grace Goddard was frantic to find a way to avoid it. Therefore, she hatched a plan with Ethel Dougherty. "What if your son marries Norma Jeane?" Grace suggested. "That would keep her out of the orphanage, and it's not as if they don't already like each other." It seemed like a good idea to Ethel, too, and so she approached her son with it.

As it happened, Norma Jeane would turn sixteen in June, the legal age to marry in California. Though Jim felt that she was too young for him, he had to admit that he liked her. She was pretty and fun. Still, dating her was one matter, marrying her an entirely different one. Many years later when talking about his thought process as a young man, Jim would say that he couldn't think of a good reason to reject the idea, especially if it meant that Norma Jeane would be saved from the orphanage.

For her part, Norma Jeane didn't have much choice in the matter. When she was presented with the idea, she agreed, though reluctantly. Not only had she never seen a marriage work out, but she was afraid of what it would mean being Dougherty's wife. She was particularly concerned about being intimate with him. When she expressed her fears to Grace, Grace tried to be understanding, telling her that she "would learn in time." It does seem, in retrospect, that Grace might have been more understanding of Norma Jeane's fears. However, in the greater scheme of things, it seems that Grace's main objective was to get the girl married as quickly as possible. Grace's friends would say, many years later, that she was just trying to do what she could to keep her charge out of another orphanage. However, some people who are more critical of her feel that Grace just wanted to marry Norma Jeane off in an expedient fashion so that she and her husband could go on with their lives with a clear conscience.

Plans quickly fell into place. At the end of 1942, the Goddards took off for Virginia. Meanwhile, Norma Jeane dropped out of high school in the middle of her sophomore year, saying that she wanted to concentrate on learning how to be a wife. She would always regret it, though, and never felt comfortable about dropping out. "She was sorry she'd done it," Jim said many years later, "and she didn't need to. It was a snap decision, I think, to just end her education. Everything was happening so fast, I think she felt she had to focus on one thing at a time."

The wedding, officiated by a minister, took place on the evening of June 19, 1942, in the home of a friend of the Goddards, Chester Howell. Howell's great-nephew, Alexander, says, "From what I have heard over the years through my family, it was a haphazard affair. The Goddards didn't even attend, which I think was a surprise. Of course, Norma Jeane's mom, Gladys, wasn't present, either. Ida and Wayne Bolender were there, though, and that was a bit of an issue, from what I understand."

Indeed, it was Norma Jeane's decision that she would not get married unless her "Aunt Ida" and "Daddy" were present. By this time, she was well aware of the animosity between Grace and Ida. However, she also knew that Grace was not going to be present at the wedding—she had just gotten to Virginia and wasn't going to turn around and drive back—so she saw no reason not to invite Ida. When she told Ethel Dougherty of her plans, however, Ethel thought it best to alert Grace. Of course, Grace was not at all happy about it. She called Norma Jeane and told her that she would prefer it if she did not invite Ida. She took no issue with Wayne's attendance, she said, but she had to draw the line at Ida's. Norma Jeane said that she was no longer going to be a party to the ill will between her two aunts, and that she wouldn't even consider marrying Jim Dougherty without Ida being present. "In fact, I'll just go back to the orphanage," she said, according to one of Ida Bolender's relatives. "What difference does it make? I was miserable before and I'll be miserable again. I can handle it." Indeed, it would seem that Norma Jeane was becoming a little more like Ida with each passing year—a determined, willful young lady who didn't like being pushed around. In the end, Grace didn't have much choice. She told Norma Jeane to do what she thought was best, but by this time Norma Jeane had already called Ida to invite her to the ceremony, so Grace's opinion was moot.

Norma Jeane not only invited Ida and Wayne Bolender, but all of her foster siblings, including, of course, Nancy Jeffrey, who recalled, "I remember the winding staircase in the living room and all of us just staring at the top of the stairs until she appeared. What a beautiful bride."

As soon as Ida saw Norma Jeane in her embroidered lace wedding dress with long sleeves and veil, she was filled with emotion and began to cry. The girl was just sixteen but she was already showing signs of the striking woman the world would one day come to know as Marilyn Monroe. Her smile was stunning, her eyes a cobalt blue. She was a brunette at this time.

After the ceremony, Ida still couldn't hold back the tears as she stood admiring Norma Jeane. That she had been kept from her former foster daughter for such a long time, and that there had been such a strong, ongoing campaign against her, had worn Ida down over the years where Norma Jeane was concerned. "Thank you so much for inviting us," she told her as she embraced her tightly. "You just don't know what this means to me. You just don't know, Norma Jeane." The bride held both of Ida's hands and looked at her with love. "This day would only be complete with you in it," she told her, now also crying. "Do you think I look pretty, Aunt Ida?" she asked her. Overcome, Ida could only nod her head. Norma Jeane then went to Wayne and hugged him. Dabbing away tears from his eyes, he smiled at her and asked, "Do you have any questions for me? You always had so many questions, Norma Jeane." Everyone laughed. "Just one," Norma Jeane said. "Do you promise to always love me, Daddy?" He smiled. "I do promise," he said. "I really do." And he seemed to mean it.

PART TWO

Transitioning

Crazy?

After they were married, Jim and Norma Jeane Dougherty eventually settled into a small four-room house in Van Nuys, California. Skipping the traditional honeymoon, Jim went back to work at Lockheed and Marilyn began her new life as a wife. She seemed to enjoy setting up the household, getting great pleasure out of deciding which meager furnishings the couple would purchase. Jim left most of these decisions in her hands. Each article was chosen with care: the drinking glasses, the cutlery, even the front doormat. She got a tremendous thrill out of establishing, for the first time, a home that included her as a primary resident. She also always made sure she was showered and dressed when her husband arrived home for supper. She wanted him to feel special, and wanted him to think of her in that way as well.

Jim has said that he felt certain that Norma Jeane was a virgin when he married her. Of course, that makes sense. Probably stating the obvious, he also said that she was extremely inexperienced—he even had to teach her how to use a diaphragm—but that once she caught on, she enjoyed having sex. "It was as natural to her as breakfast in the morning," he noted. "There were never any problems." Over the years, he was fairly indiscreet about private times shared by the couple. "Never had I encountered a girl who so thoroughly enjoyed a sexual union," he recalled. "It made our lovemaking pure joy." He even remembered having sex with her outdoors, in public places when others weren't looking. These remembrances have to be taken with a grain of salt, because Jim apparently also claimed just the opposite about Norma Jeane.

"Jim told me privately that Norma Jeane spent most of their early marriage locked in the bathroom," said Martin Evans, who was a friend of Jim's at the time of his marriage to Norma Jeane. "She had sex books and manuals that were given to her by Grace Goddard, he said, and none of them made a difference. She was scared. From my information, she even asked Grace if it were possible for her to never have sex with Jim. Could they just be friends, she wondered. She was very skittish about having sex with him and, to be honest, I don't think they had a good sex life, ever—despite what Jim later claimed."

In retrospect, we should keep in mind that Jim Dougherty's comments about his sex life with Norma Jeane were made many years after she had become famous as Marilyn Monroe. In fact, they were made many years after her death. At twenty-one, a man marries a girl who, after their divorce, goes on to become one of the greatest sex symbols of all time, a cultural icon. When asked if he was able to satisfy her sexually, is he likely to say he couldn't?

Marilyn Monroe historian James Haspiel, who knew Marilyn from 1954 until her death in 1962, had an interesting take on this subject when he observed, "It could be argued that Jim Dougherty's marriage to Marilyn Monroe was the most significant thing he ever did in his life. What I mean is that a man can live his entire life being terrific at whatever job he does, but how can anything ever top having been married to Marilyn Monroe? It's also the very thing that took him all over the world, doing TV shows and talking about Marilyn. It propelled him into international, eternal fame as her first husband. But then again, anybody who was in her life—and it was known that they were in her life—becomes a great character in history. Doughtery had a role in a classic story, and he played on it, just as he probably should have. And for all we know those may be his actual memories of her."

Here's Marilyn's view of the matter, from her memoir: "The first effect marriage had on me was to increase my lack of interest in sex."

It makes sense that Norma Jeane would have had trepidation about her sex life with Jim. After all, the truth was that she was forced by circumstances to surrender her virginity to a man she barely knew just so that she could stay out of an orphanage. That hardly seems an ideal situation for a young girl who had already experienced such trauma. In fact, Norma Jeane began to find new and inventive ways of avoiding lovemaking with her husband. Jim would later say that he was aware that many, if not all, of her phantom headaches, cramps, and assorted ailments were an attempt at sidestepping her marital obligations. For the most part, as he recalled it, he was patient with her. On one particular night, however, he was insistent. He told her he was going to take a quick shower and that they would then retire to the bedroom and make love. After his shower, Jim came out of the bathroom, expecting to find Marilyn in bed, waiting for him. He didn't. She was gone.

After a cursory search of the household, he determined that she must have quickly grabbed her coat and run out the front door. It was a balmy evening, but she had been wearing her nightgown and he assumed she wouldn't have left wearing just that.

Jim stood at the front window in the darkened living room for the better part of an hour. Then, in the black and motionless streetscape, he saw a shock of white. It was his wife, wearing only the nightgown in which he had last seen her, and she was walking very quickly—almost running—toward the house. Jim quickly moved to the bedroom and pretended to be asleep. A minute later, Norma Jeane bolted through the front door and jumped into the bed next to her husband, clinging to him desperately.

"There's a man after me," she whispered urgently.

"What?"

Norma Jeane repeated that a man was after her. She explained that she needed to leave the house, and as she was walking away she noticed someone following her. Jim said it made sense that she was being followed, given that she was wearing a nightgown. "He probably thinks you're out of your mind," he opined.

Anxiously, Norma Jeane went on to explain that the man she had seen was especially quick. He was in a tree at one point, she recalled. Then she saw him sitting in a darkened house . . . a parked car. To Jim, either this man had superhuman abilities or was, he feared, a figment of his new wife's imagination. She then asked Jim to search the house for her stalker. He disappeared for a moment and came back claiming he had done it. He hadn't, though.

He turned to Norma Jeane, who was now visibly shaking. "See? I told you, there's no one here," he told her calmly. According to what Jim Dougherty recalled to friends, this was the first time he saw his young wife as a woman with more than simple insecurities. He began to wonder if her future might hold the same terrible fate as her mother's.

"But he *was* following me," she replied.

A deep sigh escaped his lips. "Come on, Norma Jeane," Jim said. "This guy couldn't have been everywhere. Don't you see how that sounds crazy?"

Jim's last word—"crazy"—hung in the air as the young woman's anxious and alert eye contact faded. She silently lay down, her expression now blank and distant.

Gladys's Clever Plan

*N*orma Jeane and Jim never again discussed her strange stalking incident. It was just pushed aside as if it hadn't happened. In most other respects, their marriage seemed to be going fairly well into 1943. However, there were other troubling signs. For instance, Norma Jeane insisted on calling Jim "Daddy." Martin Evans, one of Jim's friends at the time, recalled, "He told me he didn't like it. It worried him, considering that she didn't know who her father was and it was an issue for her. He said, 'I don't want her to think of me as her father. I'm her husband.' He also told me that she would threaten to do herself harm if anything happened to their union. 'I'll jump off a bridge, Daddy,' she would say, and it didn't seem like a figure of speech to him. He suspected that she might actually do it. She was intensely insecure but, yes, the Daddy business bothered him the most. He felt that if he corrected her or chastised her, she would melt into tears. He was always walking on eggshells around her, I think."

During this period of time, Norma Jeane's mother, Gladys Baker, was still institutionalized. Gladys's life at the mental hospital in San Jose was, in many ways, one of fantasy. She was constantly in a state of delusion.* She desperately wanted to be released and had done everything she could think of to get out of the sanitarium, even contacting her long-lost daughter, Berniece. However, Gladys seemed to know the sad truth: No one wanted her. Rather than face this, she fantasized a scenario that included her being a part of the lives of her daughter Norma Jeane and even her daughter's father. She was clever in the way she went about trying to manifest it as well. She decided that a man from her past might just provide the ticket she needed to obtain her freedom.

By this time, Grace Goddard had moved to Chicago. During a brief visit to California, she decided to visit Gladys Baker in the San Jose sanitarium, and then visit with her friend Ethel Dougherty in Los Angeles. On the morning Grace came to visit, Gladys told her that she had some stunning news. She revealed that Charles Stanley Gifford—the man with whom she'd begun having an affair before she was divorced from Edward Mortenson so long ago—was Norma Jeane's father. Of course, as the story goes, Gladys had told Gifford that he was the baby's father seventeen years earlier when she got pregnant, but he refused to believe her. Grace was not surprised by Gladys's revelation. The two women had talked about Gifford in the past and Grace had her suspicions, but this was the first time Gladys actually confirmed them.

So what was going on in Gladys's head? What was her motivation behind confiding in Grace? It's not far-fetched that she hoped Grace

---

* An undated letter from Grace Goddard makes clear Gladys's troubled mental state. "She thinks she was sent to State hospital because years ago she voted on a Socialist Ballot," Grace wrote. "[She] sleeps with her head at the foot of the bed [so] as not to look at Marilyn's pictures—they disturb her. . . . [She] wishes she never had a sexual experience so she could be more Christ like."

would tell Norma Jeane the news and that her daughter would then track down Gifford and inform him that he was her father. Then, in Gladys's fantasy, Gifford's response would be to acknowledge his beautiful daughter and decide to start a new life with her. Once father and daughter were at long last united, who would be missing in the equation? Gladys, of course—the mother. Indeed, it would seem that Gladys found a way of possibly enrolling someone entirely new, someone yet to be approached—Charles Stanley Gifford—to get her released from the sanitarium.

After leaving Gladys, Grace didn't know how to proceed with the news. Should she tell Norma Jeane? The girl was finally happy. What would this news do to her? Should she keep it to herself? Truly, she was in a quandary. She decided to talk to her close friend Ethel—Jim Dougherty's mother and Marilyn's mother-in-law.

Ethel was certain that Norma Jeane needed the information. "She deserves to know the truth," she said, according to one account. "But what if it's not true?" Grace wondered. "Can we trust what Gladys says? And how will it affect Norma Jeane?" Ethel was certain that Norma Jeane needed to hear Gladys's news, true or not. "It should come from you," Grace told Ethel. "I think it really should come from a family member."

Of course, Norma Jeane was surprised when Ethel told her that her father was a man named Charles Stanley Gifford. "She had mixed emotions, as I recall it," Martin Evans said, according to what Jim Dougherty had told him. "She was afraid of contacting him, but she knew she had to do it."

On February 1, 1943, Norma Jeane wrote to Grace Goddard and told her that she was looking forward to actually meeting with Gifford. She'd fantasized about her father her entire life, she wrote, and felt certain that he would want to know her as well. After conducting some research, she located two former employees at Consolidated Studios who had known Gifford and from them got his telephone number. Then one night, with Jim and his mother, Ethel, at her side, Norma Jeane nervously made the call.

"This is Norma Jeane," she said, a tremulous quality in her voice.

"I'm Gladys Baker's daughter." A few seconds later, she put down the receiver. "He hung up on me," she said. She began to cry. Jim tried to console her, but, of course, it was difficult.

"That was a real blow, Jim told me," said Martin Evans. "A real blow."

Today, Charles Stanley Gifford Jr., who is eighty-five, refuses to believe that story. "It never happened," he insists. "That sounds like fiction—something she [Marilyn Monroe] created. She made up all kinds of fanciful stories about her life. What I think is that she *told* people she was making that call, and she even *dialed* some number and called *someone*, but it wasn't my father. My father would not have hung up on her. He would have wanted to know more about her, about Gladys. I think she made it up, stood there, dialed a phone . . . then made the whole thing up in front of witnesses."

"She was disappointed," Jim Dougherty said many years later—and he was actually present at the call. "Gifford missed a good chance to be a father. I didn't have much respect for him, obviously. I just gave Norma Jeane some t.l.c. and she eventually came out of it alright. But it was sad."

Trouble in Paradise

Always in the back of their minds was the reality that their marriage was not a love match, which was doubtless one of the primary reasons why Jim and Norma Jeane Dougherty decided early on not to have children. In fact, Norma Jeane was very much afraid of being a mother. She was just seventeen and, as she later put it, "terrified of the thought that I would become pregnant. Women in my family had always made such a mess of mothering." Later she would say that she always had a certain amount of dread that the marriage would end, Jim would take off, and "there would be this little girl in a blue dress and white blouse living in her 'aunt's' house, washing dishes, being last in the bath water on Saturday night."

In the spring of 1943, Jim Dougherty joined the Merchant Marine. He was soon assigned to Catalina Island, just a short cruise ship ride away from Los Angeles. Therefore, he and Norma Jeane were able to take an apartment on the island. The Dougherty marriage was in trouble by the time the couple got to Catalina, though. Norma Jeane was popular there with her little bathing suits and big smile—and he didn't like it. Also, she began to drink alcohol—though not to excess—and that bothered him too, mostly because he was afraid that it might cloud her judgment and cause her to be unfaithful. He needn't have worried, though. "My fidelity was due to my lack of interest in sex," she would later explain.

It's interesting that Norma Jeane referred to a trip she and Gladys took to Catalina in a three-page letter to her half sister, Berniece. (The trip obviously occurred sometime before Gladys was institutionalized.) Responding to the first letter Berniece had sent her, she wrote from Catalina Island. In part, she wrote:

"I just can't tell you how much you look like mother. . . . Aunt Ana [Lower] said that she could see a slight resemblance between you and I and that you looked more like my mother than I did. I have my mother [sic] eyes and forehead and hairline but the rest of me is like my dad. I don't know if you have ever heard of Catalina Island . . . my mother brought me over for the summer when I was about seven yr. old. I remember going to the Casino to a dance with her, of course I didn't dance, but she let me sit on the side and watch her, and I remember it was way after my bedtime too . . . the Maritime Services held a big dance at the same Casino and Jimmie and I went. It was the funniest feeling to be dancing on that same floor ten years later."

She continued, asking Berniece if she and her husband, Paris, would come out to California, and proceeded to give advice on what type of military service Paris should apply for: "the Maritime

Service . . . so a person can disenroll honorably on his own accord and can go about and do pretty much the way he pleases."

She ended the letter with, "I do hope you will write to me and tell me all about yourself. . . . With much love, Norma Jeane. P.S. Thank you again for the picture . . . everyone . . . asks, 'Who's that nice looking couple?' and of course I explain proudly that that is my sister and her husband."

After a year, Jim was transferred to the western Pacific. Despite any problems in the union, saying goodbye to him was still difficult on the day he set sail from San Pedro, California. Norma Jeane tried to be strong in the face of what must have seemed like yet another abandonment in her life, and for the most part she put up a brave front. She moved in with Jim's parents again and waited for word from her husband.

During this time, Norma Jeane Dougherty got her first job, at a place called Radioplane. Located in Burbank, the company manufactured drones, small planes that flew by remote control and were used as targets for war training. Her job was to spray varnish on the pieces that constituted each plane's assembly. "It wasn't an easy job," said Anna DeCarlo, whose mother also worked at Radioplane at the same time. "The hours were long, sometimes up to twelve hours a day. The varnish was smelly. It got in her hair and all over her hands and was impossible to wash away. She was late for work a lot. In fact, she started getting a reputation of being late for everything, all the time. However, she was very popular with the other employees. She was known as being very empathetic, someone you could go to with your problems."

With Jim gone so much of the time, Norma Jeane couldn't help but feel lonely. Therefore, at the end of October 1944 she decided to take all of the money she had earned at Radioplane and go on a trip by rail, first to meet her sister, Berniece, now twenty-five, who had moved to Detroit by this time, and then to see Grace Goddard in Chicago. For Norma Jeane to finally be able to meet her sibling was almost unbelievable to her. She had anticipated it for so long, and the time had finally come. When she got to Detroit she was met at the train station by Berniece, her daughter Mona Rae, and husband, Paris. Paris's sister, Niobe, was also there to meet Norma Jeane.

"Norma Jeane had written to tell me what kind of outfit she would be wearing and what color it would be," Berniece recalled. "Paris and Niobe and I walked out to the tracks and stood waiting while the train screeched to a stop. I wondered which one of us would recognize her first, or if we might possibly miss her. Well, there was no chance of missing her! All the passengers stepping off looked so ordinary, and then all of a sudden, there was this tall gorgeous girl.* All of us shouted at once. None of the other passengers looked anything like that: tall, so pretty and fresh, and wearing what she had described, a cobalt blue wool suit and a hat with a heart shaped dip in the brim."

The visit was a good one, not surprisingly. The two sisters got to know one another and spent a great deal of time talking about family history, trying to put together the pieces of stories they'd heard, and looking at photos of relatives. While studying pictures of Gladys—so beautiful in her youth—Berniece wondered what she looked like now. Norma Jeane said she was "still fairly pretty," but also told her that Gladys never smiled. She also allowed that Gladys was "a stranger" to her. "Part of me wants to be with her," she said, "and part of me is afraid of her."

They also talked about Berniece's father, Jasper, the man who had taken her and her brother from Gladys so long ago and raised them with a new wife. As it turned out, Berniece confessed, she and her father weren't close either. She cited his drinking problem as an issue. She also said that she loved her stepmother very much—the woman who had raised her in Gladys's stead.

The pleasant visit was abruptly ended when Norma Jeane learned that her husband had an unexpected leave. So she raced off to see Grace in Chicago before returning to Van Nuys. It's interesting to note that Norma Jeane was at this time sending

---

* Norma Jeane was five feet five and a half inches tall.

money to her "Aunt" Grace because apparently Grace and Doc had run into financial difficulties. Norma Jeane certainly wasn't making much at her job, but somehow she found a way to be generous with her salary to someone who had loved her very much over the years. It's also noteworthy that she seemed to forgive Grace for abandoning her when she and her family moved to Virginia without her. By this time, Norma Jeane probably knew that life has its complex twists and turns and people don't always get what they want—and that forgiveness is key to getting on with the business of living.

It was when Norma Jeane returned to California from this trip that her entire world was changed by a fluke moment, in a dramatic way that neither she nor anyone in her life could ever have imagined.

Overnight Success

At the end of 1944, when Norma Jeane Dougherty returned to work after her vacation, she and a few other women who worked with her were asked to pose for photographs by a military unit that was making a film for army training purposes. The pictures would also appear in a government magazine called *Yank*. She wasn't at all sure that she could do it, but she knew she wanted to try. For many years, Grace Goddard had told her that she was pretty, that she was special, and that one day she would be in show business. Of course, this wasn't exactly show business. However, it was definitely exciting. On the day that the photographers, including one named David Conover, came to take her picture in her work clothes—drab gray slacks and a green blouse—she couldn't have been more thrilled. It came easy to her. She wasn't at all nervous. A single moment can alter a person's entire future, and just such a moment occurred when Conover took his first frame of footage of the voluptuous yet somehow chaste-seeming Norma Jeane. Her life changed in that second. "My own future with Norma Jeane was in jeopardy the moment that army photographer clicked his shutter," Jim Dougherty once observed. "Only I didn't know it."

The phrase "overnight success story" is often used when describing the rapid ascent of certain celebrities to the upper echelons of show business. Often it's just hyperbole. In the case of Norma Jeane Mortensen—soon to be Marilyn Monroe—it happens to be the truth. The story has been told so many times, it can be easily explained by saying that she became popular with photographers and very quickly became an in-demand model. Of course, over the years it has been speculated and even reported as fact that she had sex with these photographers in order to get ahead in the business. But the motivation of the photographers who later claimed to have had romantic relationships with Marilyn has always been suspect. None ever said anything about having sex with her until she became very famous and it was considered quite the conquest to have had this great sex symbol in bed. One by one, though, stories—and even books!—by these photographers have fallen apart over the years when it comes to detail and specificity. For her part, Marilyn always gave the impression that she was not interested in sex during those years. Maybe that was just public relations malarkey on her part—but she was consistent about it just the same. It would be very surprising, say those who knew her well, to find that she actually slept with photographers in order to advance in the business. After all, it's not as if she wasn't beautiful enough to make it on her appearance alone. In fact, she became successful enough to soon be signed by a modeling agency, which sent her out on even more interviews for work. By the spring of 1946, she had appeared on more than thirty magazine covers.

Besides the speed of her success, what was also fascinating about Norma Jeane's first photo sessions was how quickly she seemed to understand the business of modeling. She was very inquisitive about the process and also highly critical of her appearance. For instance, she asked David Conover questions about lighting, about different camera lenses, about how he coaxed his models into giving their best performances. In meetings with him after the sessions, she would study the contact sheets with the kind of careful scrutiny one might expect from a professional model. She wanted to know what she'd done wrong if an exposure didn't meet with her approval. If her appearance didn't meet her high standards, the picture was rejected. Every single shot had to be perfect, or she would not be happy with it.

Maybe it's not that surprising that Norma Jeane was so intuitive about her appearance on film. After all, from a very early age, she had been attempting to win the favor of others. If Ida loved her enough, maybe she would allow her to call her mother. If she was good enough, maybe Gladys would want her too. If she was pretty enough, maybe she would be praised by Grace. The whole concept of how she was being received by others had always been foremost on her mind, fueled by her insecurity. She had been studying other people for years—those with whom she trafficked in her life, to see what they had to do to gain acceptance in the world, as well as those she didn't know in movie magazines, to see what made them so special. Now, at the age of eighteen, she could step outside of herself and view herself as if she were a separate entity. Without even realizing it, she was making an art of communicating human emotion in photographs.

At the same time Norma Jeane's exciting new modeling career was unfolding, Jim Dougherty was overseas on duty. He would have preferred it if she had been home alone, pining for him. In fact, he wrote her a very stern letter telling her that modeling was fine and good temporarily, but that as soon as he got home he expected her to get pregnant and have a family, "and you're going to settle down. You can only have one career, and a woman can't be two places at once." It was interesting that now that she had found something she enjoyed, he had unilaterally decided that they were going to have a baby.

Jim's mother, Ethel, who had always been an ally for Norma Jeane, also disapproved of her modeling. Not only did she keep her son up to date on Norma Jeane's activities (and in a way that probably made them seem like trouble in the making), but she also made it clear to her daughter-in-law that what she was doing was unseemly and could create problems in her marriage. Norma Jeane responded by moving out of the Dougherty house and back into the lower half of her aunt Ana Lower's duplex. Now more than ever, she was proving herself to be the strong, self-reliant girl Ida Bolender had tried to mold. She knew what she had to do, and she was going to do it. When Jim returned on leave in the spring of 1945, he found that he was no longer the center of Norma Jeane's world. She was busy. She didn't need him. She still loved him—maybe—but she no longer felt that she needed him to survive. The dynamic had changed between them, and he didn't like it at all.

Gladys Is Released

Gladys Baker had tried everything she could to be released from Agnews State Hospital in San Jose. Finally, in August of 1945, doctors decided that she could be discharged. The condition was that she spend a year with her aunt Dora Graham in Oregon. Norma Jeane didn't know what to make of her mother's release. She knew that Gladys still wasn't well. Her few visits with her—one at the hospital and one over lunch with Aunt Ana—had been not at all good. Berniece was much more excited about Gladys's return to the outside world. She equated it with the good news that the war had ended that same month and called Gladys's release her "personal miracle." Of course, Berniece didn't know Gladys at all. She had romanticized about her over the years and hoped to have a relationship with her. Norma Jeane had actually gone through the troubling experience that was Gladys Baker, so she was more realistic.

Soon after Gladys was released, she became completely immersed in Christian Science, which had been recommended to her by Aunt Ana, a practitioner of the faith. Christian Scientists believe in the power of prayer as the cure for emotional and physical ailments. The sect is controversial and has been so ever since it was founded by Mary Baker Eddy in 1908. Gladys could not stop reading the many books given her by Ana about the faith. It seemed to be the only thing in which she was truly interested.

Gladys's fascination with the Christian Science doctrine made sense. After all, she had known for years that no matter what people said or did, they couldn't fix her—doctors couldn't, friends couldn't, even her own mother couldn't. Perhaps she thought that by poring over Christian Science books, she might discover a certain secret or fact and then finally she would be happy.

Also at this time, Gladys began wearing a white uniform, white stockings, and white shoes every day as if she were a nurse. She never explained why, and her family could never figure it out. Perhaps she had idealized the nurses she'd known at the sanitarium and thought they led good lives. After all, they were free to leave at the end of the day and be with their loved ones while she and the rest of the patients had to remain locked up. Or maybe she just viewed the nurses as powerful and in command—as she never had been in her own life. As soon as she was out, she began taking temporary jobs in convalescent homes. Norma Jeane found it disconcerting that her mother was tending to people in any kind of medical setting. Others, like Dora, actually hoped Gladys would become a practical nurse, now that she had finally gotten the freedom she so longed for.

Gladys's Plea to Norma Jeane

*I*n December 1945, Jim Dougherty returned from his tour of duty for the Christmas holidays. He had been gone for eighteen months. In that time, things between him and Norma Jeane had definitely changed, and he knew it as soon as she greeted him at the train station. "She was an hour late," he recalled. "She told me she had a modeling job, and that was her excuse, which didn't exactly make me happy. She embraced me and kissed me, but it was a little cool. I had two weeks off before resuming shipboard duties along the California coast, but I don't think we had more than three or four nights together during that time. She was busy modeling, earning good money. It was my first inkling of her ambition."

Norma Jeane wasn't totally finished with her marriage. She still hoped that she would wake up one day to find that Jim had had a sudden change of heart. "Yes, yes, yes," he would tell her in her fantasy. "I get it now. I understand. And yes, I approve of your career!" Perhaps she hoped for just such a reaction when she showed him her recent photos taken by a rather famous photographer named André de Dienes. She hoped he would like them—she knew they were very good—and perhaps they might convince him that she had found her calling. She also displayed some of the many magazine covers on which she had appeared of late. She was keeping a scrapbook, which she also proudly displayed, thumbing through the pages and explaining where each photo was taken and for what purpose. By this time, she had even been doing pinup modeling in bathing suits—which she must have known wouldn't make him very happy. The cumulative effect of all of this accomplishment was impressive even to her, as perhaps it would have been to most people, considering how many covers she had racked up in such a short time—how could her husband not be amazed at her achievements? How could he not want her to continue? How could he not want her . . . to be happy?

"So far as I was concerned, she was turning into another human being," he later recalled. "She showed me the pictures, her new dresses and shoes—as if I cared about such things. She was proud of her new popularity at Blue Book [the modeling agency with which she had signed] and she expected me to be, too." Jim's lackluster reaction did not bode well for him or his marriage. Norma Jeane was disappointed and couldn't understand why he wouldn't at least try to act as if he were happy for her.

Jim felt that he needed time alone with his wife so that he could talk to her and try to resolve some of their issues—in other words, get her to acquiesce to his desire that she quit her career. He decided that the two of them should drive to Oregon and visit Gladys at her Aunt Dora's home. Norma Jeane agreed, though reluctantly. She knew she had to see her mother, but she also knew that every time she had done so in the past she had regretted it. She also probably had ambivalent feelings about being alone in a car with her husband for so many days, especially since they were not getting along.

The visit did not go well, according to Jim. "My first encounter with Gladys was a little of a shock," he later recalled. "She didn't seem to connect with me at all. Her mind was out in left field somewhere." Jim also was surprised at how much Gladys and Norma Jeane resembled each other. "You could almost see what Norma Jeane was going to look like when she got to be that age. Gladys was a pretty woman. With proper makeup and her hair done, she would have been a gorgeous person."

Gladys sat upright in a wicker chair and was completely unresponsive when he and Norma Jeane walked into the room. She was wearing a white nylon dress and blouse and white stockings and shoes—her "nurse's uniform." Norma Jeane knelt at her mother's feet and held her delicate hands, gazing into her vacant eyes, trying to divine what it was she was thinking, how she felt about seeing her.

"How are you, Mother? Are you happy to finally be out?" she asked her, somewhat tentatively.

Gladys smiled absently.

Still on her knees in front of her mother, Norma Jeane tried to fill the void by talking about her recent trip to see Berniece. "She can't wait to come and see you, Mother," she told Gladys. However, it didn't matter what anecdote Norma Jeane relayed, nothing seemed to interest her mother. "Mother, please," Norma Jeane said, a searching expression on her face. Gladys answered her plea with total silence. But then, suddenly, Gladys tightened her grip on Norma Jeane's hands, leaned in, and whispered in her ear that she wanted to come and live with her.

Norma Jeane looked at her, a startled expression lingering on her face. She didn't know how to respond. Truly, that was the last thing she'd expected, or even wanted. She was getting ready to leave an old life—her marriage—behind, and, hopefully, begin a new one—her career. Gladys represented a huge responsibility. No doubt, if the two had enjoyed a warm relationship over the years, she would have been much more inclined to take on such a burden. However, this woman before her was one she didn't know at all, and was also unstable and unpredictable. Yet, still, she was her mother. Quick tears came to Norma Jeane's eyes. She let go of Gladys's hands and stood up. "We have to go now, Mother," she said, gathering her coat while shooting Jim a desperate look. "I'm going to leave you Aunt Ana's address and phone number, so you know where I am. Call me anytime." Then, with tears by now streaming down her face, she bent down and kissed Gladys on the forehead. Gladys had no reaction. Norma Jeane and Jim turned and walked away.

The days driving back to Los Angeles were spent quietly, Norma Jeane deep in thought and terribly unhappy. The trip certainly did not go as Jim had planned. He didn't have the chance to really talk to Norma Jeane about his concerns relating to their marriage and her career. However, when they got back to Aunt Ana's, it all came out. "I've had enough of this modeling business," he told Norma Jeane, putting his foot down. "I'm not going to put up with it another moment. Here's what's going to happen. When I get back here in April on my next leave, I want you back in our own house. And I want you to have made up your mind that you're finished with this silliness, and then we're going to have children. Do you understand, Norma Jeane?" She nodded, but didn't say a word. She would later recall her heart pounding so much that evening, she couldn't sleep. A photographer had given her a bottle of prescription sleeping pills in case she was unable to get a good night's sleep before a session, but she was afraid to take them.

Jim Gets a Surprise: Gladys

The first four months of 1946 were busy. Norma Jeane, now almost twenty, had never worked so hard. All of the photographers who took her picture were amazed at how well they came out, and it was clear that she was no longer a novice. She'd known what she wanted in terms of results from the very beginning. Now she was getting those results. She was working nonstop—so much so that one friend, Jacquelyn Cooper, wondered if perhaps she was sleeping with the photographers. "I said she could tell me because I won't breathe a word of it if you're having affairs with these fellows," she recalled. "She said, 'Absolutely not!' And what did I think she was? Very bothered, like that, like I'd hurt her feelings even wondering if she was sleeping with these fellows. In fact, she was so bothered she didn't pay attention to me for days."

"Men who tried to buy me with money made me sick," Marilyn recalled years later. "There were plenty of them. The mere fact that I turned down offers ran my price up."

She was working a great deal. But she confided in one photographer that she would sometimes, as she put it, "get down in the dumps." She said that she would have "dark moods that came from nowhere." In those times, she said, it was as if she "didn't have the answers to anything." These particular comments from her are interesting because they call to mind what her grandmother, Della, and mother, Gladys, used to call "the doldrums." But perhaps the following terribly prophetic statement says it best about Marilyn's dark mood swings during this time in her life: "Yes, there was something special about me, and I knew what it was. I was the kind of girl they found dead in a hall bedroom with an empty bottle of sleeping pills in her hand. But things weren't entirely black—not yet. When you're young and healthy you can plan on Monday to commit suicide, and by Tuesday you're laughing again."

During this time, while Jim was away and she was working with a series of different photographers, something else happened that would change things for Norma Jeane and, in a lot of ways, for future generations of admirers. It occurred in February 1946. At the suggestion of her agent, Emmeline Snively, Norma Jeane had her hair first straightened and then stripped of its chestnut brown color and changed to a shade of golden blonde. It was all in preparation for a shampoo print advertisement. Now, more than ever, Norma Jeane Baker Mortensen Dougherty was starting to look very much like Jean Harlow. But more important, she began to look like another great screen star, one of the greatest, in fact, of all time. She began to look like Marilyn Monroe. The transformation was almost complete. Norma Jeane Mortensen was almost a woman of the past, certainly as far as her husband was concerned.

In April, Jim returned from duty—as he had promised. However, Norma Jeane did not meet him at San Pedro Bay—as she had promised. Upset, he jumped into a taxi and went straight to the small house that the couple shared in Van Nuys. After paying the cabbie, he walked toward the home and noticed the drapes open. He peeked in. All of the furniture seemed to be in place. He caught a glimpse of Norma Jeane walking by. Apparently, she had done what he had demanded. She was there, at least. Now he might have a chance to talk some sense into her, and perhaps save his marriage. He must have been relieved. However, any sense of relief was to be short-lived. Jim Dougherty put his key into the lock and opened the door. And there she stood.

Not Norma Jeane.

Gladys.

How Gladys Lost Her Children

 he's been through so much in her life," Norma Jeane told Jim. "I can't put her out on the street."

"But she's crazy," Jim said in protest.

"If you'd been through what she's been through, maybe you'd be crazy, too."

Norma Jeane had a great deal of empathy for her mother because she was privy to a story only those closest to the family knew. It was the story of how Gladys's children—Norma Jeane's half brother and sister—were kidnapped.

Back in 1922, Gladys Baker—who was twenty-two, just two years older than Norma Jeane was in 1946—had already married and divorced Jasper, her first husband. She now had custody of their children, Berniece and little Jackie. However, Jasper was concerned about his ex-wife's behavior, claiming that she was unfit due to her overactive social life and her heavy drinking. Despite his concerns, Jasper left Los Angeles and headed for his native Kentucky, vowing to return to check in on his children.

Months later, he arrived unexpectedly at his mother-in-law Della's home and found the children alone with her. He easily tracked Gladys down at a speakeasy a few blocks away. Gladys didn't see him, though, when he arrived at and then left the smoke-filled "diner." A few minutes later, one of the other revelers mentioned to Gladys that he had just seen her ex-husband. It was impossible, Gladys said, because Jasper wasn't even in town. "But I could've sworn I just saw him," her friend said. The moment hung awkwardly. Gladys shrugged and returned to her tipsy afternoon with the fellows. To hear her later recall the incident to relatives, she had convinced herself, at least for a short time, that her friend was mistaken. Yet, as she sipped on her drink, she grew concerned that maybe Jasper *had* been skulking around. As she sat thinking, her mind became flooded with terrible memories of their troubled relationship. He had told her on more occasions than she could count that she wasn't fit to be a mother. It didn't take long before Gladys's worry built to the point where she simply had to leave the diner and return home to make sure her children were safe.

As she reached her block, she began sprinting toward her home, her youth apparent as she flew down the street. When she finally got to the house, she stopped dead in her tracks. On the front steps stood her mother, Della, smoking a cigarette and weeping. Gladys bolted up the steps and burst through the front door. Her children were gone.

The first few weeks without her son and daughter were a confusing period for Gladys Baker. After she contacted Jasper's family and they convinced her that he had not returned to Kentucky, she set out on foot to find him and her two children. First she headed to San Diego, where he had once mentioned he might find work as a longshoreman. Thus began a four-month-long odyssey of hitchhiking, cheap motels, and the obligatory speakeasies that had become Gladys's only social outlet. From the road, she wrote to a cousin, "I am doing what I can. I do not know if it is enough. I don't know how I am getting by." The trip was fruitless. Gladys seemed hardened by her pointless quest, and Della decided that she would never interrogate her daughter about her awful time searching. "It was as if her smile had died," Della told one relative a number of years later. "She always seemed like a child to me before, but when she returned she was a woman. To tell you the truth, I had grown used to arguing with her. But she had no gumption left. She was just a very sad woman."

After Gladys returned to her mother's home, she found a letter from her brother-in-law, Audrey, which had been delivered in her absence. Concerned for her emotional well-being, Audrey confessed in his letter that he'd been concealing vital information from her: His brother, Jasper, had actually been living with their mother for the past four months in Flat Lick, Kentucky—with the children. He suggested that Gladys move on with her life and not attempt to contact Jasper.

Della later recalled watching tears run down Gladys's face as she read Audrey's letter. Although Della tried to lighten her daughter's spirits, there was nothing she could do for her on that day. It was spent mostly in somber silence. That night, before bedtime, Della brought Gladys a large bowl of soup. The next morning, when she went in to awaken her daughter, the dish sat on the nightstand, untouched—and Gladys was gone.

Gladys hitchhiked most of the way to Kentucky, riding the occasional bus when she grew tired of thumbing rides and being passed up. Her first stop was Louisville, where she decided to spend a day putting herself back together. She knew that the months spent traveling had not been kind and she wanted to at least appear well-rested when her children saw her for the first time.

On the day she got to Flat Lick, her plan was to march up to her mother-in-law's front door and demand that her children be handed over to her. They would all then return to Los Angeles and, hopefully, forget the events of recent months. Gladys's intentions to wrench her children from their paternal grandmother's arms did not go as she intended, however. Something had gotten in the way of her plan, something so simple—laughter.

While standing across the street from her mother-in-law's modest home, Gladys watched as Jackie and Berniece playfully chased each other. As the two giggled and ran around the yard, she couldn't help but notice little Jackie's pronounced limp. How well she remembered that injury. It had happened back in 1920, when Jackie was three. While driving from Los Angeles to visit Jasper's mother at this very home, the couple began a fierce argument. Jackie had been sitting in the backseat, unattended. In a moment almost too terrible to imagine, the toddler tumbled out of their 1909 Ford Model T roadster, a doorless vehicle, while his parents were busy arguing. When they finally arrived in Kentucky with the injured child, Jasper's family was of course horrified and wanted to know what in the world could have happened. Even though Jasper had been the one at the wheel, he told everyone that his negligent wife had been responsible for the accident because she'd not been properly minding their child. For her part, Gladys was already distraught because of what had occurred, and to now be solely blamed for it by Jasper was almost more than she could bear. She couldn't fathom that the man she so loved had turned against her that way. Meanwhile, young Jackie had suffered a serious hip injury, from which he would never fully recover.

Now the boy's limp was a reminder of his terrible accident. Gladys watched her children for a bit, unnoticed. They seemed so happy in the large yard with a tire swing amid what appeared to be acres of woods surrounding the home. Gladys turned and walked away, unseen.

However, she simply couldn't leave Kentucky without her children. But how would she ever be able to retrieve them from the place they currently called home? She knew that her deficiency as a mother would be Jasper's primary defense for having taken Jackie and Berniece. If she were going to get them back, she saw only two options. She could steal them—just as Jasper had done. Or she could prove that she was a new woman. If Jasper and his family saw her as someone capable of caring for her children, maybe they would willingly allow her to take them. So, for a time, Gladys would begin a new life in Louisville.

Within weeks, she had altered her appearance dramatically, wearing simpler, more matronly attire. She also began to go without makeup, something she hadn't done for many years. Her toned-down appearance may have helped her land the precise position she sought. She was hired as a nanny for a well-off couple, Margaret and John "Jack" Cohen, on the outskirts of town. This job would not simply be a way for her to survive financially, it would afford her the opportunity to become the kind of woman she hoped her ex-husband would approve of, a woman worthy of being called a mother.

The Cohens were a happily married couple, and their daughter, Norma Jeane, was a well-behaved three-year-old child. The new Gladys was, in this family's mind, the ideal caretaker, treating their daughter as if she were her own. However, Gladys's only goal was to one day regain custody of her own children.

Months later, when she believed her transformation had been completed, she knocked on the Bakers' front door. Her mother-in-law answered, with only a few awkward words spoken through the crack in the door. When her ex-husband appeared, he asked Gladys to come into the house. As she entered, she saw a wide-eyed little girl standing by the kitchen. However, before Gladys even had a chance to say hello, the youngster's grandmother grabbed the girl and disappeared with her into another room.

Gladys's meeting with Jasper was strained, her attempts to present herself as an improved woman falling on deaf ears. Jasper was firm in his position that she would not get the children back, no matter what she said or did to convince him that she had changed. She asked if she could at least visit them. Jasper said she could see Berniece, but not little Jackie. After months of being in agonizing pain, the boy was now in a hospital and there was no telling how long he would have to remain there. Jasper reminded Gladys that her neglect was primarily to blame for the child's desperate condition. Devastated, Gladys then spent a short time with Berniece before her ex-mother-in-law asked her to leave.

Now, back in the home of the perfect family with the perfect child, things felt different to her. She no longer saw the Cohens as role models. In fact, their very existence seemed to mock her inability to change, to truly alter the woman she had once been and become someone new, someone respectable. "Each idyllic day with that family was another dagger in Gladys's broken heart," says a cousin of hers interviewed for this book. "She couldn't help but mourn the loss of what once was, what could have been."

While Gladys did her best to appear as though nothing out of the ordinary had occurred during her weekend away—supposedly with her aunt—her sinking mood made that impossible. As had happened so many times in her past, she slipped into the dark place that was by now all too familiar to her. The progress she had made, the many joyful scenarios she had imagined, the hope she once had—all of it was gone. The "new" Gladys Baker was dying a slow death.

The First Norma Jeane

It's been written in countless Marilyn Monroe biographies that Gladys Baker's baby, Norma Jeane, was named after the actress Jean Harlow. However, this can't be true, since Jean Harlow's real name was Harlean Carpenter and wasn't changed until 1928, two years after Gladys gave birth. Other accounts have it that the child was named after another actress, Norma Shearer. Still others insist it was Norma Talmadge. None of this is true. In the 1960s, Gladys explained the derivation to Rose Anne Cooper, a young nurse's aide at the Rock Haven Sanitarium.

After her failed attempt to regain custody of Jackie and Berniece, Gladys returned to the Cohen household. The Cohens' three-year-old daughter whom Gladys had been helping to raise for the last year was named . . . Norma Jeane. It would be with *this* little girl that Gladys would finally achieve what had been expected of her with her own children. Each and every day of the year she was with her, Gladys made it her priority to see to it that the tot was nourished, entertained—loved. However, after Gladys's return from Flat Lick without her own children, things began to shift. In the simplest terms, her mind had begun to fail her. She was just twenty-three.

When Gladys's problem became apparent to the Cohens, they were alarmed, and with good reason. Here's the story, as passed down in the Cohen family:

One evening after a dinner date, Mr. and Mrs. Cohen found their child alone in the nursery. She was hysterical and the sheets were soiled, suggesting that she'd been left unattended for quite some time. When they finally found Gladys, she was crouched on the floor behind a grand piano, her knees pulled in to her chest. Her eyes were closed as she spoke quietly to herself. She was visibly upset, tears streaming down her cheeks. After a moment, she looked at Mrs. Cohen and said, "Are they gone?"

"Is who gone, Gladys?" replied the missus.

"The men."

Gladys then explained that she had seen a group of men sneaking about the house for the previous few days, but she didn't want to worry her employers.

At first the couple were deeply concerned for their own safety. However, as Gladys continued to describe her experiences, they began to have a new concern: their nanny's sanity.

Gladys told of odd happenings that were beyond reason. She said she went to retrieve something from a cabinet under the kitchen counter and found there was a man lying inside it. Another man had walked into an upstairs bathroom, she said, and when she finally got the nerve to follow him in there, he was nowhere to be found.

The Cohens had a problem on their hands—a problem that needed to be dealt with quickly.

Gladys Baker lasted a few more days—though never alone with the child—before her employers made her termination official. At that time Gladys was weaving in and out of lucidity, appearing at one moment to be just fine, and the next claiming that she heard a voice. Indeed, there were many voices—but the voices were never really there.

Gladys's dismissal was a civilized procedure, with the Cohens claiming they no longer needed a nanny.

But what about little Norma Jeane? The child had been the only constant for Gladys while she was in Kentucky during this very difficult time, and she couldn't bear the thought of leaving her. For a time, as she later told Rose Anne Cooper, she considered taking Norma Jeane back to Los Angeles with her to start a new life. However, she couldn't bring herself to do it. She had experienced the misery of losing her own children and said she couldn't inflict that kind of pain on Margaret Cohen.

After packing her things the night before she was to depart the household, Gladys recalled that she sat in her room alone. Her minimal belongings now stuffed into a tattered satchel, she crept down the dark hallway and quietly let herself into the nursery. She sat on Norma Jeane's bed and stroked the child's hair. She then kissed her on the forehead before tucking her back in. After gathering the rest of her things in the dark of night, Gladys Baker then disappeared from the Cohen family's life.

Jim's Ultimatum

*B*ut we only have two rooms here," Jim told Norma Jeane when he was told that Gladys would be staying with them. "Where are we going to put her?"

"Um . . ."

Jim took a quick look around the house. Something didn't seem quite right. There were no flowers in the vase on the table, and he knew Norma Jeane loved keeping them there to add color to the small surroundings. There were no magazines on the coffee table, and he knew she liked their guests to have something to thumb through while she fetched coffee for them. In fact, the place looked as if no one was really living there. As he scanned the room, his eye caught a framed photograph of Norma Jeane on the wall, one that he recognized as having been taken by André de Dienes. Of course, this did not make him happy. When he walked over to a closet to hang up his coat, he opened the door to a surprise. There, hanging on a rod, were just a couple of dresses. On the floor, a few pairs of shoes. Obviously, Norma Jeane and Gladys were not living in that house. "What is going on here?" he asked, now very upset.

With Gladys sitting on the bed observing everything, Jim felt that he couldn't express himself openly, so he and Norma Jeane stepped outside to talk. She explained that she and Gladys had actually been living at Aunt Ana's. She'd had a series of modeling jobs and couldn't leave Gladys alone, and so therefore it was more sensible for them to be living with Ana. "I just didn't think you'd understand, Jimmie," she concluded. Then she started crying, buckling under the pressure of the moment. Jim had had enough. In fact, he did *not* understand. She had specifically told him she was going to move back into their own home.

"That's it," he told her. "That's it, Norma Jeane. You have to choose. Me or your career. Your marriage or your career." And there it was: the ultimatum she had hoped would not be forthcoming, the one he was probably a fool to issue. She didn't say a word. She just stared at him as he walked away.

Final Confrontation

Jim Dougherty was in service in Shanghai at the end of May 1946 when he received the "Dear John" letter. He later said it had come directly from Norma Jeane personally, but actually it was much more impersonal than that: It was written by her lawyer, C. Norma Cornwall, who informed him that she had filed for divorce in Las Vegas. As it happened, Norma Jeane had made up her mind that she wanted the marriage to be ended. She wasn't sure how to proceed, but she knew of one woman who was always able to think of a solution to any problem: "Aunt" Grace. Of course, Grace had encouraged Norma Jeane into a marriage of convenience, and her plan had worked in that Norma Jeane was spared the misery of another orphanage. Now she was twenty and ready to be free. Grace knew that the quickest way to obtain a divorce was to file in Las Vegas and then live there for the six months it would take for residency to be established and the paperwork to be filed. Conveniently, Grace had an aunt there. So Norma Jeane was off to Las Vegas in early May to begin the process.

The first thing Jim Dougherty did when he got the letter announcing Norma Jeane's intention was to cut off the stipend that wives of military men received at that time from the government. He was angry. In his view, Norma Jeane had gotten what she wanted and now she was done with him. Certainly he knew what she had gotten out of the deal; he just wasn't sure how he had benefited from it. In his view, he could have been single for the last few years and enjoying the benefits of being a bachelor in the military. One thing was certain: He wasn't going to make it easy for his wife to get out of the marriage. He was determined not to sign the papers until he was able to meet with her. He later admitted that he secretly felt he could change her mind if they had sex. Many years later he still wouldn't admit that the marriage wasn't perfect. In fact, he began to insist that the reason Norma Jeane filed for divorce was because she was trying to get a movie contract at MGM and was told they'd never sign her if she was married. Why? Because she might get pregnant and the studio's investment would then be lost. Of course, this wasn't the case at all. He also said that Norma Jeane later proposed that she "just be my girlfriend" and not his wife in order to placate the studio. Again, not true. In fact, there was never a deal on the table with MGM. Yes, movie studio honchos at the time preferred their new actresses to be single, but this had nothing to do with Norma Jeane's decision. She was unhappy with him and wanted out of the marriage.

When he returned to the States in June, Jim planned to drive to Las Vegas to meet with Norma Jeane. Much to his surprise, though, she was not in Nevada. She was in Los Angeles at Aunt Ana's, where she'd been staying. When she answered the door of her apartment in Ana's duplex, the first thing Jim noticed was Gladys sitting on the bed in the one large room. She looked nervous, as if she thought there might be some sort of confrontation. Norma Jeane apologized for not being able to talk to him at that moment and asked if they could meet at another time. Jim left wondering why she hadn't apologized for wanting to divorce him. "I was losing most of my determination to hang onto her," he recalled. "She was no longer the anxious-to-please young woman I married. She was calculating, something she had never been before. She made sure that Gladys would be living there when I made my last appearance—that her mother would have my place in the only bed in that apartment. What she would do with Gladys—a woman who was only capable of looking on passively and putting her trust in God—I couldn't guess."

Jim and Norma Jeane met several times over the next few days to try to sort out their problems. At one point, Jim went directly to Ana to appeal to her. He hoped she would talk some "sense" into Norma Jeane. However, he was surprised to learn that she fully supported Norma Jeane's goals. She had always been Norma Jeane's great ally. He said later that Ana seemed "awestruck by the very notion that Norma Jeane might be a movie star." More likely, she was just very enthusiastic about Norma Jeane following her dream. Jim's appeal to Ana, though, does demonstrate how desperate he was to find a way to save his marriage—but for what reason? "He truly did not want to sign the divorce papers," says his friend Martin Evans, "but it had gone beyond love. It was now a matter of ego.

"He brought Norma Jeane to my house because he said he wanted a quiet place to talk to her. His mother was always around, or Aunt Ana or Gladys. So I said yes. When they showed up, I could see that she was miserable and didn't want to talk about it anymore. She had on a floral-print dress, I remember, and her hair was pulled back into a ponytail. To me, she looked beautiful. Jim kept saying, 'Look at her, Martin. She hasn't slept in days she's so upset.' Didn't seem that way to me, though. They sat in my living room and I was ready to leave when Jim said, 'No, stay. Maybe you can help me talk some sense into her.' I felt very awkward about it, but stayed."

Once the three were seated, Norma Jeane said, "I think you two are going to gang up on me now. And I don't like it one bit, Jimmie."

"We're not doing that, Norma Jeane," he said, according to Martin Evans's memory. "We just want you to know that acting is a tough business. You don't have the strength for it. I don't know who you have been talking to at that modeling agency, but they're filling your head with stupid ideas, Norma Jeane. This isn't for you."

Norma Jeane let his words sink in for a moment. Then, before she could respond, Jimmie verbally attacked her. He was angry, he said, because he felt she had used him to stay out of the orphanage and was now finished with him. She then asked him how many times she would have to thank him before they could just go on with their lives. He said she was unstable and, worse, that she had a lot in common with Gladys—suggesting, of course, that they were both mentally ill. With that, Jim stormed out the door leaving Norma Jeane with his friend, Martin. "She sat down and just started crying," Martin Evans recalled. He said he watched her for a bit, noting how beautiful she was, even in tears.

Finally, she turned to him. "Take me away from here," Norma Jeane said, standing tall. "Take me away from this place, and take me away from this time."

Norma Jeane Signs with 20th Century-Fox

She'd heard it from so many photographers, she had to wonder if it was possibly true: "You are made for the movies, Norma Jeane." Indeed, every man who ever took her picture seemed to want to encourage her into the film industry. It wasn't so far-fetched a notion, actually. After all, she was stunning in photographs, her unique essence easily captured by the camera lens. The thought of how her look might translate onto the big screen was a tantalizing one. Still, it was a daunting proposition, especially since she had virtually no acting experience—not even in school plays, where so many professional actresses are able to at least claim some minor experience.

"I don't even know if I can act," she told her Aunt Ana when the two of them discussed the possibility. "Honey, you have been acting your entire life," Ana, who was always very intuitive, told her. "You know what I mean, don't you?" It was true. She had spent her whole life trying to fit in, trying to be better—hoping to be someone who would be accepted. "You can do whatever you set your mind to," Ana had repeatedly told her. "You know, the initials for Christian Science—C.S.—also mean something else." Norma Jeane had to laugh. She had heard this from Ana a thousand times. "Common sense," she said, finishing the woman's thought. "That's right," Ana told her, "and my common sense tells me that if you want to act, you'll act."

Inspired by Ana and the enthusiastic approval of so many others she'd talked to about it during the early months of 1946, Norma Jeane Mortensen began to envision a future for herself in Hollywood. Years later, she would say, "I used to think as I looked out on the Hollywood night, 'There must be thousands of girls sitting alone like me dreaming of becoming a movie star. But I'm not going to worry about them. I'm dreaming the hardest.'"

Prior to Norma Jeane's final decision to divorce Jim, her modeling agent, the very efficient Emmeline Snively, had already begun to look into the possibility of film opportunities for her client. One thing led to another and soon Norma Jeane had an appointment to meet with Ben Lyon, who worked as a recruiter for new talent and director of casting at 20th Century-Fox Studios. Of course, Norma Jeane was extremely nervous, but she managed to screw up the courage to meet with the movie executive on July 17, 1946. He gave her a few pages of the script to *Winged Victory*, a 1944 film based on a successful Moss Hart Broadway play. Norma Jeane managed to get through the reading. Not much is known about it, but she must have been fairly good because Lyon arranged for her to have a film test.

Two days later, Norma Jeane found herself on the 20th Century-Fox lot, on the set of a new Betty Grable movie called *Mother Wore Tights*, where she would make her screen test. In 1946, Fox boasted an impressive list of actresses and actors already under contract. A short list of these luminaries on the lot at that time would include Henry Fonda, Gene Tierney, Tyrone Power, Betty Grable, Anne Baxter, Rex Harrison, Maureen O'Hara, and Vivian Blaine.

Cinematographer Leon Shamroy would film Norma Jeane's silent screen test. After being fitted into a floor-length crinoline gown, she was told to stand on a set in front of a camera and execute a few simple moves: saunter back and forth, sit on a stool, walk toward a window on the stage set. While she stood before a movie camera for the first time, as nervous and embarrassed as she was, Norma Jeane was suddenly transformed into a woman completely at ease, enormously self-assured, and, more important, radiant in her unrestrained beauty. "I thought, this girl will be another Harlow," Leon Shamroy once recalled of the test. "Her natural beauty plus her inferiority complex gave her a look of mystery. I got a cold chill. This girl had something I hadn't seen since silent pictures. She had a kind of fantastic beauty like Gloria Swanson, and she got sex on a piece of film like Jean Harlow. Every frame of the test radiated sex. She didn't need a sound track, she was creating effects visually. She was showing us she could sell emotions in pictures." It became clear that the studio was interested in her when they asked her to do another screen test, this time in Technicolor. It was just a matter of paperwork before she would sign a deal.

Darryl Zanuck, head honcho at Fox, was not quite as effusive as everyone else who saw Norma Jeane's test, though. (Interestingly, this man would *never* be a fan of hers—even when she was making a fortune for his company.) However, at the beginning, he decided she had enough potential to be signed to a contract—seventy-five dollars a week for six months with an option for the studio to renew at that point for another six, but at double the salary. She would be paid this amount whether she worked or not. It wasn't much, but it was a start, and Norma Jeane was thrilled.

Of course, no one was happier about this sudden turn of events in Norma Jeane's life than her "Aunt" Grace, always Norma Jeane's protector and encourager. She wasn't a star yet, but she'd come far in a short time. At this time, she was just twenty—a year too young to sign a legal contract in California. Therefore, it seemed only fitting that the woman who would cosign the contract with her, on August 24, 1946, would be—Grace Goddard.

Just before the contract with 20th Century-Fox was finalized, Norma Jeane Dougherty was called into Ben Lyon's office. There was a problem: her name. Lyon explained that, in his opinion, her last name was too difficult to pronounce. "People are going to wonder if it's *doe-herty*, or *do-gerty* . . . or, I don't know," he said, "but it has to be changed. It's too much like a child's," he told her. "We need something that will offset your vulnerability but will have some class to it." How did she feel about that? Norma Jeane didn't really know how to respond. She knew she was divorcing Jim anyway, so she certainly saw no reason to stay wedded to his last name. She agreed. Eventually, she and Lyon settled on Marilyn Monroe. Marilyn after 1920s Broadway actress Marilyn Miller, an actress he said Norma Jeane reminded him of, and also someone he had dated; and Monroe after her mother's family name.

Norma Jeane wasn't sure about the proposed name. However, Lyon was so enthusiastic, she couldn't disagree. "Well," she finally concluded with an amused glint in her eyes, "I guess I'm Marilyn Monroe."*

---

* Her friend the acting coach Michael Shaw recalls, "When the studio changed her name, she was okay with it, but not thrilled. She said to me, 'But I don't even know how to spell Marilyn!' She was so frustrated by that. In that little breathless voice of hers, she asked me, 'Honey, is there an 'i' in it?' I said, 'I think so.' But it turned out to be a 'y.'"

PART THREE

Marilyn

Marilyn Trying to Understand Gladys

$\mathcal{B}$y the summer of 1946, Marilyn's half sister, Berniece Baker Miracle, could wait no longer—she had to meet her mother, Gladys Baker. She had no memory of her at all. She had been just a little girl when Gladys left her in Kentucky all of those years ago. Now that Gladys was out of the hospital, Berniece felt the time had come for a mother-daughter reunion. Marilyn wasn't so sure about it. Gladys had been living with her and Aunt Ana since her release, so Marilyn knew that she really was not well. She seemed totally incapable of expressing love or even warmth, let alone maternal feelings. She was also quite defensive and argumentative. Marilyn didn't want to take the chance that Gladys would say or do something that would hurt Berniece's feelings. "The image in your mind of our mother is much better than the reality of her," she told Berniece. "Maybe you should just leave it be." She didn't want her half sister to be disappointed. However, there was no stopping Berniece. She wanted to see her mother and intended to stay at Aunt Ana's for an extended three-month visit. She would be bringing her small daughter, Mona Rae, along with her. Her husband would stay behind since he would not be able to leave his job for such a long time.

When the day came for Berniece and Mona Rae to arrive from Michigan, Marilyn drove Ana, Grace, and Gladys to the Burbank airport to greet them. The women waited anxiously on the tarmac for the plane to land, anticipating the sight of their relatives. There must have also been a certain amount of apprehension from Marilyn, Ana, and Grace as to how Gladys might react when she saw her long-lost daughter. As soon as Berniece and Mona Rae appeared at the top of the jet plane's metal stairs, Marilyn ran toward them. By the time they were at the bottom of the stairs, Marilyn was embracing them both. When she introduced the two of them to Aunt

Ana, the three embraced. Then, of course, Grace hugged Berniece and her daughter. "And this is Mother, Berniece," Marilyn finally said. Turning to Gladys, she said, "And Mother, *this* is Berniece." Berniece would later say she first noticed Gladys's gray hair, which was cut at this time in short curls. She also noted that Gladys stood rigid, her arms downward, and exhibited no emotion. Berniece was completely overwhelmed anyway, and hugged her mother. In response, Gladys placed her arms tentatively around Berniece's waist for a moment and patted her back. The moment hung awkwardly. Of Gladys's meeting with her daughter, Grace Goddard would later write to a cousin, "It looked to me like she was thinking to herself, why is everyone here sharing something and feeling something that I'm not sharing . . . and I'm not feeling."

Once they were back at Ana's, it was decided that Marilyn would sleep upstairs with Ana while Berniece and Mona Rae would sleep in the downstairs apartment with Gladys. That meant that Berniece and Gladys would be sleeping in the same bed, while Mona Rae slept on a small roll-away cot in the corner. In retrospect, it's easy to see how these arrangements would have been difficult for Gladys. However, it was Marilyn's idea. "She set it up that way specifically because she hoped her mother would bond with Berniece, on some level," one relative explained. "She wanted nothing more than for her mother to *feel* something. She kept waiting for some kind of emotional process to take place in Gladys—and the heart-breaking truth was that it simply was not going to happen."

As the days turned into weeks, Berniece became distressed by how often Gladys was critical of Marilyn's new career. She recalled one incident during which Marilyn was practicing the enunciation of certain words in front of a mirror. "Oh, that's just ridiculous," Gladys told her daughter. "You should be doing something worthwhile with your life. Not this." Marilyn tried to explain that she had to improve the elocution of certain words for her acting classes at the studio, but Gladys just didn't want to hear it.

After witnessing that particular scene, Berniece cornered her mother. "You should be more encouraging to Norma Jeane," she told her. "She's trying so hard to make a go of it, and you're being so difficult." In response, Gladys said something under her breath. Berniece decided to just leave her alone.

Shortly after, Norma Jeane got a scare when she got a call from her agent, Emmeline Snively, telling her, "I just wanted you to know that your mother was here." As it happened, Gladys had woken up that morning, put on her nurse's uniform, called a cab, and was taken to the Ambassador Hotel where Snively's company, the Blue Book Agency, was located. She marched into Snively's office and told her that she was very unhappy about her daughter's career and wanted her to convince Norma Jeane not to continue with it. Snively was a little surprised, but she handled it well. She said that it was a matter between a mother and daughter, not an agent and client, and that Gladys should take it up with Norma Jeane. Gladys left, but not before telling Snively, "It's very wrong for you to allow young girls to come in here and ruin their lives with picture-taking." When Snively later explained all of this to Norma Jeane, the young lady was, of course, embarrassed and upset. Gladys had asked her who was helping her with her career and Norma Jeane had mentioned Snively, but she couldn't believe that Gladys had had the presence of mind to track her down and then talk to her. That evening, she and Gladys had a contentious exchange about it, ending with Norma Jeane telling her mother to "never interfere with my career again." Gladys said, "Fine, if that's the way you want it. Do what you want to do. See if I care." She then went to her room and slammed the door so loud it echoed throughout the household. "Why is she so angry all the time?" Berniece wondered.

The only time Gladys seemed to really become invested in anything was when Ana would take all of the women in the household to Christian Science services on Sunday. Gladys's intense interest in Christian Science had not wavered since her release from the sanitarium. The subject of mind over matter fascinated her; it was as if she knew she could not manage her life and wanted to do whatever she could to seize back some control over it. At the same time, Ana and Marilyn would stay up into the early morning hours reading from Mary Baker Eddy's *Science and Health*, the most important Christian Science book. Marilyn had been interested in the belief system before her marriage to Jim Dougherty, and when the marriage collapsed she turned back to it. One person who would later know Gladys at a home in which she spent some time in the 1970s has an interesting theory about Marilyn's devotion to Christian Science:

"She had always been a student of human interaction, if you think about it: how people reacted to her if she was one way, how they would be drawn to her if she was another way. What did she have to do to make people love her? She had made a study of all this. I think it was because she always knew her mother's mind was not right. And I think she knew that she may very well have a predisposition for the same kinds of mental problems, too, because her grandmother and her mother both experienced similar fates. So the whole concept that there was a way of understanding the human brain and changing your life by changing your mind appealed to her. It was as if she was hoping to get in on the ground floor of something big, as if she was saying, 'If I study this now and know all about this by the time I'm at the age when Mother started to flip out, maybe I'll be able to control it better than she did.' I think she always feared she had a ticking time bomb inside her."

Interestingly, at this same time—the summer of 1946—Gladys sent a series of letters to Margaret Cohen in Kentucky, the woman whose child, Norma Jeane, she raised for one year in 1922. That child was now twenty-seven years old. Gladys wrote that she wanted to see the girl because, as she put it in one of the letters, "my own daughters do not understand me, nor are they willing to try." The Cohen family found Gladys's letters disturbing. First of all, they couldn't imagine how she had tracked them down. They'd moved to a different town since she worked for them so many years earlier. Secondly, they received five letters in just one week, all rambling missives about wanting to see Norma Jeane. Then they were dismayed by all of the Christian Science literature Gladys included in her correspondence. In one of these letters, she mentioned Marilyn's career. "I am sorry to say that my own Norma Jean [*sic*] has decided on the moving picture business as a career. I am very much opposed to this. However, whenever I mention it to her, she raises her hand in my face and tells me that she doesn't want to hear about it and that it is none of her mother's business. I would love to have a child who values my opinion but that is not what I have in Norma Jean." The Cohen family decided against responding to any of Gladys's letters.

It wasn't all angst in the household during Berniece's long stay at Aunt Ana's. There were some good times. For instance, Marilyn couldn't wait to show her half sister the screen test she made for Fox. She arranged for her to have a private screening of it at the studio. There were other light moments as well. Sometimes the entire family would go out to dinner together. On weekends, Marilyn would drive them around Los Angeles on sightseeing excursions to Grauman's Chinese Theatre, the Farmer's Market, the homes of certain celebrities (maps sold by youngsters on street corners were usually accurate in pinpointing these addresses, much to the chagrin of the stars), and other West Coast locales she thought they'd be interested in, including the beach. There are actually quite a few photographs of the women at Santa Monica beach. Marilyn and Berniece would chatter incessantly during these day trips; they got along famously. Meanwhile, Ana and Grace would try to engage Gladys in conversation. Sometimes, they were successful, but usually Gladys stayed in her shell. "Why can't she just have a good time? I just don't get it," Marilyn is said to have wondered.

While living in the institution, Gladys Baker had become used to each day having structure. There were certain times for eating meals, engaging in outdoor activities, reading, and then going to sleep. She had been living with those circumstances for so many years that when she left and moved in with Ana and Marilyn, she still wanted that kind of structure in her life. She wanted to know that every day was to be the same. It made her feel safe, secure. However, Berniece's arrival totally upset any routine she had been trying to establish at Ana's. For three months, she never knew from one moment to the next where she was going or what she would be doing once she got there. Still, Marilyn wanted to at least come up with activities that her mother would enjoy, and also some that might elicit some emotional response from her.

One day, she asked Grace to take them all to the home that Gladys's father, Otis Elmore Monroe (who had died by hanging himself), had built by hand. But even this potentially nostaligic excursion failed to reach Gladys; she had no reaction to seeing the old homestead.

Marilyn then asked Grace to take them all to the house in Hollywood that Gladys had bought so many years ago. It was here that Gladys had lived for a short time with Marilyn and the Atkinsons. Surely she would have some reaction to this place. It was also here that she had had the psychotic episode, and from here that she was taken to the mental hospital. The women sat in their car on the street in front of the house for a long time, telling stories of the furniture that had once been in there—the piano that Marilyn so loved and that Gladys promised she would one day play well, the flowers always in the living room, the sunny kitchen. Nothing. Gladys felt nothing.

Getting Through to Gladys?

On September 13, 1946, a few months after that ghastly confrontation with Jim Dougherty, Norma Jeane and the woman with whom she said she was living—a sixty-nine-year-old widow named Minnie Wilette—appeared in front of a judge in Reno, Nevada.

In her suit for divorce, which was uncontested by Jim (and he could have fought it, actually, since Norma Jeane clearly had not spent the required six months in Las Vegas), she had said that he'd inflicted "extreme mental cruelty that has impaired [my] health."

Now, at the hearing, her attorney asked a few questions. Did she intend to make Nevada her home and permanent place of residence? Yes, Norma Jeane answered. Had that been her intention since she arrived there in May? Yes. Was it her plan to stay in Nevada for an indefinite period of time? Yes. Then, when asked to outline the way Dougherty had mistreated her, Norma Jeane responded by saying, "Well, in the first place, my husband didn't support me and he objected to my working, criticized me for it and he also had a bad temper and would fly into rages and he left me on three different occasions and criticized me and embarrassed me in front of my friends and he didn't try to make a home for me." She said that his actions "upset me and made me nervous." She maintained that she didn't see the situation as ever improving and that there was no chance for reconciliation. The judge granted the divorce. The whole matter took about five minutes, and then Marilyn hopped on a plane back to Los Angeles.

By the time Marilyn got back to Aunt Ana's home, anyone could see that she was blissful. "She showed up at Aunt Ana's, feeling terrific," Berniece recalled. "As soon as she saw me, she threw her arms around me. 'I'm a free woman again,' Marilyn said, laughing. 'I feel like celebrating!'"

Marilyn then moved through the house and finally found Gladys, who was in a terrible mood, very angry for no apparent reason. Though she had tried to reach her mother countless times in the past and failed, this time Marilyn sensed she might be able to connect with her. Maybe it was because her spirits were soaring as a result of her new freedom and fledgling career that she believed she could get through to Gladys. Mother and daughter spent much of the afternoon and into the early evening preparing for their night on the town. As all the ladies of the house bore witness to Gladys's seeming comeback, there was a feeling in the air that salvation from her never-ending misery might finally be possible. Every time Marilyn had seen any kind of slight improvement like this in her mother, she hoped it would last. She'd always held on to the belief that Gladys could remain in a healthy mental place, if she was "managed" properly—that is, if those around her acted a certain way, exuded a particular energy. She had tried so many different tactics in the past, but with little success. However, on this night, it was as if she had dug deep within and found a character that Gladys responded to—an upbeat personality that seemed to ignite a flame of life in her mother.

That night, as the family walked into the Pacific Seas dining room in downtown Los Angeles, Marilyn continued with the persona she had created earlier in the afternoon—a mixture of confidence and naiveté . . . a dignified charm . . . a carefree exuberance. She was a little flirty . . . funny. Gladys seemed to enjoy watching her in action. Seated at the table that night were Gladys and Ana; Grace and her sister, Eunice; and Marilyn and her half sister, Berniece. Berniece's daughter, Mona Rae, was also in attendance, and has shared both hers and her mother's recollections of that evening.

Beverly Kramer's father, Marvin, managed the Pacific Seas dining room in Los Angeles. He was a good friend of Grace's husband, Doc. As it happened, Beverly worked at the restaurant as a waitress; she was about eighteen. "Grace brought the family into the restaurant a lot," Beverly recalled. "I have seen pictures of that night, so I remember it well."

"Celebrate we did," Berniece recounted. "That night, we all enjoyed a nice celebration."

Marilyn lifted a glass. "Let's have a toast! To the future, everyone," she said.

"Oh, yes, to the future," Grace agreed.

"To the future," everyone chimed in.

Smiling warmly at Gladys, Marilyn repeated, "To the future, Mother." It was then that Gladys raised her own glass in the direction of her daughter. And there it was. It was just a flash. But there was no mistaking it. Gladys smiled.

"I know that everyone was always concerned about Gladys," said Beverly Kramer, "and that anytime they brought her into the restaurant, she seemed unhappy. This night, I remember she was upbeat.

She was smiling. She seemed to be getting along with everyone, especially with Norma Jeane."

During the evening, a Polynesian-style band played island music, with a group of girls singing, surrounding a single microphone. At one point, the girls fanned out into the sea of tables to find volunteers to join them onstage for a hula dance. "I remember that before she could even be chosen, Marilyn popped out of her chair and stood front and center, waiting for the rest of the gang to be gathered," recalled Beverly Kramer. "It was a mostly comic ritual, with the patrons giving a halfhearted effort and the dining room applauding their attempts. Marilyn, however, was familiar with the song the band was playing, 'Blue Hawaii' from the Bing Crosby film *Waikiki Wedding*, and she began to sing it." Kramer remembers that Marilyn did so with such conviction that the moment became awkward for some of the others onstage. Most of the women drifted away and back to their seats. "Gladys seemed to love it, though," Kramer remembered. "I just remember her smiling. She had such a nice smile."

Just days after it seemed that Marilyn had made some headway in connecting with her mother, Gladys made a stunning announcement. Over breakfast, she looked at Marilyn with very sad eyes and said, "You know, you can't keep me here forever, Norma Jeane." It was a confusing statement. Marilyn didn't know how to react. Gladys then went to her room and started to pack her things. When Marilyn followed her, Gladys told her that she had made up her mind and that she was going to return to her Aunt Dora's in Oregon. "Won't you please stay here with me, Mother?" Marilyn said, begging her. Though she told her that she would be worried about her and didn't want her to go, Gladys was adamant. There was no talking her out of it. Marilyn asked if she would wait at least one day. Gladys agreed.

The next day, Marilyn went to a store and bought a present for her mother. She put it in a box and wrapped it gaily. That night, she presented it to her. Gladys opened the box and pulled from it a crisp white nurse's uniform. "I thought you'd like this, Mother," Marilyn said, tears in her eyes. Gladys held up the uniform and inspected it. "Are you sure this is my size?" she asked skeptically. Marilyn said that she was certain it would fit her. Gladys smiled and put it back into the box. "Then, it will do nicely," she said.

The next day, Marilyn and Berniece took their mother to the bus station, bought her a ticket to Oregon, and tearfully sent her on her way. Berniece was sure they would see her again, but Marilyn wasn't.

Two weeks later, Marilyn called Aunt Dora in Oregon to speak to her mother. Maybe what Dora had to say wasn't so surprising but, still, it was a shock. Gladys had never shown up.

Wayne Bolender's Fatherly Advice

Marilyn Monroe didn't know what to make of her recent time with her mother, Gladys Baker. She didn't know if she had made any difference in her life at all. She just hoped the time they'd spent together had done Gladys some good. However, as she would later say, she knew that Gladys wouldn't miss her or Berniece in the least, and that was a reality that penetrated her heart like a steel blade. Interestingly, she turned to her ex-husband, James Dougherty, for comfort during this time—at least in correspondence. Martin Evans, Dougherty's friend, recalled, "Jim told me he received a very impassioned letter from Norma Jeane saying that she had recently spent a lot of time with her mother and that it hadn't been easy. He said that she wrote that the woman was very mentally ill and that she had vanished without a trace. She wanted to know if it were possible for the police to begin a search for her . . . what steps they should take to have the West Coast combed in order to find her. Jim wrote back and told her that he would be happy to discuss it with her in person. He said it was too complicated to get into in a return letter. However, as far as I know, that discussion never took place."

Complicating matters at this time for Marilyn was that, during a recent gynecologist's exam, certain problems were discovered that might make having children difficult. She hadn't been able to make up her mind about whether or not she wanted a child. On some days she thought she shouldn't. What if she couldn't take care of the baby and it ended up as she had—in an orphanage? On other days she felt that she would be an excellent mother and that she would be able to do for the child what her own mother had not been able to do for her: love and nurture the baby and give him or her a good life. But then there were days when a different thought would haunt her: What if her child were to end up like her grandmother and mother? In fact, there had been times recently when she began to doubt her own sanity. Was it a good idea to bring a baby into the world under such troubling circumstances? She wasn't sure what to think about it. Therefore, she decided to go back to the place where she really felt genuine love as a young girl—to the Bolenders'—and ask for some guidance. As an excuse for her visit, she said that she needed to ask her foster brother, Lester, if he would help move some furniture that she still had at Jim Dougherty's house. She drove out to Hawthorne by herself. When she got there, Ida was not home. Wayne answered the door and let her in, and she met one of his nieces, also visiting. Her foster sister Nancy Jeffrey quoted a letter that niece wrote regarding Marilyn's visit:

"I came to see Wayne one day and Norma Jeane came in. She had asked Lester to help her move after her separation from her first husband. She had a very deep conversation with Uncle Wayne, some things that were bothering her. Her deepest thought that day was having a child and whether it would turn out like her mother. She needed to, I guess, have Uncle Wayne's blessing. He was the only stable man in her life, as far as I know."

After Marilyn explained her worry, Wayne was very clear in his advice. "You are nothing like your mother or your grandmother," he told her, according to a later recollection. "I knew Della and I know Gladys and I can tell you that you are nothing like them."

Marilyn could only hope that what her "Daddy" had told her was the truth.

Shortly after her divorce, Marilyn moved out of Aunt Ana's and into her own apartment in Hollywood. In that respect, the rest of 1946 and the whole of 1947 had moments of both frustration and exhilaration. First, the studio prepared her biography, to be sent out to the media. It said that she was an orphan who'd been discovered by a 20th Century-Fox executive while she was babysitting his child—classic movie studio malarkey. There would be other untrue press tidbits, as well—years of them, actually. It was, according to Berniece Miracle, Grace Goddard's idea to say that Marilyn's parents were both dead. What she wanted to avoid—and Marilyn certainly agreed with her about it—was the possibility of any reporter tracking down Gladys. This tactic worked . . . for a while, anyway.

Giving Up Her Soul

*D*espite the speed at which the actress was signed to a deal, there were no movies in the offing for the newly named Marilyn Monroe. In February 1947, Fox renewed her contract for another six months, though she hadn't done anything other than pose for photographers in bathing suits and negligees for press layouts.

By the time she made her first film, *The Shocking Miss Pilgrim* (1947), she was almost twenty-one years old and more beautiful than ever with her cobalt blue eyes and head of hair so silky smooth and golden blonde. There was not much of Marilyn in *Miss Pilgrim*, just a quick (and uncredited) shot of her as a telephone operator; most fans haven't been able to spot her in this film. She would be (barely) seen again in 1947's *Dangerous Years*.

("For heaven's sake, don't blink," she wrote to Berniece, "or you'll miss me!")

There would be four more films (these would be released in 1948), if you count *You Were Meant for Me*, a Jeanne Crain–Dan Dailey musical, one that some sources maintain is part of Monroe's filmography. Marilyn can also be spotted in *Scudda-Hoo! Scudda-Hay!*—a Technicolor bit of nonsense set in the Hoosier state in which June Haver vies for the affections of Lon McCallister with a pair of prize-winning mules, while a ten-year-old Natalie Wood, as Haver's bratty kid sister, just adds to the overall foolishness. It's been published many times over the years—and even Marilyn had said it and, for that matter, even Fox had claimed it!—that her one little scene was cut from the film. Not true. It's there. Just two words, but both present and accounted for. (She's also seen in a distant shot with her back to the camera, on a rowboat.)

"She was a scared rabbit," said Diana Herbert, whose father, F. Hugh Herbert, wrote the screenplay. "On the sly, I snuck her into a screening room where my father was viewing for editing, and Marilyn got to see herself in the bit part before it was trimmed. She'd had one line and whispered to me, 'Do I sound that awful?' My father, using the old adage, told me Marilyn photographed like a million dollars. He told me she was going to be a big star."

That same year, 1947, Fox exchanged bucolic Indiana for the Wyoming countryside and a pair of mules for a wild white stallion in *Green Grass of Wyoming*, with Marilyn again uncredited as an extra at a square dance. Then, in August 1947, the studio decided not to renew her contract. Her agent Harry Lipton once recalled, "When I told her that Fox had not taken up the option, her immediate reaction was that the world had crashed around her. But typical of Marilyn, she shook her head, set her jaw and said, 'Well, I guess it really doesn't matter—it's a case of supply and demand.' She understood the film business already, and she was just a novice. She knew that the studio signed many contract players and the ones who struck gold overnight stayed while those who struggled usually ended up being cut. Still, the show had to go on."

Meanwhile, there were a couple of strange incidents in Marilyn's life in 1947 that may have pointed toward some of the emotional trouble she would experience later in her life. One is told by Diana Herbert. The same age as Marilyn, Herbert got to know her while *Scudda-Hoo! Scudda-Hay!* was being filmed and remained friendly with her. She recalled that when the film was completed, she hosted a pool party at her family's mansion in Bel Air attended by her friends from UCLA. Marilyn said she would love to attend. She said that on that day, she and her new friend, actress Shelley Winters, had a class at the Actors' Laboratory—a workshop for actors, directors, and writers, mostly from New York. Afterward, she would go to the party.

On the appointed day, Marilyn arrived very late. "She came quietly with her beach bag," recalls Diana Herbert. "I got out of the pool to direct her to the dressing room. A lot of time passed . . . and no Marilyn. So I became concerned and went and knocked on the door. 'Marilyn?' I called out. 'Are you okay?' And she said, 'Yeah,' in a voice that was barely audible. 'I'll be right out, I just have to change.' So I went back in the pool. An hour went by, and no Marilyn. So, again, I went back to the dressing room and knocked on the door. 'I'll be right out,' she said. By this time, everyone was getting out of the pool, drying off, and going home. More time passed. I again went to the dressing room and knocked on the door. But . . . she was gone. She never even came out of the dressing room—except to leave." Over the years, there would be numerous incidents like this in Marilyn's life.

At the end of the year, she would very briefly engage the services of new "managers," Lucille Ryman and John Carroll. However, they weren't exactly managers. Carroll was a film actor with connections, and Lucille was director of the talent department at MGM—with connections. It's unclear as to what the terms of the arrangement were—either she was paying them to represent her (unlikely, since she didn't have much money), or they were taking a percentage of her work (also unlikely, since she didn't have any). It doesn't make any difference, really, because they came and went from her life quickly, but not before bearing witness to some unusual moments.

Lucille, Carroll's wife, has insisted that Marilyn told her and her husband that she was working as a prostitute at this time, having quick sex with men in cars in order to get money for food. "She told us without pride or shame that she made a deal—she did what she did and her customers then bought her breakfast or lunch." Lucille also said that Marilyn told her she'd been robbed in the small apartment in which she was living and that she was afraid to stay there. Things were so bad, Marilyn told her, she'd have to just continue working the streets. Moreover, she told her that she was raped at nine and had sex every day at the age of eleven. "It was her way of getting us to take her in, and it worked." They offered to allow Marilyn to live in an apartment they owned.

Marilyn was known to fabricate stories to gain sympathy. One of the problems in sorting through the Marilyn Monroe history is determining what is true and what may be the product of her overworked imagination. In short, as people in her life would begin to understand with the passing of time, one could not ever take everything Marilyn said at face value. At any rate, she did end up living in better conditions by the largesse of this couple. Then, one night in November 1947, something strange occurred. The Carrolls got a frantic telephone call from Marilyn.

"There's a kid peeping in on me," Marilyn said, her voice vibrating with urgency.

"What are you talking about?" Lucille said.

"I'm being watched."

"But how?"

"He has a ladder and he's on it and he's watching me," Marilyn continued.

"Marilyn, a ladder would not reach the third floor. You must be dreaming," Lucille told her.

"But I'm awake. *I'm awake*."

This conversation continued until, finally, the Carrolls decided they had no choice but to have her join them at their own home that night. They felt they had their hands full with her and didn't know what to do about it. "At one point, we thought about it and realized that she was running our lives, calling all the time, crying on the phone," said Lucille. "We didn't know what to do. A lot of crazy things were going on . . . it was too much. She didn't know how to handle her life . . . she fell apart. We liked her but we needed her and her craziness out of our lives."

The Carrolls were about to get their wish, because Marilyn would be out of their lives by the beginning of 1948. In February, they took her with them to a party where she met a businessman named Pat DeCicco, a Hollywood playboy once wed to Gloria Vanderbilt. He was also a friend of Joe Schenck, the sixty-nine-year-old president of 20th Century-Fox. As it happened, Schenck asked DeCicco to find him some models to act as window dressing at a Saturday night poker party at his home. DeCicco asked Marilyn if she would be interested. All she would have to do, she was told, was look pretty and pour drinks for Schenck's friends, perhaps also give them a few cigars, but that was it. It sounded easy enough and also like a great opportunity, so she agreed. Of course, that's not all that was going on at the party, as Marilyn found out once she got there. Some of the ladies present—all models and aspiring actresses—were willing and able to give themselves to any of the male guests since most of them were power players in show business. Marilyn, though, stayed close to Schenck. By the time the evening was over, he was mad for her, saying she "has an electric quality . . . she sparkles and bubbles like a fountain." The next day, he sent a limousine to pick her up and drive her to have dinner with him. That night, she had sex with him.

"I can't say that I enjoyed it," Marilyn later told her movie stand-in, Evelyn Moriarty, of her assignation with Schenck. "But I can say that I didn't feel as if I had any choice." She said that she felt the whole event had been "very tawdry" and that she felt "terrible about it. It was like giving up my soul." However, she also allowed that she was starting to understand what she called "the Hollywood game" and she knew she had no choice but to play it if she were ever to make a name for herself in show business. It was a sad realization, she said. "But it's the truth," she concluded. She and Schenck continued their relationship off and on for some time, and, by some accounts, eventually she grew quite fond of him.

Schenck persuaded Columbia Pictures head Harry Cohn to take a look at Marilyn's screen test. Cohn wasn't that interested. However, her test footage started circulating through the studio system, and eventually ended up on the desk of Columbia talent head Max Arnow. Also unimpressed by it, he asked one of the studio's drama coaches, Natasha Lytess, to take a look. She wasn't thrilled either— it seemed that no one was impressed. Lytess noted that Marilyn seemed to suffer from a lack self-confidence. However, there was still something interesting about her, Natasha thought. Her quality was difficult to describe, but it had to do with her beauty and vulnerability. She wanted to work with her, believing that "perhaps she has some potential." Harry Cohn decided to offer Marilyn a six-month contract at $125 a week beginning on March 9, 1948. Suddenly, she was signed to Columbia Pictures.

Natasha

*N*atasha Lytess, who was thirty-five in 1948, once said that when Marilyn Monroe showed up in her office on March 10, 1948, she was wearing a red wool top and a very short dress that was cut too low. Lytess referred to it as "a trollop's outfit." When she met Marilyn, her suspicions about her lack of confidence were confirmed. In fact, she said, she was "unable to take refuge in her own insignificance." Natasha was a character herself, though. Her pencil-thin figure and pale complexion suggested that something was very wrong with her health. She had dark, menacing eyes. She rarely smiled. She was a serious *actress* and *drama coach*—everything she ever said about the acting field was, in her view, of great urgency. She was self-important and judgmental of everyone in her life. That said, she was also thought of as a brilliant teacher. Marilyn needed someone strong in her life at this time—a Grace Goddard who could actually do more than just dream about what it might be like if Norma Jeane could be a star. Natasha had an impressive library of show business books in her cottage office, which Marilyn began to devour. The two women spent endless hours talking about the art of acting and how Marilyn might become better at it. Natasha worked on Marilyn's diction, her delivery—her style. Actually, some of what Marilyn would learn from Natasha would work against her in the future. The exaggerated way she would enunciate every syllable as well as the way she moved her lips before speaking were unfortunate consequences of her work with Natasha. Marilyn would have to break these habits in years to come. Fine for comedy, this style was not appropriate for dramatic roles.

At the beginning of her work with Natasha, Marilyn was pretty much a clean slate upon which could be painted any artistic vision. "As a person, she was almost totally without fortitude," Natasha would say of her. "You could say she was someone afraid of her own shadow, so terribly insecure, so socially uncomfortable and shy, and never knowing what to say. She would ask me, 'What should I say?'

"I tried to get her to draw upon herself, to go into her own experiences, but I don't believe she ever did. Marilyn denied who she really was, except for her sex appeal which she had confidence in. She knew it worked—and she was as graceful with her appeal as a swimmer or a ballerina."

"I want to recreate you," Natasha told Marilyn. "I shall mold you into the great actress I suspect—though I must say I do not know—you can be. But to do so," she told her, "you must submit to me. Do you understand?" Her Sapphic intentions were clear.

Marilyn understood. However, she was not going to comply. She had submitted to Joe Schenck and regretted it, even if it did serve a valuable purpose in her career. She quickly determined that she was not going to do the same for Natasha Lytess. Still, she didn't want to say no—not yet.

In the environment between an acting teacher and student, many emotions come into play. Student and teacher access feelings and transfer them into characters, into roles—and, sometimes, into each other. One day, according to Natasha's unpublished memoir, she embraced Marilyn and told her, "I want to love you." Marilyn's response was, "You don't have to love me, Natasha—just as long as you work with me." For years, Marilyn was used to giving women what they wanted—Ida, Gladys, Grace. It was as if she had now drawn a line.

Helena Albert was a student of Natasha's at this time, and also a confidante. "Natasha often blurred the lines," she recalled. "She did with me, as well. But when Marilyn came into the picture, everyone else paled in comparison. I felt that Marilyn should have backed away when she knew how much Natasha cared for her, but instead I think she used it to her advantage. It was torture for Natasha—but not so bad for Marilyn. She had a good teacher, a smart woman in her life—someone to emulate, to learn from. You can't blame her for wanting it to last. I actually cornered her about it."

According to Helena, she went to Natasha's office one day for a meeting. Just as she got to the cottage, Natasha was leaving it in tears. "I can't see you now," she said as she brushed by. Helena went into the cottage and found Marilyn sitting in a chair, staring into space with a faraway expression.

"Is everything all right?" she asked Marilyn.

Marilyn just continued to look straight ahead.

"Marilyn? Is everything all right?"

"No, it's *not*," Marilyn finally said, as if coming to her senses. "I'm afraid Natasha doesn't know what the word 'no' means. And I'm tired of having to say it to her over and over again. Why can't we just do what we do best—act?"

"It's more complicated than that," Helena allowed. "And you know it, Marilyn."

"No, it's not," Marilyn said. She rose and faced her. "You don't always get what you want in this life, Helena," she said. "I have wanted many things and have not gotten most of them. Do you know what I think? I think Natasha is spoiled. I think she has always gotten what she's wanted, and doesn't know how to handle it when she can't."

It was clear not only that Marilyn had lost her patience with Natasha, but also that she was cold to her and not very empathetic about her feelings. After spending so many years suppressing her emotions and trying to be what others wanted her to be, perhaps she didn't understand why Natasha couldn't do the same thing. She gathered her things and, before leaving, turned to face Helena. "If you see her, tell her I'm sorry," she said, "but there's nothing I can do about it. Tell her I hope she'll continue with me, but if not, I will try to understand." With that, she took her leave.

"The truth is, my life, my feelings were very much in her hands," Natasha Lytess said many years later. "I was the older woman, the teacher, but she knew the depth of my attachment to her, and she exploited those feelings as only a beautiful, younger person can. She said she was the needy one. Alas, it was the reverse. My life with her was a constant denial of myself."

And thus it would remain—for six more long years.

Disappointment

On March 14, 1948—just a week after Marilyn signed with Columbia—her beloved Aunt Ana passed away from heart disease. She was sixty-eight. Oddly, she was buried in an unmarked grave at Westwood Memorial Park, though a small plaque was put on it a few years later. It's been published in the past that Marilyn did not attend the services, that she was too busy with her budding career. This is not true, according to her half sister Berniece's memory. Marilyn would never have missed Ana's funeral. Actually, she and Grace and Doc Goddard had a private viewing of Ana's body, and then a tearful Marilyn slipped away before the other mourners arrived. She later said of Ana, "She was the one human being who let me know what love is." Ana left a book for Marilyn called *The Potter*, along with a note: "Marilyn, dear, read this book. I don't leave you much except my love. But not even death can diminish that, nor will death ever take me far away from you."

Marilyn Monroe would say that she was "miserable" after the death of Ana because, as she put it, "I was left without anyone to take my hopes and my troubles to." It was probably fortunate that she had her career to turn to at this time, as she began working on a low-budget musical, her first film for Columbia, *Ladies of the Chorus*. In it she had a leading role in which she sang two solo numbers— "Every Baby Needs a Da Da Daddy" and "Anyone Can See I Love You"—as well as two duets with Adele Jergens. There was also a certain amount of dancing involved in her work in this film, a real challenge for Marilyn. This was a strange little movie, just an hour long, and it took only ten days to film, but Marilyn was surprisingly good. Her singing voice was a revelation. However, when released later in the year, the film did nothing for Marilyn's career. She would be dropped from Columbia soon after its release, much to her disappointment. "I went to my room and lay down on my bed and cried," she recalled. "I cried for a week. I didn't eat or talk or comb my hair. I kept crying as if I were at a funeral burying Marilyn Monroe. I hated myself for having been such a fool and having had illusions about how attractive I was. I got out of bed and looked in the mirror. Something horrible had happened. I wasn't attractive. I saw a coarse, crude-looking blonde."

Marilyn moved into a double room at the Hollywood Studio Club in June 1948, where she paid twelve dollars a day for room and board. She needed to save money—things weren't going as well as she had hoped—and this seemed like the best way to do it. She didn't like the place, though, because it reminded her of the orphanage. She was dating a man named Fred Karger, who was the musical supervisor of *Ladies of the Chorus*, and it wasn't going well.

Though these were dark days, Marilyn tried to keep a stiff upper lip. She had been relegated to doing TV commercials by the end of the year and felt that perhaps her movie career was over. Short-lived and over. "But there was something that wouldn't let me go back to the world of Norma Jeane," she recalled. "It wasn't ambition or a wish to be rich and famous. I didn't feel any pent-up talent in me. I didn't even feel that I had looks or any sort of attractiveness. But there was a thing in me, like a craziness that wouldn't let up. It kept speaking to me."

"You never know when you'll get that big break," Natasha always told Marilyn. "And when it happens, you'll know it." Indeed, "it" would happen for Marilyn at the end of the year when she attended a New Year's Eve party at the home of movie producer Sam Spiegel. During the course of the evening, she was introduced to a William Morris agent named Johnny Hyde. In the instant she extended her hand to shake his, a major shift took place in her world . . . and things would never again be the same.

Johnny Hyde

*M*arilyn Monroe had met a wide assortment of characters in her last couple of years in show business circles, but nobody like Johnny Hyde. At fifty-three, he was barely five feet tall, of slight build with a receding hairline, not especially handsome. His head was set too close to his shoulders and he had a thin nose and not enough space between his eyes. There was something about his physical presence that seemed frail and sickly—and indeed he had a heart condition that was serious enough to require weekly visits to a cardiologist. The Russian son of a circus acrobat, he was a study in contradictions, not the least of which was that despite his un-impressive appearance and unwell demeanor, he was an extremely powerful person. Well-respected in the industry, he was manic when it came to his show business pursuits. The entertainment business was always foremost in his mind. "Everyone knew that Johnny lived and breathed show biz," one of his friends once said. Quite a few actresses owed their careers to this man, women like Rita Hayworth, Lana Turner, and Betty Hutton. He also represented Bob Hope.

When Johnny met Marilyn, it was as if his world suddenly stopped spinning. He'd never laid eyes on anyone so beautiful, and he knew he had to have her. "He was an interesting guy," said Bill Davis, who, as a young man of seventeen, worked for the William Morris Agency and often directly under Hyde. "Smart as a whip. Aggressive. Passionate. A ladies' man, even if he wasn't a looker. He fell hard for Marilyn from the very beginning, sending gifts and love letters to where she was living and really coming on strong. I imagine it would have been tough for her to ignore him or rebuff him because, after all, he was a powerful man. She was in trouble. She needed help with her career."

"I have it in my power to make you a star," Johnny told her shortly after meeting her. "And I don't mean a contract player, either. A star!"

"When I first mentioned my acting hopes to Johnny Hyde, he didn't smile," Marilyn would recall. "He listened raptly and said, 'Of course you can become an actress!' He was the first person who ever took my acting seriously and my gratitude for this alone is endless." This was hyperbole on her part, but she made her point with it.

"From my understanding, it was a straight out deal between them," said Bill Davis. "She said she wanted to be in movies. He said he could make it happen. He was influential in the business. Meeting him was, I think, probably the best thing that had happened to her up to that time. There were dozens of starlets who wanted to sleep with him just for the chance to have him in their corners. Of course, she had to have sex with the guy. I mean, he had to get something out of it, too. . . . That's the way it worked."

In January 1949, Marilyn found herself in Palm Springs with Johnny. It was there that they consummated their relationship, despite the fact that he was married. Power being the greatest aphrodisiac, Marilyn was actually attracted to him and didn't just sleep with him to get ahead in her career—though it didn't hurt. A month after she had sex with him, she found herself doing a cameo appearance in a silly Marx Brothers movie called *Love Happy*. It was a United Artists low-budget, stolen-diamond backstage romp that is significant only as the final film appearance of the legendary Marx Brothers.

The promotional tour Marilyn would embark on to promote *Love Happy* (when the movie would finally be released during the summer) was more noteworthy than the film itself. She had an opportunity to visit major cities and generate a great deal of press for herself. "I was on screen less than sixty seconds," she recalled, with typical Marilyn hyperbole, "but I got five weeks work . . . going on the tour which promoted the film in eight major cities. I felt guilty about appearing on the stage when I had such an insignificant role in the film, but the audiences didn't seem to care." During this time, she became known as "The Mmmmm Girl." The PR line had to do with the notion that some people can't whistle, so when they see Marilyn all they can do is say "Mmmmm." No such utterance would be forthcoming, however, for *Love Happy*. Certainly, with his many resources, Johnny Hyde could do better for his best girl than "sixty seconds" in a Groucho Marx movie.

"He made it pretty clear to her from the very beginning that he would bust his hump for her," said Bill Davis. "It wasn't subtle. It wasn't suggested. It was clear. I was actually in their presence shortly after they met and heard him say to her, 'You will be the biggest thing in this town if you just give me a little time to work some business out for you.' She just smiled and acted sort of coquettish. I remember thinking that she was just another empty-headed floozy, which was reductive, I know. But that's how she struck me. She didn't seem like she had any brains. All I ever heard from her was 'Yes, Johnny' and 'No, Johnny' and 'Anything you say, Johnny.' He would berate her and she would be fine with it. Sometimes she called him 'Daddy.' I remember thinking, 'Oh, his wife is gonna just love this.'"

During the promotional tour, a friend named Bill Pursel, who lived in Nevada and whom Marilyn met when she was there for her divorce, received a troubling telephone call from her. He told author Michelle Morgan for her book *Marilyn Monroe—Private and Undisclosed*, "Norma Jeane called from Chicago; she was crying . . . threatening to throw acid into her face to put a stop to the constant picture taking of her. She had no privacy, and some of the photographers were rude and demanding, as though she owed them something. I tried to console her, and even though she owed them nothing, I told her it was part of the game. I asked her to immediately contact her agent to intercede and call off the wolves or she was going to fire him immediately. . . . I offered to fly to Chicago but she said it wasn't necessary, 'cos she would be home in a few days. She finally stopped crying and settled down."

Johnny would say that he fell madly in love with Marilyn at the moment they met and remained devoted to her for the next year. She never felt the same about him. However, he was so smart, so interesting, and, of course, so powerful she felt drawn to him. Hyde encouraged Marilyn to dig deeper into the craft of acting than she had already done with Natasha. He wanted her to expand her intellectual scope by reading Turgenev and Tolstoy. She couldn't get enough of both writers. She also enjoyed both volumes of *The Autobiography of Lincoln Steffens*. Steffens (1866–1936) was one of the world's first celebrity journalists to challenge the status quo. He was so controversial in his attacks on political corruption that President Theodore Roosevelt coined a term for it—"muckraking." Johnny also suggested novels by Thomas Wolfe and Marcel Proust as well as specific books about moviemaking. She devoted herself to doing whatever he asked of her in this regard. When he gave her Stanislavsky's *An Actor Prepares*, she read it as a textbook because she knew she would be quizzed on its specifics. She had a voracious appetite for knowledge and couldn't wait to discuss with Johnny whatever book he had recommended. "You've been through so much," he told her, echoing what Natasha Lytess kept telling her. "You should draw on that for your acting." Hyde's advice was pretty much what Stanislavsky had in mind with his book.

Johnny didn't want Marilyn to waste a second of her day. For instance, she had a habit of talking on the phone for hours. That had to end, he said. "He wanted her every waking moment to be devoted to doing something progressive for her career," said Marybeth Hughes, a beautiful blonde actress who once dated Hyde. "Once you got into Johnny's whirlwind, your life was no longer your own. Most women couldn't take it. Most women didn't think it was worth the high drama he brought into their lives. You had to be pretty strong to be with Johnny Hyde."

Just as Johnny had said he had never met anyone like Marilyn, the same was true of her. All of the men she'd known in the past had been disappointments, going all the way back to Wayne Bolender, who certainly loved her but ultimately was weak when it came to standing up to his wife, Ida. She couldn't imagine Johnny being cowed by anyone. He was her protector; she felt safe in his arms. Of course, in that role, he also became a father figure to her. The reasons she sought one are obvious, and he certainly fit the bill. In the end, though, because there were so many different levels to their romance, it was complex, and thus often thorny.

Luckily for Marilyn, Johnny Hyde was as generous as he was supportive. Marilyn always had money as his girl, which was a refreshing change. Finally, she could take a deep breath and focus on her career—as he demanded—rather than on her financial woes. After he set Marilyn up financially, moving her into his new home after he left his wife and children, Hyde began to constantly pester her to marry him. He wasn't above pulling tricks that she was accustomed to doing herself, such as painting a dark picture of circumstances in an effort to gain sympathy. "I'm dying," he would tell her. "You know, it's my heart, Marilyn. I'm going and it'll be soon. And when I die, you'll be a very rich woman if you marry me." Those kinds of pleas from Johnny pretty much fell on deaf ears. Marilyn would sleep with him—he was very nice, and in a way she loved him, even if she wasn't in love with him—but she wasn't going to marry him. However, there was another wedding in the family: Gladys's.

Gladys Marries

While Marilyn Monroe was navigating delicate terrain with Natasha Lytess and Johnny Hyde, her mother, Gladys, was involved in her own little romantic escapade. Surprisingly enough, sometime in April 1948 she ran off and married a man named John Stewart Eley. Marilyn was thunderstruck by the news. Certainly, Gladys was not emotionally equipped to be in a marriage with anyone, yet she had once again done the unexpected by taking a husband. "But who is this guy?" Marilyn asked Grace Goddard. "I have no idea," Grace said, according to a later recollection. "Oh, no. Now, I'm really worried," Marilyn said. Marilyn immediately felt that she was at fault. However, she wasn't even sure where Gladys had been, and it was thus difficult to monitor her. Grace told Marilyn that it was impossible for Marilyn to have a career in show business and also be responsible for her impulsive and troubled mother. "She has to live her life," Grace said. "Oh, my God," was all Marilyn could say in response.

Still working for the William Morris Agency under Johnny Hyde, Bill Davis recalled, "I was in the office with Johnny when Marilyn rushed in looking wild-eyed. I remember she had on a white blouse that was buttoned all the way to the top with long sleeves. And she had on white slacks. The reason I remember this is because it struck me that for someone known as a sex goddess she sure didn't show much skin in her day-to-day activities."*

"Johnny, oh, Johnny. I need your help," Marilyn said, according to Davis's memory.

---

* Marilyn Monroe historian James Haspiel adds to this observation: "This woman who was supposed to be out there all the time in a sexual way, in private life, was very demure. If you look at newsreel of her in Korea, she is squatting down on the stage with a bunch of soldiers around her and she's wearing a cocktail dress. She has both hands across her chest. In other words, it's as if she is unconsciously protecting herself from being on display. This is the same lady who, of course, posed nude for the calendar. Yet, if you look at her in any of the photographs I took of her personally, or so many other photos, she's never wearing anything low-cut. Everything is always up to the neck all the time."

"Sure, doll. What's the problem?"

"My mother has married some loser and I'm very worried about her," Marilyn said, upset. She sat down in a chair, seeming exhausted. She then said that she wanted Johnny to find out anything he could about John Eley. "I cannot believe my mother would get married," she said. "Can you even believe it?"

Since Johnny had never met Gladys, he didn't have an opinion about her marriage. However, he would definitely help Marilyn, he said. And he had the right connections to be successful at it. While she sat before him, he picked up the telephone and hired a private investigator to look into the matter.

A couple weeks later, Gladys wrote to her daughter Berniece, who had just moved to Florida with her husband and child. She explained that Eley was from Boise, Idaho, and had just arrived in California "for work," though she didn't specify what kind of employment. She sent a picture of him. "He looks nice enough," Berniece told Marilyn during a telephone call. "Well, Johnny is looking into it for me," Marilyn told Berniece. "He'll get to the bottom of it. I trust him."

Soon, information from Johnny's PI began to trickle in about John and Gladys. Apparently, they had met at a bar somewhere in Santa Barbara. Eley had told his friends that he'd "landed Marilyn Monroe's old lady," and that he was waiting for the moment when he might meet the screen star. Meanwhile, he was going to try to take care of her mother, whom he described as "the craziest broad you've ever met." He said that Gladys heard voices in her head, talked to herself, and, as he put it to one friend, "scares the shit out of me." When Johnny Hyde relayed this information to Marilyn, she was angry. "That bastard," she said. "Is he trying to use my mother to get to me?" Hyde wasn't sure, but he agreed that it appeared that way. He promised to continue looking into the matter.

A few weeks later, Marilyn received a letter from John Eley, sent to her home. He wrote that he was taking care of her mother but that he needed money to do it. If she cared anything about Gladys, he wrote, then she would not ignore his request and would send him a check for a thousand dollars. She brought the letter to Johnny and asked what she should do. "Well, you can't give this sonofabitch a thousand bucks, that's for sure. That's a lot of money," Johnny said. It was decided that Marilyn shouldn't respond to the letter at all. If she did, Johnny reasoned, Eley would believe that he had a communication with her and would not stop with the money requests. All of this was very difficult for Marilyn, and it weighed heavily on her. "I think I'm going to be dealing with this kind of thing for the rest of my life," she told Johnny Hyde. He smiled at her gently. "You always said you wanted a mother, sweetheart. Well, you got one. We don't get to choose our mothers, kid."

Shortly thereafter, Berniece received a letter from Eley. Now he wondered if it would be possible for him and Gladys to move to Florida and live with Berniece and her husband and child. He said that he repaired appliances to make a living and was working out of his truck. His plan was to park his truck in front of the Miracle home; he and Gladys would live with the family as he worked. This sounded like a terrible idea to Berniece. When she told Marilyn about it, Marilyn was also skeptical. She said that she didn't know what her mother had gotten herself into with John Eley, but she was certain it wasn't anything good.

She was right.

In about a month's time, Johnny Hyde's PI came back with the news: John Eley was a bigamist—he had another wife in Idaho.

Fifty Bucks for Nudity?

*B*y May 1949, it appeared that Marilyn had reached an emotional impasse with Johnny Hyde. He still wanted to marry her and was becoming insistent about it. However, she would not be bullied into matrimony, and was just as adamant in her position. Earlier, he had taken an apartment for her at the Beverly Carlton on Olympic Boulevard in Beverly Hills, now the Avalon Hotel, while she was living with him in his home. It was just for the sake of appearances. However, by May she was living in it, and determined to pay her own rent and expenses. She needed to do something to generate income on her own, though. "I was never kept," she would say in 1962, looking back on this time. "I always kept myself. I have pride in the fact that I was on my own." In a few months, Johnny would arrange for her to make a brief appearance in a dreadful movie called *A Ticket to Tomahawk*. Again, it would not amount to much. When her car was repossessed, she knew she needed to take action.

One day, while searching through her business cards hoping that one might inspire her to seek work, she saw one given to her by a man named Tom Kelley. Marilyn had met him under strange circumstances. Back in October (of 1948), she was on her way to an audition when she became involved in a minor automobile accident. One witness at the scene was Kelley, who, as it turned out, was a former employee of Associated Press, having worked for that news-gathering organization as a cameraman. Marilyn told him she had an important audition and, because of the accident, no way to go to it, and no money for a cab either. He felt sorry for her and gave her five bucks and his business card. That was the last time she thought about him, until now finding that card.

Rather than call Tom Kelley, Marilyn decided to simply appear unannounced at his studio in Hollywood. After a brief conversation with her, Kelley told her that a model he was about to shoot for an ad for Pabst beer had called in sick. Would Marilyn like the job? Of course. He then shot a few rolls of film of Marilyn playing with a beach ball. They shook hands, he gave her a few bucks, and she left.

Two weeks later, on May 25, Tom called Marilyn to tell her that the mock poster that had been produced for the beer campaign was a hit with Pabst and had somehow gotten into the hands of a person who manufactured calendars in Chicago. He wanted her to pose nude. It would be discreet but, definitely . . . nude. She thought it over, but not for long because she really didn't have a problem with it. Thus, two nights later, Marilyn found herself writhing around on a red velvet drape, posing, preening, and pouting while arching her back to make even more obvious two of her greatest assets. Meanwhile, Tom Kelley snapped away. The photos that resulted are extremely tame by today's standards, but still she didn't want to be acknowledged as having posed for them, which is why she signed the release "Mona Monroe." She was paid just fifty dollars. (A great Marilyn Monroe quote comes to mind: "I don't care about money. I just want to be wonderful.") Years later, she would describe the experience as "very simple . . . and drafty!" And that was the end of it, as far as she was concerned.

For now.*

---

* Later, some priceless quotes were attributed to Marilyn when word got out that she was the model. When asked what she was wearing, she answered, "Chanel No. 5." And her response to what she had on: "The radio."

PART FOUR

Stardom

Unwelcome Visitors

$\mathcal{M}$arilyn Monroe's bad-luck streak in films would finally be over by the end of 1949 when she made a career-altering trip to Culver City, home of Metro-Goldwyn-Mayer. MGM, or Metro, as it was known by the cognoscenti, was the jewel in the crown of the studios constituting the motion picture industry of the day. It would be for this studio that Marilyn was cast in a new film to be directed by John Huston—*The Asphalt Jungle*, based on the novel by W. R. Burnett. Finally, Johnny Hyde had come through for her by arranging a meeting with Huston and Arthur Hornblow, the producer. Unfortunately, Marilyn thought she almost blew the audition by dressing too provocatively for the reading of the script. She knew her character was supposed to be sexy and thought she should dress the part. It was too much. It made her look as if she were relying on her body and not her acting skill to land the role. She was very nervous; the audition did not go well. Still, she was called back for a screen test. She fared much better in it, thanks to the concentrated effort she gave to preparing with Natasha Lytess. Louis B. Mayer was impressed with the result, and she was cast in the role.

This was a big career move for Marilyn, and of course there was a certain amount of anxiety about it. Even Johnny Hyde—unflappable in his belief in Marilyn—had some misgivings. "You have to break down and cry in this," he told her. "Do you think you can do it?"

"But you're the one who said I'm a star," she told him. "Are you saying you don't think I can do it?"

"I do," he told her. "But I'm just worried. Let's continue to have Natasha work on this."

It was when Natasha began coaching Marilyn on the actual script for *The Asphalt Jungle* that something so alarming happened it caused her to contact Johnny directly. A woman who had been a friend and young student of Natasha's explained how the events unfolded. "As Natasha explained it to me, the scene she was working on with Marilyn involved her character being happy and chatting about an upcoming trip. Then there was a knock on the door and she became frightened. [In the script] a bunch of men entered, and threatened her with prison if she didn't confess to having lied about something. One evening Natasha arrived at Marilyn's apartment to work on the scene. But Marilyn wouldn't answer the door. Natasha had seen Marilyn's lights on as she walked up, but after knocking on the door and waiting a few minutes, she saw the lights turn off. Natasha persisted, calling out Marilyn's name until, finally, the lights were turned back on and the door was answered.

"Marilyn said she had been hearing men outside her door all evening, and when there was a knock at the door, she just snapped and became unglued."

At first, Natasha brushed off the event, believing that Marilyn was attempting to create in her real life the fear she needed to exhibit in the film. Yet as the evening went on, Marilyn would often stop their work and tell Natasha that she was hearing voices . . . and to listen to see if she, too, could hear them. The source continued, "She'd ask, 'Did you hear that? Did you hear that?' Natasha would just reprimand her. She thought she was trying to make excuses for having forgotten her lines. However, before the session was over, Natasha began to feel that Marilyn was really on her way to having some kind of a breakdown."

A few evenings later, Natasha requested a meeting with Johnny Hyde.

By this time, Natasha believed that Johnny was using Marilyn for his own personal pleasure, and also to gain bragging rights about her in the Hollywood community. Natasha, having admitted her *own* strong romantic feelings for Marilyn, would have been happy to see him out of Marilyn's life. She believed Marilyn didn't really need Johnny anyway. She felt that if she continued to work with her, she could be the one to build Marilyn's career. Marilyn's new reputation as a fine actress would surely, in Natasha's mind, generate work for her in major films. Moreover, Johnny's presence in Marilyn's life threatened to dilute Natasha's importance. How would it look if he were the one ultimately credited with Marilyn's success? What would happen if Marilyn felt he was more important to her than Natasha? It was in this climate of fear, insecurity, and jealousy that Natasha operated. "She wanted Johnny to back off," continued her friend and student. "I think she hoped he would see Marilyn as spoiled goods if he knew she was losing her mind, then she [Natasha] could have Marilyn to herself again."

To that end, Natasha told Johnny that she was worried about Marilyn and thought he was putting too much pressure on her. She claimed that the "personal attention" he expected of her also added to her stress. At first she spoke in general terms, not becoming specific about the unusual events that had unfolded at their coaching session. However, since Johnny appeared unmoved, Natasha spelled it out for him. "She's hearing voices," she told him.

Johnny wasn't surprised by Natasha's news. It was as if he already knew about Marilyn's "voices." Perhaps she had already confided in him about them. He certainly didn't throw his hands in the air and surrender, as Natasha had fantasized. Instead, he was immediately concerned for Marilyn and wanted to do something to help her. "Johnny thought of doctors as magicians," explained a coworker of his. "He was like most everybody else in the business back then. If an actor couldn't shoot a scene, the first person to call was a doctor."

Whether to treat the flu or an anxiety attack, Johnny knew that barbiturates had become a staple in the world of filmmaking. As it would happen, he would be the first to introduce Marilyn to a brand-new reality, one formed by barbiturates. He believed that such drugs could make his girlfriend's world feel like a safer place to her. He also thought, as did many people at that time, that there was no downside to these pharmaceuticals. He viewed them as a portal to happiness and fulfillment and saw the fact that they were almost exclusively accessible to the rich and powerful as evidence of their effectiveness. Perhaps he was using as a measure of the effectiveness of drugs the example of the brilliant career of Judy Garland, who for the past decade had been like an ATM for Metro: deposit drugs—uppers, downers, whatever—and out comes money, and lots of it.

At Johnny's behest, studio doctors began prescribing drugs to Marilyn on a regular basis. She happily took them. They helped, at least in the short term. Her anxieties were decreased. The voices became softer and bothered her less. Of course, there was one problem with the new reality being entered by Marilyn Monroe. It wasn't real.

The Asphalt Jungle

*I*n the autumn of 1949, Marilyn began work on John Huston's gritty crime drama *The Asphalt Jungle*, the first so-called caper film that was told from the point of view of the criminals. Marilyn had a showy, memorable cameo—three brief appearances that comprised about five minutes—in the noir classic as Angela Phinley, the sexually arousing, libidinous mistress of an elderly, married, white-collar crook (an attorney) played by longtime MGM contract player Louis Calhern. When finally released in May 1950, the film would earn four Oscar nominations, two of which were for Huston's writing and directing, with other nominations for black-and-white cinematography and best supporting actor (Sam Jaffe). Marilyn acquitted herself well in her work on this film, demonstrating her growing ability as an actress. Her name didn't appear in the opening credits, however. It's on a list at the end of the movie—eleventh out of fifteen names. However, it was a start—a very important movie that would be the catalyst of future big events in her life and career.

"She'd worked hard and, it seemed, had been working hard on

herself for some time," John Huston would later say. "I remember the audition was interesting because the scene was supposed to be on a couch and we had no couch there, so she laid on the floor for the reading. She wasn't happy with the audition, though, and asked if she could do it again. I said, of course. Do it as many times as you like. She didn't know it, but she had the part before she even said one word.

"I just knew she was right for it before I even saw her audition for it. She was so vulnerable, so sweet, so willing, you just melted in her presence. I remember thinking, how can anyone not cast her in any movie? She was perfect for the part in *The Asphalt Jungle*. She said to me, 'I just want you to know that this will be my most important movie.' And I told her, 'Good luck.' She was worried she wouldn't be as good in it as I knew she'd be. 'What if I let you down?' she asked me. 'You won't,' I told her. 'Just be yourself and you'll be fine.' You just wanted the best for her, you know? Maybe it was a lucky break for her, I don't know. One thing is certain, she was ready for it. She was ready for it when she got lucky."

Of course, Marilyn would make sure Natasha was on the set with her every day. In fact, there's a moment in the movie where Marilyn can be seen glancing off set, presumably at Natasha for direction.

"I don't know what I did," Marilyn said when she finished her work on *The Asphalt Jungle*, "but I do know it felt wonderful!"

Years later, Marilyn Monroe noted that she first saw the finished movie with Johnny at her side, holding her hand. They didn't speak on the way home, both lost in thought about the magnitude of her achievement. "His heart was happy for me," she recalled. "I could feel his unselfishness and deep kindness. No man had ever looked on me with such kindness. He not only knew me, he knew Norma Jeane. He knew all the pain and all the desperate things in me. When he put his arms around me and said he loved me, I knew it was true. Nobody had ever loved me like that," she concluded. "I wished with all my heart that I could love him back."

All About Eve

*E*ven though Marilyn knew she'd done a good job on *The Asphalt Jungle*, it wasn't to be released for some time. Therefore, 1950 would be a year of great anticipation for her—and a certain amount of frustration as well.

In January, Marilyn filmed another awful movie that Johnny Hyde had secured for her, another bit part, this one in a roller-derby film, *The Fireball*, starring Mickey Rooney. Marilyn's role was purely decorative, with only a few scenes and lines of dialogue. Another film that received little play at this time was a fluff movie Marilyn made that same season called *Right Cross*. This one was a boxing film from MGM starring the studio's popular, peach-cheeked girl next door June Allyson and her husband Dick Powell. Marilyn was uncredited and mainly unnoticed in the tiny role of Dusky Ledoux, a bar girl who has a brief encounter with Powell's character. Then, in the spring of 1950, Marilyn was jettisoned into yet another mediocre movie called *Home Town Story*. The less said about this one the better—though it did resurface abroad as a curiosity after her death. In it, Marilyn has a two-minute scene as a receptionist in a newspaper office.

Johnny Hyde's rationale for having Marilyn make brief appearances in such terrible movies was that he hoped if she were seen enough onscreen, MGM might actually offer her a contract. That didn't happen, though. In the meantime, Marilyn would end up spending most of her free time posing for ads, pinups, and photo essays—anything to make a living while she waited to break into what she was finding to be a very tough business.

Meanwhile, Johnny continued to squire Marilyn around town. Ironically, the power had shifted in their relationship. She had gone into it feeling that she needed him. Now, a year later, he was acting as if he needed her, and he seemed to want to do whatever he could think of to keep her happy lest she walk out on him. True, *The Asphalt Jungle* was important in retrospect because it showed what Marilyn was capable of, but it was such a brief role it went unnoticed by critics. (Later in the year, Johnny would book her in a TV commercial—her first and only—for a motor oil!)

In April of 1950, Johnny Hyde took Marilyn to meet writer and director Joseph L. Mankiewicz, who was getting ready to mount a new film for Darryl Zanuck at Fox. It was *All About Eve*, and Mankiewicz cast Marilyn in a small but pivotal part based on the job she had done in *The Asphalt Jungle*. "I thought she was right for the role, which was of an aspiring theater actress," he recalled many years later, "and Marilyn was nothing if not aspiring at the time. It was suggested that the character would do whatever she had to do to get ahead, and I sensed that in Marilyn there was a certain amount of cunning as well as the innocence. I found her a fascinating mix. On one hand, she was vulnerable. But, on the other, calculating. She knew what she was doing, that one. There was never a false move with her."

The story of *Eve*, adapted from a *Cosmopolitan* short story, is well known—a ruthless, conniving ingénue, Eve Harrington (Anne Baxter), insinuates herself into the life and career of a legendary, aging Broadway star, Margo Channing (Bette Davis), wrecking the lives of all those she touches, as she claws her way to the very pinnacle of theatrical stardom. In two of three set pieces upon which the movie is based, Marilyn shone brilliantly and displayed the early promise she would later fulfill as a dominant screen personality for the next decade and a half. In a scene on the staircase at a birthday party in Margo's apartment, she is seated in the center with most of the film's stars seated or standing around her—Baxter, Gary Merrill, Celeste Holm, George Sanders, Gregory Ratoff—and it is impossible to take your eyes off her, even when other characters are delivering their lines. As has been said a thousand times, the camera loves her, and so do we. In her other scene, in the lobby of a theater, she has just fallen victim to her nerves over an audition and has gotten sick in the ladies' room. Her queasiness is unmistakable and we feel like pressing a cold towel to her forehead, her emotions spent, raw.

Today, *All About Eve* is recognized as one of the classic films of all time and certainly the best picture about the Broadway theater ever made. Entire books have been written about the movie, the best of these being *More About All About Eve*, by Sam Staggs. Anecdotes abound about this production, one of the best being that production was constantly held up due to Marilyn's lateness. She simply could never be on time.

At any rate, when released, *All About Eve* would generate fourteen Oscar nominations. It would also hold the Academy of Motion Picture Arts and Sciences' record for most nominations for a single picture until 1997, when James Cameron's disaster epic *Titanic* received the same number of nods—with *Titanic* winning a total of eleven Oscars, while *Eve* earned six, including Best Picture, Best Director, and Best Screenplay. Also, interestingly, the first and only appearance Marilyn would make at the Oscars—on March 29, 1951—was to present the award to Thomas Moulton for *All About Eve* for Best Sound Recording.

Considering her small part in *All About Eve*, one would think Marilyn would have done anything in her power to not be tardy, but that just wasn't her way. One day, actor Gregory Ratoff declared of her, "That girl will be a big star!" Celeste Holm rolled her eyes and said, "Why, because she keeps everyone waiting?" Indeed, much has been made over the years about Marilyn's penchant for being late. She was tardy for just about every appointment she made, whether it was work-related or just a coffee date with a friend. It didn't matter the occasion, everyone in her life knew she would be late for it. It was a maddening habit, but because she was who she was, most people just put up with it. To be fair, she usually made it worth their while. One thing was certain: She did light up the room with her presence. "It's not so much that I'm always late," she once quipped, "it's just that everybody else is in such a hurry!"

Dumb as a Blonde Fox

In the autumn of 1950, Marilyn—now twenty-four—went back to school. She enrolled in a ten-week program at the University of California at Los Angeles to study world literature. Fellow classmates don't have remarkable memories of her because she did what she could to fit in as a student and not call much attention to herself. "I want to expand my horizons," she explained to Grace Goddard, who wholeheartedly approved. In the last few years, as she lived her life on her own terms and met a wide range of fascinating people, she had become much more thoughtful and introspective. Anyone who thought she was a brainless blonde had been fooled by her carefully constructed image. It's true that she was still a vulnerable and scared child at heart. Norma Jeane was alive and well in everything Marilyn did—or was afraid to do—in her life and career. However, she was, at the very least, manageable. Marilyn wasn't as helpless as Norma Jeane had been, that much was clear by the time she was twenty-four. But, she also knew that her weak routine could work to her advantage. There's probably nothing more attractive to a powerful man, she decided, than a beautiful and hopelessly vulnerable young woman.

"When she would go to cocktail parties, she would put on the act for all to see," said Jerry Eidelman, an aspiring actor who knew Marilyn. "She was living in a duplex on Fountain Avenue in West Hollywood at the time with a scary acting teacher. [Marilyn had moved in with Natasha—but platonically, just to save money.] She and the teacher had a cocktail party one night and invited me because I lived in the neighborhood. When I would see Marilyn here and there, I found her to be bright . . . and interested. But when I went to this cocktail party, I was amazed by what I saw of her. She came off like she didn't have two brain cells to rub together. She was very flirtatious with anyone she thought might help her, any of the acting teacher's guests who, I took it, were casting agents. She had on a dress that was so tight there was no way she could sit down while wearing it. I noticed that she just sort of propped herself up in a corner with a martini in her hand and received admirers as if she was royalty—a princess who was just a bit drunk. She had this little girl's kind of voice, which was not very much like what I knew her to sound like in her day-to-day life. I knew she put some of that on for most of her movies, I just didn't know she did it in real life."*

Her costar in the movie *The Fireball*, James Brown, concurred. "She'd sit there batting her eyes and give you the feeling she was a pretty dumb girl, but then there was this intense, almost secret-like sincerity behind what she'd say, and that left me with the idea that this girl is a mystery. She was truly a mystery."

Jerry Eidelman continued, "The next day, I saw her walking a little dog she had, a Chihuahua, I think. I remember she had on black-and-white checked pedal pushers with a little white peasant blouse, buttoned all the way to the top. And she had on what looked like ballerina shoes—flats of some kind, made of a satin material. One thing about running into her, if you liked her as much as I did you instantly memorized whatever she had on—at least I always did. Anyway, I stopped her and said, 'You know, Marilyn, you were very different last night at the party.' She looked at me with wide eyes and said, 'Why, whatever do you mean, Jerry?' I just smiled at her and said, 'You know what I mean.' She gave me a little look. 'Marilyn, you're no dumb blonde, and you know it,' I told her. 'If anything, you're as dumb as a blonde fox.' She loved that. 'I don't even know what that means,' she said, 'but that's pretty funny, Jerry.' Then she winked at me and continued on her way with her dog."

By this time Johnny Hyde's health had begun to fail and he was for the most part restricted to his bed. For a man who had tried to

---

* Again, leave it to James Haspiel for another classic Monroe memory. He says that in the eight years he knew her, he never once saw Marilyn "drunk, not even tipsy." However, one day he showed her a photograph that was taken on a day when she had definitely had too much to drink. He handed it to her and said, "This was taken in an elevator in Marlene Dietrich's apartment building, and you were very high." Without missing a beat, Marilyn gave him a wide-eyed look and said, "What floor was I on?"

stay so vital despite his heart disease, this was a heavy cross to bear. He was still devoted to Marilyn, though she seemed less interested in him—especially when he became ill. "I don't know how to deal with it," she told one relative. "It makes me so sad to see him. I think he believes I'm heartless because I don't want to see him that way. I just don't know what to do."

At the end of the year, Marilyn finally signed a three-year contract with the William Morris Agency for representation. She'd just had a handshake deal with Johnny the entire time they'd been working together. Now it was time to make it official. At this same time, Johnny arranged for her to have an important screen test at Fox. "She was excited about that, I remember," said Jerry Eidelman. "She told me that she wanted nothing more than to do a good job, sign with Fox, and, as she put it, 'become the biggest star there is, Jerry—*the biggest star there is!*' I told her, 'You know, Marilyn, there's more to show business than stardom. There's acting.' And she looked at me squarely and said, 'Yes, Jerry, but sadly you don't get to do much unless you're a big star.' She had me there.

"The day after the screen test, she was on cloud nine. She said it had gone very well. A couple days later, she looked a little crushed when I saw her. She said she didn't get a big contract with the studio, but she did get a movie. 'It's a comedy,' she said glumly. 'I play a secretary.' I asked her what it was called. She said, 'Who cares, Jerry? I play a dumb secretary. That's not going to take me anywhere I haven't already been.' I suggested that maybe she needed a new agent. 'Great,' she said, rolling her eyes. 'I just signed with William Morris for three years.' Then she tossed her head back and laughed. 'I think my goose is cooked,' she said. 'If you see me still out here walking my own dog next month, you'll know it was a bit part, like all my other pictures.' She was disappointed but, still, there was something about her that made you know she was not going to give up. I thought to myself, you know, she's really something, that Marilyn Monroe."

The movie Marilyn referred to was to be called *As Young as You Feel*. The deal was put together for her by Johnny Hyde, of course, with an eye toward securing a contract with Fox. He was really working for her, he loved her so much. "You know, maybe you should marry him," Joseph Schenck told Marilyn. "What do you have to lose?" She usually respected Schenck's opinion, but not this time. "I'm not going to marry someone I'm not in love with," she told him. "But Marilyn, which would you rather have—a poor boy you loved with all your heart, or a rich man who loved you with all his?" She said she'd rather have the poor boy. "I thought you were smarter than that," Schenck told her, joking with her now. "I'm disappointed in you, Marilyn."

In mid-December, Marilyn and Natasha went to Tijuana to do some Christmas shopping. Johnny and his secretary went to Palm Springs for the weekend. It was there that he had a heart attack. He was rushed back to Los Angeles by ambulance. Marilyn sped back to the city as quickly as she could. Johnny's nephew, Norman Brokaw—also representing her at William Morris—accompanied Marilyn to Cedars of Lebanon Hospital (now Cedars-Sinai Medical Center), but by the time they got there, Johnny was dead. She was told that before he passed away, he cried out, "Marilyn! *Marilyn!*"

The hospital staff let Marilyn and Norman enter Johnny's room, where his body was still on a bed covered by a white sheet. Marilyn, seeming stricken, her eyes dark and shadowed in pain, walked on shaky legs to the bed and very slowly pulled the sheet down to Johnny's shoulders. Johnny had once told her that if he were to die, all she would have to do would be to hold him in her arms and he would spring back to life, just for her. Gazing down at his dead body, tears of regret and sorrow spilled onto his face as she cried out, "Johnny, I did love you. Please know that I did love you."

Suicide over Johnny?

*J*ohnny Hyde's funeral was extremely difficult; his estranged wife refused to allow Marilyn Monroe to attend it. "They thought I was awful," Marilyn later recalled. It's been said that Marilyn and Natasha Lytess disguised themselves as family servants and managed to get into the service anyway, which was held at Johnny's North Palm Drive house. Elia Kazan's yarn was that Marilyn broke into the house the night before the service and kept vigil till morning beside Johnny's coffin. Later there were published accounts that the next day at the funeral, she hurled herself onto the coffin and had to be pulled off it, kicking and screaming in agonizing grief. That story was started by Marilyn, in her own book: "I threw myself on the coffin and sobbed. I wished I was dead with him." No one remembers anything like this happening at the funeral. Rather, Marilyn was apparently subdued and contemplative throughout the burial service at Forest Lawn Memorial Park.

Afterward, Marilyn stayed at Johnny's grave site for many hours, alone with her thoughts and memories. She stayed so long, in fact, that the sun was setting and an attendant suggested that she take her leave. According to veteran Hollywood agent Norman Winters, that anecdote is actually true.

She hadn't been in love with Johnny; she was clear about it. It was just a simple matter of chemistry. She hadn't wanted to lead him on, but didn't know how to keep him in her life—indeed, in her career—without having sex with him, which, she later admitted, "was, I guess, the same as leading him on." However, they had shared so many intimate moments, she felt certain that no one knew him quite as well as she did. "No one knows the true depth of what we shared," she would later tell one of her closest friends. "When it's just the two of you in bed in each other's arms and it's pitch black in the room and you put your head on his chest and hear his heart beat, that's when you really know a man. When his heart beats for you, that's when you really know him."

"If I had never met him, he would be alive with his family," a distraught Marilyn told Natasha, according to Natasha's memory. "And now I'm alone."

"You're not alone," Natasha told her, hugging her tightly. "I'm with you, Marilyn. I'm with you."

"I had to keep telling her 'you're not alone,'" Natasha would later recall, "because I truly believed she was about to end her life."

"I hadn't seen her in some time," said her neighbor Jerry Eidelman, "and I ran into her in—of all places—the grocery store. It had to have been just a day or so after the funeral. She was buying cleaning supplies. I remember that she had on yellow slacks and a white-and-yellow angora sweater, her hair in a ponytail and horn-rimmed glasses. 'Are you cleaning the house?' I asked her. She forced sort of a thin smile and said, 'No, I don't clean, Jerry. We have someone else do the cleaning. But for her to shop for the supplies would cost more money, so I'm doing it.' Then she said, 'I need to stay busy. Did you hear about Johnny Hyde?' I told her I did. She said, 'It's so awful. I don't know how to cope with it. And then this thing with my mother, too, is driving me crazy.' I asked what she was talking about, and she said that her mother had gone off and married some creep and that she was worried sick about her. She said she was thinking of going on a trip to try to find the woman and rescue her from her husband. I said, 'But Marilyn, you can't do that. Or at least not alone. Take me with you. We'll find her together.' She said, 'I don't think I can expose you or anyone else to my mother. You don't know what she has put me and my sister through. She's very ill.' Then, in what I now view as one of those great Marilyn Monroe moments, she put her hand up to her forehead dramatically, swooned a little, and whispered, 'I'm so sorry, I simply must go now.' She then rushed out, leaving her cart of cleaning supplies behind.

"I paid for the stuff and took it to her home. I knocked on the door and she answered. She looked awful. She'd been crying and was very pale. 'Here are your cleaning supplies,' I told her. 'You forgot them.' She looked at me blankly and asked, 'What cleaning supplies?' I said, 'Thirty minutes ago, Marilyn—at the grocery store, remember?' She was very disoriented. 'Oh, that's right, the cleaning supplies,' she said. She then took the bag from me, and without saying thank you or anything else, just turned and closed the door behind her. It was very strange and, also, very disconcerting."

A couple of days after Johnny's funeral, Natasha returned home from work at the studio and found Marilyn in her bedroom. She was out cold, her cheeks puffed out and her coloring pale. Horrified, Natasha rushed to her side and forced open her mouth. It was full of dissolving pills. Natasha managed to shake Marilyn awake. By way of explanation, Marilyn told her she had taken some sleeping pills—which she had bought over the counter at Schwab's—and then fell asleep before she could wash them down. It seemed such an unlikely scenario, Natasha didn't really believe it. "She felt worthless," Natasha later remembered. "She thought she was responsible for Hyde's heart attack. If he had not loved her and cared so much about her [she thought] he would still be alive."

No, Marilyn insisted, she had not tried to kill herself over Johnny Hyde. She would never do such a thing. She later told photographer and friend Milton Greene, "I felt guilty and I had a lot of feelings to sort through—but, oh baby, I sure didn't want to die. The fact is," she concluded, sadly, "he had made certain that I had nothing to die for."

Natasha wasn't convinced. She wrote a letter to her student Helena Albert at this time in which she said she felt that Marilyn "was intent on doing herself in" and that she feared there was nothing she or anyone else could do about it. "I think that when a person wants to kill herself, she will at some point do it despite the best intentions of her friends to prevent it from happening," she wrote. She also wrote that she was determined to be loyal to Marilyn and do whatever she could to "keep her stabilized and," she added, somewhat wryly, "if there is any time for it, perhaps we will be able to work on her acting, as well."

Two weeks later, on Christmas Day, Marilyn Monroe presented

Natasha Lytess with an antique ivory cameo brooch framed in gold. On it, she had inscribed, "I just want you to know that I owe you *much* more than my life."

Marilyn Tries to Meet Her "Father"

*W*hen Johnny Hyde died, Marilyn felt that she'd lost not only one of her greatest allies, but also the closest thing she had to a father figure. She turned to Natasha Lytess to get through this difficult time. Natasha was supportive, of course, but she believed that Johnny's death could indirectly have a troubling effect on Marilyn's career. Natasha had been working with Marilyn on "deepening" her performances. She now saw that she had such great potential and wanted to make certain that she didn't fall back to the mostly hollow portrayals she had been doing in her earlier films. "I think tragic roles are her forte," she would later observe. "There is a strangeness about her . . . an un-real quality."

Though she wasn't exactly a fan of Johnny Hyde's, Natasha couldn't help but believe that Marilyn's association with him had had a positive effect on her acting. After her most recent performances, she felt certain that Marilyn was on the brink of a major breakthrough. She had seen a maturation of Marilyn as both a woman and an actress. Natasha thought that Johnny believed in Marilyn so much, it encouraged her to finally believe in herself—and thus she saw the benefits not only in her acting but in her day-to-day life. With Johnny gone, Natasha felt that they needed somehow to find another person to fill that role in Marilyn's life. Was it possible that her real father might do so? Natasha felt it was worth a try.

In Marilyn Monroe's life, there was no question in her mind about her paternity. She simply knew that Charles Gifford was her father—just as Gladys had known so many years earlier. Since this was before medical confirmation of paternity was even a viable option, there probably had been no way for Marilyn to know absolutely—yet she said she absolutely knew in her heart. When Natasha approached Marilyn about tracking down her father, saying that they should have a face-to-face encounter with him, Marilyn was agreeable.

Marilyn spent a few days doing an investigation into just what happened to her father after he left Los Angeles. It turned out he didn't go far. Gifford had moved to Northern California. After working as a contractor responsible for the building of chalets for a private resort, he went into poultry farming. He married again, to a woman who died soon after the wedding. Finally, he established the Red Rock Dairy, a five-acre farm in Hemet, where he remarried. While Marilyn had no problem finding Gifford's home address, she couldn't find a current phone number for him—though word had definitely begun to spread through Hemet that she was trying to find one. Apparently she decided that she would take a risk and drive to Hemet, hoping that maybe an element of surprise would work in her favor.

Susan Reimer, who was eight years old at the time, recalled that her family was excited that a celebrity was coming to visit their "Uncle Stan." When she asked her mother, Dolly, who was coming, the older woman put a finger up to her mouth and said, "*Shhh.* We're not supposed to tell a soul. But it's"—dramatic pause—"Marilyn Monroe." Reimer recalled, "That's when I learned about the family's secret, one that was never discussed openly and only whispered about. Uncle Stan was Marilyn Monroe's father. I was told to keep my mouth shut about it, and I did for many years." She says that when she confronted her uncle and asked him directly about his link to Marilyn Monroe, he balked and said that he didn't want to reveal anything that would hurt his wife.

Charles Stanley Gifford Jr. today says, "People have been trying to connect these dots back to my family for decades. It's not true. My father would have told me if he was Marilyn Monroe's father, too. He just would have. The press pestered him and my poor stepmother, Mary, to death because of these stories Marilyn made up. The poor woman had nothing to do with it, and yet never had a moment's peace in her life because of it."

Back in Los Angeles, Marilyn, armed only with Gifford's address, prepared to depart, assuming that Natasha would be joining her on the drive. However, Lytess seemed to think that Marilyn needed to face that powerful moment on her own. Susan Martinson, who was eighteen in 1950 and a student and friend of Lytess's, recalled, "Natasha told me that Marilyn cornered her and said, 'Please come with me. I don't want to drive up there alone. He's already hung up on me once and I'm not sure I'll be able to handle it if he rejects me again.' Natasha tried to talk her way out of it, but Marilyn insisted."

Marilyn and Natasha drove several hours to Charles Gifford's home. When they finally arrived, Marilyn reached into the backseat and fished through her purse. There she found a recent magazine that featured her on the cover. She took a deep breath, then exited the car. Did she really believe that this man could be unaware of who she was—that she needed proof that she was "somebody" to convince him she was worthy of a chance to plead her case? Possibly. She rang the doorbell, then waited, the magazine in her hand rolled into a tube.

The door opened.

Marilyn lifted her lowered head to find—a woman. Apparently, it was Mary Gifford, Charles Stanley Gifford's present wife. Marilyn's conversation with her was brief. All that came of it was a business card with Gifford's lawyer's number on it, and an awful memory of another broken dream. Gifford's son, Charles Stanley Jr., insists today that "my father would never have given Marilyn a business card." In a letter to her former student Helena Albert, Natasha was very clear that she and Marilyn definitely had made the trip, though. She wrote that it had been her idea and that "I regret now putting Marilyn through it because I think it did her no good." She also wrote that during the long drive she and Marilyn discussed "her father issues," and that Natasha had decided before they even got to Hemet that "we were making a mistake in not bringing a psychiatrist with us. I don't know what I was thinking!"

In 1962, Charles Stanley Gifford was diagnosed with cancer shortly before Marilyn Monroe's death. At that time, he supposedly tried to contact Marilyn from a California hospital. According to Monroe's friend, actor and masseur Ralph Roberts, a nurse telephoned Marilyn and said, "Your father is very ill and may die. His dying wish is to see you." To that, Marilyn was alleged to have said, "Tell the gentleman to contact my lawyer." Again, his son doesn't believe it. "Absolutely not. If you knew my father, you would know how ridiculous that is. It is not true."

Charles Stanley Gifford would die of cancer in 1965. Before his death, he supposedly confided to his Presbyterian minister, Dr. Donald Liden, that he had recently spoken to Marilyn on the telephone—impossible, of course, since she would have passed away three years earlier. When Dr. Liden questioned Gifford about it, he confessed. "My daughter was Marilyn Monroe," he said. Dr. Liden recalled, "My jaw dropped. But I didn't doubt the truth of it. He said that he felt the mother [Gladys] had been unfair. She had cut him off and didn't allow him to see the child. When he married again, it got difficult. His wife was a fine woman and he didn't want to hurt her by acknowledging he'd had a child out of wedlock. I detected it was a sorrowful thing for him."

"I was with my father every day when he was sick," insists his son, Charles Jr. "There was no deathbed confession to me, I can tell you that much. We were very close. He told me the particulars of where he wanted to be buried, how he felt about his life, his children. If ever there would have been a time for a deathbed confession, it would have been on his deathbed!

"My father and his friend Ray Guthrie lived together at the time he was dating Gladys," Gifford Jr. continues. "I once called Ray and asked him about this time. He said, 'Yeah, I remember Gladys. She used to come around and cook breakfast for us and we'd go out and do this and that, just have fun, nothing serious.' I asked, 'Well did

Dad ever say anything to you about fathering a child by her?' He just laughed and said, 'No, but if he had, he sure would have mentioned it.'

"My father's DNA is on record at Riverside Hospital," he concludes. "If Marilyn Monroe's DNA is on record at one of the hospitals she was ever in, I challenge someone to do a test and compare them, and you'll find that Charles Stanley Gifford is not her father—and I am not her half brother."

Early Films

*T*he films featuring Marilyn Monroe in 1950 and 1951 were not exactly memorable. *As Young as You Feel* found her back at 20th Century-Fox, and despite her sixth-place billing and her prominent display on the posters and lobby cards, she had but two brief scenes as Harriet, a secretary. Then there was *Love Nest*, a post–World War II sex comedy without the sex, starring June Haver and William Lundigan. Marilyn's role was described in a review as "an extended cameo," the highlight being a scene in which she emerges from a shower, draped in a towel. There was also *Let's Make It Legal*, with things only slightly better for Marilyn as regards her screen time, which is mostly spent in a bathing suit. Claudette Colbert and Macdonald Carey star in this romantic comedy "that feels overstretched even at an hour and a quarter," in one critic's appraisal.

In March 1951, the deal Johnny Hyde had been working on for Marilyn to re-sign with Fox was finally finished, without him. The William Morris Agency, Johnny's firm, wasn't interested in Marilyn after his death, so she ended up with the Famous Artists Agency, where she would be managed for the next several years by a man named Hugh French. The Fox deal was for forty weeks and $500 a week whether she worked or not—and she couldn't work for anyone else either, unless the company loaned her out. At the end of each year, the studio could decide not to renew, and if so, she would be on her own once again. However, Fox could also renew at the end of the term, and if it did she would receive $750 a week for the second year, $1,250 for the third, $1,500 for the fourth, $2,000 for the fifth, $2,500 for the sixth, and $3,500 for the seventh, if she lasted that long. It's interesting that she would now be working for Darryl Zanuck again, a man who clearly had no love for her. He only signed her because Joe Schenck, Johnny Hyde, and so many others kept pressuring him about it. Natasha Lytess also went with Marilyn as part of the deal, and would be getting $750 a week to coach Marilyn—$500 from Fox and $250 from Marilyn. So Marilyn was paying Natasha 50 percent of what Fox paid her that first year, which certainly showed how much value she placed on her work with the acting teacher. Natasha was making quite a bit more money that first year than Marilyn herself.

Another of her early films was Fritz Lang's *Clash by Night* (made in 1951, though released in 1952), adapted for the screen from an unsuccessful Broadway play by Clifford Odets, who, with the play's director, Lee Strasberg, and others, had founded the controversial, left-leaning Group Theatre in the 1930s. The play starred Tallulah Bankhead as Mae Doyle, a part assumed by Barbara Stanwyck in the film. Despite her prominent billing, Marilyn's role was minor. Still, she received excellent notices, among them these words of praise by Alton Cook in the *New York World-Telegram and Sun*: "The girl has a refreshing exuberance, an abundance of girlish high spirits. She is a forceful actress, too. . . . She has definitely stamped herself as a gifted new star. . . . Her role here is not very big, but she makes it dominant." If Fox's loaning out of its contract player to RKO was meant to test the waters as to her box-office potential, as has been speculated, the studio got its answer. Thus reassured, Fox set about finding scripts to showcase her obvious charms, pairing her with more established leading men.

Jasper Dies

$\mathscr{B}$y the fall of 1951, Marilyn Monroe had moved out of Natasha Lytess's apartment and begun sharing a home with Shelley Winters in Hollywood. There were no hard feelings, apparently, since the three women remained social together after Marilyn moved in with Shelley. That said, she would have a lot more fun with the thrill-seeking Winters than she ever did with the often maudlin Natasha Lytess. Also, at the suggestion of one of her intimates, Elia Kazan, Marilyn would begin taking additional acting classes with renowned drama teacher Michael Chekhov, known for his acting technique called "The Method." She had told Kazan that she was bored with the roles she was playing because so many of them had been basically the same kind of empty-headed characterization. She wanted nothing more than to challenge herself with more complex parts—and also wanted others to think of her as being more than a caricature. He agreed. She had a lot to give, she just needed to sharpen her skills. (It's not known how Natasha Lytess felt about Marilyn's second acting teacher.) Kazan also suggested that Marilyn take more classes at UCLA, and she did. She enrolled there for a course in "Backgrounds of Literature," described as "Historical, social and cultural aspects of various periods with an introduction to the literature, itself." Anytime she had an opportunity to broaden her mind, she wanted to take advantage of it. This time, though, she caused quite a sensation on campus, unlike her previous experience there when she wasn't as well known. She would have much preferred to blend in with the other students, but how could she?

At this same time, Marilyn received a telephone call from her half sister Berniece. Berniece's father, Jasper—who had been married to Marilyn's mother, Gladys, and who had absconded with her children so many years ago—had died. Even though Marilyn never met him, she did have some knowledge of him. When, as Norma

Jeane, she had become old enough to start asking questions about her father, Gladys had told her that he had died in an automobile accident. (Marilyn would later say that she never really believed it. Once, she said, when she pushed the issue, Gladys "went into the bedroom and locked herself in.") Gladys had kept a photo of Edward Mortenson—Jasper—on her wall, seen by Norma Jeane on the few occasions she would visit. When the young girl finally inquired as to the identity of the man in the picture, Gladys lied and said that he was her father. Marilyn then fell completely under his spell, she would later say, even if he was just a man in a photograph. "It felt so good to have a father, to be able to look at his picture and know I belonged to him," she later recalled. "And what a wonderful photograph it was. He wore a slouch hat a little gaily on the side. There was a lively smile in his eyes, and he had a thin mustache like Clark Gable. I felt very warm toward the picture." In fact, Marilyn recalled that looking at that photo of her father was "my first happy time." She said she spent many nights dreaming of him and fantasizing about the kind of man he might have been if only he'd been in her life.

Now the man Marilyn had spun so many fantasies around was gone. Jasper was the only parent Berniece had ever known. The most Marilyn could do was feel sorry for Berniece's loss and stash her conflicted feelings about Jasper in her heart—along with all of the other ambivalent feelings she had about her parents.

Soon after Jasper's death, authorities in Pineville, Kentucky, noted that he was listed on Marilyn's birth certificate as her father. This gave them a great excuse to be in contact with a movie star. Marilyn was pestered by lawyers in Kentucky for months as to whether she wanted to stake a claim on Jasper's meager estate, until finally she made it clear—via her own attorney—that she had no such interest. Also at about this time, she hired a robust woman named Inez Melson, with large round glasses and an officious demeanor, as her business manager. She was instructed to try to send money to Gladys on a regular basis—difficult to do since it was always so difficult to keep track of Gladys's whereabouts. Though she had filed for divorce from John Eley, Gladys was still with him, as far as anyone knew, and the two were traveling across the country together.

One evening, Marilyn received a long-distance collect telephone call from Gladys, though she had no idea from where it originated. Gladys said that she didn't want to be found, that she felt let down by Marilyn and Berniece, and that the two of them were "very, very disappointing daughters." She ranted on about how much she loved Marilyn and that she had only given her up because her own mother, Della, had insisted upon it. She wanted to know how much longer Marilyn was going to hold it against her. Then she said that when Marilyn was a couple of years old, she caught "the whooping cough" from her foster brother, Lester, and that Gladys had moved into Ida Bolender's home and nursed Norma Jeane back to health. "And I stayed there for a whole month with you," she told Marilyn. "And you've never even thanked me for it." Marilyn had a very vague memory of Ida once telling her about something like that, but she certainly didn't remember it happening. It was very rare for Gladys to bring up the past. Marilyn thought perhaps it meant that Gladys was showing some improvement, because her memory was quite clear, and she suggested that Gladys return home as soon as possible so that they could discuss it and perhaps work things out between them. "But that's not possible," Gladys said, "because there are people telling me what to do, and they have told me not to go back to California under any circumstances. I could be in grave danger there." Now Gladys's illness was talking again. The disturbing telephone call ended with her warning Marilyn to be careful. "You're being watched," she told her daughter. "You must believe me, Norma Jeane." Then she hung up.

Marilyn later told Rupert Allan that she cried herself to sleep that night—but not before making sure all of her shades were drawn.

Norma Jeane Mortensen was born on June 1, 1926. This beautiful baby would, of course, grow up to one day become the great film star Marilyn Monroe. (*Retro Photo*)

A sad but beautiful photo of Marilyn the woman. This picture says it all about her: Vulnerable. Tragic. Gorgeous. (*Getty Images*)

The way Gladys Baker is holding Norma Jeane—almost as if she were a baby doll—suggests that maybe she wasn't prepared to be a mother. Less than two weeks after giving birth, Gladys turned the infant over to foster parents, Ida and Wayne Bolender, to raise. (*Getty Images*)

A very rare photo of Ida and Wayne Bolender with their foster children. Ida is holding the infant Norma Jeane in her arms. (*Courtesy of Maryanne Reed Collection*)

A never-before-published photograph of the man Gladys Baker said was Norma Jeane's father, Charles Stanley Gifford Sr. His son, Charles Stanley Jr.—interviewed for this book—maintains that he and Marilyn Monroe are not related. *(Retro Photo)*

Gladys would sometimes visit her daughter at the Bolenders' and take her for the occasional outing, such as this one to the beach when the girl was about three. Still, because of her mental illness, it was difficult for her to ever forge a relationship with her child. *(Getty Images)*

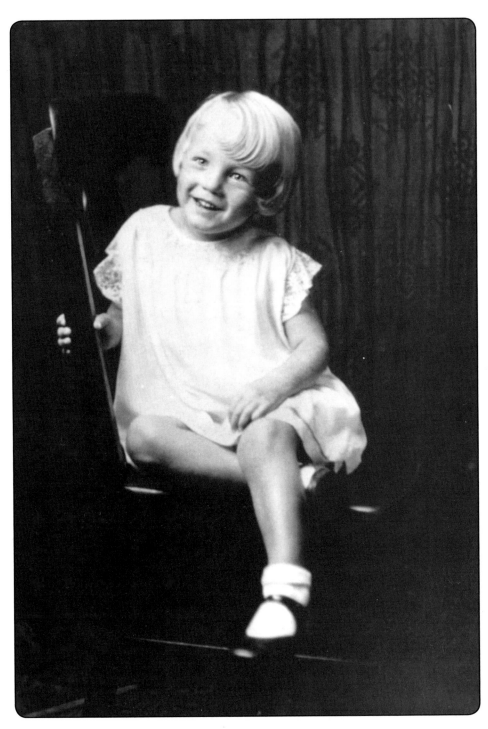

Norma Jeane at about four years of age. (*Photofest*)

Norma Jeane at age six.
(*Getty Images*)

Norma Jeane married
her first husband,
Jim Dougherty, in June
1942—but only so that
she would not have to go
into another orphanage.
(*Retro Photo*)

Norma Jeane was a highly successful model long before she ever became Marilyn Monroe. Here she is in 1944, "wearing" some of her many covers. (*Courtesy of Maryanne Reed Collection*)

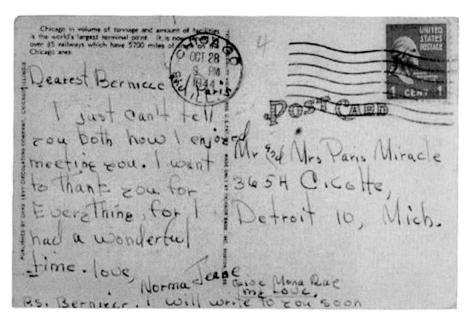

Chicago in volume of tonnage and amount of facilities
is the world's largest terminal point. It is now
over 35 railways which have 5700 miles of
Chicago area.

OCT 28
1944

Dearest Berniece

I just can't tell you both how I enjoyed meeting you. I want to thank you for Everything, for I had a wonderful time. love, Norma Jeane

P.S. Berniece. I will write to you soon

UNITED
STATES
POSTAGE
1 CENT

POST CARD

Mr and Mrs Paris Miracle
365 H Cicolte,
Detroit 10, Mich.

Give Mona Rae
my Love,

The postcard Norma Jeane wrote to her half sister, Berniece, after meeting her for the first time in October 1944. (*Getty Images*)

A very rare family photo taken at the Pacific Seas restaurant in September 1946, right after Norma Jeane was divorced from her first husband, James Dougherty. From left to right: Berniece Baker (Marilyn's half sister) and her daughter, Mona Rae; Grace Goddard (Norma Jeane's beloved guardian) and her sister, Enid Knebelkamp; Norma Jeane, Norma Jeane's "Aunt" Ana and her mother, Gladys Baker. (*Getty Images*)

The lavish production number "Diamonds Are a Girl's Best Friend," from the 1953 movie *Gentlemen Prefer Blondes.* *(Photofest)*

Marilyn married Joe DiMaggio in January of 1954, even though there were many indications that the marriage would not work out—not the least of which was his unhappiness over her career. Although Marilyn was forced to leave him when DiMaggio became physically abusive, their love for one another never died. *(Retro Photo)*

A love letter Marilyn wrote to Joe—addressed to "Dad." "I want to just be where you are," she wrote, "and be just what you want me to be." Unfortunately, what he wanted was for her to just be his wife, not one of the world's great movie stars. *(Getty Images)*

The filming of this famous scene from *The Seven Year Itch* was the catalyst to the end of Marilyn's relationship with Joe. It so enraged him that he became violent with her that very same evening. Then, as far as she was concerned, the marriage was over. *(Retro Photo)*

Three iconic poses of a legend.
(*Photofest*)

Marilyn received this very impersonal Christmas card from her
mother, Gladys, in December of 1956. She never knew just what kind
of communication to expect from her mother, who was at the Rock
Haven Sanitarium at the time. (*Shaan Kokin/Julien's Auctions*)

By the summer of 1960, Marilyn's third marriage, to Arthur Miller—
seen here on the set of *The Misfits*—was all but over. *(Photofest)*

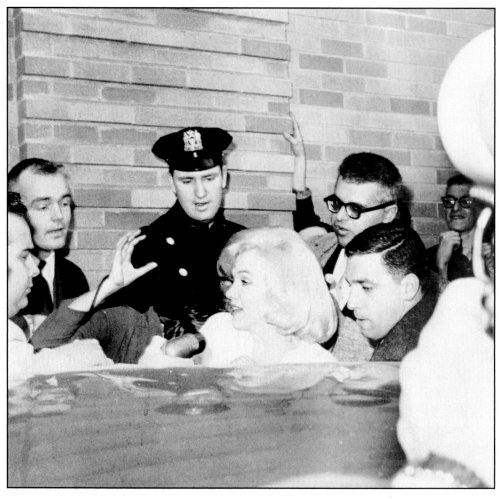

In February 1961, Marilyn was committed to the mental ward at the Payne Whitney Clinic in New York. Thanks to Joe DiMaggio's intervention, she was later moved to the Neurological Institute of Columbia University-Presbyterian Hospital, where she would remain for almost three weeks. Of course, there was the expected pandemonium when she was finally released from that facility—looking quite beautiful, as always. (*Retro Photo*)

Meanwhile, Marilyn's mother, Gladys Baker Eley, tried to commit suicide while locked behind these gates at the Rock Haven Sanitarium in California.
(Retro Photo)

According to photographer Bernie Abramson, these three photographs have never been published in any Marilyn Monroe biography. Marilyn's close friend Pat Kennedy Lawford (left in the top photo); Pat's husband, Peter Lawford; Marilyn's occasional lover Frank Sinatra; and Marilyn are seen experimenting with Sinatra's new Polaroid camera at the Lawford home in Santa Monica, California, circa 1961. (*MPTV*)

Don't Bother to Knock

At about this time, Marilyn began work on what would be her most important role to date. Fox boss Darryl Zanuck, always ambivalent about Marilyn Monroe's film future, was not quite ready to assign her to lead roles in "A" pictures and continued to look for more modest projects, budget-wise, for his contractee. He required her to screen test for *Don't Bother to Knock*, which had the following story line: Nell Forbes, recently released from a mental institution, is recommended for a babysitting job by her uncle (Elisha Cook Jr.), the elevator operator in the hotel where the action takes place, while the child's wealthy parents, Peter and Ruth Jones (Jim Backus and Lurene Tuttle), are having dinner. Dressed in a sexy negligee belonging to Mrs. Jones and wearing her jewelry and perfume, Nell begins a flirtatious, at-a-distance, slow dance of seduction for a cynical airline pilot, Jed Towers (Richard Widmark), who occupies a room across the courtyard. After Jed figures out her room number and knocks on the door, Nell invites him in, creating a situation that soon turns dangerous, with Nell alternately threatening to throw herself out the window or kill her young ward, Bunny (Donna Corcoran), now fully awake and terrified. Anne Bancroft, after a busy year acting in a series of TV programs, would make her feature film debut in this movie as Lyn Leslie, a cabaret singer in the hotel's nightclub and the ex-girlfriend of Jed.

The importance the studio placed on the film is evident in the care it gave the production artistically, assigning the studio's top composer to create the score, multiple Oscar winner Alfred Newman. The script was adapted by Daniel Taradash, who would be awarded an Oscar in 1954 for his screenplay of *From Here to Eternity*, the year's Best Picture Academy Award winner. Future Oscar winner Lucien Ballard was named director of photography; he had gained industry recognition as the creator of the Obie, a camera on which was mounted a key light, designed to eliminate any skin flaws on the face. Formerly married to Merle Oberon, he came up with the idea to disguise the imperfections on her skin that resulted from a serious car crash. The camera was named for her.

Marilyn was extremely nervous about the screen test. She knew that Zanuck wasn't a fan. She and Natasha Lytess spent hours working on the script. "I have to say that I didn't think she was ready to take on a role of this magnitude," Natasha later said. "I may have underestimated her talent in that regard. Or, at the very least, I underestimated her resolve. The time we spent on the script—two days, nonstop and I don't even remember sleeping!—was very dramatic and passionate and filled with angst, very much like Marilyn all the time. In the end, she did such a great job on the screen test that Zanuck saw fit to write her a note to congratulate her, which surprised—and thrilled—her to no end. She was so insecure and unsure of her ability, any validation at all was considered high praise."

However, Zanuck would say of her performance in the film, "She's a dumb tomato and half-crazy to boot. She's a sex pot who wiggles and walks and breathes sex, and each picture she's in she'll earn her keep, but *no more dramatic roles.*"

Marilyn's friend John Gilmore quoted Montgomery Clift, who said it best about Marilyn's relationship with Zanuck and Fox at this time: "Fox wanted to keep a tight grip on her and drain her dry. That's what they were after. The best talents, the other artists, they saw that differently and understood Marilyn had a right to make the choice of not demeaning herself. But the boss wouldn't let her. They didn't want an actress. That's what they agreed upon. They'd sit at their round table and decide that Marilyn wasn't capable of making a relevant decision."

While some critics of the day were dismissive of Marilyn's emotive skills—giving Fox's Zanuck ammunition to use against her—others would praise her, including *Daily Variety*: "[Marilyn Monroe] gives an excellent account of herself in a strictly dramatic role which commands certain attention." Studio decision makers were encouraged, and after filming concluded in January 1952, they had another film ready for her (*Monkey Business*, which began its eight weeks of production on March 5).

Over time Marilyn's acting in *Don't Bother to Knock* has been reassessed and her notices when the film was released in 2002 as part of a DVD boxed set were uniformly excellent. As film noir, the film has stood the test of time, and gives an inkling of what the future superstar would do with a highly emotional, offbeat role a year later—that of Rose Loomis, an adulterous wife, in the splashy 1953 Technicolor hit *Niagara*. When Marilyn's psychological problems eventually became known, many overanalytical parallels would be made between her and her screen character, Nell Forbes; but these parallels are unwarranted, and unfairly diminish her talent as an actress. She came to the set prepared, and though coached by Natasha Lytess, she delivered a great performance.

Still, after *Don't Bother to Knock*, the bad movies continued for Marilyn. In fact, the next year—1952—would start off on a difficult note when in March, Marilyn began work on *Monkey Business*, in which she played, much to her dismay, a stacked and dumb secretary to Cary Grant's scientist. Also at around this time, she made a movie called *We're Not Married*, which starred Ginger Rogers, Mitzi Gaynor, Eve Arden, and Zsa Zsa Gabor. Because the film is centered on three self-contained stories, there is no interaction between most of the various players, so we are denied the pleasure of seeing Zsa Zsa and Marilyn lock horns. This was another dead-end movie that added nothing much to her résumé. It was also the year *O. Henry's Full House* was released, consisting of five self-contained mini-movies, each with a separate cast, separate writers, and separate directors, all based on famous short stories by O. Henry, the acknowledged master of the literary form that always bore a touching and unexpected irony in its denouement and became the author's signature. It received a first-class production and starred some of the Fox lot's most popular actors, but there wasn't much for Marilyn to do in this one and most people don't even know she was in it.

"This is not easy," Marilyn would tell Berniece when speaking of her career. "I don't know how many bad movies an actress can make before she just becomes known for . . . bad movies!"

Joe DiMaggio

*J*oltin' Joe. The Yankee Clipper. No matter the nickname, few major-league baseball players in history had as much of an impact on our culture as the famous Joe DiMaggio. In the view of some historians, though, he may be as well known for his relationship with Marilyn Monroe as for his skill as a New York Yankees center fielder (for his entire professional career, 1936 to 1951).

Born Giuseppe Paolo (Joseph Paul) DiMaggio Jr. on November 25, 1914, Joe was the eighth of nine children of Sicilian immigrants in the small town of Martinez, California. When he was a year old, the family moved to San Francisco. He was raised with strict Catholic values in a household that stressed a strong work ethic and, above all, pride in their Sicilian heritage. At the same time, like most children of immigrants back then, the DiMaggio children were taught by their parents that nothing was more important than successfully merging into the American culture and being thought of as American. When he was a young boy, around six, he was forced to wear a leg brace due to a congenital weakness in his ankles. When the brace came off after two years, he was shy and withdrawn but also determined to excel at some physical activity. His brothers Vincent and Dominic played baseball—both went on to the pros—and he was thus inspired to also play the game. Joe dropped out of high school in the tenth grade—like Marilyn. His father, Giuseppe, had wanted him to be a fisherman—crab fishing had been a family trade for generations—but Joe couldn't stand the smell of fish and cleaning them made him sick to his stomach. For many years, his father would view him as "good for nothing" as a result of his decision to do something other than fishing for a living. Joe's brother Vince played for the San Francisco Seals, and it was he who persuaded the team's management to bring Joe, then eighteen, on as a shortstop in 1932. He wasn't such a great shortstop but he could definitely hit. By the age of twenty-one, he was batting .398. It wasn't long before he became known as a reliable hitter for the team. He made his major-league debut with the Yankees in 1936, batting ahead of Lou Gehrig. From the start, he was a wonder on the field. It had been four years since the team had been in the World Series, but thanks in large part to DiMaggio, the Yankees would find themselves winning the next four fall classics. Joe joined the team in 1936 amid a great deal of publicity and attention. He was viewed as the greatest thing to happen to the sport in a long time. Paid $15,000 a game, he used the money to set his family up in a nice home as well as to invest in his own seafood restaurant on Fisherman's Wharf called Joe DiMaggio's Grotto. He had a fifty-six-game hitting streak, from May 15 to July 16, 1941, that is thought of as the greatest in baseball history. Then, after going hitless for one game, he bounced back and hit in the next sixteen games for a total of seventy-two out of seventy-three.

Joe DiMaggio was more than just a baseball player, though. He was a cultural icon during the Great Depression, a desperate time in our history during which Americans sought out public figures for inspiration and motivation. He elevated the sport, but he also elevated the country. Watching DiMaggio in action was a thrill because of his grace and agility, but also it felt like a validation of the American dream. Injuries got the best of him, though, and by the late 1940s there were times when he could barely walk, let alone play the sport. Still, in 1949, he signed a contract with the Yankees for $100,000—an enormous amount of money in the sport at that time. He was deeply depressed after surgery on his foot and the breakup of a marriage—his first, which brought forth one child, a son named Joe Jr. So his heart wasn't really in the sport at this time. Still, even in his darkest hours, he was an amazing player. That year he had four home runs in three games and was rejuvenated. He went on for another year or so playing the game in historic ways as the country watched, mostly amazed by his exploits: He played in 139 games in 1950, scoring 114 runs and three home runs in a single contest! By 1951, though, his injuries (as well as persistent ulcers and painful arthritis) began to take a toll on him. He announced his retirement at the end of 1951 at just thirty-six. By the time he gave up the sport, he had the fifth most career home runs (361) and the sixth highest slugging percentage (.579) in history. He's the only player in baseball history to be selected for the All-Star Game in every season he played. He's still considered one of the best professional baseball players to ever walk out onto a field.

Joe DiMaggio was a complex person, a study in contrasts. Like many celebrated people, he could be charismatic in a room full of people yet distant and sullen behind closed doors. Also, like many celebrities—especially in the sports world—he was accustomed to getting whatever his heart desired when it came to the opposite sex.

What follows is the oft-reported story of how Marilyn Monroe met Joe DiMaggio. It's true that the two did meet at this time; however, new interviews for this book reveal that this really was not the *first* time they met.

First, the accepted story:

After seeing Marilyn in a dazzling series of photos she made with the White Sox, Joe decided that he wanted her. Or at least he wanted to meet her, and then take it from there. Marilyn had done the photo shoot with the Sox during their spring training that year at Brookside Park in Pasadena as a publicity gimmick set up by the studio. She posed with popular baseball player Gus Zernial in one of the pictures. After Joe determined that he wanted to know Marilyn, he contacted a mutual friend, David March, and the date was set for March 8, 1952, at Villa Nova, an Italian restaurant.*

* Villa Nova is now the Rainbow Bar & Grill, on Sunset Boulevard. There's a gold plaque outside the very popular establishment with Marilyn's likeness on it to recognize her first date with Joe. (In her memoir, Marilyn recalled first meeting Joe at Chasen's restaurant.)

Marilyn wasn't exactly eager to meet Joe. She didn't quite know who he was, and didn't much care. She figured he was just an egotistical baseball player—or maybe a football player, she wasn't sure—and since she knew little about the sport she couldn't imagine what they would have in common. So while Joe DiMaggio sat waiting with David March and an actress named Peggy Rabe, Marilyn did what she did best in these kinds of social situations—she was late. ("It was a balmy night, and I was late, as usual.") In fact, she kept them waiting for almost two hours. Of course, when she appeared, the table was more than happy to see her, especially given that she had on a revealing, low-cut white blouse and a tight little blue skirt that made sitting down just a tad perilous. She didn't know it, but DiMaggio was apprehensive about meeting her.

Marilyn later said that if she hadn't known he was a baseball player, she would have picked him out as "either a steel magnate or a congressman." He was quiet and thoughtful, not at all the boastful sports hero she had expected. He didn't say much. Instead, he just stared into his glass of vodka, straight with lime. "You know, there's a blue polka dot right there in the middle of your tie," she mentioned, trying to make small talk. "Did you fix it so that it would be like that—right in the middle like that?" He shook his head and tried to avoid her steady gaze. She later recalled thinking that he was adeptly playing one of *her* best games—the one where she is enigmatic and elusive, and as a result inspires great curiosity from everyone in her midst. However, she did wonder how two could play such a game and quickly concluded that not much would ever be said between them.

What most impressed Marilyn about Joe on this night was that despite his quiet, almost sullen demeanor, he somehow still managed to command the table. In fact, the whole room. Sitting there in his white silk shirt, pearl-gray silk tie, and black trousers, he seemed more like a movie star with the golden tan of a playboy than some jock from New York. He wasn't good-looking: His face was all sharp angles, his teeth not only bucked but haphazardly arranged, his eyes too close together. He was lanky and spindly. He didn't walk, he lumbered. It didn't matter, though. He was still power personi-fied; it seemed to emanate from him, that's how much attention he generated just by his mere presence in a booth in the back of the restaurant. Marilyn was used to getting that kind of rapt attention from onlookers, but on this night she was just . . . another fan. Or, as she so perfectly put it, "Sitting next to Mr. DiMaggio was like sit-ting next to a peacock with its tail spread, that's how noticeable you were." There was no doubt in her mind that she was fascinated.

After their meal, Marilyn apologized, said she was exhausted and needed to get to bed. "I have to be at the studio in the morning," she explained. When Joe offered to walk her to her car, she didn't turn him down. In fact, she hoped it might give her a little more time to learn more about him. A bevy of smiling faces saw the couple out of the restaurant, all fans of Joe's—a few of Marilyn's too, but hers seemed a lot less excited than his.

Once in the parking lot, Joe asked her to drive him back to his hotel, the Knickerbocker. In her memoir, she recalls that she ea-gerly agreed because she didn't want the evening to end just yet. She remembered that when they got back to the hotel, they agreed that it had been such a lovely evening, it was a shame to end it. So they tooled around Beverly Hills for three hours—and anyone who knows Beverly Hills knows that it's not exactly a metropolis. Indeed, any two people driving about there for three hours are not looking at the sights but rather are preoccupied with each other.

For the record, the two had actually met a couple years earlier. Back in 1950, when Marilyn was with Johnny Hyde, his nephew, a young William Morris agent named Norman Brokaw, booked her on an NBC program called *Lights, Camera, Action*, a thirty-minute variety show hosted by actor Walter Wolf King. Marilyn had a brief walk-on part in a sketch—it was just a way for Brokaw to get some televised footage in order to possibly secure future bookings for her. After the show, Norman and Marilyn walked down Vine Street from the affiliate KNBH studio—now KNBC in Los Angeles—to the famous Brown Derby restaurant. As they had dinner, the actor William Frawley (Fred Mertz from *I Love Lucy*) came over to the table. After Norman introduced him to Marilyn Monroe, Frawley said, "You know, I'm sitting over there with Joe D. He really wants to meet this young lady. But he's very shy . . ." Norman said, "Sure. On our way out, we'll come by and say hello." After Frawley left, Marilyn turned to the agent and said, "So, who's Joe D.?" He said, "That's Joe DiMaggio, one of the greatest baseball players of all time." It meant nothing to her. Then he said, "But I guarantee you that if I introduce you to him, he's going to want your telephone number. Is that okay?" She said it was fine. As they were leaving the Derby, Norman took Marilyn to Joe's table. "Joe, this is Marilyn Monroe," he said, "a young lady we have a great feeling about for the future. I think she's going to be a big star." Joe looked at her warmly, but he was clearly bashful. Barely able to meet her gaze, he said, "Well, listen, you're in the right hands with Norman. He's a great agent." They shook hands, said goodbye, and that was the extent of it.

"Sure enough, the very next morning, one of my first calls was Joe DiMaggio wanting her telephone number," Brokaw recalls. "I gave it to him. Then I called her up and said, 'Marilyn, what'd I tell you. I just gave your telephone number to Joe D.'" It is not known whether Joe called her.

After their dinner in 1952, something began to stir in Marilyn Monroe. She'd never really experienced it before, at least to hear her tell it. She most certainly hadn't been in love with Jim Dougherty. Joe Schenck was kindly and influential, but that wasn't love either. And as much as she wished she could have been in love with Johnny Hyde, the emotion simply never materialized for her. However, the sudden warmth for and pull toward this new fellow, Joe DiMaggio, felt different, unlike anything she'd ever experienced with any other man. Indeed, with this one, it would definitely be . . . *different*.

The Nude Calendar Scandal

*W*ithin weeks of meeting Joe DiMaggio, Marilyn Monroe faced a career crisis when the nude photos taken by Tom Kelley a couple of years earlier—when Marilyn signed off as "Mona Monroe"—finally surfaced. Actually, they first had come to light on the John Baumgarth 1951 calendar. However, the connection between the naked model and Marilyn Monroe hadn't been made—she wasn't that famous yet, and the photos went unnoticed. By 1952 she was much more of a celebrity, with a few more movies under her belt and much more publicity from the studio. The Baumgarth company decided to use Monroe's photos again for the 1952 calendar—and this time they would not be missed by anyone. When word of the photos began to circulate, the executives at Fox knew they had a big problem on their hands. No actress had ever done anything quite like this before, at least not in anyone's recent memory. "I was sure that it would put an end to my fame and that I would be dropped by the studio, press and public and never survive my 'sin,'" Marilyn later recalled.

She certainly had good reason to be concerned. The Hollywood studio system was incredibly puritanical, and had been since censorship regulations came into play in 1934. Film studios such as 20th Century-Fox had stringent moral clauses in their contracts that were designed to intimidate actors and actresses. They were forbidden to do anything immoral that might affect their image or that of the studio for which they worked, or they would be put under suspension. Not that this ever stopped most actors who were inclined to such behavior anyway. The moral clauses hadn't informed certain decisions made by the likes of Elizabeth Taylor or Frank Sinatra or many other celebrities. They did what they wanted to and just accepted the suspension, considering it a vacation. But none of them had ever posed nude and then had the pictures distributed to a startled nation. Making it much worse for all concerned, this period in American history was particularly volatile due to Senator Joe McCarthy's widespread fearmongering about Communism and its imminent infiltration of the United States due to the country's loose sense of ethics and morality. In the midst of such caution came forth Marilyn Monroe, posing on a red velvet drape with her breasts—and nothing else, by the way—proudly exposed. By today's standards, it's difficult to imagine how these pictures could have caused such a sensation. They were just typical "cheesecake" fare—Marilyn striking an uncomfortable-looking pose with her arms extended over and behind her head, her perfect breasts perky and round, her back arched seductively, and her bent legs and hip discreetly covering her nether regions. However, in 1952, this kind of photography of a celebrity was definitely not the norm—and the reaction from Fox was quick panic. Marilyn was called into the studio and asked if, indeed, the photographs were of her. Yes, she admitted, they were. "But I really think Tom [Kelley] didn't capture my best angle," she added. Marilyn's surprisingly nonchalant comment to Fox's brass about the photographs demonstrates her savvy as a public relations strategist and also her ingenuity under pressure.

As it happened, Marilyn was already scheduled by the studio to be interviewed by Aline Mosby of United Press International. Should the interview now be canceled because of the release of the nude photos? No, Marilyn decided. Not only would she meet with Mosby, she also would use the encounter as a platform to explain herself. On the specified day, she dutifully sat for the interview and photo session. Afterward, she pulled the reporter aside. "I need to discuss something with you," she whispered to Mosby. Then she let her have it—the whole Marilyn Monroe spiel. She'd been using it for many years, telling anyone who would listen how difficult her life had been and all she'd had to do to survive it. "A few years ago, when I had no money for food or rent," Marilyn told Mosby, "a photographer I knew asked me to pose nude for an art calendar. His wife was there, they were both so nice, and I earned fifty dollars I needed very bad. That wasn't a terrible thing to do, was it?" she asked, her eyes welling up with tears. She paused for dramatic affect. "I *never* thought anybody would recognize me," she continued, her eyes wide with astonishment, "and now they say it will ruin my career. They want me to deny it's me." Then she added, "But I can't lie. What shall I do?" Aline Mosby didn't know what Marilyn should do, but she certainly knew what *she* was going to do—and it was to write a big feature called "Marilyn Monroe Admits She's Nude Blonde of Calendar." That story, which ended up being picked up by every wire service and circulated around the world, was one of Marilyn's most masterful strokes, and it was basically honest (unlike some of her tales). The reaction was swift and immediate national forgiveness. Not only that, but the sensation of the pictures, her interview, and all of the attendant controversy made her an even bigger star. Eventually one of the photos would even end up on the cover of the first issue of *Playboy*, thereby launching that magazine into the stratosphere as well.

Marilyn never apologized for the photos. "I want a man to come home after a hard day's work, look at this picture, and feel inspired to say, 'Wow!'" she said. Indeed, she accepted the photographs and any ensuing scandal, just as she'd had to accept all manner of turmoil in her young life—and truly this imbroglio paled in comparison to what she'd faced in the past. She then exploited the pictures in the same way she'd often exploited her history. Frank Sinatra said it best: "If ever a broad knew how to make lemonade from lemons, it was Marilyn Monroe." In this case, she managed to make lemon meringue pie.

From this point on, Marilyn Monroe's image as a sex goddess was set in stone. For years to come, magazine covers—such as one for *Life* shortly after the nude pictures surfaced—and provocative photo layouts would underscore her steamy sexuality in a way that had never been seen from any other actress. She was never vulgar, either, which was part of her genius. Sometimes she came very close, but she knew just where the line of decency ran and never crossed it. Many others tried to imitate her—actresses like Jayne

Mansfield and Kim Novak, for instance—but they couldn't pull it off in quite the same way.

Many people have come forth over the years claiming to have "discovered" Marilyn Monroe. Perhaps the man who really deserves the honor is the guy who gave her five bucks for a cab—and his business card—on a day she was so broke she couldn't figure out a way to get to an audition: Tom Kelley, the photographer who truly exposed Marilyn to the world.

Gladys: "I'd Like to Have My Child's Love"

Marilyn Monroe had just successfully coped with the surprising release of her nude photography when another scandal broke out around her. For years, she had told the world that she was an orphan, that her parents were both deceased. Where her father was concerned, this may as well have been the case because he played no role in her life. But her mother was a different matter.

In May 1952—right before Marilyn turned twenty-six—part of the story of her mother leaked out and caused a painful public relations quagmire for her. A reporter named Erskine Johnson from the *Hollywood Reporter* learned that Gladys was indeed alive, and he found her. He assumed in his report that she had just been released from Agnews State Hospital, but by this time she'd been out for seven years. In a story he called "Marilyn Monroe Confesses Mother Alive, Living Here," which ran in the *Reporter* on May 3, 1952, he reported that Gladys was working at a private nursing facility in Eagle Rock, California, called Homestead Lodge. The thrust of the story wasn't so much that Gladys was alive as that Marilyn had lied about it. It caused no end of problems for Marilyn in the media. For instance, she had just done an interview with a reporter for *Redbook* about her sad childhood, being raised an orphan after both her parents died. It was too late for the magazine's publisher to pull it from circulation. The story—"So Far to Go Alone"—not only made Marilyn look like a fabulist but also jeopardized the credibility of the publication and the writer of the feature, Jim Henaghan. Henaghan phoned Fox and complained to the publicity department, calling Marilyn a liar; he was very upset. Marilyn did what she did best—she handled the matter openly and honestly. She wrote a letter to *Redbook* for publication, stating, "I frankly did not feel wrong in withholding from you the fact that my mother is still alive . . . since we have never known each other intimately and have never enjoyed the normal relationship of mother and daughter."

Since becoming famous, Marilyn had still been in constant communication with her half sister, Berniece. When her nude calendar made headlines, her first impulse was to call Berniece and warn her about it. (Berniece's husband, Paris, had already come home from work with a dozen publications featuring the photos.) The two sisters then discussed how at the time Marilyn posed for the pictures, one of her greatest fears had been that her Aunt Ana would one day see them. How would she have explained them to Ana? In her mind, that would have been much tougher than explaining them to America. Ana was gone now, so it was a moot point, but others in her life were still alive and could be affected by the scandal. Marilyn knew her Aunt Grace—now more devoted to Christian Science than she had been even when Ana was alive—might take issue with the photographs, but she also knew that Grace understood show business and public relations and would eventually reconcile all of it in her head. Gladys was another story. Marilyn and Berniece just hoped that Gladys wouldn't see the pictures. It turned out that in 1952, Gladys had more important problems.

Four years earlier, when Marilyn had learned from Johnny Hyde that her mother's new husband was a bigamist, she had immediately called her Aunt Grace to tell her the startling news. Grace in turn told Gladys. "And who told you this?" Gladys wanted to know.

"Norma Jeane," said Grace. That was all Gladys needed to hear to become convinced that Marilyn was trying to ruin her marriage, "because that's how much she hates me. She'll do anything to ruin my life because she still believes I ruined hers." There was no talking Gladys out of her point of view. She insisted that John did not have another wife and that it was all a lie that Marilyn had come up with, "like the rest of her stories."

Gladys had other problems with Eley, though. The man was a heavy drinker and emotionally abusive. In 1951, Gladys decided to file for divorce. However, before the paperwork could be completed, Eley became ill with heart disease. Gladys felt she had no choice but to stay at his side and utilize her belief in Christian Science to possibly heal him.

In the winter of 1951, Gladys got the job at Homestead Lodge, referred to in the *Hollywood Reporter* story about her. Then, on April 23, 1952, John Eley died at the age of sixty-two. Gladys moved in with Grace Goddard. After a time, she decided to look up Ida Bolender, and proceeded to move in with her. "Mother could never turn anyone down," said Ida Bolender's foster daughter Nancy Jeffrey. However, once she was at Ida's, Gladys said that she was sorry she had moved in with her. The two women just did not get along. Gladys wanted to leave the Bolender home, but apparently Grace didn't want her moving back with her. On top of all of this, Marilyn hadn't acknowledged John Eley's death with a sympathy card. Even though Marilyn was sending Gladys a monthly allowance, Gladys was still unhappy about what she perceived as her daughter's indifference, and she wrote her this stinging letter:

Dear Marilyn,

Please dear child, I'd like to receive a letter from you. Things are very annoying around here and I'd like to move away as soon as possible. I'd like to have my child's love instead of hatred.

Love,
Mother

Though Marilyn found the letter very upsetting, she would keep it as a memento. She also kept a framed photograph of Gladys on her nightstand.

Gladys had been talking for some time about going to Florida to visit Berniece. There was some trepidation about this possibility from all quarters. Berniece wanted to know her mother and welcomed the notion of a visit, but Marilyn and Grace had strong reservations about it because they knew Gladys a lot better than Berniece and weren't so certain it would be a good experience. Still, Berniece wrote to Gladys and said she was open to a visit from her and hoped she would come to Florida as soon as possible. Even though she had her doubts about the wisdom of such a visit, Marilyn decided that she would pay for all of Gladys's traveling expenses. The matter was then left up in the air; no one knew what Gladys was going to do next.

During the summer of 1952, while Gladys worked at Homestead Lodge, her daughter was getting more attention and publicity than ever before. It was impossible to miss her on the cover of some magazine or on television in a news report, especially after her many movies and personal appearances, the calendar scandal, and her budding romance with Joe DiMaggio. Gladys would go to work and often be confronted by the image of her daughter in a newspaper or, especially, on the TV set in the "television room" where the guests of the home would while away the hours.

Ever since Gladys started working at Homestead, she had been telling people she was Marilyn Monroe's mother. According to two women who worked at the facility at that time, Gladys would insist, "I'm telling you that Marilyn Monroe is my kid. I don't know why you don't believe me." In turn, she was inevitably told that she was being ridiculous because everyone knew that Marilyn's mother was dead; Marilyn had said so publicly—repeatedly. From all available evidence, it seems that Marilyn and Grace—who together had the idea to proclaim Gladys dead in an effort to protect her from the media—had never told Gladys their PR strategy. She became defensive about it and believed her integrity was called into question when people at her job felt she was lying.

Soon, according to one of two women on duty at that time at Homestead Lodge with Gladys, "She came in one day with photos of her and Marilyn Monroe—or at least a girl who looked like she could have been Marilyn Monroe except that she was young and had dark hair. 'See, this is me and Marilyn Monroe,' Gladys said, very proudly. 'Do you believe me now?' No one knew what to think. This was some big news, let me tell you. Yes, it had to be true, everyone decided. I mean, she had *pictures*. Gladys felt better, and everyone went about his or her business. However, we all looked at Gladys a little differently at that time. We certainly wondered how it came to pass that this woman, Marilyn Monroe's mother, was working here at an old folks' home. It seemed very odd . . . very sad."

Like ripples in a pond, the repercussions of Gladys's revelation were sure to spread out far and wide from Homestead Lodge to . . . the world. It was just a matter of time before someone would tell someone else—who would then tell someone else—that Marilyn Monroe's mother was alive and working in Eagle Rock, California. It's not known who called Erskine Johnson with the tip, and Johnson would never reveal his source. While this backstage drama was going on, Fox renewed its contract with Marilyn. Now she would be receiving $750 a week. At about the same time Homestead Lodge was abuzz over Gladys's revelations, Marilyn was in the hospital having her appendix removed. While she was still recovering, Johnson's article about Gladys appeared in the *Hollywood Reporter*. The surprising news that Marilyn's mother was alive traveled around the world at the speed of light. Fox was unhappy about it. Marilyn was told that her mother's existence should have been kept a secret, and some of the executives blamed her for allowing the news to come out. Marilyn disagreed. "The cat's out of the bag now," she said. "The secret is no more." Then, taking the matter into her hands quickly, the first thing she did was call Erskine Johnson from her hospital bed. She would repeat what had worked so well with Aline Mosby of United Press International when the nude calendar scandal broke. She gave Johnson an exclusive interview.

"Unbeknownst to me as a child," Marilyn said, "my mother spent many years as an invalid in a state hospital. I was raised in a series of foster homes arranged by a guardian through the County of Los Angeles and I spent more than a year in the Los Angeles Orphans' Home. I hadn't known my mother intimately, but since I have become grown and able to help her, I have contacted her. I am helping her now and want to continue to help her when she needs me."

Marilyn would later say of Gladys, "I just want to forget about all the unhappiness, all the misery she had in her life, and I had in mine. I can't forget it, but I'd like to try. When I am Marilyn Monroe and don't think about Norma Jeane, then sometimes it works."

Because it seems that Gladys hadn't been told Marilyn was keeping her existence a secret, it also would seem that Gladys wasn't trying to hurt Marilyn in revealing her existence.

As mentioned earlier, Erskine Johnson's May 1952 story assumed that Gladys had just been released from Agnews State Hospital (whereas she had been released seven years prior); and because Marilyn *never* set anyone straight on this detail, the public has formed a lasting impression of Marilyn Monroe as a heartless person who had disowned her mother from the time Gladys had been committed to the mental hospital, right up through 1952. In all the years since 1952, the true date of Gladys's release from the hospital still hasn't become widely known. This biography sets the record straight: Marilyn's PR decision to portray her mother as deceased had nothing to do with her being ashamed of Gladys. On the contrary, we now know that Marilyn throughout her life did everything she could to help her mother.

Marilyn and Joe: Tumultuous Already?

During the summer of 1952, Marilyn Monroe and Joe DiMaggio began to date more regularly. He had a job at that time broadcasting for the Yankees on television, as well as at the games themselves. He wasn't very confident in the role and, in truth, wasn't very good at it. He simply didn't have the personality for that kind of on-air position. Obviously, Marilyn—who turned twenty-six on June 1—could have helped him a great deal in his new endeavor, if only in terms of his presentation. But he didn't want her help, and in fact wasn't very nice about rejecting it. Marilyn was quickly learning that Joe felt she had a "place," and that she should find it . . . and stay there.

Indeed, red flags were being raised all over the terrain of Marilyn's new relationship with DiMaggio. For instance, he was clearly jealous of the attention she generated from other men wherever she went. When she was at the stadium with him, of course she would be the subject of great fascination. She had always attracted men, but never like in the 1950s. By this time, she was in full-fledged Marilyn Monroe mode, meaning that the transformation from Norma Jeane had been total. The way she spoke—a honeyed voice so whispery and seductive. The way she moved her lips—a kiss always imminent. The way she moved her body—a striptease always a possibility, but never quite a reality. When she was in public in front of her adoring fans and the ever-present glare of the photographers' flashes, she instantly became *Marilyn Monroe*. She didn't even have to think about it anymore. The persona she had created was now such a part of her being it just . . . *was*. She was quickly becoming a rising sex symbol for an entire generation. It was only going to get worse for him (and for her!), not better, as her star continued in its ascent. Yet the heart wants what it wants, and the couple ventured forth anyway. Of course, Natasha Lytess had a strong opinion about it. "This man is the punishment of God in your life," she told Marilyn, disguising neither her contempt for him nor her disapproval of their relationship.

In July, Joe took her home to meet his family. Once there, she clearly saw why Joe wanted his wife to be domestic—women stayed home, raised children, cooked and cleaned, and it had always been that way in the DiMaggio family. Marilyn was not that kind of woman at all.

At the end of the summer of 1952, Joe dropped a real bomb-shell: He thought it would be best if Marilyn abandoned her ca-reer. It only caused her great stress anyway, he argued, so why do it? It was becoming abundantly clear that this was a man who didn't understand Marilyn. Her career—meaning fame—was her great-est passion. Acting was important to her and she did whatever she could to improve her skills. However, Marilyn Monroe wanted to be famous. In just a few months she would tell her stand-in on *Gentle-men Prefer Blondes*, "I want to be a star more than anything. It's something precious."

"I didn't want to give up my career," Marilyn later recalled, "and that's what Joe wanted me to do most of all. He wanted me to be the beautiful ex-actress, just like he was the great former ballplayer. We were to ride into some sunset together. But I wasn't ready for that kind of journey yet. I wasn't even thirty, for heaven's sake."

The physical attraction between Joe and Marilyn was intense, and it definitely contributed to their desire to be with each other. However, it was clear that they had very different values. The many differences between them can be boiled down to this: He was con-servative. She was not. And neither was willing to compromise. Given these facts of their personalities, there seemed no way a ro-mance between them was going be anything but tumultuous.

Gladys's Surprise Visit

Though Gladys Baker had been saying for some time that she wanted to visit her daughter Berniece in Florida, Berniece and Marilyn were really not sure she was serious about it. When Mari-lyn offered to take care of her expenses for such a trip, all was quiet with Gladys.

Then, true to form, Gladys—always one for a surprise appearance or disappearance—showed up in Florida without warning during the first week of September 1952. How she got the money for her trip (and by airline, no less, because Marilyn intended to send her by railway) remained a mystery. She definitely did not get the funds from Marilyn, though, because if she had, Marilyn would have warned Berniece about her impending arrival. Instead, Berniece's daughter, Mona Rae, picked up the telephone one morning and it was Gladys on the other end telling her she was at the airport—and why wasn't anyone there to pick her up? When Marilyn found out about it, she was frantic with worry. She couldn't imagine how Gladys had made the trip. The mere fact that she was capable of such surprise maneuvers was something Marilyn found very troubling. "I don't know how to keep an eye on her," she said. "It's becoming more than I can handle."

The same could have been said for poor Berniece, because the next few weeks would prove to be very difficult. Gladys wasn't exactly the ideal houseguest. The apartment in which Berniece and her husband, Paris, and daughter lived was very small, and now there was a fourth occupant. Not surprisingly, Gladys was demanding and difficult, argumentative and disruptive. She wouldn't help with any household duties and spent her days complaining and making long-distance telephone calls. Berniece did everything she could to make Gladys happy, but nothing worked. Gladys's emotional problems were complex. She needed to be managed very carefully, and Berniece simply didn't have the skills necessary to do that. Ultimately, she was at a loss, especially when she got the bill for the first month of telephone calls—long-distance costs were unbelievably exorbitant back then and Paris was very unhappy about the charges. When Berniece asked Gladys about the phone calls, she became defensive and explained that she had simply forgotten to mention them. Confused, Berniece called Marilyn to ask if she thought Gladys was being forgetful or just plain inconsiderate. Marilyn decided it was probably a little bit of both.

From an analytical viewpoint, Marilyn found the unhappy interaction between Gladys and Berniece interesting because for years she had wondered if it was just she who could not get along with Gladys. Maybe she should have tried harder, she often thought. Maybe she hadn't been as patient as she should have been, or as understanding. However, when she learned of Berniece's troubles with Gladys, she felt at least somewhat vindicated. From a practical viewpoint, what were they going to do about Gladys now? Marilyn had an idea: What if she paid for Gladys to move into an apartment near Berniece? Since Gladys did seem to like Florida, perhaps she could live there, Marilyn would take care of her expenses, and Berniece could keep an eye on her. The sisters agreed that this was a good idea and they felt certain that their mother would approve of it. However, when Berniece approached Gladys with the idea, she wasn't happy about it at all. She became very angry because she felt that Berniece and Paris were just trying to get rid of her. Her feelings now hurt, she didn't want to discuss it any further—and, moreover, it seemed as if she were not going to be ending her stay with Berniece anytime in the foreseeable future.

While Gladys was with her, Berniece took the opportunity to ask her about Marilyn's father. Gladys came out very bluntly with the information that Edward Mortenson was not Marilyn's father. Did Marilyn know? Yes, Gladys said, she knew because Grace told her. (Here, she was probably referring to the time Grace visited her in the sanitarium and Gladys told her that Charles Gifford was Marilyn's father.) Berniece wondered how Marilyn had reacted to the news. Gladys said she had no idea (which was true—she had been in the hospital when Grace gave Marilyn the news). As Berniece pressed on about the subject, Gladys became increasingly agitated. Finally, she snapped at her daughter, "Look, if you want to know all of the details, ask *Marilyn*." Berniece dropped the subject.

After almost two months of domestic turmoil, Berniece—feeling terrible about the entire situation—called Grace Goddard on October 30 to ask her advice. Grace sympathized with her. She had known Gladys for many years and she knew how difficult she was. She assured Berniece that Gladys didn't mean any harm, that she was just sick and there had never been anything anyone could do about it. Grace had been using Christian Science as a tool in the healing of Gladys's mind, but that didn't seem to be working at all. Just two days earlier, she had sent Berniece a note telling her that Gladys "did not get a complete healing." She wrote that she was afraid they were going to have to send her back to Agnews in San Jose, or maybe they should place her in the Rock Haven Sanitarium in La Crescenta, California.*

In fact, Grace and Marilyn had recently visited Rock Haven, Grace wrote, and both agreed that it was "not terrible as such places go, about as good as they get, I suppose." She wrote that Marilyn was so traumatized by the visit, however, she didn't sleep well that night and "had to take some sleeping pills, which did not make me very happy." Moreover, she indicated that if it Gladys were to end up at Rock Haven, "at least it will be easier for Norma Jeane and I to visit her, though I'm not sure how many such visits Norma Jeane could make. It's a very upsetting place for her. However, a parent must be cared for and we are all doing the best we can for Gladys."

"Let's please mail Mother a train ticket to come back to Los Angeles," Marilyn finally suggested. She then telephoned Gladys and said that she wanted her to return to California. Of course, Gladys stood her ground. She wasn't going anywhere. In fact, she told Marilyn to concentrate on her "moving picture career" and to leave her alone. She said she was tired of being told what to do, that she had her own agenda and was going to live her life exactly as she pleased. Then she slammed down the phone. The next day, Marilyn paid for a train ticket and mailed it to her mother in Florida.

---

* This sanitarium has most often been described in Marilyn Monroe biographies as having been in Eagle Rock, California, and Verdugo City, California. However, it was in La Crescenta. For many years it served as a women's rest home until closing down in 2006.

Niagara

$\mathcal{M}$arilyn's 1953 films, three carefully constructed, big-budget, high-profile properties in gorgeous, eye-popping Technicolor—*Niagara*, *Gentlemen Prefer Blondes*, and *How to Marry a Millionaire*— would define the Monroe screen persona and secure her place in the firmament of Hollywood for the next decade, always billed above the title and more often than not in the top spot. The films would also propel Marilyn to the number five spot in Quigley's Top Ten list of the year's box-office stars. "The time when I sort of began to think I was famous, I was driving somebody to the airport," she would recall in 1962, "and as I came back there was this movie house and I saw my name in lights. I pulled the car up at a distance down the street—it was too much to take in up close, you know? And I said, 'God, somebody's made a mistake!' But there it was, in lights. . . . And I sat there and said, 'So, that's the way it looks' . . . it was all very strange to me."

Charles Casillo, an author and Marilyn Monroe historian, best summed up Marilyn's appeal this way: "Marilyn Monroe was beautiful. Marilyn Monroe was sexy. Marilyn Monroe was delicious . . . always delicious. Everyone knew that. She wasn't just a sex symbol. She was *the* sex symbol. But it was a certain kind of sex appeal, initiated, developed and perfected by her. Her appeal was childlike, innocent, tempting, glowing—bursting forth and available like a dish of fresh strawberries arranged in cream. . . . The creation of Marilyn Monroe had made an unwanted girl of the streets the most desired, written about, analyzed, gossiped about, wondered about and longed for woman of her era."

For the first of these landmark movies, *Niagara*, the studio lavished the film with an impressive team of Oscar-honored artisans and craftsmen, with veteran Fox director Henry Hathaway, who had just directed Monroe the previous year in *O. Henry's Full House*.

Joseph Cotten played Loomis, a mentally damaged Korean War

vet who, with his wife, Rose (Monroe), makes a trip to Niagara Falls in an attempt to repair their broken marriage. In Rose's mind, the marriage is beyond repair and she uses the trip to continue an adulterous affair with her lover, Patrick, who agrees to murder George. The plot to kill George backfires when he hurls Patrick into the falls to his death. Rose escapes and begins a deadly game of cat-and-mouse with George, played out against the awesome beauty and deafening power of the falls. George's pursuit of Rose moves furtively in and out of Niagara's watery veil. We teeter between horror and relief as George corners the beautiful Rose in the belltower and chokes the life out of her.

Since the beginning of her film career, Marilyn had striven to win the approval and respect of those in her profession. She studied her craft and worked with coaches from day one. She had the adoration of millions of fans yet somehow felt her beauty got in the way of her being recognized as a serious actress. There is evidence that some movie critics felt the same way. But occasionally there would be favorable comments about her acting chops, and her films would also get a thumbs-up. Even Pauline Kael, the feared film critic of the *New Yorker*, would praise her with faint damns, as she did when writing about *Niagara*. "This isn't a good movie," she wrote, "but it's compellingly tawdry and nasty . . . the only movie that explores the mean, unsavory potential of Marilyn Monroe's cuddly, infantile perversity." Of the same movie, a critic at the *New York Times* wrote, "Seen from any angle, the Falls and Miss Monroe leave little to be desired."

Gentlemen Prefer Blondes

$\mathcal{I}$'m trying to find myself now, to be a good actress and good person," Marilyn said as 1952 came to a close. "Sometimes I feel strong inside, but I have to reach in and pull it up. It isn't easy. Nothing's easy, as long as you go on living."*

Toward the end of 1952, Marilyn leased a house in Beverly Hills so that she and Joe could have some peace and quiet away from the swarm of paparazzi that gathered whenever they left their suite at the Hotel Bel Air, where they had been spending much of their time. However, it was neither peaceful nor quiet at the new home. On October 1, they had a fight—it's not known about what—and Joe stormed out after what Marilyn later called "a lot of name calling." They had known each other for only seven months. A major problem in Marilyn's relationship was presented by Natasha Lytess, who disliked Joe very much. She couldn't understand why Marilyn would be interested in him. In her view, he had no personality, was dense, and maybe even dimwitted (which was not true). Apparently, she had called Marilyn one day only to have Joe pick up and tell her that if she wanted to speak to "Miss Monroe" she should call "Miss Monroe's" agent. In Joe's view, she was a controlling shrew who had too much influence over his girlfriend. "She's an acting teacher, for Christ's sake," he had told Marilyn. "Why do you treat her like she's

---

* She really was "a good person," too. Consider this, from James Haspiel: "A famous story about her happened on a night she went for a walk in New York, when she was living on East 57th Street. At the end of 58th is a very small park with a small bridge. As she stood on that bridge, she watched two teenage boys with nets on long poles catching pigeons and then putting the birds in a big cage. She went down and asked them what they were doing. They explained to this blonde woman they didn't know that they were catching as many pigeons as they could so that they could then take them to the market where they would be paid 25 cents apiece for them. [This sounds like something these boys made up. What would any market want with their pigeons?] After a pause she said, 'Well, if I sit on this bench and wait until you're done, and I pay you for the pigeons, will you then free them?' They agreed to do this. After they were done, she gave them a quarter for each pigeon they freed. Then she asked, 'What nights do you come here?' They said, 'Thursdays.' She said, 'I'll try to be here next Thursday night.'"

a psychiatrist?" Marilyn said that he just didn't understand. She was right about that—he didn't. Pretty much from the moment Joe and Natasha met, it was all-out war between them.

From November 1952 through February 1953, Marilyn Monroe would be at work on one of her most memorable movies, *Gentlemen Prefer Blondes*.

Fox spared no expense in its transfer of *Gentlemen Prefer Blondes* from stage to screen—from choreographer Jack Cole's staging of the spectacular pre-credits opening number with Jane Russell and Monroe singing and dancing to "We're Just Two Little Girls from Little Rock," identically gowned head to toe in shimmery red sequins, to the reprise of the song in the final scene where the two stars are again dressed identically for a double wedding ceremony in blinding white gowns of figure-hugging lace appliqué, both by costumer Travilla, who surely must have been Bob Mackie's inspiration in his career. Russell was billed above Monroe in all the film's posters and publicity and in the opening credits. Russell was also first in money earned for this film, $400,000 to Monroe's $11,250 ($1,250 per week for nine weeks). Fox wasn't exactly kind to Marilyn. "I couldn't even get a dressing room," she would recall in 1962. "I said, finally—I really got to this kind of level—I said, 'Look, after all, I *am* the blonde and it is *Gentlemen Prefer Blondes*. Because still they always kept saying, 'Remember you are not a star.' I said, 'Well, whatever I am, I *am* the blonde!'"

Throughout the shoot, Jane and Marilyn got along famously, with the five-years-older Russell protective of the insecure Monroe in the way of a big sister. Often all it took for Marilyn to be coaxed out of her trailer was a word from Jane. "She would be afraid to come out, she was so shy," Russell said, "but it was understandable in the sense that she never had to sing so much, dance so much. Then, of course, she had the acting teacher [Natasha Lytess] on set every moment, a woman who was such an annoyance, running Marilyn's life the way she did. I'm sure Marilyn did not need her on this movie . . . she would have been fine without her, if only she had more confidence in herself."

They may be just two little girls from Little Rock who come from the wrong side of the tracks, but Lorelei Lee (Monroe) and Dorothy Shaw (Russell) easily change their status to the right side of the tracks after they conquer Paris in search of a couple of men of means. Veteran director Howard Hawks guides the large cast through the tune-filled story of a beautiful blonde with a weakness for diamonds, and her equally lovely enabler. Lorelei's erstwhile fiancé Esmond (Tommy Noonan) has financed the trip to Paris to test her fidelity. Suspicious of Lorelei's motives, Esmond the elder hires private eye Ernie Malone (Elliott Reid) to spy on the girls and report any suspicious activity back to him. And there's plenty to report, including charges leveled at Lorelei of grand larceny of a valuable tiara. Of course, she's guilty, and it remains for a French judge to set things right, but not before Dorothy shakes things up by posing as Lorelei. When her true identity is called into question as she testifies in court, Jane Russell mounts a perfect impersonation of Marilyn's Lorelei, which includes a devastating, dead-on version of "Diamonds Are a Girl's Best Friend."

Marilyn's rendition of this song is the most lavish of all the production numbers in the film, again with choreography by Jack Cole, and with what seems like an army of tuxedoed chorus boys, one of whom turns out to be a teenage George Chakiris, with gray brushed into his temple hair. Though the picture was photographed with 35–millimeter film, studio head Daryl Zanuck ordered the "Diamonds" production number to be reshot later in CinemaScope for use in a demonstration of the new process, held on the Fox lot in March 1953. Zanuck told *Daily Variety* that the CinemaScope reshoot was done in three and a half hours, as opposed to the four days it took for the original version. That would stand to reason, considering the number had already been blocked and rehearsed.

What's clear with this movie is not only Marilyn's sense of humor about herself but also her ability as a comedic actress. Monroe biographer Donald Spoto put it this way: "She put a twist on sexiness. It was not something wicked and shameful and shocking and dirty and embarrassing. It was something which was terribly funny. And Marilyn enjoyed it."

Hugh Hefner, founder of *Playboy* magazine, added, "In retrospect, although the fifties is clearly a time of very real political repression and social sexual repression, you can see those early signs of changing values, and Monroe was clearly a part of that."

Gentlemen Prefer Blondes premiered on July 15, 1953, with both Jane's and Marilyn's hand- and footprints enshrined in the forecourt of Grauman's Chinese Theatre. It opened nationwide three days later to great reviews and big box-office returns, earning more than $12 million in its initial run.

Gladys Threatens Grace

In November 1953 Gladys Baker received a ticket, arranged and paid by Marilyn, for transportation from Florida back to Los Angeles. Grace Goddard had followed Marilyn's direction to book the arrangements, but it was her own decision to have Gladys travel by rail, not air. She may have been attempting to delay her friend's arrival in California since she would need to have her home prepared for it. Grace also needed to emotionally steel herself and her family for the possibility that Gladys might be bringing with her a trunkload of paranoia and confusion. She had heard from Berniece that Gladys had been having some "episodes." The long train ride turned out to be a torment for Gladys. As soon as the cab pulled up in front of Grace's house, she and Doc heard Gladys's screams. They ran to the front window and saw the poor cabdriver take her bags from the trunk of his vehicle, drop them on the front lawn, get back into his cab, and speed off as quickly as he could. It appeared that he didn't even wait to be paid! Gladys then marched toward the Goddards' front door, shouting nonsensically about her awful train trip. "Torture!" she exclaimed. "Grace Goddard, you wanted to torture me, and you succeeded! Now it's my turn."

Grace told Doc to get away from the window so that they could pretend they weren't home. Then she drew the curtains in a flash and ran for the telephone, dialing Marilyn's number as quickly as she could. Marilyn happened to be home and having a meeting with an accountant named Wesley Miller who worked for Wright, Wright, Green & Wright, the law firm that represented Marilyn at the time. When Marilyn answered, Grace quickly explained what was going on, that Gladys had just pulled up and was frantic. She said that she had never seen her in such bad shape. Then she held the phone up to the front window so that Marilyn could hear her mother's shouting: "I'll show you torture, Grace! Open up this door!"

"I recall that Marilyn and Grace stayed on the phone for a time," said Wesley Miller, "with Grace reporting Gladys's every move. Marilyn said she hoped her mother would eventually calm down, and I think she did. However, from what I later gathered, when Grace walked toward the front porch, she could clearly hear Gladys speaking, as if in a one-sided conversation. She was mumbling something about being 'put on a train like a child,' with all of the other passengers staring at her for the entire trip. 'Eyes everywhere, for days on end . . .' is what Marilyn later told me she was repeating, nonstop."

The story continued, as per the recollections of the principal players:

After whispering her report of the unfolding events, Grace stopped and listened. "Wait," she said, "someone else is out there. Hold on." Grace and Doc each peeked through a curtain and watched as a nearby resident, who had obviously heard the commotion, approached. Gladys greeted him angrily. The neighbor explained that he had grown concerned when he heard all the shouting. At that, Gladys became even more irate, asking if the man "owned" Los Angeles and demanding to know "is this your air I'm breathing, too?" Grace listened as Gladys's voice trailed off. She then followed the man off the property. Doc ran to the kitchen and out the back door saying he would try to keep on eye on Gladys.

"Meanwhile, Marilyn asked Grace not to call the authorities, saying she would be right over," recalled Wesley Miller. " 'Just don't let her leave,' she said of her mother before clicking off. I said, 'You are not going there alone, Marilyn. I'm coming with you.' And she said, 'No. This has to do with me and my mother. I can handle it on my own.' She then ran out of the house. I sat in her living room thinking, 'Oh, I should definitely have insisted. I should have insisted . . .' "

Marilyn jumped into her car. After speeding through stoplights and weaving in and out of traffic, she finally reached her destination: a Los Angeles police precinct. She screeched onto a lot that was meant only for official vehicles.

"It's not every day people came in that way," explained a retired Los Angeles police officer. "When she got out, I actually drew my gun—but as soon as you saw her you knew who she was."

Marilyn asked the patrolman to direct her to "whoever the man in charge is," and despite her illegal and alarming arrival, the awestruck officer brought her inside the building and to a police captain.

"She was crying when she walked in the office," explained the officer. "She said her mother was sick and that she'd been sent to a mental hospital before, so I knew where this was headed."

Marilyn further explained that Gladys was easily frightened. She asked if the captain could simply call an ambulance to quietly approach Grace's home and collect her mother without too much angst. "He felt bad for her, but there were procedures," the officer recalled of the captain. "He had to send a [patrol] car first . . . try and talk to her first—and that was me." The captain also explained to Marilyn that a specific officer was trained to respond to what he called "psych calls," and then he directed the officer to contact that specialist. "I called Teddy [the 'specialist'], who was supposed to be going to a kid's ball game that day, and told him that Marilyn

Monroe was sitting across from me," said the officer. "He said he'd have his uniform on before he hung up the phone."

While waiting for the responding officer to arrive at the precinct, Marilyn called Grace. Gladys was still in front of the house, she reported, and neighbors had been calling, asking if she was all right. Marilyn explained that there would be two patrol cars arriving, with *no* sirens. "She just wanted it quiet," the officer recalls. "I told her she could see for herself that everything would be okay. We'll follow Teddy and his partner, I told her, and she could see how good he was. He had a talent, that guy."

In a matter of minutes, two police cars were rolling toward Grace Goddard's home. In the first was Teddy and his partner, and in the second a police officer and a movie star. "When we turned onto the block we slowed the cars," the officer explained, "Marilyn just kind of slid down in her seat." The two vehicles parked one house away from Grace's, from which vantage point they could see Gladys sitting on the front steps, arms crossed and appearing calm. The officer from the first car—Teddy—then approached her. The captain and Marilyn couldn't hear what was being said, but it was quickly evident from Gladys's expression and tone that she was now agitated at the sight of the uniformed patrolman. "I picked up the radio right away and called [for an ambulance], and I told Marilyn it was gonna be quick," recalled the officer who had been sitting with her.

Marilyn sat quietly watching as the other officer successfully calmed Gladys.

"I got out of my car to give Teddy a quick signal that the ambulance was on the way," the first policeman remembered, "and by the time I got back, the street was filling up."

Indeed, neighborhood residents who had witnessed Gladys's antics of the past hour from behind pulled curtains were now brave enough to get a closer look. As the first officer returned to his vehicle, he saw an odd sight: Marilyn had taken the jacket of an extra police uniform in the car and pulled it up over her head.

When he got back into the car, Marilyn asked urgently, "Did they see me?"

"No, they're here to watch me," he said, "they're rubberneckers." He then asked Marilyn if she'd like to get out of the vehicle and speak to her mother. She decided against it, saying that Gladys was clearly not herself at that moment, "and what good will it do?"

The two then waited as an ambulance drove up quietly. "Did you ask them not to use their sirens?" Marilyn asked. He said that he had. She then placed her hand on his knee. "You're a kind man," she told him. They watched as Gladys Baker—still very upset—was strapped onto a gurney and lifted into the ambulance. As the ambulance slowly passed their car, for just a moment they could hear the shouts of an insane woman coming from inside it. Marilyn winced and pulled the coat still on her head tightly down over her ears.

As the police officer and Marilyn followed the ambulance, not a word was said between them. Finally, Marilyn took the jacket off, studied it carefully, and softly brushed away some locks of hair left on its lining. "I asked her if she was okay," recalled the policeman, "and she just kind of laughed for a moment." They watched while the ambulance made a right turn, toward its destination.

As they drove back to the police precinct, the policeman and the actress continued to maintain their silence. Finally, Marilyn sighed deeply. "No one understands," she said, her voice softening, "some people just can't help who they turn out to be."

Gladys's New Home

On February 9, 1953, Marilyn Monroe was scheduled to attend the Photoplay Awards, where she was being honored as "Fastest Rising Star." A relative recalls that she didn't want to go: "She didn't think she could pull it off, be what was expected of her—become Marilyn Monroe—under the circumstances of what else was going on that day."

Indeed, it was a difficult day.

That very same morning, Gladys was moved to Rock Haven Sanitarium at 2713 Honolulu Avenue in La Crescenta, California. It was a sprawling, Mexican-style complex on three and a half lush acres behind two gigantic iron gates with the metal words "Rock Haven" on top of the impressive entryway. Marvina Williams was eighteen at the time and had just been hired as an aide there. "It was a wonderful place," she recalled. "Actually it was also called the Screen Actor's Sanitarium, even though not a lot of movie stars stayed there. The only ones we all knew of were Frances Farmer and Florenz Ziegfeld. We got fan mail for them for years after they were gone. [Note: Actress Billie Burke, who had been married to Ziegfeld and was known for her role as Glinda the Good Witch from *The Wizard of Oz*—was also a patient in the 1960s.] When I worked there, we had forty-two guests—we called them guests, by the way. We had forty-two beds, too, so it was full. Just before Gladys came in, someone had died—virtually the day before, actually. Gladys had been on the bottom of a very long waiting list, but when they found out she was Marilyn Monroe's mother, they moved her to the top—not fair, but the truth."

Though it was many years ago, Williams has distinct memories about Gladys because, as she put it, "There was something about her—you just felt so badly for her, I guess because you knew she was Marilyn Monroe's mother. When I heard that she had been out of a sanitarium for seven years, I simply couldn't believe it. I don't think she was being properly medicated when she was on her own. On the day she showed up, I remember her saying that she had called her daughters—one, I think, was in Florida [Berniece], and she said the other was Marilyn Monroe. She said she had talked to Marilyn that day and that Marilyn said she was coming to get her. 'I won't be here long because Marilyn Monroe is coming for me,' she kept saying. It seemed so tragic, the way she kept referring to her daughter as 'Marilyn Monroe.' I remember that there were some people who didn't believe it was true that Marilyn was her daughter. Then someone came in with a newspaper article and we passed it around. There was a lot of astonishment about it."

"Marilyn had, that same morning, agreed to pay for Gladys's care in the new facility," recalled accountant Wesley Miller. "However, she didn't want to see her mother in a mental hospital any more than Gladys wanted to be there, but there was no alternative. It was this second stay—the one that happened in 1953—that really tore at Marilyn.

"She told me that she remembered visiting Gladys at the other institution when she was a young girl, and she never forgot how horrible it had been. She told me that there were patients in the hallways in beds and that the place smelled of urine. She said that everyone was dazed and on drugs, that she heard people screaming and that she just wanted to get her mother out of there. She said that she had nightmares about it all the time, that the memory of her mother in that place haunted her. She didn't want her to end up back in a place like that, she said. Also, she said that the whole thing brought back memories of her own time in an orphanage, memories she said she had been working to forget.

"Apparently, she and her aunt Grace had earlier visited Rock Haven and thought the conditions were much, much better. She said that there were fresh flowers on all of the tables—very lovely. But, still, the patients were frightening and, she said, so drugged they were 'walking around like zombies.' She said that she spoke to one woman who recognized her and told her that she was 'evil' for making the kinds of movies she made.

"'I don't know how to deal with this,' she told me. 'I don't know how to do what I have to do, have my career and all it takes and have Joe and all he takes, and do this, too, with Mother.' I actually thought, for the first time, that she was on the verge of a nervous breakdown. It was too much. She was developing a strange nervous twitch and stuttering a lot. The trouble she had with Gladys this time . . . it really was too much for her to handle. I don't think Berniece was a lot of help. When I asked Marilyn about that, she said, 'She's got a family. I don't. I never have had one.

So, let her live her life. I'm forced to live mine, and my mother is my burden.'"

Despite the awful circumstances of the day, Marilyn decided that she couldn't disappoint all of those who were expecting to see her at the Photoplay Awards. The show had to go on, she decided, even if she would have to force herself through it.

To accept her award that night, Marilyn decided to wear a slinky gold gown with a plunging neckline—of course—that was so form-fitting its designer, Travilla, had to actually sew her into it. In fact, he suggested that she not even wear this particular dress because, in his opinion, it wasn't flattering on her. (Incidentally, Marilyn was very briefly seen in it in a long shot in *Gentlemen*.)

That very same week, Marilyn had made a deal with Joe that she would not wear gowns that were so revealing if he in turn laid off her where her career was concerned—and also about her relationship with Natasha. He said he would try if she would try, and she agreed. Apparently, she was about to break the deal. In fact, to make the dress even more provocative, she had decided on no bra and no panties. It was as if she were purposely defying Joe—and that's exactly how he took it when he found out about her plans. He was supposed to attend the show with her, but stormed away and took a plane to San Francisco. "I have enough on my mind," Marilyn said at the time. "Why *this*, too? Why do I have to do *this* with him?"

How to Marry a Millionaire

*I*n mid-March 1953, at the same time that Marilyn moved into a new apartment on Doheny Drive in West Hollywood just outside of Beverly Hills, she began work on her next picture, *How to Marry a Millionaire*. The picture was shot in about six weeks (March 9–end of April 1953).

How to Marry a Millionaire has a provenance that goes all the way back to 1932 when Sam Goldwyn purchased the movie rights to Zoe Akins's Broadway play of the previous season, *The Greeks Had a Word for It*, about three beautiful young gold diggers who set out in New York City to get their hooks into three wealthy men, reel them in, and navigate them down the bridal path. When the project was announced, it was said to be based on Doris Lilly's best seller of the same name, but the only thing the studio used was the book's title.

The studio powers knew they would have to dress up the familiar plot with something spectacular, and that they did: Technicolor, CinemaScope, and stereophonic sound. In fact the film marked the first use of the new widescreen process, but the studio's prestige picture of 1953, *The Robe*, filmed after *Millionaire*, was released to theaters before it, thus its claim to being the world's first Cinema-Scope film. Another untried tactic was used to give the picture heft, to make it feel "important"—Alfred Newman, the studio's musical director for twenty years by this time, was filmed conducting the 20th Century-Fox Symphony Orchestra on a soundstage dressed to look like an amphitheater, replete with Greek columns and blue sky, where they performed Newman's classic paean to Manhattan, the soaring "Street Scene." It had been written for the film version of Elmer Rice's Broadway play of the same name twenty years earlier, and later became a musical signature for New York. After completing the conducting of "Street Scene," Newman turned and bowed to the camera, turned back to the orchestra, and gave the downbeat on the musical score of *How to Marry a Millionaire*, as the film's credits rolled.

The film was produced and cowritten by Fox mainstay and Oscar-nominated screenwriter of *The Grapes of Wrath*, Nunnally Johnson, and directed by Jean Negulesco, also Oscar-nominated, as director of *Johnny Belinda*. Costumes were by Travilla under the direction of wardrobe supervisor Charles LeMaire, with both eventually receiving Oscar nominations.

When this movie was announced, the Hollywood press rubbed

its collective hands together, practically salivating for a dustup between the queen of the Fox lot, Betty Grable, and the pretender to the throne—Marilyn Monroe. But they would be disappointed. They had not calculated the genuine unselfishness of Grable toward her ten-years-younger costar. In fact, she told the press that Marilyn "was a shot in the arm for Hollywood."

Later, on the set during the shoot of *Millionaire* in front of witnesses, Betty reportedly told Marilyn, "Honey, I've had it. Go get yours. It's your turn now." If Betty now felt she was playing second fiddle to the upstart Marilyn, it was something she apparently felt no need to articulate.

The situation with Lauren Bacall was different. Only two years older than Marilyn, Bacall was a disciplined actress; she had been a star since she was nineteen and was said to be put off by Marilyn's constant tardiness on the set, but she remained quiet and did not make an issue of it. But in her autobiography, *By Myself*, Bacall wrote about how irritating it was with Marilyn, prompted by Natasha Lytess sitting just off camera, calling for take after take, "often as many as 15 or more." She wrote that she didn't dislike Marilyn; that she had no meanness in her, no bitchery. "There was something sad about her," Bacall wrote.

Still, Marilyn's comic genius was on full display in *How to Marry a Millionaire*, as she achieved a level of physical comedy so subtle as to be almost invisible. Playing her nearsightedness for all it was worth, her sexy vulnerability raised the humor to new heights as she tripped over stairs and bumped into walls, her dignity intact. *How to Marry a Millionaire* would premiere in New York on October 29, and open nationally on November 5. It would wind up as the second highest grossing movie of 1953, after Columbia's *From Here to Eternity*. The picture was a success with both the public and the critics, with Marilyn being singled out in the reviews for her beauty and comic timing. Over the years, Marilyn's biographers and industry insiders have maintained that her true calling was comedy, and when one reassesses the Monroe filmography, it is hard to argue against that point.

River of No Return

Also at about this time, Marilyn made another film, *River of No Return*, with Robert Mitchum, directed by Otto Preminger.

Earlier, in 1949, the movie's producer, Stanley Rubin, had been coaxed by film editor Danny Cahn to audition Marilyn for a TV show he was manning called *Your Show Time*. It was a series of short stories dramatized for television. After her reading, he thought Marilyn was beautiful, of course, but extremely nervous and inexperienced, thus he didn't give her a job. However, he remembered her when it came time to cast this film. In fact, he says that he realized how much she'd improved after seeing some of her recent movies, and had the part in *River* written with her in mind. When he contacted her, Stanley says that she didn't want to do the movie, "because she didn't want to do what she thought was a western. I told her I thought of it as a piece of Americana, but she still figured it to be a western. However, when I sent her a tape of the songs she would be singing in the film, she said, yes, she would do it. So, really, she did it so that she could sing those songs more than for any other reason."

Those who predicted the oil-and-water lack of chemistry between the autocratic Austrian-born director Otto Preminger and the sensitive, shy, insecure Marilyn would be right—to a point. Curiously, the director began the film seemingly quite pleased with Monroe as a person and artist, treating her on the set with truly European courtliness. However, by this time, Natasha Lytess had Marilyn reading her lines with exaggerated facial gymnastics, enunciating every syllable like a robot—and while no one liked it, no one could change it, either, not even Preminger. Again, the big problem on this set was the same as always—Natasha telling Marilyn how to act and usurping the director's influence over her. It caused major problems between Marilyn and Preminger.

Set in the American Northwest during the gold rush, *River of*

No Return depicts Matt Calder (Robert Mitchum), his young son Mark (eleven-year-old Tommy Rettig), and saloon gal Kay Weston (Marilyn) as they follow her ex, a handsome horse thief and gambler, Harry Weston (Rory Calhoun), who needs to get upriver to Council City to register a claim on a gold mine he has cheated another gambler out of. With no transportation and time running out, Kay and Harry make the trip via raft. The trip is fraught with gripping, heart-stopping action, including a swamping of the raft in the treacherous river rapids. Wringing wet, out of sorts and out of breath, Marilyn is still a vision.

Shot on location in two national parks in the Canadian Rockies—Banff Springs and Jasper in Alberta—in Technicolor, CinemaScope, and released initially in 3–D, *River of No Return* gives Marilyn, sexier and more sensuous than ever, a chance not only to flex her dramatic acting muscles, but to prove her real muscles are up to the physicality the script demands of her character, as she raft-rides the swirling, potentially deadly whitewater of the river of the movie's title. Marilyn also sings four songs in the film and performs them admirably. She's more than admirable in her acting. She's forceful and vulnerable by turn as she comes to realize what a no-good rat Harry is and what a good man and father Matt is.

The ninety-minute film began shooting on July 28, returning to Hollywood on September 29 to complete the shoot. *River of No Return* would open toward the end of April 1954, to generally favorable reviews.*

---

* A funny story relating to this movie: One day, when Marilyn was to get a massage, the crew wanted to play a joke on her. So one of the jokesters asked a young production assistant—seventeen years old—to go to her trailer and give her a message. "Don't knock," he said. "Just walk right in. She likes that." The youngster did what he was told. He opened the door, and there was Marilyn Monroe, lying nude on her stomach on the massage table, waiting for her masseuse. Completely nonchalant, she asked the red-faced teen, "Did they put you up to this?" He said, "Yes, ma'am." She said, "Okay. Well, close the door, sit down, and stay for twenty minutes. Then the joke is on them!"

PART FIVE

Difficult Times

Grace's Upsetting Secret

*O*ne day in May 1953, Marilyn Monroe returned home from a day of shopping to find Grace Goddard's car parked in front of her house. Grace was not in the habit of dropping by without calling first, so Marilyn must have suspected that something was wrong. "They were pretty inseparable during this time, after Gladys went back into the institution," Grace's stepdaughter, BeBe Goddard, confirmed. "I think Marilyn called her every single day. She still depended on her. Grace was doing office work for her, arranging her schedule, keeping things organized. Marilyn was always filling her in on what was going on at the studio or in her personal life with Joe. Grace loved hearing her stories, especially the show business stories. Everything that the two of them had dreamt about so long ago had come true. It almost seemed unfathomable that Norma Jeane had become this . . . *sensation*."

After inviting Grace inside, Marilyn listened in stunned silence while her aunt shared a secret that she had been hiding from everyone in her life—she had cancer.

The concept of a life-threatening illness and its treatment was quite complex for Grace. She had been a Christian Scientist for a long time, and in recent years passionate about it. One of the core beliefs of the faith is that doctors are unnecessary. The body, as devout believers claim, has within it everything it needs to remain healthy. However, Grace had been feeling under the weather for many months and, despite her long-standing opposition to the medical profession, had secretly sought help at a Los Angeles clinic. That's how she learned the devastating news that she had uterine cancer. Sadly, she was embarrassed by her condition and not sure how to cope with it. In the 1950s, many women felt uneasy about openly discussing so-called "feminine issues," especially with the men in their lives. Marilyn had recently been diagnosed with endo-metriosis and practically no one knew about it. In Grace's case, her husband, Doc, wasn't aware that anything was wrong with her.

Marilyn was concerned, of course, but more than that, she was determined—determined to fight. She had become a firm believer in the medical profession, as doctors were an important part of the studio system at that time. Actors needed insurance, which required physicals, and they often needed (or believed they needed) treat-ment for conditions that were by-products of their stressful lives. There's little doubt that Marilyn was dependent on sleeping pills by this time—doled out to her without concern by the studio physi-cians—and had also become used to the idea of taking other drugs to calm herself during times of stress. Marilyn convinced Grace that she needed to put her metaphysical beliefs aside for the time being and allow Western medicine the chance to heal her.

"I believe that Marilyn loved Grace more than anybody in the world," BeBe Goddard would observe. "Grace had been a second mother from the time she was born and had been such a fair per-son, and as much a mother, or more so, than Gladys. Grace was the single most consistent factor throughout Marilyn's life."

After years of focusing on her own career, her own happiness, her own life, Marilyn decided it was time to change. A debt needed to be repaid. This wonderful woman, who had always worked so tirelessly to solve the problems of others, needed her—and Mari-lyn wanted to make certain she was going to receive the best care money could buy. It was to be a delicate dance, however, because Grace did not want Doc or the rest of her family to know pre-cisely what was going on. As much as possible, they would hide Grace's condition and the fact that she was seeking help from doc-tors. While she eventually would admit to receiving treatment, she would never explain just how intensive her medical quest had been. In some respects, there would be a covert aspect to the journey the two women would take—but this was something with which Marilyn had become quite familiar. Marilyn had come to believe that the "truth" was something abstract, malleable—and she easily enrolled Grace in that belief. After all, they were simply trying to save her loved ones from anguish and worry.

While Marilyn had nothing but the best of intentions, Grace Goddard's experience in the following months would prove to be ghastly. Marilyn arranged for Grace to see numerous physicians, all of whom needed to examine her, of course. For a woman not familiar with any kind of medical examination to now have doctors studying the most intimate parts of her body was torturous. The experience was so draining, in fact, that after one day of tests, Grace told Marilyn that she could not go home to face her husband, Doc. Marilyn suggested that she stay with her for much of the summer. "We'll have fun, just you and I," Marilyn suggested. "It'll be like the old days."*

Grace Learns About Marilyn's Troubles

*B*ecause Grace Goddard was now spending so much time at Marilyn Monroe's home, Marilyn felt more freedom to share with her some of the problems she was having in her career. She was unhappy with Fox, she told her, and she didn't know what to do about it. Grace, according to a later recollection, was clear in her advice. "You have to stand up for yourself, Norma Jeane," she told her. "Don't let them push you around." Marilyn didn't know if she could do it, she said, because Darryl Zanuck disliked her so much. He'd always believed that he was dealing with a stupid, very foolish

---

* Marilyn Monroe's accounting ledger for this time frame indicates two payments to "Mrs. G. Goddard"—Grace—made in May and June of 1953. The first is for $851.04, and the second is for $300.00. Both carry the notation "medical." For years, it's been speculated that these checks were used to cover an abortion Marilyn may have had—though no one can explain why, if this were the case, the checks were made out to Grace. The truth seems clear: These checks were obviously drawn by Marilyn to help pay for Grace's medical crisis at this time.

actress, and she'd never been able to disabuse him of that opinion, no matter how hard she tried. She said that she'd hated every movie she'd made for him thus far because each one was "shit"—an exaggeration, obviously, but one made in the emotion of the moment. No matter the scope of her complaint, though, Grace was firm. She told Marilyn that she had come too far to let Zanuck push her around. "Don't forget who you are," she said. "Don't forget where you came from." Marilyn told her that there were times when she definitely wished she could forget, some of the past had been so bad, so painful. "But it brought you here," Grace reminded her with a gentle smile. "And that's not so bad now, is it?" Marilyn had to agree with her. It wasn't so bad . . . most of the time. Grace was adamant, as always, that Marilyn was more powerful than she even realized. She'd already demonstrated such courage and spirit in her life—certainly now was not the time to stop. "You already have everything in you that you need," she told Marilyn, echoing an integral aspect of Christian Science. "As you see yourself, so will others. Believe in yourself," she concluded, "and others will follow."

On June 1, Marilyn spent her twenty-seventh birthday with Grace, BeBe, and Bebe's brother Fritz. That night, they called Gladys at Rock Haven. She didn't realize it was Marilyn's birthday. "I don't remember giving birth to you," she told her daughter. Then, unfortunately, she began to rant once again that she wanted her release from the sanitarium. If Marilyn and Grace really cared about her, they would see to it that she had her immediate freedom. The phone call ended badly, as most did with Gladys. Marilyn vowed never again to call her mother on her birthday, saying that she never wanted to have another birthday ruined such as her twenty-seventh.

At this time, Grace wrote to Berniece to tell her that all was as well as could be expected and that she had been organizing a filing system for Marilyn in order that she might keep track of her appointments (and, perhaps, not be late for them—though that wasn't likely). "I really mean it when I say that next to President Eisenhower, she is next in line as far as the demands of her time are concerned," Grace wrote of Marilyn. (And it's interesting that she often referred to her as Marilyn. If even Grace sometimes was calling Norma Jeane by her new name, then the transformation had to be complete.) She also said that she and Marilyn spent a great deal of time trying to catch up on her fan mail, but to no avail. Regarding her health, Marilyn had earlier suggested that Grace open up to Berniece about her cancer. She had done that, and was happy about it. Now she told Berniece that she'd been to a doctor who told her the cancer was under control but that she would soon have to have a hysterectomy. She predicted that after she had it she would "feel human again."

On June 26, Marilyn received an honor that probably meant more to her than any she'd received since becoming famous: her hand- and footprints in cement at Grauman's Chinese Theatre. The occasion was really a promotional event for *Gentlemen Prefer Blondes*, and Marilyn was joined by her costar Jane Russell for the ceremony; they wore matching white polka-dot dresses. She and Jane had become fast friends. "The biggest disappointment to her, though, was that Grace was too sick on this day to be able to accompany Marilyn," said Wesley Miller from the law firm of Wright, Wright, Green & Wright. "Certainly, they both would have enjoyed the moment so much. Marilyn told me it seemed like just yesterday when Grace took her, as little Norma Jeane, to Grauman's. She said she would place her small hands and feet into imprints left by the major stars of her youth as Grace stood behind her and watched. The two would go from one cement square to the next . . . and the next . . . each dedicated to a movie star who they had seen in motion pictures. Now, of course, Norma Jeane—as Marilyn Monroe—was in that same constellation of stars. In fact, she was a bigger star than many of the ones she and Grace once admired. For me, at the time, it was astonishing to consider how much she'd achieved, especially considering her unstable background. 'This is as much for Aunt Grace as it is for me,' she told me. 'If it wasn't for Aunt Grace, I don't know where I would be, but I know it wouldn't be where I am today.'"

Throughout July, Marilyn was ill with bronchial infections.

Grace insisted on taking care of her. She would take the telephone out of Marilyn's bedroom and bring it into the living room and bury it with pillows so Marilyn wouldn't hear it ring and disturb her sleep. Then she would dutifully take all messages for her.

It was at around this time that Grace became alarmed because of Marilyn's reliance on sleeping pills. She saw that Marilyn couldn't sleep at night without them and that she couldn't even take an afternoon nap unless she was medicated. Then there were the "uppers" Marilyn was taking to stay awake during the day after what she called "a sleeping pill hangover." It was all too much, Grace decided. When she finally confronted Marilyn about it, Marilyn told her that she knew what she was doing, "and I'm very careful, Aunt Grace. I've been taking these things for at least ten years." That was news to Grace. She also noticed that Marilyn was drinking—bourbon and soda—much more than she ever had in the past. Moreover, Marilyn believed that as a consequence of the stresses in her life, she was eating more and thus gaining weight. It's true that she was a tad rounder at this time, but not much. However, every pound mattered when wearing those skin-baring gowns for which she was becoming so famous. At a loss as to what to do, she began using colonic irrigation—basically, enemas. If she had to get into a dress that she didn't think would fit, she would endure as many enemas as it would take to squeeze into it Eventually, she would succeed, too; she could actually lose inches in just a day. Though it was an extremely dangerous way to control one's weight, Marilyn would swear by it for the rest of her life. This was almost more than Grace could process. In fact, she didn't believe it was true. As it happened, Wesley Miller mentioned it to her when he dropped by to deliver some documents for Marilyn to sign. He said that Marilyn had confided in his wife that she was using enemas for the purpose of weight loss. "I simply have never heard of such a thing," Grace told Miller. "Well, it's true," he said. "Ask Marilyn. I'm worried about it. It's not good. Someone needs to talk to her about it." Grace agreed. "I can't believe that Joe would allow such a thing," she said. Grace then called Berniece to ask her if she were aware of her half sister's bad habits. "I never knew a thing about sleeping pills," Berniece said. "And bourbon? It just can't be! Not Norma Jeane. It makes me wonder what else we don't know."*

A Graceful Exit

*W*hile Grace Goddard lived with Marilyn Monroe, she witnessed the beginning of her battle with mood-altering substances. However, by August, Grace too was self-medicating in order to help her deal with the great pain she was in as a result of the spreading cancer. Despite her best efforts, Marilyn was not able to convince her to undergo chemotherapy. Doctors brought in by Marilyn urged Grace to undergo a hysterectomy, and she does seem to have considered it briefly, but in the end she would never allow that surgery to happen. As much as Marilyn might have tried to convince her, Grace was adamant.

It was a losing battle on all counts. There was nothing that could be done to encourage Grace to listen to the advice of the many doctors Marilyn had arranged for her to consult. By this time, Marilyn was getting ready to leave to begin filming *River of No Return*. Without treatment and Marilyn's constant intervention, there seemed little doubt that Grace would die. Still, she believed that her Christian Science principles would heal her. At a loss as to how to proceed—other than just to pray for the best outcome—the two women would often go through numerous bottles of wine in a single evening. It was as if the alcohol allowed them to forget, even if just temporarily, that one of them was dying. On certain occasions, a distraught Marilyn would end such binges with a handful of

* High colonic irrigation was part of the daily routine of Mae West for all of her adult life, not for weight control, but for cleansing purposes. She is said to have used coffee laced with herbs for her routine.

pills to make her sleep. The longer Grace stayed with Marilyn, the more Marilyn's medicine cabinet filled with different kinds of pain pills—prescriptions from different doctors, some intended to help Grace's cancer or its collateral conditions, and some to make life "more bearable" for her. At this same time, both women were being treated for their anxiety, each having prescriptions of barbiturates, including phenobarbital. Marilyn eagerly took hers. Grace didn't. She just puts them aside, promising to take them later.

The day finally came at the end of July when Marilyn had to leave the state to begin working on the movie. Grace needed to return to her family. They both knew that Grace was going home to die. On September 23, while Marilyn was away making the movie, Grace Goddard passed away. She was just fifty-nine.

A Shocking Discovery About Grace

Grace Goddard's husband, Doc, told Marilyn and Berniece that her death had been very sudden—as he put it, "the cancer just took over." He hadn't been aware of how long Grace had been battling the disease. "Grace's death seemed terribly sad and needless to Marilyn and me," said Berniece years later, "and we never really got over it."

Of course, the funeral, on October 1, was very difficult for Marilyn. "I feel an anchor is gone," she told Berniece in a tearful telephone call after the funeral. She said that it seemed that "life is just one loss after another."

Berniece said she hoped Joe DiMaggio could be of some comfort. Marilyn told her that without a doubt, he was more important to her now than ever before.

After the funeral Marilyn had a warm telephone call from Ida Bolender. It had been many years since the two last spoke. Marilyn's life had taken so many twists and turns, she'd actually lost touch with the Bolenders. However, Ida and Wayne were alive and well, and still living in Hawthorne. In speaking to Marilyn, Ida explained that she and her husband had moved next door to the house in which Marilyn was raised. They had turned the old residence into a boarding house for employees of a nearby factory. With that income, she said, they were doing quite well. "I hope you know that if you need anything at all, money or anything, I would love for you to call me," Marilyn told her, according to what Ida later recalled to her foster daughter Nancy Jeffrey. "You did so much for me. I would love to help you." Ida said she appreciated the offer but they were doing just fine. "I wanted you to know how sorry I am about your Aunt Grace," Ida told her. Ida then acknowledged the long-smoldering grievances between her and Grace and said, "Truly, I don't know, to this day, why she disliked me so much. I don't know what I ever did to her. Do you know?" Marilyn said that it was probably best for them to not even try to figure it out all of these years later. "I know that you both loved me, and that's what's important," she concluded. Ida also told Marilyn that she was unhappy about the way Marilyn's life at the Bolenders' had been recently depicted in the press. "They are saying that we were mean to you and that we were poor," Ida said. "I don't understand that, Norma Jeane." Ida said that she had read somewhere that Marilyn recalled Grace bringing her a birthday card with fifty cents in it. Apparently, Marilyn told the reporter that Ida took the money from her because she had dirtied her clothing. "But that never happened, Norma Jeane," Ida said. "You know that never happened, don't you?" Ida said she would never have done such a thing and that it broke her heart to read about it. Marilyn then tried to explain show business public relations to her foster mother, telling her that she shouldn't believe anything she read, "especially," she said, "when it comes to Marilyn Monroe," referring to herself in the third person. In truth, though, Marilyn constantly fed the flames of controversy about her times with the Bolenders by painting a more dismal picture than was true, and she also never did anything to rectify any falsehoods. The phone call ended with both women expressing their love for each other and promising to stay in touch.

After speaking to Ida, Marilyn apparently called Gladys to tell her that her old friend Grace had died. Gladys said that it was probably for the best. According to a later recollection, she said that Grace had been being followed for years and that if she hadn't died when she did, "someone was going to kill her." Marilyn listened patiently, trying not to become upset. By now, she thought, she should be used to hearing these kinds of upsetting proclamations from her mother. She'd hoped that Gladys would be upset by her friend's passing. Maybe such sadness would have suggested a bit of a healing on Gladys's part, but that was not the case. Marilyn told her mother that she intended to visit her very soon. "I'll believe it when I see it," Gladys said. Then she hung up.

Many years later, long after even Marilyn's death, it would be revealed that Grace Goddard had actually committed suicide. The death certificate reads, "Death by barbiturate poisoning—ingestion of phenobarbital." Apparently, Grace, a woman who always had the solution to everyone's problems, had finally come up against one for which she could not find a solution—cancer. At the very end of her life, the biggest dilemma she faced was how to end the suffering her family would experience by watching her slowly waste away. So she ended her life quickly to save others from continued sadness, in the same selfless fashion as she had lived.

After the funeral, Marilyn Monroe was taken by limousine back to her apartment. She was once again alone in the place where she had attempted to nurse Grace back to health and had failed. Her Aunt Grace was gone forever. The one woman Marilyn could always depend upon had receded into the family history. Now it seemed that all that remained of Grace Goddard in Marilyn's home was what might make the loss just a little easier to handle: bottles and bottles of pills.

Marilyn's Rebellion

The end of 1953 saw Marilyn Monroe close to total collapse. She had been working hard, the relationship with Joe DiMaggio was draining (though she would never think to leave him), she was still upset about Grace's death, worried about Gladys, and now she was also having tremendous problems with 20th Century-Fox. The studio announced that her next movie was to be *The Girl in Pink Tights*. From the title alone, Marilyn felt that she was in for another dumb-blonde role, and she didn't want to do it. If she had looked beyond the title, she would have discovered that it was a movie based on a recently closed Broadway musical of the same name starring French singer/dancer Zizi Jeanmaire. "Directors think all I have to do is wiggle a little, not act," she complained to one reporter. To another, she was even more specific about her unhappiness. "I'm really eager to do something else," she said. "Squeezing yourself to ooze out the last ounce of sex allure is terribly hard. I'd like to do roles like Julie in *Bury the Dead*, Gretchen in *Faust* and Teresa in *Cradle Song*. I don't want to be a comedienne forever."

Ever since the advent of sound movies, studio contractees were forced to take part in whatever movie was thrown at them by their studio, and they had to be happy about it. When it came to *The Girl in Pink Tights*, Marilyn displayed nerve and shrewdness unheard of at the time—she demanded to see the script. Darryl Zanuck, who had never made a secret of the fact that he didn't like and, even more unfortunately, didn't respect Marilyn, said that there was absolutely no way he would consider giving her script approval. She didn't actually want "approval," though—she just wanted to see the script. Of course, if she didn't like it, she would then not want to do the movie. Zanuck said that the production was going to cost Fox more than two million dollars and that the role was "written and designed" for Marilyn. He couldn't understand her problem. *The Girl in Pink Tights* obviously had not been "written and designed" for Marilyn, because the property had tried and failed on Broadway.

It got worse. When Marilyn found out that Frank Sinatra was making $5,000 a week to her $1,500, she became even more dissatisfied with Fox. "I've been in this business a long time, and I know what's good for you," one executive told her. Her response was, "I've been in this business a very short time, but I know what's better for me than you do."

Later, she would say of *River of No Return* and (the soon-to-be-filmed) *There's No Business Like Show Business*, "I was put into these movies without being consulted at all, much against my wishes. I had no choice in the matter. Is that fair? I work hard, I take pride in my work, and I'm a human being like the rest of them. If I keep on with parts like the ones Fox has been giving me, the public will soon tire of me."

At this same time, Marilyn began confiding in a very good friend, the excellent photographer Milton Greene (who would go on to take many of the most amazing photographs of her). She told him that she was very unhappy about the ridiculous amount of money Fox was paying her at this time—$1,500 a week. She said that the roles she was playing "are all the same, all dumb-blonde types with sex appeal," and "it's too much tedium. I'm sick of it." Greene suggested that perhaps the two of them should start their own production company. She could then choose her own roles, select her own films, and work in tandem with the studio system instead of strictly *for* the system. Today, of course, major actors and actresses develop their own projects or, at the very least, cherry-pick their roles carefully to suit not only their tastes but also whatever image they have cultivated to present to their public. Most major stars have their own production companies through which such projects are developed and even financed. While the biggest male stars of that time did in fact have their own production companies—Jimmy Stewart, Kirk Douglas, John Wayne, and Burt Lancaster, to name a few—and thus exerted creative and financial control over their careers, that was not the case with female stars. But Marilyn Monroe was about to change that. This was the only way to go, and Marilyn and Milton had decided their goal would be to create their own company. They began discussing the matter with her attorneys. It was definitely one way to avoid the "dumb blonde" kind of movie.

Marilyn was supposed to report to work on December 15. She didn't. When the studio sent executives to her home on Doheny to try to convince her to change her mind, they were met by an enraged Joe DiMaggio, who ordered them off the premises.

Joe and Marilyn were having their own problems at this time. He was still unhappy about the demands of her career. In his view, she wasn't even the same woman he had met a year earlier. She was constantly distraught, run-down, anxious. She could not sleep without pills. Then she would be lethargic for much of the next day. He felt she needed a break—a long break. However, there was no chance of that happening anytime in the near future. She had a tight schedule of TV appearances, photo shoots, rehearsals, and, of course, movies.

"Joe was sick and tired of Marilyn's career," said Stacy Edwards, who was a sportswriter at the time in Philadelphia and knew Joe well. "I know he went with her to Canada when she made *River of No Return*. He called me from there to do an interview. 'I hate it up here,' he told me. 'They treat her like she's a princess and if you want to know my opinion,' he said, 'I think she's getting to be too spoiled. She expects everyone to treat her like these people on these movie sets, and this ain't real life.' He said he wanted to get her out of the movies. 'We'll buy a nice home in San Francisco and just live a simpler life,' he told me. I said, 'Joe, are we talking about the same Marilyn Monroe—I mean, the movie star? Because she ain't quittin' the movies. She looks like she loves it too much for that.' He said, 'Yeah, well, we'll see about that.'

"I knew Joe and I knew what he was about deep down, and it wasn't just Marilyn's career. The attention she got, he was used to getting. When he walked into a room with her, he disappeared.

He wasn't used to that at all. He was used to being the center of attention. But with Marilyn, no man could ever be the center of attention. She drew focus wherever she went. Joe couldn't accept that."

Natasha Continues Her Dual Purpose

Of course, Natasha Lytess was still a permanent fixture in Marilyn Monroe's life. Most observers felt that she was determined to keep Marilyn under her control by reinforcing the notion that she was indispensable to her. "She is not a natural actress," Natasha said in an interview in 1953. "She has to learn to have a free voice and a free body to act. Luckily, Marilyn has a wonderful instinct for the right timing. I think she will eventually be a good actress."

"There wasn't a single moment on the set of any film Marilyn made during this time that Natasha wasn't there," said Jane Russell, Marilyn's costar in *Gentlemen Prefer Blondes*. "I felt that Marilyn was using her too much as a crutch. After she would do a scene she would look over to one side or another to see Natasha's reaction. Directors didn't like it, I can tell you that much. At one point, [Natasha] was removed from the set of *Gentlemen Prefer Blondes* because the director just had enough of her presence."

Only a select few people, however, knew that Natasha had a dual purpose in Marilyn's life—she was her acting teacher, certainly, but she was also the one person who could calm Marilyn when "the voices" became too loud in her head.

In *Gentlemen Prefer Blondes*, Marilyn had a scene with Charles Coburn in which his character, "Piggy," was reciting to Monroe's character, Lorelei, a line in Swahili. "The actor was speaking gibberish, of course, and in each take Coburn read the line a bit differently," Natasha wrote in a letter to her former student Helena

Albert. For some reason, his pattern of speech was something Marilyn could not get out of her head, Natasha wrote. Apparently, days after the shooting of this scene, Marilyn locked herself in her dressing room and refused to speak to anyone but Natasha. The director, Howard Hawks, adjusted the shooting schedule and then sent for the acting coach, who arrived quickly. According to Natasha's memory of events, Marilyn explained to her that she couldn't stop her mind from playing and replaying Coburn's Swahili impression. "It was as if she had become haunted by it," Natasha wrote. "Marilyn told me she couldn't even bear to look at Charles Coburn. Prior to this time, she had adored him. They had appeared in *Monkey Business* together."

Somehow, after less than an hour with her star client, Natasha managed to get Marilyn back in action. It was as if nothing had ever happened. Natasha knew how to bring Marilyn out of these kinds of episodes. "Whenever Marilyn works herself into a panic about something, only I have the cure," Natasha wrote, rather cryptically.

Similarly, during the making of *How to Marry a Millionaire*, Natasha was ordered off the set. The next day, Marilyn didn't show up for work, claiming she had bronchitis. Marilyn would often cloak her mental breakdowns with excuses of physical illnesses. When the studio sent a doctor to her home, which was the procedure at that time, she insisted on speaking to Natasha. Not surprisingly, Marilyn soon returned to work, and Natasha was brought back in—at an even higher salary. Nunnally Johnson, who worked with Marilyn on that film (in March 1953), recalled, "Natasha was really advising her badly by this time, justifying her own presence on the set by requiring take after take and simply feeding on Marilyn's insecurity. 'Well, that was all right, dear,' she often said to Marilyn, 'but maybe we should do it one more time.'

"I'm not sure, but I think Joe felt that Natasha was more important to Marilyn than he was—and he may have been right."

"If it were up to me, Morticia would take a long walk off a short pier," Joe DiMaggio told Stacy Edwards. "Maybe I could get through to Marilyn if I didn't have this broad to deal with. This broad is gonna ruin her, I'm telling you."

Mrs. DiMaggio

Marilyn Monroe knew that she would be put on suspension by Fox for not showing up for work on the set of *The Girl in Pink Tights*. She didn't care. She was exhausted by the last year. It had been one drama after another. What was done was done, she decided. She had taken a firm stand against the studio and wasn't going to now look back with regret. She knew that her Aunt Grace would have wholeheartedly approved of the way she'd handled Darryl Zanuck. Grace would not have wanted Marilyn to stand by and just allow Zanuck to walk all over her, "I don't care who he is."

Marilyn would later say she felt sure that she needed a new beginning, a fresh start in the new year of 1954. Was it to be with Joe? She felt that he was all she had, now that Grace was gone. That night, at 11:45, Marilyn took a plane to San Francisco—to Joe.

Once safely ensconced in San Francisco, Marilyn stayed with Joe and his sister, Marie DiMaggio, in Joe's home. She fit in well with the family, eager to help out around the house—washing dishes, cleaning up with Marie after Joe and his brother Dom; whatever was necessary was what she wanted to do. Indeed, whenever a family environment presented itself to Marilyn and she was asked to join in, she was eager to do it. One morning, she prepared a big breakfast for Joe and his family members and friends—and it was good, too. Marie had given her a lot of assistance. This was the Marilyn Joe DiMaggio wanted her to be—domesticated, calm, and at peace with her household chores and wifely duties. Of course, this was just a fantasy life for Marilyn. She may have been unhappy with the way her career had been unfolding lately, but there was no possibility of giving it up. Still, this was a good time and there was no point in her reminding Joe that it was all just temporary. She enjoyed seeing him happy and noticed that when she was relaxed, he was as well. They went fishing together, washed his car, took long walks. It was a wonderful week. Then, on New Year's Eve 1953, Joe asked her to marry him. It was easy for both of them to forget their differences in the idyllic world they had created that week. It must have felt to them that they were completely compatible. It was all an illusion, though. In the romantic moment, of course Marilyn said yes, she would marry him. They decided to keep the news of their engagement a secret from the media for the time being and just enjoy their private time with Joe's family, all of whom were delighted by the news.

Fox finally relented and sent Marilyn the script to *The Girl in Pink Tights*. This was a little victory for her. It was probably the first time she'd gotten her way with Darryl Zanuck. However, as expected, when she took a look at the script, she realized that her instincts were right. It was ridiculous and cliché-ridden and she didn't want to do it. As soon as she informed Fox of her decision, the studio put her on suspension, meaning she would not be getting her salary. She could live with that; it wasn't as if they were paying her a mint, anyway.

Meanwhile, Marilyn began work on a three-part magazine article with writer Ben Hecht. Hecht went to San Francisco to interview the star over a period of four days for a piece about her life—or, really, the story of her life as she wanted to present it at the time—for *Ladies' Home Journal*. Eventually, Hecht's notes would end up in book form and be touted as Marilyn's memoir, *My Story*, published many years after her death (and in fact, after Hecht's death).

My Story is not a terrible book, though it's disjointed and filled with inaccuracies. The reader gets the sense, however, that Marilyn wanted to be thought of as a victim, and she framed her stories with an eye toward that goal. One anecdote that was excised from the book upon its release was that Marilyn said she had tried to commit suicide twice—both times over relationships with men. One episode may have been a reference to the incident with Johnny Hyde when she was saved by Natasha Lytess. The other remains mysterious to this day, although she told Hecht that she was very angry when she was saved the second time because she definitely wanted to die. "But now I'm glad it happened the way it did. I'm glad I'm alive. I hope to stay glad for a long time."

Some people in Marilyn's life completely disavow this book—like her half-sister Berniece, who calls it "half-baked." It's not known where the money goes from proceeds of this book, but likely not to any family members. What must irk Marilyn's intimates even more is that a document does exist that memorializes an agreement Marilyn made with Ben Hecht—dated March 16, 1954—which clearly states that the material "shall not be put into book form by you and you shall have no right to the use of the material for anything except one magazine article to be published in the *Ladies' Home Journal* magazine." Like it or not, *My Story* is the book of record— ostensibly, Marilyn's own words about her life. Reading it today, it does seem accurate, it just doesn't seem complete.

On January 14, 1954, Marilyn and Joe were wed in a quick civil ceremony before a judge in San Francisco. Much of her public, and the media, felt the marriage to be somewhat anticlimactic, that a star like Marilyn (in a dark brown suit with an ermine collar on this day) should have had a grander affair. However, there were hundreds of fans and reporters at City Hall waiting for them to arrive, because Fox had put out the word, unbeknownst to Marilyn, who had been considerate enough to inform the studio but asked for confidentiality. An affair any bigger would have been more than Marilyn could have handled at this intense time in her life. She made a strange request of Joe, though. If she died before him, would he promise to place flowers at her grave every week? He promised, giving her the same vow that William Powell had once given Jean Harlow.

The DiMaggios honeymooned in the small seaside town of Paso

Robles—not much of a honeymoon. The couple then left for a vacation/business trip (for Joe) to Japan in early February. At the airport, the press noticed that Marilyn's finger was bandaged and in a splint. It appeared to have been broken. She said that she "bumped it" and that Joe was a witness. "He heard it crack." It seemed suspicious.

When they got to Tokyo, they were surprised by the absolute mob that awaited them there—thousands of fans in what was the most chaotic scene Marilyn had ever seen built around her. Her international appeal was obvious, if not also a little frightening. As for Joe, he wasn't happy about it at all. It was clear that her popularity eclipsed his, even in a foreign country. The realization just made him more surly and disagreeable. At a press conference that had been arranged in his honor to promote the exhibition games for which he had traveled there, matters got worse. Practically every question was directed to Marilyn. He sat at her side looking more than a little peeved.

While the couple were in the Far East, an invitation came from General John E. Hull's Far East Command headquarters for Marilyn to entertain the troops in Korea. She wanted to do it, but Joe was against it. The two had a heated discussion which ended with him saying, "It's your honeymoon. Go if you want to go." She did.

The brief tour began on February 16. Of course, the servicemen went wild for Marilyn everywhere she appeared as she sang songs such as "Kiss Me Again" and "Diamonds Are a Girl's Best Friend." Appearing before more than one hundred thousand military men in just four days, she was a smashing success. What was interesting about this brief series of concerts is that she was on her own—there was no Natasha Lytess in the wings telling her what to do, no Darryl Zanuck over her shoulder telling her how to be, and no Joe DiMaggio at her side telling her she couldn't do it. She proved to herself that she could stand before an audience and entertain using her own instincts and judgment—and while singing, too, which she was never really comfortable doing, let alone in front of people. It was a big win for her, and she had never felt better about herself.

She wasn't the least bit nervous, either. It was as if when left to her own devices she knew she could soar, and she did. "I felt I belonged," she would later say. "For the first time in my life, I had the feeling that the people seeing me were accepting me and liking me. This is what I've always wanted."

"And now I'm flying back to the most important thing in my life—Joe," she told the troops at the end of her last show. "And I want to start a family. A family comes before a career."

When the DiMaggios returned to America on February 24, 1954, it was business as usual—meaning one problem after another. It hadn't been going that well between them. There was still a sense that DiMaggio could not reconcile himself to Monroe's stardom. For instance, when talking about her tour of Korea, she exclaimed, "You've never heard applause like that!" He responded, "Yes, I have." He seemed to always want to remind her that she wasn't the only star in the family. He definitely didn't want her to become any bigger a celebrity than she already was, he said, because he didn't believe she could handle it. So they fought about their future— about her career and how it fit into their plans as a married couple. Still, Marilyn tried to stay optimistic. "I love you till my heart could burst," she wrote in a love note to Joe in March 1954. "I want someday for you to be proud of me as a person and as your wife and as the mother of the rest of your children. (Two at least! I've decided.)"

At around this time, during a trip to Los Angeles, Joe telephoned his friend the agent Norman Brokaw who had first introduced him to Marilyn in 1950. Joe said he needed to see him. They met at the Polo Lounge of the Beverly Hills Hotel. As the two took a back booth, DiMaggio seemed very unhappy. "I don't know what to do, Norm," he said, according to the agent's memory of the conversation. "I love her. But I can't accept her career. I want her to quit, but she won't do it."

Norman mulled over his friend's problem for a moment and said, "Joe, let me explain something to you, as an agent in this town. There's no actress in this business who is going to give up Clark Gable or Tyrone Power or Spencer Tracy for any man. In fact, I don't know any actress who would be willing to give up her career when she's on her way to the top any more than you would have given up your baseball career before its time." He continued, "What if when you were shooting to break the record of fifty-seven hits, a girl came into your life and said, 'No, you need to stop at fifty-six. You can't go for fifty-seven because I won't allow it.' How would you have handled it?"

DiMaggio thought about it for a second. "I never looked at it that way," he said. "That makes sense to me."

"Well, that's the way it is, Joe," Norman concluded. "That's the field you're playing on, my friend. She's not going to give up her career any more than you would have before you were ready to do it. So you have to get used to it, Joe. Or, honest to God, you're going to lose her."

Joe thanked Norman for his advice. He would try to follow it . . . but it wouldn't be easy. Not long after this meeting with Norman, Joe wrote in his personal journal about Marilyn, "No jealousy. . . . Don't forget how lonesome and unhappy you are— especially without her."

There's No Business Like Show Business

*I*n March 1954, Marilyn Monroe's victory against Fox seemed complete when the studio decided that she didn't have to appear in *Pink Tights*. Instead, they offered her a supporting role in *There's No Business Like Show Business*. She was also scheduled to appear in a more major role in *The Seven Year Itch*. Plus, the studio promised to give her a new contract in August and a huge $100,000 bonus. It definitely seemed as if Darryl Zanuck had blinked—or, at the very least, realized that he had a good thing in Marilyn Monroe and didn't want to lose her.

Marilyn began work on *There's No Business like Show Business* in May. This big, splashy musical all dressed up in CinemaScope, stereophonic sound, and color by Technicolor, with its star-heavy cast, classic tunes from the Irving Berlin songbook, and Oscar-nominated costumes, had "blockbuster" written all over it. After all, it would star Ethel Merman, Donald O'Connor, Dan Dailey, Mitzi Gaynor, and pop singer Johnnie Ray. In these waning days of the big studio musical, Fox's decision makers knew it lacked the one ingredient that would send moviegoers stampeding through the nation's theater turnstiles: Marilyn Monroe. And though the part was not even yet written into the script, it was added with Marilyn specifically in mind after the *Pink Tights* debacle.

To lift a line from the film's title song in describing the movie, "Everything about it is appealing." It clocks in at 117 minutes and with sixteen musical numbers, at least half of them so elaborately staged, it's hard to imagine that anything comparable would be possible today—even with CGI (computer graphics and imaging). The film chronicles the saga of the Donahue family, both on and off the stage, from 1919 to 1942. As evidenced by a whole slew of successful movie musicals, from Hollywood's Golden Age up to the mid-sixties, stories about showbiz families were audience favorites—from the Cohans and the Foys to Gypsy Rose Lee and the von Trapps—and it didn't seem to matter if the stories were true or not.

Terry and Molly Donahue (Dailey and Merman), vaudeville headliners, incorporate their three kids, one by one, into their act from toddlerhood to teenager. The first time we see all five Donahues performing together is at the New York Hippodrome in an overwrought and overlong production of "Alexander's Ragtime Band." We are soon treated to the sight of Marilyn in an abbreviated French maid's costume as she makes her first appearance—as Victoria Hoffman, a nightclub hat checker. Two minutes later, she is auditioning for producer Lew Harris, singing and dancing to "After You Get What You Want (You Don't Want It)." Dressed in a white, see-through, skin-revealing gossamer gown, with embroidered, jewel-studded appliqués strategically placed on the slit-to-the-hip, formfitting costume, and wearing a crown of snowy egret hackle feathers, Marilyn is breathtakingly beautiful.

The film unfolds as complex relationships evolve between Victoria and the Donahues. Tears and heartbreak give way to reconciliation and apologies all around—and then a big number for the Five Donahues, "Alexander's Ragtime Band." That number segues into "There's No Business like Show Business," with the Five Donahues and Vicky descending an imposing staircase, marching in unison and singing in harmony. Merman is in a draped, strapless white evening gown. Gaynor is gorgeous in a slinky red floor-length gown. And Monroe is elegant in a silver-sequin-spangled, powder blue number with a modest décolletage. Of course, she is—as always on film—dazzling. There is much to admire in this film, with Marilyn more than holding her own with old pros Ethel Merman, Dan Dailey, and Donald O'Connor.

However, the shoot was fraught with problems, mostly from Marilyn. She was ill with bronchitis for part of it and was also diagnosed with anemia. Moreover, her growing addiction to sleeping pills and barbiturates had become a real issue in her life, affecting her performance. She was sluggish and unhappy most of the time. Naturally, she was also late very often.

Natasha Lytess—who was on the set with Marilyn every day, of course—later claimed that Joe was beating Marilyn during this period and that Marilyn had confided in her details of the terrible confrontations. It would be difficult to trust Lytess's word given her animosity toward DiMaggio, but others close to Marilyn concur—and even some close to Joe. "He was smacking her around, yes," said one of his closest friends. "He didn't seem too ashamed of it, either. He said that she brought the worst out in him, that he wasn't usually that kind of man. He said she was spoiled and very self-centered and it drove him crazy. He told me he was sick of coddling her, tired of her 'woe is me stories,' as he put it. I said, 'Joe, maybe you two should get divorced.' He looked at me as if I was crazy. 'I ain't letting her go,' he said. 'Hell if I'm letting her go.'"

In marrying Joe DiMaggio, Marilyn may have repeated a pattern in her life of becoming fixated on a man who would not support her desires or her ambitions. The concensus is that he was physically abusive to her. He also could be insensitive and dense. For instance, Marilyn once gave him a gold medal as a gift that she'd had inscribed with a quote from *The Little Prince* by Antoine de Saint-Exupéry: "True love is visible not to the eyes, but to the heart, for eyes may be deceived." He took one look at it and said, "What the hell does *this* mean?"

"When he came onto the set of *Show Business*, it happened to be the day we were doing Marilyn's big 'Heat Wave' number. She had worked so hard on it with [her vocal coach] Hal Schaeffer, and I know she was proud of it. He just stood there, a big lug of a man, so unpleasant and unsupportive," said one person who worked on the movie's production team. "She would come in with bruises here and there that they would cover with makeup. If you cared about Marilyn, and I think everyone there really did, you wanted to say to her, 'Dump this guy. Now!' You just wanted to hold her and keep her safe, that's the way she affected you."

The Seven Year Itch

In August, Marilyn began work on *The Seven Year Itch* in New York. Like no other of her films before or after, *The Seven Year Itch* established Marilyn's iconography as the world's number one sex symbol and burnished her image as a contemporary love goddess, much as Rita Hayworth had been a dozen years earlier.

The film's roots were planted on the Broadway stage at the Fulton Theatre on November 20, 1952, and flourished for 1,141 packed-house performances. The play was written by George Axelrod and starred Tom Ewell, who won the year's Best Actor Tony Award. It was originally acquired by Paramount as a Billy Wilder project, but when Wilder left the studio he took the screenplay with him to 20th Century-Fox, where he became the picture's director, cowriter, and coproducer.

In the movie, Ewell is Richard Sherman, a thirty-eight-year-old publishing executive, left alone in his New York apartment while his wife of seven years and son spend the summer in Maine. Subleasing the upstairs, non-air-conditioned apartment is a gorgeous blonde, a television pitchwoman identified only as "The Girl" (Monroe), who soon becomes the object of Sherman's fantasies. A couple of brief encounters with her is enough to set Sherman off on a Walter Mittyish, wild-goose chase in which he imagines himself romantically involved with The Girl in a series of improbable situations. The "relationship" becomes so serious in Sherman's mind that he becomes paranoid that his vacationing wife, Helen (Evelyn Keyes), is aware of his imagined infidelity. The rest of the plot doesn't really matter—the movie falls apart halfway through. Suffice it to say, Marilyn is stunning in every scene.

Filming commenced on September 1, 1954, at Fox's L.A. studio. The first location scene in New York was the "flying-dress sequence" on September 15, at 1 a.m. The shot of Monroe in the Travilla-designed ecru halter-top dress, standing on a subway grate, the accordion-pleated skirt a-flying as she gleefully but vainly tries to anchor it, is firmly imprinted on the collective cerebral cortex of moviegoers for all time. Five thousand onlookers watched the filming of it at 52nd and Lexington near the Trans-Lux Theatre. Unfortunately, Joe DiMaggio was one of them.

Prompted by Walter Winchell, who, it would seem, was trying to get a good reaction from Joe for his column, Joe found himself on the set that night. Watching his wife perform in such a provocative—even if very obviously staged—moment infuriated him. Billy Wilder described the look on DiMaggio's face as "the look of death." Even though Marilyn wore *two* pairs of panties for modesty, under the klieg lights there was still more visible than what Joe would have been comfortable with. James Haspiel was present for the filming, and he recalled, "I must confess I had no trouble seeing through Marilyn's sheer panties. Most of the published photographs from that night do not illustrate this intimacy. I think they shot the scene fifteen times so it was a very exciting, intimate situation being played out over and over again before my eyes. Nonetheless, I could fully appreciate DiMaggio's anger. Indeed, Joe stood there sour-faced. In defense of Monroe, I am reasonably convinced that in her dressing room she did not see what the powerful klieg lights then put on display."

DiMaggio rushed back to the St. Regis Hotel and waited for his wife to join him there at the end of her workday. Then he took out his rage on her, slapping her around the room. The altercation was so noisy, in fact, that other hotel guests reported it to the hotel's management, afraid that someone was getting badly hurt. Natasha, in the room next door, was alarmed enough to pound on the door to the DiMaggios' suite. "Is everything okay in there?" she shouted out, knowing, of course, the answer. The door swung open and there was Joe, eyes blazing, face reddened. "Get outta here," he told her brusquely. "Mind your own business, for once." Later that night, Milton and Amy Greene had dinner with Joe and Marilyn. They noticed bruises on Marilyn's back. The next day, Gladys Witten, a studio hairdresser, noticed bruises on Marilyn's shoulders, "but we covered them with makeup," she said.

"That was the last straw," recalled Stacy Edwards, who met Joe in New York earlier in that day. "The way I heard it, Joe let her have it. It was pretty bad. After he hit her, she told him she'd had enough and wanted out of the marriage. I spoke to Joe maybe three weeks later and asked him about that night. He said, 'Things got out of hand, I admit it. But she pissed me off so much. She didn't care what I thought about anything, she just wanted to do what she wanted to do.' That was DiMaggio. He could be a sweetheart if everything was going his way. If not, he was pretty mean. To tell you the truth, I lost a lot of respect for Joe when I found out he hit Marilyn Monroe. I thought to myself, 'How could any man hit such a beautiful creature?'"

Years later, Marilyn admitted to her hairdresser, Sydney Guilaroff, very famous in his time for his work with Hollywood stars, "Joe beat me up twice. The first time, I warned him. 'Don't ever do that again.' I'm not going to stand for it. Then, after he witnessed me filming a sexy scene for *The Seven Year Itch*, he slapped me around the hotel room. I finally screamed at him, 'That's it.' I don't know what makes a man beat a woman—vulnerable and weak—I just don't understand it."

The DiMaggios left New York on September 16. The next day, Marilyn did not show up for work at the studio. Her doctor said she was home in bed with the flu. It would be four days before she could return to work. Even Darryl Zanuck—arguably a cruel man himself, with his comments about his star Monroe—felt badly about what was going on in her private life. He sent a note over to Billy Wilder assuring the director, "Others could give a good performance, but nothing could make up for Marilyn's personality in this film."

Billy Wilder summed up Marilyn's appeal best when he told her biographer Donald Spoto, "She had a natural instinct for how to read a comic line and how to give it something extra, something special. She was never vulgar in a role that could have become vulgar, and somehow you felt good when you saw her on the screen. To put it briefly, she had a quality no one else ever had on the screen except Garbo. No one."

What's most stunning about Marilyn's performance in *The Seven Year Itch* is that she was able to rise to the occasion despite the misery of her private life. That's what real movie stars do—they give all they have when on camera, even when they seemingly have nothing left to give. She inhabited the role of The Girl as if born to it. With her arresting beauty, she is totally aware of the effect she has on men, even joking about it. But the jokes are on her, not the men. Melissa Anderson of the *Village Voice* wrote, "So arresting is Monroe's presence that when she's not on-screen, we wait impatiently, wondering, 'Where have you gone, Mrs. DiMaggio?' " She wears white throughout most of the film, appearing in a pastel pink shorts outfit briefly and in a slinky evening gown in one of Sherman's fantasy sequences. It is apparently meant to point out the character's virginal purity and her total lack of guile. Her short, curly hairdo by Helen Turpin is timeless and the one most closely associated with Marilyn for the rest of her life.

That said, Marilyn's emotional problems took their toll during filming. This, along with her tardiness and ill-preparedness—by one report as many as forty takes for a single scene—was said to have added over a million dollars to the film's $3.2 million budget. It still managed to earn a nice profit, taking in $12 million at the box office for Fox. The still shot of the famous billowing-dress scene that so infuriated Joe became the film's graphic signature, and Fox's marketing team decreed that it be blown up to a height of fifty-two feet. The enormous Monroe image was then cut out and placed in front of Loew's State Theatre in Times Square when the movie opened. It caused a sensation.

Marilyn Divorces Joe

She knew what she had to do—but that didn't make it any easier for her. The much-reported story is that she called her attorney, Jerry Geisler, and told him that she wanted a divorce. However, Marybeth Cooke worked for Geisler at the time and she tells a different story. She recalled, "We all knew that Marilyn Monroe was still crazy in love with Joe, but that he was beating her up. Still, she did not want to let him go. I have to say—and Jerry would not have wanted anyone to know this at the time—that Marilyn called him from New York and told him that she might want a separation from Joe, but she wasn't sure. When she got back to Los Angeles, she was not calling Jerry to ask him to file divorce papers. She thought maybe he knew someone who could talk to Joe and make things better. She was desperate to find a way to save her marriage. It was Jerry who said, 'Look, I like you a lot, Marilyn. As a friend, I have to tell you—you have to get this creep out of your house.' That was not like Jerry. He represented the biggest names in Hollywood and never injected his personal opinions. But with Marilyn Monroe, it was different. When he found out what was going on, he was very upset, I remember him saying, 'God damn it, I'm a big fan of Joe DiMaggio's, too. Or at least I *was* a fan.'"

On October 4, Jerry Geisler—middle-aged, stout of frame, and balding above a ruddy face—was ready to serve "Joltin' Joe" DiMaggio with divorce papers. Marybeth Cooke continued: "I remember him saying, 'Christ, almighty, I just called Marilyn to ask her where Joe was so I could serve him myself out of respect and guess where he is? At home with her!' It turned out he was still living in the same house, though I believe in separate bedrooms, or maybe on separate floors. He went to the house and gave Joe the papers. He told me DiMaggio glanced at the papers, said, 'Thanks a lot,' popped a beer, and then went back to watching television. When he got back to the office, Jerry sank into a chair and looked drained. I asked him, 'Are you okay?' He said, 'I just told Joe DiMaggio that Marilyn Monroe is divorcing him. How do you think I feel?' I think at about that same time, he and Marilyn sent a memo to Darryl Zanuck telling him that DiMaggio wasn't allowed on the property. So, it was really over.

"The next morning was chaos at Marilyn's home on Palm Drive in Beverly Hills. I had to meet Jerry there and give him some papers, but I couldn't even get into the house there was so much media in front of it, just camped out and waiting for the next shoe to drop. I finally got into the house and it was just teeming with people. It was also a mess. I couldn't believe the clutter—it looked as if it hasn't been tidied up—ever! There was food left out in the kitchen and on plates in the living room. There were crushed, empty beer cans on the floor . . . clothes strewn about . . . ashtrays filled with cigarettes . . . I mean it was really a pigpen. Someone who worked for Marilyn—I can't recall who wouldn't let me upstairs to her room, where I knew Jerry was. I was told she was too sick to be disturbed, or, as it was put to me, 'She has taken to her sick bed.' So, I left.

I spoke to Jerry that night, who told me, 'The kid is sick, she's on drugs, she's sad . . . she's a mess.' The next day was the press conference. I didn't go. It was a zoo."

Marilyn Monroe emerged from her home on the morning of October 6 to meet the press wearing an all-black ensemble: a skintight black sweater with a matching gabardine skirt and heels along with a black leather belt. She leaned on Jerry Geisler for support as he told the assembled reporters that "Miss Monroe will have nothing to say to you this morning. As her attorney, I am speaking for her and can only say that the conflict of careers has brought about this regrettable necessity." While reporters shouted questions at her, Marilyn seemed ready to faint. "I can't say anything today," she said, her voice almost a whisper. "I'm sorry. I'm so sorry." She then broke down and began to cry, her head on the attorney's shoulder. Never in any reporter's fantasy could the scene have been any more melodramatic—and newsworthy. Even when she didn't intend it, Marilyn Monroe always gave a good show. Photographs from that brief press conference appeared all over the world that night and the next day. It wasn't an act. "She was at the end of her rope that day," said Marybeth Cooke. "Jerry had to take her straight to a doctor's office where she was given more pills to get through the rest of that day. Then he took her back to her house where she went right to bed. She didn't want to speak to anyone. I remember thinking, this girl is only twenty-eight. How much longer can she endure this kind of life?"

Indeed, Marilyn was very difficult to reach during this difficult time and even her beloved half sister, Berniece, could not get through to her. Therefore, on October 8, she sent her a letter:

Dear Marilyn,

The news about you and Joe came as a shock and we were very sorry to hear it. I know you are lonely—do try and come visit us and it may help you over the cloud. You are very busy and all, but if you could fly here for a few days I'm sure you would feel better.

We three are just the same as when you saw us last, except a little fatter and older, ha ha. Mona Rae is very busy in school and loves it. She is trying hard to become a cheerleader for the football team this year. We love you loads and hope to see you soon.

Your sister,
Berniece

If Berniece had known of some of the bizarre situations unfolding in her half sister's life, she might have tried even harder to get her to Detroit. However, Marilyn was keeping a lot of the sadness of her life from Berniece. First, she didn't want to worry her. Second, she just didn't want her to have the information in case any reporter ever tried to trick it out of her. Every time she talked to Berniece, she would say the same thing to her before ending the call: "Please promise me that you won't give out stories about me." One might have thought, given all they shared, that Berniece would be the last person Marilyn would feel she'd have to worry about in terms of discretion. However, that wasn't the case. A sister of Jim Dougherty's gave a story about Marilyn to the press, and even though it would be flattering, Marilyn would still be very unhappy about it. It was getting to the point where she felt she couldn't trust anyone.

Sinatra

One of the people Marilyn Monroe did trust during this time was Frank Sinatra. Lena Pepitone, her maid and sometimes seamstress, once recalled that while Marilyn's divorce from Joe DiMaggio was being finalized, she went to live with Sinatra for a couple of weeks so that she could regain her emotional bearings. Much of what Pepitone recalled in a book she wrote with William Stadiem titled *Marilyn Monroe—Confidential* has been called into question. However, this memory of hers is in fact true.

It's difficult to determine when Frank and Marilyn first met. She had always been a fan of Sinatra's. His friend Joey Bishop recalled the time Marilyn went to see Frank at the Copacabana, "sometime in the fifties. I'm doing my act, and in the middle of it in comes Marilyn Monroe walking into the room like she owns the joint," Bishop remembered. "Of course, I lost the crowd. Who's gonna pay attention to me when Marilyn Monroe walks in? There wasn't an empty seat in the house, so they pulled a single chair up for her to sit in and stuck it ringside, about four feet away from me. I looked down at her and I said, 'Marilyn, I thought I told you to wait in the truck.'" Like many people's memories of their star-crossings with Marilyn, Joey's is a little off. What actually happened was that Marilyn was with a group of friends in New York when she decided she wanted to see Sinatra perform at the Copa. However, the show was sold out. "So?" she asked her friends. "What does that have to do with me? Of course we can get in." Marilyn and her group then took a cab to the nightclub. As soon as the management saw her, they made quick arrangements. They brought a table into the packed club—Sinatra was already onstage, not opening act Bishop—as the Copa staff put white linens on the table and moved it right to the front of the nightclub in an empty corner. Frank stopped his song, winked at Marilyn, and continued with the show.

At this time—in 1954—Frank Sinatra was miserable about the slow erosion of his marriage to actress Ava Gardner, said to be the love of his life. Now the two consoled each other over their losses: Frank's over Gardner and Marilyn's over DiMaggio. Another friend of Frank's, Jimmy Whiting, recalled, "Marilyn was real dependent on Frank. There were many late-night phone calls to him. She used to say, 'If I have any problem in the world about anything, there's only one person I know can help: Frankie.' Frank's feeling was hey, if I can help out the dame, I will. She's a good kid."

Jim Whiting has a funny memory regarding Sinatra. "He heard that Marilyn's . . . you know what . . . was visible underneath her panties in that scene in *The Seven Year Itch* where her dress blows up. So he got an early 'screening copy' of the film and invited a whole bunch of guys over to see her . . . you-know-what. We all sat in his darkened screening room watching the film and waiting and waiting and waiting for this one scene. Finally, the dress starts blowing up and every neck and head in the room craned forward. The dress is up and up and up . . . nothing . . . no you-know-what. You couldn't see it! Frank said, 'Goddamn it! If she wanted to sell tickets to this movie, all she had to do was show her . . . you-know-what.' Except he didn't say 'you-know-what.'"

After they began living together, Frank and Marilyn both admitted to still being in love with their estranged spouses. Therefore, for a time there was nothing sexual going on between them. They were just sharing a vast, common loneliness. Frank wasn't interested in anything more, though it was difficult for his friends to fathom that he had one of the most beautiful and sought-after movie stars living in his apartment with him and was not intimate with her.

As it happened, Marilyn had a habit of not wearing clothing around the house. Everyone who knew her well knew that this was the case. She always said she would rather be naked; her friends and staff were used to seeing her au naturel. When she stayed with Frank during this time, she did not change that behavior. One morning, according to one friend of Sinatra's, he awakened, went into the kitchen wearing just his shorts, and found Marilyn standing in front of the open refrigerator with her small finger in her mouth, trying to decide between orange juice and grapefruit. She was naked. "Oh, Frankie," she said, probably feigning embarrassment, "I didn't know you got up so early."

"That was the end of anything platonic between the two of them," reported Jimmy Whiting. "He told me that he took her right there in the kitchen, up against the closed refrigerator. 'Man,' he told me, 'I never had sex like that. She is one fantastic woman.'

"Actually, Frank had been going through this whole impotency trip at this time. Way too much sauce [liquor]. The booze was completely ruining his sex life. He was getting too old to drink like that and then expect to also perform in the sack. He was frustrated by it because one thing Sinatra always prided himself on was his ability to satisfy a woman."

Apparently, Marilyn cured Sinatra of his impotency, at least for a while. She said that she didn't care how long it took; she was determined that he was going to acquit himself in bed with her. They were sexually innovative. For instance, according to Sinatra's friends, he and Marilyn engaged in intimacies one night on the roof of the Sands Hotel, above the Las Vegas strip. Interestingly, a memo dated May 30, 1959, from Jack Entratter to the hotel's security staff, confirms as much. It reads, "Please be advised that Mr. Frank Sinatra is permitted twenty-four-hour access to the roof of the Sands Hotel. Mr. Sinatra will use his own discretion in choosing to entertain any guest on those premises. Thank you."

"What I heard around the office was that Marilyn and Frank had an argument when she drunkenly confessed to him that while she was attempting to cure him of his impotency, she had been 'faking it,' not achieving sexual satisfaction herself," recalled Wesley Miller from Wright, Wright, Green & Wright. "Frank was upset about that revelation and, apparently, said, 'Jesus Christ, if I can't satisfy her, then what the hell am I doing with her? Why'd she even have to tell me that? Did I have to know that? Hell, no, I did not.'" (While Frank took Marilyn's confession as an affront to his masculinity, others who knew her well said that she rarely felt satisfaction during sexual relations and that this problem was the consequence of her many psychological problems.)

Despite any problems with her, Frank always felt that Marilyn was intelligent, witty, sexy, and exciting. "Frank said that Marilyn was like a shooting star," observed actress Esther Williams, "and you couldn't help but be fascinated by her journey. While you knew she was going to crash and burn, you didn't know how. However, you knew it was going to be a merry ride. The only reason Sinatra wouldn't allow himself to become more serious about Marilyn, he had said, was because he was still so wracked with pain about Ava.

It was too soon. Also, he would never end up with another actress. He had made that promise to himself."

As much as they got along, Marilyn and Frank did argue from time to time. Once, she almost absentmindedly walked naked into a poker game he was having with friends, which infuriated him. "Get your fat ass back in your room," he scolded her, always the charmer. However, he could never stay angry at her for long. He truly loved Marilyn—though he was not in love with her—and he understood her frailties. Obviously, she was weak and delicate, traits he was usually not fond of in a woman. He would never allow any of his women the luxury of vulnerability, but with Marilyn it was different. She was special.

After that poker-game incident, when his friends had departed, Sinatra went back into her bedroom, as Marilyn later remembered it, "kissed me on the cheek, and made me feel like a million. From then on I always dressed up for him, whether or not anyone was coming over."

The Wrong Door Raid

Marilyn's time at Frank Sinatra's did not last long. They could never really connect romantically, though they did love each other. She soon moved out of his apartment and was on her own again. At around this time, another gentleman came into her life as a potential suitor, but this too would not work out for her. He was Hal Schaeffer, the musical coach of her recent films. He actually arranged the highlight of *Gentlemen Prefer Blondes*, Marilyn's stunning routine of "Diamonds Are a Girl's Best Friend." The two had a flirtation going on for some time. Schaeffer, who sounds as if he had his own emotional issues, was so distraught that Marilyn did not want to take things any further with him, he reacted by trying to kill himself. Schaeffer may have been hoping Marilyn would rush to his side if he tried to do himself in, and of course she did. However, the time she spent at his bedside in the hospital was just more time for Joe to act out in a jealous rage. Now that he clearly no longer had a hold on Marilyn and Sinatra was also out of the picture for the time being, she was adrift emotionally, and she turned to Hal. It's difficult to imagine that what the two of them shared was serious for her, though it was to him. It was brief and definitely a diversion for her. By this time she had become so dependent on sleeping pills—freely given to her by the studio's physician—it's likely her judgment was impaired. That said, Schaeffer was kind, gentle, and understanding, and he was also creative—about as opposite to DiMaggio as possible.

When Joe DiMaggio heard about Hal Schaeffer in Marilyn's life, he simply could not accept it. How dare his estranged wife replace him so quickly? What right did she have to move on without him? For a couple of weeks, he and his best friend, Frank Sinatra, did what best friends often do when faced with love lost in their lives—they began to commiserate about it. "We dagos gotta stick together," Frank told Joe. "So let me take care of this thing. Let me come up with something that'll screw with the divorce. Then she'll see the light and you'll be in like Flynn."

The next day, Frank made a few telephone calls and was eventually referred to a company called City Detective and Guard Services. Joe Dougherty (no relation to Jim Dougherty) was one of the detectives working for the company. He recalled, "The divorce hearing was set for October 27. Sinatra hired us about a week earlier. He said, 'I want you to follow Marilyn and this bozo she's screwing—Schaeffer somethin' or others—and take pictures of them in the act. Then, Joe DiMaggio is gonna use it against her and get that broad back in his life.' I was thinking, 'If this doesn't piss off his wife, I don't know what will. So how's he going to get her back doing this thing is beyond me.' But a job is a job and so, fine, we signed a deal and got right to work.

"We did what we were paid to do. We followed Marilyn Monroe

all over the goddamn city waiting for her to hook up with this guy. She knew we were on her tail, too, which must have rattled her because once she almost crashed her car into a tree trying to evade us. Another time, she ran a red light and almost hit an old woman walking across the street with a shopping cart. When she got out of the car and started apologizing to the woman, we started snapping away thinking, well, at least we got some good pictures of Marilyn Monroe maybe we can sell or something later on. Looking back on it now, it was a dirty business. We bugged her car. We bugged her apartment. We bugged his car. We bugged his apartment. I don't know what they had going on but I can tell you that we didn't get one goddamn thing to use against her. If they were hooking up, I don't know where they were doing it."

Hal Schaeffer confirms, "We were followed everywhere. It was sick and twisted. She was absolutely scared to death. How a man could do that to a woman, I don't know. It just confirmed to her that she had made the right decision in letting him go."

On October 27, Marilyn—again in all black except for white gloves and pearls—stood before a judge and detailed her reasons for her divorce petition. "Just the night before, Joe had shown up at her house to try to talk her out of it," said Marybeth Cooke. "Jerry [Geisler, her attorney] couldn't believe his nerve, and was especially surprised that Sidney Skolsky had arranged the meeting. That made no sense. Everyone who cared about Marilyn wanted it over—not extended. But, luckily, Marilyn stood her ground. She told Joe it was over. He left, angry as ever."

In court, Marilyn said that DiMaggio was "cold and indifferent" to her and that days would go by when he wouldn't speak to her. "Cold and indifferent"? That wasn't DiMaggio. The problem was that he was just the opposite, a hothead who was furious because he couldn't have her in his life the way he wanted her.

The stress of being married to him had made her sick on numerous occasions, Marilyn continued. She said she even offered to give up her career at one point, but that nothing would have satisfied him. She wasn't even allowed visitors when he was around, she claimed. Inez Melson, Marilyn's business manager, then took the stand and testified that she had witnessed DiMaggio "push her away and tell her not to bother him."* Natasha Lytess had earlier stated that she had a few things on her mind and hoped to have her day in court, too, but Melson told her that it wasn't the time or place for whatever she had to say about the Monroe-DiMaggio alliance. Joe DiMaggio didn't make an appearance. The divorce was granted— final decree to be effective in a year's time. End of story? Not quite.

"We figured our job was over when the divorce was granted," said Joe Dougherty. "But Sinatra and DiMaggio still had plans for Marilyn. DiMaggio said that she probably hadn't hooked up with Schaeffer because she was too smart to do it before the divorce was granted. Now that it was a done deal, he was sure that she and the guy would start having sex. And he still wanted to catch them in the act. 'Why?' I asked him. He said, 'Who are you to ask me questions? I just want to screw with her, that's why. Satisfied now?' Well, that wasn't a good enough reason for me, so I pulled out of it. The company I was working for, though, wanted the money so they just replaced me with another guy, and the surveillance of Marilyn Monroe continued."

To fully understand just how jealous Joe DiMaggio was, consider the details of what has, over the years, become known as "The Wrong Door Raid." It happened on the night of November 5, 1954. Frank, Joe, and Frank's friend Hank Sanicola were eating at a favorite Italian restaurant called Villa Capri when the maître d', Billy Karen, came to the table and said that there was a phone call for Sinatra. Sinatra went to take the call and, according to Hank Sanicola, returned saying, "Let's go, fellas. They found Marilyn and that little jerk at some dame's apartment in Hollywood." The fellows, who'd had a few too many drinks by this time, took

---

* It's been widely reported over the years—even by *Vanity Fair* in its cover story on Marilyn dated October 2008—that Inez Melson was hired by Joe DiMaggio to be a "spy" for him in the Marilyn Monroe camp and that she was "secretly" working for Joe. It's true that Melson came into the picture at around the same time as DiMaggio. However, her testimony against Joe on this important day would seem to suggest that she wasn't exactly loyal to him, if in fact she was even hired at his recommendation.

off without paying their bill. As they walked out of the restaurant, the maître d' came running after them. "We'll pay it later. Christ almighty," Sinatra exclaimed. "The hell with that," said Billy Karen, "I'm comin' with you guys. I want in on this thing."

Five minutes later, Sinatra, DiMaggio, Sanicola, and Karen met two detectives in front of the building in question. The bunch of them then walked up to the apartment and, with a good kick from slugger DiMaggio and a hearty shove from crooner Sinatra, broke the door right off its hinges. All of them then rushed into the apartment, one person shouting out, "Get your paws off Marilyn Monroe!" and another hollering, "We caught you red-handed. The jig is up!" But guess what? Wrong apartment. Thus "The Wrong Door Raid." The poor woman who actually lived in the unit had been snugly tucked away and probably counting sheep by this time. Suddenly awakened by the sound of a crashing door and a bunch of goons screaming at her while shining flashlights in her face, she sat up in bed, gathered her bedclothes at her chest, and then screamed so loud that people three blocks away would complain about the ruckus the next morning.*

Today, more than fifty years later, Hal Schaeffer says that he and Marilyn actually *were* in the apartment building together—just obviously not in the apartment that was raided. "I think I'd be dead today if they had found me in there with Marilyn," he says. "They came in there and started destroying things, I mean, these guys were thugs. We heard the whole thing from the apartment we were in—which belonged to a student of mine. Marilyn was scared to death. She said, 'Jesus Christ, Hal. We gotta get out of here. If Joe finds us here, he'll kill us both.' We managed to get out through a back door when all attention was focused elsewhere. I can't say I have good memories of that night."

Frank Sinatra was terribly embarrassed by this chain of events. After all, he was the one who had hired the detective company that

---

* This woman later sued DiMaggio and Sinatra for $200,000 and ended up getting $7,500 out of them.

botched the job. "He came down to our office the next day and was so pissed, honest to God, I was afraid for my life," said Joe Dougherty. "He had three henchmen with him and said, 'You guys are lucky we don't tear this goddamn building apart brick by brick.'"

A controversy exploded years later over this raid as a result of a retrospective report about it in *Confidential* magazine. In February 1957 the sensational magazine would publish a story entitled "The Real Reason for Marilyn Monroe's Divorce from Joe DiMaggio." As a result, the California State Senate Investigating Committee would begin a probe to determine just how those kinds of stories about celebrities were leaked to scandal publications, and what the practices of certain unethical private detectives had to do with any of it. As part of the investigation, Sinatra would be called to testify about his participation in the raid. Of course, he was furious about being dragged into any investigation by the media. He despised publications like *Confidential* and could not have cared any less how its reporters gathered their information. Though he wanted nothing to do with any of it, he was still compelled to testify.

Under oath, Sinatra swore that he had only driven Joe DiMaggio to the scene of the break-in, where they then met two private detectives who had been hired by DiMaggio to keep Marilyn under surveillance. Frank lied and claimed that while he stood by his car having a smoke, DiMaggio, Sanicola, Karen, and the two private investigators broke into the wrong apartment. DiMaggio, though, insisted that he didn't break into the apartment either. In fact, eventually all of the principal players began denying involvement in the raid, as if none of it had ever occurred and it was all a figment of someone's wild imagination. Because of so much conflicting testimony, a grand jury convened and compelled Frank to testify again. He had his story, though, and he was sticking to it. He didn't change a word, except to add that, yes, he did pay the $800 for the surveillance. He had to admit this much, because the detective agency presented his check as evidence. However, he said he had only advanced the money for DiMaggio, and was paid back by him. Everyone was lying about this event, though, it would seem—even

Sheila Stewart Renour, whose apartment Hal Schaeffer and Monroe were using for their assignation. She claimed that it was she, not Hal, who was in the apartment with Marilyn. Unless she was watching TV while the other two were in the bedroom, then she was lying under oath, too. The notion of perjury didn't seem to mean much to any of these witnesses.

One more postscript to "The Wrong Door Raid": This ridiculous bit of business marked the end of Frank Sinatra's friendship with Joe DiMaggio. It rankled Sinatra that since he was a Los Angeles resident he was forced to spend hours testifying in a Los Angeles courtroom while DiMaggio, a Florida resident, was not compelled to testify. Sinatra had to bear the brunt of the investigation, whereas DiMaggio was able to walk away from it with nary a problem— especially galling to Sinatra since he had orchestrated the whole matter as a favor to DiMaggio.

Marilyn in New York

It was time for a change. After her marriage to Joe DiMaggio, Marilyn felt engulfed by so much sadness and confusion that she would say she believed she had no one to whom she could turn. She missed her Aunt Grace terribly. It seemed that everywhere she looked in Los Angeles, there were memories of Grace. Though she and her half sister, Berniece, were close, it was really a telephonic relationship. There was only so much she felt she could explain under those circumstances. Moreover, Berniece had her own family and her own problems as well. Marilyn didn't want to burden her. As for Natasha Lytess, she was so possessive of Marilyn it had become impossible to be around her without the outbreak of some kind of turmoil. She wanted to direct Marilyn not only on the soundstage, but also in her life. It was exhausting work trying to placate Natasha. On one hand, Marilyn was fed up with her. On the other, Natasha had seen to it that her student had become so dependent on her, Marilyn wasn't even sure she could act without her. Hal Schaeffer was a kind and understanding man, but he'd just been a temporary diversion. The Wrong Door Raid had been embarrassing to Marilyn and she could barely face Hal after it; she felt that she brought chaos into the lives of anyone who came into her world. Meanwhile, she was being bombarded by letters from her mother, Gladys. They were showing up almost every day—pleadings for Marilyn to secure her release, along with books and pamphlets on Christian Science.

In November 1954, Marilyn went into the hospital to have an operation intended to solve her painful problems with endometriosis. She wasn't sure it would be successful, but she knew she had to try because the condition had just gotten worse in the last year. After she was released, she made an important decision: She was moving to New York. Manhattan promised new vistas for Marilyn Monroe, a fresh start. She would move into the Gladstone Hotel, meet new friends, go to the theater, and enjoy the freedom of a new and exciting environment.

On January 7, 1955, Marilyn held court at a major press conference to announce her future plans, begin a new phase in her career. As eighty members of the media feverishly took notes and photographs—and she did look stunning in a white satin dress and matching ermine coat, her hair now platinum—she formally announced the establishment of a new company. She and her friend photographer Milton Greene, were starting a new production company, Marilyn Monroe Productions. She would be president, he vice president. She explained that she wanted to find plum roles for herself in worthwhile projects and, if possible, even produce them. "We will go into all fields of entertainment," she said, "but I am tired of the same old sex roles. I want to do better things. People have scope, you know."

At this same press conference, Marilyn's lawyer let it slip that she was no longer under contract to Fox. He would later say he had found a loophole in her contract. The executives at Fox begged to differ, though, and promptly held their own press conference to say that Marilyn was still legally bound to the studio, whether she and her attorney liked it or not. Moreover, they had a new role for her. As if to put her in her place, the studio came up with a vehicle called *How to Be Very, Very Popular* in which she would play—a stripper. Marilyn, of course, had other ideas. At this same time, in early 1955, she began to tell the press that she was dreaming of essaying the female lead in Dostoevsky's *The Brothers Karamazov*. This was a surprise, to say the least. Indeed, there was some cynicism about it, too. Later, at a different press conference, a reporter asked her if she really thought she was up to the task. She said, "I don't want to play the brothers, I want to play Grushenka. She's a girl." With a raised eyebrow, the writer then challenged Marilyn. "Spell that name, Grushenka," he said. A flicker of annoyance crossed her face and she said, "Look it up."

Natasha Lytess was still in Los Angeles wondering when Marilyn would be sending for her. Or, as she wrote to Helena Albert, "I am being kept from Miss Monroe by 3000 miles and a circle of vultures. I don't know how to reach her and I must say the situation is dire." What Natasha didn't know was that Marilyn had screwed up the courage to break free of her. She began taking private acting lessons with Constance Collier,* and, shortly thereafter, with Lee Strasberg, who ran the Actors Studio, specializing in so-called "method acting." Indeed, it was Strasberg who began to convince Marilyn that, if she put her mind to it, she could be the kind of actress who would be accepted in a Dostoevsky role. But was such a thing really possible?

In the 1950s, there was a certain segment of movie stars who were considered classic, highly talented actors—and that would include women such as Elizabeth Taylor, Joan Crawford, Bette Davis, and Katharine Hepburn. When people thought of them,

---

* Collier was an English-born, classically trained character actress of stage, radio, and films who turned to teaching and coaching as acting roles began to dry up. She worked with Marilyn for only a few months, dying at the age of seventy-seven in April 1955 in New York.

they thought of classy, well-bred women. However, that's not what came to mind when people thought of Marilyn Monroe—and she knew it. What drew people to Marilyn wasn't her classic acting ability or her regal bearing—it was her sex appeal. Crawford and Hepburn were as much known for their complex thoughts as they were for their acting. No one thought Marilyn was complex, just sizzling hot. No one was looking for depth from Marilyn, they were just looking for cleavage. In some ways, Darryl Zanuck was right about her. What she did, she was the best at doing it—and any-thing more was a risk. She was willing to take the risk—indeed, she *wanted* to take it—but would others allow it? A couple of her roles along the way suggested that there was more to her than what met the eye, but some people felt that she should just be satisfied with her success and leave well enough alone. That wasn't Mari-lyn. She was restless. She was imaginative and not willing to settle for the status quo.

Her sense of dissatisfaction bled into the rest of her life. Because she felt she was viewed as just a bubble-headed blonde, she not only thought she couldn't have the career she wanted, she also believed she couldn't have the kind of relationships she wanted—indeed, the kind of *life* she wanted. "She realized that she would have to ease into a new image," noted Charles Casillo, "an image that would allow her to age and continue to grow in her work and still remain 'Marilyn.'"

Now, at twenty-eight, she was determined to do something to rectify her image, both professionally and personally. Thus her con-nection with Lee Strasberg in 1955.

Lee Strasberg's version of "The Method"—inspired by the teach-ings of Stanislavsky—required an actor to use "sense memory," drawing from his own past experiences. The concept was that in doing so the actor would create a character with more depth and interest. Strasberg's devout belief in sense memory would become quite controversial. It would be the reason why some other found-ing members of the Group Theatre, like Stella Adler and Sanford Meisner, rejected Strasberg's concept and would teach their own versions of Stanislavsky's method. Though these new instructors' concepts were also based on Stanislavsky's system, Strasberg and his devotees would not budge from their position that self-examination and reflection upon one's past was integral to the creation of a fine actor. Many noteworthy actors would come through the studio at different times during their careers, including James Dean, Marlon Brando, Robert Duvall, Montgomery Clift, Sally Field, Dustin Hoffman, Paul Newman, and Sidney Poitier.

"My father wanted to arouse everything undealt with, everything repressed about Marilyn's past, and to tap all her explosive energy," Lee Strasberg's daughter, Susan, once explained. "To bring all that up, he said she'd have to work on it in a formal, professional setting." Strasberg's acting theories appealed to Marilyn. After all, it was familiar terrain for her in that Natasha Lytess had always wanted her to draw from her own life and then imbue her performances with aspects of her sadness and confusion—and even come to terms with her past in order to be a better actress. The difference, of course, is that Natasha, being the controlling woman she was, actually dictated to Marilyn what experiences she should draw from and, moreover, even attempted at times to manipulate those experiences—such as when she encouraged her to meet her father in order to then extract from that relationship what might benefit her acting. But Lee Strasberg presented his own set of problems, too. Though Marilyn made every attempt to follow his instruction, he didn't believe she was successfully accessing her past emotional pain.

"Lee was particularly hard on Marilyn," says a classmate of Monroe's. "I think he saw her as a way to rebuild his reputation."

Indeed, when Strasberg became artistic director of the Actors Studio, he claimed to have trained a number of actors who didn't actually study under him. When Sanford Meisner, the acting teacher and founder of the highly respected Neighborhood Playhouse, heard that Strasberg was claiming responsibility for the success of actors Meisner himself had taught, sparks flew. Meisner, seeking to set the record straight, spoke often of Strasberg's attempts to take credit where credit was not due, and the two would have an animosity for each other that would last the rest of their lives. "I think [Lee's] feeling was that if he could make Marilyn Monroe a great actress, people would see him as a miracle worker. She wasn't considered a 'real actor' in the New York theater community, and he tried like hell to turn her into one."

"He was mean to her," recalls another classmate. "He'd say things like 'that's how someone who's never felt before would do the scene, now try to do it like someone who can experience emotion.'"

Still, Marilyn dedicated herself to Strasberg's classes—at the studio, and also privately at his home—even though she sometimes felt that the other students looked at her more as a curiosity than as a real actress.

As part of Marilyn's new life in New York, she began to undergo analysis with a therapist named Margaret Hohenberg. She'd been recommended to her by Milton Greene, but it was at Lee's insistence that she underwent such psychotherapy. Moreover, Hohenberg was a psychiatrist whom Lee Strasberg said he approved of, which suggests that maybe he was having a little too much influence on Marilyn. Some even began to wonder if perhaps he was to be "the new Natasha." Only time would tell. One thing was certain: Lee Strasberg may have been a capable acting teacher, but privately his life was as much a mess as those of some of his troubled and conflicted students—including Marilyn. "Our household revolved around my father, his moods, his needs, his expectations and his neuroses," recalled his daughter, Susan. "He was teaching people how to act, but that was nothing compared to the drama in our house . . . our entire family were intimate strangers."

While Marilyn had been in analysis in the past, she was more determined than ever to now understand herself and her mother as well as other influences in her life. She had seen so much emotional and mental deterioration in her family, she'd always believed that if she faced problems head-on on a psychiatrist's couch, she would have an advantage that had been out of reach for her ancestors. In other words, if she ever felt she was losing her mind, at least she would have some recourse and would be able to do something about it, unlike Della and Gladys. That may have been a logical and worthwhile pursuit in and of itself, but coupled with the kind of introspection going on every day in Strasberg's acting classes, it was definitely too much, too quickly.

Many people in Marilyn's new life whom she had known prior to this time—such as Arthur Miller, the playwright whom she had met a few years earlier and with whom she had stayed in close contact over the years—were concerned about subtle changes in Marilyn's personality that were becoming evident during this time. Indeed, the combination of Strasberg's influence to dig deep within herself for her acting along with Hohenberg's insistence that she do the same thing for her life was turning Marilyn into a different kind of person—a darker and often more morose person. She had long believed that her focus on her earlier pain and misery was a destination in and of itself, that there was a payoff in it. Now, at long last, those feelings were being confirmed for her. Yes, she *should* concentrate on her past. Yes, she *should* bring it all to light on a daily basis and identify herself with it. And why not exaggerate it, too? It was as if she had found the key to becoming a better person and a better actress—her pain. Therefore, she began to concentrate daily on her darkest self, her saddest self. Though she may have thought this was a treasure trove of dramatic interest—and maybe it was—the problem was that she wasn't able to just turn off all of those emotions when she wished and go about her day. Indeed, in the months and years to come, she would become more depressed than ever as the misery of her past weighed heavily on her mind. After a day of dealing with her personal pain in such an intensified setting, how could anyone expect her to just drift off and go to sleep? No. She had to have sleeping pills. Then, the next day, she would need more medication to function. If it went particularly badly in class or in therapy, she would need something else for her anxiety—a sedative would do nicely. She was so dependent on pills by this time, it's a wonder she could function at all. "I remember that she would ask me, 'Do you want a pill?'" recalled her friend John Gilmore, "and she would reach into her purse and come out with a handful. She'd just put them all out on the table and say, 'You can take this one to sleep and this one for anxiety and this one for . . .' It was very disconcerting." It should be noted, though, that in the 1950s, many actors and actresses depended on drugs to get through the day. Everyone from Elizabeth Taylor to Marlon Brando to Montgomery Clift to Tallulah Bankhead was addicted to one drug or another. Their lives and careers were not enhanced either by such excessive self-medicating.

It now seems ironic that in Marilyn Monroe's quest for clarity, her mind became even more clouded. Some of the notes she took during therapy at this time reveal her to be conflicted and, as always, terribly insecure—but also not necessarily cogent. "How or why I can act," she wrote one day, "and I'm not sure I can—is the thing for me to understand. The torture, let alone the day to day happenings—the pain one cannot explain to another." She also wrote, "What is there I'm afraid of? Hiding in case of punishment? Libido? Ask Dr. H." And another: "My problem of desperation in my work and life—I must begin to face it continually, making my work routine more continuous and of more importance than my desperation."

Marilyn's half sister, Berniece, would notice troubling changes in Marilyn's personality and blame them more on her therapy than on her acting classes—but that's because Berniece didn't understand Lee Strasberg's methodology. "She couldn't handle all of that therapy," Berniece would say. "It made things worse, not better."

In fact, throughout 1955, as Marilyn's studies with her acting teacher intensified, she began to rely even more on her psychiatrist. Marilyn's increasing reliance on Dr. Hohenberg suggests that, on some level, she may have felt she was ill-equipped to handle her own life. She may have started therapy at Strasberg's insistence, but she could have done it by seeing the doctor once a week. However, by the end of 1955 she was going at least three times a week, and also telephoning her constantly for advice and direction.

Almost as a backdrop to Marilyn Monroe's search for herself in both her life and career was the legal warring that was going on between her and Fox. It continued throughout 1955. However, by the end of the year, Marilyn would, at long last, be the victor. "Fox offered her a new contract—four more movies over the next seven years," said Wesley Miller from Wright, Wright, Green & Wright. "If memory serves, she would get $100,000 per upcoming film and $500 a week for expenses. She would also have subject, director and cinematographer approval—a huge win for her. Finally, she would be able to veto a nonsensical movie if it came her way. She would also be able to work in television and onstage if she wanted to do so."

As for "Marilyn Monroe Productions," its first of two new projects would be the film version of William Inge's Broadway play *Bus Stop*, for Fox, of course. Also on tap, a film version of Terence Rattigan's *The Sleeping Prince*. Both of these were not only worthwhile projects, they were worthy of the time and energy Marilyn had put in to reclassify herself in the minds of those with whom she and her lawyers had negotiated at Fox. What she learned was that she didn't have to settle for just being a brainless but pretty face, even if that would have been the easier way to go. "There is persuasive evidence that Marilyn Monroe is a shrewd businessman," a writer for *Time* magazine noted after the deal was announced—high praise for someone who'd been thought of as a dumb blonde.

Maybe her Aunt Grace was right, after all . . . about a lot of things. Indeed, no matter how complicated Norma Jeane's life would become, Grace Goddard was someone who had been able to grab her "niece" by the collar and force her to simplify things and think in a less complex manner. Whereas Lee Strasberg would chastise Marilyn and tell her that she wasn't *thinking* enough or wasn't *feeling* enough, Grace would tell Marilyn that she was fine just as she was at any given time. In a sense, Strasberg kept trying to add complexity to a woman whose mind was too busy to begin with, while Grace had sought to quiet that mind by offering straightforward and effective advice. Her wisdom may have seemed pedestrian to someone like Lee Strasberg, but, it could be argued, it was far more valuable and maybe even prescient. "You already have everything in you that you need," Grace had told Marilyn the summer before she died. "As you see yourself, so will others. It's not so complicated, Norma Jeane. Just believe in yourself," she concluded, "and I guarantee that others will follow."

Arthur Miller

*I*n the spring of 1955, Marilyn began a new chapter in her story with a man who would become one of the great loves of her life, the playwright Arthur Miller, whose drama *A View from the Bridge* was currently playing in New York. (Marilyn saw it three times and loved it.)

Miller was tall and thin, almost Lincolnesque in bearing. His face somehow seemed full of wisdom. His large spectacles and serious expression made him appear humorless, but this was misleading. He was gregarious, thoughtful, and not as bookish as most people expected. Rather, he was a sports enthusiast and enjoyed the outdoors. He could not be considered handsome, at least not by the standards of the day, but he had an imposing presence. What was interesting about Marilyn's choices in men was that they were almost always of the "everyman" variety, which was perhaps one of the reasons why she was so beloved by men in this country in the 1950s. The perception was that any "normal" guy in America could have a chance with the most beautiful woman in the world because, after all, look at the men with whom she had been involved: Jim Dougherty, Johnny Hyde, Joe DiMaggio . . . even Frank Sinatra wasn't considered a strikingly handsome man. She went for depth, always, not appearances.

Marilyn first met Miller in August of 1951 on the Los Angeles set of her film *As Young as You Feel*, when he showed up there with Elia Kazan. Kazan hoped to direct Miller's screenplay of *The Hook*, a politically charged story about waterfront workers and racketeers. The two men were in town to try to secure a movie deal for it. (The movie would never be made, however, because the work was viewed as anti-American during a time when the shipping of military men and weapons was vital to the Korean War.) Miller—who was ten years her senior—would later recall of his first meeting with Marilyn on the set, "The shock of her body's motion sped through me, a sensation at odds with her sadness amid all this glamour and technology and the busy confusion of a new shot being set up."*

Novelist/playwright/essayist Arthur Asher Miller was born in New York City's Harlem in November 1915. In 1944, he won the Theater Guild's National Award for *The Man Who Had All the Luck*. Despite critical acclaim in New York, the play closed after only six performances. A few years later, he published his first novel, *Focus*, about anti-Semitism, to little acclaim. He then adapted George Abbott and John C. Holmes's *Three Men on a Horse* for television. However, his first major breakthrough came in 1947 when his *All My Sons* was produced in New York at the Coronet Theater. The play was directed by Elia Kazan, with whom Miller would have a long-term personal and professional relationship. *All My Sons* won the New York Drama Critics Circle Award and two Tony Awards in 1947. The work for which he is best known, though, is *Death of a Salesman*, which premiered on Broadway in February 1949, also directed by Kazan. *Salesman* won the Tony Award for Best Play as well as a Pulitzer Prize. He was

---

* The occasion of Marilyn's and Arthur's first meeting has become like *Rashomon*, with so many versions reported on. Most seem to agree on one point: It took place on the set of *As Young as You Feel*. In dispute is how all the players happened to be gathered there at the same time. In Elia Kazan's 1988 memoir, *A Life*, he writes that Charles Feldman was hosting a party in Miller's honor, that Kazan was not able to attend, and that he then asked Miller to take Monroe. Then there's the version of events detailed in Miller's 1987 memoir, *Timebends* (Grove Press). Miller wrote that his visit to the set of *As Young as You Feel* was at the request of his father, who asked him to call on actor Monty Woolley ("my father's *bete noire*"), who had a principal part in the movie. Unknown, as far as we could tell, is Marilyn Monroe's version of her first meeting with Miller.

married when he met Marilyn and lived on the East Coast with his wife and their two children.

At the time that Arthur Miller and Marilyn Monroe began secretly dating, he was having a great deal of difficulty in his life, constantly hounded by the House Un-American Activities Committee (HUAC). It's difficult to trace Miller's problems with HUAC. Some reports say that he was being investigated as far as back at 1944 simply because he was viewed as a powerful and influential left-wing writer and public person. When he wrote *All My Sons*, the FBI called it "party line propaganda" just because it had to do with someone selling defective parts to the United States Air Force. In 1949, the FBI declared his *Death of a Salesman* "a negative delineation of American life." It was felt that the FBI had something to do with his story *The Hook* meeting a dead end in Hollywood. J. Edgar Hoover had it in for Arthur Miller, that much was certain, and he turned the heat up after Miller's play *The Crucible*.

The Crucible had been inspired by the experience of Miller's friend Elia Kazan, who had appeared before HUAC in 1952. Under fear of being blacklisted from Hollywood, Kazan named eight people from the Group Theatre—a popular theater company in New York—who, he said, were just mildly interested in Russian history, particularly in the Russian Revolution. HUAC took Kazan's naming of names to mean he was fingering members of the Communist Party, which he most certainly was not doing. In discussing the extent and effects of HUAC's activities, Miller developed the idea for *The Crucible*, an allegorical play in which he compared HUAC's activities to the witch hunts in Salem. The play opened on Broadway in January 1953. After its debut, Miller was, more than ever, viewed by HUAC as a Communist sympathizer, hell-bent on overthrowing the government by his work on the stage and also because he had attended Communist writers' meetings in the 1940s.

There was such paranoia at this time, Americans living in a constant state of fear about Communism. The panic was fueled by the media and certain government officials like Hoover. In fact, at that time all a public person had to do was suggest that he knew anyone who was Russian or appreciated anything of Russian culture and he was branded anti-American and a Communist sympathizer, his life then made a living hell. Miller went farther than that, though. As an intellectual and a liberal thinker, he did know some party members and was interested in learning more about Communism—and that was enough to brand him right there. When Miller ended, for a time, his friendship with Kazan because of Kazan's testimony, it convinced certain members of the conservative press that he was sympathetic to those Kazan had named—which he was, but only in the sense that he thought they shouldn't have been named, not because he thought they were Communists.

Between HUAC and the FBI's constant surveillance of and investigations of public figures such as Arthur Miller, it's a wonder there was time for any official business to be conducted in this country. Even Lucille Ball was investigated at one point. As pernicious as HUAC and the FBI were during the early 1950s in the pursuit of those alleged to have Communist leanings, the hunt for "pinkos" and Communist sympathizers reached its zenith with the rise of McCarthyism as practiced by Senator Joseph McCarthy of Wisconsin, who used his chairmanship of the Senate Committee on Government Operations as his personal stage to launch attacks on citizens, in places both high and low, as being "soft on Communism." His fall from grace was as ignominious as his rise had been spectacular, with his censure by the U.S. Senate in 1957.

After *The Crucible* opened, Miller was denied a passport to go to its opening in London, and that was just the beginning of his trouble. When he defended his actions through the play *A View from the Bridge*—the plot of which has a dockworker informing on two illegal immigrants—the response from HUAC was more surveillance and harassment. Walter Winchell, who was Joe DiMaggio's friend and the man who made it possible for Joe to see the scene in *The Seven Year Itch* that was the catalyst for his beating of Marilyn, couldn't wait to weigh in when Arthur Miller announced in February 1956 that he and his wife were divorcing: "America's best known blonde moving picture star is now the darling of the left-wing intelligentsia."

Why Marilyn Was Investigated by the FBI

*M*any have wondered over the years how Marilyn Monroe ever ended up being the subject of so many years of FBI investigations. It seems preposterous, especially given her dumb-blonde persona, that she was viewed as a serious threat to this country's security. So how did it start?

Actually, there are reams of documents filed with the FBI concerning Marilyn. In October 2006, ninety-seven more were released under the Freedom of Information Act, most of which are marked "Internal Security." As research for this book, all of these voluminous documents were carefully reviewed, and, based on them, it's clear that surveillance of Marilyn by the FBI began in 1955 because of her growing relationship with Arthur Miller.

Judging from his files, it seems clear that J. Edgar Hoover had pretty much lost his mind by the 1950s, at least when it came to his obsession with celebrities and what they may have had to do with Communism. Of course, it wasn't just Marilyn whom Hoover was interested in—it was just about all of Hollywood, including Abbott and Costello (who knew that Bud Abbott had fifteen hundred porn movies in his possession?). And of Marilyn, consider this, from file marked 100–422103 and dated June 1, 1956: "Miss Monroe is expected to move to New York sometime during the later part of 1956. . . . Marilyn Monroe will according to present plans complete her present assignment in the motion picture entitled *Bus Stop* on or about May 25, 1956. Further, that on or about July 6, 1956, she will proceed to England where she tentatively plans to make a motion picture starring Laurence Olivier." Hedda Hopper couldn't have done a better job!

Later, when she would begin her association with John F. Kennedy, her files would increase tenfold, not only in pointless paperwork but also in foolishness. Most of the files have names and places redacted, as if the country would surely be taken over by Commies should it be revealed that she had dinner with Mr. X and Mr. Y.

Here's the truth: None of it means a thing. Much of the FBI activities back then had more to do with rumormongering than truth-gathering. Any wacky "informant" could say anything about a celebrity and it would end up in the FBI's files as fact. This is one of the reasons why these files are so tantalizing to some historians. They are rife with seeming scandal, if one can read beyond the redacted segments. However, how much of it was just J. Edgar Hoover's paranoia being passed down to his agents, all of them out there in their trench coats with flashlights following Marilyn Monroe to the set of "*Bus Stop* on or about May 25, 1956." The less one relies on the FBI's accounts of anything having to do with Marilyn Monroe, the better.

Marilyn Monroe and Arthur Miller—both hounded by government agencies—became very close quickly. So close, in fact, that in Marilyn's will, which she signed on February 18, she bequeathed to him $100,000. That was a lot of money for someone she was just dating, so it at least suggests that she felt she had some kind of a future with him.*

---

* This same will stipulates that her mother, Gladys Baker Eley, should have her sanitarium expenses paid "for the rest of her life"—but not more than a total of $25,000.

Bus Stop

$\mathscr{I}$n February 1956, Marilyn Monroe returned to Los Angeles to begin work on her next film, *Bus Stop*. This would be the first co-production of her newly formed Marilyn Monroe Productions in partnership with 20th Century-Fox. Marilyn and MMP vice president Milton Greene and his wife, Amy, and their baby son, Joshua, rented a house in the Westwood section of Los Angeles. The next month, in March (the twelfth), she made it legal—her name, that is. Norma Jeane Mortensen officially became Marilyn Monroe. "I am an actress and I found my name a handicap," she said in the hearing to finalize the name change. "I have been using the name I wish to assume, Marilyn Monroe, for many years and I am now known professionally by that name."

In April, *Bus Stop* would begin shooting in Phoenix. Marilyn felt it would be her most important role—a big stretch for her as an actress—and she sought to do her best to make sure the powers that be at Fox were not sorry they had acquiesced to her contractual wishes. After scoring big with *The Seven Year Itch*, the studio honchos had wisely acquired the Tony Award–winning comedy of 1955, William Inge's *Bus Stop*, for their new box-office queen. The Harold Clurman–directed play opened at the Music Box on March 2, 1956, and starred the redoubtable Kim Stanley as Cherie, the haunting, vocally challenged saloon singer. It ran for 478 performances and closed at the Winter Garden on April 21, 1957.

After Fox acquired the movie rights, it assigned George Axelrod, author of *The Seven Year Itch*, to write the screenplay, which he adapted from Inge's play. Broadway director Joshua Logan was then selected to guide the cast through its paces. For reasons unknown, the play's setting was moved from Kansas City to Phoenix and Sun Valley–Ketchum, Idaho, for the movie's exteriors, perhaps due to financial considerations. Joining Marilyn in the cast was Don Murray, making his film debut as the obnoxious, hunky cowboy Bo, a role for which he received an Oscar nomination. Besides theater vets George Axelrod and Josh Logan, the film's casting director went to the Broadway talent pool for the supporting parts—Arthur O'Connell (Virgil), Betty Field (Grace), and Eileen Heckart (Vera).

The plot of *Bus Stop* can be summed up in just a few sentences: A macho, twenty-one-year-old cowboy, naïve to the ways of the world, travels from Montana to Arizona for a rodeo event and while there finds his "angel," tarnished though she may be. She is turned off by his crude, clumsy attempts to woo her, her rejection making him only more determined. He kidnaps her and takes her on a bus ride back to his ranch, pulling into a bus stop along the way. She is horrified, but weakens when he reasons that with her (carnal) experiences with so many men and his lack of experience with even one woman, doesn't that kind of average things out? "That's the sweetest thing anyone ever said to me," she sobs to him, as she accepts his marriage proposal.

Marilyn's "look" was significantly altered for this role, though her beauty and sex appeal are not affected in the least. Cherie is a saloon singer who works at night and sleeps in the day, hence her pale complexion, which her personal makeup artist, Allan Snyder, achieved by a dusting of white, cornstarchy face powder and pale pink rouge. A touch of mascara and light brown eyebrow pencil complete the transformation, which is in sharp contrast to the tanned-by-the-sun-and-wind skin of Bo (Murray), the bronco-riding, lovesick braggart. Hairstylist Helen Turpin transferred Marilyn's platinum-colored hair to Cherie's more subdued honey blonde. The role also required that Marilyn forgo her studio-trained, how-now-brown-cow dulcet tones and deliver her lines in Cherie's corn-pone Arkansas drawl. She also had to learn to become a bad singer, which she cannily demonstrates as she stands center stage, her soul laid bare, skimpily clad, singing "That Old Black Magic."

Marilyn fully realizes the role of the desperate, lonely, abused, and confused Cherie, whose pain is often in sharp contrast to the good humor and laughter displayed by some of the other characters.

In the words of one critic, "[Monroe] creates a complete and deeply moving character." Another hailed it as Marilyn's breakthrough role. It's true. She had never been better on film and some film historians maintain that it's her best work. It's worth seeing—repeatedly.

Natasha Non Grata

*M*arilyn's return to the West Coast marked the first time she'd set foot in California in more than a year. There was at least one person more than a little anxious to see her: Natasha Lytess.

It had been just a few weeks into Marilyn's stay in New York that Lytess had a strained telephone conversation with her. "Marilyn told her she needed a 'new beginning,'" recalls an actress friend from New York. "She had been feeling constricted by Natasha, and Lee was trying to loosen her up."

Marilyn made no secret of the fact that Natasha had unrequited feelings for her, and most everyone in Marilyn's New York world saw that as a roadblock to growth. "If your goal as an actress is to be as authentic as possible, imagine how difficult it would be to rehearse scenes with someone who's told you she's in love with you," actress Maureen Stapleton once observed. "Every role Marilyn played was sexy. I can't imagine how she could have felt comfortable exploring her own 'sexiness' with a woman who actually had a sexual attraction to her. Any actor would agree that would be a recipe for a superficial performance."

Whatever Marilyn's reasoning, over time it became clear that Natasha Lytess's usefulness in her life, and at 20th Century-Fox, was drawing to a close. The time Marilyn had spent in New York was humiliating for Natasha. The few friends that Lytess had at Fox had begun to drift away, and her regular paychecks from the studio were suspiciously late. On one occasion, she went to the studio to have the bookkeeping division issue her a check that was overdue, and she saw for herself that word had been spreading about her— not just word of her difficulty with Marilyn, but much more. From the giggles Lytess heard while on the lot, it wasn't difficult for her to recognize that people at the studio knew more than she would have liked.

Natasha, a woman who had been well-respected as a dramatic scholar, was now feeling the chill of her disappearing welcome at the studio. It wasn't long before it was made official. She would no longer be on the payroll of 20th Century-Fox. Since her calls and letters to Marilyn were not being answered, if she wanted an immediate response from Marilyn, she would have to go to New York and confront her. However, Natasha must have known that her sudden appearance in New York would only solidify people's image of her as a pathetic woman obsessed with a movie star. Therefore, she chose to wait in Los Angeles and began to tutor clients privately, if through clenched teeth. To a woman who had once wielded the power to halt production of a multimillion-dollar film, it must have felt humiliating to now be handed cash as hopeful actors left her apartment, maybe with dreams of being the *next* Marilyn Monroe.

Despite the awful circumstances in which Natasha found herself, she loved Marilyn dearly and was concerned for her former friend's well-being. She had been a stabilizing factor for Marilyn, even if some may have viewed their dynamic as somewhat bizarre. She worried that whoever Marilyn would find to replace her wouldn't have the ability to navigate her out of her complex emotional disturbances. Her career hopes and income aside, Natasha couldn't help but view Marilyn as a helpless soul. Without her, Natasha believed, Marilyn would spiral downward.

Now back in Hollywood, Marilyn appeared to be a changed woman in many ways. She had gone to New York with every intention of leaving the past behind. Grace Goddard's death, the divorce from Joe DiMaggio, and a seemingly endless string of misery as far back as she could remember made that "new beginning" a requirement. Her time in New York was well spent, she believed. She had aligned herself with Lee Strasberg, which she viewed as a positive move, even if it may have led her down the dangerous road of self-exploration. She now had her own production company with Milton Greene—and she owned 51 percent, incidentally, a controlling interest. She'd been in intensive therapy. Strasberg's wife, Paula, had become one of her best friends, and also her new personal acting coach. Paula and Marilyn would go over the script to *Bus Stop* line by line, working on it day and night—much the way Natasha and Marilyn had worked on *Don't Bother to Knock*. Indeed, the last year had been one of sweeping changes for Marilyn Monroe—out with the old and in with the new. Unfortunately for Natasha Lytess, she had fallen into the former category. "She was a great help to me," Marilyn concluded during a cocktail party at her new home, possibly understating Natasha's importance in her life. "Whatever road leads to growth, you take."

When Natasha became aware that Marilyn had returned to Los Angeles, she wanted desperately to see her. She drove to the studio and convinced an employee from the press office that she had misplaced Marilyn's new phone number, and she left the studio with what she needed. She then called the new Westwood residence dozens of times—to the point where it could have been viewed as, if not outright stalking, then certainly harassment. Marilyn had made a firm decision, however—she wanted nothing to do with Natasha Lytess. In the last year, she had done very well without Natasha, and even managed to get Fox to do for her what, arguably, Natasha had never really done: take her seriously as an actress.

"I think Marilyn, on some level, felt that Natasha had been largely responsible for her earlier, sillier performances," Marilyn's friend Rupert Allan once said. "Natasha wanted Marilyn to be some cutesy doll, and she was kind of sickened by it."

But in Natasha's defense, history views these performances as near perfection, and it was Natasha's direction that made them so specifically innocent and childlike. It was as though she took Marilyn's vulnerable, sensitive essence and magnified it to near caricature. It's a great testament to Marilyn's onscreen presence that we, the audience, found her so engaging. For example, her appearances before she met Natasha, such as in *Ladies of the Chorus*, for example, might be considered provocative, but not the least bit "childish or naïve." Even while singing "Every Baby Needs a Da Da Daddy" there's a come-hither maturity to her performance. Compare that to the first film on which Natasha coached her, *Asphalt Jungle*. In that one, Marilyn's character seems wide-eyed and vapid. Though not yet the fine-tuned, baby-talk performances that followed, as in *Gentlemen Prefer Blondes* and *Seven Year Itch*, her acting in *Asphalt Jungle* shows that Natasha was beginning to mold Marilyn more and more into a childish performer. Even after Marilyn's association with Natasha ended, directors wanted "that Marilyn," and she would grudgingly deliver—but none of those performances would be as precisely honed as the ones that Natasha had helped create.

Now, with a year away from her career and a few concurring opinions about Natasha's influence on her, Marilyn believed that her New York colleagues were right—that, in a sense, Lytess had probably been carving Marilyn into Lytess's own fantasy. Now Marilyn was left to reverse the image and change the way Hollywood viewed her, if she could. She certainly wanted to try.

Natasha continued to pursue contact with Marilyn. Finally, when she simply would not back off, Marilyn had her attorney, Irving Stein, telephone her. Stein told Lytess in no uncertain terms that she should not call or visit Marilyn Monroe under any circumstances. In response, according to the attorney's notes, Natasha delivered this soliloquy to him on the telephone:

"My only protection in the world is Marilyn Monroe. I created this girl. I fought for her. I was always the heavy on the set. I was frantic when I called the house and she would not speak to me. I am her private property, she knows that. Her faith and security are mine. I'm not financially protected, but she is. I'm not a well person. I would like very much to see her even with you, if only for one half-hour."

The answer was no.

"She's surrounded by these people who don't let her do anything by herself," Natasha said—and one could argue that she would know. "They're afraid to lose her. She never goes anywhere alone; they're stuck to her like glue."

In a very interesting letter to her former student Helena Albert, Natasha put it this way: "I, for years, have seen Marilyn's ability to cut people out of her life. I have even encouraged it. Imagine my dismay in finding that I am now one of those people. I suppose it was inevitable, yet it pains me so much I can't bear it another moment."

In one last-ditch effort, Natasha revealed that she was dying of cancer. When Marilyn's lawyer told her the news, Marilyn appeared to be unmoved by it. However, later, she discreetly sent Natasha a check for a thousand dollars, at least according to a correspondence from Lytess to Albert. "It is very generous of her, yet it does not take the place of a simple and courteous telephone call," she wrote. Indeed, when she received that money, Natasha must have known it was Marilyn's farewell gift—but she may also have seen it as suggesting that Marilyn still cared. On March 5, despite the attorney's warning that there would be "trouble" if she continued her pursuit of Marilyn, Natasha showed up unannounced at the Beverly Glen home. MCA agency president Lew Wasserman, who represented Marilyn, happened to be there, meeting with Milton Greene. He refused to allow Natasha entry into the house, telling her that Marilyn didn't want to see her and had no plans to intervene on her behalf with the studio.

"You don't understand, Marilyn needs me," Natasha told him.

"Marilyn Monroe needs no one," Wasserman snapped, slamming the door in her face.

Dejected, Natasha walked back to her car. When she turned to open her vehicle's door, she noticed a quick flash in an upstairs window of the house. There, next to a curtain, was Marilyn, staring down at her with a vacant expression. The two women looked at each other for a long moment. Then Marilyn closed the drapes.*

---

* Natasha Lytess died of cancer in 1964—two years after Marilyn Monroe.

PART SIX

Voices

The Misery of Arthur Miller

One of the major components in the Arthur Miller–Marilyn Monroe relationship was that Miller loved how well Marilyn Monroe listened to him, the way she hung on his every word. One mutual friend of the couple's put it best: "She was all about listening and receiving and he was all about talking and sending. He lectured her constantly. She was mesmerized by him. She drank him in like a sponge and let him affect her through osmosis."

Arthur Miller could do no wrong, as far as Marilyn was concerned. He was smart and interesting. He was invested in social change and had a real conscience. He was also supportive of her ambition—unlike her last husband. However, despite all of his good qualities, she was reluctant to marry him. In fact, she didn't want to encourage him to divorce his wife—even though his mind was made up about that. She didn't want him to break up his family for her, because she wasn't sure she was right for him. He could continue to dazzle her with his intelligence, but on some level she must have known that he would eventually need some input from her. How did *she* feel about literature, about culture . . . about the world? She was a smart woman, smarter than even she knew. However, she was so insecure in herself, she never thought of herself as intelligent. She always felt that she was less than . . . whoever she was with at any given time. She confided in friends that she didn't think she had the tools to really meet Miller at his intellectual capacity, "and what will he do when I'm found out," she fretted. "I'm a good actress, but I don't know that I'm *that* good." Her great fear was that he would wake up one day and believe that he was with someone who didn't know a lot about anything that mattered to him.

During production of *Bus Stop*, she leaned on him during times of great stress. That he was there for her meant the world to her.

Desperate late-night telephone calls had become a recurring theme to their relationship. She could never seem to sleep, no matter how many pills she took, so inured had she become to their effects. Sometimes she would wash them down with champagne, and then not only was she wide awake, she was also inebriated. There was no telling what she might say in such telephone calls. "I can't do it. I can't work this way," she cried to him in one call during production of *Bus Stop*. "I'm no trained actor. I can't pretend I'm doing something if I'm not. All I know is real. I can't do it if it's not real." She was talking about her role in the movie, but it also seemed as if she were referring to her role in his life.

On weekends, the two would meet at the Château Marmont Hotel in Hollywood for a romantic rendezvous. For days afterward, she was miserable. "I don't know what is happening to her at this time," Berniece wrote to another relative. "She thinks too much about every little thing. She doesn't seem to want to just jump in and live, like Norma Jeane used to. Instead of making her more courageous, all of that therapy has made her more timid. I am definitely worried about her."

Berniece may not have been a highly educated woman, but she knew her half sister well and she had pinpointed a major problem in her. "All of that therapy" had definitely caused Marilyn to want to think and rethink every move she made—whether in real life or her reel life. Nothing seemed left to chance anymore. Everything had to be the orchestrated result of looking within in a quest to develop her inner life. That would have been fine had she not at the same time been constantly coached to conjure up bad memories. As a result, she was miserable much of the time. Ironically, from outward appearances, anyway, she had little reason to be in pain at this time in her life. She was on top of the world. She was a success. She had money. She had an interesting and challenging role in what could become a very good movie. However, she also had a new therapist on the West Coast—and that was the problem. She would constantly ruminate over her sad childhood, her troubled relationship with Gladys, her arranged marriage to Jim Dougherty, the nightmare of Joe DiMaggio, and anything else that could be dredged up from her past. Whether drawing from it as an actress for her role in *Bus Stop* or as a woman for her self-improvement, she always found herself in a terribly dark place, never moving past it. Now she was also faced with the prospect of being involved with someone she knew was intellectually superior to her, and that, too, hurt. Whether looking backward or ahead, attached to it was a sense of dread. She *was* her pain, now—there seemed no escaping it.

Marilyn and Arthur Marry

*I*nterest by the House Un-American Activities Committee in Arthur Miller came to a head on June 21, 1956, the day he was summoned to appear in Washington and answer questions about his alleged association with certain Communist front organizations. The committee had done everything it could to find some kind of link between Miller and the USSR, even calling upon J. Edgar Hoover in the hope that maybe some of Hoover's rumor-filled files would hint at something that could be used against him—but to no avail. If Hoover couldn't come up with at least some kind of innuendo, Miller was definitely clean. Still, he was compelled to appear, and he dutifully did to address all concerns. Not much came of the hearings, though. He didn't name names—mostly because he didn't know any "names." For instance, he confirmed that back in the 1940s he had attended a few Communist Party writers' meetings, but he would not provide the names of anyone he ever saw there, risking a contempt of court charge.

The testimony was a little dull—Miller wasn't exactly charismatic—but he did say a few things of interest. He mentioned that he wanted to have his passport returned to him because "I have a production which is in the talking stage in England, and I will be there with the woman who will then be my wife." This was a big surprise to everyone—including Marilyn, who was sitting home watching on television. (In the end, Miller did get his passport back.) During a break in the proceedings, Miller was told that a pending contempt charge against him that had been spearheaded by Congressman Francis E. Walter could very easily "go away" if Miller did one thing: Persuade Marilyn to take a picture with Walter. That this was even suggested says a lot about these hearings. Miller refused, of course. (Congress would issue a contempt citation against him in July.)

Marilyn wasn't sure how she felt about the proposal of marriage Miller had made on national television during the very strange HUAC proceedings. On one hand, she was impressed that he felt so strongly about her he would make a point of it on national television. However, she also wished he had discussed it with her first. His audacity bothered her. He hadn't taken her feelings into consideration at all. How could he be so presumptuous? She *was* Marilyn Monroe, after all, and she could have any man she desired. Was he so cocky he just assumed he was the one for her and that was the end of it? "He does have a lot of nerve," she told Milton Greene. "I mean, I wish he had told me of his plans to marry." No matter how conflicted she was, though, she also didn't want to be alone any longer. She so loved being in love, she said, that she just hoped what she was feeling for Miller was the real thing. It felt like an obligation now. She'd been told what was expected of her, and—proving perhaps that Norma Jeane was still alive and well—she was going to do it. On June 22, she held a press conference in which she said that, yes, she would marry Arthur Miller. Just prior to this press conference, a car traveling behind Marilyn and Arthur had crashed into a tree, killing the New York bureau chief of *Paris Match* magazine, Princess Mara Scherbatoff. Marilyn was very shaken by the accident. It was everything she could do to get through the press conference.

That night, during a very quick and perfunctory private service—four minutes long!—Marilyn and Arthur were married before a judge at the Westchester County Court House in White Plains, New York. Then, on July 1, a second ceremony was planned, this one a Jewish ceremony performed before friends. Unbeknownst to most people, Marilyn took a quickie course in Judaism, which allowed her to marry in the faith (though she would never really practice it.)

In the two days that passed after the first ceremony, Marilyn began to have serious reservations about the wisdom of her decision. "She wasn't sure that she loved him," said one of her relatives, "but she wasn't sure that she didn't. At the core of her confusion, though, was her sense that she was in over her head with this man. Her insecurities were running wild by this time. She couldn't help but wonder what this intellectual wanted with her, and it was driving her crazy. Was he just looking for a trophy wife, as Joe [DiMaggio] had? What was really going on here?"

Before the second ceremony, which was to be held at the home of Arthur's agent, Kay Brown, Marilyn was in bad shape. Tears sprang to her eyes whenever anyone would offer her congratulations. She was not at all the happy bride. Milton Greene told her that she didn't have to go through with it if she didn't want to. The guests would be told to go home, he said, and everyone would just have to deal with it. The embarrassment was better, he suggested, than another bad marriage. Marilyn agreed. The second ceremony would not take place, and the first one would be annulled. For about a minute, she felt better. Then she realized she couldn't do it—she couldn't let Arthur Miller down and also humiliate him that way. So the second ceremony went forward. Afterward, Marilyn was all smiles at the wedding reception. Indeed, she *was* a good actress.

The Prince and the Showgirl

*M*ost of the summer of 1956 would be devoted to filming Marilyn's next movie, *The Prince and the Showgirl*, which would star her with Laurence Olivier and be set in London. Marilyn and her new husband, Arthur, would be ensconced in Parkside House, a large manse in Englefield Green. Rehearsals for the movie began on July 18 and continued until August 3. Filming would commence on August 7 and continue through November.

Laurence Olivier's original connection to the movie was when he appeared on the London stage in the Terence Rattigan play *The Sleeping Prince*, on which the film was based. Sir Larry starred with his wife, Vivien Leigh, forever remembered as Margaret Mitchell's beautiful, resourceful heroine Scarlett O'Hara in *Gone with the Wind*.

Set in London in 1911 during the coronation of King George V, the plot has us spend an evening with Grandduke Charles (Olivier), the prince regent of Carpathia, who's come to town for the royal proceedings to take place the following day. Taking advantage of his one evening off, the grandduke, a notorious womanizer infamous as a seducer of chorus girls for one-night stands, attends a musical at the Coconut Girl theatre and is immediately charmed by a beautiful American understudy, Elsie Mariner (Monroe). He orders his British attaché to invite her to the embassy for a private supper. It plays like a French farce disguised as a Victor Herbert operetta, with neither the sex of the former nor the music of the latter. Elsie is led to believe she's being invited to a party, not a one-on-one, intimate late-night repast. Foreplay consists of the grandduke's attempts to get Elsie sloshed and then in bed. He succeeds in the first and fails in the last. The sub rosa political shenanigans going on behind closed doors, involving the competition between the grandduke's seventeen-year-old son, Nicolas, the king-in-waiting, and the grandduke, are too complicated to go into. What is important to know is that despite all odds, Elsie and Charles manage to fall in love, but their future plans must be put on hold while Carpathia fights for its survival in the Balkan Wars.

Marilyn's longtime friend Milton Greene executive produced the film, along with Marilyn. It would be the second project for Marilyn Monroe Productions, following *Bus Stop*, and would be filmed at Britain's Pinewood Studios. There was widespread speculation as to how Marilyn's well-known neurotic behavior—tardiness, absenteeism, ill-preparedness, insecurities—would play against the professionalism and discipline of the classically trained Olivier. Those who predicted the worst got it right. Olivier, as director and leading man, bore the brunt. He reveals in his 1983 autobiography, *Confessions of an Actor*, that preparatory to beginning production on the movie, he was convinced he was going to fall in love with Marilyn. During the shooting of the picture, he must have wondered where he ever got such a notion. However, he was very enthusiastic about her, admitting she was "wonderful in the film, the best thing in it," her performance overshadowing his own and the final result worth the aggravation. (This is essentially what Billy Wilder said after his experience with Marilyn in *Some Like It Hot*.) Olivier goes on to say, "There are two entirely different sides [to Marilyn]. You would not be far out if you described her as a schizoid, the two people that she was could hardly have been more different. She was so adorable, so witty, such incredible fun and more physically attractive than anyone I could have imagined, apart from herself on the screen." Of her acting, Olivier called her "a professional amateur."

Also interestingly, regarding this film, James Haspiel observes, "[In this film] Marilyn is as close to being her off-screen self as she ever was. That is her real voice. It's the way she spoke in person. Her hair is the real color of her hair. I think that's what's most fascinating about this one movie."

Mable Whittington, who worked at Parkside House as a maid under the direction of the main housekeeper, Dolly Stiles, recalled of this time, "There was a great excitement about the arrival of the Millers. I remember that someone [Milton Greene] had the walls of the master bedroom painted white in Marilyn's honor. There was an increase in all security measures. We were all on alert, so to speak. What did I think of them? I thought Mrs. Miller was a bit pampered. She was used to a certain way, let's just say. Everything had to be just so. I remember she complained about the pillowcases being too starched, but what she required was minor. Too many pills, though. I remember being surprised by the number of bottles on her nightstand. I didn't know what they were for, exactly—but there were a lot of them. There were always empty bottles of champagne in her room, too. Also, I have to say that she was a bit untidy. She would step out of her clothes and there they would lay on the floor until I or someone else picked up after her. The bathroom was always a sight—makeup everywhere, personal belongings everywhere. I recall that she had a way of transforming herself that was almost magical. She was lovely but not necessarily glamorous in her day-to-day. But at night, if they were to go to a show—which they did often—or if she needed to be dressed for a dinner, she would become an entirely different person. It wasn't just the makeup and beautiful gowns and gloves and furs, though they were a big part of it. It was the attitude. When she dressed like Marilyn Monroe she *acted* like Marilyn Monroe. The star quality was there, I guess—in the Marilyn persona. Her personality as Marilyn Monroe was entirely different than as . . . I don't know . . . the *real* her, maybe.

"Arthur Miller? I found him to be insufferable. He didn't want to speak to the help and, in fact, would get angry if we even looked at him. He would say, 'Must you look at me?' I recall that two household employees were approached to give secrets about the Millers to the press. When he found out about it, he became raving mad. 'I demand that they be fired,' he kept saying. Of course that was to be the case, anyway—though I don't recall that they actually sold their stories. Marilyn wasn't very upset about that turn of events. I recall that she said, 'What else is new?'

"As a couple, they seemed happy at the start but as the months wore on, less so. He was constantly nagging her about one thing or another, usually how he felt she should prepare for the day's work. I remember that there were a lot of press conferences during their stay and that, afterward, he would tell her that she had answered this or that question in the wrong way. He picked on her a lot. She seemed to really want to know his opinion, though. However, I think that there was a point when she'd had enough of it, especially when he began to criticize her acting when she was practicing from her script. I recall her having trouble memorizing her script. I remember thinking, goodness, for an actress who has made so many movies, I can't understand how she can't remember her lines. She would walk around the house trying to remember a simple line, repeating it to herself over and over. I remember that he was annoyed by the way she was trying to memorize something and he kept correcting her. She snapped at him and said, 'When you begin making pictures, we can discuss this. Until then, let me act, and you just do what you do.'"

Possible evidence of marital discord at this time comes from a letter Marilyn sent to Berniece from England. In it, she never once even mentions Arthur Miller, and refers to herself only in the singular, from "I am having a wonderful time," to "I have been sightseeing," to "I am staying very busy."

Also at this time, Marilyn continued to receive letters from her mother, Gladys, even while in England. Gladys seemed somewhat better judging from one she wrote, dated July 25: "I am very unhappy, daughter. I wish there was some way to join you in England where I am sure we would have a lovely time. May God be with you and may He find a way for us to be together again very soon. Love, Mother." However, a week later, on August 2, she seemed to be not as well: "I have decided that the sooner I am able to leave here the better. I know I am a big topic of discussion here and it's not because of you, Marilyn. There seems to be a lot of interest in me, as well. Perhaps when I am released I will tell you about it though I doubt you would be interested in anything that has to do with me, your only Mother. Love, Gladys Baker Eley." It's not known if Marilyn responded to any of the mail she received from Gladys while in England. However, it is known that she was informed by the sanitarium staff that Gladys had also begun writing letters to J. Edgar Hoover at the Justice Department. This Marilyn found quite disturbing. As soon as she heard about it, she called Inez Melson long distance and asked her to look into the matter. Marilyn certainly didn't want Gladys giving any information about her to Hoover. In fact, she didn't like that Hoover knew where Gladys was, and how to communicate with her. Melson quickly reported back to Marilyn that when she asked Gladys what was going on, Gladys told that she was just sending Christian Science literature to Hoover, just as she had also sent some to the president of the United States. She said that she believed Marilyn to be friends of those two government officials and that she felt she could use Marilyn's name as an en-trée to them. She wondered why every time she attempted to reach out to people, her daughter was always "the first one to try to stop me." She also demanded that Melson tell Marilyn to stop thwarting her attempts to have communication with "the people running our country." Again, all of this was very disturbing. Gladys didn't realize that anything she said to someone like Hoover could be used against her daughter somewhere down the line. Marilyn shot off a letter to Melson telling her that any missive sent to any government officials written by her mother should be immediately confiscated by the sanitarium officials and not mailed. She wrote that she didn't want to censor her mother's communication, but that she felt she had to "draw a line somewhere, and this is as good a place as any, I think."

Meanwhile, while Marilyn was dealing with her mother, prepro-duction negotiations for the film continued. There was one surprise in this regard that, in retrospect, maybe shouldn't have been so surprising. Lee Strasberg—Marilyn's new acting guru—demanded that his wife, Paula—Marilyn's new on-set acting coach—receive what was then a huge amount of money for her work with Monroe: $2,500 a week for ten weeks' work, plus expenses and double that amount for overtime. This was more than most of the actors were making. Donald Spoto, in his Monroe biography, published a cor-porate memorandum from Irving Stein, Marilyn's lawyer, regarding the demand. It said, "Lee doesn't care that this money would really come from Marilyn's pocket. Joe [Carr, Marilyn Monroe Productions accountant] and Milton carefully explained the shaky finances, but Lee was adamant. He kept emphasizing Marilyn's emotional weak-ness—and then he said he would be willing to settle for a percentage of the picture! He also wanted George Cukor to direct, not Larry. Paula, he said, is more than a coach—therefore he doesn't care what other coaches get. He absolutely rejects Paula's *Bus Stop* salary."

When Marilyn heard about the demand, she decided to allow some of the money to come from her own salary because, as far as she was concerned, Paula was absolutely necessary on the set at all times. Thus, after all was said and done, Paula Strasberg would be making more than anyone else involved in the picture besides Marilyn and Laurence Olivier! It would seem that Marilyn had replaced one Natasha Lytess with another, especially given Arthur Miller's feelings about Paula. Like DiMaggio before him, who loathed Natasha, Miller had this to say about Paula: "She was a hoax, but so successful in making herself necessary to people like Marilyn that she created this tremendous reputation." He also said she was "poisonous and vacuous."*

Moreover, to Arthur Miller's great dismay, Marilyn's psychiatrist—Dr. Hohenberg, who had been sanctioned by Lee Strasberg—somehow ended up involved in the negotiations for *The Prince and the Showgirl*, and saw to it that Paula received the money that had been demanded by her husband. One wonders how much the doctor may have received in return. Moreover, since when did acting teachers like Lee Strasberg have a say in who directed a movie starring one of their students? Marilyn may have thought she was in charge when she started Marilyn Monroe Productions, but she continued to fall under the sway of domineering colleagues.

Arthur Miller's Damning Journal

*I*n July 1956, shortly before filming was to begin on *The Prince and the Showgirl*, something happened that would change the course of Marilyn's new life with Arthur Miller. She happened to see a journal of his on a table in the living room, glanced at it—and then decided

---

* Susan Strasberg defended her mother this way: "My mother literally sat with her for twenty-four hours on those films, holding her hand, trying to get her to take less pills. . . . The incredible insecurity that she [Monroe] had that she needed to be pampered and reassured. My mother gave her life's blood, in a way. And got blamed on top of it, for Marilyn's unprofessional behavior."

to read the pages that were opened. She was in for a terrible shock. On those pages, Arthur confessed that he had second thoughts about having married her. She wasn't what he'd thought she was—she was just a child, not a woman. She wasn't as intelligent as he had hoped and, in fact, she was someone he pitied. Moreover, he thought his own career might be jeopardized by his new association with her, and he wasn't sure what to do about it. He had heard that Laurence Olivier thought she might be a spoiled brat, and he didn't know how to respond to that since he basically agreed. Olivier had been hired by Marilyn—the movie was being produced by her company—but wasn't exactly grateful. He couldn't have been any less patient or understanding. Of course, that Miller seemed to be siding with him was devastating to Marilyn. It was the realization of her worst fear—that she would be "found out," that she wasn't as smart or as talented as she had made him think she was, and now he knew the truth about her.

"It was a terrible thing for her to find, that journal," Susan Strasberg would say many years later. "It would set her back a great deal. She lost so much confidence in herself when she read that. The question in my mind was this: What was it doing out? Everyone is entitled to their private thoughts, of course. But to leave it out and open like that? It made me wonder when I heard this . . . it made me wonder."

It felt to many people at the time that Miller had left the journal open and available to his wife on purpose. As a playwright, he certainly recognized the power of the written word. He had to have known how much his thoughts, once committed to paper, would hurt Marilyn. Some thought he was acting like a coward who was afraid to divorce her and just hoped she would leave him instead. One does have to wonder about Miller's character. After all, he married Marilyn after having convinced himself that he and she were a good match, and mere weeks later he made the decision that she was not for him. It suggests an enormous immaturity on his part and lack of judgment. Whatever the case, it seems safe to say he left the diary out on purpose. Why he did so would be a question only he could have answered—and he didn't. Marilyn would later tell her half sister, Berniece, that the marriage was never the same from the moment she read the journal. When she told her that Miller had written that she was "a bitch," Berniece was shocked. She couldn't believe, she said, that Arthur would be so cruel. However, Marilyn then clarified that what he wrote was that he agreed with Olivier that she *could* be a bitch. Somehow that didn't seem much better to Berniece—nor to Marilyn. Marilyn told her that she wished she could get past it, but she was certain she would never be able to do so. She wanted to tell Arthur that he should try acting with the capricious Olivier and see how that worked out for him, and she would sit on the sidelines and write about it, but "I don't have the nerve."

As upsetting as the discovery was, it still would not be the catalyst for Marilyn to actually leave Arthur. "She had decided that no matter what happens, I'm staying married to this person," said her friend Rupert Allan. "I don't think she realized it was going to have to kick in so soon. If something like this had happened after her first marriage, she would have divorced him. But I think she felt she had something to prove with this third marriage. But I also think she decided, [Miller] will never again get all of me. He will only get the part of me I will allow him to get. Now, I will be careful around him and that shall be his punishment. He will now be getting a percentage of who I am. The rest that he would never again see would be the part of her that was vulnerable."

Mable Whittington recalled an incident that occurred at around the time Marilyn found Miller's journal. "I knew about the incident with her finding the diary, or whatever it was. Everyone in the household knew about it. We didn't know what had been in it, only that Mrs. Miller saw it and read it and was very, very upset about it. That same week, I heard a sound in the kitchen and went down to investigate. There was Mrs. Miller, sitting alone at the kitchen table, having a cup of tea and a good cry. I just peeked into the kitchen and stood there watching for a long while. I thought many things. First of all, I was struck by just how beautiful she was. She had on a pink robe with marabou feathers at the neck and sleeves. Her hair, so blonde . . . just so pretty, I thought. I decided not to go into the room, to just leave her to her privacy. Then, I thought, my, how sad she is. There was a deep sense of sadness about her, and that's what I remember most. The sadness. I distinctly recall that, one day, her psychiatrist showed up from New York. I went into the living room and there was a strange woman in there reading. I asked someone who it was and was told, 'That's Mrs. Miller's analyst.' She did seem somewhat better when the doctor arrived, that was certain.

"I can also say that she was nicer to people when she first arrived. With the passing of time, she became more brittle and snappish. She seemed to never have a nice expression on her face around the house . . . she was always deep in thought, frowning. Also, I recall that she was late to the set almost every day. Hours late, in fact. The reason I know is that this was a never-ending source of annoyance to Mr. Miller. There were many arguments about her being late. Also, she didn't get along with Laurence Olivier and, I have to say, from my vantage point—which was, admittedly, on the outside looking in—it seemed that she disliked him a lot. I also remember that Mr. Miller felt that she didn't understand Olivier and wasn't trying hard enough to fit in with him. So, there was a lot of turmoil."

Just three weeks into the marriage and, as far as Marilyn Monroe was concerned, it was over. How could she remain with this man now? She would have to focus her energy on making the movie and do what she could to put in a good performance. However, with her heart broken, it would be very difficult. "It seemed to be raining the whole time," she would later say of her experience in England. "Or maybe it was me."

Quiet Before the Storm

After returning to the United States following production of *The Prince and the Showgirl*, Marilyn Monroe and Arthur Miller took a lease on a spacious thirteenth-floor apartment in New York on 57th Street. They'd recently purchased a large farmhouse in Roxbury, Connecticut, but it was being refurbished. Meanwhile, they would live in the city and spend the next few months trying to get their marriage back on track. In her spare time, during the first part of 1957 Marilyn fancied herself a housewife, preparing meals for her husband—breakfast every morning had become a specialty of hers—as well as grocery shopping and running errands that made her feel, as she put it in an interview at the time, "as if I have a real purpose in this world. I don't mind it at all. In fact, lately, I think I prefer this kind of more simple life." (One wonders what Joe DiMaggio might have thought if he'd read that comment from his ex-wife.) Often the couple would retire to a summer cottage they rented on Long Island where Marilyn would go horseback riding or spend her time painting with watercolors. It was actually a very pleasant year, 1957, perhaps the quietest she'd ever had in her life. Her career wasn't that far from her mind, though. She was still studying with the ever-present Strasbergs, but she did have a new psychiatrist, Marianne Kris, recommended to her by Anna Freud, daughter of Sigmund and also the founder of child psychoanalysis.

Marilyn saw Dr. Kris as many as five days a week, which at this time most people believed was too much. "Every single day she would sit in that office and lament her childhood or her marriage," said one person who was close to Marilyn at the time. "Afterward, she would be upset for hours. Then, just as she was regaining her equilibrium, she would be back on that damn couch. Some thought she was on a quest to learn more about herself, to set right the past. I didn't. It was, I thought, a form of self-abuse. She simply would not allow there to be any peace in her life. If there was a lull in the drama, she would create something new upon which to fixate, and most of those creations at this time came from her sessions with Marianne Kris. That, along with Strasberg's constant nagging of her to draw upon her childhood for her acting . . . well, it's no wonder she was not an emotionally well woman. As Berniece used to put it, 'Why can't she just leave well enough alone?'"

Why? Because Marilyn Monroe wanted nothing more than to,

once and for all, come to terms with the sadness of her childhood. She knew she had significant emotional problems stemming from her youth, from not being wanted, not feeling loved—and she felt it necessary to explore those areas and see what she could learn from them, or at the very least find a better way to confront her demons. The constant stream of letters from Gladys—at least one a week—probably didn't help matters. It was as if Marilyn always had one foot firmly planted in the distant past, the other in the uncertain present. The problem was that there were never any new revelations. There was never a sense of closure. Rather, the same questions were asked time after time, with the same answers being given and no progress ever made. Perhaps it was, as many people believed, a case of too much therapy. Perhaps she needed to live the present rather than constantly analyze the past.

Also at this time, Marilyn and Milton Greene—partners in Marilyn Monroe Productions—ended their relationship. The two had been having problems for many months with Greene attempting to control, at least in Marilyn's view (shared by many observers), too much of her business affairs. Money was always an issue with Greene—he never seemed to have enough and always seemed to be looking to MMP to bail him out. Also, there were any number of creative issues between them over *The Prince and the Showgirl*. When he suggested that he be recognized as executive producer of the film, Marilyn balked. That she took issue with it suggested she was really finished with Milton Greene by this time, because he, by rights and by contract, had every right to be recognized as an executive producer. In the end, Greene blamed Arthur Miller for any problems, not Marilyn. The two men didn't like or trust each other. Greene felt that since Miller had Marilyn's pillow-talk ear, there was nothing he could do to redeem himself from whatever Miller had accused him of at any given time. Moreover, Greene couldn't stop himself from criticizing Miller in Marilyn's presence, which made her uncomfortable and left her feeling that she had to take sides. Once she decided that she had to choose her husband, there was nothing Greene could have done to rectify the situation. After some wrangling, Marilyn made a decision to eject him from the company on April 11. She issued a very unkind statement saying that he had mismanaged MMP and had even entered into secret agreements about which she knew nothing. When Greene acted as if he didn't know what had happened to cause such a schism, Marilyn issued another statement that sounded suspiciously not like her—but a lot like Arthur Miller: "As president of the corporation and its only source of income, I was never informed that he had elected himself to the position of executive producer of *The Prince and the Showgirl*. My company was not formed to provide false credits for its officers and I will not become a party to this. My company was not formed merely to parcel 49.6% of all my earnings to Mr. Greene, but to make better pictures, improve my work and secure my income." After much legal wrangling, Marilyn settled with Greene for $100,000, which was just the return of his original investment in MMP. She never spoke to Milton about what had happened, simply refusing his telephone calls much as she had with Natasha Lytess. These decisions were not like Marilyn. It was as if she were doing anything she could do to impress Arthur Miller, who had made his loathing of both Lytess and Greene quite clear.

In June 1957, *The Prince and the Showgirl* opened at Radio City Music Hall. Marilyn, of course, attended with Arthur. The reviews were favorable and it seemed as if there might be a new appreciation of her ability as an actress, which somehow made all of the angst in England worthwhile, or at least most of it. What's perhaps most interesting about this film is the active role Marilyn took in its production and how far she had come as a thoughtful and, indeed, imaginative artist with a keen eye toward filmmaking. When she was unhappy with Fox's final cut of the film, she expressed her dissatisfaction to Jack Warner, MCA, and Laurence Olivier's production company. What she had to say and how she expressed it says so much about who she was at the time: "I am afraid that as it stands it will not be as successful as the version all of us agreed was so fine. Especially in the first third of the picture the pacing has been slowed and one comic point after another has been flattened out by substituting inferior takes with flatter performances lacking the energy and brightness that you saw in New York. Some of the jump cutting kills the points, as in the fainting scene. The coronation is as long as before if not longer, and the story gets lost in it. American audiences are not as moved by stained glass windows as the British are, and we threaten them with boredom. I am amazed that so much of the picture has no music at all when the idea was to make a romantic picture. We have enough film to make a great movie, if only it will be as in the earlier version. I hope you will make every effort to preserve our picture." Does that sound like the critique of an empty-headed movie star? In the end, no changes were made to the picture. It came out as Fox and MCA saw fit, but not for lack of trying on Marilyn's part.

In July, Marilyn would learn that she was pregnant. She wanted nothing more than to have a baby, but now she wasn't sure how she felt about this child's father. However, she had to admit that the last six months with Arthur had been very relaxing. She wasn't sure that she had his respect, but she knew he cared about her. Still, it was difficult for her to get past what she'd read in his journal. "My little girl is always going to be told how pretty she is," Marilyn said when she learned of the pregnancy. She was sure it would be a girl. "When I was small, all of the dozens and dozens of people I lived with—none of them ever used the word 'pretty' to me. I want my little girl to smile all the time. All little girls should be told how pretty they are and I'm going to tell mine, over and over again."

Unfortunately, on August 1, Marilyn would be diagnosed as suffering from an ectopic pregnancy. She was about five or six weeks along at that point. She was extremely saddened by the loss of the baby. "My heart is broken," she told her half sister, Berniece, in a telephone call from the hospital. She could, she said, "try again," and she intended to—"but not now."

The first six months of the year had been peaceful, but that changed after Marilyn lost the baby. Some in the family say that a letter she received from Gladys set in motion a chain of events that could have proven deadly. Apparently, Gladys sent a heartless note to her daughter in which she in effect said that, in her view, Marilyn wasn't ready to be a mother. She told her that along with motherhood came certain responsibilities, "and you, dear child, are not a responsible person." One relative recalled, "Marilyn was, I think, as upset about that letter as she was about losing the baby. She began to drink a lot more after that, and with the pills it all got to be too much. She started to say that she was hearing voices in her head. This was very scary and very reminiscent of her mother and grandmother. 'I could never be like them,' she said, 'because at least I know the voices are not real.' She was acting very strangely. Arthur told me that he was at a restaurant one night and the maître d' came over to tell him that he had a phone call. It was Marilyn. She was out of it and asked him to come home to save her. Luckily, he rushed home. She had taken an overdose. I don't know if it was on purpose, or not. No one ever knew. Afterward, no one ever discussed it, which is why there's a lot of mystery around it. It simply was never discussed."

Marilyn's Depression

The year after Marilyn Monroe's ectopic pregnancy was difficult. August 1957 through about July 1958 found her in perhaps the deepest depression of her entire life. In her mind, she had already failed as a mother just by virtue of the miscarriage. Her marriage was not fulfilling. She had lost interest in her career, and especially, it would seem, in Marilyn Monroe Productions. Arthur Miller spent the year writing—or attempting to write—a screenplay, *The Misfits*, based on one of his short stories. He believed that it would have a plum role for his wife, if only he could pull it together. But faced with writer's block, he found it impossible to break through, one draft after another ending up in the trash can. Frustrated with the work and exasperated with himself, he took it out on Marilyn. He was short and temperamental with her, despite regular visits to his psychotherapist to try to work his way through his own emotional problems. Marilyn—now thirty-two—gave as much as she got, if not more.

"It doesn't overstate it to say that she was never the same after the miscarriage," said Edward Lovitz, a struggling screenwriter in New York at this time, who had known Arthur Miller for many years. "Arthur told me that he thought she needed psychiatric help, that she would start to scream at him for no apparent reason. He wasn't sure if it was the drugs she was taking, the alcohol she was drinking, or just her mind breaking down on her. He told me that she had stopped going to her psychiatrist after she lost the baby. He wanted to try for another baby, but that was difficult if they weren't even getting along. He slept in a guest room, he said, many nights if not most nights."

"The fact that Arthur was not able to write at this time is probably not surprising, given the stresses in his life," added Rupert Allan. "However, Marilyn blamed herself for his lack of vision. She told me that she feared she no longer inspired him. 'If I inspired him at all, he would have finished by now,' she told me after a few months of nonproductivity on his part. 'Oh, the hell with it,' she decided. 'It doesn't matter to me anymore. I'm sick of him.' What I think she was really sick of was his judgment against her. She felt it strongly."

The longer this cold war continued between spouses, the deeper into her depression Marilyn seemed to sink. Nothing had worked out for her the way she had hoped, she said. She desperately wanted this marriage to be a success. She told one relative that she believed there were "people out there" who felt they had "won" when her marriage to Joe DiMaggio had failed. "'Ah-ha! See, she's not happy at all,' they said about me," Marilyn observed bitterly. "'She's stupid and talentless and she can't keep a husband.' But this one is going to last," she continued, "because I don't want people to have the satisfaction of seeing me suffer." She also wanted to prove to herself, as well as to the public, that she could be a good wife and mother. However, it now appeared that she could be neither. Her disappointment in herself combined with the drugs she was taking to sleep and then to awake caused her to exist in a clouded state of mind that made it impossible for her to reason out her problems. Add alcohol to the mix—champagne for the most part since most other drinks made her sick to her stomach, though that didn't always stop her—and the combination was potentially lethal. She had gotten to the point where she would pour herself a glass of champagne with trembling hands, snap open a capsule, and then pour the contents right into the glass for a quicker high. Or, for an even faster effect, she would just pour the crystals under her tongue. Because she had lost interest in so much in her life, she began to gain weight. She didn't care. She had been struggling to stay thin for so many years, she felt she deserved the right to be fat. She gained about twenty pounds during this time.

There was no telling how one might find Marilyn—seeming happy and content or morose and depressed. Still, people obviously wanted to be around her, wanted to be in her presence.

Two separate visits at this time tell differing stories:

The first involved Marilyn's half sister, Berniece. Marilyn called her one day seeming desperate. "I tried all day to call you, yesterday," she told her when she finally reached her. "And this morning I tried three times!" She made it clear that she needed to see Berniece. In speaking to her, she kept talking about how much she admired Berniece's marriage to Paris Miracle. It was clear to Berniece, as she would later tell it, that Marilyn was having problems in her marriage. Berniece made plans to go, but then, at the last minute, her husband forbade her to travel alone. Paris later said that he had a trip planned for New York, where Marilyn lived. Berniece wanted to go with him, of course, and use that opportunity to visit Marilyn. Paris said no. It was a business trip, he said—no wives allowed. But then while he was in New York, *he* went to visit Marilyn, and took his business associates with him! At any rate, Marilyn could not have been nicer to Paris and his friends. She appeared after having bought flowers, her arms full of dogwood blossoms. Everyone had cocktails, which she served, and she signed pictures for the entire group—"Love and kisses from your sister-in-law to Paris." One of Paris's friends tried to sneak out of Marilyn's home with a highball glass, which was apparently too large to fit under his jacket. In the midst of all this, Marilyn seemed fine.

A couple of days later, Marilyn's psychiatrist, Dr. Marianne Kris, came to visit. The story was a very different one, as told by Barbara Miller (no relation to Arthur), the daughter of a friend of Dr. Kris's. She, her mother, brother, and Dr. Kris all arrived at the same time to visit Marilyn and Arthur. "It wasn't pleasant," she recalled. "I was about twelve, but I remember it well. I was a big fan of Marilyn Monroe's and couldn't wait to meet her. She was a lot heavier than I thought she'd be, but still she was very beautiful. She came swooping into the living room to greet us in a floral-printed caftan that was just lovely. She had her hair long, to her shoulders—very blonde. I remember she had the most delicate hands with tapering fingers, her nails painted red. She was very nice, but seemed . . . I guess tipsy would be the word."

Barbara Miller recalls what happened after everyone was seated in the living room:

"Would you like a Bloody Mary?" Marilyn asked the adults. "And a soft drink for you?" she offered, looking at the young girl. The adults said they would all prefer soft drinks. "Fine," Marilyn said with a smile. "I generally don't like to drink alone, but I'll make an exception today." She then called out the name of their maid. When no one appeared, she called again. Finally, she screamed out, "Arthur, where is the goddamn maid?" Still, no answer. She shook her head and rolled her eyes. "My secretary, Mary [Reis], isn't in today and my husband is somewhere trying to write," she said, according to Miller's memory. "He's having a difficult time, though."

According to Miller, Dr. Kris studied Marilyn carefully and said, "Dear, is there someplace where you and I might talk? I'd like to speak to you alone."

Marilyn eyed the doctor suspiciously and said, "I think we've done enough talking, Doctor, don't you? I'm fine, really I am. All I need is a Bloody Mary if I could just get the goddamn maid to come in here. Jesus Christ," she concluded. "I'll go get it myself, and the soft drinks too." She rose.

"You don't seem fine," the doctor said, while the other two guests sat in awkward silence.

"Goddamn it," Marilyn snapped, now standing and facing the doctor, her eyes blazing. "Why can't you leave me alone? I've had it with you. I'm sick of going over and over and over the same things. *I'm not going to do it anymore.*" With that, she turned and walked out of the room, leaving her guests in stunned silence. They wondered whether or not she would return. Or should they just go? Ten minutes later—just as everyone was preparing to depart—Arthur Miller appeared. "My wife asked me to apologize to you all," he said, looking very contrite. "She's not been well. It's just been awful, and I hope you'll accept our sincere apologies and come back another time." Then, turning to the doctor, he said, "Could you please call me later? I must speak with you. It's urgent." Dr. Kris said that she would certainly make the call. Everyone then agreed that it was best for the visit to end. However, just as the small group got to the front door, Marilyn came walking out from one of the back rooms. In her hands was a tray of drinks. "Wait," she said, gazing at them with astonishment. "You're leaving? But I have drinks! Wouldn't you like to sit down and talk?"

"She was a totally different person," said Barbara Miller. "She was smiling and cheerful and it was as if she had no memory at all of what had occurred earlier. We said, no, we have to run. She looked disappointed. Then she gave each of us a hug. As we were departing, she smiled and told Dr. Kris, 'Okay, I'll be calling you tomorrow. Bye-bye.' When the door closed, I remember the adults standing in the hallway looking at each other with worried expressions. Then, in the cab, no one said a word. Everyone just sat and stared straight ahead."

Some Like It Hot

*B*y May 1958, Arthur Miller had convinced Marilyn that she needed to return to work—or at least that's what he told his friends. It's also possible that Marilyn had come to terms with the fact that as she put it to one intimate, "someone needs to bring some money in this house," so it might as well be her. She put her agents to work on finding the right project. After a few false starts, Billy Wilder submitted a two-page proposal to Marilyn for a film he was writing called *Some Like It Hot*. On July 7, Marilyn departed for Los Angeles to begin work on the movie.

Every single person who contributed his or her talent to *Some Like It Hot* can be assured that it was the group collaboration that made it the comedy classic it is, and arguably one of the best pictures ever made. They can also be assured that without Marilyn Monroe and Billy Wilder, it would have been just another funny film. Wilder lifted the central premise from an obscure German movie musical, *Fanfares of Love*—that of two unemployed musicians who resort to cross-dressing in order to join an all-female band—and stretched it into two hours of unmitigated hilarity. Adding the subplot of the St. Valentine's Day Massacre and its fallout is the engine that drives the train. (Wilder's writing partner on this and many other scripts was I. A. L. Diamond, and the film earned them an Oscar nomination for best adapted screenplay.)

Now that they had a script—or at least they had one in mind—the next concern was how to cast it. According to one source, Wilder early on envisioned Danny Kaye and Bob Hope as the drag duo. Tony Curtis received a verbal pitch for the film from Wilder himself and agreed to sign on. Then when Frank Sinatra expressed an interest in the project, Wilder toyed with the idea because he needed a "name" to get studio financing. He was actually relieved when Sinatra dropped out, though, because Ol' Blue Eyes was well known for following his own rules—shooting nine to five, limited retakes, and other special treatment. Wilder was happy to keep it A Billy Wilder Film. Meanwhile, Mitzi Gaynor was being considered for the role of Sugar Kane, due mainly to her excellent showing in the recently released *South Pacific*. But then Marilyn launched a campaign for the part. Her box-office pull had placed her on Quigley's list of Top Ten stars for three years, and though she had been absent from the screen for the two previous years, attending drama classes at the Actors Studio and trying to shore up her disintegrating marriage, her popularity with the fans was at an all-time high.

Marilyn's legendary reputation for causing delays apparently was overlooked and she was signed for the film for $200,000 plus 10 percent of the gross over $4 million. In its initial release, the movie earned $25 million, which comes to $215.4 million in today's dollars, enough to place it at number 150 in the top-grossing films of all time. Marilyn's share: $2.3 million

The first actual footage filmed was a scene that took place at the standing train set at MGM Studios in Culver City. It is twenty-four minutes into the film and we see Sugar Kane (Marilyn) for the first time as she walks along the side of the train with the all-girl band, the Sweet Sues, to board. It went off without a glitch and Marilyn was letter perfect. During the setup prior to the shot, Wilder observed a woman hovering beneath an umbrella out of view of the action. When the scene was over, he called out to the woman, "How was that, Paula?" He recognized her as Paula Strasberg, a constant presence on every Marilyn set, just as Natasha had been before her. From that deferential moment on, Wilder controlled the set.

After getting the go-ahead from Wilder, Tony Curtis (Josephine), and Jack Lemmon (Daphne) went to couturier Orry-Kelly, Monroe's costumer, and asked him to make their outfits. Of course, there were problems with two straight men playing transvestites that had nothing to do with how well the clothes fit. The actors had to *become* women, believable as such in their walk, talk, attitude, actions, the way they stood, the way they sat. But their problems paled compared to those Wilder (and the rest of the cast and crew) had with Marilyn: Her problems in her marriage and her lack of self-confidence as an actor drove the production costs up, according to Wilder, adding another $750,000 to the $2.9 million budget. He said, "Sometimes [Marilyn's lateness, demand for constant retakes, etc.] would stretch out to three days, something that we could have completed in an hour because after every bad take, Marilyn began to cry and there would have to be new makeup applied." In addition, she couldn't remember her lines. They would have to write them on cards and place them where Marilyn could read them. The simple line "Where is that bourbon?" had to be shot and reshot as many as forty times.

"There were days when I could have killed her, I admit it," Billy Wilder added. "I knew, of course, that she had serious problems. I hate to say it, but at the time, I couldn't give a rat's ass about her problems. I was trying to make a movie and she'd been paid a good deal of money to be in it. But, that said, there were a lot of marvelous days, too, when she would do something we all knew was golden."

Yet somehow, Marilyn got through it all with unbelievable results onscreen. Watching her magical performance, there is no hint of the nightmare making the film was for her. Maybe her friend Jeanne Martin put it best: "I treasure every moment of that film, but without Marilyn it would have been nothing."

During the publicity blitz for the film, Curtis was asked repeatedly and relentlessly by the press what it was like to kiss Marilyn Monroe. "What was I supposed to say, 'It was like skiing down a snow-covered mountain and being launched into the air by a ski jump and then floating to earth on gossamer wings?' C'mon, kissing the most desirable woman in the world and then being asked repeatedly what it was like is a no-brainer and it began to annoy me. Whether the Hitler comparison came out as irony or sarcasm, which is the way I meant it, the press preferred the sound-bite and refused to print the whole story." The following few days, Curtis was bombarded with phone calls asking him to verify the report. For forty years, he denied he ever said it—and actually became hostile when confronted about it when appearing on a Larry King show with Marilyn Monroe historian James Haspiel—but he came clean to Leonard Maltin in an interview taped for inclusion in the deluxe DVD two-disc set of *Some Like It Hot*, released as part of "The Marilyn Monroe Collection."*

The number of "best" lists accorded *Some Like it Hot* continues to grow every year. The American Film Institute named it number one on its list of the 100 Funniest Movies of All Time. AFI has also ranked it variously as number 14 and number 22 Greatest Movie of All Time. The film's last line, "Well, nobody's perfect," was voted number 48 on AFI's list of Greatest Movie Quotes. *Entertainment Weekly* readers voted it the 9th Greatest Film of All Time and the Greatest Comedy of All Time.

During production of this movie, on Friday night, September 12, 1958, after a long and emotional telephone conversation with Arthur, Marilyn took another overdose of sleeping pills. Had it not been for Paula Strasberg coming to her rescue, she might have died. As always, she said that she hadn't intended to commit suicide.

"She had so much to live for," said Rupert Allan, "but she didn't see it that way. That said, the way I heard it, it happened when Arthur arrived in Los Angeles and he was the one who took her to the hospital. Typical of Marilyn's overdoses, no one could ever get the story straight. However, yes, she definitely overdosed. When and how she got to the hospital doesn't matter. Arthur came in imme-

---

* Author Charles Casillo notes: "It's only in the last decade or so that Tony Curtis tried to rectify his nasty comments about Marilyn. I don't blame him for being furious after working with her. It's easy to make excuses for her now, but almost everyone who made a movie with her has said that Monroe was terribly difficult to work with. Actors have huge egos and Marilyn was always favored in the final takes, which infuriated Tony Curtis. There is no denying he despised her after the movie—and his loathing lasted decades after her death. Yet, as her legend grew and her value to every movie became more and more undeniable, Curtis has tried to revise history and defuse his derogatory comments about her. But even Marilyn—in her last *LIFE* interview—addressed the "Hitler" remark: "I don't understand why people aren't a little more generous with each other. I don't like to say this, but I'm afraid there is a lot of envy in this business.... For instance, you've read there was some actor that once said that kissing me was like kissing Hitler. Well, I think that's his problem. If I have to do intimate love scenes with somebody who really has these kinds of feelings toward me, then my fantasy can come into play. In other words, out with him, in with my fantasy. He was never there.""

diately from New York to be at her side," said Allan. "I can't say that helped, though. In fact, I think it may have made things worse."

Once Arthur Miller arrived in Los Angeles and had a chance to take in the terrain, he realized that practically everyone connected with *Some Like It Hot* found his wife to be incredibly unprofessional. That she was able to eventually turn in a brilliant performance didn't seem to matter much at the time. Miller was again embarrassed for her, and also for himself. It caused him to be angrier with her than ever. "My feeling about Arthur Miller was that he was a little too resentful of his wife," Billy Wilder recalled. "I wasn't married to her. I didn't have to be patient and loving. But he was her husband and I thought he could have been more understanding. I remember saying at the time, finally, I have met someone who resents Marilyn Monroe as much if not more than I do."

Rupert Allan recalled, "Marilyn told me and Susan [Strasberg] that [Miller] lashed out at her one day and said, 'You should be ashamed of yourself. How dare you not know your lines? How dare you be late? Who do you think you are?' Instead of being her support, he had turned into her enemy. It was very unkind of him. I can't say I know what he was thinking. Anyway, Marilyn said, 'He can kiss my ass, Rupert. As far as I'm concerned, he can just kiss my ass.' So, really, things were, shall we say, a bit on the tense side."

One might have thought that things would have taken a turn for the better when, in October, Marilyn learned that she was once again pregnant. Of course, she was overjoyed by the news. She had been scheduled to accept a film award in France, but was happy to have a good reason to decline. In a two-page Western Union telegram to the Académie du Cinéma in Paris, dated November 26, 1958, she said in part, "I had greatly looked forward to coming to Paris and receiving the honor which you so graciously awarded me (stop) However nature intervened and I am expecting a baby (stop) Because of some recent complications in regards to the pregnancy my doctor has forbidden travel of any kind."

It's not clear what Arthur Miller thought of the pregnancy, though he didn't seem very happy. "At this point, I think Marilyn put Arthur out of her mind and began to think, okay, I can have this child and go on with my life without my husband, and at least I won't be alone," said Rupert Allan. "A big problem for her, though, with the pregnancy was all of the drugs she was taking . . . that was a problem."

During this time, Marilyn was taking—among other prescriptions, such as Nembutal—a barbiturate to calm her nerves as well as allow her to sleep. Her gynecologist, Leon Krohn, was against all drugs in her system, but he realized that there was no way she would be able to function without them. He warned her against drinking on this and other medications and hoped to monitor her closely— he was on the set every day—but, truly, she was not manageable. When it came to pill-taking, Marilyn Monroe would always find a way if she felt the need.

After the movie was completed on November 6, Billy Wilder— who was not speaking to Marilyn by that time—went on record as having made a few unkind statements about her. For instance, when one New York reporter asked if he would ever make another movie with her, his response was, "I have discussed this project with my doctor and my psychiatrist and they tell me I'm too old and too rich to go through this again." To another reporter he said, "She's very good, obviously. But is she worth it? I don't know."

Marilyn was stung by his remarks. In her view, yes, she had presented some problems—what else was new?—but in the end she did turn in a good performance. She felt that Billy Wilder could have shown some gratitude by having a little more tact in discussing her with the media. One afternoon, after deliberating over it for a while, she had a few drinks and then picked up the telephone to talk to Wilder, calling from New York to Los Angeles. His wife, Audrey, answered the phone. Marilyn asked if she could speak to Billy. She was told that he wasn't at home. "That's fine," Marilyn said. "I wonder, Audrey, if you could give him a message for me." Audrey said, "Of course." Marilyn continued, "Would you please tell him that Marilyn called . . . and that she would like it very much if he would . . . go and fuck himself." There was silence on the other end of the phone. "Oh, and Audrey," Marilyn concluded sweetly, "my warmest personal regards to you."

A Sign from God?

On December 16, 1958, Marilyn suffered a miscarriage. She would say that she felt more alone than ever before. She also felt a tremendous sense of guilt about the drugs she had been taking during the pregnancy and was afraid that she was responsible for the baby's death. "Could I have killed it?" she asked one friend. "I felt she was slipping away," her half sister, Berniece, would say of this time. Indeed, on December 24, Marilyn received a letter from her mother, whom she had not seen in some time. "Have I pushed you away, dear daughter?" she wrote, probably knowing the answer. "I would love a visit from you." Then, in a heartrending understatement, she concluded, "The holidays are so sad. So very sad." She added, "I have tried to reach you so often but it is very difficult. Please do me the favor of a telephone call or a return letter. May God bless you." She signed it, "Mrs. Gladys Eley."

Marilyn didn't work in 1959. She was too sad and never really recovered emotionally from the miscarriage. In April, she received a note from Berniece, addressed to "Mrs. Marilyn Miller." She wanted to visit. "Please phone or write me as to when you will be home, and the best time to come. Give my regards to Arthur." Marilyn didn't respond. Now was not a good time for a visit.

In June, she had to undergo a series of operations to determine if it were possible for her to have children. It was decided that, no, it could never happen for her. Vanessa Steinberg, daughter of Dr. Oscar Steinberg, who performed one of the surgeries, told Marilyn Monroe historian Michelle Morgan, "Marilyn had also had numerous pelvic infections that had gone untreated, which had contributed to the scar tissue and infertility problems. [The operation] was a dismal failure. My father had the unfortunate task of telling her that she would never be able to have children. Apparently he walked into her room, she looked up at him and said: 'Thank you doctor, I already know.' He told her that if he ever had a daughter he would name her after her, which he did." She was very, very sad. I know he was worried about her. She took it very badly."

She didn't give up hope, though. Later that year, she would go to see singer Diahann Carroll at the Mocambo in Los Angeles and, recalled the singer, "I was pregnant with my daughter, Suzanne. Marilyn, so sad and so beautiful, came backstage to say hello. 'May I touch your tummy?' she asked me. I was delighted, of course. I took her hand and put it on my stomach and said, 'You pat right here, sweetheart, and say a prayer and a wish, and I'll hope with all my heart that your dream comes true.' She looked at me with tears in her eyes and said, 'Oh, I do, too. I do, too.'"

There seemed to be no end to her melancholy at this time in her life as one terrible moment seemed inevitably to give way to another. Though she signed on to begin filming a new movie in 1960, a musical comedy called *Let's Make Love*, Marilyn was feeling anything but lighthearted. Her marriage would most certainly not last another year, and she knew it. She refused Berniece's telephone calls that holiday season—the first time that had ever happened. Throughout all of the vicissitudes of her life, she had never felt so low. Indeed, as Marilyn told one close friend, "As hard as I tried, the amount of time and energy I spent on this thing . . . I think now that it must be a sign. God must not want me to have children. Of course. Why should he allow me to have children? I can barely handle my own life."

One evening after Marilyn got home from the hospital, she and that friend went through Marilyn's closet, looking for something she might be able to wear to dinner. "I don't like to wear fancy clothes," she told her friend. "They take away from me, from who I am. I don't want people to be distracted when I walk into the room. So let's find something very simple." As she was talking and thumbing through a row of blouses, she came across a maternity top. She stopped for a moment. Then she took it off the hanger and handed it to her friend. "Please get rid of this for me," she said. Then, a few moments later, she came across another. "Oh, no." Finally, with tears streaming down her face, she decided to just take the time to get rid of all of the maternity clothes in the closet. "This isn't even what I set out to do," she said, very upset. "I just wanted to wear something pretty for dinner." After cleaning out the closet, she and her friend put all of the maternity outfits in a large box. The next day, Marilyn had her secretary send them all to her half sister. "Maybe Mona [Berniece's daughter] will have better luck than me," she concluded sadly.

PART SEVEN

Slow Death

Giving Voice to the Voices

The second week of January 1960 found Mr. and Mrs. Arthur Miller in Los Angeles, ensconced in bungalow number 21 of the plush Beverly Hills Hotel, next door to the French actor Yves Montand and his wife, actress Simone Signoret. Montand had been cast to star opposite Marilyn in *Let's Make Love*, replacing Gregory Peck, who had decided—wisely, as it would turn out—that making this film was a very bad idea. It was a new year and Marilyn seemed determined not only to make the movie an enjoyable experience, but also to somehow save her marriage in the process. Diane Stevens, an assistant to John Springer, who worked for Marilyn as a publicist at this time (through the Arthur Jacobs agency), recalled, "I remember thinking, no, she is not in shape to do a movie. Unlike Elizabeth Taylor—whom John also worked for and with whom I had a great deal of contact—Marilyn was not able to bounce back after personal tragedy. Rather, she seemed to lose herself in the personal chaos. It was as if she had no coping skills or, at the very least, it was as if she had exhausted her supply. I thought she should have been in a hospital by this time, not on a soundstage."

In fact, Marilyn was primed to make this film a big success. How could it fail with the legendary "woman's" director George Cukor at the helm, a script by the Oscar-honored writer Norman Krasna, songs by the triple-Oscar-winning tunesmiths Jimmy Van Heusen and Sammy Cahn, and with Gregory Peck as her leading man? But Peck left the project early on because he felt the script was terrible. Other big male stars who turned down the role were Cary Grant, Charlton Heston, Rock Hudson, Yul Brynner, and James Stewart. French actor/singer Yves Montand had no such misgivings, though. He had recently made a big success in a French-language film version of Arthur Miller's play *The Crucible*. Married to Simone Signoret, an

Academy Award Best Actress winner in 1960, he signed on to join Marilyn as her leading man in *Let's Make Love.*

A strange thing occurred during the early part of rehearsals for the film, something that greatly impacted Marilyn's marriage to Arthur. A Writers Guild strike had broken out, causing a problem for the film, the script of which was already such a mess Marilyn barely wanted to appear in it. There was some hope from her that the strike might cause the cancellation of the film as no union writer would be available to work on it. The film's producer, Jerry Wald, asked Arthur Miller if he would mind doing some rewrites on the script. Miller agreed. In effect, he not only consented to rewriting the movie—an endeavor that, to most observers, seemed far below his station as a Pulitzer Prize winner—but also to break ranks with the guild. Marilyn was surprised. "She had always thought of Arthur as someone who championed the rights of the underdog," said Rupert Allan, who was in Los Angeles visiting the Millers at the time. "For him to snub his nose at the strike first confused her and then made her lose respect for him. She had thought of him as a principled person, an Abraham Lincoln. And he suddenly turned on her. He became much hated, too, on the set. He would lord his wisdom and knowledge over everyone involved in the movie, to the point where people didn't want to be around him. Suddenly Marilyn was ashamed of him. My, how the tables had turned."

Actually, there was somewhat more to Marilyn being upset with Arthur than met the eye. She wasn't upset with him just because he had betrayed his own ideals, though that was part of it. She also suspected from the start that he had taken the writing job just to put her in her proverbial "place." After all, she signed on to do the movie at least partly because no one in the household was making any money. Arthur Miller may have been at least a little embarrassed by this situation. Then, suddenly an opportunity presented itself to him to not only bring in a paycheck but perhaps also to be the person responsible for the words his wife had no choice but to recite on camera. It may have seemed as if he were getting back at her. According to people who knew him best, that was his intention. Or, as one person put it, "It was an in-your-face 'screw you' to her." It's no wonder she was beginning to resent him as much as he seemed to resent her.

Of course, there were the usual problems with Marilyn during production of *Let's Make Love*, having to do with her tardiness and pill-taking. Often, she seemed stabilized and well-balanced—her medication probably working—but other times she looked dazed and loopy. Tony Randall, also in the film, recalled, "You have to understand, we would all be in makeup and ready to roll in the morning and here she would come strolling in sometime in the early evening. It got to be tiring after a while. There were days when she seemed barely able to function. Still, she somehow managed to get through it, just as always, I suppose." It should be noted that Marilyn was acutely aware of her constant disruptions on the set. After the film was over, for instance, she sent choreographer Jack Cole $1,500 with a note telling him she realized she had been "awful." She suggested he take the money and use it for a vacation, "and act like it all never happened." A couple of days later, she sent him another $500 and the suggestion that he "stay three more days."

During production of this movie, Marilyn and Yves Montand at first formed a close bond of friendship. As it happened, he was insecure about his role in *Let's Make Love* and about his grasp of the English language. (Actually all of his dialogue ended up having to be meticulously rerecorded.) In this kind of insecurity, he shared Marilyn's own apprehensions. She was never sure she was very good as an actress, and to have a costar who had his own self-doubts was a provocative development in her life. She liked him very much and wanted him to feel the same way about her. However, Marilyn being Marilyn, she couldn't help but be late to the set, which was a bit of a problem for Montand. One day when she didn't show up for work, he left a terse note under the door of her bungalow:

Don't leave me to work for hours on end on a scene you've already decided not to do the next day. I'm not the enemy. I'm your pal. And capricious little girls have never amused me.

She was horrified when she received his little missive. In fact, she felt so terrible, she overreacted and couldn't leave her bungalow until Mr. and Mrs. Montand went to comfort her and tell her that it was all right, they would all survive. The shoot went on. Then . . . *it* happened in mid-April 1960. Montand was concerned about Marilyn because she was too exhausted to attend a rehearsal. Arthur Miller was in Nevada with John Huston scouting possible locations for *The Misfits*. Montand's wife, Simone, was in Europe working on a film. Paula Strasberg suggested that Yves go to Marilyn's bungalow to say hello and make her feel better about her absence. He did. So, there he was, asking her how she felt and hearing her tell him she would be fine when—one thing led to another. According to what he later wrote in his memoir, he couldn't help himself and leaned over and kissed her, and then . . . they made love.

The affair lasted for just two months, from April until June, when the film wrapped. When it ended, the Montands tried to put the pieces of their marriage back together. It was difficult, though, because anytime someone tumbled into bed with Marilyn Monroe it ended up front-page news. The Montands had their hands full not only with their broken marriage but with an avalanche of publicity about it. Yves Montand and Simone Signoret proceeded to make statements that surprised the American public. They suggested it was perfectly fine for Yves to have had an affair with "someone like Marilyn Monroe" because that is how the machinery of marriage works. It was just that Marilyn mucked up the works by taking it all too seriously.

From Yves: "[Marilyn] is a simple girl without any guile. Perhaps I was too tender and thought she was as sophisticated as some of the other ladies I have known. Had Marilyn been sophisticated, none of this ever would have happened . . . she is known throughout the world, but she is still a child. Perhaps she had a school girl crush. If she did, I'm sorry. But nothing will break up my marriage."

From Signoret: "Let us say Marilyn felt Yves' charm. Who doesn't? But everything that might be natural among us is twisted and deformed right from the start by publicity and talk. The real problem is that when a woman feels the physical attraction of a man who is not her husband, she must also feel she is in love to justify it. It is no longer casual even in passing. A man, on the other hand, doesn't feel he has to confuse an affair with eternal love and make it a crisis in his marriage."

When reporter Alan Levy read Mrs. Montand's comment to Marilyn, she said softly, "I think this is all some part of her problem, not mine."

"It was all very hurtful," said Rupert Allan. "It was despicable of Yves Montand to say what he did. And I'm not sure Yves came out looking much better. Of course, Marilyn was wracked with guilt and embarrassment. I remember her saying, 'I shouldn't have done it because he's married.' I think she felt shame about it. Of course, she was married, too, but that seemed a secondary concern. You can imagine her reaction to all of this if she wouldn't come out of her bungalow because he had chastised her for being late. This kind of public thrashing took a lot to get over. It was as if the Montands were saying, 'Well, *of course* he had sex with her. She's Marilyn Monroe after all. Then, silly girl, she thought it meant something. How stupid of her. Now, let's just all move on, shall we?' It was very reductive."

Rupert Allan's observation that Marilyn felt guilt about the affair rings true in that, generally, she was conflicted about her feelings relating to marriage. On one hand, she had great respect for the notion of wedded bliss and constantly told her half sister, Berniece, how fortunate she was to be married to the same man for so many years. She even mentioned the Montands to Berniece as a couple she very much admired for their commitment to each other. On the other hand, she seemed to not have a problem with having affairs with married men. Simply put, she seemed to believe that if a man would have sex with her then he must not be happily married—and therefore he was fair game.

The premise of *Let's Make Love* has Marilyn portraying musical comedy actress Amanda Dell, appearing in an off-Broadway revue that satirizes celebrities, including the fictional Jean-Marc Clement (Montand), a French-born billionaire industrialist who is now headquartered in New York City. Clement attends a performance just as Amanda is going through Cole Porter's "My Heart Belongs to Daddy," a full-on production number with a half dozen chorus boys, staged by Jack Cole. He is instantly smitten by Amanda's beauty and sets in motion a plan to win her heart without revealing his identity as the super-rich businessman being parodied in the revue. The balance of the film follows the development of Jean-Marc's pursuit of Amanda, complete with the two rehearsing the musical numbers, and also including acting out love scenes together. As expected, the sexy continental wins the heart of the musical comedy star without ever revealing his true identity.

It's clear from Marilyn's work in this movie that she was trying to expand her horizons, yet it was difficult for her. She wrote these words in a notebook in her dressing room:

What am I afraid of? Why am I so afraid? Do I think I can't act? I know I can act, but I am afraid. I am afraid and I should not be and I must not be.

She actually had no reason to be afraid of this movie, this script. She was much better than the film deserved, actually, and that may have been the problem. The weak script forced her to fall back on her tried-and-true image of sexy blonde bombshell in order to make the movie work. In other words, Arthur Miller did her no favor with this one. Still, it was well received. In fact, *Daily Variety* gave it a surprisingly rave review, which read, in part, "After the film is underway about 12 minutes, the screen goes suddenly dark . . . and a lone spotlight picks up Marilyn Monroe wearing black tights and a sloppy wool sweater. She announces with appropriate musical orchestration, that her name is Lolita and that she isn't allowed to play (pause) with boys (pause) because her heart belongs to daddy (words and music by Cole Porter). This not only launches the first of a series of elegantly designed [by Jack Cole] production numbers and marks one of the great star entrances ever made on the screen, but is typical of the entire film—which has taken something not too original (the Cinderella theme) and dressed it up like new."

Let's Make Love would be released September 8, 1960, and gross $3 million at the box office. It would also be nominated for an Oscar for the best scoring of a musical.

In the summer of 1960, Marilyn stayed on in Los Angeles while Arthur was busy with preproduction of *The Misfits*. Yves and Simone were back in Europe. Feeling more confused than ever, Marilyn did what perhaps she should not have—she continued with her therapy. Her New York psychiatrist, Marianne Kris, had recommended that when Marilyn was in Los Angeles she begin seeing a colleague named Dr. Ralph Greenson, which Marilyn agreed to.

Marilyn and Pat

In the spring of 1960, while Marilyn was in Los Angeles, she met a woman who would not only go on to become a good and trusted friend but would actually alter the course of her life, even if inadvertently—Pat Kennedy Lawford. In some ways, Pat may be the consistently missing link in all accounts of Marilyn's relationship with the Kennedy family. While she is referred to in many biographies as having been Monroe's "best friend" during the 1960s, this might be overstating their relationship a bit—and little concrete information has ever been reported. In some ways, it was an unlikely alliance between the two women.

As we have seen, Marilyn had been the unwanted love child of a woman who had gone insane. She'd spent her childhood being passed from foster home to foster home, never knowing what it felt like to belong, to be loved. Despite her fame, she never had much money; she always lived beyond her means. Privately, she longed to know the comfort and protection of a real family. In stark contrast,

Patricia Kennedy Lawford—"Pat"—was the sixth of Joe and Rose Kennedy's nine children, a member of the closely bound and influential Kennedy family. Her privileged background allowed her to live an affluent lifestyle, educated in the finest convent schools and graduating from Rosemont College, a private women's liberal arts school in Pennsylvania. She traveled the world over and wanted for nothing, always under the protective and watchful eye of her wealthy family.

Pat, who was thirty-six when she and Marilyn became friends, was outgoing and friendly. She wouldn't have been considered beautiful, but she was arresting just the same. She had a resolute-looking face that was a bit longish, with deep blue eyes, a sharp nose, and, of course, that toothy Kennedy smile. She was athletic, again like her relatives, her tall, slender body moving with easy grace as she tossed the pigskin about with her brothers. Always eager to forge an identity separate and apart from her famous family, she was a TV producer for a while before having her children. She had loved being in show business and wished it could have continued, but a Kennedy woman's first responsibility was always to family, not career. Still, Pat was a very independent person. In fact, she was known in the family as "the Hollywood Kennedy," the least politically motivated of the Kennedy sisters, the one who—as Jeanne Martin, Dean's widow, put it—"loved a good time, loved show business, was a lot of fun and well liked by the stars she had met through her husband: Judy Garland, Jackie Cooper, Lauren Bacall, Humphrey Bogart, Martha Raye, Jimmy Durante, and dozens of others. You could depend on Pat. She was an absolutely fabulous person. She could be a great friend. She was, to Marilyn." (Note: Pat was godmother to Jeanne and Dean's daughter, Gina Caroline.)

When Peter Lawford first introduced Marilyn to Pat, two words came to mind: Grace Goddard. "She reminds me of my Aunt Grace so much I can't even believe it," Marilyn said at the time. "She has the exact same personality. When she laughs, it's Grace's laugh." Any similarity Pat had with Grace may have been one of the reasons Marilyn felt so close to her so quickly. Definitely, Pat had

Grace's energy. She was always busy, always moving—always on the go and excited about going there. She was also wisecracking and had a sarcastic sense of humor. For those to whom the memory of Pat Kennedy doesn't strike an image, think Jane Russell in *Gentlemen Prefer Blondes. That* was Pat Kennedy.

Pat had met her husband, the British actor Peter Lawford, in 1949 in London. They married in 1954. By this time, Pat was thirty and had a personal fortune of $10 million. Peter, at thirty-one, was worth about $100,000 and was accused by some Kennedy loyalists of being a gold digger. Kennedy patriarch Joe certainly did not approve of him. "If there's anything I'd hate more for a son-in-law than an actor, it's a *British* actor," he said. That Peter was Protestant didn't help matters. Christopher Lawford, Pat's son, recalls his mother saying that Joe Kennedy sent her on a trip around the world in order that she might forget Peter. "It didn't work," she told her son. I got to Japan and turned right around." Joe Kennedy called J. Edgar Hoover and asked him to check out Peter's background. Imagine it. Your potential father-in-law has the pull to have you investigated by J. Edgar Hoover. "He found out that I wasn't homosexual and that I wasn't a Communist, so I guess I was okay in those respects," Peter would later say. "Still, Joe Kennedy wasn't a fan of mine. It took Pat a lot of courage to marry me when her old man disapproved so much. I think she was very brave to do it, actually."

Though Pat loved Peter, the marriage was troubled almost from the start, partly because of Peter's personal demons, his drinking habits, and, later, his obsession with trying to fit in with Frank Sinatra's notorious Rat Pack, but also because he never felt that he fit in the Kennedy fold, either. Whereas the husbands of Pat's sisters, Eunice and Jean, both became involved in the Kennedys' financial empire, Peter never did; he simply wasn't interested. It may sound absurd in retrospect, but the fact that he couldn't play football made things worse for him with the family. After all, he was unable to participate in the family's greatest free-time ritual. "Never played in my life," he said in 1981, "and that was bad news to the Kennedys. I was an outcast from the start."

Immediately after they married, Peter began seeing other women—even during Pat's pregnancies. However, Pat was accustomed to the idea of the philandering husband; her father and brothers had long ago exposed her to the notion of the unfaithful spouse, and of course, her mother, Rose, had endured a roaming husband in Joe. Pat did, too, but she was angry about it, not collected. She didn't even try to fake it. Much like her sister-in-law, Jackie, she felt that the best she could do was to make sure her husband didn't think she was a complete idiot, and then go about the business of making a good life for herself. She took it a step further. She insisted that she and Peter have separate bedrooms. She decided early on that she'd just as soon not sleep next to someone she knew was having sex with someone else. An oft-told "inside story" among Marilyn's and Pat's friends was that shortly after they met, Marilyn was at the house having lunch when Peter walked into the room. Pat took a sandwich from a platter in the middle of the table and handed it to Peter. "Ham and cheese," she said. Then, in the next breath and very nonchalantly, "And that little brunette you were [expletive deleted] last night? I want her out of the picture. She called the house. And that's where I draw the line. You got it?" She met Peter's stunned expression with a stern one of her own. He just nodded and left the room, embarrassed. Then Pat went back to her conversation with Marilyn as if the scene had never happened. Later, Marilyn said, "She's probably the strongest, most confident woman I have ever met. I wish I had her balls."

In the spring of 1960, these two very different women—Marilyn and Pat—became close friends. It was an ironic meeting in the sense that Marilyn had dated Peter for a short time back in 1950. Peter was crazy about her, Marilyn not so much him. In some ways, the friendship between Marilyn and Pat made sense, though. Pat was drawn to the glamour and glitz that was all Marilyn's, whereas Marilyn had always longed for the security and financial stability enjoyed by Pat. In other ways, the friendship seemed surprising. For instance, Pat was puritanical. While Pat was rather plain and ordinary in appearance, Marilyn was . . . well, *Marilyn*. While it was said that Pat made the sign of the cross whenever she had to have sex with Peter, Marilyn was . . . well, *Marilyn*.

"I don't know when it happened exactly, but I know that Pat started to become very, I don't know what the word is for it, really—infatuated, I guess, with the idea of knowing Marilyn Monroe," says Pat Brennan, who met Pat in 1954 and remained friends with her through the 1960s and 1970s. "I think it's safe to say that she was starstruck by her. Suddenly, everything was 'I just spoke to Marilyn and she said that . . .' It was as if she had a best friend overnight. I found it strange.

"I remember calling Pat once in the spring of 1960 and she said, 'I'd like for you to speak to someone here.' The next thing I knew, I was hearing this breathy voice on the other end of the phone. Marilyn. 'Pat says you are her dear friend,' she told me. 'Well, I am, too. Maybe we'll meet one day.' I said, 'Fine, let's do.' Finally Pat came back on the line. 'So what do you think of *that*?' Pat said. She was definitely impressed by Marilyn and wanted to impress others that she knew her."

Very quickly, the two women became close. Pat's son Christopher recalled of his mom and Marilyn, "[Marilyn] had a quiet voice and she would smile at me and head out to walk on the sand with my mom. My mother told me Marilyn was like her 'little sister.' It surprised her that Marilyn was so open with her. My mom didn't come from an environment where emotions and feelings were openly shared. Marilyn Monroe trusted my mother's love for her."

As they got to know each other, they began to share details of each other's life while commiserating about their joys and sadnesses. For instance, Pat had three children—Christopher, Sydney, and Victoria. In a year, she would have a fourth, Robin. Marilyn, of course, desperately longed for children. Sometimes the stories Pat told Marilyn about her family would leave her with her mouth wide open, such as this one:

"After Peter and I had Christopher, Peter was very unhappy because the baby cried all the time and the house smelled like shit," Pat told Marilyn in front of other friends.

"Oh, well, I guess that's what happens when you have a baby," Marilyn said. "So what did you do?"

"Well, we decided it would be best if Christopher had his own apartment across the street."

"*What?* How old was he?"

"Well, he was about two months old, actually. So, anyway, we rented an apartment for him and the nanny and he slept over there. It was just a lot easier on everyone."

Indeed, Pat Kennedy Lawford was of a rare breed. Her story about Christopher aside, she was the best mother she knew how to be to her children. Of course, the Lawfords had a live-in nanny, but when the brood was a little older Pat would give the nanny one week off a month so that she could be a full-time mom to them. She would turn the clocks ahead an hour so that the kids would go to sleep a little earlier—but after spending the day running after four small children she probably figured she deserved the break.

Then there was this story:

"You will never guess what my dad gave me when I turned twenty-five."

"A new outfit?" Marilyn asked.

"No, guess again."

"A car?

"Nope. Guess again."

"What? What?

"One million dollars," Pat said with an impish grin.

Again, Marilyn couldn't believe her ears. "But why?" she asked.

Pat laughed. "Oh, who knows? I guess because he loved me. It was quite generous, wasn't it?"*

Marilyn had to agree.

---

* Pat's humor is legendary in Kennedy circles. Here's a funny story from Ted Kennedy's 1980 presidential campaign: A frazzled campaign worker called Pat one day and said that he needed her immediately at a political gathering, if she could possibly make it—in an hour. "But I haven't done my hair yet," Pat exclaimed. "And I don't have any makeup on. And I just have this old dress. I'm a total wreck. Why, it's just impossible! I just can't do it!" When the frantic campaign worker continued to press her by saying no one else was available, Pat relented. "Okay, fine, then," she said. "I'll just come as Eunice."

The friendship with Pat had an interesting dynamic in that Pat wanted to share it with others while Marilyn chose to keep it to herself. "She liked Pat, I know that much, but other than that, I don't know a lot," said Ralph Roberts. "She was not effusive when it came to Pat. I remember thinking that it was mostly a telephonic relationship. I think Marilyn began to call her when she had problems—as she did all of us. And I think Pat enjoyed that. I think she wanted to help Marilyn, though I'm not sure why except that, well . . . everyone wanted to help Marilyn. She had that kind of vulnerability that made you want to take care of her, and I think Pat Kennedy Lawford was struck by it, too."

In July 1960, Pat invited Marilyn to be present when her brother, John F. Kennedy, accepted the Democratic Party nomination for president of the United States. Marilyn wasn't sure she could make it. She said she had prior commitments with *The Misfits*. However, Pat told her that if she missed it she would be "missing something very historical." So Marilyn agreed that she would be there. She would be out of town, she said, but she would fly in for the convention and fly right back out that night.

On the night of July 15, 1960, Marilyn and many other celebrities joined a packed house at the Memorial Coliseum in Los Angeles and watched in rapt attention as John Kennedy spoke of his New Frontier. "The new frontier of which I speak is not a set of promises," he intoned, "it is a set of challenges, it sums up not what I intend to offer of the American people but what I intend to ask them." His aide Peter Summers, who was responsible for coordinating much of the television coverage of Kennedy's campaign, recalled, "It was a magical moment like no other I can remember. When he came to the podium, the applause was thunderous but then, as he spoke, you could hear a pin drop. Chills were going up and down your spine. Yes, Marilyn was in the audience, along with many other stars. That night, I think a strong friendship began to develop between her and Jack Kennedy. She was free, but Jack Kennedy wasn't."

Marilyn did see Kennedy backstage after his speech. It was Pat who introduced them. Actually Marilyn and JFK had met once before, in the 1950s at a dinner party, but hadn't had a chance to talk or get to know one another. They wouldn't on this night, either. There was too much going on—the scene was chaotic and Marilyn had to fly out of Los Angeles that night anyway. However, something strange did happen as a result of that evening. It was clear to some observers that the two were flirtatious toward one another, and there was concern about it. Because Kennedy was known for his voracious sexual appetite, red flags went up in his campaign quarters anytime he flirted with a movie star. "Some people on staff said products are sold by star endorsement," Peter Summers recalled, "and that maybe a closeness [between JFK and Monroe] of this nature will be a benefit to him getting elected. The other side was that you're not going to elect someone president who is perhaps ignoring his wife or cheating on his family. So, yes there was concern. Marilyn was spoken to very frankly about it. The president was spoken to very frankly about it. There was great concern at the time. It could have destroyed him."

In fact, Marilyn was spoken to—by Pat. One Kennedy relative recalled, "What happened was that someone from the Kennedy campaign told Peter Lawford that JFK had been flirting with Marilyn. They wanted to nip it in the bud before something happened. Would he talk to Marilyn about it? Peter thought it was unfair to approach Marilyn Monroe with a warning since nothing had even occurred. Still, he decided to ask Pat to at least mention to her that there was concern about it. So, from my understanding of it, Pat called Marilyn and said, 'Look, I know this is ridiculous, but everyone is going nuts because they think my brother was flirting with you the other night. Do you think he was?' Marilyn said, 'Well, of course he was. And I was flirting back. But it meant nothing. It was just flirting.' Pat said, 'Fine. I just wanted you to know that they were worried about it.' Marilyn asked, 'About what?' And Pat said, 'Just that something might happen between you and my brother, that's all. It's very silly.' Marilyn agreed. 'Oh Pat, that is silly,' she said. 'It's just ridiculous.'"

The Misfits

$\mathcal{B}$y the end of July 1960, Marilyn Monroe was in Reno, Nevada, for location shooting on *The Misfits*, which, as it happened, was the last movie she would complete. Entire books have been written about the various miseries surrounding the production of this film. Suffice it to say, not one thing seemed to be in balance, not the least of which was Marilyn's mental and physical condition, which continued to deteriorate by the day.

"*The Misfits* should never have happened," Marilyn's makeup artist, Allan "Whitey" Snyder, once said to the "All About Marilyn" fan club. "She wasn't feeling well when they insisted on starting shooting, and there were so many script changes in her part that Arthur made so often, she became less and less happy with her role and character." In another interview, he added, "The drugs had pretty much taken over by this time. She was having a terrible time. Everything was going wrong. It was like a snowball going down a mountain, the problems just accumulating.

"Marilyn and Arthur so loathed each other, I'm not sure how either of them got through this movie. Everyone felt the pressure of it all. Marilyn was more paranoid than ever before. She believed Arthur was having an affair with someone on the set, a script supervisor I believe. He wasn't. After what had happened with Yves Montand, though, it was surprising that she was so angry. Everything was out of whack. He had written a movie that seemed very personal, that drew from elements of the real Marilyn's personality and her relationship with him, so that made it even more difficult for her. Honest to God, there were lines in that movie that were right out of her experience with Arthur Miller. Why he did that, I don't know. To be mean, maybe? I don't know. Then he would change the lines just before she had to film them. He kept her off balance the entire time. To me, it felt like a punishment. I have never said that before, but that's how I feel. I have bad memories of this time. It was as if Marilyn was close to the edge, and her husband was the one pushing her over it."

Can Marilyn Monroe be considered Arthur Miller's muse? Or was she more like a wounded, unwitting victim of the playwright's exploitation? An examination of two of Miller's literary creations—a play and a movie script—would seem to point to his former wife as having been a bit of both. In Miller's 1964 play *After the Fall*, which opened at New York's ANTA Washington Square Theatre in January 1964, only eighteen months after Marilyn's death on August 7, 1962, the protagonist is a middle-aged lawyer ruminating upon his relationships with the three women in his life and how the marriages to two of them ended, the first in divorce, the second in the suicide of his wife, an actress, and the third a work in progress. Though Miller always denied the genesis of the play, if he thought of it at all, he must have acknowledged to his private self the parallels with events in his own life, not only concerning his women but also his personal experiences in the mid-1950s with HUAC's spurious search for alleged Communists in the government, which he used as the inspiration for *The Crucible*.

Miller's screenplay of *The Misfits*, adapted from his *Esquire* magazine short story, was the only thing he wrote during his four-year marriage to Marilyn. He points out in his autobiography, *Timebends*, that he wrote the screenplay as a gift to her and as she read an early draft she would "laugh delightfully at some of the cowboys' lines but seemed to withhold full commitment to playing Roslyn." Perhaps Marilyn should have listened to her instincts, for she grew to hate the script and her character, which she regarded a caricature of her. Making Roslyn a recently divorced dancer and a needy clinging vine, whose very existence was reliant upon the approval of the men in her life, Miller seemed determined to show the character in all its flaws, and by extension Marilyn, who is limning the character. Marilyn was as smart as she was sensitive, and none of this was lost on her. Despite her misgivings, the reassurances of director John Huston and others whose opinions she valued gave her the will to continue. When Arthur sent the first draft of the script to Huston in Ireland, he agreed to direct it. With her *Asphalt Jungle* director at the helm, and a dream cast assembled by MCA über-agent Lew Wasserman—Clark Gable, Montgomery Clift, Eli Wallach, Thelma Ritter—Marilyn came around and agreed to be in the film.

In the story, Roslyn Taber (Monroe) has come to Reno to get a divorce and taken a room with Isabelle Steers (Ritter), who accompanies her to divorce court as a witness. Celebrating Roslyn's freedom at a bar, they meet Guido (Wallach) and Gay (Gable), a late-fiftyish, still roguishly handsome onetime cowboy. Their chemistry established, Roslyn and Gay move in together in a house Guido is building. Like Gay, he too falls for Roslyn. Guido hatches a plan to round up wild mustangs, called misfits because they are too small to ride, on the Nevada salt flats and sell them. Joining them in the enterprise is Perce (Clift), a beaten-up, down-on-his-luck rodeo rider. The three, accompanied by Roslyn, head out to the salt flats to corral the mustangs. It is only after they arrive at the site that Roslyn learns of the mustangs' fate: They are to be sold to a dog food manufacturer. Horrified at the thought—just as Marilyn, always a pet lover, would be—Rosalyn begs Gay to spare the six horses. At first he refuses, but in the end, so struck is he by her passion to save the mustangs, Gay cuts the ropes and frees them. This act of compassion also allows Gay and Roslyn to come to a better understanding of each other as they head off to a future together.

Marilyn threw herself into the role, determined to make the film work. Despite the demands of the part, both physically and emotionally, she was able to rise to the occasion again and again. She was given a look that was quite different from the one her fans were used to. Famous Hollywood hairstylist Sydney Guilaroff styled a wig that was smoother, sleeker, and longer than what she usually wore. Gone were the bedhead curls that had become her trademark. Jean Louis—who would go on to create the skintight, sparkly "Happy birthday, Mr. President" gown—came up with several outfits that revealed Marilyn's curves to wonderful advantage. The halter-top white cotton dress splattered with large, quarter-size polka dots was worn without any discernible foundation garment and worked so well that Marilyn selected it for personal appearances when she promoted the film. She was photographed in color for an *Esquire* pictorial and the polka dots turned out to be red, not black as they appeared in the film. Her longtime personal makeup man, Allan Snyder, was on location to apply the powder, lipstick, mascara, and blush sparingly in keeping with the film's rustic, open-air setting. It is almost unbelievable that Marilyn's beauty remained unmarred by the angst, the stress, the drugs and alcohol, and the rough-and-tumble action of the film.

The long, four-month shoot in the harsh Nevada landscape was difficult, made more so by Marilyn's erratic behavior and her insecurities about the project. There was also her abuse of booze and drugs and her unhappiness about her marriage to Miller, which was coming to an end. "I don't even think he wanted me in it," she said at the time of her husband and his movie. "I guess it's all over between us. We have to stay with each other because it would be bad for the film if we split up now. Arthur's been complaining to [John] Huston about me, and that's why Huston treats me like an idiot with his 'dear this' and 'dear that.' Why doesn't he treat me like a normal actress?"

In sharp contrast to Marilyn's on-set conduct with her repeated delays in arriving on the set and the now legendary demands for retakes was the professionalism of Montgomery Clift, who memorized the entire script before arriving on location in Nevada. As Miller notes in his autobiography, "Indeed, [Clift] never missed an hour's work . . . and was always on time despite the long delays in finishing the picture." Gable also exhibited extreme empathy for Marilyn, but was clearly frustrated at the situation. He took out his frustration by insisting on doing his own dangerous stunt work.

By this time, of course, Natasha Lytess was long gone and now replaced by Marilyn's other guru, Paula Strasberg. Marilyn wouldn't so much as make a move on camera without Paula's consent. However, there was a big difference in their relationship as compared to that with Natasha. Paula had a husband and children. She had other responsibilities. Natasha only had Marilyn. Whereas Natasha was devoted to keeping Marilyn's moods from swinging out of control and made sure she was on the right medication in the right doses, Paula just coached her acting. Indeed, without Natasha, Marilyn would fall into great despair during the filming of *The Misfits*.

By the end of August, Marilyn could take no more. The stress had gotten to her to the point that she began to complain of hearing "voices" again. The drugs were not working, so the dosages were increased. Ralph Greenson prescribed 300 milligrams of the barbiturate Nembutal. The maximum dose was supposed to be 100 milligrams. "Doctors had gone along with her demands for new and stronger sleeping pills," Arthur Miller later remembered, "even though they knew perfectly well how dangerous this was. There were always new doctors willing to help her into oblivion."

"He was giving Marilyn three times the dosage she should have been given," said Rupert Allan (who was on the set every day) of Ralph Greenson. "I found it shocking, just shocking, that any doctor would prescribe that much Nembutal for insomnia. It made her absolutely paranoid in her waking hours. She told me she always felt as if she was being followed. Everything was closing in on her." Allan recalled Marilyn splitting open Seconal capsules and letting the drug dissolve in her mouth during breaks in filming. "I would say that by this time she was, I'm sorry to say it, a drug addict. That would not be overstating it." Her makeup artist, Allan Snyder, recalled applying her makeup in the morning while she was still flat on her back in bed. "There was no other way," he said. "It would take her so long to get up in the morning, we had to start with the makeup before she was out of bed."

The result of such drug abuse, on top of the desert heat and all of this stress, was that Marilyn was flown to Los Angeles, where she was admitted to Westside Hospital. The press was told that she was suffering from "extreme exhaustion." That wasn't the case, though.

"She had a nervous breakdown," said Evelyn Moriarty, her stand-in on this film. "There was a lot of concern about her health and well-being. She was in bad shape. Some of us didn't think she would be able to find her way back from it. There was also talk that the whole movie would have to be shut down. All of her friends went to Los Angeles to be with her—Paula [Strasberg], May [Reis, her secretary], 'Whitey' [Snyder, her makeup man]. I really thought the movie was over for all of us, and I felt terrible for her. I was very worried. If you knew Marilyn as I did, this kind of thing really made you feel just dreadful. You wanted her to pull out of it, you really did. . . . You just wanted her to be okay. She was trying so very hard, but the odds were always against her. Every time she took a step forward, something happened to knock her back again.

"Then there were a lot of stories on the set that John Huston had run the budget into the ground with his gambling—he was a terrible gambler!—that he needed time to raise more money, and that the movie was going to be shut down anyway, and that he had convinced doctors to admit Marilyn into the hospital in order to use her as a scapegoat. I now think it was a little of both—that she needed to be hospitalized and that Huston took advantage of her illness so that he could blame the delay in filming on her. I thought that was awful."

Pat Brennan recalls a visit that Pat Kennedy Lawford paid to Marilyn. "Pat wanted to visit Marilyn but she didn't want to cause a spectacle by doing it," Brennan recalled, "so she arranged with the hospital to sneak in after visiting hours and wore a silly black wig and glasses in order to not be recognized.

"She said that when she showed up in Marilyn's room, she was sound asleep. She remembered Marilyn as being white as a sheet, so much so that for a moment she actually thought she was dead. 'I had never seen a woman look like that who was not in a casket,' she told me. She stood at the foot of Marilyn's bed and just stared at her for ten minutes wondering how in the world it had come to this for her. 'I knew I was coming in at the end of a long story and was so sorry I had not been around to help her,' she told me. She said that Marilyn stirred and finally awakened. 'Then she looked at me,' Pat remembered, 'and said, somewhat angrily, "Who the hell are you?"' She took off the disguise, and Marilyn burst out laughing.

Suddenly, she was Marilyn Monroe again. A glow just came over her, Pat said. Her color returned, her personality returned. Marilyn said, 'Well, this is the first time you have ever seen me in the hospital, Pat. How do I look?' Pat said, 'Marilyn, I swear to God, you look like shit.' And the two had a good laugh. 'So, can we get a couple of martinis in here, or what?' Pat asked."

"I guess about a week later, she was back on the set," Evelyn Moriarty recalled, "and you just had to wonder how she ever did it."

"I had to use my wits," Marilyn would later explain, "or else I'd have been sunk—and nothing's going to sink me. Everyone was always pulling at me, tugging at me, as if they wanted a piece of me. It was always, 'Do this, do that,' and not just on the job but off, too. God, I've tried to stay intact, whole."

Indeed, as Ralph Roberts put it, "Under all that frailty was still a will of steel."

Just before filming for the movie moved back to Los Angeles for the final shooting, Marilyn and her coterie of friends, including Paula Strasberg, Ralph Roberts (now also her masseur), and May Reis, went to San Francisco to attend an Ella Fitzgerald concert. While she was there, Marilyn decided to pay a visit to the DiMaggio family. She had always gotten along well with them, even if not so much with Joe toward the end of their marriage. Though Joe was out of town, she had a chance to visit with his brother and sister and, it would seem, rekindled her friendship with them. Maybe it had something to do with the DiMaggios, or maybe not, but as soon as she got back to Los Angeles the fights started again with Arthur Miller. The two argued so loudly at the Beverly Hills Hotel, Marilyn's friends felt sure that the marriage was over—and this time it really was. Miller soon moved out of the hotel, leaving Marilyn alone there. Now it was just a matter of formal divorce papers being drawn up for the battling couple.

On October 21, Marilyn's director of *Niagara*, Henry Hathaway, saw Marilyn on the Paramount soundstage. She was crying. "All my life, I've played Marilyn Monroe, Marilyn Monroe, Marilyn Monroe," she told him. "I've tried to do a little better and when I do, I find myself doing an imitation of myself. I so want to do something different. That was one of the things that attracted me to Arthur when he said he was attracted to me. When I married him, one of the fantasies in my mind was that I could get away from Marilyn Monroe through him, and here I find myself back doing the same thing, and I just couldn't take it. I had to get out of there. I just couldn't face having to do another scene with Marilyn Monroe."

Marilyn's statements to Hathaway have a sad, tortured irony to them. Long ago, she had buried Norma Jeane Mortensen in favor of being reborn as Marilyn Monroe. She celebrated the day, eager to free herself from the shackles of her sad youth. Now, all of these years later, she wanted nothing more than to kill off Marilyn Monroe.

No Relief

As if things were not bad enough for Marilyn Monroe as the year 1960 blessedly wound down, news of a death in the cast of *The Misfits* plunged her back into the deep depression that had recently caused her to be hospitalized. She had always admired Clark Gable, all the way back to when she found a photo of Edward Mortenson and thought he looked like Gable. She regretted that she'd caused the distinguished actor so much grief by her behavior on the set of *The Misfits* and hoped he would forgive her and try to remember her fondly. She never had a chance to tell him how she felt about him, though. "I don't know how he would have reacted if he had known how important he had been to me all these years," she later said.

On November 5, Clark Gable suffered a massive heart attack. He would die on the sixteenth at the age of just fifty-nine. Before his death, Gable had seen *The Misfits* and had judged it one of his best movies. Still, rumor had it that he had been so annoyed at Marilyn's behavior on the set, it ultimately caused him the stress that precipitated his attack. Perhaps it was a theory that would have held more credence had he fallen ill during the production instead of after it. Moreover, Gable had a three-pack-a-day cigarette habit that couldn't have done much for his well-being. At any rate, the story circulated around the world that it was Marilyn Monroe who was responsible for his death. "I kept him waiting—kept him waiting for hours and hours on that picture," Marilyn told Sidney Skolsky. Then, as if parroting something that had obviously sprung from one of her five days a week with Dr. Ralph Greenson, she added, "Was I punishing my father? Getting even for all of the years he kept me waiting?"

Marilyn would later tell her half sister, Berniece, that people would shout at her from passing cars as she walked down the street in Manhattan, "How does it feel to be a murderer?"

"It upset her so very much," said Diane Stevens from the John Springer office. "This was the last thing she needed. I called her when I heard the news about Clark because I knew how she'd probably react. She picked up the phone—she was back in New York by this time—and sounded like a shell of her old self."

"I'm not doing so well," Marilyn told Diane, according to her memory of the conversation. "I feel so responsible. I know it's my fault he's dead."

"But it's not," Diane told her. "You have to stop thinking that, Marilyn. It will just make you worse."

"I don't see how things can get any worse," she responded, her voice sounding heavily medicated. "My marriage is over. I have no one. Now this. I don't think I can go on." With those chilling words, Marilyn hung up the phone.

"Frantically, I tried to call her again, but she never picked up," said Stevens. "I was scared. I called my boss, John [Springer], and told him about the conversation. He said, 'My God, what now?' as if he had been waiting for the other shoe to drop. He then called May Reis and asked her to check on Marilyn. She told him, 'Oh, no, I recently quit. I no longer work for her. I just couldn't take it.' I swear, not a thing seemed to make sense in Marilyn's world. There was always a surprise right around the corner. He said, 'I don't care if you work for her or not, get your ass over there and find out if she's still alive.' Finally, he called me back about an hour later and said May had told him Marilyn was sleeping and that all was well. John and I knew better. 'All is not well,' he told me. 'I'm becoming very afraid as to how this whole thing is going to end.' I shared his fear."

It would seem, though, that all Marilyn needed was a break from the pressure of her life in order to turn things around. "She seemed a lot better once she got to New York," says one relative. "I know she called Gladys as soon as she got to New York."

After Marilyn received another very strange Christmas card from her mother—she had one every year—this one signed, "Loving good wishes (whether or not they are warranted), Gladys Pearl Eley, your mother," she felt compelled to reach out to her.

"Gladys had been calling the office for weeks trying to reach Marilyn," recalled Diane Stevens. "I so dreaded hearing her voice. She always said, 'This is Mrs. Eley calling for Miss Mari-lyn Monroe—she pronounced it like Mary-lynn.' John's position was always the same: If she calls, be polite but firm that Marilyn would call her back when she was ready to do so—and then tell her to call Inez Melson, who was really responsible for dealing with Gladys. However, the last time I spoke to Gladys—when she heard that Marilyn was in the hospital and was trying to track her down—she became very irate and accused me of not passing her message on to her daughter. In fact, I hadn't passed those messages on because I felt that Marilyn was already under so much strain. When I finally told her that Gladys had been calling, she sighed and said, 'Oh, gosh. I have been meaning to call her, really I have. But I just haven't had the strength to cope with her right now. I haven't called Berniece back, either, and I feel terrible about it.' Then she said, 'Have you told anyone at Fox about this?' I hadn't. She said, 'It's so funny because they are trying to keep it a secret from the press about Mother, and we're trying to keep it a secret from Fox. Where my mother is concerned, I would say there are enough secrets to go around, wouldn't you?' I had to agree. I know there was always concern at the studio that someone would track Gladys down again and she would say or do something that would cause a scandal. It was one of the reasons we tried not to antagonize her. We didn't want one of her voices telling her to do something that would be totally destructive to Marilyn's career or reputation."

Coincidentally, just before Christmas, Marilyn finalized her new will—which would be signed in January 1961. In it, she provided a $100,000 trust fund for Gladys—up from the previous will's $25,000 allocation (and so much for those who have claimed over the years that Marilyn had no interest in her mother). However, she only bequeathed $10,000 to Berniece, whom she was a lot closer to than Gladys. Interestingly, she also wished to bequeath her psychiatrist, Marianne Kris, with a full 25 percent of her estate and—more surprisingly—Lee Strasberg with the other 75 percent.*

"Finally, she called Gladys when she got back to New York," says Diane Stevens. "From my understanding, it was a fairly good conversation. Gladys seemed a little better to Marilyn and, in fact, Marilyn said she enjoyed talking to her. She had avoided visiting her when she was last in Los Angeles and said that she would definitely see her when she returned. 'She's a very strange link to a past I have worked so very hard to forget,' she told me. 'But, still, she is my mother, isn't she?'

"I think that her miscarriages made her feel somehow more warmly toward Gladys. She also told me, 'You know, my mother's

---

* Lee Strasberg's second wife, Anna, was his sole beneficiary when he died in 1982. He married Anna—forty years his junior—in 1967, a year after his first wife, Paula, died. Today, Anna Strasberg holds the bulk of Marilyn's estate, which, according to *Forbes* magazine's most recent list of income generated by dead celebrities, ranks Marilyn at number eight, with $8 million accumulated in royalties and merchandising in 2007. It should be noted, though, that when Marilyn died, she did not die a wealthy woman. Millions accumulated for her estate after her death as a result of merchandising of her name, as well as money generated from her films. Strasberg—who guards the estate with famous determination—says she was "acquainted" with Marilyn before Marilyn's death. (Most accounts have it that the two met at least once.) "Anna thinks about and handles" Ms. Monroe's image "from the moment she wakes up," says William Wegner, her attorney. "My husband, Lee, was her teacher, her mentor, but most of all Marilyn's friend," Anna Strasberg has said. "I am not only protecting her legacy and image, I am honoring my husband's wishes."

children were kidnapped from her by her ex-husband. I think I can now understand how terrible that must have been for her. I actually don't know how she could have survived such a thing. I wonder,' she said, 'if that's what made her lose her mind. I think I would lose mine if that ever happened to me.' The interesting thing to me about Marilyn, though, was that just when you thought all was lost with her, she would rally. By Christmas, she looked and sounded better to me."

During this period, Marilyn renewed her friendship with a publicist named Pat Newcomb, a woman who had worked with her on *Bus Stop* and whom Marilyn rehired at the end of 1960. Rupert Allan, a good friend of Princess Grace Kelly, had decided to spend more time with the princess in Monaco. Newcomb would take his place as Marilyn's personal publicist. "At the core of her, she was really much stronger than all of us," Pat Newcomb recalls of Marilyn, "and that was something we tended to forget, because she seemed so vulnerable, and one always felt it necessary to watch out for her."

Marilyn actually spent Christmas with Pat, gifting her with a mink coat for the holiday. She also decided to rekindle her relationship with Joe DiMaggio after he sent her poinsettias for Christmas. When she asked him why he had sent them, he said that he did so because he knew she would call him to thank him. "Besides," he said, "who in the hell else do you have in the world?" When Marilyn allowed him to visit her on Christmas evening, some in her circle were concerned about it. After all, it had not ended well with DiMaggio. Most people felt that he was the last thing she needed at this desperate time in her life. (In just a short time, DiMaggio would turn out to be a savior in her life.)

Marilyn's divorce from Arthur Miller would be the first order of business to be taken care of in January 1961. Along with her publicist, Pat Newcomb, and attorney, Aaron Frosch, Marilyn would fly to Mexico on January 20—picking the day of John Fitzgerald Kennedy's inauguration specifically because it was sure to have the attention of all media—where the divorce would be quickly granted. There would be no alimony for either party and the house they owned in Roxbury would go to Miller since he used the money from the sale of his previous home to buy it.

With another marriage over, and especially after the affair with Montand, Marilyn's image was now, maybe more than ever, that of a hussy, a homewrecker. The perception was that she had used Arthur Miller to write movies for her—*Let's Make Love*, for example—then dumped him. Considering that it was because of Miller's alleged ties with Communists that Marilyn would be forever tailed by the FBI, maybe it was appropriate that even the Russian media got into the act. "When you speak of the American way of life," commented the Russian magazine *Nedyela*, "everybody thinks of chewing gum, Coca-Cola and Marilyn Monroe. She found in Arthur Miller what she lacked. She exploited him without pity. He wrote scripts for her films and made her a real actress. Marilyn paid him back. She left him. Another broken life on her climb to the stars."

When a reporter read that commentary to Marilyn, she couldn't contain her anger. "Listen!" she exclaimed. "I know Arthur Miller better than the Russians and I've learned from Arthur Miller more than the Russians. I've learned from Arthur Miller that he does not believe in a Communist State. That's what I've learned from Arthur Miller. The Russians can talk all they want about my climb to the stars, his broken life and what I've done to somebody. But I know the man. They're talking about an idea. They can have their ideas. I had the man."

Earlier, Marilyn had told Joe DiMaggio, when he visited her, that she was looking forward to returning to Los Angeles so she could continue her treatment by Dr. Ralph Greenson. At the end of the month of January, as if to bid a final and respectful farewell to Arthur Miller and her life with him, she would happily attend the New York premiere of *The Misfits* with Montgomery Clift.

Marilyn Is Committed

I opened my living room window as wide as I could and I leaned out. I knew that I had to make up my mind inside the room. If I climbed out onto the ledge, someone below would be certain to recognize me and there'd be a big spectacle. I squeezed my eyes shut at the open window, clenched my fists. I remembered reading somewhere that people who fall from heights lose consciousness before they hit the ground. Then when I looked down, I saw a woman walking along the sidewalk near the building awning. She was wearing a brown dress and . . . *I knew her.*"

Those were Marilyn Monroe's words to her friend Ralph Roberts, when she described to him her decision to commit suicide in February 1961. It was a startling admission. Marilyn told Roberts that she had been so depressed about any part she might have played in the death of Clark Gable that she had considered leaping from her thirteenth-floor apartment window. Luckily, she changed her mind at the last moment.

After her divorce from Arthur Miller, Marilyn began once again to sink into the deepest of depressions, some of which were so bottomless it seemed to those who knew and loved her that there was simply no reaching her. Clearly she wasn't eating much, and by the beginning of 1961 she looked gaunt and sickly. She wasn't even washing her hair, once so vibrant and luxurious but now dull and lifeless. It was as if she no longer cared about anything. With the exception of her daily visits to her psychiatrist Dr. Kris's office, she secluded herself in her New York apartment, refusing most guests and expressing no interest in socializing. Socializing had become an ordeal for her especially as she got older. Monroe historian Charles Casillo explains it best this way: "There was no place for lines in her face with that kind of persona. Let's face it, we all want to look nice when we go to a party, but imagine every person you meet inspecting every inch of you, judging you on your appearance only? Does she have freckles? Is she tired? Is she thin? Is she really *that* beautiful? Marilyn had to face that kind of scrutiny every day, with every person who faced her. She knew what her major attraction was. She even admitted that at times she was invited to a party 'to dress up the dinner table.' Would the invitations keep coming if the dessert wasn't so appetizing?"[*]

Those who managed to reach her by telephone couldn't help but note the abject despondence in her voice. She had taken such a sharp turn for the worse, there was genuine concern about leaving her alone, yet she refused to allow anyone to stay with her. Though Dr. Kris had been trying to find a proper pharmaceutical strategy for managing not only Marilyn's depression but also her increasing anxiety, nothing seemed to work. She had been taking so many drugs for such a long time, it had become difficult to find one that would have a true impact on her condition.

During a session, Marilyn relayed to Dr. Kris the same chilling story she told Ralph Roberts about her near suicidal leap. Obviously, it piqued the doctor's concern. After all, sitting before Dr. Kris was an important patient she had been trusting to follow her orders when it came to proper drug dosage and frequency. Kris was well aware that if Marilyn had genuine interest in killing herself, she could easily do so with the pills already in her possession. She wouldn't have to leap out of a window to get the job done. There was no question about it—the doctor needed to take action.

Dr. Kris suggested to Marilyn that she check into a private ward at New York Hospital for some rest and relaxation under medical supervision. Reluctantly, Marilyn agreed. Therefore, on Sunday, February 5, Dr. Kris drove her to Cornell University–New York Hospital. Marilyn checked in using the pseudonym of "Faye Miller," in order to keep her presence there unknown. However, when it came time to take her to her room, she was mysteriously escorted to another clinic on the expansive premises.

---

[*] Casillo cites an interesting comment from her, made shortly before her death, to *Life* magazine's Richard Merryman: "Sometimes I'm invited places to kind of brighten up a dinner table like a musician who'll play the piano after dinner, and I know [I'm] not really invited for myself. You're just an ornament."

From the moment Marilyn entered this strange new wing, it was obvious to her that there was something very different about it. She had been to hospitals over the years, and none of them were quite like this one. For one thing, the orderlies escorting her seemed distant and forceful. Her journey deeper into the ward involved passage through numerous steel doors, most of which required a key from both sides. Suddenly, it all became clear, and fear swept through her at the realization: Those doors were meant to keep people *in*, not keep people out.

Marilyn realized that Dr. Kris's description of what awaited her had been misleading: "a place to relax and rest," she had said in a soothing voice. Yet this place, these people, this environment—all of it felt uncomfortably familiar to Marilyn. In fact, this was exactly like the sanitariums where her mother had spent so many years of her life. Indeed, she was in the Payne Whitney Clinic, the psychiatric division of the hospital.

If Dr. Kris had had any notion that Marilyn would relax in this place, she had been sorely mistaken. In fact, for starters, Marilyn threw an emotional tantrum, screaming to be let go, crying that she was frightened and insisting that it was all a big mistake—which, of course, only served to make her appear even more disturbed. "What are you doing to me?" she hollered out as she was dragged down a long hallway. "Where are we going?" She shrieked in horror as she was forcibly thrown into a sparse padded room with barred windows and, in the corner, another smaller room with a sign on it that said simply "Toilet." A steel door closed with a terrible sound, and was locked. She would later recall the cell as being "for *very disturbed* [her emphasis] depressed patients, except I felt I was in some kind of prison for a crime I hadn't committed . . . the violence and markings still remained on the walls from former patients."

"You Are a Very, Very Sick Girl"

*H*ow had it come to this? Had she gone completely mad and not realized it? Was she destined to spend her last days in an asylum, just like her grandparents, and maybe her mother, too?

Though Marilyn Monroe screamed for someone to come and release her, it was useless. Finally, she broke down into wracking sobs, as she later recalled it, feeling now more than ever that all hope was lost. Then she began to repeatedly bang her fists against the hard metal door until finally both were battered and bruised. At last, two nurses entered Marilyn's cell, their eyes blazing. If she persisted, they warned her, she would be put into a straitjacket. They then stripped her of her clothing and forced her into a hospital gown. Their angry work done, they took their leave, but not before turning off the light, leaving their stunned patient in total blackness with her confused thoughts and desperate fears—and without her medication.

The next day, Marilyn was told that she would be allowed out of her room if she agreed to mingle with other patients and "socialize." She complied, knowing by now that it would be the only way she'd ever be able to obtain her freedom from the padded cell. Once in the hallway, she happened upon a young, sickly-looking woman standing in the hallway who, as she later recalled, "seemed such a pathetic and vague creature." The patient may have viewed her visitor in the same light because she suggested that Marilyn would be much less depressed if she could talk to someone on the telephone, a friend perhaps. Marilyn agreed but said it was impossible since she was distinctly told that there were no telephones on the floor. The woman's face registered surprise and she said, "But that's not true. Who told you such a thing? In fact, I'll take you to one." She then escorted Marilyn to a pay phone, reached into her pocket and gave her a nickel. However, when Marilyn reached out to make a call, a security guard suddenly grabbed the receiver from her hand. "*You can't make any phone calls*," he told her.

Not knowing what to do next, Marilyn headed back to her room and, as she later recalled, tried to imagine how she would handle such a situation if she were doing an improvisational sketch in one of her acting classes. After giving it some thought, she knew what she would do in that situation, which was to make the biggest noise she could make in the hope that someone new would be summoned, someone who might actually take pity on her and help her. To that end, she picked up a chair and, with everything she had left in her, hurled it against the glass on the bathroom door. It didn't break. She picked up the chair and hurled it against the door again and again until, finally, the double-thick glass cracked. She then reached out and carefully extracted a small, sharp sliver from the cracked window. Because she had made such a racket, an entire team of doctors and nurses burst into her room. And there she sat before them on the bed, holding the jagged glass to her wrist. "If you don't let me out of here, I'll kill myself," she threatened. Later, she would rationalize this horrifying moment by explaining that she was actually just playing out a scene from her movie *Don't Bother to Knock*—"only [in that movie] it was with a razor blade." It didn't appear to the medical staff, though, that she was playacting. The staff took quick and decisive action. Two large men and two hefty women lifted the wriggling patient from the bed right into the air, kicking and screaming, until she dropped the shard of glass. They then carried her to the elevator stretched out and facedown as she fitfully sobbed the entire way, her tears leaving a small trail. Once in the elevator, they took her to another floor. There, after she calmed herself, she was commanded to take a bath, though she had taken one that morning. "Every time you change floors you have to take a bath," she was told. Finally, after what seemed an endless time, a young doctor came in to see her.

Through her tears, Marilyn told the intern that she had been betrayed by her psychiatrist and admitted to this mental hospital "even though I don't belong here." "Why are you so unhappy?" he asked her, ignoring what she had just told him. Marilyn looked at him squarely and answered, "I've been paying the best doctors a fortune to find out the answer to that question, and you're asking *me?*"

After speaking to Marilyn for a while longer, the doctor studied her face carefully and, as if making a profound statement, said with great authority, "You are a very, very sick girl. And you've been very sick for a long time." Marilyn didn't know how to respond to the obvious. After all, she had been hearing voices for years. She had also felt paranoid—always suspecting that someone was watching her or was after her—for just as long. It had been a secret shared by just a few, such as her first husband, Jim Dougherty; her lover and Svengali, Johnny Hyde; her acting teacher, Natasha Lytess; and, most certainly, her psychiatrists. However, her secret was out of her control now—and this doctor, a total stranger, seemed to know it.

The doctor, his brow furrowed in concentration, continued, "You know, I don't see how you ever could have made a movie being so depressed. How can you even act?" Marilyn was astonished by his obvious naiveté. After all, she had been doing just that for as long as she could remember, concealing her true feelings—portraying a reality very different from the one in which she existed from day to day. "Don't you think that perhaps Greta Garbo and Charlie Chaplin and Ingrid Bergman had been depressed when *they* worked?" she asked him. She'd recently had a conversation with her half sister, Berniece, along these same lines. She had asked Berniece if she ever became depressed. Of course, Berniece said, she had experienced the blues in the past. Marilyn wondered what she did about it if she didn't take pills—and Berniece didn't. Berniece told her that she prayed. That sounded like a good answer. It just never worked for Marilyn. How could Berniece, a housewife in Florida living a peaceful existence with her husband of many years, ever truly relate to Marilyn's extraordinary problems, or to the vastness of her depression? The doctor had no answer to Marilyn's question. So he ignored it. Instead, he jotted into his notes that, in his view, Marilyn was "extremely disturbed" and also "potentially self-destructive."

Then he left her without giving her any indication that he would ever return. That evening, she couldn't sleep. The sounds of shrieking and wailing and moaning and sobbing echoed all night long through the hallways—anonymous voices, the mentally ill. She would never be able to forget these sounds. She would never forget this awful night.*

On Tuesday morning, another doctor showed up in Marilyn's cell and suggested that she spend the day with the other patients in what he referred to as "OT"—occupational therapy.

"And do what?" Marilyn asked.

"You could sew or play checkers," he suggested brightly, "even cards, and maybe knit."

Marilyn shook her head at his pathetic presence. "The day I do any of that," she said through gritted teeth, "will be the day you'll *really* have a nut on your hands."

"Why is it you feel you are so different from the other patients?" he asked.

She simply stated, "I just am."

"I'm Locked Up with These Poor Nutty People"

The rest of Marilyn Monroe's experience at Payne Whitney was more of the same—a story characterized by one indignity after another, all heaped upon a woman used to being treated with much

---

* Later Marilyn recalled in a letter to Dr. Ralph Greenson, "There were screaming women in their cells—I mean they screamed out when life was unbearable for them, I guess—and at times like this I felt an available psychiatrist should have talked to them, perhaps to alleviate even temporarily their misery and pain. I think they (the doctors) might learn something, even—but they are interested only in something they studied in their books. Maybe from some life-suffering human being they could discover more."

more reverence. It felt to her as if she'd been locked away simply because no one knew quite what to do with her. Doctors and nurses would stop by her door and peer into the little square window as if she were a caged animal at the zoo. Some seemed astonished, as if they simply couldn't believe their eyes. At one point, out of frustration, Marilyn ripped off her hospital gown and stood before them naked, just to give the sightseers "something to really look at."

Marilyn spent most of Wednesday begging anyone who would listen to her for a piece of paper and a pen so that she could write a note to someone, and so that her plea for release could be heard. It must have struck her that she was now in a situation eerily similar to one in which her mother, Gladys, often found herself. How many rambling manifestos had Gladys written over the years explaining why she shouldn't have been institutionalized, pleading with the disinterested to intervene on her behalf and obtain release? Finally, a young nurse agreed to allow Marilyn to make contact with someone by mail. But who? Marilyn would later recall thinking that Berniece would be too stunned to know what to do, and besides, she was out of state. She also didn't feel close enough to any of her ex-husbands to ask for help, and besides, it would have been too humiliating. Certainly, Natasha Lytess would have come to her aid, but that bond was long broken, and besides, she was in California, too. Who? Finally, she decided to appeal to her friends Lee and Paula Strasberg. She sat down and wrote this letter to them:

Dear Lee and Paula,

Dr. Kris has put me in the hospital under the care of two idiot doctors. They both should not be my doctors. You haven't heard from me because I'm locked up with these poor nutty people. I'm sure to end up a nut too if I stay in this nightmare. Please help me. This is the last place I should be. I love you both.

Marilyn

P.S. I'm on the dangerous floor. It's like a cell. They had my bathroom door locked and I couldn't get their key into it, so I broke the glass. But outside of that I haven't done anything uncooperative.

The note was delivered that same day. Lee Strasberg, when he received it, immediately called Dr. Kris. He was told that Marilyn had been suicidal and that this was the reason for her hospitalization. That was all he needed to hear to make the decision that his star student was exactly where she needed to be. Neither of the two Strasbergs would interfere with her doctor's orders.

On Thursday morning, once Marilyn at least acted as if she was calm, she was allowed to make one phone call. At a loss as to whom to call, she knew she would have to contact someone who would move heaven and earth to get her out of that place. Who was the most obstinate man she knew? Who would not take no for an answer? The answer was clear to her: Joe DiMaggio. Their marriage hadn't ended well, that was true. However, based on the kind of man he was and the way he reacted when faced with defiance, she knew she would be able to count on him. So she placed the call to him in Florida.

His friend Stacy Edwards recalled, "I believe Joe was in Florida because he used to coach the Yankees down there during training. He told me, he's sitting in his motel room having a cold beer and watching TV when the phone rings. It's Marilyn, sobbing that she's in a nut house in New York and she needs him to get her out of there. He thought it was a joke. He said she was making no sense, at all, and he thought, surely, it was a prank, or she was high on pills and delusional. But then, after he calmed her down, she told him the whole story. She needed him. How she ever tracked him down in a fleabag motel in Fort Lauderdale, I'll never know, but she needed him. That was all he needed to hear. He jumped on the next plane."

Joe DiMaggio showed up at Payne Whitney that very night and demanded that Marilyn Monroe be released in his custody the next morning. He said that he didn't care who had to authorize the matter, he just expected it to be done. He was told that only Dr. Kris would be able to obtain her patient's release. "I don't care who does it," Joe said brusquely, "but if someone doesn't get her released from this place, I swear to Christ, I'll take this hospital apart brick by brick." He was then put on the phone with Dr. Kris, who had locked away her patient four days earlier and hadn't come by to say hello or ask how it was going. The doctor said that if Marilyn was unhappy at the facility, perhaps she would feel more comfortable in another hospital. Joe would later say that he couldn't believe his ears, or as he told Stacy Edwards, "I got to thinking the doctor was the one who shoulda been locked up. She was acting like Marilyn had her choice of resorts. To get what I wanted from her, I said, yeah, fine, we'll do that. But let's just get her out of here, first. Please." The release was hastily arranged for the following day.

"How Dare You Betray Me!"

*E*arly Friday afternoon, February 10, Ralph Roberts, Marilyn's good friend and masseur, picked her up from a back entrance of Payne Whitney and then secreted her away, with Dr. Kris in the backseat. In the car on the way back to Marilyn's apartment, she let Dr. Kris have it. "How dare you betray me!" she shouted at her. "I trusted you. How could you do that to me? And you didn't even visit me? *What is wrong with you?*" Roberts recalled, "Marilyn was screaming at the doctor as only she could. She was like a hurricane unleashed. I don't think Dr. Kris had ever seen her like that, and she was frightened and very shaken by the violence of Marilyn's response.

"We dropped Marilyn off, and I wound up driving the doctor home. There was a lot of traffic, so we inched down the West Side Highway overlooking the river, and Dr. Kris was trembling and kept repeating over and over, 'I did a terrible thing, a terrible, terrible thing. Oh God, I didn't mean to, but I did.'"

Some people question Roberts's recollection of Marilyn's release. As a close friend of Marilyn's, he may have had a vested interest in portraying the psychiatrist as remorseful. He may have known that Marilyn would have wanted this short bit of her history minimized. If Dr. Kris admitted to doing something terrible, then perhaps Roberts could believe Marilyn had been of sound mind the entire time and shouldn't have been hospitalized at all. In any case, this is how Roberts recollected it, and therefore many people have chosen to view the Payne Whitney chapter in Marilyn's life as just a tremendous mix-up, or a misdiagnosis from an incompetent doctor.

"Once Joe got Marilyn situated in her apartment, he realized that perhaps Marilyn's shrink may have had the right idea—just the wrong way of going about it," said Stacy Edwards. "Marilyn wasn't well. She was crying and disoriented. Without her pills for those few days, her entire system was out of whack. He also could not believe how thin she'd gotten. After calming her down, he convinced her to allow him to take her to another hospital, Columbia University–Presbyterian. She said she would go but he had to promise her that he would not leave town and would come to visit her every day she was in there. He agreed to that."

At about five 'o clock that afternoon, Marilyn was admitted to the Neurological Institute of the Columbia University–Presbyterian Hospital, where she would remain for more than three weeks, until March 5. The first thing she did, once settled into her new hospital room, was to contact her attorney, Aaron Frosch. She demanded that he draft a document that would prevent any one person from ever having the power to commit her again without first consulting Joe DiMaggio.

When she was finally released from the second hospital, Marilyn was descended upon by such an excited mob of reporters and photographers that the scene became riotous. What was perhaps the most revealing element of such chaos, though, was how much she seemed to relish it. Except for a few occasions in the past, such as when she announced her divorce from Joe, Marilyn generally lit up whenever the media was present. She loved the public's rapt attention, even if her private life was falling apart. Moreover, she knew what her job as a movie star entailed, which was to look and act like Marilyn Monroe, even when she didn't much feel like her. No matter the present travail, she usually managed to play the part. In fact, by this time—1961—it had become second nature to her.

When she got home, though, Marilyn was in for a shock. First of all, she got a telephone call from Doc Goddard, Grace's husband. She hadn't heard from the man in many years. In fact, she couldn't remember the last time she had talked to him. After exchanging a few pleasantries, he said that he was tired of reading in the press that it had been Grace's idea that Marilyn marry James Dougherty. He was going to write a book, he said, tell the truth—which, he said, was that Marilyn had been the aggressor in that relationship, and in fact had asked Grace's help in convincing Dougherty to marry her. He was tired, he said, of being blamed for that first marriage since it was due to his job transfer that the Goddards had to leave Norma Jeane behind. Marilyn truly didn't know what his angle was, but she didn't like it. She told him that if he wrote a book about her, she would sue him. She also told him that Grace would be very disappointed to hear that he was planning such a venture. The conversation ended in an unpleasant way with Marilyn hanging up on him.

Gladys's Sheets, Soaked with Blood

The very week that Marilyn Monroe was suffering through her experiences at Payne Whitney in New York, her mother was having similar problems in the Rock Haven Sanitarium in California.

Gladys Baker Eley, who was now sixty, had by this time been officially diagnosed as paranoid schizophrenic. It had been clear for many years that this was the case with her. She was extremely unhappy at Rock Haven; indeed she had never been happy at any sanitarium over the years. No one at Rock Haven seemed to believe in or understand Christian Science, which was something Gladys simply could not accept. She was as devout about the religion as ever, sending pamphlets and brochures about it to everyone she knew on a weekly basis, including her daughters, Marilyn and Berniece. Now, with her mental illness affecting her intensely, she'd become firmly convinced that the doctors at Rock Haven had been poisoning her food. She wrote to her daughters that she needed to be released very soon or, as she noted to Berniece, "I will most certainly die in here from all of the poison." She also believed she was being sprayed with insecticides while she slept. Moreover, because of her faith, she steadfastly refused to take medications that had been prescribed to control her schizophrenia. Therefore, there was no relief for her; her mental state worsened with each passing day.

One evening during the time that Marilyn was in Payne Whitney, Gladys saw a news account of her daughter's apparent mental breakdown on the television that was watched by the patients at the sanitarium. Apparently upset by what she had seen, she retired to her room. When nurses went to check on her a couple of hours later, her bedsheets were soaked with blood. Gladys was unconscious. Apparently, she had slit her left wrist with a razor blade—where she got it would always remain a mystery. However, instead of slicing her wrist horizontally, which would cause the most blood flow and thus result in a quick death, she cut it in the other direction. Therefore, the bleeding was slower and eventually led to her unconscious state. She was rushed to Huntington Hospital in Pasadena, where she spent three days. Berniece was called. However, she asked that the hospital not contact Marilyn because she felt her half sister already had enough to worry about. Berniece didn't want to burden her.

Rose Anne Cooper, a nurse's aide at Rock Haven, recalls, "I personally tried to contact Marilyn Monroe to tell her what had happened. I somehow ended up talking to a man named John who said he was her manager. [Note: Likely this was John Springer, Marilyn's publicist.] He was very abrupt with me. 'Is she alive?' he wanted to know. I said she was. 'Fine,' he told me, 'then Miss Monroe doesn't need to know this news right now. She has enough problems.' He told me to call Inez Melson [Marilyn's business manager]. I did. She was worse. 'You are being paid handsomely to make sure Mrs. Eley does not hurt herself,' she said angrily. When I told her that we couldn't monitor her twenty-four hours a day, she asked, 'Why not? I would think you would be able to do that. If not, then why are we paying you?' It was all very unpleasant. Finally, I asked if she would please tell Marilyn that her mother had tried to commit suicide, and she said, 'I most certainly will do no such thing. I am not going to upset her with this news.' She told me that it was incumbent upon me to keep very secret anything having to do with Gladys being in Marilyn's life. She said, 'This is a secret we have been trying to keep for years, and we expect you to act with great discretion where this is concerned because the studio will otherwise be very upset with the sanitarium.' I didn't know what she meant by that and before I had a chance to ask, she hung up. Eventually, I tracked down Gladys's other daughter, Berniece. She was a lot more sympathetic, but even she said she was not going to give Marilyn the news. 'I don't think she could handle it right now,' she told me. Then she told me to contact Fox's publicity department. That made no sense to me. If I was supposed to keep this a secret, why would I call the studio's publicity department? It felt like no one knew what they were doing . . . so I dropped it."

When Gladys was finally returned to the sanitarium, she remained heavily sedated for many weeks, never leaving her room. Much later, when she was no longer sedated, she was taken on an outing. Rose Anne Cooper recalled, "A group of women—including Gladys—had been authorized to leave the premises with two nurses as chaperones in order that they may shop for some personal items at a local drugstore. At one point, a nurse realized that Gladys was missing."

A frantic search commenced to find Gladys. Luckily, a half hour later, they found her sitting at a bus stop. Gladys explained that she was headed to Kentucky. "I need to find my children," she said. "My husband has kidnapped my children."

Returning to the Safety of Sinatra

*I*n the months following her release from the hospital, Marilyn Monroe reconciled with the man she now considered a savior, Joe DiMaggio. Both decided, however, not to make their relationship official but rather to keep it informal and without strings. Over the years, it has been reported in biographies that the two planned to wed again. It simply isn't true. In fact, a major obstacle between them was that Marilyn was interested in reviving her career at this time, and Joe was still steadfastly against her having one. No one in Marilyn's life at the time felt she was going to revisit that problem with him. It would only be many years after the fact that certain people who didn't know her well began to speculate that she would have remarried DiMaggio. As we will later see, she even began to date Frank Sinatra again during this time, so clearly she wasn't thinking of marrying Joe. Moreover, none of the baseball great's friends or associates interviewed for this book felt that he was interested in another marriage to her, either. However, that said, he had definitely changed in certain ways. Whereas in their marriage he was cold and distant and even abusive, now he was caring and loving and seemed to want to do whatever he could to make her happy. He told her that if he had been her a few years back, he would have divorced him, too. Moreover, he said that it was because of a psychotherapist that Marilyn had recommended that he was able to become a better and more well-adjusted person. Still, at times he could be alarmingly possessive and—as in old times—jealous of the attention she received everywhere they went together. Also, he was still quite invasive of her privacy. For instance, according to Berniece Miracle, he would go through her trash, looking for receipts to see just how much she had paid for certain items. Always the penny-pincher, if he thought the amount was too high, he would angrily confront her about it, receipt in hand. Inevitably, Marilyn would snatch the paper from his hand and tell him to mind his own business. "How dare you go through my trash!" she'd say, very upset. This exchange usually ended in a loud argument. Marilyn tried her best to ignore such moments, but it was difficult for her.

In March 1961, the couple took a relaxing vacation to a secluded resort in Redington Beach, Florida. Marilyn certainly needed the break. Just before they left, she became very upset about an article that was published that quoted Kay Gable (wrongly, as it would happen) saying that she believed Marilyn was responsible for her husband's death. "John [Springer, Marilyn's publicist] told me, 'Do not send this to Marilyn, whatever you do. If she sees this, I don't know what she'll do,'" said Diane Stevens. "'So, just send it over to Aaron [Frosch, her lawyer.]' That's what I did. Then, somehow or another, Marilyn saw the clipping. I think she was in Aaron's office and it was on his desk. She became unglued over it. 'How dare you keep this from me!' she asked me on the phone. 'I need to know what is going on. I'm the only one who doesn't know what the hell is going on! You tell John that I am very, very angry about this. I should fire him over this.' I tried to explain that we were just concerned about her, but she didn't want to hear it. 'God damn it,' she said. 'Everyone is so concerned about poor, screwed up Marilyn. Poor, poor Marilyn is going cuckoo and can't handle her own press. I don't want to hear it. *I just don't want to hear another word about it.*' Then she slammed the phone down. By that time, I was shaking. I told John and he called her right away. Then she let him have it. It was clear that she was very much on edge and not well at all."

Shortly after, Marilyn received a letter from Kay Gable. It was clear that Gable did not blame Marilyn for her husband's death. In the letter, dated April 11, 1961, she wrote, "I miss Clark each day more, I'll never get over this great loss, but God has blessed me with my three great children and precious memories. . . . Went to confession after 24 years (hope the priest did not call the cops), seriously, you do not know how much this has helped me." Marilyn would soon visit Kay as well; there were certainly not hard feelings from Kay, though that didn't seem to assuage Marilyn's own sense of guilt.

At the end of April, Marilyn decided to take another apartment in Los Angeles. It was then that she learned the news that her friend Pat Kennedy Lawford was pregnant with her fourth child. "I remember Pat saying, 'I don't even know how to tell Marilyn this news, considering what's going on in her life. I'm afraid it'll make her even sadder,'" said a relative of Pat's. "'I already have three kids. She just wants one.' Of course, she had no choice but to tell her when Marilyn was back in Los Angeles. By that time she was about six months pregnant. She told me later that when Marilyn laid eyes on her, she jumped into the air with excitement. Then she wrapped her arms around Pat and started to cry, she was so happy. It added another dimension, I think, to Pat's friendship with Marilyn when she realized that Marilyn was able to put aside her own sadness, at least in the moment, and share in Pat's joy. She told me, 'I think she's a wonderful woman and would make such a great mother. I pray every night that she has a child soon. I know it would change her life if she had someone else to be worried about.'"

During this time, as mentioned earlier, Marilyn rekindled her romance with Frank Sinatra. It's not known how Joe DiMaggio felt about Marilyn and Frank, or even if it mattered. Clearly, Joe and Marilyn had an understanding about their relationship as it stood at this time, because Marilyn would likely not have been dating

Frank if Joe had strenuously objected to it. For his part, though he was dating Juliet Prowse at the time, Frank was still attracted to Marilyn and, according to those who knew them well, couldn't resist her. "He was in love with her, no doubt about it," said Milt Ebbins, who was a good friend of Sinatra's and also vice president of Peter Lawford's production company, Chrislaw.

"By 1961, though, his feeling about her was more protective than passionate. I remember that there was an incident involving President Kennedy, who was new in office at the time. Peter and I arranged a luncheon for Kennedy, and Frank was invited. We had a special chef flown in from New York to cook fettuccine Alfredo, veal picatta, and a salad and ice cream at the end. Sinatra's secretary called at the last minute and said he couldn't make it, that he had a cold. I was astonished. This is JFK. He can't stand up JFK. I knew Frank loved that guy, had campaigned for him, organized his inaugural entertainment, so it seemed strange. I found out later that what happened was that Marilyn was staying with him for the weekend and had left the house without telling him where she was going. He was frantic with worry. So he spent the day driving around trying to find her, and he did. She was out shopping. So that shows you how much he cared about her, if he was willing to miss a luncheon with the president so that he could figure out what the hell happened to Marilyn."

Rupert Allan confirmed, "I always thought of Frank and Marilyn as star-crossed lovers. In a different time and place, they would have been together. He loved her a lot. However, by 1961, she was in so much turmoil, I think he was annoyed with her a lot of the time. He just thought she should have worked harder to pull it together so, yes, sometimes she pissed him off. Also, Sinatra certainly didn't want to be involved with anyone who would be considered weak or vulnerable."

Indeed, women like Marilyn were usually too much trouble for him. He liked his "dames" to have more inner strength and self-reliance, like Ava Gardner and his mother, Dolly Sinatra, both of whom represented his ideal of the total woman. He often didn't have the patience necessary to deal with someone as conflicted as Marilyn. Just recently released from a mental hospital, Marilyn was not on sure footing when she was with Sinatra, and he wasn't exactly tolerant with her. For instance, at one gathering at his home, Marilyn began to become emotional, was sharing sad childhood stories to guests. She seemed on the verge of an intense crying jag, only to be cut off by Frank. "Look, Norma Jeane," he said, "we don't want to hear it. Toughen up, baby, or get the hell out. I ain't no babysitter." She got up and bolted to her bedroom.

Some people in Sinatra's circle thought that the only reason he was with her was because he felt sorry for her. "If Marilyn Monroe wanted sex, and she did constantly to make herself feel desirable, Mr. S. would play Sir Galahad and rise to the occasion," said his longtime valet, George Jacobs. "He would rarely turn a good friend down. It fit in with his padrone self-image to give rather than receive. [However,] Mr. S. had a ton of misgivings about Marilyn. She was a total mess."

People who were in his circle back then still talk about what happened on June 7, 1961—six days after her thirty-fifth birthday—when Frank invited Marilyn to Las Vegas. He was appearing at the Sands and was also planning a party for Dean Martin's forty-fourth birthday that day. From the Sands interdepartmental correspondence between Jack Entratter, president; Al Guzman, publicity director; and Al Freeman, advertising and promotional director, we can glean that there was a great deal of preparation for the Dean Martin party, some of it concerning Monroe and Sinatra.

One memo, from Entratter to Guzman and Freeman, dated June 6, 1961, states, "Please be advised that under no circumstances is any backstage photographer permitted to photograph Mr. Sinatra and Miss Marilyn Monroe together at the cocktail reception to follow the performance on 7 June. Any photographer who attempts to do so will be permanently barred from the hotel. Be advised that this is not only a Sands requirement, it is a requirement of Mr. Sinatra's and, as such, will be absolutely enforced. Thank you."

Another memo, from Entratter to "All Concerned," also dated June 6, 1961, states, "Marilyn Monroe will be Mr. Sinatra's guest. It is Mr. Frank Sinatra's intention that Miss Monroe be accorded the utmost privacy during her brief stay here at the Sands. She will be registered in Mr. Sinatra's suite. Under no circumstances is she or Mr. Sinatra to be disturbed by telephone calls or visitors before 2 p.m."

Marilyn's friend Pat Kennedy Lawford brought her sister, Jean Smith, to Vegas for the opening night. It's not known whether Pat was aware of what was going on between Marilyn and Frank. Pat and Jean spent the day with Marilyn, getting facials and manicures while gossiping, so perhaps Marilyn mentioned it. "Pat told me she was most concerned about Marilyn," says Pat Brennan. "She said she was already pouring herself glasses of champagne by noon. Pat was a drinker, too, but at least she waited until cocktail hour. In Vegas, though, Pat wasn't drinking at all because she was eight months pregnant. 'When you're not drinking,' she told me, 'you see what everyone else is like when they're loaded, and it's not pretty.'" According to what Kennedy Lawford relayed to Brennan, she pulled Marilyn aside and told her that she believed her drinking was getting out of hand. "Marilyn, as your friend, I think you should know that when you're drunk you're not very becoming." At first, Marilyn was insulted. But after a few moments, she seemed to realize that Pat was right. "It's the only way I can keep the voices in my head from getting too loud," she told her. Pat's reaction to that startling admission is not known, but likely she was concerned. However, it didn't stop her and Marilyn's good time.

Pat had her two-and-a-half-year-old daughter Victoria with her in Las Vegas. Her other two children were to arrive the next day. She was having them carted by stretch limousine from California to Nevada. That day after their beauty treatments, Marilyn and Pat took Victoria gambling. Of course, children weren't allowed in the casino, but overlooking this rule was the least of the perks afforded the Kennedys whenever they were in Vegas. To Marilyn's fascination, Pat sat the little girl right on top of the blackjack table and said, "Okay, here's the deal. If I lose, I'm leaving this kid right here. But if I win, I'll take her as my prize." She sat down and played a hand, with Marilyn standing directly behind her. When she lost, she said, "Okay, that's it. You get the kid." And she rose and walked away. "But Pat . . . *Pat!*" Marilyn shouted after her, very alarmed. Of course, Pat turned around and retrieved her daughter. "She loved doing things like that just to get a reaction from Marilyn," said Pat Brennan. "She liked to keep it light and easy when she was with Marilyn because she knew Marilyn had so much sadness in her life."

Also present for Sinatra's Las Vegas opening that evening were Elizabeth Taylor and her husband Eddie Fisher, as well as, of course, the birthday boy Dean and Jeanne Martin, with whom Monroe sat. "What can I say about Marilyn that night?" Eddie Fisher remarked. "We all knew that she was having a thing with Sinatra, so it was definitely hands off. But she was so drunk that night, I can tell you that she was an embarrassment to him. It wasn't good."

"She was beautiful, a vision with a great smile, lots of teased blonde hair, and a dress that was so low-cut you couldn't take your eyes off her bosom," said a Las Vegas photojournalist who, along with a photographer for Wide World Photos, was one of the few reporters granted access to the opening-night party in Sinatra's suite. "From a distance, it was wow, she's a knockout. But up close it was . . . oh, no, she's knocked out! She didn't look well, and she also acted very strangely. She seemed a little crazy to me.

"At the party, I remember her whining, 'Oh, Frankie, c'mon, let's make out for the photographers. I love you, Frankie. I want the whole world to know.' I remember that she was standing behind him and had her hands around his waist, almost as if she was leaning on him for support."

According to the journalist, when Frank pulled away rather than be photographed with her, Marilyn almost lost her balance. After giving her a concerned look, he told one of his bodyguards, "Keep an eye on her. I don't like the way she's wobblin'. Let me know if she faints, or something."

The reporter continued, "Marilyn still wanted a picture taken with Frank. She sidled over to him like a kitten and motioned my photographer with her index finger, indicating that he should take the shot while Sinatra wasn't looking. She was being very playful and coy.

"Just as my photographer was about to take the picture, Frank's bodyguard grabbed the camera. He gave it to Frank and whispered something in his ear. Then Frank walked to where we were standing and hissed, 'Next time you try that, I'll crack your skull open with this goddamn camera, the both of ya.' I remember that he talked out of the corner of his mouth, like a gangster.

"At that moment, Marilyn came over and, with wild eyes, said, 'Frankie, I'm gonna throw up.' He looked alarmed and said, 'When?' and she said, 'Now. Right now. I mean it, Frankie. *I'm gonna throw up.*' He said, 'Oh, Jesus Christ, Marilyn, not again.' And he got her out of there, quick."

Elizabeth Taylor, who happened to be standing right next to the reporter, observed the entire scene. Afterward, she turned to the photojournalist and said, "Marilyn shouldn't drink if she can't hold her liquor. Now, me," she added, sounding confident, "*I* know how to hold my liquor." With that, Elizabeth flashed her famous violet eyes and threw back a martini. However, when she saw that the reporter had written her comment on his notepad, she grabbed the pad out of his hand, smacked him playfully on the back of the head with it, and said, "Now, *that* was strictly off the record, buster."

A Reunion with Berniece

At the end of June 1961, Marilyn was diagnosed with gallstones and an inflamed gallbladder. There seemed no end to the physical and emotional crises she was facing at this time. The operation on

June 29 was successful. Joe DiMaggio was at her bedside when she awakened, looking down at her with devotion. It was decided that her half sister, Berniece, would come to New York and be present for Marilyn's recovery. Joe wasn't particularly happy about it, though. Marilyn would later learn that he was very suspicious of Berniece and her husband. "What if they want money from you?" he asked Marilyn. "I think that's what's going on here." His suspicion was shared by Marilyn's secretary, May Reis, who was now back on the job with Marilyn. Marilyn couldn't believe Joe would think such a thing about Berniece. "I've known her a lot longer than you," she told him angrily. "And besides, if she did want my money, she can have it. What am I going to do with it when I'm gone?"

Despite Joe's ambivalence about Berniece, Marilyn seemed almost desperate to reconnect with her after her gallbladder operation. Therefore, as soon as Marilyn was released from the hospital, Berniece flew to New York from Florida and checked into the Park Sheraton Hotel, where she was to await a phone call from May. When told the coast was clear of reporters, Berniece was to take a cab to Marilyn's apartment on East 57th Street. Berniece's husband had been against the visit. He was always very strange when it came to the subject of Marilyn. He wanted to be around her as much as possible—thus his recent trip to see her behind his wife's back—but didn't seem to want Berniece to have time with her. For his part, Joe was also unhappy about the sisterly plans—for his own reasons, having to do with Marilyn's money, but also because he was afraid that Berniece might go to the press with details about his and Marilyn's life together. Berniece knew better, of course. Still, it had to bother her that, after all of this time, Marilyn kept reminding her not to talk to the press. It didn't escape Berniece that Marilyn still concluded every telephone conversation with that very warning.

When Berniece arrived at Marilyn's thirteenth-floor apartment, she was greeted by May Reis. May could not have been more chilly. However, it would seem that Berniece took her aloof attitude to be professional rather than rude. When Marilyn appeared, the reunion was noisy and exciting. "I can't believe you're finally here," Marilyn squealed. "Finally! We're together again!" After embracing, they stood back and took a long look at each other. They'd known each other since they were young women. Now Marilyn was thirty-five and Berniece forty-one. However, both agreed that they'd only gotten better with age, even though Marilyn was clearly weak from the surgery and not at all well. She was wearing a cream-colored summer dress and high-heeled sandals. She'd had her hair styled before leaving the hospital because she knew she'd be photographed on her way out and wanted to look her best. So when she saw her half sister, she looked very put together.

Marilyn's life was anything but ordinary, and Berniece must have gleaned as much when she learned that the first order of business every day for Marilyn's maid, Lena Pepitone, was to hand wash the beige lace bra Marilyn had worn the previous day. When recalling this visit, Pepitone had an interesting observation about Berniece— whom she described as being "blonde, even blonder naturally than Marilyn . . . slightly shorter and thinner, yet her figure was definitely on the voluptuous side":

"In a way, Berniece seemed far shyer than Marilyn, who was now in an outgoing phase. All the hustle and glitter of Manhattan seemed to scare Berniece. She seemed in a daze, caused by New York as well as Marilyn. . . . Yet the way Marilyn sat at attention holding Berniece's hand and listening to every detail about where Berniece shopped in Florida, what she cooked, how she ran her home, and raised her sons [Note: Berniece did not have sons, just a daughter] made me think that Marilyn could easily be tempted to trade in all her fame and become a housewife, too."

After just a few days with her, Berniece was concerned about all of the drugs Marilyn was taking. People who were around her all the time had grown accustomed to the constant pill-taking, which usually resulted in unsure footing about an hour or so later. She was never quite coherent. She always seemed a little . . . off. Marilyn's friends and daily associates were used to this troubling demeanor, but newcomers were always stunned by it.

Every night, Marilyn's doctor would come by the house to check on her. This, too, was odd. Every night? Was that really necessary? During each visit, Marilyn would fix him a stiff drink, which he enjoyed—again, odd. Then he would begin to dispense all sorts of pills to Marilyn in what could only be considered "generous" quantities. Sometimes he would give her an injection of who-knows-what, but she definitely enjoyed its effect on her. Berniece seized the opportunity, while the doctor was present, to ask him about the pills. "Truly, does she need all of these sleeping pills?" Berniece asked him. "This is extreme, don't you think?" The doctor didn't have time to answer before Marilyn glanced at her sharply. "Yes, I *do* need these pills," she said, her temper quickly rising. "*I need my sleep.* So, the answer is *yes*, Berniece. That's the answer. *Yes.*" There was an awkward silence. After a moment, the doctor continued with his offering of different pharmaceuticals without missing a beat.

Berniece also took note of Marilyn's relationship with Joe DiMaggio. He was clearly still in love with her. However, Marilyn seemed unsure of her feelings for him. Perhaps the best indicator of how she felt was that she was planning a trip to California in less than a month and told Berniece that she was going to stay with Frank Sinatra. She made Berniece promise not to mention the trip to Joe. She intended to go, she said, and just not tell him. How she was going to manage that, considering that he was with her every single day, was a mystery to Berniece. According to Lena Pepitone, Sinatra would call Marilyn often and she would speak to him, not at all concerned that Joe might walk into the room at any moment. When it came to Sinatra, she was determined to do whatever she liked.

Also, Berniece couldn't help but notice how paranoid Marilyn had become. For instance, at one point in the visit, an Italian restaurant that had just opened in the neighborhood sent over a complimentary meal to Marilyn. Marilyn told Lena to throw the food away. She didn't even want it in the household. Berniece assumed that Marilyn didn't want the food because she was watching her weight, or maybe because she'd been told that she shouldn't eat spicy foods after her surgery. Either would have been an acceptable reason. However, Marilyn's reasoning was more troubling. "It could be poisoned," she told Berniece, very seriously. "I never eat anything that's been prepared by strangers."

Indeed, in about a month, when Marilyn was back in Los Angeles under the care of Dr. Greenson, he would write to a colleague that in her sessions with him she expressed a "feeling of mistreatment, which had paranoid undertones."

Other friends of Marilyn felt that her paranoia, especially about food, was out of control. "Once, during a late night at the office, we sent out for Chinese food," said Diane Stevens from John Springer's office. "Marilyn and Joe were there. When the food came, Marilyn refused to eat it. She and Joe got into a big fight about it. 'If it was poisoned, I'd be dead now because I just ate some,' Joe told her. 'So, what the hell is going on with you?' Marilyn looked at him very seriously and said, 'I'm the one they want to poison, Joe. Not you.' We all sat there with our mouths open, trying to figure out how to respond. 'But it's all the same food,' John finally said. Marilyn was not going to bend, though. 'Enjoy it. See if I care,' she said. 'But I'm not taking a chance.' It made me think of Gladys, I have to admit. I mean, that's the first thing that came to my mind—Gladys believing that the doctors in her mental hospital were poisoning her food."*

---

* Despite all of the confusion in her life, Marilyn always managed to be kind to her fans. Also, despite all of the upset in her life, she still managed to keep her sense of humor. Here's a good story: Back in 1960, the first-ever biography of Marilyn Monroe was published by Harcourt, Brace and Company, written by Maurice Zolotow. She wasn't happy with it—just on principle; she probably didn't read it. Her friend and longtime fan James Haspiel had Zolotow sign a copy of the book to him. Afterward, he wanted nothing more than to have Marilyn sign it as well. Therefore, when he felt the time was right—in June 1961—he asked her if she would do so. She frowned, then said she would sign it—and that it would be "the only copy of this book I will ever sign." She opened to the page Zolotow had signed. It said, "To Jim Haspiel—who could have written a better book on MM—Sincerely, Maurice Zolotow." Then she took a pen and scrawled right below it, "That's right! Marilyn Monroe xoxo."

Greenson's Diagnosis

$\mathscr{D}$r. Ralph Greenson is not a popular figure in Marilyn Monroe history. Born Romeo Samuel Greenschpoon in 1910 in Brooklyn, he was one of fraternal twins—his sister was named Juliet. He studied medicine in Switzerland before practicing as a psychiatrist and psychoanalyst in Los Angeles. He was the president of the Los Angeles Psychoanalytic Society and Institute (LAPSI) from 1951 to 1953 and dean of education from 1957 to 1961. He was also clinical professor of psychiatry at the UCLA Medical School. In his paper "Unfree Associations: Inside Psychoanalytical Institutes," Douglas Kirsner writes of Greenson:

"The author of a classic clinical textbook, *The Technique and Practice of Psychoanalysis* (1967), and over sixty papers and articles, Dr. Greenson was unusual in moving outside the ambit of his analytic colleagues to give many public lectures. His psychoanalytic interests were wide-ranging. He was most concerned that analysts with different theoretical approaches seemed to talk at each other. . . . Upon graduating as an analyst, Greenson quickly became a major influence in the Los Angeles psychoanalytic scene. He soon became an important figure nationally and later internationally . . . he wielded a good deal of power and influence within LAPSI. [Greenson] was nationally and internationally well known not only for his numerous psychoanalytic writings but also for his real flair for lecturing and teaching. His institute seminars were especially highly regarded at LAPSI. Hilda Rollman-Branch [a director of LAPSI] felt that although Greenson was 'a character' and 'narcissistic,' his tactlessness could be forgiven because of 'his enthusiasm and inspiration. He was without a doubt the best teacher of psychoanalysis any of us have ever had.' Greenson was a passionate man with strongly held views. Three analysts each reported to me that after a disagreement Greenson did not speak to them for years. He was given to irrational fits of anger. Elisabeth

Young-Bruehl, Anna Freud's biographer, aptly described Greenson as 'a hard-living man of passionate enthusiasm and even flamboyance, a man for whom psychoanalysis was . . . a way of life.'"

Despite his credentials and reputation, Dr. Ralph Greenson has been much maligned in books about Marilyn over the years, and for many reasons, some of which are valid. Most of Marilyn's friends and associates agree that Dr. Greenson exerted far too much control over her life and career. As these people began to give interviews for biographies of the star, Greenson's reputation as a psychological Svengali became set in stone. He has practically been blamed for his patient's mental disturbances, as if there was no chance she might have been genetically predisposed to such problems.

What has not been clearly stated in the past is that Dr. Ralph Greenson had very specific opinions about Marilyn's mental problems. At first, he had described her in a letter to Anna Freud as a "borderline paranoid addictive personality." He wrote in his letter that Marilyn exhibited "classic signs of the paranoid addict," including a fear of abandonment and also a tendency to rely on others too heavily (Natasha Lytess and Paula Strasberg) to the point where she refuses to allow these people to live their own lives. Also, those suffering from this disease are prone to wanting to commit suicide. It was very difficult to treat such problems in patients, let alone someone as famous as Marilyn. He also said he was working behind the scenes to get her off of some of the drugs she was taking, but that it was an uphill battle. "Short of searching her person every day, it is impossible to know what she is taking and when," he wrote in a different letter to Freud. "I'm not sure how to monitor someone like her. She's very crafty." Indeed, when a person would turn his back, she would pop a pill just that fast.

Dr. Hyman Engelberg added to Greenson's diagnosis in an interview in 1996. He stated that he and Greenson had also diagnosed Marilyn as having been manic-depressive. "It is now known as bipolar personality," he said, "but I think manic depressive is much more descriptive. Yes, she was definitely manic depressive. That's just one of the many things we were up against."

Apparently, there was more. After Dr. Greenson began to treat Marilyn more intensively, he started telling colleagues that she'd begun to exhibit strong and growing signs of borderline paranoid schizophrenia, just like her mother and, possibly, her grandmother before her. Three psychiatrists interviewed for this book, who requested anonymity since all are still treating patients in Los Angeles, say that when they were younger and studying in the city Greenson shared with them (on separate occasions) his concern about borderline paranoid schizophrenia in the case of Marilyn Monroe. "He was very specific," said one of the doctors. "He was concerned, very much so. He felt it would get worse as she got older unless it was treated in a specific way. He also said that Marilyn knew and that she was looking into ways to treat it herself, and that he was trying to discourage that. He didn't want her out there medicating herself, but he suspected that this is what was going on behind his back."

It's not known if Dr. Greenson shared his views of her different problems with Marilyn. In notes regarding her case, he is specific about being careful to give her information "only in small portions." He wrote that, in his view, telling her "too much, too soon" could only lead to "other more significant problems."

What also comes from fresh research for this book is Marilyn's determination to get the drug Thorazine, which was used to treat paranoid schizophrenia. "Dr. Greenson had prescribed it to her," said one of the psychiatrists. "I know for a fact that he did because he told me that he had. However, he wasn't sure he liked her reaction to it. For some reason, he changed his mind about Thorazine. He said, however, that she wanted more than he wanted to give her and that he was afraid she was going about the business of getting it from other doctors. A major frustration for him was that he knew he was not the only one giving her drugs. She was such an expert doctor shopper toward the last couple years of her life, there was no way to be sure what she was taking, what she was mixing."

According to what Dr. Greenson would later remember in his papers stored at UCLA, he had insisted that Marilyn "get rid of her unhealthy connection to the past." Her half sister, Berniece, her business manager, Inez Melson, and many others were convinced that therapy—not her mental state—was ruining Marilyn Monroe. In a letter to Greenson, Melson wrote that she was concerned about Marilyn spending "too much time thinking about her problems." She added that she didn't see how it was doing Marilyn any good and, in fact, "I think quite the contrary. It is not my place to tell you how to treat your patient," she wrote, "but, truly, I am concerned that she is languishing in her misery."

Part of Marilyn Monroe's sickness had to do with her paranoia. However, complicating things was that, in many ways, she had actually good reason to be paranoid. As we've seen, she *was* being followed and she was well aware of it. Consider this story, from Diana Herbert, daughter of the man who wrote *Scudda-Hoo! Scudda-Hay!* She and Marilyn stayed in touch over the years, and she encountered Marilyn in New York during this period. "I was coming up out of the subway and there she was," recalled Herbert. "Dressed very casually, she was stunning, in a coral beige ensemble. She looked a little lost, but she perked up when she recognized it was me. We went to a little health food sidewalk cafe in Midtown. She spoke about how much she loved New York and the Actors Studio, but she told me something bizarre. She said, 'I'm so uncomfortable here in New York because I am being followed.' I said, 'Well, Marilyn, that's because you are a star, you are beautiful, of course people are following you.' She said, 'No, that's not it.' Her voice became lower, whispering, 'I'm being followed by the FBI.' I thought, 'Well, she's totally flipping out!' Marilyn said, 'I'm being followed because of my connections with the Communist Party.' She told me she was very proud of herself because she became adept at losing the FBI agents. She said she started figuring out how to evade them when she became a movie actress and learned how to 'become invisible.'"

While the FBI's episodes of surveying Monroe did happen, there were also times when she was not under their watch yet still concerned about a plot to know her every move—and at times, she believed, her every *thought*. Maureen Stapleton was a contemporary of Marilyn's at the Actors Studio. In an interview in 1995,

Stapleton recalled that while she was dining with Monroe one evening, an odd thing happened. "[Marilyn] thought the waiter was reading her mind. At first, she said he was a secret agent or something, she said, 'He's one of the bad guys,' and then she said, 'He knows what I'm thinking now, we have to leave.' Now, you have to keep in mind we were *all* [New York actors] a little loopy back then—but that was particularly strange."

Others in Marilyn Monroe's life at the time were more categorical. "I think Marilyn was a very sick woman, a classic schizophrenic," said Johnny Strasberg, son of Lee and Paula. "She was dedicated to love. It's a thing schizophrenics talk about, love. They'll do anything for love and, additionally, they are totally infantile; they have no ego, no boundaries, as the rest of us have. The amazing thing about her is that she survived as long as she did. There was enough capacity for life that had she been lucky enough to find a therapist who could treat her problems, she might have . . . That's the tragedy. People loved her. But nobody could say no to her. No one would or could take responsibility for her. They had to cut her off or abandon her, which is the thing she expected. With Marilyn, you're dealing with an abandoned infant who's not an infant anymore."

A Second Opinion

*F*resh research now establishes that Dr. Ralph Greenson was not alone in his belief that Marilyn Monroe was probably suffering from borderline paranoid schizophrenia. Rather than work in a vacuum, Dr. Greenson obtained a second opinion by consulting psychologist Dr. Milton Wexler.

Born in San Francisco in 1908, Dr. Wexler trained as a lawyer before switching to psychology. After taking a doctorate at Columbia University, studying under Theodor Reik, a disciple of Freud, he became one of the country's first nonphysicians to set up in practice as a psychoanalyst. Also a member of the Los Angeles Psychoanalytic Society, Dr. Wexler would go on to become a pioneer in the study and treatment of Huntington's disease, forming the Hereditary Disease Foundation. Wexler also felt strongly that Marilyn Monroe suffered at least from borderline paranoid schizophrenia after sitting in on three sessions with her in Dr. Greenson's home. "Yes, I treated her," he said in 1999. "I won't discuss that treatment but will say that I agreed with Dr. Greenson that she presented borderline symptoms of the disease that had run in her family. I found her to be very proactive in wanting to treat those borderline symptoms, as well. One misconception about her treatment is that it was Dr. Greenson's idea that she move in with his family. She never moved in with the Greensons. Instead, it was my suggestion that she spend as much time there as possible in order to create the environment that she lacked as a child. That was my theory at the time and Dr. Greenson agreed. Also, I felt it would alleviate her separation anxiety if she knew she had a place to return to."

All of these many years later, to ignore the findings of these two doctors or act as if those findings did not exist makes no sense. It's certainly not what Marilyn Monroe did over the years. In the year and a half after Greenson's and Wexler's diagnosis, Marilyn did everything she could to perform beyond her illness. She always had. She'd always soldiered on, even knowing that something wasn't quite right with her.

Dr. Greenson's different opinions of what Marilyn was dealing with in her life have been, it would seem, purposely overlooked in Marilyn Monroe history for many years. Some biographers have written that his findings were egregiously misguided and couldn't possibly have been true. As one put it, "[Greenson] even spread lies about his patient to the professional community, including the unsubstantiated report that she was borderline paranoid schizophrenic." It would seem, though, that if a psychiatrist treats a patient—in Monroe's case, just about every day of the week—and comes to a conclusion about that person's state of mind, it is not an "unsubstantiated report." It's a diagnosis.

Unfortunately, Dr. Greenson would become so zealous in his treatment of Marilyn, and thus so overbearing in her life, that he would lose credibility, especially with the passing of the years. Historically, he seems like a quack because he invited Marilyn into his home, had her sleep over, integrated her into his family. It was felt that he had lost all perspective where Marilyn was concerned. However, in the 1950s and 1960s, all sorts of vanguard treatments for mental illness were being tested. In fact, in Greenson's opinion, welcoming Marilyn into his home was the only alternative to putting her in a mental hospital. In his notes about the case, he is specific that he was trying to figure out any way he could to keep her from being "committed once again, for I know she will not survive it a second time." Douglas Kirsner confirms, "Greenson decided to offer his family as a substitute for the family Monroe never had because she would have killed herself sooner if he had committed her to a mental hospital."

Marilyn's Drugs of Choice

By late August of 1961, Marilyn Monroe was back in Los Angeles permanently and living in her apartment on Doheny and Cynthia in West Hollywood. There was also word that she would be making a new film for Fox called *Something's Got to Give*. She wasn't thrilled with the script, felt it needed a lot of work, and wasn't even sure it could ever result in a decent movie. Still, she was contractually obligated to do one more film for Fox, and this would have to be it.

In September, Marilyn joined Frank Sinatra in entertaining guests on his yacht for a four-day cruise to Catalina Island. "They were definitely a couple," said one of the partygoers. "She was acting as if she was the hostess, not a guest. She seemed in good spirits, but definitely not quite right. I had heard that there'd been some trouble getting her there. Everyone knew she was not well, that she was under the care of doctors."

At this time, Marilyn's primary physician working with Dr. Greenson was Dr. Hyman Engelberg. However, Marilyn had become so adept at the art of "doctor shopping" that the two doctors were unable to keep track of the medications in her system. When she would demand confidentiality from another doctor, she would always get it because of her celebrity. She would then stock up on as much medication as she could from him before that doctor would refuse her any more. Then she would simply "shop" for a different doctor. Greenson and Engelberg did attempt to control Marilyn's doctor-shopping habit, though perhaps not in the best possible way. "The idea was that she was never to be said no to when she wanted a prescription," said Hildy Greenson, Dr. Ralph Greenson's wife, "because the only thing that would happen was she would procure medication elsewhere and not inform her primary physicians about it. So whenever she asked for a drug she would usually get it." That "idea" apparently did not work. The list of drugs she was taking by the end of 1961 was staggering.

After Greenson's and Wexler's diagnosis of Marilyn Monroe as suffering from BPS, she began taking the barbiturate Thorazine. At the time, Thorazine was a new drug, developed in the 1950s to treat the disease. When she would take it, however, she would gain weight, and therefore she didn't like it. As soon as she was off the medication, she would lose weight quickly. However, she would also lose her grip. Historically, whenever she looked her best—as in her last film, *Something's Got to Give*—it was because she was not on Thorazine. Certainly the problems she would later have on the set of that movie suggested that she was off her meds.

Marilyn was also taking the narcotic analgesic Demerol as well as the barbiturates phenobarbital HMC and Amytal, along with large quantities of Nembutal. Of course, she had been taking

Nembutal to sleep for many years, and truly it had become an addiction. Dr. Engelberg insists that the most he and Dr. Greenson gave her was twenty-four Nembutal at a time. However, Marilyn went through the drug like candy, so she must have been getting it elsewhere.

Marilyn was also taking Seconal, and no one knew where she got that drug from either. Moreover, she was taking chloral hydrate to sleep, and Dr. Engelberg emphatically states that he never prescribed it to her, nor did Dr. Greenson. In fact, Engelberg would say that he was amazed at the number of drugs found in her system when she died—including the aforementioned chloral hydrate, which he now presumes she bought when she was in Mexico just before her death. There were fifteen bottles of pills on Marilyn's night table when she died.

Though Engelberg consulted Greenson on all of the sleep medications he prescribed to Marilyn, he didn't on other drugs. If she got an infection, for instance, and needed an antibiotic, Engelberg would not pass it by Greenson for approval. Also, Marilyn very often received injections of vitamins to boost her resistance to colds and sinus infections—a recurring problem for her. Often she would receive such injections a few times a week. By the end of 1961, though, Marilyn had developed the alarming habit of giving herself injections. Many people witnessed that she had syringes with her and bottles that had been premixed—by whom, no one knows. A source who was very close to the actress recalls that the concoction was of phenobarbital, Nembutal, and Seconal. "Marilyn referred to it as 'a vitamin shot,'" said the source. "I think I know who gave her this combination of drugs, but I'd rather not say because I am not one hundred percent certain. I can tell you that after she would give herself this injection, she would be gone—no longer able to function."

Indeed, Jeanne Martin recalled that prior to their leaving Frank's home for the cruise that August 1961, Frank asked her to help get Marilyn dressed. She was too disoriented from all of the medication she was taking to do so herself. "I had to pick out each item of clothing and practically dress her," Jeanne recalled. "I kept asking her, 'Marilyn, are you all right? Because you don't look good to me.' She would just sort of look at me with her eyes half-closed and say, 'Oh, I am just fine. I couldn't be better.' I was worried. I remember thinking, who is giving her all of these drugs? What kind of doctor would keep her in this kind of state? She was really, shall we say, glazed."

During the weekend, Marilyn drank plenty of champagne every night, as always. The more she drank, the more disoriented and even boisterous she became. "It was such a sad sight," Jeanne Martin recalled. "I didn't take my eyes off her for a second because I was afraid she would slip and fall. You can't know how difficult this was unless you knew Marilyn and what a lovely woman she was, how nice she was to everyone. You wanted her to be all right, but on this day during this party, it struck me that she was not all right. Not at all."

Gloria Romanoff, also a guest for the weekend, recalled, "She was very unwell that weekend. Sleeping pills were her downfall, I'm afraid. The poor girl simply couldn't even take a nap without them, she was so addicted. She didn't even need water or anything to wash them down. She could just take a handful of pills and swallow them, dry. Then, of course, all of the alcohol just made things worse."

As the afternoon wore on, Frank became frustrated and embarrassed by Marilyn's behavior. One of his former associates recalled, "To tell you the truth, Frank couldn't wait to get her off that boat. She was embarrassing him. He told me, 'I swear to Christ, I am ready to throw her right off this goddamn boat.' Instead, he called one of his assistants at the end of the trip, when they were ashore, and had her taken back to his place. He told me later that when he got home, she was sound asleep on the couch. He picked her up, he said, and moved her to the bedroom. He undressed her and put her under the covers where she slept soundly through the night. He was worried about her."

When that same associate asked Frank Sinatra if he was going to stop seeing Marilyn Monroe, he said, "By now I would have cut any other dame loose. But this one—I just can't do it."*

What's most interesting—and telling—about this time is that despite the unhappiness she felt, the photos Marilyn took during this period for publicity purposes, especially those by Douglas Kirkland, are perhaps the best of her career. Kirkland, who shot her in November 1961, described her as "amazingly pleasant and playful, like a sister, and not at all intimidating as I had imagined her to be. She sat beside me, laughed easily and made small talk, putting me at ease. I was young and did not know how to ask her to pose for the sexy images I hoped to get, but she simplified it all by suggesting, 'I should get into bed with nothing on but white silk.' We discussed the details and Marilyn said she wanted Frank Sinatra music and chilled Dom Perignon." She never looked lovelier than she does in Kirkland's photographs. (It should be stated, though, that based on how Kirkland later described the session, with Marilyn saying, "I think I should be alone with this boy," and then asking everyone else to leave—and then even inviting him into bed with her—it doesn't sound like a very platonic situation. However, he insists that nothing happened between them—except for the amazing photos that resulted from the session.)

How Marilyn was able to turn on *Marilyn Monroe* when she needed to for professional purposes at the same time that she was so terribly troubled remained a true mystery to her friends and associ-

---

* In February 1962, Frank Sinatra would announce his intention to marry the dancer Juliet Prowse. While promoting his third memoir, *Why Me?* Sammy Davis Jr. said that the engagement was Frank's way of putting distance between himself and Marilyn. "Marilyn was a sweetheart, but Frank had his hands full with her," Sammy recalled. "Next thing I knew, I get a call from him telling me he's involved with Juliet and going to marry her. I know it had to do with Marilyn in some way; him trying to break from her."

"[The Sinatra-Prowse engagement] drove Marilyn up the wall," said George Jacobs. "It also drove her to her mirror. That Juliet was a decade younger than Marilyn was bad; that her legs were perfect was worse. Both Marilyn and Ava [Gardner] were ridiculously insecure about their legs. Too short, too fat, was the whine. Marilyn must have stayed in front of the mirror for days, trying on a hundred pairs of high heels, asking whoever she could grab which ones made her legs look best. No one took rejection harder than Marilyn."

As it turned out, Frank Sinatra's engagement to Juliet Prowse only lasted six weeks.

ates. It was as if she only found her true bliss in front of the camera as the perfect vision of herself. Everything else—her real life, the one she led in private—paled in comparison. The truth, of course, is that one quick way for her to feel like Marilyn Monroe was to stop taking her Thorazine, as she had during this period. In her mind, as long as she was slim and sexy . . . she was Marilyn Monroe. In just a few months, when asked by reporter Alan Levy if she was happy, her response would be, "Let's put it this way. I'm slim. And I can always get very gay. It depends on the occasion or the company."

The Douglas Kirkland sessions provide an excellent opportunity to contrast experiences with Marilyn. Her publicist Michael Selsman tells the story of what happened when he and his wife, the actress Carol Lynley, were to meet Kirkland at Monroe's Doheney apartment to go over the proofs of the session. "Carol was nine months pregnant, due any moment," he says. "I couldn't and didn't want to leave her at home by herself, so I took her along to Monroe's apartment," he recalls. "I knocked on her door, as Carol stood shivering beside me. MM opened the door and looked at Carol, whom she knew, since they had adjacent dressing rooms at the studio, and said, 'You come in,' motioning to me, 'but *she* can wait in your car.' This was unexpected and I was momentarily stunned. Carol and I exchanged glances, and I assured her I'd be out in fifteen minutes."

At some point, the two were joined by Douglas Kirkland. Selsman continues, "Every other actor I worked with would use a red grease pencil to put an X through the negatives they didn't like, but not Marilyn on that day. She took a scissors and cut out every one she did not like, then cut those into tiny splinters and threw them in the wastebasket. This laborious process took three hours, during which I repeatedly got up to leave, but Marilyn kept ordering me to sit down. It was my first evidentiary of Marilyn Monroe's capacity for cruelty. Doug told her that the negatives and proofs were his property—that he could be trusted to keep them locked up if that was her wish. That didn't deter her. Poor Doug. She just mopped up the floor with him. He would say, 'But I like this one.' She would say, 'No! I don't. I don't want to be seen like that. That's *dead*.' "

Douglas Kirkland's memory of that night is totally different. "Yes, she cut the proofs and negatives into little pieces—and that was disturbing," he says. "It was shocking, actually, the way she went through them, cutting them up. However, she was extremely clear about what she thought was best for her and the ones she killed, for the most part, were not good. She was thorough and professional. She wanted photos that the Everyman could enjoy. Or, as she put it to me when she saw one shot she really loved, 'I like this one because [Marilyn] looks like the kind of girl a truck driver would like to be in there [the bed] with. That's who this girl appeals to—the regular guy.'

"I absolutely agree, though, that she was a darker personality than the one I had shot the day before," says Kirkland. "The day before, she had been sexy, vibrant, and exciting, but twenty-four hours later, she was drawn, tired, and disturbed. She answered the door with a scarf on her head and dark glasses on. I don't know what could have happened in such a short period of time to change her personality but it was totally, totally different. However, was I horrified? Did I think she was awful? Oh my gosh, no. Absolutely not. No, no, no. She was *Marilyn Monroe*, after all." *

---

* Perhaps Marilyn Monroe historian Charles Casillo best put these events into perspective: "Clearly, Michael Selsman showed poor judgment in bringing Carol Lynley to Marilyn's house uninvited. Imagine! Bringing a beautiful younger blonde actress (from the same studio) to a private meeting to discuss publicity photographs with Marilyn Monroe? And Carol was pregnant, to boot! He knew that Marilyn had been unable to have children. Bad call. Bad judgment. Also, maybe it wasn't so outrageous that Marilyn destroyed the negatives by cutting them into tiny pieces. With any other star, it would have sufficed to simply cross them out with a red grease pencil. With Marilyn, any scrap of her was valuable and would eventually be exploited. No one understood that better than Marilyn herself. Look at what happened after she scratched out the photos she disliked taken by Bert Stern on the negative. Soon after she died, he released them—all scratched and crossed out! And years after that, they were digitally retouched so that her mark of disapproval was erased forever."

Dr. Greenson in Control

At the end of 1961, Marilyn Monroe purchased a house for about $77,000. She had wanted a house that looked as much like Dr. Greenson's as possible, and she found one. She had been searching for some time. Once, she and Pat Newcomb found a home that Marilyn liked very much. The two were standing outside near the pool talking it over when the owner, a woman, came out, stared at Marilyn for a long time, and finally said, "I know who you are! Get off my property immediately!" There seemed no justification at all for such an outburst, but it suggested that Marilyn's reputation was by now a mixed one among her public. There were people who loved her, but also definitely people who had a judgment on her. Choked with tears, Marilyn and Pat quickly left the premises.

With three bedrooms and two baths, Marilyn's new house was a surprisingly small—by show business standards—hacienda-type, one-story home on Fifth Helena Drive outside of Brentwood, California. The living room was so small, just three pieces of furniture would fit. The bathrooms were extremely small, as was the kitchen. Basically, it looked like a small, very modest apartment. It did feature a swimming pool and a lush garden area, and the entire property was walled from the street at the end of a cul-de-sac. It seemed very private. Below the front door was a tile with the engraving CURSUM PERFICIO. Over the years, some have translated this Latin motto to mean, "My journey ends here"—suggesting that Marilyn had a death wish of some kind and may have had this tile installed to send a message. However, the literal translation is "I complete the course," and it has been used in the doorways of European homes for many years as a way of welcoming guests. It was installed when the house was built, some thirty years before Marilyn took ownership. Marilyn said she was looking forward to furnishing the house with Mexican-style furnishings that she hoped to purchase during her trips to that part of the world. Despite the important purchase, though, by the end of the year Marilyn was in terrible shape. Her spirits had plummeted and there seemed no way for her to rebound. She was scheduled to go before cameras in 1962 with a new movie, *Something's Got to Give*, but she was far from interested in it.

Whereas she had been more or less fine—at the very least her emotional illness seemed to have been stabilized—when she was with her half sister Berniece in New York, in Los Angeles she was not well at all. Those in her circle who did not know about her diagnosis attributed this change in her demeanor to the constant therapy she was receiving from Dr. Greenson. She was with him almost every day. Then, at night, she would often have dinner with the Greenson family. Sometimes she would stay overnight. Doubtless, the biggest problem Dr. Greenson faced was the damage he did to his image with certain aspects of his advice and behavior. Some of what he did *was* strange, was suspicious, and did not put him in a very good light. For instance, consider this story:

One of Marilyn's best friends was Ralph Roberts, an actor and her personal masseur, who had the nickname "Rafe." Because he was a constant companion of Marilyn's, she had sent for him to be in Los Angeles with her. She thought of him as a brother. One day, Dr. Greenson announced that Roberts had to go. "There are one too many Ralphs in the picture," he told Marilyn. She couldn't believe her ears. "But he's one of my best friends," she said in protest. "I don't care, he's got to go, Marilyn," Greenson said. "But I call him Rafe, not Ralph," she said, now becoming hysterical. It would appear that she actually thought the problem was in her friend's name—not in his presence. "Rafe! Rafe!" she said over and over again. Greenson concluded, "I don't care what you call him. You are much too dependent on him." That night, Marilyn told Ralph that he had to go back to New York. According to people who knew her best at that time, she sobbed all night long. Still, she felt she was powerless to do anything about it; that's how reliant she had become on Dr. Greenson.

Another example of Greenson's seemingly territorial nature where Marilyn was concerned can be found in a letter he wrote to a colleague (in May 1961): "Above all, I try to help her not to be so lonely, and therefore to escape into the drugs or get involved with very destructive people who will engage in some sort of sadomasochistic relationship with her. This is the kind of planning you do with an adolescent girl who needs guidance, friendliness and firmness, and she seems to take it very well. She said for the first time, she looked forward to coming to Los Angeles, because she could speak to me. Of course, this does not prevent her from canceling several hours to go to Palm Springs with Mr. F.S. [doubtless, Frank Sinatra]. She is as unfaithful to me as one is to a parent."

It seems true that Marilyn felt inclined to explain her romantic experiences to Greenson as if he had a right to sanction them. For instance, in March 1961, she wrote a letter to him in which she described "a fling on a wing" with someone she did not name. She said he was unselfish in bed but that she knew Greenson would not approve of the relationship. Many reporters over the years have suggested that she was referring to one of the Kennedy brothers. She may also have been referring to Frank Sinatra.

Making the situation all the more uncomfortable to observers at the time was that Marilyn's new attorney was Mickey Rudin—Ralph Greenson's brother-in-law. Rudin was also Frank Sinatra's lawyer and, moreover, Greenson was Sinatra's therapist. "Why in the world Sinatra would have Greenson as his shrink fully knowing the condition of his other famous patient, Marilyn, was a mystery to everyone," said one of Marilyn's friends at that time. "It was all just a little creepy. There was just too much Greenson everywhere you looked."

Pat Kennedy Lawford was one of those who did not support Marilyn's relationship with Dr. Greenson, and she made that clear during a luncheon with Marilyn. Her father, Joseph, suffered a stroke in the fall of 1961, and she was having a difficult time coping with the fact that it had left such a vibrant man paralyzed. Marilyn and Pat arranged to have a drink and catch up at the Beachcomber restaurant in Malibu, a favorite haunt of Pat's. When she had her son Christopher in 1955, she and Peter stopped there to celebrate on the way home from the hospital. They just plopped the infant right down on the bar in his little bassinet, ordered a couple of dirty martinis, and drank up. That was a happy, if not also crazy, day. However, on this later day, Pat was feeling melancholy and sad. According to Pat Brennan, who joined the two for drinks, Pat cried about her father while Marilyn watched, almost distantly.

"Do you love your father?" Marilyn asked Pat, who was shocked by the question.

"Of course I do," Pat replied.

"Dr. Greenson says I don't need a father," Marilyn said. "They're optional—not everyone has one."

If Marilyn had been trying to console Pat, it certainly wasn't working. More likely, however, Monroe was simply free-associating her conversation, without much of an agenda. This wasn't one of Marilyn's good days.

"You are seeing too much of that guy," Pat replied coolly, "he's got you under a spell or something."

"But he's like a father to me," Marilyn confided, "and I can trust him not to tell anyone."

"Tell anyone what?" asked Pat.

Marilyn had been confiding in Pat about her need to "quiet her mind" for quite some time, and she believed Pat had to know what she was talking about.

"That I'm like my mother," Marilyn said.

Pat's face hardened. Later she would say that it dawned on her that Greenson had convinced Marilyn her condition was serious enough that she needed him—indefinitely. "Now you listen to me," she said, according to Brennan's memory of the conversation. "That man doesn't know what he's talking about. Your mother is a very sick woman."

"So am I," Marilyn said quite plainly.

There was silence between the two. Pat Brennan watched the scene play out without saying a word. Everyone just looked at each other for a long moment, until Marilyn finally began to cry.

"Don't be angry with me," she said, as she stood and started to collect her belongings.

"Why would I be angry? Sit down, where are you going?"

"Just don't be angry with me. I couldn't take that."

Marilyn headed for the door, and the two Pats—Lawford and Brennan—followed. They caught up with Marilyn in front of the restaurant, still visibly upset. Pat Kennedy Lawford hugged her.

"This is all that damn doctor's fault."

"No it's not," Marilyn said. "But it's not my fault either."

"Let's just talk about this," Pat insisted.

"No. I've upset you both," Marilyn said. She gave Lawford a quick peck on the cheek and Brennan the same. Then she looked the former in the eye and said, "I swear, this isn't my fault."

Marilyn, again on the verge of breaking down, walked off toward her car while both women were left to try to make sense of what had just happened.

Eunice Murray

*D*r. Ralph Greenson replaced the other Ralph in Marilyn's life—Roberts—with perhaps the strangest character who had ever come into the picture—another reason he is so maligned by historians. She was fifty-nine-year-old Eunice Murray, a dowdy, bespectacled woman with not much personality who called herself a "nurse," but who had no medical training whatsoever. She had a very stern face and hard features. In fact, Marilyn hadn't had anyone in her life like this since Ida Bolender. The difference between the two, though, was that Ida had great warmth beneath the cold exterior whereas Eunice didn't, or at least not that anyone was ever able to discern. Because she had "homemaking skills," she was installed as Marilyn's companion—sometimes she spent the night, sometimes not—much to the dismay of almost every person who knew Marilyn, it's safe to say. It seemed to Marilyn's friends and associates that there was nothing Marilyn could do during her private time at home that wasn't immediately brought to Dr. Greenson's attention by Murray. Indeed, in their view, he had a new spy in the household. Even Marilyn's publicist and friend Pat Newcomb, not usually one to make waves and who went along with practically every decision made on Marilyn's behalf, was suspicious of Eunice Murray. Saying she was frightened of her, she didn't even want to be around the woman. "She keeps giving me that fishy stare," Pat told John Springer, "and I don't like it one bit."* In Greenson's defense, however, he believed strongly that Marilyn needed to be monitored as much as possible. He didn't care if people thought he was spying on her via Eunice Murray, as long as he knew what his patient was up to every moment of every day.

"I heard that she [Murray] was constantly on the telephone, whispering information to him," said Diane Stevens, who came to Los Angeles with John Springer for business meetings at that time. "Marilyn couldn't have guests over without Greenson knowing who they were, how long they stayed, and what they wanted. This woman was always peering around corners, taking mental notes, and then reporting back to the doctor. I met her once. I had to drop some paperwork at Marilyn's house and when I did, this woman came to the door. 'Who are you?' she demanded to know. 'Why haven't I seen you around here before? What business do you have here?' Oh my God, I was horrified by her attitude. I thought to myself, she's a housekeeper. What right does she have to talk to anyone like this? So I said, 'Who are *you*? Why haven't I seen *you* around here before? What business do *you* have here?' She looked at me with an angry face and then slammed the door in my face. I told John about it and he said, 'Oh no. What has Marilyn gotten herself into now?'"

At the end of 1961, Dr. Greenson wrote in his notes of what he

---

* A classic Newcomb/Murray story is this one: Eunice Murray, in the last months of Marilyn's life, said to her, "Pat Newcomb is going all over town telling everybody she's your best friend." In her peculiar genius, Marilyn retorted, "Eunice, if she were my best friend, she wouldn't have to tell anybody." Of course, as interesting as that story is, it does come via Eunice Murray, and there was definitely no love lost between her and Pat.

called "a severe depressive reaction" to something that had happened in Marilyn's life. He wasn't clear as to what had transpired. "She had talked about retiring from the movie industry, killing herself, etc." Certainly it's not good news when a psychiatrist becomes so used to hearing a patient's threats to commit suicide that he adds "etc." to his notes about it, suggesting that he's heard it all before. "I had to place nurses in her apartment day and night," he wrote, "and keep strict control over the medication since I felt she was potentially suicidal. Marilyn fought with these nurses, so that after a few weeks it was impossible to keep any of them."

After hearing her voice on the telephone, Joe DiMaggio decided that he'd better fly to Los Angeles to spend Christmas with Marilyn. She was happy to see him. As difficult as he was at times, she knew he loved her and she felt safe in his arms. "Joe was there maybe thirty minutes when he figured out that things had gotten much worse with her," said his friend the sportswriter Stacy Edwards. "Let me put it to you this way. He took one look at that Mrs. Murray and knew she was trouble. From what he told me, he said to her, 'I don't want you knowing anything about me or my business. You work for Marilyn, but you are not her friend. And you are not my friend. If it were up to me, you wouldn't even exist.' He was very direct with her. I'm sure she had a lot to tell Greenson about him."

Joe wanted to make certain that Christmas Day would be happy for Marilyn. To that end, he had purchased a large tree and had decorated it for her. He was as solicitous and as romantic as he could be, doing whatever he could think of to make the day festive. He purchased gifts and even had them wrapped at the store. "He told me it was a great day," recalled Stacy Edwards. "He said she seemed okay, not too manic. I'm pretty sure the housekeeper wasn't there, though I don't know where she was—or where he sent her, I should say. Everything was going well . . . until that night, anyway."

Earlier in the day, Marilyn announced that they were having dinner with . . . the Greensons. Joe hadn't met the doctor, but already he wasn't a fan. However, he was anxious to spend time with him and come to his own conclusions. It didn't take long for him to make a determination, though. Joe had always thought that Natasha Lytess had too much influence on Marilyn, and he certainly felt the same way about Lee and Paula Strasberg. However, that night—after just thirty minutes of watching his ex-wife act as if Ralph Greenson was her long-lost father and Greenson's family was the one she'd never known—Joe DiMaggio would say that he had a sick feeling in the pit of his stomach. "You know what it's like when you're in a car with someone and they run a red light and you know you're gonna crash but you're not driving so there's nothing you can do about it?" he asked Stacy Edwards. "That's how I felt that night. I felt like Marilyn was about to crash, but I was no longer in the driver's seat anymore . . . and there was nothing I could do about it."

Joe wasn't the only one worried about Marilyn. Others who were not aware of her disease had no frame of reference for her strange behavior. "'She's not well.' 'She's acting strangely.' 'What's wrong with her?' That's all I kept hearing by the beginning of 1962," said Diane Stevens from John Springer's office.

"Pat Newcomb and a young publicist named Michael Selsman were mostly handling her from the Arthur P. Jacobs Company by this time. She was paying them $250 a week, I think, which was $50 more than she'd been paying John Springer's firm. Every now and then we still had to field a press request, and it wasn't easy. She had become difficult and argumentative. Once you got her there, she was okay. But getting her there was hell. She'd have an appointment to do an interview and just not show up. It had been her custom to be late, but to not show up was not her. Then, she was saying the strangest things. For instance, she said that the reason she bought her new house was because it reminded her of the orphanages in which she was raised. After spending the better part of the last decade bemoaning the orphanages she was sent to—and I believe it was just one, by the way—to now suddenly start making that statement seemed more than odd. The word was out that she was sick, a drug addict. I was scared."

PART EIGHT

The Kennedys

Kennedy Style

It was late January 1962. "You have just got to meet him," Pat Kennedy Lawford told Marilyn Monroe. "You'll never know anyone quite like my brother." She was taking about her brother, Bobby, now attorney general of the United States.

One thing is certain, anytime Marilyn had the opportunity to be around the Kennedys, she took advantage of it. She was much more politically minded than people knew. What follows is a remarkable letter she wrote to journalist Lester Markel, a *New York Times* editor she had met and with whom she enjoyed lively discussions about politics. It was written before JFK won his party's nomination for president:

Lester dear,

Here I am still in bed. I've been lying here—thinking even of you. About our political conversation the other day: I take it all back that there isn't anybody. What about Rockefeller? First of all, he is a Republican, like the New York Times and secondly, and most interesting, he's more liberal than many of the Democrats. Maybe he could be developed? At this time, however, Humphrey might be the only one. But who knows since it's rather hard to find out anything about him. (I have no particular paper in mind!) Of course, Stevenson might have made it if he had been able to talk to people other than professors. Of course, there hasn't been anyone like Nixon before because the rest of them at least had souls. Ideally, Justice William Douglas would be the best President, but he has been divorced so he couldn't make it—but I've got an idea— how about Douglas for President and Kennedy for Vice-president, then the Catholics who wouldn't have voted would vote because of

Kennedy so it wouldn't matter if he [Douglas] is so divorced! Then Stevenson could be secretary of state.

It's true I am in your building quite frequently to see my wonderful doctor [here she is referring to her psychiatrist, Dr. Marianne Kris] as your spies have already reported. I didn't want you to get a glimpse of me though until I was wearing my Somali leopard. I want you to think of me as a predatory animal.

Love and kisses,
Marilyn

PS Slogan for late '60
"Nix on Nixon"
"Over the hump with Humphrey" (?)
"Stymied with Symington"
"Back to Boston by Xmas—Kennedy"

Back to Boston by Christmas? It doesn't sound as if Marilyn—a registered Democrat—had much confidence that JFK could win the election. She was well-read and knowledgeable enough to have an opinion, though, and could definitely hold her own in any political conversation. As they got to know one another, she and Pat also had lengthy discussions about civil rights, a subject about which Marilyn had become quite passionate. She identified with the underdog, and began to realize that Pat and her dynastic family shared those ideals. When the two would discuss coverage of world events in the press, Marilyn always took the position that important stories that made the country look bad—such as certain riots taking place in urban areas—were not given enough prominent space. "Sometimes I think the government is running the media," she told Pat in front of friends. "I don't trust anything I read these days." Pat was certainly not ashamed to have Marilyn Monroe mixing with her peers because she viewed her as a woman of substance. Pat especially enjoyed having her visit when her siblings were present because she also knew that Marilyn never really had a family. Therefore, it gave her pleasure and satisfaction to share hers with her new friend.

Of course, as is well known, the Kennedys were a raucous bunch totally devoted to each other. It seems that when they weren't running the country, they were having a good time at Peter and Pat's. One writer once opined, "The problem with the Kennedys is that they have no problems." Of course, history has shown us that this wasn't the case—but it certainly seemed like it to the outside world back in 1961. "You're a Kennedy now," Pat told Marilyn shortly after having met her. Pat didn't throw around the designation easily, either. For instance, when JFK won the Democratic nomination, all of the Kennedys were to join him onstage at the convention in Los Angeles at the Coliseum. When Peter Lawford started to walk out with the rest of them, his wife, Pat, stopped him. "You're not actually a Kennedy," she told him, "so I think it's not right." JFK overheard what was going on and stopped his sister. "He's married to you so that makes him a Kennedy, don't you think?" he asked her. She shrugged. "Besides, he's a good-looking movie star," he added with a wink at Peter. "So we can certainly use him up there." Poor Peter had even taken the citizenship test just to become an American so he could cast his vote for JFK. If Pat still didn't think of him—her own husband—as a Kennedy, she must have really taken to Marilyn to have awarded her with the appellation. Of course, Marilyn loved being around the Kennedys—the joyous laughter, the intense rivalry, the crazy drama that informed everything they ever did . . . the many children, more than she could count . . . and all of the dogs. The Lawfords always had at least a half dozen dogs running around the property, chasing and yapping at whichever team of Kennedys was playing touch football on the beach. Because Pat was deathly allergic to the animals, she kept her distance. Peter pretty much ignored them. In his view, they were just part of the grand scenery that surrounded him. However, Marilyn took to the pets and made sure they were bathed and well fed whenever she was around. "Why, they're just like little people," she would tell Pat. "Oh yeah?" Pat would shoot back. "Well, little people don't shit on my white carpets, now do they?"

Parties at Pat and Peter's home at 625 Palisades Beach Road in

Malibu (now Pacific Coast Highway) were practically legendary at this time. Originally built by Louis B. Mayer in 1926, it was quite a showplace, an enormous marble and stucco Mediterranean-Spanish structure. It was built on thirty-foot pilings to prevent it from being swept away in a tidal wave—not that there has ever been one in Santa Monica. The walls were a foot thick to ensure that the house remained cool in the summer. Its best feature was its large, curving living room with windows facing the ocean and wrought-iron balconies onto which French doors opened. There were thirteen onyx and marble bathrooms, but just four bedrooms. Of course, it also had the standard-issue fifty-foot pool, always heated and glistening. It was easily accessible from the street—with no gate or any kind of security entryway, it sat right off the highway.

Behind the main house was Sorrento Beach, popular for its volleyball tournaments. The surf pounded this coastline day and night, the rising tides littering it with brown seaweed. The Lawford children often brought the slimy plants into the house and played with them in their bedrooms, much to the fastidious Pat's dismay. The neighbors on one side of the Lawfords' property were the actor Jeffrey Hunter and his family. On the other, there was a vacant lot. It was all that remained after the home that once stood there was demolished. Pat joked to Marilyn that she had the house blown to smithereens when she learned that a family of Republicans had purchased it. Or, at least Marilyn *thought* Pat was joking.

Matthew Fox was a friend of Jeffrey Hunter's son, Steele. The two boys were eight in 1961. "These parties, man, you've never seen anything like them," recalled Fox. "The Kennedys had style. I mean, those people knew how to throw a party, let me tell you. Sometimes they would have afternoon barbecues, which I loved. If I had a sleepover with Steele, I would wander over there the next day just to snoop around. Once, I saw Angie Dickinson baking in the sun in a bikini that was so revealing I think it was the first time I ever got a boner. I'd always see Mrs. Lawford—Pat—tossing a football around with her brother, the president. Bobby would be there. Teddy. Judy Garland would be there, doing the twist on the sand in her bare feet, just about as drunk as she could be. And there'd be Frank Sinatra with Dean Martin and Sammy Davis with Peter, walking on the beach, chain-smoking like mad and tossing their cigarette butts into the ocean as if to say, 'Screw Mother Nature. As far as we're concerned, the whole world is our ashtray.'

"And Marilyn. I think from 1961 on, she was there a lot. I remember I would just see this shock of blonde hair from a distance and I'd run over to stare at her up close."

Fox remembered Marilyn as "the most beautiful woman, no, goddess, I have ever seen," as she stood on the beach, always shielding her eyes against the spray and the sand. He recalls her walking on the hot sand with Pat's dogs and stopping to admire the deep blue ocean so flecked with whitecaps. Sometimes she would toss a ball into the water and then squeal with delight as one of the animals retrieved it and returned it to her.

"Once, I walked out to the beach with my little Brownie camera and asked if I could take a picture of her," continued Matthew Fox. "She said, 'Oh no! Not today. I don't have my makeup on and I don't even look like Marilyn Monroe. Come back tomorrow and I'll be all ready for you.' So the next day I went back with my camera. She was made up as if getting ready to make a movie—heavy mascara, red lipstick, big hair teased out to there—the whole Marilyn bit. I said, 'Wow, just look at you!' And she said, 'I did all of this just for you, Matty, so let's take that picture now, shall we?' And we did. I shot a few pictures and then Pat took a picture of the two of us together. Afterward, Marilyn kissed me on the forehead and said, 'You come back in about twenty years and we'll be better friends, okay?' Then she winked at me and walked back into the house. And I thought, 'Oh my God. *I am in love with Marilyn Monroe.*' Even then, I knew that most people in the world didn't have these kinds of experiences."

Marilyn and Bobby

𝒪ne of the biggest problems faced by Pat Kennedy Lawford in the early 1960s was her and Peter's reputation. Peter and his Rat Pack friends had used her home so often for their sexual escapades with women that some wise guy renamed the place "High Anus Port." Jeanne Martin, Pat's good friend, said, "I truly don't know what Peter was thinking. How could he put himself and Pat in that position? It was always a mystery to me. He was not a careless man, but to do that to his wife . . ." Indeed, when Pat heard about the nickname, she was embarrassed. However, there wasn't a lot she could do about it. Her brother, Jack, was president of the United States, and if he wanted to meet girls at her home when he came into town, she felt she had no choice but to allow it. "Obviously, Pat was not clueless," said George Jacobs. "She was just resigned. [But] Pat must have hated that her house was being used as a brothel for JFK."* The only thing she believed she could do to keep her place of residence dignified was the occasional classy dinner party—which she usually had when Bobby and Ethel were in town. No one seems to remember an occasion when she had such a party for JFK and Jackie, the reason being that when JFK came to the West Coast, he preferred leaving Jackie behind since her presence at his side usually cramped his style. The latest Kennedy gathering organized by Pat was to take place on February 1, 1962. Again, Pat was hosting for Bobby and Ethel since they were in Los Angeles on the first leg of a fourteen-country goodwill tour.

With the telling of events leading up to this party, one can also begin to understand one of the reasons behind all of the rumors about Marilyn and Bobby. Prior to this evening, Marilyn—always one to embellish an already interesting story—spent at least two

---

* Jacobs says that his boss, Frank Sinatra, never indulged in dalliances at Pat's home, "because he had too much respect for her . . . more, I guess, than her own brother."

weeks calling people such as Danny Greenson (the doctor's son), Jeanne Martin, Henry Weinstein (producer of *Something's Got to Give*), among others to tell them exciting news: "I have a date with Bobby Kennedy."

Henry Weinstein recalled, "I get a call one day from her and she says, I have a very important date with a very important man. And I want to know from you what kinds of things I can say to him, what kinds of questions I may be able to ask him, that will be impressive. So I said, 'Fine, but who's the man, so I can think of topics for you.' She said, 'It's Bobby Kennedy.' I was a little floored. 'Seriously?' I asked. 'Yes,' she said, 'I have a date with Bobby Kennedy.' So, I said, 'Okay, well, we're right in the middle of the civil rights business, so ask him what he's doing to calm down the riots, how he feels about Martin Luther King, that sort of thing.'"

In subsequent years, sources who have said Marilyn told them she was "dating" Bobby Kennedy weren't fibbing. Apparently, *she* was fibbing. In this case, it most certainly wasn't a date. It was a dinner party at Pat's, and she was just one of the guests. However, people heard from her that it was "a date," and then passed that information on to reporters many decades later. Each person has told the same story: She wrote down all of the questions she was given on a napkin, so that she could remember them. They were inquiries about civil rights, about the country's support of the Diem regime in Vietnam, and also about the House Un-American Activities Committee.

Marilyn showed up at Pat's that night dressed to kill. Years later, Joan Braden, who was present that night, recalled, "Bobby turned and I turned and there she was—blonde, beautiful, red lips at the ready, clad in a black-lace dress which barely concealed the tips of her perfectly formed breasts and tightly fitted every curve of the body unparalleled." Joan whispered in Bobby's ear, "Bobby, this is *the* Marilyn Monroe, the genuine article." Then Pat came over and said, "Bobby, I'd like you to meet Marilyn."

While Bobby was mildly interested in meeting the screen star, his wife, Ethel, was much more starstruck. Unlike many of the Kennedys, Ethel was down-to-earth, not at all pretentious. She enjoyed a good time, loved playing football with the men in the family, and was considered something of a tomboy. She was also the life of any party, pretty much like her sister-in-law Pat. She'd wanted to be a nun before meeting Bobby, but then of course went on to marry Kennedy and give birth to eleven children by him. She was well-liked within the family, though she and Jackie often butted heads. Ethel, always one to speak her mind, was devoted to the Kennedy family and was Bobby's biggest supporter when it came to his political ambitions. Whereas the other women who'd married into the family—Jackie and Joan—had to apply themselves in order to be invested in their husband's careers, Ethel absolutely loved politics and hoped to one day be First Lady.

Ethel had wanted to meet Marilyn ever since deciding a year earlier that the actress should play her in a screen version of Bobby's book *The Enemy Within*, which was about his investigation into the illegal activities of Jimmy Hoffa and the Teamsters union. It was presently being developed into a movie by Marilyn's studio, 20th Century-Fox. Budd Schulberg, who had written the screenplay for *On the Waterfront*, was adapting the Kennedy work. In the end, it would not see completion, but Ethel's choice to have Marilyn play her in the movie is interesting just the same. On its face, it seems odd. The two were not at all alike, after all. Whereas Marilyn was a sex kitten, Ethel was earthy and a more motherly figure. However, Ethel had seen many of Marilyn's films and was interested in her not for her looks but rather because she saw what a lot of people saw in Marilyn, a very good actress. "I think she's underrated," she told Joan Braden, a friend of the Kennedy family's. "I think she's done some very good work and I'd be honored to have her play me in the movie." Ethel's appreciation of Marilyn didn't last long after she actually had a chance to meet her—and see her interact with Bobby.

Joan Braden recalled, "Bobby ended up sitting right next to her at dinner, with Kim Novak, Angie Dickinson and me at the table. Who the men between us were, I can't remember. I can only remember the women and the dresses, which showed off their bosoms."

Of Marilyn and Bobby, Braden continues, "They had an instant rapport, not surprising in that they were both charismatic, smart people. Bobby enjoyed talking to intelligent, beautiful women, and Marilyn certainly fit the bill. She was also inquisitive in a childlike way, which I think he found refreshing. I found her to be delightful, and everyone at the party was completely enthralled by her and rather dazzled by her presence."

After dinner, Marilyn pulled out her little napkin of questions and started asking them to Bobby. She really didn't need the crib sheet, though. She certainly knew how to engage in an intellectual conversation with someone like Bobby Kennedy. Soon, the two retired to the bar to discuss J. Edgar Hoover. Marilyn said she felt he was out of control. "Spying on this one and that one. He even spies on me, and what do I ever do?" she asked, according to Jeanne Martin, who was also at the party and overheard the conversation. "All I ever do is shop and make movies, yet he has his goons following me!" Marilyn had long felt she was being stalked. There was the incident where she called her pseudo-manager Lucille Carrol to tell her that someone was peeping in on her in her bedroom, even though no available ladder would have reached the third floor. There were many other times, as well. In fact, there's a very good adage that applies here: Just because you're paranoid doesn't mean someone's not following you. The fact that Marilyn actually *was* being followed, and by Hoover's "goons," had to have fed into her sense of paranoia. Bobby said that he and his brother Jack felt the same way about Hoover—and they should have because he had agents tailing their every move as well!—but there was nothing they could do about it yet.

It should be noted that there have been many different accounts of Marilyn's first meeting with Bobby, going all the way back to dates in 1960. However, on the basis of information assembled for this book, February 1, 1962, marked the first meeting. Immediately afterward, on February 2, Marilyn wrote a letter to Isadore Miller, Arthur's father. She began it, "Dear Dad," and wrote of meeting Kennedy, "he seems rather mature and brilliant for his thirty-six years, but what I liked best about him, besides his Civil Rights program, is he's got such a wonderful sense of humor." She also wrote to Arthur's son, Bobby, to whom she was close. "When they asked him who he wanted to meet, he wanted to meet me," she wrote. "So I went to the dinner and sat next to him, and he isn't a bad dancer either." Based on Marilyn's words ("he wanted to meet me"), the two had not met before this evening. She wrote that she'd asked Bobby questions about the civil rights movement and that she was impressed with his answers. She further stated that Bobby had promised to send her a letter that would summarize their conversation. She promised to send Miller a copy of it, "because there will be some very interesting things in it because I really asked many questions that I said the youth of America want answers to and want things done about."

"Afterwards, we all started dancing and I remember Marilyn teaching Bobby how to do the twist," recalled Joan Braden. "The two were laughing and having a very good time together. That, I think, was really pushing it as far as Ethel was concerned. I remember wondering how Bobby could be so blatantly flirtatious with another woman knowing that Ethel was watching, and I was also worried about Ethel's feelings. People always thought Ethel Kennedy could take care of herself, more so than the other Kennedy women. But I always thought that underneath Ethel's bravado was a very sensitive, and often very hurt, woman."

It's been reported countless times over the years that Marilyn Monroe became so inebriated on this night that she could not drive herself home. Therefore, Bobby and his press aide Ed Guthman supposedly did so. Guthman has even been quoted as saying that this was true. Perhaps that happened on some other night—it's never been proven, though—but definitely it did not occur on this night.

Fresh research now establishes that Marilyn did not drive to the Lawford home. She was picked up at 8 p.m. by the Carey Cadillac Renting Company of California from her apartment on Doheny Drive and then taken to the Lawfords'. She stayed until three in the morning and then was driven back to her home. A receipt exists from the Carey Cadillac Renting Company proving as much.

Edward Barnes, who now owns his own valet service, was a young parking attendant at the Lawfords' that evening. He says that while Marilyn was waiting for her driver, there was a bit of chaos in front of the Lawford home. "One of the other valets broke a cardinal rule and asked Miss Monroe if he could take a picture of her," says Barnes. "She said, 'Of course.' And that very second, a Secret Service agent appeared from nowhere and grabbed the guy's camera. It stunned everyone. Marilyn was surprised, too, and she said, 'Wait a second. *Who the hell are you?*' He said, 'Secret Service, ma'am.' Just then, a Kennedy aide who I later learned was Ed Guthman said, 'We have agents here, Marilyn. It's okay.' And she said, 'Well, it is not okay to steal someone's camera.' She then turned to the agent and said, 'You give back that camera right now.' And he did! Then she posed for the picture. Everyone stood there with their mouths open, it was such a moment. I will never forget it. I thought to myself, Holy Christ, I can't believe that Marilyn Monroe just went up against the Secret Service . . . and won!"

"The next day, I asked her how the date with Bobby Kennedy went," recalled Henry Weinstein, "and she said it went great, and 'Guess what? I have *another* date with him.' So I thought, wow, that's very nice. A few days went by and I didn't hear from her. I called her and said, 'So? How is it going with Bobby Kennedy?' She said, 'Well . . . let's put it this way. I don't need any more questions.'"

JFK: *"Finally! You're Here!"*

At the end of February 1962, Peter Lawford invited Marilyn to a dinner party in New York that was being held to honor President John F. Kennedy. Kennedy loved the Hollywood culture and was enamored of celebrities, especially beautiful actresses, or, more specifically, especially beautiful *blonde* actresses—though, as was well known about him, he never tossed a brunette or redhead out of his bed either. Though Marilyn had met Kennedy back in the 1950s when he was a senator, she never had a chance to speak to him in depth. After having had the opportunity to meet Bobby, she was eager to know his brother Jack. She had no romantic designs on JFK. Not yet, anyway.

The party was to take place at the home of Fifi Fell, the widow of a wealthy industrialist. Milt Ebbins, who was Peter Lawford's partner in his production company, recalled:

"Dave Powers [a presidential aide] and I were supposed to escort Marilyn to the party. Dinner was at eight. We showed up at her place at 7:30. Of course she was nowhere near ready. Her maid came out of the bedroom and said something about her not being able to make up her mind about what to wear. Also, she had this hairdresser [Kenneth Battelle, her hairstylist] combing and teasing and combing and teasing. Finally, Dave said, 'I'm not going to sit here when I could be with the president.' So he took the car back to the party and then sent a limousine for us.

"The limousine arrived at 8:15 and she still wasn't ready. At that point, Peter called and said, 'What the hell is going on? Does she realize that she's keeping the president waiting?' And when he said that to me, something clicked in my head and I thought, 'Hmmm, I wonder if that's the whole idea.'"

At 8:30, still no Marilyn—but the hairdresser came out of the bedroom very casually as if he had not a care in the world. Before breezily taking his leave, he said to Milt, "It's worth the wait. Believe me. She looks *fabulous*."

At 8:45, another call came in from Peter to Milt. By now, Peter was frantic and, with Dave Powers cursing in the background, hollered into the phone, "Get her over here, God damn it. The president wants her here, *now*." Milt replied, "I'm trying, *I'm trying*." Peter bellowed, "Well, try harder," before slamming down the phone.

At 9 p.m., the telephone rang again and the maid said it was Peter. Milt told her to say they'd already left the premises. By now totally exasperated, he burst into Marilyn's bedroom. There she was, with her back to him, sitting at her vanity, staring into the mirror and, with what looked to Ebbins like an eyeliner pencil, darkening her famous beauty mark (a little mole on the right cheek of her face). "Marilyn, Jesus Christ, almighty!" Milt said. "Do you realize you're keeping the president waiting." She rose to face him. She was completely nude except for a pair of black high heels. "Oh, calm down, Milt," she said casually. "My goodness. Just help me put this dress on." After taking a casual sip of sherry, she lifted a little beaded and sequined number off the bed and put it over her head. Then she shimmied it down over her breasts, to her hips.

For the next ten minutes, Milt Ebbins attempted to assist Marilyn into what he described as "the tightest goddamn dress I have ever seen on a woman. We couldn't get it past her hips. Of course, typical of Marilyn, she wasn't wearing underwear either. So there I was, on my knees in front of her, my nose an inch from her crotch, pulling this dress down with all my might trying to get it past her big ass. And she kept saying, 'Keep pulling, Milt. Keep pulling. You can do it. *You can do it.*'"

Finally, with one final tug, the dress gave way past Marilyn's hips and down to her knees. "Ah, perfect," she squealed. "I knew you could do it, Milt." She then put a red wig over her hair and sunglasses over her eyes and then . . . back to the vanity where she sat down and began studying herself again. "Finally, I just grabbed her by the elbow," Milt recalled, "and said, 'That's it. We're leaving.'

"We got into the limousine and made it to Park Avenue. When we got out of the car, the place was mobbed with photographers waiting to see who the president's guests were. Not one person recognized her. We went up to the floor he was staying on and two Secret Service agents met us as soon as we got off the elevator. They escorted us to the apartment."

Standing in front of the closed door, Marilyn took off her wig and handed it to one of the agents. After fluffing up her halo of blonde hair, she took the glasses off and handed them to the other agent. Then she drew a deep breath, smoothed down her dress, and said,

"Okay, shall we?" One of the agents opened the door and Marilyn walked into the apartment, followed by Milt Ebbins.

"When she walked in, Christ almighty, it was like the parting of the Red Sea," Ebbins recalled. "There were about twenty-five people in there, and the crowd divided into halves as she walked through the room."

The actress Arlene Dahl, who was married to Fernando Lamas and is actor Lorenzo Lamas's mother, was also at that party. "Marilyn walked in with her agent and, I'll never forget it, everything stopped, everyone stopped. It was magical, really. I've never seen anyone stop a room like that. The president turned around and noticed her and you could see that he was immediately attracted to her. 'Finally! You're here,' he said with a big smile as he walked over to her. 'There are some people here who are dying to meet you.' Then, she was descended upon. People just wanted to stand near her, smell her fragrance, breathe the same air as she."

JFK took Marilyn's arm and off she went with him. But not before turning to Milt Ebbins and giving him a wry little smile and a wink.

As it happened, JFK was immediately taken by Marilyn that night in New York—no surprise there. Before she left, he asked for her phone number. Of course, she gave it to him. He called her the very next day with a suggestion. He explained that he was going to be in Palm Springs on March 24. He would be staying with his friend and, as he understood it, hers as well—Frank Sinatra. Why not join him there? Oh, and incidentally, he told her, "Jackie won't be there."

Notorious Players

*W*asn't it remarkable enough that Marilyn Monroe had made plans for a romantic getaway with the president of the United States? Did fate also have to decree that their assignation would occur in the center of a big melodrama involving both Kennedy brothers, Frank Sinatra, and Peter Lawford, the husband of Marilyn's friend Pat?

Everyone who knew Bobby Kennedy knew one thing about him: He was determined to bring down the underworld. Not only that but, as he had earlier indicated to Marilyn, he felt that J. Edgar Hoover was involved in certain illegal activities, too, and that he was using mob informants to beef up his scurrilous files on the Kennedy family. The scrappiest and most volatile of the brothers, Bobby spent most of 1960 and 1961 looking into these kinds of hunches. The irony was that pretty much everyone knew that his father, Joseph, had all sorts of underworld connections—and is there any doubt that a man as shrewd and savvy as Bobby knew about them, too? Still, in February 1962, his investigation of the underworld was completed and a report compiled by the Justice Department. Basically, it claimed that Sinatra was in so deep with the mob, he was practically running his own little syndicate.

Matters became even darker for Sinatra when, on February 27, 1962, FBI agents reported to J. Edgar Hoover that a woman named Judith Campbell Exner was sleeping with President Kennedy. Exner was one of the many girlfriends of leading Mafia kingpin Sam Giancana. It didn't take long for Hoover to figure out that Sinatra was the one who had introduced all these notorious players to one another. Finally, the FBI got it right!

As JFK had mentioned to Marilyn, he was scheduled to stay with Sinatra at his Palm Springs home. As it happened, Sinatra idolized JFK (whom he referred to as TP—The President) just about as much as he did any mobster he knew. Sinatra had spanking new cottages built on the property for JFK's visit. He also hung pictures of the Kennedys all over the main house, and even put up a gold plaque in the president's bedroom that said, "John F. Kennedy Slept Here." He had new phone lines installed for the Secret Service as well as a new helipad.

However, Sinatra was in for a rude awakening. Bobby told his brother Jack that due to the circumstances of Frank's mob ties, there was no way the president of the United States could stay in his home. JFK concurred. Of course, this sanctimonious reasoning was the height of hypocrisy, since one of the reasons Bobby and JFK agreed that Sinatra should be ostracized was because he was friends with Sam Giancana and his girlfriend, Judith Exner—a woman with whom JFK was having sex! "President Kennedy liked to live on the edge and he liked to take chances," observed retired Secret Service agent Lawrence Newman, "and I think he was walking on the edge of issues that were dark and dangerous."

Poor Peter Lawford was the guy chosen by Bobby to break the news to Sinatra. Peter never had a chance, especially when he told Frank where JFK would be sleeping in Palm Springs. As expected, Sinatra hung up on him. Then Sinatra dropped the phone to the floor. Staring out at the hot desert, he said to his valet, George Jacobs, "You want to know where he's staying? Bing Crosby's house, that's where—and he's a Republican!" After that, Frank dropped Peter from two upcoming Rat Pack films, *Robin and the 7 Hoods* and *4 for Texas*. As far as he was concerned, Peter Lawford was history.

Pat Kennedy Lawford was angry about this turn of events. Lately, Frank hadn't been on her list of favorite people anyway. That hadn't always been the case, though. In fact, it had been due to Pat that Sinatra and Peter Lawford reconciled after a spat in the 1950s over (Sinatra's) ex-wife, Ava Gardner. That argument marked the *first* time Sinatra gave Lawford the heave-ho and didn't speak to him for a couple of years. But then he met Pat one night at a dinner party at actor Gary Cooper's home in Holmby Hills. Even though she was pregnant, she and Frank flirted a bit. Apparently, it then occurred to Sinatra that his former friend, Lawford, was actually *married* to one of the daughters of a family that had the potential to become one of the most powerful in the world. Sinatra always had his sights set on getting into politics and began to hope that the Kennedy family might assist him in that regard. The next thing everyone in his circle knew—voilà!—he and Peter Lawford were best pals again. When Pat had the baby, sure enough, she and Peter named the girl Victoria Francis—after Francis Sinatra. Pat even put up her own Kennedy dollars to option the script of *Ocean's 11*, thinking it would star Peter with Frank. But guess who ended up starring in it? Frank. With Dean, Sammy, oh, and . . . Peter. "But after what Sinatra did to Peter where JFK was concerned, she was done with him for good," concluded her friend Pat Brennan.

Marilyn's Weekend with the President

On Saturday morning, March 24, 1962, Marilyn prepared for her date with presidential destiny.

As the plumbing wasn't functioning at her home, Marilyn had to race over to Dr. Greenson's to wash her hair on the morning of the twenty-fourth. Then she returned to her own home and got dressed. Meanwhile, Peter Lawford paced back and forth in her living room waiting for her to finish so that he could drive her to the desert. That Peter was still involved in any of this business suggests he was hopelessly hooked to the Kennedy-Sinatra-Monroe story and really didn't want it to end for him. Marilyn finally emerged from the bathroom with a black wig over her newly washed and styled hair. Lawford and Monroe then made the two-hour drive to Palm Springs.

In order to comprehend how Marilyn felt about this date with the president, one has to understand the woman Marilyn had become, and what she was accustomed to in her life. She had been much sought after for many years, the poster girl for human sexuality in this country since the mid-1950s. She was long used to being the center of attention, to being the one focused on anytime she showed up at a party. In fact, it usually wasn't a party until she showed up! Also, she was used to being around smart and powerful men—such as Joe DiMaggio and Arthur Miller—and also used to them falling for her. So, while one might have thought she would be thunderstruck by the idea of meeting the president of the United States for a date while his wife, the First Lady, was not on-site, that wasn't really true. To her, it was . . . interesting—just another mad day in the mad life of a mad actress. This attitude is borne out by a couple of credible sources.

Diane Stevens from the John Springer office recalled, "I telephoned her on March 22 to ask her a question about *Something's Got to Give* and said, 'So, what have you got planned for the weekend?' Very casually, she said, 'Oh, I'm going to Palm Springs to spend the weekend with Frank Sinatra and Jack Kennedy.' [Apparently, at this time, Marilyn didn't know that the locale for the party had been changed.] She was so casual about it, it was a little strange. I said, 'Wow! Marilyn, that's really something.' And she said, 'Really? Is it?' I said, 'Well, yeah!' And her reaction was, 'Well, you know, Bobby and I have had a couple of dates'—which was news to me—'and I met Jack in New York recently. He's a nice guy, so I'm just going to go and see what happens.' I hung up thinking to myself, wow. What a life!"

Philip Watson, who was a former Los Angeles county assessor, actually met Marilyn while she was with Kennedy in Palm Springs, and he says she seemed quite calm and casual wearing what he described as "kind of a robe thing." He further recalled, "There were a lot of people poolside, and some people were wandering in and out of a rambling Spanish-style house. Marilyn was there and the president was there and they were obviously together. There was no question in my mind that they were having a good time." He added, "She obviously had a lot to drink. It was obvious they were intimate, that they were staying there together for the night."

While Marilyn was with JFK in Palm Springs—Jackie was in India—she telephoned her friend Ralph Roberts. The three had a conversation that suggests that she and the president either didn't understand how troubling it could be to so many people if word of their tryst got out, or they just didn't care. Marilyn told Roberts that she was with "a friend" who was having certain back problems. The two—she and Roberts—had previously discussed certain muscle groups and she believed these were the specific areas troubling her friend. She also wanted to ask him about the solus muscle, which she had read about in a book called *The Thinking Body* by Mabel Ellsworth Todd. She wanted Roberts to talk to him. He agreed. The next thing he knew, he was talking to a man who sounding exactly like the president. They had a few words and Roberts hung up thinking that his friend Marilyn was, once again, up to no good. Later, she told him that it had most certainly been Kennedy and that he appreciated Roberts's quick diagnosis of his back problem.

Marilyn spent two nights with President Kennedy. It's not known that they were intimate on even one of those nights, let alone both. It can be presumed that they were, though, if only because JFK was used to having relations with a variety of beautiful women—and Marilyn was, no doubt, on top of any man's list of most desirable women, especially in 1962. Also, for her part, Marilyn would have found it hard to resist Kennedy. He was strong, powerful, and good-looking. Not only that, he *was* the president. Indeed, to think that these two passionate people did not find themselves in the throes of passion would be a little naïve. Rather, the question is whether it was on one or on both nights. As it would happen, though, this assignation would be the first and last for Marilyn where Jack Kennedy was concerned. "That was really the end of it," Ralph Roberts recalled many years later. "She told me very specifically that they were together that one weekend, and that it was the only time. It wasn't until many years later that I had begun hearing rumors to the contrary, but I just didn't believe them because she was so specific in what she said back then when it happened." Indeed, according to Roberts and a number of other credible sources, including Secret Service agents whose job it was to keep track of the president's activities, this weekend was the only one ever shared by the movie star and commander in chief. One agent who asked for anonymity put it this way: "If there had been an affair, I would have known about it. There was no affair. Sorry. There just wasn't. It was one weekend, and that's it." Another agent further stated, "At the time [1962], we all knew about the weekend. It wasn't until she [Monroe] and the president were both dead that people started talking about an affair. Trust me, no one was saying anything about an affair in 1962. What we knew was that JFK and Marilyn had sex at Bing Crosby's, and that's it. We didn't think it was a big deal. He had sex with a lot of women. At the time, looking back on it now, she was just one of many and it wasn't that noteworthy. If there was more to it between them, they [Kennedy and Monroe] somehow managed to keep it from us—and I don't think you can keep something like that from the Secret Service."

Indeed, contrary to decades of speculative reports of a long, protracted relationship with him, what Marilyn really shared with JFK was either one or two nights of—maybe—passion. Of course, it's always possible there was more. Obviously, anything is possible. However, there's just no credible evidence to support the existence of a long affair between them. Anything more to tell about it would be strictly the product of many an overworked imagination.

Something's Got to Give

Marilyn Monroe owed Fox one last picture under her 1956 contract and they wanted it in 1962. That one would be *Something's Got to Give*, a moderately budgeted remake of *My Favorite Wife*, the 1940 screwball classic that starred Cary Grant, Irene Dunne, Randolph Scott, and Gail Patrick.

At this time, the Fox executives were panicked because the studio was close to bankruptcy due to its losses on *Cleopatra*, the epic being filmed in Rome. Though Elizabeth Taylor was paid a million dollars to make that film—ten times what Marilyn was making for *Something's Got to Give!*—it would suffer numerous delays due to its leading lady's many different illnesses and missing days on the set. The studio couldn't afford any more problems on the set of one of its major films. It had already sold off its back lot to finance *Cleopatra* and it desperately needed the operating capital that a Marilyn Monroe picture would provide. Unfortunately, there was simply no way such an endeavor was going to be smooth sailing. Making a movie with Marilyn was quite often an ordeal under the best of circumstances due to her habitual tardiness. At this time, she was obviously not well at all, emotionally as well as physically.

As it turned out, there have been entire books and DVDs based on the troubled production of *Something's Got to Give*, that's how much of a mess it was from the start. As many as five different writers worked on the script, culminating with Walter Bernstein's final work, which was anything but stellar. The movie was over budget almost before it even began filming! Making matters even more confounding, Dr. Ralph Greenson found his way into this aspect of Marilyn's life as well, even if not completely by design. Fox studio head Peter Levathes must have known that his star Marilyn was going to cause all manner of problems on the production considering her condition, so he recruited Greenson as the point man responsible for making sure she showed up on set every day. Apparently, all Greenson needed was an invitation to participate, because before anyone knew what had happened, somehow producer David Brown had ended up being replaced by Greenson's friend Henry Weinstein—much to director George Cukor's outrage.

Marilyn had the director of her own choosing, George Cukor, and the leading man of her choice, Dean Martin. She had Jean Louis creating her costumes. Her personal makeup man Whitey Snyder was on hand, as was MGM's Sydney Guilaroff, who gave her hair a flattering bouffanty flip and a stunning new platinum color. What she didn't have was the will to fight the demons that would keep her off the set for sixteen of the first seventeen days of filming. She would blame a slew of maladies for her nonappearance: sinusitis, insomnia, virus, loss of voice, physical exhaustion. The studio engaged three doctors to remain on the set daily—an ear, nose, and throat specialist, an internist, and a psychiatrist.

To watch the DVD of the documentary *Marilyn: Something's Got* to Give—a comprehensive look at the making of this movie—is difficult, made more so when one considers what Marilyn's life and career might have been had she not been so bedeviled with self-doubt, insecurities, unhappy relationships, paranoia, despondency, and drug dependency. Remarkably, though, Cukor was able to get a few excellent sequences on film, and Marilyn was—and this is without exaggeration—more beautiful, more appealing . . . indeed more Marilyn Monroe, than ever. How she always looked so ravishing on film despite the nightmare of her private life remained, until the very end, one of the biggest mysteries about her. In fact, she dropped eighteen pounds before appearing on this set for makeup and costume tests, and as a result her figure was astonishingly young and toned. Of course, she was off her medication, which accounted for some of the weight loss (not to mention some of the problems she had on the set). Her trim figure gave her much more confidence. She was playful, like a little girl, as she posed for the camera in some of the outfits designed for her by Jean Louis. She walked with a new elegance. It's quite amazing to see. The test footage was included in the documentary mentioned previously. Also included are the scenes Cukor shot. Indeed, for years it was thought that there was nothing left of the film, but in 1982 in a cluttered studio warehouse, eight boxes of raw film were discovered, some of its color faded, but in good enough condition to be useful. Some forty years after Fox fired Marilyn and closed down production, the studio salvaged thirty-seven minutes of film time and included some of it in the documentary, which was shown as a television special.

What also has to be stated about this production is how cooperative Marilyn was on the days that she did show up. Certainly her selection of Cukor as director was one she regretted. She knew he was a good director and respected his work, but she also knew that he didn't have much regard for her, so in a sense it was very brave of her to hire him. Given that she had approved of Cukor as director of Let's Make Love two years earlier, one would have to wonder why she would repeat that experience with him. "The mother was mad, and poor Marilyn was mad," he would later say of her. After she realized she would have a problem with Cukor, she tried to bring in screenplay writer Nunnally Johnson to replace him, but to no avail. "But the girl was neurotic beyond description," Johnson would recall. "Even if they were nutty enough to let me take George's place, two weeks later something would happen and she would come to hate me as much as she hated him. Marilyn kept retreating farther and farther from reality." In the end, Cukor had Marilyn doing the most ridiculous scenes over and over—such as one with a dog that would amount to just a few seconds in the final product. Her time could have been so much better utilized. Even in scenes where she was shot from behind—where her stand-in, Evelyn Moriarty, could easily have done the work—Cukor insisted that Marilyn be present and on set to do take after take after take. Never once did she lose her temper, though.

Incidentally, 20th Century-Fox made the aborted film the following year with Doris Day and James Garner filling the Marilyn and Dean roles, and a new name, *Move Over, Darling*. What's funny about this finished film is that in scenes where Marilyn was dressed in the finest of cocktail dresses with the most bouffant of hairstyles, Doris is seen in blue jeans with her hair pulled back in an ordinary ponytail—thus the personality differences between two great actresses, Misses Monroe and Day.

Marilyn's Fascination with the President

It's safe to say that Marilyn's mind wasn't really on *Something's Got to Give*, even though she tried to do her best. Since her weekend in Palm Springs with him, Marilyn Monroe seemed to have only one preoccupation—President John Fitzgerald Kennedy. On the basis of newly assembled information it's clear that she wanted to see him again. Rupert Allan recalled, "All I know is that she seemed fixated on the president. It started to become unclear as to what was going on between them, even though I thought it wasn't much. She was acting like she wanted more, though." One Secret Service agent working for the Kennedy administration added, "She was calling, or trying to call him. A lot. She wanted to see him. She made that clear. Everyone knew it."

It's certainly not difficult to understand why Marilyn invested so quickly in President Kennedy. Suffering from borderline paranoid schizophrenia, she obviously had severe bouts of paranoia. We know she was being followed by the FBI. There may have been other political eccentrics after her too, just based on her affiliation with Arthur Miller. How could she not be concerned? In JFK, perhaps she thought she had found the ultimate of protectors. After all, he was a man who was in control of the entire nation's defense department. If there was anyone in the world who could protect her from real or imagined enemies, it had to be John Fitzgerald Kennedy. He was, bar none, the most powerful man she had ever met. The other noted men in her life—DiMaggio and Miller—had personal presence. Their power was in how they ruled a room—how people would react to them in a social situation. However, Kennedy was powerful on a global scale. He didn't command a room—he commanded the world.

In understanding Marilyn Monroe's overnight obsession with JFK, one has to also remember that she was a woman who was, above all things, scared when she was alone. Unfortunately, the circumstances of her life had arranged themselves so that she was, for the most part, by herself. There's little doubt that by 1962, the choices she was making were out of fear. They were made when she was by herself, alone in the dark, scared of what was to happen to her, what new ordeal she would face with the rising of the morning sun. If Dr. Greenson felt she would trust Eunice Murray, he was wrong. Years later, even Murray herself would have to admit that she didn't know a thing about the Kennedys in Marilyn's life, even though she was living right there in the house with her and snooping about trying to gather information. The people Marilyn trusted were people such as Pat Newcomb, her publicist—and she wasn't always sure about her, either—Joe DiMaggio; Pat Kennedy Lawford; *maybe* Pat's husband, Peter; Ralph Roberts; and a few others. She'd kept a tight circle and her world was becoming even smaller in 1962. Even her half sister, Berniece, was on the outside looking in at this point. Lately, when the two talked on the phone, it was superficial. There's little doubt that Marilyn felt she needed help—maybe on some level she felt JFK could be her savior. Also, there was obviously a certain level of respect that could be achieved by such an association. Unfortunately, she would be the least of President Kennedy's concerns. He wasn't even returning her calls to the White House.

Frank Sinatra's friend and valet George Jacobs enjoyed many conversations with JFK back when the president felt comfortable at the Sinatra home. "I spent enough time with the man to know that no woman, not even his wife, was sacred to him. His need was like that of Alexander the Great, to conquer the world. To him Marilyn was one more conquest, a trophy—maybe the Great White Shark of Hollywood, but still a record, not a romance."

"Jack was pretty much done with her after Palm Springs," said Senator George Smathers [Democrat of Florida], Kennedy's good friend. "I think he only saw her one more time, and that was when she came into Washington unexpectedly and we—he, I, and a few others—including Hubert Humphrey, if you can imagine it, took her sailing on a motorboat down the Potomac River. Marilyn and Hubert Humphrey—now that was funny. The two of them didn't have much to say to each other. We got back at 11:30 at night. She didn't stay at the White House, she stayed somewhere else. There was no hanky-panky between her and JFK that night, I know because I asked him the next day and he would have happily said so. But, anyway, Jackie knew about that trip. In fact, we were dancing at a White House ball and she said to me, 'Don't think I'm naïve to what you and Jack are doing with all those pretty girls—like Marilyn—sailing on the Potomac under the moonlight. It's all so sophomoric, George.'

"Jackie was accustomed to Kennedy's indiscretions, but this one bothered her. She knew from what she'd heard and read that Marilyn was a troubled woman. 'Have some pity' on her, she said, according to what he later told me. It wasn't so much that she was angry as it was that she was just disgusted. So, Jack told me, 'It's not worth it, George. I have a free ride here with Jackie. She gives me great latitude. So, if this one is going to be an issue for her and cause me other problems with respect to her dealing with the other women I am interested in, then, fine, I can live without this one. I can live without Marilyn Monroe. No problem. So, look, let's just end it with Marilyn before it's too late.'

"I was surprised. I knew Jackie had influence but not *that* much influence, not so much that she could cause the end of the president's relationship with a movie star. But, apparently, she did. So I called someone I knew, a friend of Marilyn's I could trust, and I said, 'Look, I need you to put a bridle on Marilyn's mouth and stop her from talking so much about what's going on with Jack. It's starting to get around too much.' That's all I did to end things, my little contribution. But I know what Jack did. He stopped taking her calls, if he ever took any. As far as he was concerned, he was done with her. But, Marilyn . . . well, she wouldn't be so easily rid of, let's put it that way."

"If Kennedy had handled Marilyn differently, things might not have turned out so badly," said Rupert Allan. "But just ducking her as he did. Not good."

Moreover, JFK had apparently issued somewhat of a challenge to Marilyn in Palm Springs. George Smathers recalled: "JFK told me that they were talking about one thing or another and he happened to say something to her like, 'You're not really First Lady material, anyway, Marilyn.' He said it really stuck in her craw. She didn't like hearing that."

Kennedy never actually told Marilyn that he was finished with her and that whatever he shared with her in Palm Springs would be the extent of their relationship. As sources now indicate, he simply did not return her calls to the White House. It should also be noted, in his defense, that the man was running the country. He had other things on his mind. Marilyn, however, had him on her mind. "Marilyn was a very obsessive and neurotic person," said Diane Stevens. "She was mentally ill, let's face it. She was on drugs and not thinking clearly and just went over the edge when it came to this man and, truly, I do not know why. It had just been a weekend, after all. But for some reason, it became, looking back on it now, the catalyst to her total ruination. The fact that he would not return her calls drove her mad."

Marilyn's Surprise Visit to Pat

Pat Kennedy Lawford had never before had a surprise visit from Marilyn, but on April 8, a couple of weeks after Marilyn's weekend with her brother Jack, she showed up unannounced. "Marilyn was cheery and upbeat," recalls a friend of Lawford's who was present. "She was wearing an orange silk blouse and black slacks and a matching black scarf with cat-eye sunglasses. I thought she looked absolutely marvelous. I know she told Pat that she had been trying to call but her phone was busy."

Pat may have suspected that there was a reason for Marilyn's visit. Earlier, her brother-in-law Bobby called to ask her a series of cryptic questions about Marilyn. Had she seen her? What had she been talking about? Did she mention Jack? Of course, Pat wanted to know what the interrogation was really about. Bobby then told her that Marilyn had been calling the public number to the White House. Since that phone was mainly a message center for the executive branch, not a reliable way to actually speak to the president, Marilyn never got through. JFK, however, did hear about her numerous calls. "Pat was immediately suspicious," says Pat Brennan. "She asked Bobby why Marilyn would be trying to call Jack. He didn't have much of an answer. She knew something had happened, and she anticipated the worst. She made a few calls and it didn't take her long to find out what had happened in Palm Springs. She wasn't happy about it, I can tell you that much."

According to a friend of Pat's who was present that day, Marilyn "bounced onto the beach," while Pat was on the sand winning an intensely competitive game of volleyball, leaping and flailing about without peer on her team. She stopped playing and walked over to Marilyn to embrace her. After a few minutes of small talk with Pat remaining uncharacteristically quiet, Marilyn brought up the subject of her brother, Jack. She said that Pat had been right, her brother *did* have a powerful presence. Pat just stared at Marilyn.

The full details of this tense conversation between Marilyn and Pat remain unknown because the two went into the house, alone. What is known—because Pat later disclosed it—is that Marilyn finally asked Pat for her brother's direct phone number at the White House. Pat refused to give it to her, explaining that the only number she had for him in Washington was his personal number, or as she called it, "his *family* number."

Marilyn backed off the topic a few times, but always returned to it. This obsession about Jack's number frustrated Pat, who later said she had "never seen Marilyn so hyper and manic." Finally, when Marilyn asked if Pat thought her brother was happily married, Pat reached her breaking point. "Why don't you ask him yourself?" she said, grabbing a pen and paper. "I don't want to have anything to do with this." She wrote down a number and handed the paper to Marilyn. After taking it, Marilyn asked Pat if she were angry at her. Without specifically addressing what she now knew happened in Palm Springs between her friend and her brother, Pat was still able to be painfully clear. According to what she later recalled, Pat said, "I can get past it. You and I will be able to continue our friendship. But my family? My sisters and my sisters-in-law? I don't know . . . I just don't know."

It's not known if Marilyn used the number she got from Pat Kennedy Lawford to call President Kennedy's private residence. However, something did occur at this same time that suggests that she may have done so, for it was in the spring of 1962 that Kennedy dispatched his attorney general, Bobby Kennedy, to inform Marilyn that she was not to call the White House. Also, he was told to make it clear that the relationship—or whatever it was she thought she had with him—was over, and that she should move on with her life. Bobby gave Marilyn the message.

An Overdose Because of JFK?

On April 10, 1962, Marilyn Monroe was scheduled to meet with the screenwriter of *Something's Got to Give*, Henry Weinstein. The day before, while at Fox for makeup and costume tests, she looked absolutely beautiful and performed quite well for many hours. However, for her follow-up meeting with Weinstein, she was late. That wasn't surprising. When he telephoned her to find out when she might be arriving, he was alarmed to find that there was no answer. After repeated attempts, she finally picked up the phone. "Oh, I'm just fine . . ." she told him. However, she didn't sound "fine" to him at all. Her voice was slurred and she seemed to be drifting in and out of consciousness. Alarmed, Weinstein told her that he would be right over and hung up. Then he called Dr. Greenson and the two rushed to Marilyn's Brentwood home. There they found her in bed, out cold.

"She was almost naked," Weinstein recalled. "And she was almost dead, as far as I could see. She was at least in a drug coma. I couldn't imagine what it was that had happened, why she did this to herself. The fact that she had been so upbeat one day and then in this state the next day was very disconcerting. Somehow, Dr. Greenson revived her. I was so shaken, I could not get over it. He kept coming over to me and saying, 'Don't worry, she'll be fine.

She'll be fine.' It was as if he had seen this so many times, he was not alarmed by it. But for me, it was traumatic."

Later, it was determined that Marilyn had taken what could have amounted to a deadly combination of Nembutal, Demerol, chloral hydrate, and Librium. "Immediately afterward, I tried to get Fox to delay the movie. I said, 'Look, this girl is in no shape to make a movie. She needs time. She's very sick. She has severe mental problems.' The studio said, 'No. The movie goes on. If we had stopped production of a film every time Marilyn Monroe had a crisis, we would never have gotten a single movie out of her.'

"I don't think I ever got over the shock of finding her that way," said Weinstein. "You don't get past something like that easily. I spent hours trying to understand what had gone so wrong. I thought, well, [George] Cukor hadn't shown up to direct the costume tests the day before and maybe she was unhappy about that. Maybe she thought it was a slap in the face, or a rejection. But . . . I don't know . . . it had to be something more."

It was something more. One source who was close to Marilyn Monroe at that time and who asked for anonymity rather than risk the possibility of retaliation from any member of the Kennedy family summed it up this way: "JFK. That's what was wrong. She'd just been jilted by the president of the United States. Do you really think that after all she'd been through with moviemaking she was going to try to kill herself because a director hadn't shown up for a day's work at the studio? It was Kennedy. That's why. Kennedy."

Were Marilyn and Bobby "The New Item"?

$\mathcal{I}$t was clear to Marilyn that President John Kennedy was finished with her. There wasn't much she could do about it, especially since he was not going to take her calls. However, a very popular story concerning Marilyn and the Kennedys claims the following: When Bobby told Marilyn Jack was done with her, he couldn't help himself and he, too, ended up falling for her. The two then had a passionate affair and Marilyn felt more strongly about him than she had about his brother. This scenario has been repeated in count-less books over the years by many respected historians. Could this have happened? Were these people just that capricious and, dare it be said, foolish? Well, actually, in many ways, they were . . . but, that said, it simply doesn't appear to be true. New research now reveals that Bobby, who—at least at first—apparently decided to not be quite as coldhearted as his brother, felt sorry about the way Marilyn had been treated. He had enjoyed the times he met her, thought she was witty and intelligent as well as beautiful, and didn't feel the need to be cruel to her. "I think he told her, look, don't call the White House, call me," said the veteran entertainer Andy Wil-liams, who was one of RFK's best friends. "Bob was that way. He was a compassionate person. He wasn't a jerk. He had no reason to be mean to the poor woman. I mean, why would he do that? What was the harm in giving her a friendly shoulder to lean on when she was in so much trouble?"

At around this time, Marilyn did indeed tell certain people that she and Bobby were involved. These people, of course, believed her. It's interesting in that many of them never believed anything she ever said about anything else, but *this*, they believed. Could she re-ally be trusted, though? Was she a reliable source for this kind of information, especially in the last six months of her life when she was in such a desperate emotional state and also addicted to drugs? Remember, this is a woman who first began creating fictions about herself years earlier. In 1958, for instance, she made this statement to a reporter: "When I lived with the minister and his wife, they told me that if I went to a movie on a Sunday, God would strike me dead. The first time I dared to sneak away and go to a Sunday movie, I was scared stiff to come out. When I did, it was raining. There was thunder and lightning and I ran all the way home, expecting to be dead any minute. Even after I was home and in bed underneath the covers, I was terrified." Marilyn never lived with a minister and his wife—she was obviously speaking of the Bolenders, with whom she lived during the first seven years of her life. If anyone believed Ida would have let her out of her sight at that age long enough for her to "sneak away" to the movies—about two miles from the Bolenders' home—they did not know Ida very well. As we've seen time and time again, for a variety of reasons, Marilyn often embellished the truth, and not just to the press, which would have been an acceptable form of public relations, but to her friends as well. Her publicist Pat Newcomb put it this way: "Marilyn told several people a lot of things, but she never told anybody everything." Indeed, just as recently as a few months earlier she had told many of her friends that she and Bobby Kennedy were about to go on "a date." It turned out, of course, that it was a dinner party attended by many others, not a date.

Still, some people were very convinced that she was in love with Bobby, even Michael Selsman, who was another in a string of publicists. "Oh, please, of course it was true," he says. "Everyone knew it even then, but the press was much more protective. It was our job to steer them away from it, anyway. But she couldn't stop talking about it. With Bobby, it was more serious than with JFK."

"Sometimes I think, yes, Bobby did end up with Marilyn Monroe," says Andy Williams. "But then I think, wait. Based on what? I know he never told me. Ethel never told me, and she's one of my best friends. Not that Bobby was a saint. He was like the Kennedys when it came to women. I know that Ethel was aware of it and, in some ways, maybe didn't have a problem with it. She would call me and say, 'Bobby is coming to town. Will you have him to dinner? And find the best-looking girl for him, as a dinner partner?' But where Bobby and Marilyn are concerned, the only people I ever heard that from was from those who, I guess, heard it from Marilyn. And now, all of these years later, I have to say I don't know . . . I never met the woman and wouldn't want to be critical of her but I think she was telling tales."

Then again, maybe she wasn't the only one. Consider this very strange letter Marilyn received after meeting Bobby Kennedy, from his own sister, Jean Kennedy Smith:

Dear Marilyn,

Mother asked me to write and thank you for your sweet note to Daddy. He really enjoyed it and thought you were very cute to send it.

Understand that you and Bobby are the new item! We all think you should come with him when he comes back East.

Again, thanks for the note.

Love,
Jean Smith

This letter (which was found by Marilyn's business manager, Inez Nelson, after Marilyn's death) has been used several times over the years to support the claim of an affair between Marilyn and Bobby. There are a few problems with it, though. The way Kennedy women operated, they didn't confirm the affairs had by the men in the family. They ignored them. They certainly didn't cheerily write about them in correspondence, committing to paper what could one day be used against them. The family members were always cognizant of their place in history and knew that whatever they said, did, or wrote could one day become part of the historical record. That said, it is strange that Jean Smith would have written the note at all, knowing that it could be one day misinterpreted if read by someone other than Marilyn. She would have done it only if she truly thought the story was so absurd that no one would take it seriously, even with the passing of time. Of course, another possibility is that the letter is a forgery. Comparing the handwriting to that of Smith, it appears to be legitimate. The fact that it's not dated, though, makes it impossible to place it in the proper time context. Whatever questions there are about this letter, its mere existence is a primary reason it's so widely believed Marilyn and Bobby were "the new item!"

It's clear that Bobby Kennedy regarded Marilyn with at least a little affection and that she felt the same way about him. The two did have telephone conversations. "He didn't mind talking to her," said George Smathers, a longtime Kennedy political ally and a former governor of Florida and U.S. senator from that state. "There was no harm in it. She was sad and lonely and she would call, so, yeah, he would talk to her and calm her down. There was no affair with Bobby, though. I can tell you that Ethel had her doubts at first, only because the rumors started right away. But Bobby told Ethel they were not true and she believed him. Marilyn had it in her head that she wanted to be First Lady—JFK's wife—not Bobby's. She wasn't interested in Bobby that way. Anyone who says otherwise doesn't know what he's talking about."

Ed Guthman was a good friend of Robert Kennedy's and was with him and Marilyn on at least two occasions. "I know there was no affair," he maintains. "It's not even a question in my mind. I was there. I saw what was going on. And I'm telling you that there was no affair." Another close friend of RFK's, Kenneth O'Donnell, said, "I knew this man as well as anybody. I was intimately associated with him for years and knew everything he ever did, and I know for a fact that this Marilyn Monroe story is absolute bullshit." Pat Newcomb—admittedly not the most reliable source for information considering that her job as Monroe's publicist was to protect her—also weighed in on journalists who have bought into the Marilyn-Bobby romance: "Are they crazy? I knew Bobby very well, better than Marilyn did in a lot of ways. However, you didn't even have to know him well to know that he would never have left Ethel. And with all of those children? Come on!"

"Let me be clear," added Milt Ebbins, who of course knew Marilyn and RFK. "Marilyn was a lot of things, but she wasn't a slut. What kind of character would she have, going from one brother to the next? She was a sexual creature, yes, but she would not have done it. I'm certain it never happened."

Peter Lawford's friend Joseph Naar concluded, "When I hear

Bobby Kennedy was her lover, I say, 'bullshit.' Absolute and complete bullshit."

One more anecdote about Marilyn and Bobby comes from a Kennedy relative who requested anonymity, "because this is still such a sore subject with the family." She was married to one of the family members, though—she will allow that much. She says that she called Pat Kennedy Lawford in the spring of 1962 to ask if she had heard the stories about Marilyn and Bobby. "Okay, this has got to stop right here," Pat said, annoyed. "Either Marilyn is making up stories about Bobby in order to get Jack to change his mind about her, or she's doing it to show Jack what he's missing—or maybe both. Either way, it's adolescent behavior and I will talk to her about it. I asked Bobby very specifically if something was going on with Marilyn and Jack," she added. "He said he did not feel comfortable answering that question. I then asked him if anything was going on between him and Marilyn. He said absolutely not. And I believe him."

Of course, it can be said that for every person who believes the affair didn't happen, there are bound to be people who believe it did—including a number of FBI agents, it would seem.

Because of the ongoing contentious relationship between Bobby Kennedy, who as the attorney general was head of the Justice Department, and J. Edgar Hoover, director of the FBI, who considered the younger Kennedy an upstart and not someone he wanted to answer to, it is entirely possible that promulgating and perpetuating the "romance" between Bobby and Marilyn was a campaign of disinformation ordered by Hoover, a notorious lover of gossip, making it up and spreading it. Actually, some of the FBI's files on Kennedy and Monroe sound as if they were written by a lovesick schoolgirl, especially in that the key players are described by their first names. One missive, released in October 2006 under the Freedom of Information Act, notes that "Robert Kennedy was deeply involved emotionally with Marilyn Monroe." The relationship is described as "a romance and sex affair." The paperwork reports that Bobby "has repeatedly promised to divorce his wife to marry Marilyn. Eventually, Marilyn realized that Bobby had no intention of marrying her." According to whom, though? The "former special agent" who wrote the report and whose name is deleted admits that he doesn't know the source for the information, nor can he vouch for its authenticity. However that didn't stop his report from being duly documented in the FBI's files, on October 19, 1964.

Bobby: "The President Wants It and I Want It"

In May 1962, the relationship between Marilyn and the Kennedy brothers would take yet another strange twist. A celebration was being planned on May 19 for JFK's forty-fifth birthday—a big, overblown, televised spectacle that was to take place at Madison Square Garden. (His actual birthday would be on May 29.) It had been Peter Lawford's idea to have Marilyn Monroe sing "Happy Birthday" to the president. Of course, it was probably the height of arrogance that Peter felt he could get away with such a thing. It was almost as if everyone was so accustomed to getting away with so much where Marilyn was concerned, now they wanted to push the envelope and flaunt the relationship in front of the entire country—and on television!

One question that's never asked in regard to Marilyn's invitation to perform for the president is this: *What in the world were Bobby and JFK thinking?* "This manipulation of Marilyn, already so sick, was as low as it got," said Jeanne Martin, wife of Dean Martin, who was costarring with Marilyn in the beleaguered *Something's Got to Give*. Jeanne was not only still a very good friend of Marilyn's but had also remained friendly with the Kennedys through the years. However, even she realized that the brothers had crossed a line. "This was shameful, it really was," she said. "There was no excuse for it."

Perhaps Marilyn needed the president in her life now more than ever. After all, she was rattled at this time by a series of events that had occurred just a month earlier.

In February, Marilyn had gone to Mexico to purchase furnishings for her new home. While she was there with Pat Newcomb and Eunice Murray, it again became clear that she was being followed by FBI agents. It couldn't have been a more ludicrous pursuit. The agents had it in their heads that she was involved with someone named Fred Vanderbilt Field, who had apparently served nine months in prison for not naming Communist friends. He moved to Mexico in 1953. Now, all these years later, a friend of a friend introduced him and his wife to Marilyn and—voilà!—the FBI was tracking her every move in Mexico. For a woman who was already thought to be borderline paranoid schizophrenic by her doctor, such pursuit had to have been extremely frightening.

There are actually many allegations presented as fact in the FBI files concerning Monroe and Field, none of which appear to be true and none of which therefore are worth enumeration. In these same FBI files that detail her every move in Mexico, there is mention of her meeting with Bobby Kennedy in October 1961. She was definitely being watched—and she knew it.

At about this same time, Marilyn was in desperate trouble with 20th Century-Fox. In April and May 1962, as she continued to slip deeper into the darkest recesses of her mind, she placed the production of *Something's Got to Give* in even greater jeopardy. It was impossible for her to begin rehearsals and camera tests for the film. She was constantly late, if she showed up at all. She always had an excuse, as she would for absences during the entire production, whether it was a cold, a sinus infection, or some other malady. All of it was true—she was a very sick woman. But she was also scared to death of George Cukor, and that didn't help matters either. Moreover, it was thought by most observers that Paula Strasberg, Marilyn's acting coach (who was being paid $5,000 a week), had become very intrusive. Sidney Guilaroff, who styled Marilyn's hair for the film as he had for many others, put it this way: "Dressed all in black, including a black gypsy scarf and thick stockings, Paula haunted the set—sometimes directing Marilyn with hand signals behind Cukor's back. Marilyn was so dependent upon her that she could barely read a line without Strasberg's specific brand of coaching."

Harvey Bernstein once recalled a meeting he had with Marilyn at her home to discuss the script. She answered the door in hair curlers. There was no furniture in her living room, just a chair on which he sat while she sat on the floor. "Many of her ideas [for the script] were good for her and not so good for the story," he recalled. "But if I hinted at this, her face would go blank for a second, as though the current had been turned off, and when it was turned on again, she would continue as though I had said nothing. . . . Sometimes she would refer to herself in the third person, like Caesar. 'Remember you've got Marilyn Monroe, you've got to use her,' she told me. . . . I left feeling like a deckhand on a ship with no one at the helm and the water ahead full of rocks.'"*

The last thing executives at 20th Century-Fox would approve of was Marilyn taking more time off to fly to New York City to sing for the president. Even though she had earlier been given permission, Peter Levathes reversed his position based on her poor attendance on the set of the film. He didn't want her to be distracted. In fact, the studio threatened to sue her if she took off for New York (and actually would file suit against her). When Bobby Kennedy heard of the possibility of a lawsuit against Marilyn, he decided to take matters into his own hands. He called Levathes to appeal to him that Marilyn's appearance for the president was *very* im-

---

* On her revised script for *Something's Got to Give* (dated February 12, 1962), Marilyn recognized that the story was still not a good one. She wrote on the title page, "We've got a dog here—so we've got to look for impacts in a different way, or as Mr. [Nunnally] Johnson says, the situation." On page 12, she noted, "The only people on earth I get on well with is [sic] men so let's have some fun with this opening scene." And on page 23, she commented on Cyd Charisse's character, "Let's remember she is frigid—We all know what Kinsey found out about most females."

portant and would mean a lot to JFK. Levathes stood firm that he would not approve it. Annoyed, Bobby went over Levathes's head to his boss, Milton Gould. Gould has recalled that Bobby told him, "'The president wants it, and I want it.' He was very abusive. I was surprised at his total lack of class. I told him we were very much behind in our schedule and would not release her. He called me a 'no-good Jew bastard,' which I didn't appreciate. Then he slammed down the phone. I have to say I was surprised that they wanted her so badly that he was willing to humiliate himself like that."

As it would happen, it didn't matter to Marilyn whether or not the studio approved of her going to New York. She'd made up her mind that she was going, and that was the end of it. Her priority was to be in New York with the Kennedy brothers. Twentieth Century-Fox could wait. At some point during this time, she apparently became melancholy about President Kennedy, because she painted a single red rose in watercolor on a sheet of paper. Then, in blue ink, she signed at the bottom left, "Happy Birthday Pres. Kennedy from Marilyn Monroe." She additionally signed and inscribed below the first signature, in black ink, this time mysteriously signing her name twice, reading in full: "Happy Birthday June 1, 1962/My Best Wishes/Marilyn/Marilyn." Of course, June 1, 1962, would be her last birthday, her thirty-sixth. (Decades later in 2005, this artwork would sell for $78,000 in a Julien's auction of Marilyn's possessions.)

Marilyn left Los Angeles for New York on May 17, telling the media, "I told the studio six weeks ago that I was going. I consider it an honor to appear before the President of the United States." The cast and crew of *Something's Got to Give* were stunned by her decision. "It was very surprising," recalled her stand-in, Evelyn Moriarty. "We all just felt like things couldn't get much worse. It was all so unpredictable and awful. But she did have permission, even if they took it away from her."

Dean Martin's manager, Mort Viner, said, "That was poor form on her part. It showed where her priorities were, anyway, didn't it? But Dean told me, 'Hey, you can't blame her, Mort. Look, if Jackie

Kennedy had asked me to fly cross country and sing Happy Birthday to her, I woulda gone.'"

New research now establishes, however, that perhaps the decision wasn't as easy for Marilyn as previously believed. She was conflicted, and she turned to her friend Pat Lawford for advice. According to people who knew Pat well, Pat told her that she now believed her brothers were being unfair to Marilyn, and maybe even trying to make a fool of her. This was likely not easy for Pat to admit. After all, she was a loyal Kennedy and almost always supported her brothers. However, as Marilyn's friend, she may have felt compelled to tell her how she truly felt about the matter. It's a testament to her, actually, that she was able to put aside her feelings of betrayal by Marilyn in order to help her friend achieve some clarity over the situation.

"She was worried about her," said a Kennedy family member. "She knew her brothers. She loved them, but she knew them well. She didn't think Marilyn could handle them. However, Marilyn thought that maybe if she went to New York, it would show the family that she was being supportive. She was putting her career on the line to do it, too. I mean, she was risking everything. There wasn't much Pat could say to that, I guess. It was a tough situation for everyone."

It also should be noted here that Marilyn no longer felt compelled to confide in her half sister, Berniece. Marilyn loved Berniece but had always felt that she had her own life and problems and was not necessarily a person she could turn to in times of trouble. What was Berniece to do on the other side of the country when Marilyn was in crisis mode? As a demonstration of the superficial nature of their relationship at this time, when the two talked about the upcoming Madison Square Garden appearance, Marilyn told her that her only apprehension was that she didn't feel she was up to the task of singing in public. She said that she felt her voice was not up to her standards. She didn't invite Berniece to the show, and apparently Berniece didn't ask to go.

By 1962, Marilyn had done everything she could to see to it that her mother—seen here at Rock Haven Sanitarium—received the proper medical attention for paranoid schizophrenia. However, because her religious beliefs restricted the use of most medications, Gladys's mental illness was never under control. (*Courtesy of Maryanne Reed Collection*)

Not at all well. In these two rare photographs, taken on January 20, 1962, Marilyn is seen at a party hosted by Harvey Weinstein, producer of her movie *Something's Got to Give*. In the first, she sips on a cocktail while talking to poet Carl Sandburg. In the second—published here for the first time—she is seen dancing while still holding a drink. (Note how thin she is in this picture.) (*Getty Images*)

Marilyn first met Bobby Kennedy on February 1, 1962, at a dinner party at Pat and Peter Lawford's home. This receipt disproves the long-reported story that Marilyn became so drunk that night she couldn't drive herself back home and had to be driven by RFK and a friend. That maybe happened some other time, but on this evening she was definitely driven to and from the Lawford home by Carey Cadillac. (*J. Randy Taraborrelli Collection.*)

CAREY CADILLAC RENTING CO. of CALIF., INC.
9641 Sunset Boulevard
Beverly Hills, California

Date 2/1/62

Charge to: *Marilyn Monroe*
882 N. Doheny
West Hollywood
Calif.

For use of:

Limo # *83*   From *882 N. Doheny*

Miles	Hours	*625 Oceanfront–Santa Mon.*
In *11618*	*3:60A*	to *882 N. Doheny*
Out *11591*	*8:00P*	
Net *27*	*7*	

THE WHITE HOUSE
WASHINGTON

April 11, 1962

Dear Miss Monroe:

Many, many thanks for your acceptance of the invitation to appear at the President's Birthday Party in Madison Square Garden on May 19.

Your appearance will guarantee a tremendous success for the affair and a fitting tribute to President Kennedy.

With every good wish,

Sincerely,

Kenneth O'Donnell
Special Assistant to the President

Miss Marilyn Monroe
12-305 Fifth Helena Drive
Los Angeles 49, California

Certainly Kenneth O'Donnell, special assistant to JFK, couldn't have known the sensation that would be caused by extending this invitation to Marilyn! (*J. Randy Taraborrelli Collection*)

Another photo that has never before appeared in a Marilyn Monroe biography, of Marilyn and her publicist, Pat Newcomb, arriving at Madison Square Garden for JFK's birthday party in May 1962. (*J. Randy Taraborrelli Collection*)

Taken at a party following her performance, this is the only known photograph of Marilyn with both Bobby (left) and President John F. Kennedy. *(Cecil Stoughton/Life Magazine, Time-Warner Inc.)*

Marilyn performed for JFK wearing what she described as "a dress only Marilyn Monroe could wear." *(Photofest)*

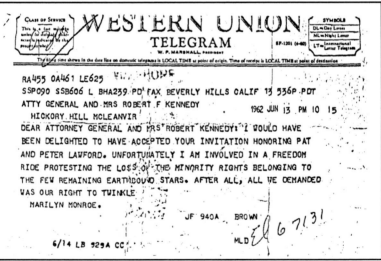

Marilyn sent this telegram to Mr. and Mrs. Robert Kennedy, declining an invitation to attend a party in honor of Pat and Peter Lawford in June 1962. Some have speculated that Marilyn declined because she was having an affair with Bobby. Others have wondered if Ethel would have invited her at all had she thought Marilyn was involved with her husband. In fact, it doesn't seem as if Marilyn and Bobby were anything more than friends. (*J. Randy Taraborrelli Collection.*)

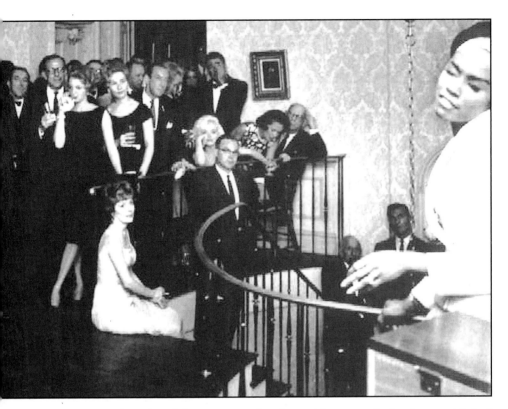

This fascinating photo hasn't been seen in decades and has never before been published in any Marilyn Monroe biography. It, too, was taken at the after party following the Madison Square Garden event. Marilyn—on the right, watching Diahann Carroll perform—is holding a glass of champagne, her arm dangling carelessly over a railing. Seated on the far left is President John F. Kennedy. Against the wall, under the stairs, one can spot Ethel Kennedy and Pat Kennedy Lawford, Marilyn's close friend. Peter Lawford is directly behind Marilyn, leaning against the wall. *(The Kennedy Library)*

The Lost Weekend: Marilyn and Peter Lawford at the Cal-Neva Lodge in July 1962, the weekend Marilyn was perhaps at her worst—the weekend that changed the lives of just about everyone involved: Peter, his wife, Pat, Frank Sinatra, and, of course, Marilyn. *(MPTV)*

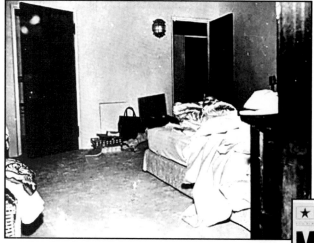

It's difficult to believe that one of the greatest movie stars of all time died in this sparse, disheveled bedroom. It's been said that she hadn't had time for interior decorating, even though she'd moved into the house almost six months earlier. *(Retro Photo)*

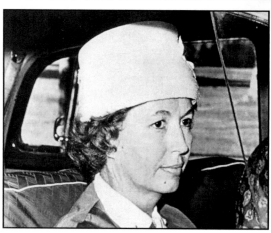

Berniece Miracle leaves the funeral home after having made final arrangements for her half sister. *(Retro Photo)*

A sad—and shocking—headline. *(Retro Photo)*

Marilyn's final resting place, at Westwood Memorial Park. *(J. Randy Taraborrelli Collection)*

A never-before-published letter from Gladys Baker Eley to Marilyn's business manager, Inez Melson, written after Marilyn's death in 1962. "She is at peace and at rest now," Gladys wrote of her daughter, "and may God help her always." Gladys affixed to the letter a newspaper notice of the probate of Marilyn's will. *(Shaan Kokin/Julien's Auctions)*

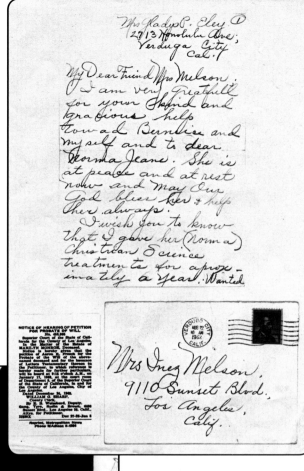

Gladys lived another twenty-two largely unhappy years after the death of her famous daughter. *(Photofest)*

"She should have been made of iron or steel, but she was only made of flesh and blood." Like many of the photographs in this book, this one is so rare it may never have been published before, and certainly not in any previous Marilyn Monroe biography. *(Frank Worth Estate and International Images, Inc.)*

"*Happy Birthday, Mr. President*"

$\mathcal{B}$ackstage at Madison Square Garden in New York City on May 19, 1962, Marilyn Monroe was extremely anxious, and with good reason. No doubt the gravity of the situation finally hit her. She was about to honor someone who had just rejected her, and he was the president of the United States. She had left Los Angeles against the wishes of her bosses at Fox, risking her starring role in a movie. Complexities most people could never imagine, yet this was Marilyn's life, for better or worse (and, lately, it would seem, mostly for worse).

Earlier in the month, producer Richard Adler expressed concern over what Marilyn might decide to wear to such an important, televised event. She told him not to fret. She said she planned to wear a sophisticated black satin dress with a high neckline that had already been designed for her by couturier Norman Norell. However, she secretly had other plans. She asked designer Jean Louis to design a dress "that only Marilyn Monroe could wear," and that's exactly what he did. "Marilyn had a totally charming way of boldly displaying her body and remaining elegant at the same time," he later recalled. "So, I designed an apparently nude dress—the nudest dress—relieved only by sequins and beading." Incidentally, the gown was not lined, and Marilyn did not wear undergarments—of course! She was actually stitched into the dress by its designer. (This is the gown that sold at auction in 2007 for $1.27 million.)

After she was introduced by Peter Lawford, he took her ermine stole from her and Marilyn went on to breathlessly sing "Happy Birthday" to the president. "She handled the lyrics well enough," said producer Richard Adler, "but you couldn't hear them anyway. For the crowd was yelling and screaming for her. It was like a mass seduction." Most people with even a passing interest in Marilyn Monroe have seen footage of Marilyn singing "Happy Birthday" on this evening. Less seen was the rest of her number, a special tribute to JFK written by Adler and performed by Monroe to the melody of "Thanks for the Memories." Afterward, Marilyn had the audience join her for another round of "Happy Birthday."

"I was honored when they asked me to appear," Marilyn later told Richard Merryman of *Life*. "There was like a hush over the whole place when I came on to sing Happy Birthday—like if I had been wearing a slip, I would have thought it was showing, or something. I thought, 'Oh my gosh, what if no sound comes out . . .' I remember when I turned to the microphone, I looked all the way up and back and I thought, 'That's where I'd be—way up there under one of those rafters, close to the ceiling, after I paid my $2 to come into the place.'"

Making her performance that night as provocative as possible was definitely an odd choice for Marilyn, especially if one considers her career up until that point. How many years had she spent complaining about her dumb-blonde image? How many fights had she waged against 20th Century-Fox for roles that would break her from the mold? How many years had she spent studying acting so that she could be revealed as a different kind of performer? Why, one has to wonder, did she decide to throw away any chance she would ever have of being thought of in a different way and appear on this very important, high-profile night as the very character she had worked so hard to bury? She certainly wasn't doing the "dumb, sexy blonde" act in *Something's Got to Give*, the movie she was currently making, so we know she was doing serious work. It was a choice. Most people in her circle were unhappy about it. During a rehearsal of her song, Paula Strasberg said, "It keeps getting sexier and sexier. If she doesn't stop, it will be a parody." In fact, Richard Adler, who had written the special lyrics for the "Thanks for the Memories" part of the medley, was so uncomfortable about Marilyn's presentation, he called Peter Lawford about it. Lawford called JFK and told him, "Marilyn's going to be over-the-top sexy." JFK's reaction? "Sounds good to me." There was nothing anyone could say to Marilyn that would encourage her to tone it down.

Based on the footage we've all seen over the years from this evening, it would appear that Marilyn is extremely far from the president as she performs for him. Engulfed in blackness, she seems to be gazing into a great void. We've never actually seen whatever was in front of her. Actually, less than a foot away from her was the orchestra pit with about twelve musicians in it, all in tuxes and looking up at her with big smiles on their faces. Behind them was a walkway that was about two feet wide. Then, directly behind that, was the first row with the president sitting directly in front of Marilyn. In all, he's not more than about twelve feet away from her. According to people who were present, he at first seemed a bit thunderstruck by Marilyn's appearance, but then quite happy—not embarrassed, as other accounts have had it. For his part, Bobby—in the third row—grinned like a Cheshire cat. Ethel—in the second row sitting in front of her husband—also looked happy. In fact, judging from photos of her as she watched Marilyn, she seems as if she couldn't have been enjoying it more. However, Pat, in these same photos, looks more concerned than anything else.

Jeanne Martin, seated in the VIP section of Madison Square Garden, says she watched with horrified fascination. "To be really honest, as much as I loved Marilyn, I thought it was the height of distastefulness," she said. "Nothing against Marilyn. She was being Marilyn, doing what Marilyn does. She couldn't be blamed for being herself.

"I remember squirming in my seat and turning away, but you also couldn't help but watch," said Martin. "It was such a spectacle. The footage we've all seen doesn't do it justice. In person, it was pretty shocking, especially for the times. For Bobby to organize this thing and for the president to sit there and allow it, well, I must say, I thought at the time that it was very disrespectful to the presidency, and also to the First Lady. I remember thinking, 'My God, what if Jackie sees this? What will she think?'"

Jackie was not present. Her absence made quite a statement. After all, she was the First Lady, it was the president's birthday celebration, and the event would be broadcast on television. That she decided to absent herself spoke volumes about how she felt about the situation regarding her husband and the movie star. She knew about it, and was annoyed by it. In fact, she told her Secret Service agent Clinton Hill, "I'm not going to sit and watch that. If you ask me, I think this administration is completely out of control with all of this Marilyn business." Hill had no opinion on the matter, or at least not one that he would think to tell the First Lady. After an awkward silence, Jackie may have realized that she'd gone too far by expressing her own view of the matter because she told him, "Forget I ever said that, please."*

"I can now retire from politics after having had Happy Birthday sung to me in such a sweet, wholesome way," Kennedy said when taking the podium after Marilyn. Was he joking? Or being sarcastic?

"I hurt for her," Susan Strasberg said of Marilyn that night. "From what she'd told me, each time she caricatured herself, she chipped a piece out of her own dream." Susan's father, Lee—Marilyn's acting coach—must have known it would be difficult to sit through such a performance because he refused to attend.

After the performance, there was a small party hosted by Arthur Krim, president of United Artists, and his wife, Mathilde, a scientist who would later be known for her work in the fight against AIDS. Marilyn, Bobby, and JFK were in attendance. Anthony Sherman was one of the Secret Service agents at work that night. He recalled, "Oh, boy! I'll never forget that night. I was assigned at the checkpoint at the private home where the party took place. I remember the car pulling up very vividly and the door opened and out walked this unbelievably beautiful woman, Marilyn Monroe, with this older man [Isadore Miller, Arthur's father and Marilyn's "date" for the evening—a man she adored and called "Dad"]. She

---

* Nunziata Lisi, a friend of Jackie's sister Lee Radziwill, recalled, "Lee told me that there wasn't a big fight between Jackie and JFK over the matter of Marilyn at Madison Square Garden. She just made a quiet decision that if he wasn't going to care about her feelings— if he didn't care that she would be humiliated—then, fine. She just wasn't going to go and there would be nothing he could do to persuade her otherwise. She told Lee, 'Life is too short to worry about Marilyn Monroe.' She would take the children to the Glen Ora retreat, a couple hours outside of Washington, where she enjoyed riding her horses."

had on this dress—or whatever it was—it was more like a see-through thing—that she, apparently, had worn on stage. What a knockout. Everyone was stopped dead in their tracks as she got out of the car and walked toward the entrance. She walked up to me, I had a list of people who had been invited, and she said, 'Hello, sir. I'm Marilyn Monroe.' And I stood there thinking, you're Marilyn Monroe, all right. We smiled and as I let her pass, I thought, wow. I was working for the president of the United States so every moment was history. But this? *This*, for me, was history."

At the party, Marilyn walked up to the president and said, "This is my former father-in-law, Isadore Miller." Then, embarrassed for a second, she said, "I'm so sorry. I should have said, 'Happy Birthday, Mr. President,' but I was so excited about Dad, I introduced him first." It was an odd encounter. It was that impersonal, as though Marilyn and Jack didn't really know each other at all. Marilyn spent maybe five minutes with JFK and Bobby, if that long. For the rest of the party, she doted on her former father-in-law. Seventy-seven years old, he was tired; she managed to get him a chair. "Sit down, Dad, please," she begged him. Then she knelt beside him to talk. He later recalled, "She was very beautiful."

"It's certainly her beauty I remember most," recalled Diahann Carroll, who performed at the Krim party. "As I sang, I distinctly remember being somewhat distracted by her gaze. Her tragic beauty, so vulnerable . . . so lost."

It has been reported numerous times over the years—thanks to the FBI's report of the evening in its files—that Marilyn spent the night with JFK at the Carlyle Hotel after the show. Even more sensationally, it's also been even reported that after JFK was finished with her, he sent her over to the room next door where she then had sex with Bobby. Marilyn's actual itinerary that night was as follows: The show started at 8 p.m. Marilyn didn't get onstage until at least one o'clock, being the thirty-fifth of thirty-nine appearances made onstage that night. Then she went to the Krim party with Isadore Miller. Afterward, she accompanied him to his home in Brooklyn. She kissed him goodbye at the elevator and began to walk away. He recalled that just before he got into the elevator, she turned around and said, "Dad, come back to the coast with me tomorrow." He smiled. "Later, Marilyn," he promised. "Maybe in November." She blew him a kiss and walked away—and that would be the last time he would ever see her. She got home at about four in the morning, where she was met by her friend James Haspiel, who had earlier attended the performance. He recalled, "I looked at Marilyn, not knowing that this would be our last time together. Now she wasn't on stage, she was here just at arm's length away from me, and I could touch her. Her face was incredibly beautiful, movingly vulnerable. Her hair looked like white spun gold. My eyes descended to the rhinestone-like gems sewn onto her dazzling gown, now eliciting flickers of light, those beams bouncing off the flesh colored material encasing her magnificent body."

One might argue that somewhere between dropping off Isadore Miller and meeting up with James Haspiel, Marilyn could have slipped off for a quick interlude at the Carlyle with JFK . . . but all of my years of research indicate that this did not happen.

That said, Marilyn did not do a very good job of hiding her feelings for the commander in chief. Rupert Allan, who was present at the after-party, recalled, "When Marilyn finally moved close to the president, I suddenly realized that she had fallen in love with him. It frightened me because I knew Marilyn never did anything by halves."

Neither did Jackie Kennedy, apparently. In fact, multiple sources now report that Jackie made it clear to JFK that she was unhappy about the Madison Square Garden performance and that if he didn't assure her that it was truly over with Marilyn, she would take action. She threatened to file for divorce immediately before the next presidential campaign, thereby jeopardizing his chances of being re-elected. "Oh, and she meant business," said George Smathers. "She wasn't fooling around. But Jack was already done with Marilyn, anyway, by that time. He had this other girl named Mary Meyer he was playing around with, and there was always Judith Exner . . . and there were others, one of whom was rumored to be [actress] Angie

Dickinson. His view of Marilyn was that she was a very sweet girl, but to him sweet girls were a dime a dozen. There was no shortage of sweet girls in his life, and Marilyn was trouble. She began to ask for opportunities to come to Washington, come to the White House, that sort of thing. So, he told Jackie, 'Look, it really is over. It was nothing, anyway.' I don't know if she believed him."

PART NINE

Sad Endings

Marilyn Fired

*W*hen Marilyn Monroe returned to Los Angeles, she was scheduled to get back to work on the set of *Something's Got to Give*. However, Dean Martin had a cold that day—May 29, 1962—and Marilyn felt that if she caught it she would not be able to work for the rest of the week, so she stayed home. "That, to me, was the funniest goddamn thing in the world," said Mort Viner, Dean Martin's manager. "This girl is home almost every day with some crazy sickness holding up the whole production. Then, the one day Dean has a cold, he goes to work anyway because he doesn't want to let the cast down—and *she* doesn't show up because she doesn't want to catch his cold? That night, Dean and I had a good laugh about it. Dean said, 'She's got some nerve that one, you gotta hand it to her. When she doesn't want to work, she will find a way to not work.'"

Marilyn did return to the studio the next day for what turned out to be an incredible day of shooting a nude scene in a swimming pool. It was the first time an American actress had ever done such a thing, and of course, it would be Marilyn doing it. The plan had been for her to wear a skin-colored bodysuit. However, she lasted a very short time in it until she took it off and decided to just be nude. The set was closed, however, with only those most required to be there allowed access. Footage from that day's work reveals her to be in good spirits. Her body, toned and voluptuous, probably never looked better. She appeared to be in her mid-twenties, certainly not a woman on the verge of turning thirty-six. Monroe historian Charles Casillo astutely observes, "It was part of the schizophrenic, contradictory view she had of herself at the time. Part of her was ready, even eager, to move into serious roles, yet another part of her realized what was still expected of her. She'd have to transcend gradually into the new image while still having to occasionally play to the legend. So if displaying her calendar girl figure would add a little fire to a mediocre movie and keep the public interested—buy her some more time—then she was willing. God, she felt like she needed a hit."

Her friend the acting coach Michael Shaw, twenty-two at this time, saw her at the Fox studio and his comments show that Marilyn, when she did manage to get to the studio, was a pro: "I was studying with [acting coach] Sandy [Meisner] on the 20th lot and Marilyn came up to me in the parking lot, and said, 'Peaches'— that's what she called me—'why don't we meet and have lunch,'" he recalled. "She was wearing a pair of pedal pushers and a pair of flat shoes and a scarf and nobody paid her the slightest bit of attention because she looked like she was fourteen! She went to her dressing room, and said, 'Well, time to put her together.' She went into her dressing room and about forty minutes later . . . *Marilyn Monroe* walked out. It was just a total transformation.[*]

"So, we walked into the commissary. She stood in the doorway as we were waiting to go into the private section of the dining room. All of a sudden there was total, complete silence. People were in the process of eating. They had forks of food halfway up to their mouths and they stopped. She was such a knockout. She looked so great. She had lost weight, in the best health that I had seen. We had lunch. She seemed very excited about Joe DiMaggio again. I wanted to meet him. I had met him very informally. I was looking forward to seeing him again. I was a big DiMaggio fan. She said, 'Well, then, we've got to have you over for dinner when I'm cooking . . .'

"Then, I guess it must have been a week or so later, a few of my classmates, we were at lunch in the commissary. Marilyn came in. She was wearing pink-and-white Capri pants with a matching top

---

[*] Marilyn Monroe historian James Haspiel recounts this story: "[The actress] Sheree North told me that when she was at 20th Century-Fox one day, she ran into Allen 'Whitey' Snyder, who was pacing outside of a closed door, very frustrated. She asked him what was wrong. He said, 'Marilyn is in there and she won't let me in. She's making up her own face.' I'm not saying Whitey never made up her face. Of course, he did. But there were times when all he needed to do was make a touch-up. She—Marilyn—was the real master of that look."

with a little white lace eyelet around the neck and the sleeve. She also had on white ballet slippers. She came over and greeted me with 'Peaches!' And she pulled me back in the chair, planted a big one on my mouth, and said, 'I *love* this guy!' Of course, I felt like a half million dollars! And, that was the last time I ever saw her."

On Monday, May 28, Marilyn called in sick, again. Apparently, she'd had a very difficult weekend. It's not known what happened, but any hope that she would be able to continue the kind of good work she'd done the last time she was at the studio was dashed. When she returned on Tuesday, she was in terrible shape, not really able to concentrate. Her thirty-sixth birthday was on June 1. There was a birthday cake for her on the set, which she appreciated, and that afternoon she made a charity appearance at Dodger Stadium. When she went home that night, things spiraled further downward. Later that night, Marilyn showed up at the Greensons' home in such bad shape, his children didn't know what to do with her. Dr. Greenson and his wife, Hildy, were on vacation in Rome.

"This woman was desperate," Greenson's son Danny recalled. "She couldn't sleep and she said how terrible she felt about herself, how worthless she felt. She talked about being a waif, that she was ugly, that people were only nice to her for what they could get from her. She said life wasn't worth living anymore."

The doctor that Greenson had asked to cover for him while he was out of town rushed over to the house and felt that Marilyn was suicidal. He attempted to confiscate any pills she had and hoped she would be okay long enough for Dr. Greenson to return, which he did as soon as he heard how poorly his star client was faring.

After she missed yet another day of work, the cast and crew of the film were pretty much finished with her. Dr. Greenson met with the Fox executives to tell them that Marilyn would do whatever he wanted her to do, and he could guarantee that she would return to work. He wasn't believed. On June 8, Fox fired her from the film and then filed a half-million-dollar lawsuit against her. Some thought it was George Cukor the studio should have gotten rid of, and perhaps with him gone Marilyn would have shown up for work. It was difficult to say, though, because she was so removed from reality at this time—especially off her Thorazine—that all bets were off. For instance, she wanted Cyd Charisse's hair dyed a darker color since, in her view, there should only be one blonde in the movie and Charisse "unconscious wants it [her own hair] to be blonde." Even more outrageous, Marilyn viewed the rushes of a bedroom scene between Dean Martin and Charisse, wearing a revealing negligee. She accused the actress of padding her bra and threatened to walk off the picture if the padding was not removed. It was another instance where Monroe's paranoia surfaced; Cyd Charisse's bra was not padded. In the end, Marilyn had showed up for only about a third of the movie's production days thus far. The film was a million dollars over budget.

Naturally, Marilyn was upset about being fired. In her view she had been loyal to 20th Century-Fox for sixteen years and was now being treated without regard for the legitimate problems she faced in her life. In Fox's view, those had not been sixteen good years. Yes, she made a great deal of money for the studio—and, truly, was underpaid in a way that even today seems shocking—but almost every movie she ever made caused so many problems for everyone involved that some people had begun to wonder if she were worth it. Of course, the same could be said for Elizabeth Taylor and practically every other actor and actress working in the business at that time. That said, Marilyn was a woman whose aspirations had always been very basic. All she ever wanted was to be an actress and to be good at it. Oh . . . and she wanted to be famous. That was about it. There was never a monetary motivation. Money and prestige meant pretty much nothing to her. The modest house she'd just bought is evidence of her simple and, really, very charming taste. How her dreams got so screwed up was probably beyond her comprehension at this time, especially given her mental illness.

Marilyn wouldn't take it all without a fight, though. As soon as she was dismissed, she began to orchestrate a major campaign to make sure the public knew she was alive and well. Her public relations venture included a cover story in *Life* magazine that was, no doubt, the best and most thought-provoking interview she'd ever given. Richard Merryman had told her that he wanted to discuss not only the legend of Monroe, but also the woman. In what now seems like an eerily prescient moment, Marilyn quipped, "The legend may become extinct before publication day. Not the woman, but the legend."

Reading the article today, one senses that Marilyn was such a nice, decent person, it makes her travails all the more tragic. She certainly wasn't one of those celebrities who resented her success or her popularity. About her public, she told *Life* magazine's Merryman, "In the morning the garbage men that go by 57th Street when I come out the door say, 'Marilyn, hi! How do you feel this morning?' To me, it's an honor, and I love them for it. The working-men—I'll go by and they'll whistle. At first, they whistle because they think, oh. It's a girl, she's got blonde hair and she's not out of shape, and then they say, 'Gosh, it's Marilyn Monroe!' And that has its—you know, those are the times it's nice, people knowing who you are and all of that, and feeling that you've meant something to them."

Of course, Marilyn being Marilyn, she also couldn't resist the dramatic "exaggeration," like this one: "Some of my foster families used to send me to the movies to get me out of the house and there I'd sit all day and way into the night—up in front, there with the screen so big, a little kid all alone, and I loved it." That likely never happened. But it's a nice image, anyway.

However, regarding her feelings for Fox, she was very clear: "I think that when you are famous, every weakness is exaggerated. This industry should behave like a mother whose child has just run out in front of a car. But instead of clasping the child to them, they start punishing the child. Like don't you dare get a cold—how dare you get a cold! The executives can get colds and stay home forever, but how dare you, the actor, get a cold? You know, no one feels worse than the one who's sick. I wish they had to act a comedy with a temperature and a virus infection. I am not an actress who appears at a studio just for the purpose of discipline. This doesn't have anything to do with art. I myself would like to become more disciplined within my work. But I'm there to give a performance and not be disciplined by a studio! After all, I'm not in military school. This is supposed to be an art form not just a manufacturing establishment. The sensitivity that helps me to act also makes me react. An actor is supposed to be a sensitive instrument. Isaac Stern takes good care of his violin. What if everybody jumped on his violin?"

She would also do her first layout for *Vogue*, with excellent photos by Bert Stern. It must have rankled her, though, that he wanted her to pose nude. She was trying to break away from that cheesecake image, or so she kept saying. Was she really, though? After the skinny-dip scene in *Something's Got to Give* . . . maybe not. It's clear that she was very confused at this point as to what her image was to be, and where she should draw the line. Some of the partially nude shots she took with Stern are stunning, though. Others, not so much. In those, she definitely looks exhausted, troubled, and not well. She even looks *older*, and *that* was unusual for her. She ended up doing more shots for *Vogue*, these in high-fashion wear and in moody black-and-white. However, even in that sitting, Stern somehow managed to get her to take off her clothes for more nude shots, this time draped with a sheet in a hotel bed. In the end, *Vogue* chose to publish the black-and-white fashion shots—a very wise (and gracious) choice.

As for the movie? The studio decided to replace Marilyn in *Something's Got to Give* with actress Lee Remick. "That was the end of it as far as Dean was concerned," said Mort Viner. "He called me and said, 'Get me the hell out of this movie. Jesus Christ, this is the biggest three-ring circus in show business and I'm the clown in the middle of it all.' So we referenced a clause in his deal that said he would only work with Marilyn. And he quit the film saying, 'No Marilyn. No Dean.' It was bullshit, really. The real reason is that he didn't want to start over with another actress and do all that work, again, on a movie that was not that great to begin with. He felt bad for the crew. A lot of people worked hard on that goddamn movie.

It was a shame. But it was jinxed from the start. On the very first day she didn't show up for work, the very first day, Dean said, 'That's it. This picture will not get made.'"

In 1995, Dean Martin recalled, "I met Marilyn in 1953, before she met Frank, before she met Peter, before she knew any of us. I met her before she was all screwed up, so I knew what she was like then and what she had become, and I felt badly for the kid. At the same time, I was a little tired of all the bullshit. There was only so much you could take. In fact, no one had an easy life. We were all screwed up in our own ways. We all had problems. We were all doing drugs, let's face it. I was no saint, either. But I showed up for work. You had to show up for work. That was the priority. You had to be glad you had a job and you had to show up for work. I'm not saying she wasn't sick all of those days. Who knows? I wasn't following her around like the FBI, I was just sitting on my ass waiting for her to show up at the studio. So, when I had my chance to get out, I did. However, the few scenes we did, I enjoyed, but getting to them . . . oh my God, I mean, the takes, one after the other, it would drive any man crazy. But . . . look . . . I liked her. She was a good kid. But when you looked into her eyes, there was nothing there. No warmth. No life. It was all illusion. She looked great on film, yeah. But in person . . . she was a ghost."

Gladys: "I Don't Say Goodbye"

*W*hen she first moved back to Los Angeles from New York, Marilyn was excited to rebuild the life she once lived in the sunnier, more tranquil locale. Yet there were elements to her life that had drastically changed since she last resided in California. Certainly, the difficult times she endured in recent weeks had made her even more famous than ever before—but for the wrong reasons.

The public had already been made aware of her admittance to the mental hospital in New York, and now, as a result of her being fired from the movie, there was growing interest in her emotional state. Worse, her daily trips to see Dr. Ralph Greenson were now being noticed by some members of the press and even fans who had begun following her every move.

Her time with Dr. Greenson—controversial as it was, even back then—had begun with a certain amount of frustration. While in New York, and under the care of numerous physicians there, Marilyn had come to believe that a certain pharmaceutical had been helpful in stabilizing her: Thorazine. It had begun to represent hope to her that she might be able to regain control of her often chaotic thought processes. Yet when Dr. Greenson heard Marilyn's request for Thorazine, for some reason, he refused. Greenson had quickly become the one doctor Marilyn would trust and speak with openly, and he served that purpose well. Yet he knew all too well that Marilyn would at times have her own agenda when it came to her chemical treatment. It may have simply been that she was asking for more than he would have recommended, or that he didn't want her to take it at all—but it was clear to her that she would need to find this wonder drug elsewhere, especially when her Los Angeles physician, Dr. Hyman Engelberg, also refused to prescribe it to her. Therefore, Marilyn continued her doctor-shopping ways with medics she had seen previously, most of whom had been starstruck by her and had given her whatever prescription drugs she requested.

"She was waiting in the lobby," recalls one of the doctors to whom she had paid a visit during the summer of 1962. "I guess she had her head down in a magazine as the last client of the day left, and then she just walked right into the office. She was a knockout—lots of teased-out blonde hair . . . red lipstick. I remember she was wearing a cream-colored coat that looked like satin to me. She had on a white dress and I specifically remember that she was wearing white stilettos. I mean, she was dressed to kill in all-white. Very impressive . . . very movie star."

Though Marilyn would address this doctor by the name of his previous employer—making it clear that she had so many doctors she didn't even remember what they looked like!—it would quickly become apparent that he was a total stranger to her. Indeed, the man who had previously treated Marilyn had died and the one who now stood before her was his protégé and successor, the much younger Dr. Schwartz.*

"I knew her immediately, of course," says the doctor, "and I even knew that she had seen [the deceased doctor] for a time. I had only been an intern for a short time before he died. There was no one to continue his practice, so his wife asked me to stay on and at least help some patients through the transition.

"She wanted Thorazine," explains Dr. Schwartz. "I was wary of taking her on as a patient. Most doctors were afraid of treating a famous patient who had been suspected of attempting suicide. No one wants to be mentioned in a patient's obituary as their last doctor."

Though Marilyn persisted in trying to convince the young doctor that her experience with Thorazine had been a positive one, he was still reluctant. "When you're fresh out of med school you're under real scrutiny," he explains, "overprescribing could get you into all kinds of trouble. Not with the authorities so much, but it can leave a doctor with a bunch of drug-dependent patients. Some doctors would like that, because it kept people coming back—but I didn't [like it]."

Marilyn spent some time detailing her need for confidentiality —which made it easier for this young doctor to help her. While he refuses to detail what financial arrangements the two made, he doesn't deny that he was compensated for the services he would provide. "There were a bunch of old prescription pads [from the deceased doctor]," Schwartz explains, "and since she wanted them [the prescriptions] written to a pseudonym anyway . . . I just did it. I wasn't just doing it for the money, though. She actually seemed

---

* Because of the nature of his service to Marilyn Monroe, this doctor asked for anonymity. Therefore, we are using a pseudonym to protect his identity.

to be making sense to me. She convinced me it was in her best interest."

The young doctor was rightfully anxious about his dealings with Marilyn Monroe, and so when he received a phone call from her a few weeks later, he was leery of further involvement. Despite his concern, though, she seemed to be doing well. "She said she felt better than she had in ages, and asked how much I charged for a house call," explains Schwartz. "I told her I wouldn't visit her at home but she said that she didn't want me to. She wanted me to go with her to see her mother."

Marilyn's mother, Gladys, was at this time still being cared for at Rock Haven Sanitarium in La Crescenta, about a thirty-minute drive from Marilyn's home and Schwartz's office. Marilyn wanted the doctor to meet her there to try to convince Gladys, and also her doctors, that Thorazine could be an effective treatment for her. Again, after an undisclosed financial arrangement, Schwartz agreed to meet her at Rock Haven.

"When I got to Rock Haven, the front desk was empty, which is unusual in such a place," Schwartz recalls, "then I turned and looked down a hallway and all of the staff seemed to be congregated in one area. I knew she—Marilyn—was already there."

As odd as it may seem, Marilyn was actually early for the appointment. Schwartz found her—cloaked by a black-and-white scarf and wearing black-checkered pants—sitting across from an administrator and two doctors on staff. She seemed upbeat and hopeful—at least at first. (Note: These well could have been the "famous" black-and-white-checkered JAX pants worn by Marilyn in countless photos. She owned them for at least twenty years—even in photo sessions as Norma Jeane—and wore them very often.)

"Guess what? She's already taking it," Marilyn told Schwartz as he approached. "Thorazine," Marilyn added with a big smile. "Mother has been on it for a while."

"She's being *given* it, anyway," clarified one of the physicians present.

"What does that mean?" asked Marilyn.

The doctor then explained something that Marilyn already knew, that Gladys was a very stubborn woman. It seemed that the staff had often caught her attempting to avoid taking her medication. Marilyn said that she didn't understand how that was possible. She thought a nurse would have stood in front of Gladys and waited while she took her pills. It turned out that a member of the staff *would* witness her pop the pills into her mouth, and would even wait while she drank a cup of water. Gladys would even be told to open her mouth to show that it was empty. However, she seemed to have mastered the ability to quickly tuck her pills between her teeth and inner cheek. That was at least what the staff assumed, since she seemed relatively unaffected by any of the drugs she was supposed to be taking. "She can't do that," Marilyn said, "you just can't *let* her." The doctor told her that it happened all the time. When he questioned Gladys about it, he said, she told him that the one or two times she actually took the medication, it stopped the voices in her head, "and then she missed them." Therefore, she wouldn't take the medication, and, he concluded, "if someone doesn't want help, they won't *get* any."

That statement angered Marilyn. "She isn't well enough to *know* she wants help," she said. "Why don't you give her injections of it? She can't spit those out."

The doctors seemed to find that proposal absurd. Marilyn was told that the staff did not administer drugs intravenously at that facility. If a patient needed that kind of care, she was told, then she needed to be somewhere else. "Then she *will* be," Marilyn threatened. "Just tell me where to take her."

It was then that one of the other doctors told Marilyn that Gladys had indeed been moved to other facilities numerous times, after episodes of extreme violence or threats of suicide. However, once her mother showed improvement, after having been given intravenous medication for a few days, she would always be released back to Rock Haven. He said he was surprised that Marilyn didn't know about this. Perhaps he was referring to Gladys's recent suicide attempt. "Not as surprised as I am," Marilyn said, now very upset.

"You wouldn't want her spending the rest of her life in a hospital, would you?" he asked.

"What do you call this?" Marilyn shot back.

"To your mother," he answered, "it's home."

Marilyn didn't know how to respond to that.

According to Dr. Schwartz's memory, Marilyn was most unhappy with the staff's blasé attitude about Gladys's avoidance of treatment. Also, it's likely their description of a couple of her stays in two other facilities reminded Marilyn of her own experience at Payne Whitney. The last thing she wanted to do was make Gladys's life more difficult. Therefore she decided that she would not remove her mother from Rock Haven but would instead at least make an attempt at personally convincing her to take her medication.

Marilyn and Dr. Schwartz were then led out to the grounds by a nurse. He remembers the facility as being surprisingly bucolic, with sprawling, well-manicured lawns and numerous oak-tree-shaded areas in which patients could relax and roam. They found Gladys sitting at a picnic table, wearing a fur stole around her neck. She was a small-boned, frail woman now, with silver hair pulled back from her face and tied in a small knot with what appeared to be a simple rubber band. The doctor recalls thinking that she looked very much like what he might imagine Marilyn to look at age sixty-two. Moreover, he would also recall Marilyn later confessing that when she laid eyes on her mother she experienced a strong and unexpected feeling of bittersweet nostalgia sweeping through her. A large purse sat in front of Gladys on the table. It appeared as if she was searching inside it for something. Marilyn approached carefully. "Mother?"

"I'm here," Gladys said rather loudly, as if a nurse was taking attendance.

Marilyn sat across from her mother. "Mother, I'd like you to meet a friend of mine," she said. "This is Dr. Schwartz."

Dr. Schwartz distinctly remembers Gladys pulling her purse closer to her for a moment.

"You're new," Gladys said, eyeing the visitor suspiciously. Then, turning to her daughter, she said, "I don't know him."

Marilyn then explained to her mother that she and the doctor had come to tell her something very important. She looked to the doctor and said to him, "She won't listen to me, so you tell her."

There was an awkward moment as Marilyn waited for the doctor to tell Gladys why she should take her medication. "It was a little bizarre," he recalled, years later. "I wasn't a psychiatrist, I wasn't even her doctor, but [Marilyn] seemed desperate, so I did my best."

The doctor then spoke to Gladys about the importance of taking her pills, but it was mostly for Marilyn's benefit. As he spoke, Gladys continued rummaging through her purse. When he was finished, Gladys looked up at him and asked him if he were a doctor. He nodded. "Well, I'll say a prayer for you and you can say one for me," she said pointedly. "That's more powerful than anything. Norma Jeane knows that."

"No. Mother, no," Marilyn insisted. She then explained that perhaps they'd all been wrong about Christian Science since neither of them had thus far been healed by the religion. She said that she now believed they needed more than just faith—they also needed medication. Then she briefly explained that she too had lately endured some very difficult times—she was probably referring to her stay at Payne Whitney—and that she now truly believed that both of them would benefit from Thorazine.

Gladys listened intently until Marilyn stopped talking. Then Gladys looked at Schwartz. "I don't know what you've been filling this child's head with," she said, according to his memory of the conversation, "but Norma Jeane knows that the path to heaven is through prayer and devotion."

"But maybe these drugs *are* an answer to your prayers," Marilyn said. "*Our* prayers." She continued pleading with her mother so vehemently, so passionately in fact, that she soon began to cry. "Can't you listen to me, just this once?" she said through her tears. She said that "after all of these years" she now finally realized how truly torturous Gladys's life had been and that she wanted to help her.

"Please, I never ask you to do anything," she continued, "but I'm begging you now."

Gladys watched her daughter with a distant gaze. Finally, she asked Marilyn exactly what it was she wanted her to do. Marilyn said that all she wanted was for Gladys to take Thorazine for at least a week, or maybe even a month, if possible. "I know you'll feel better," Marilyn said.

"And *then* what?" Gladys asked.

"Then you can leave here," Marilyn answered, "and get your life back."

Gladys leaned in to her daughter. "And what life is that, dear?" she asked. "This place is all I've known for years."

"I just want you to get better," Marilyn said.

"You want me to get better for you," Gladys responded, "and I thank you for that." Then, staring intensely into her daughter's eyes, she added, "but, Norma Jeane, I want *you* to get better for you." Mother and daughter just looked at each other for another long moment. Then Gladys suddenly changed the subject. She turned to the doctor and, touching the fur that was wrapped around her neck, told him that Norma Jeane had given it to her. When he said he thought it was beautiful, she looked pleased. She said that the hospital staff rarely let her have it. However, when the weather got cold, she'd ask for it, and usually the staff would give it to her. She suggested that he touch it. The doctor cautiously reached out and began to stroke the pelt, but when he did, Gladys winced and pulled back forcefully. "You have an evil touch," she said, her face suddenly darkening. All of this was just too much for Marilyn. With that, her tears began to flow again, unchecked. "You've upset Norma Jeane," Gladys told the doctor. "She can be very sensitive."

Just then, according to the doctor's memory of these events, an elderly woman walked up behind Gladys. Oddly, the woman reached toward Gladys's hand and held it. Without saying a word, she just stood there.

"Who's this?" Marilyn asked, forcing a smile.

"This is Ginger," Gladys replied. "She's my friend."

"Hello, Ginger," Marilyn said. "Would you like to join us?"

Gladys began to stand. "Ginger doesn't like visitors," she said, her voice now suddenly flat and devoid of expression. "We've got to go back inside."

As Gladys began to pick up her purse, Marilyn said, "No. Wait a moment." She reached into her own pocketbook and pulled out a small flask. Quickly, she slipped it inside her mother's purse.

Gladys, after a pause, seemed to perk up again. She gave her daughter a childish grin. "You're such a good girl, Norma Jeane," she said finally. "A very good girl." She smiled. Marilyn beamed back at her. Then Gladys turned and began to walk away.

Marilyn and the doctor watched as Gladys and Ginger made their way across the expansive lawn. Though they didn't know it, it would be the last time mother and daughter would ever lay eyes on one another. "I don't say goodbye," Gladys announced loudly, her back still to her daughter.

"She never has," Marilyn said quietly. "Maybe that's why I have to say it so often."

Pat: "My Friend Is Dying"

At about this same time—in mid-June 1962—Marilyn Monroe was scheduled to participate in a number of photo shoots for *Vogue* and *Cosmopolitan* magazines. She decided to keep those commitments. For one of the sessions, she wanted to use as a setting the beach behind Pat Kennedy Lawford's home. Therefore, she and Pat met for lunch to discuss the shoot and also to catch up as friends. "At this point, Pat didn't know what was going on with Marilyn and her brothers," said a Kennedy relative. "And she was afraid to ask . . . she was actually afraid to know."

As soon as Marilyn showed up at her home, Pat could see that she was in terrible condition. According to a later recollection, Marilyn told her friend that she was "humiliated" by what had happened at Fox. She said that she had never before had so much anxiety in her life, but that she was now trying to focus on the future. "What's next?" she remarked. "That's what I want to concentrate on from now on." She indicated that she believed *Something's Got to Give* would go back into production. In fact, she said that she had sent telegrams to many of the actors apologizing to them and asking them to return. "However, I would like it if the entire crew was new," she told Pat, "because I don't know that I can face them. I let them all down and I think they probably hate me by now." She also told Pat that she felt that she was "on the brink of understanding what my problem is," and that all she needed was "more time. I know I can overcome this," she said cryptically. "I just need everyone to give me a little more time."

Pat was worried. Marilyn seemed manic. A few of Pat's friends were having lunch on the patio when Marilyn arrived. Pat suggested that the two of them go out and join the group. "Maybe some sun will do us all some good," she offered. "Would you like a whiskey sour?" Marilyn, of course, said she would love a whiskey sour, but first she wanted Pat to do her a favor. "Please tell [the guests] that I am here and see their reaction. If it looks like they would hate it if I joined them, I won't." It seemed like such an odd request. However, there was little about Marilyn that made sense on this particular day. When she began mouthing words that Pat couldn't even make out, she decided it would be best if Marilyn didn't join the others, after all. Instead, as she later recalled it, she sat down with her friend at the bar and tried to have a serious discussion with her about the medication she was taking, and whether or not she was abusing it. It's not known what specifically was said during this talk, only that Marilyn became very upset. "I thought I was getting better," she told Pat as she rose to leave the house, "but now I see that I'm not. I'm worse, Pat. I'm worse than ever. Maybe I'm even worse than my mother, and she's pretty bad, Pat!" She then left in tears.

"After that, Pat was shaking all over," said the same Kennedy relative. "It was then, I think, that she decided that being forthright and honest with Marilyn was not a good idea. 'I now think I need to be like everyone else in her life and just tell her that everything is fine,' she said, 'because I don't think she can handle the truth.' Pat said that if it had been any other woman who was that troubled, she would have immediately called that friend's husband. But Marilyn had no one—just that creepy psychiatrist, and Pat didn't trust him at all. So she picked up the phone and called Joe [DiMaggio]. I don't know what she said to him, and I don't know his response. I only know that Pat was left with a feeling of dread. 'I felt that it was inevitable,' she said. 'I felt my friend is dying and that there wasn't a thing I could do about it.' "

In mid-June, Bobby and Ethel Kennedy were hosting a party at Hickory Hill, their home in Virginia, for Peter and Pat Lawford. Knowing that Marilyn was very close to Pat, they decided to invite her. One wonders, if Ethel believed Marilyn was having an affair with her husband, would she have invited her into her home? It seems doubtful. If Bobby was having relations with Marilyn, it also seems doubtful he would host her at Hickory Hill. A Kennedy relative recalls that the only trepidation about that evening had to do with how many people were, by now, well aware that Marilyn and JFK had been intimate. What would happen if Jackie decided to show up at the party? She wasn't invited, but what if? It was a risk. Maybe not one Marilyn was willing to take, though. She decided not to go, realizing that she would be seeing Bobby anyway at the end of the month at another party at Pete and Pat Lawford's. She sent this telegram to Ethel and Bobby on June 13, 1962:

Dear Attorney General and Mrs. Robert Kennedy: I would have been delighted to have accepted your invitation honoring Pat and Peter Lawford. Unfortunately, I am involved in a freedom ride protesting the loss of the minority rights belonging to the few remaining earthbound stars. After all, all we demanded was our right to twinkle. Marilyn Monroe.

On Wednesday June 26, 1962, Bobby Kennedy was scheduled to return to Los Angeles—without Ethel—and Peter and Pat planned to return the favor and host another party for him at their home. "I want Bobby to see my new house," Marilyn told Pat on the phone earlier that week. "Really?" Pat asked. "But why?" Marilyn didn't really have an answer. She just wanted him to see it, she said. Pat tried to explain that, logistically, it would be complicated. After all, Bobby was coming straight to their house from the airport. She could think of no reason to bring him to her home. "Well, there would a reason if you had to come and pick me up," Marilyn suggested. Of course, Marilyn could have driven to the Lawfords' home herself. She wouldn't let it go, though. So Pat gave in. On Monday, June 25, telephone records document that Marilyn called Bobby's office in Washington to confirm that he would be at the Lawfords' on Wednesday, and also to invite him to have a drink with her in her new home. She spoke to his secretary, Angie Novello, for one minute. And that's how the very unlikely situation unfolded that saw Peter Lawford driving his wife, Pat, and Bobby Kennedy to Marilyn Monroe's home on the twenty-eighth. Once there, Marilyn invited them in and showed Bobby around—Peter and Pat had previously been there.

How very curious that Marilyn had no pretense about her environment whatsoever. She was incredibly down-to-earth, especially when one considers how big a star she was at the time. Her home was quite modest, just a few rooms. It wasn't any bigger than the house the Bolenders owned in which she was raised. In fact, it was smaller! Yet she had no reservations at all about showing it off to Bobby Kennedy, a wealthy man who lived in an absolute mansion in Virginia on a sprawling estate. Her home was her home, and she was proud of it—no matter how small and inconsequential it may have seemed to outsiders—and she was eager to show it off. There were bigger concerns, she felt, than how much money she had or how well she displayed it. And in terms of housing, she was working on a more important structure. "As a person, my work is important to me," she said during an interview this very same month. "My work is the only ground I've ever had to stand on. Acting is very important. To put it bluntly, I seem to have a whole superstructure with no foundation. But I'm working on the foundation."

After just about a half hour, during which they sipped on glasses of sherry, the foursome got into Lawford's car and then drove to their oceanfront home. At the end of the evening, Bobby Kennedy's driver took back Marilyn Monroe back home—alone.

The Lost Weekend

*P*at Kennedy Lawford didn't know what to do about Marilyn Monroe. She didn't know if the stories she had heard through the grapevine about her brothers and her friend were true. Marilyn had definitely been saying that she was dating Bobby. However, Pat knew that one of those "dates" had actually been a dinner party at her home in her brother's honor, and that Marilyn had just been a guest. Whom could she believe? Certainly Marilyn had never been the most reliable source of information. She also couldn't depend on her brothers to tell her the truth. After all, it wasn't as if the Kennedy men were ever honest about their indiscretions. One thing seemed true, though. Bobby had told Marilyn to stop pestering his brother Jack, and she was very unhappy about it. Had she built up her in her mind her relationship with JFK to be something it wasn't? And if so, maybe she did have the poor judgment to somehow end up sexually involved with Bobby. By this time, it was beginning to seem as if anything was possible, everyone's reality was just that skewed. "It was as if we were all caught in Marilyn's nightmare," said one Kennedy relative. "Everything sort of satellited around Marilyn's sickness and no one knew what was true and what wasn't, who was lying and who wasn't."

Desperate for some direction, Pat Kennedy Lawford telephoned

Frank Mankiewicz, Bobby's press aide.* "I told her, Pat, you should know better than to believe this nonsense," he recalled years later. "She said, 'Honest to God, Frank, I don't know what to believe anymore between what I hear Marilyn is saying and what everyone else is saying.' I said, 'Well, hear what I'm saying, Pat. It's not true. If it was, I would know and I don't, so it's not true.' She was so grateful. She said, 'Oh, thank you so much. Thank you so much.'"

At this same time, Frank Sinatra called Pat—unusual, in that they seldom spoke—to say that he was sorry he had targeted her husband after President Kennedy decided not to stay at the Sinatra home in Palm Springs. He said that he wanted to invite the Lawfords to his resort, the Cal-Neva Lodge, for the weekend. (Though Frank and Peter were still not on good terms, for business reasons better left to a Peter Lawford biographer to explain, they tolerated each other from time to time.) Sinatra told Pat that he was performing in the main room and singers Buddy Greco and Roberta Linn were working in the lounge.

Cal-Neva, located exactly on the California–Nevada border, boasted a beautiful showroom (where the same performers who frequented Las Vegas—Frank's friends, for the most part—appeared), an enormous dining room, plus about twenty furnished cottages that cost about fifty dollars a day. The luxurious gambling casinos were located on the Nevada side of the compound. It was advertised as "Heaven in the High Sierras." Pat was against the idea of flying to Nevada to see Sinatra. However, she felt she had to at least mention the invitation to her husband. He, of course, couldn't wait to go. If Frank wanted to mend fences, Peter was going to be at his side with a hammer and nails. "Pat and Peter had a bit of a disagreement about it," said Milt Ebbins. "All I can tell you is that Pat didn't want to go and Peter said, 'We can not turn down an invitation by Frank Sinatra. If Frank wants us there, we have to go.' Pat hated hearing

---

* Frank Mankiewicz was the son of screenwriter Herman J. Mankiewicz, who cowrote *Citizen Kane* with Orson Welles. They both won Academy Awards for Best Original Screenplay for the 1941 film.

that kind of stuff from Peter. But she buckled, and they went." Marilyn also said she would like to go. Upset about something that had just occurred with her mother at Rock Haven—it's unknown what, exactly—she said she could use a weekend away.

Therefore, against Pat's better judgment, she, Peter, and Marilyn departed for Nevada on July 27, 1962, in a private plane provided by Sinatra and copiloted by Dan Arney. "She had no makeup on," Arney recalled of Marilyn, "and I didn't realize who she was until we got into the airport and George [Jacobs, Sinatra's valet] came out in the station wagon and said, 'You know, that's Marilyn.'"

When the trio—Peter, Pat, and Marilyn—arrived, Sinatra greeted them and then installed Marilyn in Chalet 52, one of the quarters he always reserved for special guests. He then asked Peter and Pat to leave so that he could have some time with Marilyn. George Jacobs says that Frank had heard she was "having a crisis" in her life and wanted to know more about it. "He knew what was going on," said Jacobs, "I think, with the Kennedy business. Or, at least he heard rumors. He knew she was upset. He wanted to know more."

Mickey Rudin—who was both Marilyn's and Frank's attorney —said in 1996, "Frank is a very, very compassionate person. He brought Marilyn to Cal-Neva to give her a little fun, a little relief from her problems. If she was upset during the time, well, she could have a crisis over what she was having for lunch, she was that emotional and high-strung. She could have had an *imagined* crisis, in fact."

However, Joe Langford, a Sinatra security employee at Cal-Neva, said that Marilyn's crisis that weekend seemed to not be of the imagined variety suggested by Mickey Rudin. "When Frank saw her, he was pretty shocked at how depressed she was," he recalled. "As soon as he got her settled in, he got on the phone with her psychiatrist [presumably Dr. Greenson] and started in on the guy. 'What the hell kind of treatment are you giving her? She's a mess. What is she paying you for? Why isn't she in a sanitarium?' He hadn't seen her in a while and he couldn't believe how broken-down she was."

It's true that Sinatra was known to have great concern for his friends. However, that said, one of the biggest problems with him was that he also had terrible judgment when it came to some of those friends—many of whom were underworld characters. Moreover, he didn't seem to care whom he exposed his mob pals to, which was one of the big problems at Cal-Neva that weekend. About three hours after Pat and Peter Lawford arrived with Marilyn, they found a surprise waiting for them in the Cal-Neva lobby: Sam Giancana, one of the world's leading gangsters, who was deeply involved in all sorts of underworld activity, some of it reputedly having to do with the Kennedy brothers. As it happened, Sinatra had sent his private jet back to Los Angeles to pick him up and bring him to Cal-Neva. For Sinatra to have invited him to the resort at the same time as the president's sister and her husband made no sense. Naturally, Pat was upset. She wanted to turn around and fly right back to Los Angeles. In fact, according to a witness, as soon as she saw Giancana, she said, "That's it. We have to go."

Peter, who seemed embarrassed because Pat had spoken loudly enough to have been heard by Giancana, walked over to the mobster and shook his hand, then began conversing with him. The two repeatedly glanced at Marilyn while they spoke, as if they were taking about her. Because Marilyn just looked at Giancana with a dazed expression, it's not known if she recognized him or not. "I don't feel well," she told Pat. "I can't fly again. We can't leave now."

Pat put her arm around Marilyn's shoulder and whispered something in her ear. However, whatever she said upset Marilyn. "I don't care," she said, now raising her voice. "I don't care about any of it. I just need to go and lie down, right now. Take me to my room, Pat. *Right now.*"

With that, Peter walked quickly over to the two women and said something to them in an angry tone. Pat gave him a long, piercing look. Then, without saying a word to him, she led her friend away, her hand on the actress's elbow.

Roberta Linn, who was entertaining at Cal-Neva along with Frank Sinatra and Buddy Greco, recalled, "I remember that her hair was in disarray the entire time, sometimes hidden under a scarf. She was very sad and she seemed out of it. She was at Sinatra's show every night—he was performing in the main room, and she would sit in the back looking very unhappy. I thought it was such a shame, this girl who had everything in the world, yet nothing, really. It was very hard to see her in this condition."

Sinatra's friend Jim Whiting recalled, "Jilly [Rizzo, another close friend of Sinatra's] told me that Marilyn had some kind of bad reaction to alcohol while she was at Cal-Neva. It sounded like alcohol poisoning to me. She was also having stomach problems then and the booze along with the pills was, I guess, having a bad effect on her."

There was more to it than just pills and "booze," though. As earlier stated, Marilyn had developed the alarming habit of giving herself injections of phenobarbital, Nembutal, and Seconal—which she referred to as "a vitamin shot." Joe Langford confirmed, "On the day she opened her purse and pulled out those syringes, I was standing right there with Mr. Sinatra and Pat Kennedy Lawford. Marilyn was very casual about it. She was looking for something else and just pulled them out and put them on the table. Sinatra went white, like a sheet. He said, 'Marilyn. Jesus Christ. What are *they* for?' She said, 'Oh, those are for my vitamin shots.' She was very nonchalant about it. Pat looked like she was going to faint. 'Oh my God, Marilyn,' she said. 'Oh my God.' Then Marilyn said, 'It's all right Pat. I know what I'm doing.'

"[Marilyn] was still going through her purse until, finally, she found what she was looking for: a pin. As we all stood there with our mouths open, she opened a bottle of pills and picked one out. Then—and I had never seen anything like this before—she put a small hole at the end of the capsule, and swallowed it. 'Gets into your bloodstream faster that way,' she said. She turned back to Pat and said, 'See, I told you I knew what I was doing.'"

Later that night, after Sinatra's performance in the main show-room at Cal-Neva, the Lawfords and friends shared a few cocktails. Marilyn had only one drink. Still, she excused herself from the group, saying that she wasn't feeling well and needed to rest in her room. Sometime later Pat went to check on her. According to a later recollection, Pat knocked on Marilyn's door for a while before a wobbly Monroe let her in, then flopped back down on her bed. She was nauseous, she said. Pat grew concerned and asked Marilyn if she had taken another of her "vitamin shots." At some point, Marilyn became violently ill. Pat later said she knelt next to her, holding her friend's hair back as she threw up into the toilet. After this episode, Pat helped Marilyn change into a different outfit because the white blouse Marilyn had been wearing was stained with vomit. Marilyn then asked Pat to throw the top away in a trash can on the premises, claiming that "people will be going through the garbage in my room later."

Obviously, it turned out to be a very difficult weekend for all concerned at Cal-Neva, made even more so by the swarms of FBI agents due to Sam Giancana's presence. As a result of Sinatra's poor judgment, much fiction has been spun from the stories that have circulated—most of which are not true—about those couple of days in July 1962. Place Sinatra in a room with a Kennedy, a mobster, and a movie star, and what else can one expect but rumors, gossip, and innuendo? Add the FBI to the mix—with its theories presented as "fact" in its files—and it's a sure recipe for confusion. In fact, Marilyn Monroe aficionados refer to this brief period as "The Lost Weekend," because there have been so many conflicting stories about it.

What we do know is this: Marilyn Monroe was dreadfully sick, emotionally and physically, the entire time she was at Cal-Neva. Whenever she was left alone for even fifteen minutes, she would pop a couple more pills, take another "vitamin shot," and make herself even sicker. At one point during the weekend, Pat Kennedy Lawford raided Marilyn's purse and got rid of all of the syringes. "She's a very sick woman," Pat told Peter. That was an understatement. In fact, between July 1 and August 9, Marilyn had twenty-seven appointments with her psychiatrist, Greenson, and thirteen with her internist, Engelberg.

"Frank Sinatra didn't know what to think about any of it," said his valet, George Jacobs. "He was upset, though. He loved Marilyn, yes. But this was pushing it. For her to maybe *die* at Cal-Neva while he was there? That would have been terrible. So, after he'd seen enough, he said, 'Get her out of here and get her out of here now.' And that was it. We had to do what he said, get her out of there. You know, you felt bad about it, yeah. I mean, the woman was sick. But as compassionate as Sinatra was, he had a line and she crossed it. He didn't want her dying at Cal-Neva, and that's just the truth of it."

Ken Rotcop, who was a guest at Cal-Neva, recalled seeing Marilyn leave the resort. "She was shaking, she had chills, she looked very very sick." Stacy Baron, another guest of the hotel, recalled, "I was in the lobby and I saw Peter Lawford on one side of her and Pat on the other side and they were practically carrying this woman out of there. I recognized the two of them but I couldn't figure out who the woman was because she had her head down and was just sort of groggy. Then she raised her head and I got a real shock. It was Marilyn Monroe. I was stunned. And as I was standing there with my mouth open, I heard Pat say to Peter, 'This is all your fault, Peter. This is all your fault.' And Peter said, 'Not now, Pat. Jesus Christ, not now.'" I just watched them leave, thinking, my God! Marilyn Monroe looks like death."

"Maybe"

After Marilyn Monroe returned from Cal-Neva on July 29, 1962, she spent so much of the next few days alone behind the walls of her modest home in Brentwood, it made monitoring her state of mind a near impossibility. Only Eunice Murray and her doctors—Greenson and Engelberg—seemed to know what was really going on with her, and they weren't exactly forthcoming to her friends. "After Cal-Neva, Pat was worried to death for her," shared a friend of Mrs. Kennedy Lawford's. In the days after their return from Nevada, Pat tried to call Marilyn, with no success. Finally, she asked Peter to run an errand for her. Pat had salvaged the blouse Marilyn soiled in Reno and now saw its return as an opportunity for Peter to check in on her troubled friend. Therefore, Peter dropped by Marilyn's, and as Pat later reported, he found her in "better than good spirits." Pat was relieved. That evening, Pat telephoned Marilyn, who finally answered. Now she seemed distant and depressed, and this was mere hours after Peter's pleasant visit with her.

During their conversation, Pat questioned Marilyn about what she had done that day. Marilyn said that she had seen her doctor (not specifying which one), and, she claimed, the only other person she had come into contact with the entire day was Eunice Murray. Pat, knowing that her husband had spent the better part of an hour at Marilyn's, found her withholding of this information to be very odd. Peter had said he spent long enough time at her home to enjoy a cocktail with her at the pool, and he even described her as having been in a "silly mood." However, Marilyn now painted a picture of her day without Peter as a part of it. Pat challenged Marilyn, explaining that she knew that Peter had been there to return the blouse, and she was baffled by Marilyn's reluctance to voluntarily discuss Peter's visit.

Though Marilyn apologized for not telling Pat about Peter's time there, Pat was more interested in *why* she decided to withhold the information. Marilyn, when pressed, explained that she didn't want Pat to feel jealousy over Peter's visit. That explanation angered Pat and she let Marilyn know it. Marilyn, who was not used to Pat's clipped manner, began to cry and reassure her friend that nothing was going on between her and Peter. "I didn't think for a moment anything *was*," Pat told Marilyn, "and I still don't—because he's not attracted to you, Marilyn." Pat then went on to say that Peter didn't see Marilyn as a sexual being, but more as a wounded child. "She told Marilyn that she thought it was sick that Marilyn viewed every man as wanting her and every woman as being jealous of her," this same intimate of Pat explained many years later. "Pat said that she thought Marilyn behaved like that because she had no important men in her life—no father, no brothers."

From this trustworthy source's account, it would seem that Marilyn took a browbeating from Pat that night. The call ended abruptly, at Pat's initiation. Unfortunately, this confrontation between good friends would never be fully resolved. However, it may have been that conversation that led Marilyn to reach out during this period to a man from her past she still called "Daddy."

"The phone rang one day when my mother was at the grocery store," recalled Nancy Jeffrey in an interview for this book. "Daddy [Wayne Bolender] answered. It was Marilyn. He wanted to know how she was doing, he had heard that she was having a hard time. She said that she was fine. She would never have shared with him any of her sorrow, though. My parents would watch things on TV and get very upset. I think they felt that maybe she should not have gone into show business, that maybe her life would have been better. Anyway, somewhere in the conversation, I know that she asked my father, 'Daddy, are you disappointed in the way my life has turned out?' And all he said was, 'Norma Jeane, I promised you on your wedding day that I would always love you—and I will keep that promise until the day I die. I still love you, Norma Jeane.' That's what he told me he told her, just like that."

Marilyn then revealed to Wayne Bolender the primary reason for her call. She asked if he had any paperwork from her time at his home so long ago that might help convince Stanley Gifford Sr. and his son, Stanley Gifford Jr., that she actually was related to them. He explained that, unfortunately, there was no such documentation. It's been said that he also attempted to discourage her from contacting the Giffords again. He believed it would only lead to more disappointment for her. However, Marilyn wrapped up the call apparently undeterred. She would contact the Giffords again, she insisted. The next time she did so, they would listen. The next time she did so, they would believe her claim to be "one of them" was the truth.

While Stanley Gifford Jr. believes to this day that he is not related to Marilyn Monroe, there is no telling what five minutes in her presence could have done to sway him and his father. Even if they hadn't believed they were blood relatives, they could have been convinced to take Marilyn under their wings. There was at least a possibility that they may have seen in her what so many others already had—a woman who simply wanted what so many other people already have: a place to belong. Marilyn ended the phone call with her "Daddy" on an optimistic note. "Maybe that's what I need," she concluded. "Maybe if I find my brother, that will change everything."

As had happened so many times before, Marilyn Monroe's hopes for happiness in her future hinged on one word: Maybe.

Final Curtain

She is at peace and at rest now and may our God bless her and help her always. I . . . gave her Christian Science treatments for approximately a year . . . wanted her to be happy and joyous . . .
—Gladys Baker Eley on the death of her daughter, Marilyn Monroe, in a previously unpublished letter, circa 1962

August 4, 1962. While there's no way to know with certainty what Marilyn Monroe's state of mind was on this day, she had every reason to at least be happier. Just a few days earlier, on August 1, she had signed a one-million-dollar contract with Fox for two pictures. Moreover, her attorney, Mickey Rudin, also settled the conflict with the studio over *Something's Got to Give*. The movie was back on track and would begin filming again in October.*

Yet despite the bright possibilities that may have lain ahead, by most verifiable accounts, this Saturday had not been a good one for Marilyn Monroe. She was experiencing extreme emotional highs and lows, and her contact with others during her depressive moments would leave many baffled by just why she was in such a state. Since most all of the principal players have contradicted each other, it may be impossible to establish who came and went from the Monroe household that day, and at what time. It is known that at some point, Dr. Greenson was called to the house by Eunice Murray. When he arrived, he found Marilyn in a drugged, depressed condition. A day earlier, Marilyn had filled a prescription (by Dr. Engelberg) for twenty-four—some have said twenty-five, but he said twenty-four—Nembutal, and it was believed that she had taken more than necessary. At another point, while Greenson was with Marilyn, Peter Lawford called. Marilyn said that she wished to talk to Bobby, but Peter was known to try and steer Marilyn away from that topic.

"Yes, I think she was fixated on Bobby that day," Peter Lawford would say years later. "I'm not sure why. One thing led to another, one obsession to another you might say until, I think, she had worked herself into a deep despondency over the Kennedys." Lawford continued with this observation. "The Kennedys may have been the subject of her great sadness," he said, "but the thing about Marilyn is this: While it may have been the Kennedys in that moment, in the one before it, it may have been *Something's Got to Give*, and in the moment after, Joe [DiMaggio]. Or maybe all three at the same

---

* Of course, Elizabeth Taylor had just been paid a million for only one film—*Cleopatra*—but that was an unprecedented deal in the business. Considering that Marilyn was only compensated $100,000 for *Something's Got to Give*, this new contract was quite amazing and also one of the biggest in show business up until that time. Beyond its obvious financial reward, it marked a big personal win for her, too. That she and Fox were able to come to these terms despite everything that had occurred on the set of her most recent film suggests that the studio had finally begun to understand just how valuable a property Marilyn was to them—at whatever financial inconvenience it may have been when she worked on a movie.

time. There was no way to account for her mood swings . . . for her deep depressions. You can't blame the Kennedys. They were just a facet of a much bigger problem."

Marilyn had heard that Bobby was in San Francisco that weekend, scheduled to give an address the following Monday to the California Bar Association. When she called Pat Kennedy Lawford, she was told that Bobby and his wife, Ethel, were staying at the St. Francis Hotel in San Francisco. It turns out, however, that they were staying at the ranch of John Bates, president of the Bar Association, some sixty miles south of the city. It's unclear whether or not Pat was also attempting to shift Marilyn's focus off of the Kennedys. The closest of Marilyn's friends, the ones privy to her obsessions and their consequences, knew it was crucial to deflect her attention from the Kennedy brothers whenever possible.

At approximately 7 p.m. on August 4, Dr. Ralph Greenson left Marilyn's home, requesting that Eunice spend the night there to keep an eye on his patient. Around the time of Greenson's departure, Peter called to invite Marilyn to a dinner party at his home. She declined, which wasn't unusual for Marilyn—she had been known to take to her room on nights like this one, when she was attempting to endure one of her many emotional plunges. Marilyn brought a telephone into her bedroom and closed the door. It appears that the rest of this evening, indeed the rest of Marilyn's life, would be spent alone in this room, thus destroying any hope of detailing precisely what transpired that night within those four walls.

So, then, how did Marilyn most likely spend her last hours? She was undoubtedly becoming more and more affected by drugs. Whether they were the ones provided her by Dr. Engelberg or ones she took herself, the barbiturates that entered Marilyn's body that night were of a massive volume.

If she had taken these willfully, she either intended to kill herself or had become so desperate to quiet her mind that she tossed reason aside and experimented with higher doses and possibly different delivery methods. It might be reasonable to assume that Marilyn, a woman who had administered numerous enemas to herself in the past, may have used this mode to ingest some of her dissolved Nembutal capsules. Yet, no matter how these drugs entered her system, Marilyn's consciousness had to have been growing increasingly compromised throughout that night.

It seems that she continued making telephone calls—but the number of calls is up for debate as well. Some people's claims that they had spoken to Marilyn on this night have been viewed with skepticism, the theory being that they had an interest in being remembered as a part of the mystique of the events that followed.

Later that fateful night, Peter called again. This time, he could sense Marilyn wasn't well. According to Peter, it was during this call that she said, "Say goodbye to Pat. Say goodbye to the president, and say goodbye to yourself because you're such a nice guy." Obviously, this was distressing and would seem to indicate that she was thinking about taking her life. Alarmed, Peter called Marilyn yet again; the line was engaged. He mentioned to his business partner, Milton Ebbins, that he was worried about her. He wanted to go to the house, but Ebbins was afraid that Marilyn had overdosed again and didn't want Peter—the president's brother-in-law—to be the one to find her. Ebbins called Marilyn's attorney, Mickey Rudin, who then rang the house at 9 p.m. He spoke to Eunice, who told him that Marilyn was fine, but whether or not Murray was able to confirm this (or even had an interest in doing so) is unknown.

The conflicting accounts of Marilyn's passing occur after this time frame. The most oft-told version is this one, the events and timings based on official statements by Eunice Murray and Dr. Greenson.

At around 2 a.m., Eunice Murray called Dr. Greenson, alarmed because Marilyn's door was locked and she couldn't get into the bedroom. Greenson showed up five minutes later and went around to Marilyn's window. He saw the actress on her bed, frozen and lifeless. Breaking the glass, he let himself into the room. Once inside, he realized that she was dead, lying facedown, holding her telephone in her right hand with numerous open bottles of pills on her nightstand.

With the passing of the years, many murder theories developed. Some involve Marilyn being killed by Bobby Kennedy, or at the orders of Bobby. Some implicate Peter Lawford. Some the FBI. Dr. Greenson. Eunice Murray. The Mafia. Of course, it's very easy to pin murders on dead people and intelligence agencies. It has to be noted here that the mystique of Marilyn's death would become a lifelong obsession for some, and the conspiracy theories born of it would serve an important purpose for these individuals. The belief that Marilyn had fallen victim to any one of a number of dastardly plans provides a macabre solace for those who felt her loss most deeply. The possibility that her death was at another's hands, or that its details will never be fully known, makes it a mystery virtually without a chance of being solved. If the way Marilyn met her end is unknown, in an odd way that keeps her alive—there's still more she has to reveal. In fact, debates about the circumstances surrounding that evening may never end, and whether or not they choose to admit it, that's just how many people want it.

Are there suspicious circumstances around Marilyn's death? Absolutely. For instance, the doctors and Murray waited almost two hours to contact the authorities. Why? No one has ever sufficiently answered that question. More intriguingly, Eunice would later say that there was no lock on Marilyn's door. If that's the case, then the entire story of how she was found seems to fall apart. There was very little drug residue found in Marilyn's stomach—and what was found wasn't properly analyzed. Also, there was some discoloration in her lower intestine. Do these facts support the theory that maybe she was given a lethal enema by . . . someone? Not really. Marilyn was a drug addict. It is a medical fact that an addict's stomach becomes accustomed to the drugs of choice and that they easily pass into the intestines. Many addicts die without a trace of pills in their stomachs. Also, an empty stomach does not preclude the possibility that pills were ingested over a number of hours, and the high levels of barbiturates found in Marilyn's liver testify to this. Perhaps if the autopsy had been more thorough, though, who knows what might have been concluded? Certainly, if she died today, with current science, there would be no mystery.

So, as always . . . the question remains: Suicide or murder?

All the byzantine theories of Marilyn's death share one common denominator: They involve an often frightened, vulnerable, unstable woman who had been spiraling deeper and deeper into her own mental illness. She was in a state of confusion, panic, and despair, and had been off and on for most of her life. If she had been a stable woman who had never overdosed in her lifetime, then, yes, one might legitimately question the circumstances of her death. However, this was a woman who over the years had overdosed more times than people in her circle could even recall—sometimes, it seemed, intentionally, sometimes maybe not. She could have died on any number of those occasions were it not for people like Natasha Lytess, Arthur Miller, Susan Strasberg, and the others who found and revived her. In fact, she overdosed twice just in the month before her death—at Cal-Neva and then at her home—and was saved both times. However, that night of August 4, tragically enough, no one came to her aid. Perhaps the only real question about her death is whether or not it was intentional.*

It's been argued that Marilyn's upcoming prospects were so promising, she couldn't possibly have taken her own life. She supposedly had too much to live for. However, what was probably going on inside her mind had little correlation to those factors. When we consider her last moments on earth we need to focus on an unwell brain, not simply the enticing rewards of a movie star's existence.

---

* "At the side of her bed was a lot of Seconal, which I had never given her," said Dr. Engelberg. "Also, her liver showed that she had a lot of chloral hydrate. I never gave her chloral hydrate and I don't think any doctor in the United States gave it to her. She must have bought it in Tijuana.

"I believe she was in a manic phase," speculated Dr. Engelberg, "and something happened that caused her to suddenly plummet into an extremely depressed state. Of course, I have no idea what that was. But whatever it was, in reaction to that, she did what she often did: she grabbed as many pills as she could, as were at her bedside, and she took them. So, in that sense, [her death] was intentional. But then, I think she thought better of it, and that's why she called Peter Lawford. So while it was at first intentional, I do believe that she changed her mind. If Peter had rushed to her side when she called him, she might have lived."

Marilyn's day-to-day happiness was not affected by a desire for more fame, more wealth, more success. To believe that her will to live could have been reclaimed by finishing *Something's Got to Give* or even by a million-dollar contract with Fox is absurd. To do so is to greatly underestimate the formidable opponent she faced—her own mental illness. To accept this unfortunate truth doesn't negate all that this woman was in her lifetime—it just forces one to accept that Marilyn's story isn't simply one of glamour and fame. In fact, it may not even be a story about "Marilyn Monroe" at all.*

This is the story of a girl named Norma Jeane Mortensen. She thrived despite seemingly insurmountable obstacles and almost impossible odds. She created and became a woman more fascinating than even she believed possible. And in the face of her own failing mind, she battled to keep that creation alive—not for her, but for us. Indeed, Marilyn Monroe *did* exist. Even though the woman inside her was at times doubtful of that fact, we knew it better than she did. She spent so much of her energy, her own will, projecting an image of impossible beauty and ultimate joy. Yet, as the end neared, her experience of who she truly was drifted farther and farther from that ideal—until she found it impossible to pretend anymore. Her choice, as awful as it may have been, was this: Admit to the world that Marilyn Monroe had become nothing more than smoke and mirrors, or die.

On August 5, 1962, Marilyn Monroe gave the world all she had left to give—the knowledge that she was, and always would be . . . ours.

---

* While Marilyn may have had certain projects in the offing, the fact remains that she was still in financial straits at the end of her life. In a letter dated June 25, 1962, her attorney, Mickey Rudin, warned her, "I feel obligated to caution you on your expenditures since at the rate you have been making those expenditures, you will spend the $13,000 in a very short period of time and we will then have to consider where to borrow additional monies." As stated earlier in this text, Marilyn *always* had financial problems.

APPENDICES

AFTER MARILYN

AFTER MARILYN'S DEATH

Miss Monroe has suffered from psychiatric disturbance for a long time. She had often expressed wishes to give up, withdraw and even to die. On more than one occasion in the past when disappointed or depressed, she had made a suicide attempt using sedative drugs. On these occasions, she had called for help and had been rescued. From the information collected about the events of the evening of August the fourth, it is our opinion that the same pattern was repeated—except for the rescue.
—Theodore J. Curphey
Los Angeles Coroner's Office
August 1962

Obviously, the repercussions of Marilyn Monroe's death on many of the principal players in her life would be profound. She was much loved by those in her close-knit circle. Unfortunately, her half sister, Berniece Miracle, received the news of Marilyn's death many hours after most people in the country already knew about it. She had been on a vacation, driving for hours with a broken radio. When she finally returned home and was called, she immediately flew to Los Angeles. Though overwhelmed by grief, she still managed to plan the funeral with her ex-brother-in-law, Joe DiMaggio.

As is by now well known, it was DiMaggio's decision to prohibit just about everyone in Marilyn's life from attending the services that took place on August 8, 1962, at the Westwood Village Mortuary Chapel. He felt strongly that the Kennedys and Frank Sinatra had let Marilyn down and, in some way, even contributed to her death. Therefore, he lashed out by excluding them from the services—as well as most of Marilyn's other friends in show business. During this time of grief, DiMaggio wasn't even sure what to make of Marilyn's publicist and friend Pat Newcomb, because he knew she had known the Kennedys before Marilyn, and still had a relationship with the family. According to Gary Springer, DiMaggio asked his father, John Springer, to handle the bulk of public relations for Marilyn's funeral.

Some of the choice few who were allowed to attend the services for Marilyn Monroe were Pat Newcomb, Berniece Miracle, Inez Melson, Milton Rudin, Ralph Roberts, Allan "Whitey" Snyder, Sydney Guilaroff, Joe DiMaggio Jr., Dr. Ralph Greenson, and his family. In all, there were just twenty-six names on the approved guest list. Lee Strasberg read the eulogy, describing Marilyn's "luminous quality—a combination of wistfulness, radiance, yearning—that set her apart and made everyone wish to be a part of it."

Certainly, in the coldness of death, no one looks as they did in life, and especially not a woman who had been as vital as Marilyn Monroe. Still, she appeared at least serene in a simple green dress of nylon jersey, her blonde hair (a wig, actually) styled pretty much as it had been in the ill-fated *Something's Got to Give*.

George Jacobs, Sinatra's valet, says that Frank Sinatra was very upset over Marilyn's death. Surprisingly, he even joined DiMaggio in the finger-pointing. "Mr. S. began to suspect Lawford and his brothers-in-law of possible foul play," Jacobs recalled, "but since at that point, he would get suspicious of them for a rainstorm, I didn't put much stock in it. Marilyn was one of Mr. S.'s favorite people. He loved how much she loved him. Without that love and admiration she constantly showered onto him, he was deeply wounded. The healing of that wound made him harder and colder than ever before."

For her part, Pat Kennedy Lawford was obviously also devastated by Marilyn's death. She and Peter showed up at the chapel in Westwood only to be turned away at the door. Even Eunice Murray, who wasn't fond of most people in Marilyn's circle, insisted to Berniece Miracle that Pat should be invited to the services. However, Berniece really didn't have much input in that decision, it was all in Joe DiMaggio's purview. This had to have been especially trying for Pat in that the last conversation she had with her friend had been an angry one. It was the one during which Marilyn said she feared Pat might be jealous of her friendship with Peter Lawford.

Pat's friend Pat Brennan says, "It doesn't overstate it to say that Pat was never the same woman. After Marilyn's last weekend at Cal-Neva was when she really began to change. I think she saw firsthand the destruction her husband's lifestyle could wreak on a person. Even though she had enjoyed some of the parties herself, and was also a drinker from time to time, she had never seen anything like Marilyn at Cal-Neva. That weekend marked the beginning of the end of her marriage to Peter. After Marilyn's death, she decided that she wanted out of the marriage. Indeed, the good times in Santa Monica ended with Marilyn's death."

In fact, the Lawfords decided to stay together until after JFK's reelection bid in 1964, but, of course, he was assassinated in 1963. Shortly after her brother's murder, Pat filed for a legal separation. The couple would divorce in 1966. She would never marry again. Peter died in 1984.

Pat, who battled alcoholism for many years after Marilyn's death, worked with the National Center on Addiction. She was also a founder of the National Committee for the Literary Arts. She died at age eighty-two in New York from complications of pneumonia. She is survived by four children and ten grandchildren.

It's impossible to know what President John F. Kennedy thought about Marilyn Monroe's death. It would seem she didn't mean that much to him after all. In his mind, she was likely not much more than a one-night stand. In fact, according to the Secret Service gate logs of the White House, the night after Marilyn's death—August 6, 1962—another of his mistresses, Mary Meyer, paid him a visit at the White House while Jackie and the children were on their way to Ravello, Italy, for a vacation. Meyer showed up at 7:32 p.m. At 11:28, Kennedy called for a car to meet Mary Meyer at the White House's South Gate to take her home.

Robert Kennedy also went on with his life and political career, never mentioning Marilyn publicly. He was assassinated in 1968.

Ida and Wayne Bolender heard the terrible news of Marilyn's passing on television, like most of America. "Ida went straight to church to pray for the soul of Norma Jeane," said one of her relatives. "She never stopped loving her. In her mind, she would always be that little girl she raised. Wayne was sad for many months. It was like losing a daughter for the both of them, it really was." Ida Bolender survived Marilyn Monroe by ten years. She died in 1972. Wayne lived two more years, until 1974.

Respected Marilyn Monroe historian and author Charles Casillo should have the last word on Marilyn here:

"Many decades after her death, Marilyn Monroe is still able to reach from the grave and entice, enthrall and inspire. The living Monroe had inspired a love affair with the world, through death she has inspired a sort of mass necrophilia. Yes, she had and maintains the astonishing fame that many still crave—but beyond that she had an incredible sweetness that touched us and a genuine soul that blazed. Now that she's gone, we're still reaching for that glow . . . willing to grab what light we can."

GLADYS'S LIFE AFTER MARILYN

Shortly after Marilyn's death, Inez Melson received a two-page handwritten letter on personalized stationery from Gladys Baker Eley, sent from the Rock Haven Sanitarium. Published here for the first time, it said:

> *My Dear Friend Mrs. Melson;*
>
> *I am very grateful for your kind and gracious help toward Berniece and myself and to dear Norma Jeane. She is at peace and at rest now and may our God bless her and help her always. I wish you to know that I gave her (Norma) Christian Science treatments for approximately a year; wanted her to be happy and joyous. God bless you and all your goodness. I am getting ever so much good out of the fan and I am indeed most thankful and grateful to you and Berniece and all. May the love of our God bless you and keep you. Miss Travis told me you'd be here to see me this weekend so I am anticipating and hoping to see you soon.*
>
> *Love, Gladys*

When Gladys refers to giving Marilyn Christian Science treatments, she's likely not suggesting that she was praying *with* her daughter (because that had never been the case) but rather praying—or to use Christian Science vernacular, "treating"—*for* Marilyn. Of course, she did not attend the funeral.

When Gladys's other daughter, Berniece Miracle, went to visit her mother at Rock Haven Sanitarium in La Crescenta, California, in August 1962, after Marilyn's funeral, she was distressed to find that Gladys's biggest concern was as it had always been: She wanted her freedom. During that visit, Gladys was dressed in her nurse's uniform, all white—including stockings and shoes. At this point, she was sixty-two years old. She was still attractive with her aquamarine blue eyes and snow white hair, which she wore tied into a tight knot on the top of her head. She had Marilyn's fine bone structure and would have been an absolutely striking older woman if she had taken care of herself, or had any interest in doing so. It's not known what her private reaction was to Marilyn's death, but with Berniece and others who came to visit, she seemed to not be upset.

Mira Bradford's mother was Gladys's friend Ginger—whom Marilyn met the last time she saw her mother at Rock Haven. "I went to visit my mother after Marilyn's death and I saw Gladys," said Mira Bradford. "She was watching television. I remember that she was wearing her nurse's uniform—all in white from head to toe. I went to her and said, 'Gladys, I am so sorry about your daughter.' She looked at me with cold eyes and said, 'She shouldn't have been taking sleeping pills. I told her many times that I could help her sleep with prayer, but she wouldn't listen to me.'

"I was very upset. I had never met Marilyn Monroe, but I thought she deserved more from her own mother than that. Of course, I understood Gladys's illness because my mother was just as disturbed. But, still, I thought I might be able to get through to her. So I sat in front of her and held her hands in mine. I remember they were very cold, very bony. I said, 'Gladys, you know that Marilyn loved you very much, don't you?' She shook her head. 'No,' she said. 'I don't think Marilyn loved me at all.' I wasn't prepared for that. I couldn't hide my surprise. I instinctively let go of her hands. But then I saw a flash of humanity. Suddenly looking very sad, she said, 'Marilyn didn't love me. Norma Jeane loved me, and I loved her. She was a good girl.' Then she just went back to her television. I got up and walked away so that I could cry. It broke my heart."

Marilyn provided $5,000 a year in her will for her mother's care for the rest of her life. Unfortunately, Marilyn did not die a wealthy woman. It's difficult to imagine where all of her money went, but it certainly wasn't in any of her bank accounts. Eventually, the estate would accumulate enough money to care for Gladys, but in 1962 there was only about $4,000, not even enough to continue to care for Gladys at Rock Haven. Berniece left Los Angeles at the end of August to return to Florida and begin the process of having Gladys's conservatorship transferred from Inez Melson to herself. It would be some time, though, before Gladys would be moved to Florida. Then, shortly after her sixty-third birthday, she did the unthinkable.

"It was shocking," recalled Mira Bradford. "I went to visit my mother and there was chaos at Rock Haven. Police were everywhere. Gladys had tied bedsheets together, nailed them to a windowsill on the third floor, and climbed out the window to the ground floor. Then she somehow managed to scale the high fence around Rock Haven. They didn't know she was gone until the next day. I was astounded at her will to be free. The police searched all of Los Angeles for her. She was gone a couple of days. They found her about fifteen miles away, sound asleep in the basement of a church. It was so sad. She was then returned to Rock Haven. I saw her there about a month later. Her eyes were cold as steel. I thought she was worse. Much worse. After that, she was transferred to Camarillo State Hospital, which was far, far worse than Rock Haven in terms of its conditions. It was very sad, how this woman suffered."

In 1967, Gladys was finally released into Berniece's care in Florida.

In 1970, she was considered sane enough to live in a retirement home not far from Berniece.

In April of 1971, Marilyn Monroe historian James Haspiel spent time with Gladys. He explained, "My wife and I were traveling through Gainesville, Florida. I found Gladys's number in the telephone book and just called her. She picked up the phone. Obviously, I wanted to meet her. She asked me if I was a Christian Scientist. I said, 'No, but I'd be interested in exploring that.' I eventually persuaded her to let me come to visit her if she could give me literature on Christian Science. I took my wife and two little sons with me to the apartment building. She wasn't frail. She was almost a little weighty. What was so striking about her was that she had Marilyn's face. But more significantly, she had Marilyn's laugh. I couldn't get over the laughter.

"En route to her apartment, I decided that I would only call her daughter Norma Jeane, not Marilyn. So for the hour and a half I was there, I called her Norma Jeane. But she called her Marilyn. She was very intense on the subject of Christian Science. She gave me a bunch of pamphlets before we left. She asked me to call her back, and I did. Gladys's displeasure with Marilyn's profession was very evident to me. She called it the moving picture industry. In fact, she said her work, what she did as a Christian Scientist, was 'diametrically opposed to what Marilyn was doing in the moving picture industry.' She said that she never wanted Marilyn to be in that business, but, as she put it, 'I never told her one way or the other. I never told her a word.'"

Gladys continued to live in Florida, spending infrequent time with her daughter Berniece—at her own decision—for many more years. She was known to ride a tricycle around town with a red flag on the handlebars that read, "Danger." Around 1977, she finally began receiving money from the estate of Marilyn Monroe.

Gladys Baker Eley died of heart failure in Gainesville on March 11, 1984—almost twenty-two years after her famous daughter. She was eighty-three years old.

PERSPECTIVE: MARILYN AND THE KENNEDYS

Six months. That's all it was, just six months. It would appear that Marilyn Monroe's in-depth experiences with the Kennedys comprised just six months out of thirty-six years of her life. Despite such a brief span of time, a plethora of books and documentaries have resulted that have sought to stretch those months into many years and, thereby, make them the central focus of all sorts of romantic intrigue and FBI espionage. However, fresh research now establishes that it's simply not true. Of course, it's always possible that two people can slip away and have secret rendezvous that no one else could ever know about. That's a little harder to do when the two people are as high-profile as Marilyn Monroe and either of the Kennedy brothers. That said, here is all we know with absolute certainty based on fresh research for this book:

Marilyn met JFK at a dinner party in the 1950s. She met him again at the Democratic Convention in July of 1960. Those meetings were passing and perfunctory.

A year and a half went by.

Then the six-month time clock began:

Marilyn met Bobby Kennedy on February 2, 1962, at Pat and Peter Lawford's home.

She saw JFK in March 1962 at a dinner party in New York.

She slept with JFK on March 24 and possibly March 25, at Bing Crosby's home.

She performed at JFK's birthday celebration at Madison Square Garden in May 1962.

She saw Bobby at another dinner party at Pat and Peter Lawford's in June 1962.

Other than telephone calls she placed to JFK—which he apparently did not take—and to Bobby—which he and his secretary apparently did take—that's it. Anything else just cannot be proven. Of course, that doesn't mean it didn't happen. JFK and Bobby could also have been secretly living in her guesthouse, too—and that can't be proven or disproven either.

Over the years, so much has been said and written about these colorful characters, it's become accepted wisdom that Marilyn was romantically involved with both brothers. However, this writer interviewed Peter Lawford in 1981—before most of the fiction about Marilyn and the Kennedys took root—and was told, "All of this business about Marilyn and JFK and Bobby is pure crap. I think maybe—and I'm saying *maybe*—she had one or two dates with JFK. Not a single date with Bobby, though, and I swear to Christ that's the truth."

But then, of course, a number of years later, an ex-wife of Peter's came forward and added to the confusion. She said that Peter finally confessed all to her "when he was kind of high." The next day, Peter was so confused about what he may have said while up on his cloud, he called the ex-wife and told her to just forget about all of it. He was stoned and, he observed, "Who knows what I was talking about?" Of course, she didn't forget. However, to take the secondhand recollection of someone who was "kind of high" as gospel truth is perhaps not the wisest course of action in matters so historical.

Sadly, Peter Lawford—a kindhearted even if conflicted man who many say would never have betrayed a friend—has been widely quoted about Marilyn and the Kennedys decades after his death. It's as if the man couldn't stop talking about them during the last months of his life. But did he really make all of those statements, especially to ex-wives? "If you knew Peter like I knew Peter," Dean Martin told this writer when I wrote a book about Frank Sinatra, "you would know that he would never have said those things about Marilyn and the Kennedys—*especially* if those stories were true."

Of course, it's easy to see how Marilyn and the Kennedy brothers became eternally linked to so many sensational and lurid tales. The confluence of these powerful and historical men with one of the most legendary movie stars of her time has been too compelling to ignore. The Kennedy regime was viewed as a special time in history—Camelot, it was called after the fact—during which idealistic men came into power with an eye toward changing the way people thought of government. Both brothers were known philanderers, though it wasn't reported at the time because, pre-Watergate, the press was much more protective of those in government. Marilyn's publicist Michael Selsman recalls, "I spent a lot of time saying to reporters, 'The president? What? You must be joking!' Knowing all the while that it was true. I was also good with, 'Pills? What pills?' And, 'Drinking? Of course not. Marilyn is just a social drinker.'"

Sometimes, though, JFK's nature was at least suggested in the press, and as a result, innuendo about him and Marilyn can be traced all the way back to 1960. For instance, in July of that year, after learning that Marilyn had been asking questions to her friends about Kennedy's policies, Art Buchwald wrote, "Let's be firm on the Monroe Doctrine. Who will be the next ambassador to Monroe? This is one of the many problems which president-elect Kennedy will have to work on in January. Obviously, you can't leave Monroe adrift. There are too many people eyeing her, and now that Ambassador Miller has left, she could flounder around without any direction." Such wink-and-nod reporting was going on way back in 1960 where JFK and Marilyn were concerned, and she'd only met him twice by that time.

One of the major leaps toward national fascination where this subject is concerned happened in the 1970s with a lavish Marilyn Monroe biography by Norman Mailer that actually involved the Kennedys in her death and, for the first time, linked Marilyn with Bobby. Of course, rumors about whether or not Marilyn had been murdered didn't begin in the 1970s. Michael Selsman put it this way: "The rumor that Marilyn had been murdered happened immediately after she died. Within five minutes of her body being found. The first thought was, 'Is there a movie in this?' That's this town [Hollywood]." When this writer spoke to Mailer, though, he indicated that he wasn't proud of his murder theory. "Not my best work," he said of his book, "and not my best research. In hindsight, maybe I shouldn't have allowed its publication." He'd also said that he "needed the money" and that this was why he allowed to be published details about Marilyn and the Kennedys that were not verified, and that have gone on to be considered fact. That's difficult to believe of a gifted Pulitzer Prize winner, yet apparently true. After Mailer's book was published another came forth from syndicated gossip columnist Earl Wilson, which was the first to formally reveal that Marilyn and JFK had been in a sexual relationship. That work opened the floodgates, and since that time there have been many, many books whose premise has been different variations on the Kennedy theme. Truly, stories involving Marilyn and the Kennedys have been circulating for many decades.

Also being written about for just about as long as Marilyn has been dead are the many different tapes that supposedly exist implicating people in her death. If one is to believe all that has been published in the last few decades—and entire books have been published based on these supposed recordings—poor Marilyn was being bugged by everyone from the Teamsters, the FBI, the CIA, Howard Hughes, the Kennedys, and the Mafia to her own movie studio, 20th Century-Fox. The woman must have had so many different wires and recording devices in her homes, it's a wonder she was able to get a decent radio or TV signal. Even her answering service was supposedly tapped. She wasn't the only one, of course. Peter and Pat Lawford, the Kennedys, Frank, Sammy, Dean . . . all of them were supposedly also the subject of wiretapping that resulted in audio documentation of a plethora of shocking secrets. There's even supposed to be a tape recording of Marilyn and Bobby Kennedy having a violent argument just hours before her death over a diary in which she supposedly kept all of the secrets of state revealed to her by the Kennedy brothers. "I want that diary, Marilyn. *And now, damn it!*" Yet, in almost fifty years, not one single tape has ever seen the light of day.

The fact of the matter is that no matter how many people claim to have heard these tapes—and there are dozens—until the rest of us have the opportunity to do so, they simply don't matter. "You could hear the voices of Marilyn and JFK," Peter Lawford supposedly said of one of the tapes, "in addition to Marilyn and RFK. In both cases you could make out the muted sounds of bedsprings and the cries of ecstasy. Marilyn, after all, was a master of her craft." Ignoring the fact that Lawford would never have made such comments—not to mention that the notion of a ménage à trois between Marilyn and the Kennedy brothers is preposterous—it's at long last time to accept the truth: These tapes do not exist.

THE FBI'S FILES ON MARILYN

In October 2006, under the Freedom of Information Act, the FBI released a number of new files on Marilyn Monroe, referenced in the text of this book. One is truly extraordinary and has to do with Marilyn Monroe and Bobby Kennedy. This three-page document—called simply "Robert F. Kennedy" and referenced in this book's chapter "Were Marilyn and Bobby 'The New Item'?"—has never before been mentioned, despite hundreds of articles, books, and documentaries about Marilyn Monroe's death. It was written by an unnamed "former special agent" supposedly working for the then governor of California, Democrat Pat Brown, and forwarded to Washington by Curtis Lynum, then head of the San Francisco FBI. Though this paperwork is like all of the FBI's documentation of Marilyn and the Kennedys in that it can't be substantiated—and this one even states that the source of the information is unknown and the information can't be verified—it was circulated to the FBI's most senior officers, including Director J. Edgar Hoover's right-hand man, Clyde Tolson. Despite its specious nature, it's interesting just by virtue of the fact that this report—classified for decades—was written and filed back on October 19, 1964, years before people started gossiping that the Kennedys may have had something to do with Marilyn's death.

As earlier stated, this file announces that Marilyn and Bobby were having a "romance and sex affair" and that Bobby promised to divorce Ethel and marry Marilyn. However, according to the report, she soon figured out that he was lying. At this same time, according to the report,

"Marilyn also had an intermittent lesbian affair with [name deleted] while Robert Kennedy was carrying on his sex affair with Marilyn Monroe," and also "on a few occasions John F. Kennedy came out and had sex parties with [name deleted] actress." Moreover, "During the period of time that Robert Kennedy was having his sex affair with Marilyn Monroe, on one occasion a sex party was conducted at which several other persons were present. Tape recording was secretly made and is in the possession of a Los Angeles private detective agency. The detective wants $3000 for a certified copy of the recording, in which all the voices are identifiable."

The details in the paperwork continue by stating that Marilyn began to call RFK "person-to-person" to complain to him about her problems with Fox and the ill-fated movie *Something's Got to Give*. Bobby "told her not to worry about the contract—he would take care of everything." Later, they had "unpleasant words" and she became upset and "threatened to make public their affair." The report continues, "On the day that Marilyn died, Robert Kennedy was in town and checked into the Beverly Hills Hotel. By coincidence, this is across the street from the house in which a number of years earlier his father, Joseph Kennedy, had lived for a time, common-law, with Gloria Swanson."

Moreover, the document maintains that Peter Lawford made "special arrangements" with Marilyn's psychiatrist Dr. Ralph Greenson—who, it says, was treating her to "get her off of barbiturates"—to give her sixty tablets of Seconal on her last visit to him, "unusual in quantity especially since she saw him frequently." (Note: The truth is that the day before her death she was given Nembutal, not Seconal, and twenty-four of them, not sixty, and by Dr. Engelberg, not Dr. Greenson.) It says that "Peter Lawford knew from Marilyn's friends that she often made suicide attempts and that she was induced to fake a suicide attempt in order to arouse sympathy."

The report states that Marilyn's publicist, Pat Newcomb, and her housekeeper, Eunice Murray, conspired with Peter Lawford and Dr. Greenson "in a plan to induce suicide." (In return for her assistance, Newcomb was "put on the federal payroll.") The report suggests that the principals deliberately gave Marilyn the means to fake another suicide attempt by making sure—via Eunice Murray—that the pills were on her nightstand before she went to bed. It's not clear why they believed she would want to try to kill herself that night, but the implication is that they were going to do or say something that would drive her to want to at least act as if she were going to kill herself, and then "[she] expected to have her stomach pumped out and get sympathy for her suicide attempt." But this time, she was allowed to die rather than be saved just in time, as had often happened in the past. After the deed was done, RFK telephoned Peter Lawford "to find out if Marilyn was dead yet." It goes on to state that Joe DiMaggio knew exactly what was going on but was powerless to stop it; he "is reported to have stated that when Robert Kennedy gets out of office, he intends to kill him."

Bits and pieces and different variations of the above scenario have appeared in a number of books and magazine articles over the years having to do with Marilyn's death, but none of it is verifiable. Still, it's very interesting that what was once just gossiped about by secondhand sources and then reported by a slew of biographers turns out to actually be material found in the FBI files. It does give all of those who believe that RFK was involved in the death of Marilyn Monroe a little more certainty in their beliefs.

So, what does all of this mean? Unfortunately, not much. There are a couple of possible scenarios as to why the report exists in the FBI files. It's well known that J. Edgar Hoover strongly resented Bobby Kennedy and perhaps intended to use the report to discredit him at some point along the way, maybe before the 1968 election. One wonders, though, what might have happened if the document had been leaked in 1968. It might have done some damage just by virtue of the fact that it's an FBI document. But how seriously anyone would have taken it given its gossipy nature—and the fact that it's not sourced at all—is questionable. What's laughable is that the report refers to all of the principal players by their first names; the document reads as if it were written by a Hollywood gossip columnist.

In truth, if in 1965 the FBI truly believed that Robert Kennedy, Peter Lawford, Eunice Murray, and Pat Newcomb conspired in the death of Marilyn Monroe, wouldn't they all have been charged? Obviously, that never happened. Was it because the FBI didn't believe its own files?

Also very interesting is that this latest Marilyn Monroe release from the FBI refers to a "sex tape" supposedly featuring Marilyn Monroe. The memo is titled "interstate transportation of obscene matter." It says, "[Deleted] . . . at his office ran a French-type movie which depicted

Marilyn Monroe, deceased actress, in unnatural acts with an unknown male. [Deleted] informed them he had obtained this film prior to the time Monroe achieved stardom and that subsequently Joe DiMaggio attempted to purchase this film for $25,000. This information should not be discussed outside the bureau."

In April 2007, someone—not named by any news reports—supposedly purchased this fifteen-minute tape (which allegedly shows Marilyn having oral sex with an unidentified male) for $1.5 million. The anonymous purchaser is quoted by the person who says he brokered the deal—someone named Keya Morgan who was apparently making a documentary about Marilyn—as saying he would not release the tape, and that he only bought it to keep it out of circulation because he is trying to protect Monroe's legacy. Likely, though, it won't be shown because it does not exist. The timing is just too convenient. It's likely that someone came up with the idea of saying that the video described in the latest FBI document actually exists and, not only that, was just purchased? What was the intent of doing such a thing? Who knows? In truth, though, not one shred of evidence has been brought forth to prove that the sale was even made—no seller has been named, no buyer identified, no receipt either. Yet the story received national attention, demonstrating if nothing else that the public's hunger for interesting stories about Marilyn Monroe has never waned. However, like all of the other audio- and videotapes of Marilyn Monroe supposedly having intimate encounters with the Kennedys or others, if this one ever actually surfaces it'll be a first.

THE JOHN MINER TRANSCRIPTS

John Miner, now about ninety years old, is the former deputy district attorney of Los Angeles County and the founder and head of the medical-legal section of that office. He claims to have heard hours of secret tapes of psychiatric sessions between Marilyn and Dr. Ralph Greenson, and while doing so took copious, "nearly verbatim" notes—many, many pages—reconstructing word for word every statement she made during the sessions. Entire books have been based on these notes, which include in-depth and very personal comments from Marilyn about her affairs with both Kennedys, her sex life, her career aspirations, and so on. This writer spent six hours with Miner and reviewed all of his handwritten notes.

"You are the only person who will ever know the most private, the most secret thoughts of Marilyn Monroe," she told Greenson, according to Miner's transcript. "I have absolute confidence and trust you will never reveal to a living soul what I say to you." Would Marilyn really speak like that? Would she really find it necessary to make such statements to a doctor she had been seeing almost every day?

Miner says, "I kept my promise to Dr. Greenson to respect the confidentiality of his interview with me and the contents of Miss Monroe's tapes, I kept that promise in spite of incredible pressures from reporters, authors, and official investigators to relate this information. It is only after [authors] Donald Spoto, Marvin Bergman, and others accused Dr. Greenson of being responsible in some way for causing Marilyn Monroe's death that I approached Dr. Greenson's widow to ask for a release from my promise to her husband. She wishes to do whatever is possible to clear his name and granted my request."

Miner's explanation that he reconstructed his copious notes from memory is troubling. It takes a leap of faith to believe his verbatim recollection of so many quotes. Here, he provides a synopsis of what he says he heard on these tapes:

"She explains that she has recorded her free associating (saying whatever comes into her mind; a necessary technique used in psychoanalytic therapy) at home because she could not do it in office sessions. She hoped this would assist in her treatment. And she believes that she has discovered a means of overcoming the resistance which patients have in being unable to comply with the psychiatrist's request to free associate because the mind becomes a blank.

"She tells how she plans to become the highest paid actress in Hollywood so that she can finance everything that she wants to do.

"She says that she aspires to do Shakespeare and that she will pay Lee [Strasberg] to coach her in Shakespeare as his only student for one year.

"Laurence Olivier, she says, had agreed to polish her Shakespearean training after Strasberg finished, and she would pay him whatever he asked.

"She says she would pay Dr. Greenson to be his only patient while she was undergoing the instruction in Shakespeare.

"She says that when she is ready she would produce and act in all of the Shakespeare plays that she would put in film under the rubric Marilyn Monroe Shakespeare Festival.

"For those many writers who maintain that she was going to blow the whistle on JFK about their sexual relationship, she shoots down such speculation when she expresses utmost admiration for the President and explicitly says she would never embarrass him.

"Her remarks disprove those who claim that she killed herself because Robert Kennedy broke off their relationship because it was she who broke it off.

"She strongly asserted that she wanted to rid herself of Eunice Murray, her housekeeper, and requested Dr. Greenson's assistance in so doing.

"She says that she never had an orgasm before becoming Dr. Greenson's patient but that he had cured her of that infirmity for which was she was forever grateful."

John Miner maintains that Marilyn was murdered with a lethal enema of Nembutal, which he believes was administered by housekeeper Eunice Murray—who, oddly, *was* doing the laundry when the police arrived in the middle of the night. It's been maintained by many people that Eunice Murray customarily gave Marilyn Monroe enemas. (*Why?* Isn't this something a woman would want to do for herself? Is a housekeeper really necessary for this kind of duty?)

The bigger question, perhaps, is: Why would Marilyn Monroe have had to explain the background and history of each person mentioned in her long narrative, editorializing as if she and Dr. Greenson had never met? She had been seeing him almost every day.

It would seem that John Miner, a very nice, congenial man, would have no reason to lie. It therefore comes down to a simple matter of choice as to whether or not a reporter feels he can rely on his notes. In fact, no one has ever heard these tapes, other than John Miner—not even Ralph Greenson's wife or children. John Miner believes that Greenson, who died in 1979, destroyed all of the tapes. In other words, there is one and only one source for all of this information . . . and, believe him or not, that's John Miner.

ACKNOWLEDGMENTS

THE AUTHOR'S SUPPORT TEAM

During the course of years of production on a book such as *The Secret Life of Marilyn Monroe*, many people become invested in the project, from researchers and investigators to copy editors and fact checkers to designers, publicists, and, yes, even attorneys. My colleagues at Grand Central Publishing have always made it possible for me to utilize all of the resources available to me—no matter how complex the working situation or how many people necessary to complete the task at hand. In fact, an author could not ask for a better and more nurturing environment than the one I have been so fortunate to have at Grand Central for the last ten years of my career. In short, it's been terrific. As with all of my books, this one is a collaborative effort. None of it would be possible, though, without my publisher at Grand Central, Jamie Raab. As a publisher—and an editor—she is without peer. I want to thank her for her patience and trust in me as she shepherded this project along for the last couple of years. She had to make more than a few concessions for me along the way with this work, and she always did so happily. What more can an author ask for? Thanks also to Jamie's wonderful assistants, Sharon Krassney and Sara Weiss. I would also like to thank Frances Jalet-Miller for her conscientious work on this book and for helping me to shape its story. I really appreciate her help so much and look forward to working with her again. Interior production of this book was handled by Tom Whatley; the amazing jacket was designed by Flamur Tonuzi, with print coordination handled by Antoinette Marotta. I thank them all, and thanks also to Anne Twomey. Special thanks also to Bob Castillo for his work in managing editorial, to my able copy editor, Roland Ottewell, and proofreaders Richard Willett and Lisa Nicholas.

The Secret Life of Marilyn Monroe—my fifteenth book—was, without a doubt, my most challenging, primarily because its development took so many years. I first began to work on it in 1995 at the time I was writing *Sinatra: A Complete Life*, my biography of Frank Sinatra. Then, in 1998 and 1999, as I wrote *Jackie, Ethel, Joan: Women of Camelot*, I continued to keep the Monroe project on the back burner. I always knew that many of the interviews I would conduct for books about Sinatra and the Kennedys could and should be utilized in a book about Marilyn Monroe. I was very fortunate to draw from these interviews because, in the intervening years, many of those valuable sources would pass away. However, I believe that each is well served on these pages.

Also, I am very fortunate to have been associated with the same private investigator and chief researcher, Cathy Griffin, for the last twenty years. Much to my great advantage, Cathy has also worked on a number of books about Marilyn Monroe in the past. Therefore, I was able to rely on her many years of research, including invaluable interviews she conducted in the past, again with people no longer with us.

I must acknowledge my domestic agent, Mitch Douglas. He has been a very important person in my life and career for more than ten years, and I thank him for his constant and enthusiastic encouragement. He went the extra mile for me, especially with this book.

Dorie Simmonds of the Dorie Simmonds Agency in London has not only been an amazing agent for me in Europe for the last ten years, but a loyal and trusted friend. I so appreciate her dedication to me and to my work. Dorie manages to perform miracles for me on a daily basis, and I don't know how she puts up with me. However, I do know that an author could not ask for better representation, or a better friend.

My capable fact checker and editor, James Pinkston, has worked for me on my last five books. He reviews everything I write long before anyone at Grand Central ever sees it—thank goodness! I can't imagine what kind of book we would be publishing if not for Jim's tireless quest for accuracy. Working with him on *The Secret Life of Marilyn Monroe* has been a true honor and joy.

THE TRUE EXPERTS

Whenever I write a new book, I am fortunate to meet people who have devoted their lives to better understanding my present subject. If an author such as me is lucky enough to be able to call upon true experts in the field in which he's working, it just makes for a better and more comprehensive book. Happily, I had the good fortune of being able to call upon one of the greatest, I think, experts in all things Marilyn, and that's James Haspiel. I thank him for the time he gave in setting straight some of the myths about Marilyn. Mr. Haspiel was not only a fan of Marilyn's, he became a close friend of hers. In fact, if I had to recommend any of the many books that have been published about Marilyn over the last forty years, I would wholeheartedly recommend Haspiel's two books, *Young Marilyn: Becoming the Legend* and *Marilyn Monroe: The Ultimate Look at the Legend*. They're both revelatory not only because they are so personal in scope but because the many photographs of James as a youngster with the stunning Marilyn in her prime are absolutely priceless. I was truly inspired by James's devotion to Marilyn and by the way he brought her to life in his books. No doubt, every author's vision of a subject is different, and so I am therefore not sure how James will feel about my "take" on his greatest star—but I have so loved his. Mr. Haspiel was interviewed on March 17, 1998, and again in April 2008.

I also have to thank my very good friend of many years, Charles Casillo. Charles is another "ultimate" Marilyn Monroe fan who understands her character and personality so well. He also brought her to life in a different way, a fictional telling of her story called *The Marilyn Diaries*. It's a terrific book and I would recommend it as well. I want to thank Charles for setting me straight on so many details about Marilyn's life. To show you how long Charles and I have been thinking about Marilyn's life and career, he and I actually interviewed Kennedy hairdresser Mickey Song more than ten years ago—he touched up Marilyn's hair for her "Happy Birthday" performance at Madison Square Garden in 1962. I had completely forgotten that we collaborated on that effort until I found the tape recording of the interview while researching this book. Whereas I, apparently, have a bad memory for such things—thank goodness for tape recorders!—Charles does not. He remembers virtually everything having to do with Marilyn Monroe, and for that I thank him. This is a much better book because of him.

Maryanne Reed allowed me access to her complete collection of Marilyn Monroe memorabilia, most of which was culled from the files of the newspaper *Hollywood Citizen-News* and the *Woman's Home Companion*, both of which are now defunct. I am so grateful to her. This material was invaluable to me in that it provided many leads and also included the unpublished notes and interviews of reporters who were covering Marilyn for the *News* and *Companion* in the 1950s. I listened to and utilized in this work thirty-five previously unpublished taped interviews and conversations with Marilyn intimates such as Jim Dougherty, Ida Bolender, Wayne Bolender, and costars such as Jane Russell, Betty Grable, and Lauren Bacall, all of which Ms Reed generously had transferred from reel-to-reel format to cassette for my convenience.

Also, Maryanne Reed has on file many documents associated with Inez Melson's relationship with Gladys Baker and Marilyn Monroe. This includes correspondence between Ms. Baker and Ms. Melson, as well as rare published interviews such as one that appeared with Melson in *The Listener* (London) on August 30, 1979. Acquired through a private purchaser, they became key to my research. Importantly, Ms. Reed also obtained from a private source tapes of interviews conducted with Eleanor "BeBe" Goddard that were made in or around January 1991. She also provided me with documents relating to Emmeline Snively, including a rare interview with her that was published in the *Los Angeles Daily News* on February 4, 1954. Working with Maryanne was a real pleasure and I am eternally grateful to her for everything she did for me while I was working on *The Secret Life of Marilyn Monroe*.

GENERAL RESEARCH

Over the course of years I have devoted to *The Secret Life of Marilyn Monroe*, a great number of people went out of their way to assist me, literally hundreds of relations, entertainment journalists, socialites, lawyers, celebrities, show business executives and former executives, associates, and friends as well as foes, classmates, teachers, neighbors, newspersons, and archivists. However, at the very beginning of this project, I sat down with my researchers and investigators and posed the very important question: What is there about Marilyn Monroe that has not been reported in about a hundred other books about her? It took us some time to answer that question, and we had a few false starts over the years—as my publisher well knows! However, it was the relationship between Marilyn and her mother, Gladys Baker, that began to most fascinate me as we continued our research, and I soon realized that it was one of the stories I most wanted to tell on these pages—because it had never before been told. I must thank my amazing researcher Michael Stevens, who uncovered much of the information on the Rock Haven Sanitarium and of Gladys Baker's time there. What a wonderful job he did for me on this book! He dedicated himself to Ms. Baker's memory and was truly a champion of hers during this entire process. Together, we went on an amazing fact-finding journey, and I thank him so much for the experience. I'll never forget a moment of it. Also, he obtained from a private collector more than twenty-five files from Rock Haven regarding Gladys's treatment there, most of which were invaluable to my research.

Also important, I must acknowledge all of the fine people at Julien's Auctions for making available to me so many of the letters and notes from Gladys Baker that were utilized in this book and, I might proudly add, for the first time in any Marilyn Monroe biography. Also, my researchers obtained a treasure trove of material—including correspondence from Gladys Baker, Berniece Baker, BeBe Goddard, Arthur Miller, Joe DiMaggio, Dr. Ralph Greenson, and, of course, Marilyn Monroe—from the following auction houses: Bonham's, Butterfields, Christie's, Hunt Auctions, and Sotheby's.

I've had many investigators and researchers over the years, but none who have been as consistent as Cathy Griffin. Cathy is also a fine journalist in her own right. It would be easy with a subject as popular as this one to simply reinterview those people who have told their stories to others and hope for an occasional new angle. However, Cathy always manages to locate people who have new, previously untold stories—such as the story of Charles Stanley Gifford Jr., the man Marilyn believed to be her half brother. Gifford broke his silence for the first time on these pages, and I thank him for his interview of May 9, 2008. How Cathy ever locates people like him, I'll never know, but I'm very glad she does. This particular work represents our seventh book together. I thank her for her assistance over the years, her tenacity, and, most of all, her friendship.

Thank you, also, to Jane Maxwell, a terrific pop culture historian who allowed me to have access to all of her notes and files concerning Natasha Lytess. Her assistance was invaluable. She also gave me access to all of the documents that were culled from her research using "The Milton Greene Papers."

Also, I would like to thank Juliette Burgonde, Cloe Basiline, Maxime Rhiette, Suzalie Rose, and especially Mary Whitaker in London, who helped with the UK research.

Thanks to Samuel Elliot for helping us with all of the Bolender family history. What a tangled web that was to sort through, and I could not have done it without Mr. Elliot.

Of course, I reviewed every one of Marilyn Monroe's films, as well as all of the made-for-television movies and miniseries about her and, obviously, scores of documentaries. I would not have had access to all of this material had it not been for the efforts of Nick Scotti in the United Kingdom. I definitely owe him a debt of gratitude for procuring all of this important research material for me. Also, I reviewed—and it took months, I might add—the vast 20th Century-Fox collection at UCLA, which contains detailed letters from executives about all of Monroe's movies at the studio, legal and production files pertaining to same, as well as daily production reports. This material was also important to my research in all areas of this book.

Thanks also to the staffs of the Hans Tasiemka Archives in London and the Special Collections Library of the University of California in Los Angeles.

As always, Marybeth Evans in London did a terrific job at the Manchester Central Library reviewing reams of documents for me and pointing me to just the ones I needed for this book.

Thanks also to Suzalie Rose, who did research for me in libraries in Paris. She and Carl Mathers spent so much time thinking about Marilyn and coming up with new ways to tell her story.

I also have to thank the fine folks at Photofest for some of the terrific photographs that are found in this book. I go to Photofest first whenever I begin the process of selecting pictures to illustrate my books. They always come through for me, and I thank them.

Bernie Abramson, who was a personal photographer for President John Fitzgerald Kennedy, had photographs of Marilyn with Peter Lawford, Pat Kennedy Lawford, and Frank Sinatra that he'd taken and that I had never before seen. I am so grateful to him for allowing us to publish them here, for the very first time in any Marilyn Monroe biography.

I want to thank all of the dedicated people at the Margaret Herrick Library of the Academy of Motion Picture Arts and Sciences for their assistance on this and all of my books. I must also thank James Pinkston for all of the time he spent at the Academy Library for me.

I also owe a debt of gratitude to Donald Spoto, the best-selling author of the excellent *Marilyn Monroe: The Biography*, for his having donated all of his interview tapes for that project to the Margaret Herrick Library of the Academy of Motion Picture Arts and Sciences. His generous donation made it possible for me to obtain background and quotes from Marilyn Monroe's publicist, Patricia Newcomb, and also from other sources who are either dead or were simply not available to me at this time. I also must acknowledge Maurice Zolotow, who wrote the first in-depth biography of Marilyn Monroe—*Marilyn Monroe*—published in 1960, before her death. Mr. Zolotow stored many of his papers in a collection at the University of Texas, and his impeccable research was vital to my own. As a side note, I have always been moved by the poignant last passage in Zolotow's book about Marilyn. He wrote, "Now, at thirty-four, Monroe has it all . . . [but her] great achievement has been the making of herself and the imposition of her will and her dream upon the whole world. . . . In one sense, then, her life is completed because her spirit is formed and has achieved itself. No matter what unpredictable events may lie in her future, they cannot change who she is and what she has become. And there will be many surprises and alterations in her life ahead; there will be, in Hart Crane's phrase, 'new thresholds, new anatomies.' In her heart is a questing fever that will give her no peace. . . . her soul will always be restless, unquiet."

I would be remiss in not mentioning the other preeminent Marilyn Monroe biography, and that is, of course, Anthony Summer's *Goddess*. It's one of the first books historians most often turn to when trying to understand Miss Monroe—and rightly so.

Numerous other organizations and institutions provided me with articles, documents, audio interviews, video interviews, transcripts, and other material that was either utilized directly in *The Secret Life of Marilyn Monroe* or just for purposes of background. Therefore, I would like to express my gratitude to the following institutions: the American Academy of Dramatic Arts; the American Film Institute Library; the Associated Press Office (New York); the Bancroft Library (University of California, Berkeley); the Billy Rose Theater Collection in the Library of the Performing Arts, Lincoln Center, New York; the *Boston Herald* Archives; the Beverly Hills Library; the University of California, Los Angeles; Corbis-Gamma/Liason; the Ernest Lehman Collection at USC; the Glendale Central Public Library; the Hedda Hopper Collection in the Margaret Herrick Library, Academy of Motion Picture Arts and Sciences, Beverly Hills; the Lincoln Center Library of the Performing Arts; the Kobal Collection; the *Los Angeles Times*; the Los Angeles Public Library; the Louella Parsons Collection at the University of Southern California; the Margaret Herrick Library (Academy of Motion Pictures Arts and Sciences); the Museum of Broadcasting, New York; the former Metro-Goldwyn-Mayer studio archives, now part of the Turner Entertainment Group, Los Angeles; the Museum of the Film; the National Archives and the Library of Congress; the New York City Municipal Archives; the New York University Library; the *New York Daily News*; the *New York Post*; the *New York Times*; Occidental College (Eagle Rock, California); the Philadelphia Public Library; the *Philadelphia Inquirer* and the *Philadelphia Daily News*; the Time-Life archives and Library, New York; the Universal Collection at the University of Southern California; the University of Southern California; and, finally, Rex Features.

SOURCES AND OTHER NOTES

In all of my books I provide documentation of firsthand sources, which I think is very important to most readers. I also usually set forth the hundreds of other books, periodicals, magazine, and newspaper articles consulted by myself and my researchers. After careful deliberation, I've finally come to the conclusion that the listing of such material is nothing more than typing practice for all concerned. In truth, in my twenty-five years of authoring books about public figures, I have encountered very few people who have ever actually paid attention to such material. Therefore, with this, my fifteenth book, I am going to dispense with the customary page-after-page accounting of secondary source material, if only for the sake of space and time considerations. In a few cases, I will mention secondary source material in the notes that follow if I think it's important to understanding my research. Generally, though, I can assure my readers that many books about Marilyn Monroe, the Kennedys, Frank Sinatra, and others were reviewed as part of my research, as were countless newspaper and magazine articles.

Also, in writing about a person as popular and also as beloved as Marilyn Monroe, a biographer is bound to find that many sources with valuable information prefer to not be named in the text. This is reasonable. Throughout my career, I have understood that for a person to jeopardize a long-standing, important relationship with a celebrity or a famous person's family just for the sake of one of my books is a purely personal choice. Nevertheless, I appreciate the assistance of many people close to Marilyn who, over the years, gave of their time for this project. I will respect the wish for anonymity of those who require it, and, as always, those who could be identified are named in these notes.

The following notes and source acknowledgments are by no means comprehensive. Rather, they are intended to give you, the reader, a general overview of my research.

PART ONE: THE BEGINNING

I relied heavily on the interview with Nancy Jeffrey, only surviving foster daughter of Ida and Wayne Bolender, conducted on May 21, 2008. I thank her so much for her trust and confidence.

I'd also like to thank Louise Adams for her insight into the lives of Gladys Baker and Ida Bolender. Also, Rose Anne Cooper—who worked at the Rock Haven Sanitarium in La Crescenta, California—was extremely helpful and spent more hours with me in 2007 and 2008 than I'm sure she cares to remember. She even had photographs of Rock Haven, key to my understanding of the environment there. I owe a real debt of gratitude to both Ms. Adams and Ms. Cooper, both of whom I interviewed on February 1, 2007, April 10, 2007, June 15, 2007, and January 3, 2008.

I must give special acknowledgment to Mary Thomas-Strong, whose mother was a close friend of Ida Bolender's. I interviewed Ms. Thomas-Strong on April 1, 2008, April 3, 2008, and April 10, 2008. She also provided me with boxes of material invaluable to my research and to my understanding the complex relationship between Ida, Gladys Baker, and Norma Jeane. This material included correspondence files between her mother and Ida Bolender. It also included *The Legend of Marilyn Monroe*, a rare film source of information from 1964, from David L. Wolper Productions, Inc. This documentary features what I believe to be the only televised interview with Ida and Wayne Bolender. Ms. Thomas-Strong also provided for me the medical files of Della M. Monroe from the Norwalk State Hospital, including her death certificate (#4081). Moreover, she provided me with a copy of the documentary *Marilyn: Beyond the Legend*.

Special acknowledgment must be extended to the family of Bea Thomas, who knew Grace Goddard. Ms. Thomas was interviewed in January 1990 by Elvin Summer for a family history. I obtained that history from a private source.

Thanks also to Esther Thompson, whose mother, Ruth, worked with Grace McKee at Consolidated Studios. Ms. Thompson spent many hours with me reconstructing certain events for this book and I thank her for the interviews I conducted with her on July 2, 2007, and February 1, 2008.

Mary Robin Alexander's father, Albert, was a close, personal friend of George and Maud Atkinson's. I thank her for sharing her dad's memories of the Atkinsons and Norma Jeane Mortensen with me on July 2, 2007, and August 11, 2007.

Dia Nanouris's mother was an assistant film editor at Columbia who worked with Grace Goddard at that company. She provided absolutely invaluable insight in my interview with her on December 15, 2007.

Also, Eleanor Ray's mother knew Grace Goddard and Ms. Ray spent many hours with my researchers in preparation for this book. I interviewed her as well on February 1, 2008. Also, she provided me with details of Grace Goddard's suicide found in California State File #53–087308.

Thanks to Elliot Ross for providing us with the files of the Los Angeles Orphans' Home having to do with "Norma Jeane Baker," including correspondence from 1937 relating to Grace Goddard, Ida Bolender, and the orphanage's headmistress, Sula Dewey. Also, Magda Bernard's stepbrother, Tony, was at the orphanage at the same time as Norma Jeane, and Ms. Bernard provided me with a terrific amount of background and color when I interviewed her on March 2, 2008, and April 13, 2008.

For many sections of this book, I also relied on voluminous correspondence between Norma Jeane and her half sister, Berniece, which has fallen into the public domain as a result of its placement in public auctions over the years.

Marybeth Miller-Donovan's aunt, Ethel, was Ana Lower's best friend. She provided me with great detail and insight into Norma Jeane's time with her beloved aunt when I interviewed her on March 11, 2008.

I also referenced personal correspondence that had been exchanged between the Bolender family members, obtained from a private source.

I referred to the many notes and transcripts of Ben Hecht, the original ghostwriter for Marilyn's autobiography, *Marilyn: My Story*. All of Hecht's notes and other paperwork regarding this book are found in his personal collection at the Newberry Library in Chicago.

I interviewed James Dougherty, Norma Jeane's first husband, in May 1999 and utilized parts of that interview in this work. I also referred to Jane Wilkie's interview with Mr. Dougherty for "Marilyn Monroe Was My Wife," *Photoplay*, March 1953. Moreover, I referenced Mr. Dougherty's 1976 memoir, *The Secret Happiness of Marilyn Monroe*.

I also referred to "Body and Soul: A Portrait of Marilyn Monroe Showing Why Gentlemen Prefer That Blonde," by Barbara Berch Jamison in the *New York Times*, July 12, 1953.

Moreover, I referenced: *The Divorce petition of Della Monroe Graves vs. Lyle Arthur Graves*, Superior Court of Los Angeles County, Petition #D-10379; *Gifford vs. Gifford*, Superior Court of the State of California, Divorce Petition #D-24788. *Divorce Petition of Baker vs. Baker*, Superior Court of Los Angeles County, Petition #D-10379; *Mortensen vs. Baker*, County of Los Angeles, File #053720; Gladys Baker/Edward Mortensen, California State Board of Health, Bureau of Vital Statistics, register no. 13794; Death Certificate of Tilford Marion Hogan, Missouri State Board of Health, File #17075; *Norma Jean Dougherty, Plaintiff vs. James Edward Dougherty, Defendant*, #31146, Eighth Judicial District Court of the State of Nevada, Clark County, July 5, 1946.

PART TWO: TRANSITIONING

Charles Stanley Gifford Jr.—son of Charles Stanley Gifford (who Gladys Baker said was Norma Jeane's father)—was very helpful in filling in details of these early years. He was interviewed on May 9, 2008.

Alexander Howell, the great-nephew of Chester Howell, was helpful in helping us reconstruct Norma Jeane's wedding to James Dougherty. I interviewed him on June 10, 2007.

Martin Evans was a close friend of James Dougherty's. His memory was vital to understanding Dougherty's marriage to Norma Jeane, and I appreciate the interviews I conducted with him on May 20, 2007, July 30, 2007, and April 11, 2008.

Anna DeCarlo's mother, Florence, worked at Radioplane during the time that Norma Jeane was employed by that company. I interviewed her on May 22, 2007, and her stories were vital to my research.

I also relied on Mona Rae and Berniece Miracle's wonderful book, *My Sister, Marilyn*, for certain details in this section and in others in this book.

I had a number of sources with connections to the Agnews State Hospital in San Jose, California, who asked for anonymity, and I will of course respect their wishes. I also obtained from a private source all of Gladys Baker's medical records from that hospital.

John Leonard's father, Mack, was a friend of Gladys Baker's, and he was vital in reconstructing Gladys's search for her children. I interviewed John Leonard and his wife, Marcia, on November 11, 2007, and November 20, 2007.

I must acknowledge sources in the Cohen family who asked for anonymity and who provided information having to do with Gladys Baker's work for Margaret and John Cohen. Also, these sources provided the correspondence between Gladys Baker and the Cohens, which is referenced in Part Three of this book.

Marilyn's friend Michael Shaw was also very helpful in reconstructing certain events in this section of the book, and I thank him for his enthusiastic cooperation. He was interviewed by Cathy Griffin on April 17, 2008.

I also referred to "The Mystery of Marilyn Monroe" by Maurice Zolotow in *American Weekly*, October 23, 1955.

PART THREE: MARILYN

Norman Brokaw, the esteemed entertainment agent, provided details for this and other sections of the book. He rarely grants interviews, and never about Marilyn Monroe and his uncle, Johnny Hyde. Therefore, I thank him for his trust. His cooperation was invaluable. Cathy Griffin interviewed him on May 14, 2008, and May 16, 2008.

Beverly Kramer's father, Marvin, managed the Pacific Seas dining room in Los Angeles, which was frequented by Grace and Doc Goddard. I thank her for her memories and also the family photographs she shared when I interviewed her on May 11, 2007.

Diana Herbert, whose father, F. Hugh Herbert, wrote the screenplay to *Scudda-Hoo! Scudda-Hay!*, was very helpful in providing details for this and other sections of the book when Cathy Griffin interviewed her on April 10, 2008, and April 15, 2008.

Helena Albert, a student of Natasha Lytess's, provided many of the details of the relationship between Natasha and Marilyn for this and other sections of the book. Susan Martinson was also a student and friend of Lytess's and was key in the writing of many parts of this book. I interviewed Ms. Albert on June 15, 2007, and Ms. Martinson on January 4, 2008. Ms. Martinson was also interviewed by Marybeth Evans on May 15, 2008. Also, I referred to Jane Wilkie's interview with Ms. Lytess. Moreover—and maybe most importantly—I relied heavily on a manuscript of Natasha Lytess's unpublished memoir, which can only be found at the University of Texas but a copy of which was purchased by a private party who then allowed me to carefully review it for this book.

Bill Davis worked at the William Morris Agency with Johnny Hyde and was key to understanding Hyde and his romance with Marilyn Monroe. Mr. Davis was interviewed by Marybeth Evans on December 1, 2007, and by me on March 11, 2008.

Marybeth Hughes once dated Johnny Hyde and was instrumental in this and other sections of the book. I thank her for her trust and for her interview of February 28, 2008.

Susan Reimer is the niece of Charles Stanley Gifford. She was very helpful in compiling information for this and other sections of the book. I interviewed her on January 12, 2008.

I also referred to *Screenwriter: The Life and Times of Nunnally Johnson* by Tom Stempel.

PART FOUR: STARDOM

Jerry Eidelman was a friend of Marilyn Monroe's and was very kind to share his memories of her with us for this and other sections of the book when I interviewed him on August 1, 2007, September 13, 2007, and January 10, 2008.

Rupert Allan was one of Marilyn's closest confidants. I had the opportunity to meet with him several times, first on March 13, 1985, then again in 1988 and 1989. I used my interviews with him in my book on Grace Kelly and Prince Rainier, *Once Upon a Time*, since he was Monaco's counsel general in Los Angeles as well as a very close friend of Ms. Kelly's. I also utilized his comments in *The Secret Life of Marilyn Monroe*. Primarily, I also used transcripts of Bruce Ebner's interviews with Mr. Allan as the foundation of much of my research for this book. I also conducted a telephone interview with the ailing but always cooperative Allan in the summer of 1992.

My thanks to John Gilmore for his interview, conducted by Cathy Griffin on April 10, 2008. He was another good friend of Marilyn's and contributed greatly to this book.

Thanks again to Norman Brokaw for his anecdotes about his friend Joe DiMaggio, utilized in this section of the book.

Also, I interviewed two women who worked at Homestead Lodge during the time that Gladys Baker was an employee at that Eagle Rock, California, facility. Both sources asked for anonymity, and I will grant it. However, they know who they are and how much I appreciate their cooperation with this book.

PART FIVE: DIFFICULT TIMES

My thanks to Wesley Miller, who as a young man worked as a paralegal for the firm of Wright, Wright, Green & Wright, the law firm that represented Marilyn in the 1950s. He was very helpful to me when I interviewed him on March 2, 2008, and March 20, 2008. I value his friendship as well.

The police officers who cooperated with me in this section of the book asked for anonymity. I appreciate their kindnesses and memories very much.

As a teenager, Marvina Williams worked as an aide at Rock Haven Sanitarium in La Crescenta. She spent many hours with me on December 11, 2007, December 12, 2007, December 20, 2007, and January 12, 2008, reviewing her memories of Gladys Baker's time at that facility. I thank her for her time and also her many photographs.

Thanks to Stanley Rubin, producer of *River of No Return*, for his interview, conducted by Cathy Griffin on April 24, 2008, a very rare treat.

Special thanks to the lovely Jane Russell for her interview, conducted by Cathy Griffin on April 20, 2008. We also referred to Ms. Russell's appearance on *The Sally Jessy Raphael Show*, April 15, 1992, as well as her memoir, *Jane Russell: My Paths and My Detours*.

I interviewed the inimitable Joey Bishop on May 5, 1997.

I interviewed Esther Williams on May 16, 1997, a lovely lady.

Stacy Edwards was a close friend of Joe DiMaggio and I don't think this section of the book could have been written without his cooperation. I thank him very much for the interviews I conducted with him on April 11, 2007, June 1, 2007, July 13, 2007, and March 1, 2008. Regarding DiMaggio, I also referenced *Joe & Marilyn* by Roger Kahn; *Where Have You Gone, Joe DiMaggio?* by Maury Allen; and *Joe & Marilyn: The Ultimate L.A Love Story* by Maurice Zolotow.

Sydney Guilaroff's comments are extracted from Cathy Griffin's many interviews with him in 1995. I also referred to his autobiography, written with Ms. Griffin, *Crowning Glory: Reflections of Hollywood's Favorite Confidant*, published in 1996. Guilaroff's five decades in the motion picture business and intimate friendships with the biggest stars of Hollywood's Golden Age made his memoirs the most eagerly awaited autobiography of its kind. Cathy first met him in 1993 when she interviewed him for an A&E documentary on Elizabeth Taylor. She allowed me to review copious notes and transcripts from her work with Mr. Guilaroff, which I utilized in this and many other sections of *The Secret Life of Marilyn Monroe*.

Marybeth Cooke worked for Marilyn's attorney, Jerry Geisler, and was very helpful with all aspects of this book. I thank her for spending so much time with me on November 1, 2007, December 12, 2007, and April 11, 2008.

Research material regarding The Wrong Door Raid—including my interview with Hal Schaeffer (conducted on November 1, 1996)—was conducted for my book *Sinatra: A Complete Life*, and now also utilized in *The Secret Life of Marilyn Monroe*. My interviews with Frank's friend Jimmy Whiting were conducted on April 2, 1995, and May 4, 1996. I interviewed Joe Dougherty, who worked for City Detective and Guard Services, on January 11, 2008. I also had access to Cathy Griffin's taped interviews with the late private investigator Fred Otash for background material regarding The Wrong Door Raid, as well as the *Confidential* magazine report in February 1957 and many court documents relating to that particular case. I also reviewed notes and other unpublished material from the *Los Angeles Examiner*'s file on the "raid" and on subsequent hearings about it.

I also referred to "The Strange Case of Marilyn Monroe vs. the U.S. Army," by Robert C. Jennings, *Los Angeles Magazine*, August 1966.

Finally, I also referred to many interoffice memos to the staff at Famous Artists Agency, found in the Charles K. Feldman Papers at the American Film Institute in Los Angeles, as well as the rest of Feldman's papers, including his many appointment books.

PART SIX: VOICES

Importantly, I had the distinct pleasure of interviewing Arthur Miller in 1987 when he was on his book tour for his memoir, *Timebends*. I found him maddeningly difficult and not at all open, despite the fact that his book is incredibly candid. I even wondered at the time if he had written his own memoir! Of course, I was sure he had—though one would never know it if judging from his evasive demeanor, especially when it came to discussing his marriage to Miss Monroe. However, I did draw upon that interview for this book. In retrospect, of course, it was an honor to interview such a literary icon.

I also turned to the Arthur Miller Collection at the University of Texas, which I found very enlightening—mostly, though, in regard to his plays, including *The Crucible* and *After the Fall*. Also, the Joseph Raugh Collection at the Library of Congress in Washington, D.C., proved invaluable in confirming certain details about the Monroe-Miller alliance. I also referred to the John Huston Collection at the Academy of Motion Picture Arts and Sciences in Beverly Hills.

I also referred to "The Un-American Activities in California—The (California) Senate Fact-Finding Committee on Un-American Activities, Third, Fourth and Fifth Reports" (Sacramento, California, 1947), which is on file at the Margaret Herrick Library of the Academy of Motion Picture Arts and Sciences.

I reviewed the personal papers and files of columnist Sidney Skolsky and the files of the Production Code Administration, also on file at the Margaret Herrick Library.

Thanks to Mable Whittington, who worked at Parkside House in London, for her memories of Marilyn and Arthur Miller, which she shared with me on March 12, 2008.

I interviewed Susan Strasberg in June 1997. I also referred to her memoirs, *Bittersweet* and *Marilyn and Me: Sisters, Rivals, Friends*. What a delightful woman. She is missed by many.

I also referenced Lee Strasberg's 20th Century-Fox legal files.

Edward Lovitz was a personal friend of Arthur Miller's who spent many long hours with me discussing Miller's marriage to Marilyn on September 1, 2007, and September 15, 2007. I so appreciate his assistance.

I interviewed the delightful Mitzi Gaynor in January 1997 for my Sinatra biography. I interviewed Billy Wilder in February 1997 as well, a charming fellow and quite helpful.

Cathy Griffin interviewed Jeanne Martin (Dean's wife) on October 22, 1998, and then again in 1999 and in 2001, and parts of those interviews were used in this volume.

I interviewed Tony Curtis in January 2000 and appreciated his help very much.

My thanks to Melissa Steinberg for her assistance in this section as well, and for the interview she granted me on May 11, 2007.

I also referred to the 1988 documentary *Remembering Marilyn*, narrated by Lee Remick and directed by Andrew Solt.

Cathy Griffin interviewed Diahann Carroll on April 21, 2008. A side note: I also interviewed Ms. Carroll on July 24, 1975—one of my first interviews after moving to Los Angeles to become a reporter. I didn't even have a driver's license yet—but I did have a tape recorder! I never had the opportunity to thank her for granting a young writer such an important interview, so I'd like to do that right now: Thank you so much, Miss Carroll, for being so kind to me way back when.

PART SEVEN: SLOW DEATH

Regarding Dr. Ralph Greenson, Dr. Milton Wexler, and Dr. Marianne Kris:

Cathy Griffin conducted interviews with Dr. Greenson's widow, Hildy, on June 4, 1991, and on June 24, 1991. I directly and indirectly utilized both lengthy interviews in *The Secret Life of Marilyn Monroe*.

I also referred to *The Technique and Practice of Psychoanalysis* by Dr. Ralph Greenson and *On Loving, Hating and Living Well: The Public and Psychoanalytic Lectures of Dr. Ralph Greenson* by Dr. Ralph Greenson, as well as scores of the doctor's papers and correspondence, all found in the Greenson Collection at the UCLA library. Among this collection is Greenson's complete and unpublished memoir, "My Father the Doctor," which proved absolutely invaluable to my research. I also referred to "Special Problems in Psychotherapy with the Rich and Famous," dated August 18, 1978, and found in the UCLA Collection.

A number of highly respected California psychiatrists who either once worked with Dr. Greenson or who were otherwise associated with him were also interviewed for this book and requested that I preserve their anonymity. Moreover, I had two independent and invaluable sources in the Greenson family who asked for anonymity as well.

Additionally, I obtained through a private purchaser more than fifty letters written by Greenson not found in the UCLA collection.

Also extremely helpful to me where Greenson is concerned was the paper "Unfree Associations: Inside Psychoanalytical Institutes" by Douglas Kirsner. I also referred to "Interview with Leo Rangell, M.D.," from the *Los Angeles Psychoanalytic Bulletin*, Special Issue honoring Leo Rangell, M.D., Winter 1988.

Dr. Greenson's deposition to the Estate of Marilyn Monroe was vital to my research and can be found in the UCLA collection.

Also important to my research was the Anna Freud Collection at the Library of Congress in Washington, D.C. It is here that one can find many of the letters Freud wrote to her friend Greenson, in response to his correspondence. Those missives not found in Greenson's UCLA collection are inevitably found in Freud's Library of Congress collection.

I interviewed Dr. Milton Wexler in 1999. The reason I tracked him down was simply this: He is mentioned in passing on page 107 of Eunice

Murray's book *Marilyn: The Last Months*. Indeed, in that book, he is simply referred to as "a Doctor Wexler [who was] on call for Dr. Greenson's patients." According to Murray, Greenson was in Switzerland the week after Monroe's birthday when she became unglued. Wexler was summoned. "When he came out to visit Marilyn," wrote Murray (via her ghostwriter Rose Shade), "he took one look at the formidable array of sedatives on her bedside table and swept them all into his black bag. To him, they must have seemed a dangerous arsenal." That's the most that had ever been published about Dr. Wexler—not even his first name!—and thus I found it intriguing. When I began work on *Sinatra: A Complete Life* in 1994, I hired a private investigator to track down the mysterious Dr. Wexler. He was unsuccessful. Then, five years later, we tried again when I was researching *Jackie, Ethel, Joan: Women of Camelot*. This time, persistence paid off—but past the deadline for that book, unfortunately. Finally, in this work, *The Secret Life of Marilyn Monroe*, the full scope of Dr. Wexler's participation in Dr. Greenson's treatment of and diagnosis of Marilyn Monroe can be placed in its proper context.

I also interviewed Dr. Hyman Engelberg—Marilyn Monroe's physician—for *Sinatra: A Complete Life* in 1996 and then again for *Jackie, Ethel, Joan* in 2000. Comments from those interviews were utilized in this book as well. Moreover, I obtained from a private source notes, correspondence, and other material relating to his work with Dr. Greenson. I also referred to his comments found in "Report to the District Attorney on the Death of Marilyn Monroe by Ronald H. Carroll, Assistant District Attorney; Alan B. Tomich, Investigator."

I also consulted "Tribute to Marianne Kris" by Edward A. Gargen, *New York Times*; and "In Memoriam: Marianne Kriss" by Henry Nunberg, *The Psychoanalytic Study of the Child, Vol. 1*. I referred to Dr. Kriss's obituary in the *New York Times*, November 25, 1980. Additionally, I consulted a number of letters written to Dr. Kris by Dr. Greenson concerning his opinion of and treatment of Marilyn Monroe.

Barbara Miller relayed her memories of Dr. Marianne Kris's relationship with Marilyn when I interviewed her on March 29, 2007, and August 11, 2007. I so value her help, and that of her wonderful family, too.

I interviewed Peter Lawford twice in October 1981 when I was working for a magazine in Los Angeles called *SOUL*. It was a black entertainment publication and Lawford was at the time taping a voice-over spot for the sitcom *The Jeffersons*. Truly, it's impossible to imagine the strange ways a reporter and a celebrity's paths can cross in this town! Though I only spent two full afternoons with him—maybe ten hours at most—and exchanged a number of telephone calls, I still found Lawford to be extremely charming and erudite. I also have never believed any of the quotes attributed to him after his death concerning Marilyn Monroe and the Kennedys. While interviewing Sammy Davis Jr. and Dean Martin for my biography of Frank Sinatra, I learned that both found it very difficult to imagine Peter ever implicating the Kennedys in Marilyn's death—*especially* if it was true (and it's not, as I have explained in this book's text). He was just no such teller of tales, despite the way he has been portrayed since his passing. In fact, in a deathbed interview he gave to the *Los Angeles Times* on September 29, 1985, he was very clear that even if all of the rumors were true—and he maintained that they were not—he would certainly not be the one to confirm them. Some very skilled and respected reporters over the years decided that he was just covering for the Kennedys with that interview. Every reporter is entitled to his opinion, of course. I choose to take Mr. Lawford at his word—his words while he was alive, that is, rather than what he was purported to have said after he was no longer around to confirm or deny. I hope I am able to do justice to his true relationship to Marilyn and the Kennedys in this book, as well as that of his wife, Pat, to Marilyn. A bit more opinion here, if I may: Peter Lawford was a great guy. I liked him very much. I'm happy that I knew him, even for just a sliver of time.

Peter's comment regarding Marilyn Monroe having said, just before she died, "Say goodbye to . . . the president," etc., is from his official statement to the Los Angeles Police Department in its continuing investigation into Monroe's death, October 16, 1975.

Pat Brennan met Pat Kennedy Lawford in 1954 and remained friends with her through the 1960s and 1970s. I am eternally grateful for the many hours she spent with me discussing Pat and Marilyn on April 12, 2007, April 15, 2007, April 28, 2007, and June 1, 2007. The subject of their friendship has fascinated me for many years since it has never been fully explored in any biography of Miss Monroe. It's only because of Ms. Brennan that I was able to write about that relationship as I have. This wonderful woman passed away very suddenly in the spring of 2008.

Truly, I had never been more saddened about the death of anyone connected to one of my books. I only hope she is somewhere "out there" right now, happy with the way that she, Pat, and Marilyn are portrayed in these pages.

Diane Stevens, assistant to John Springer, was first interviewed by me for my Elizabeth Taylor book on October 2, 2006, because Springer handled Taylor's publicity concerns. Because her boss also handled Marilyn Monroe, I interviewed her again on April 15, 2007, August 1, 2007, and September 11, 2007, for *The Secret Life of Marilyn Monroe*. Special thanks also to John Springer's son, Gary, for his time—on both books. He was interviewed by Cathy Griffin on April 11, 2006, and also on May 1, 2008. Also, my thanks to Rose Marie Armocida, who was the personal secretary to John Springer. She was interviewed by Cathy Griffin on June 1, 2006.

I had the opportunity to interview Yves Montand in the spring of 1989 while in Paris. He was very open about his affair with Marilyn Monroe, and at the time was working with a writer on his memoir (which was eventually published and called *You See, I Haven't Forgotten*). He was charming and accessible and I'm happy to be able to draw from that interview in this book.

I thank my friend Bruce Ebner for transcripts of interviews he did with Allan "Whitey" Snyder, Marilyn's very good friend and makeup artist, and Ralph Roberts, Marilyn's friend and masseur. These transcripts were very invaluable to the research for this section of the book, as well as many others. (Incidentally, Roberts was interviewed on March 2, 1992.)

I referred to the *New York World-Telegram*'s report of Marilyn's stay at Payne Whitney, February 10, 1961.

The letter from Marilyn to Dr. Ralph Greenson regarding her stay at Payne Whitney is found in the Ralph Greenson Collection at the UCLA library.

The letter Marilyn wrote to the Strasbergs from Payne Whitney was printed in an abbreviated version in the *Daily Mirror*, August 5, 1981. The version used in this text is the letter in its entirety.

Marilyn's "stand-in" Evelyn Moriarty was interviewed by Cathy Griffin on May 2, 1997, and again on June 1, 2007.

Memos from Jack Entratter to his staff at the Sands Hotel are from the Sands Hotel Papers found in the University of Nevada, Las Vegas.

These papers include many interoffice memos (some of which were utilized in this work) as well as newspaper clippings, photographs, negatives, brochures, press releases, audiotapes, news clips, interview transcriptions, and correspondence, all of it stored in forty-nine boxes. The papers were donated to the James R. Dickinson Library of the University of Nevada, Las Vegas, in December 1980 by the Sands Hotel through the office of Al Guzman, director of publicity and advertising. The collection comprises essentially the files of Al Freeman, director of advertising and promotion for the Sands Hotel from 1952 until his death at the age of forty-eight in 1972. My thanks to Peter Michel, head of special collections of the Dickinson Library, for his assistance with this material.

My special thanks to Joseph D'Orazio, a friend who was close not only to Frank Sinatra but to Hank Sanicola and Emmanuel "Manie" Sachs. He and I became pals during the course of my five years of research on my Sinatra biography and became reacquainted when I had to again turn to him for this book. I thank him for so many hours of interviews on May 22, 2007, June 1, 2007, July 15, 2007, and January 10, 2008. "Joey Boy" is one of a kind.

Michael Selsman, one of Marilyn's publicists, was interviewed twice by Cathy Griffin, first on October 2, 1998, and then again on May 22, 2008. I interviewed his wife, the actress Carol Lynley, on June 9, 1997.

I interviewed Douglas Kirkland by telephone on May 23, 2008, to counterpoint Michael Selsman's comments.

I interviewed Maureen Stapleton in November 1995.

As earlier stated, I interviewed Sammy Davis Jr. several times for *SOUL* magazine. As the former editor in chief of that magazine, I had the opportunity to interview him in 1976, 1980, 1984, and 1989. Mr. Davis was a kind and generous man who is deeply missed. I also referred to his autobiographies *Yes I Can!*, *Hollywood in a Suitcase*, and *Why Me?*

I interviewed Mickey Rudin on October 31, 1992, and then again on July 1, 1995, for my book about Frank Sinatra, and his comments about Marilyn are included here. Rudin was a powerhouse in his day. To say he was intimidating is an understatement. However, underneath his brash exterior, I found a very sensitive and kind man.

Dorothy Kilgallen's husband, Richard Kollmar, donated seventy of his wife's scrapbooks to the Lincoln Center Library of the Performing Arts. They are filled with her articles, columns, unpublished notes, and other material that she personally accumulated over her lifetime, including her rough drafts of articles about Marilyn Monroe. I reviewed them all thoroughly as part of my research.

Hedda Hopper's personal notes and unpublished material are housed in the Margaret Herrick Library of the Academy of Motion Picture Arts and Sciences. I utilized many of her papers throughout this book, especially those concerning Marilyn's romances. Most helpful were her unpublished notes. Any biographer would be grateful for such a find, and I must thank my friends at the Margaret Herrick Library for making all of this material available to me, and the estate of Hedda Hopper for having the vision to donate it.

I also had access to the complete library of *Photoplay* and *Look* magazines from the 1950s of a generous person who wishes to remain anonymous, which was incredibly beneficial to my research. Thanks also to that same benefactor, for giving me access to hundreds of notes and transcripts from Louella Parsons concerning Marilyn Monroe and Joe DiMaggio.

Over the years, I met many lawyers who worked alongside of Marilyn's trusted attorney, Aaron Frosch, and I conducted informal interviews with most of them for background purposes only. Because of the sensitive nature of Mr. Frosch's work with Marilyn, these sources do not wish to be acknowledged in these pages, or even quoted in this book. For those who worked with Mr. Frosch, I respect their wishes and remain appreciative to them for the time they spent with me. They know who they are, and know that this acknowledgment is directed at them.

PART EIGHT: THE KENNEDYS

I referred to a number of FBI documents for this section of the book, which were recently released under the Freedom of Information Act. My thanks to Tommy diBella for helping to make them available to me. With the most recent release of FBI documents utilized as research for this book, there are now ninety-seven pages that have been declassified concerning Marilyn Monroe—thirty-one documents in her main file and sixty-six in a cross-referenced file—beginning with the FBI's account of Marilyn applying for a visa and the history of her previous two years.

Much of the FBI's files on Marilyn—as I stated in the book—are remarkable only for titillation value. However, occasionally something slips through that is quite interesting. For instance, a file dated February 21, 1962, describes Marilyn's trip to Toluca, Mexico, and notes that her entry into the country was "reportedly arranged by Frank Sinatra through former President Miguel Aleman." It goes on to state that she was accompanied by "an agent, a hairdresser and an interior decorator. The latter was identified as Eunice Churchill, a part time interior decorator [who] also claims to be an assistant of Dr. Wexley, Monroe's analyst." This mention is obviously of Eunice Murray and Dr. Wexler—but, typical of the FBI where Monroe is concerned, the names are not accurate. (It should be noted that Churchill isn't even Eunice's maiden name—that would be Joerndt.) Also, this is the only mention of Wexler in the FBI's records, he being the psychiatrist Dr. Greenson turned to for a second opinion about Marilyn's condition of borderline paranoid schizophrenia. This document suggests that Eunice Murray was in contact with someone who was an informant for the FBI—or maybe even Murray was the informant, who's to say?—in that it continues, "According to Churchill, Monroe was much disturbed by Arthur Miller's marriage on 2/20/62 and feels like a 'negated sex symbol.' Churchill said that the subject 'has a lot of leftist rubbed off from Miller.' Monroe reportedly spent some time with Robert Kennedy at the home of the Peter Lawfords in Hollywood. Monroe reportedly challenged Mr. Kennedy on some points proposed to her by Miller." Note that the FBI has Arthur Miller giving Marilyn ideas on how to converse with Kennedy. If this is true, it's likely she told him the same thing she told many others—as explained in the text—that she had "a date" with RFK.

The February 21, 1962, file also notes that Eunice says Dr. Wexley—again, no doubt, Wexler—"did not like what was happening in the relationship between Monroe and [deleted] and said that Monroe must get out with other people at once." One has to wonder if the deleted name was not Dr. Greenson's. Is it possible that Wexler did not really approve of how much Greenson stifled his patient, even though it had been at least partially his idea that Marilyn spend so much time at Greenson's home? It's an interesting thought, but we'll never know for certain since the name is redacted. Eunice also supposedly told the FBI informant that "Monroe is very vulnerable now because of her rejection by Arthur

Miller and also Joe DiMaggio and Frank Sinatra." The file goes on to say that Marilyn asked Sinatra to "come and comfort her" while she was in Mexico, but that he declined. Again, who knows if this is true or not?

One more admittedly cynical note about the FBI documents: On October 23, 1964, two years after Marilyn's death, the bureau was still gathering information about her. One file with that date includes this classic anecdote: "During the period of time that Robert F. Kennedy was having his sex affair with Marilyn Monroe, on one occasion, a sex party was concocted at which several other persons were present. Tap [sic] recording was secretly made and is in the possession of a Los Angeles private detective. The detective wants $60,000.00 for a certifiable copy of the recording, in which all the voices are identifiable."

Suffice it to say, this tape has yet to surface.

I also consulted Sam Giancana's Justice Department file, obtained through the Freedom of Information Act, as well as transcripts of federal wiretaps and Justice Department files on President John F. Kennedy and his brother Bobby Kennedy.

I want to thank Bernie Abramson—the aforemention photographer who took countless pictures of Peter Lawford, Frank Sinatra, and President Kennedy during his career—for the time he spent with me and Stephen Gregory on May 9, 2008, and for his many memories and also photographs.

Special thanks to Matthew Fox for his memories of the Kennedys and Lawfords. I interviewed Mr. Fox on January 8, 2008.

My appreciation to the late Don Dandero, an AP photographer working at the Cal-Neva Lodge during the Monroe-Sinatra years. Mr. Dondero was most helpful in giving me leads and ideas. My thanks also to his daughter, Debbie.

I interviewed Walter Bernstein in March 2000.

I interviewed Joan Braden in April 1999.

In March 2007, I had the pleasure of meeting the venerable investigative journalist and USC professor Ed Guthman during an evening honoring him for his many achievements and his imminent retirement, at the Annenberg School for Communication. Guthman, of course, was Robert Kennedy's press secretary. In the midst of the hoopla surrounding him that night I was able to ask him just a few questions about Marilyn and RFK. "I know there was no affair," he told me. "It's not even a question in my mind. I was there. I saw what was going on. And I'm telling you that there was no affair." With that, he was cut off by Tom Brokaw, who quipped to me, "Only one question about Marilyn Monroe and RFK is allowed per journalist lucky enough to get in here tonight." Guthman's other comments are found in this text.

My thanks to Edward Barnes for his memories of Marilyn at the Lawford home, which he shared with me on January 4, 2008, and January 28, 2008.

I interviewed Henry Weinstein in May 2000, and I thank him for his time.

I interviewed Milt Ebbins on August 6, 1992, and again on July 1, 2000. Milt was a wonderful man with an amazing memory for detail. I think his story (told in this book) of getting Marilyn ready for her appearance at a party honoring JFK is classic Ebbins. Milton, who was one of a kind, is much missed. Milt was partner in Peter Lawford's production company and also a very close friend of Peter's. He too agreed that much of what has been attributed to his friend over the years makes no sense, considering Lawford's temperament and personality. Also, I referred to Donald Spoto's interview with Ebbins, found in his papers at the Margaret Herrick Library. Moreover, I also referred to Spoto's interview with Joseph Naar.

Senator George Smathers was interviewed by Cathy Griffin on September 14, 1998, and again by me on October 1, 1998.

The great entertainer Andy Williams was interviewed by Cathy Griffin on May 4, 2007. It's certainly an honor to include his comments about his best friend, Bobby Kennedy, on these pages for the first time.

I interviewed Peter Levathes by telephone on February 3, 2000.

I interviewed Nunziata Lisi on June 12, 1999, and I thank her for her time. Her stories have been key in this volume just as they were in *Jackie, Ethel, Joan: Women of Camelot*.

PART NINE: SAD ENDINGS

Regarding Dean Martin: I must admit that I practically stalked Mr. Martin in the summer of 1994 when I learned that he ate regularly at La

Famiglia, an Italian restaurant in Beverly Hills. I simply had to interview him, not only because I was writing a book about his pal Sinatra, but also because I had such admiration for him. After a week of visits to the restaurant without seeing him, he finally showed up on the night of June 23. I watched as he ate alone in a corner, seeming very sad and alone. When he finished, I approached and asked if I might one day interview him. After some banter back and forth about both of us being Italian-Americans, he agreed to be interviewed the next night. I returned and, true to his word, he gave me the interview. To be candid, it was a somewhat odd and disjointed affair. He wasn't himself—a little drunk, a little ill, and very much on the decline. That said, it was quite a thrill for me to have even a few hours with Mr. Martin, and he certainly did have his very amusing moments. I have used some of his comments about Marilyn Monroe and *Something's Got to Give* in this book. "At the time, I was a little pissed off at her," he told me when discussing her many absences during the filming of that movie. "The only other person who ever kept me waiting that much was Sinatra. I hated waiting. Still do. But now, looking back on it, I get it about Marilyn. She was a sweet kid who probably would have been better off marrying a nobody from the suburbs and then living happily ever after with a bunch of kids. Maybe she was just too real, too honest to be in this business." He was a class act. I think we all miss Dino.

Again, Michael Shaw's comments are culled from Cathy Griffin's interview with him on April 17, 2008.

I interviewed Mort Viner on March 11, 1996, and again on July 2, 2002.

Cathy Griffin and I interviewed John Miner on May 22, 1991. I interviewed him again on May 12, 1998, and then again on June 2, 1999.

Cathy Griffin interviewed Roberta Linn on May 5, 2008.

I interviewed Stacy Baron on June 5, 2007.

Cathy interviewed Janet Leigh on July 1, 1991, and we utilized much of it here for background purposes.

I interviewed Frank Mankiewicz on August 27, 1998, and on October 5, 1998. Cathy interviewed Frank's son, Chris, in May 1999. Of interest to the reader may be that Frank Mankiewicz completed nine interviews for the Robert F. Kennedy Oral History Project: RFK#1: 6/26/1969; RFK#2: 7/10/1969; RFK#3: 8/12/1969; RFK#4: 9/30/1969; RFK#5: 10/2/1969;

RFK#6: 11/6/1969; RFK#7: 11/25/1969; RFK#8: 12/4/1969; and RFK#9: 12/16/1969. Each is stunning in scope and can be found at the John F. Kennedy Presidential Library and Museum in Washington.

The following Secret Service agents assigned to President John F. Kennedy were also interviewed: Anthony Sherman on September 29, 1998; Larry Newman on October 1, 1998, and October 13, 1998; and Joseph Paolella on September 12, 1998.

I interviewed Arlene Dahl on October 5, 2002.

I'd like to mention that once it became known that I was writing this book, many people contacted me and my researchers to tell me of their experiences with Marilyn Monroe. It was impossible to work all of their stories into this volume because of space considerations. I feel badly that they so graciously gave of their time, only to then not appear in the text. Therefore, I would like to generally thank anyone who participated in this project, named in the text or otherwise . . . and—who knows—maybe their stories will find their way into the paperback edition.

Specifically, I interviewed James Wright, Sinatra's chauffeur on April 16, 1997; Kennedy hairstylist Mickey Song twice—with Cathy Griffin on April 24, 1997, and with Charles Casillo on July 16, 1998. Cathy also conducted her own interview with him on August 17, 1991. Also, Cathy interviewed entertainment manager Jess Morgan on May 2, 1997; the talented Tony Martin and the beautiful Cyd Charisse on April 15, 1997; private investigator Fred Otash on August 29, 2001; Danny Cahn on April 28, 2008; and the wonderful Miss Ruta Lee on May 19, 2008. I also interviewed Cyd Charisse on June 1, 2007, regarding her role in *Something's Got to Give*. Jackie Bouvier Kennedy's cousin John Davis was interviewed in March 2008. No quotes from those sources were utilized in this book, but I referred to their stories for background purposes and certainly do thank them all for their time.

Cathy Griffin would like to thank the following people for helping to make her work on this project so much easier and worthwhile: Greg Shriner (of the "Marilyn Remembered" fan club), Harrison Held, Kathleen Hughes, Harlan Boll, Jayne Meadows, Larry Billman, Scott Fortner, Tanya Somova, Senator William J. Raggio, Dave Spencer, John Morris, Joshua Greene, and the Nevada Federal Bureau of Investigation.

And, in conclusion, James Pinkston wishes to acknowledge the following people for their help with his work on *The Secret Life of Marilyn*

Monroe: Linda Harris Mehr, director of the Margaret Herrick Library of the Academy of Motion Picture Arts and Sciences, and her dedicated staff, including Susan Oka; Jan and Ray Boyle (a.k.a. Jan Shepard and Dirk London); Armando Munoz, VideoWest; Robert T. Crane; Lisa and Chris Bonbright; Ron Parish; Meg Woodell Gregory; Hart Henson; David Streets, gallery director, Celebrity Vault; Marian Silverman; Gabriel Rotello; Cherry Vanilla; Hotch and Nita Rippere; Robert Schear; Joe Harvey; Hamilton Powell; Maude Schuyler Clay; Elizabeth Bowman Woolverton; Sandra Shafton; and Richard and Robert DuPont.

PERSONAL ACKNOWLEDGMENTS

I want to thank Stephen Gregory for his priceless contribution to this book. He has been one of the most important people on my team for many years, and his understanding of the human mind continues to astound me. His own talent as a storyteller and writer has made his counsel during the production of this, and many of my books, invaluable. I thank him sincerely for always reminding me that my goal is to treat everyone represented in all of my books with compassion first and foremost. I am honored to have him as a coworker, and proud to call him my friend.

My sincere thanks to Jonathan Hahn. Not only is he a brilliant writer and my personal publicist, he also happens to be my best friend. I thank him for so many years of support in all of my endeavors, both personal and professional. We have had an amazing run, and I think the best is yet to come. I would also like to acknowledge his wife, Alysia Garrison, also a trusted and loyal friend to me.

As I have often stated, without a loyal team of representatives, an author usually finds himself sitting at home writing books no one reads. Therefore, I thank all of those from "USA Team JRT" who mastermind the chaos in my office: attorneys Joel Loquvam and James M. Leonard; C.P.A. Michael Horowitz of Horowitz, McMahon and Zarem in Southern California, Inc.; Felinda deYoung, also of Horowitz et. al.

I must thank Jeff Hare, a vice president of Dreamworks, for being such a good and trusted friend. I can always count on Jeff to read my books, and I truly appreciate that.

Brian Evan Newman, George Solomon, Frank Bruno, and Jeff Cook have been such good pals to me, and I would like to acknowledge as much here. Also, I would like to especially thank Andy Hirsch for his invaluable contributions to my life. In fact, it means the world to me to be blessed with so many good friends, including: Al Kramer, Richard Tyler Jordan, Steve Ivory, Hazel and Rob Kragulac, Bruce Rheins and Dawn Westlake, Manuel Gallegos, Lisa Reiner, Matthew Barasch, Steve Ridgeway, Andy Skurow, Billy Barnes, Scherrie Payne, Lynda Laurence, Barbara Ormsby, John Passantino, Linda DeStefano, Mr. and Mrs. Joseph Tumolo, Daniel Tumolo, Charles Casillo, John Carlino, David Spiro, Mr. and Mrs. Adolph Steinlen, David and Frances Snyder, Abby and Maddy Snyder, Maribeth and Don Rothell, Mary Alvarez, Andy Steinlen, Jared Murphy, Mark Bringelson, Hope Levy, Tom Lavagnino and little Sam, Michelle Caruso, Leslie Miller, Roman D'Angelo, Yvette Jarecki, Scott Allen, Phil Filomowicz, Jonathan Fousek, Master Aaron Lawrence of Quest Martial Arts, as well as Nolan Blackford, Erik Rodriguez, Brandon Visco, Magda Vamos, and Daniel and Erika Feser.

There are two other fellows who have meant more to me than I can say over the last few years—G.C. and B.P. They know who they are and the impact they've had on my life. Both have my undying loyalty. Also, I want to thank D.B. and V.B. for their many kindnesses along the way.

I have always been so blessed to have a family as supportive as mine. My thanks and love go out to: Roslyn and Bill Barnett and Jessica and Zachary, Rocco and Rosemaria Taraborrelli and Rocco and Vincent, and Arnold Taraborrelli. Special thanks to my father, Rocco, who has always been my inspiration. He has encouraged me in ways too numerous to mention.

My mom, Rose Marie, would have loved this book as she did pretty much everything I ever wrote. She was my biggest fan, and I was most certainly hers. We miss her very much.

Finally, I must also acknowledge those readers of mine who have loyally followed my career over these many years. As I have often said in the past, the reason that I write about people such as Marilyn Monroe is to bring about an exchange of ideas concerning how others have lived in the hope that we may learn by their choices. Never did I dream that I would have a global audience for such communication. I am indebted to each and every reader who has stuck by me over the course of my career. I receive so many letters from people who have enjoyed my books—as well as from those who have taken issue with certain aspects of my work. Whatever the response, I am eternally grateful to anyone who takes the time to pick up one of my books and read it.

Thank you so much,
J. Randy Taraborrelli
Winter 2008

MARILYN MONROE FILMOGRAPHY

The Shocking Miss Pilgrim (1947)
Betty Grable, Dick Haymes, Anne Revere
Boston and the Gay Nineties provide setting and period, as Grable
strikes a blow for women's rights while learning the typewriter.
In Technicolor. Monroe appears (unbilled) as a telephone operator.
85 minutes.
20th Century-Fox
PRODUCER: William Perlberg
DIRECTOR/WRITER: George Seaton
CINEMATOGRAPHER: Leon Shamroy

Dangerous Years (1947)
Billy Halop, Scotty Beckett, Marilyn Monroe (waitress)
A half dozen former child stars play overage juvenile delinquents
in this low-budget exploitation film. They seem unwilling to be
rehabilitated, but we don't really care. Marilyn has a bit as a waitress
at the Gopher Hole, a juke joint where the juvies hang out.
62 minutes.
20th Century-Fox
PRODUCER: Sol M. Wurtzel
DIRECTOR: Arthur Pierson
WRITER: Arnold Belgard
CINEMATOGRAPHER: Benjamin Kline

Scudda-Hoo! Scudda-Hay! (1948)

June Haver, Lon McCallister, Marilyn Monroe (girl in canoe)
June Haver competes with a pair of prizewinning mules for the
affections of farmboy Lon McCallister in rural Indiana, all dressed
up in Technicolor. Marilyn can be spotted in two scenes. 98 minutes.
20th Century-Fox
PRODUCER: Walter Morosco
DIRECTOR/WRITER: F. Hugh Herbert
CINEMATOGRAPHER: Ernest Palmer

Green Grass of Wyoming (1948)

Peggy Cummins, Robert Arthur, Marilyn Monroe (extra at square
dance)
A second sequel to Mary O'Hara's beloved story My Friend Flicka—
a boy, a girl, and a wild white stallion, photographed in the lush
Wyoming countryside. Charles G. Clark was Oscar-nominated for
his Technicolor cinematography. 88 minutes.
20th Century-Fox
PRODUCER: Robert Bassler
DIRECTOR: Louis King
WRITER: Martin Berkeley
CINEMATOGRAPHER: Charles G. Clarke

Ladies of the Chorus (1948)

Adele Jergens, Marilyn Monroe (Peggy Martin)
Beautiful blonde Adele Jergens is a former burlesque queen who
aims to see that her daughter (Monroe) avoids the same mistakes
she made. Marilyn is impressive in her first lead, sings two songs. 61
minutes.
Columbia Pictures Corp.
PRODUCER: Harry A. Romm
DIRECTOR: Rick Karlson
WRITERS: Joseph Carole and Harry Sauber
CINEMATOGRAPHER: Frank Redman

Love Happy (1950)

Harpo Marx, Groucho Marx, Marilyn Monroe (chorus girl)
This is mostly Harpo's show (he wrote the original story), and is
remembered mainly as the sad cinematic swan song of the legendary
Marx Brothers. A low-budget backstage romp, involving an

impoverished theatrical troupe trying to put on a Broadway show. Detective Groucho is the story's narrator, his trademark zaniness reined in, as he tries to solve the theft of a Romanov diamond. 85 minutes.

United Artists
PRODUCER: Lester Cowan, Mary Pickford (as a founder of UA)
DIRECTOR: David Miller
WRITERS: Ben Hecht, Frank Tashlin (story by Harpo Marx)
CINEMATOGRAPHER: William C. Mellor

A Ticket to Tomahawk (1950)

Dan Dailey, Anne Baxter, Marilyn Monroe (Clara)
A race between a train and a stagecoach will determine the owner of the rights to the passenger route to Tomahawk, Colorado. Comic, colorful actioner, set against the towering Rockies near Durango. Marilyn has a bit part as one of Madame Adelaide's showgirls. 90 minutes.

20th Century-Fox
PRODUCER: Robert Bassler
DIRECTOR/WRITER: Richard Sale
COWRITER: Mary Loos
CINEMATOGRAPHER: Harry Jackson

The Asphalt Jungle (1950)

Sterling Hayward, Louis Calhern, Marilyn Monroe (Angela Phinlay)
A major jewelry heist by a group of career criminals goes off as planned, but all the principals are either dead or in custody as the gritty film noir's end credits roll. Told from the criminals' point of view. Marilyn stands out in a small part as the mistress of an elderly, crooked lawyer, played by Calhern. Nominated for four Oscars, including writing, directing, and cinematography. 112 minutes.

Metro-Goldwyn-Mayer
PRODUCER: Arthur Hornblow Jr.
DIRECTOR/COWRITER: John Huston
COWRITER: Ben Maddow
CINEMATOGRAPHER: Harold Rosson

The Fireball (1950)

Mickey Rooney, Pat O'Brien, Marilyn Monroe (Polly)
Thirty-year-old Rooney plays a teenage fugitive from an orphanage

who struggles before becoming a skating star in the roller derby, very
big on early TV. Father O'Hara (O'Brien) tries to save him from
himself, much as Father Flanagan did for Whitey Marsh in *Boys'
Town* fifteen years earlier. 84 minutes.
20th Century-Fox
PRODUCER: Bert Friedlob
DIRECTOR/COWRITER: Tay Garnett
COWRITER: Horace McCoy
CINEMATOGRAPHER: Lester White

All About Eve (1950)

Bette Davis, Anne Baxter, Marilyn Monroe (Claudia Casswell)
A ruthless, conniving ingénue insinuates her way into the inner
circle of a legendary, aging Broadway star, leaving wrecked lives and
shattered relationships in her wake, as she claws her way to the very
pinnacle of theatrical stardom. Of the set pieces, Marilyn shines
in two of them, earning kudos from the critics. Widely considered
the best film about the theater ever made and, by the American
Film Institute, among others, one of the best films of all time. The
script contains a number of memorable lines, not the least being
Davis's warning to her captive audience to "fasten your seatbelts."
Nominated for fourteen Academy Awards, winning six, including
Best Picture, Best Director, and Best Screenplay. 138 minutes.
20th Century-Fox
PRODUCER: Darryl F. Zanuck
DIRECTOR/WRITER: Joseph L. Mankiewicz
CINEMATOGRAPHER: Milton Krasner

Right Cross (1950)

June Allyson, Dick Powell, Ricardo Montalban, Marilyn Monroe
(Dusky LeDoux)
Anglo-Latino romantic entanglements are unresolved as they
play out against the story of a Chicano fighter (Montalban) trying
to hang on to his boxing career after a hand injury leaves him a
noncontender. Allyson is in his corner, but not necessarily in his
bed. Marilyn plays a bar girl who has a brief encounter with Powell,
Montalban's best friend. Pretty dull going, but good production
values help. 90 minutes.
Metro-Goldwyn-Mayer
PRODUCER: Armand Deutsch

DIRECTOR: John Sturges
WRITER: Charles Schnee
CINEMATOGRAPHER: Norbert Brodine

Home Town Story (1951)

Jeffrey Lynn, Donald Crisp, Marilyn Monroe (Iris Martin)
After losing a hard-fought reelection bid to the legislature, Jeffrey
Lynn assumes control of the hometown newspaper and launches a
bitter attack on the man he holds responsible for his defeat, Donald
Crisp, the powerful head of the town's biggest business. The film
was made on the MGM lot by General Motors' public relations
department, which rejected the final result as substandard. Metro
deemed it unworthy of copyright renewal and it languished in the
public domain until Marilyn's fans rediscovered it. She has a two-
minute scene as a receptionist in the newspaper office. 61 minutes.
Metro-Goldwyn-Mayer
PRODUCER/WRITER/DIRECTOR: Arthur Pierson
CINEMATOGRAPHER: Lucien Andriot

As Young as You Feel (1951)

Monty Wooley, Thelma Ritter, David Wayne, Constance Bennett,
Marilyn Monroe (Harriet)
A sixty-five-year-old factory worker (Wooley), forced into an
unwanted retirement, impersonates the company president and saves
the firm from bankruptcy, proving his worth and saving his job.
Solid cast makes the story believable, with Marilyn in small role as
an office worker. Marilyn devotees know this is the film where she
and Arthur Miller first met. 77 minutes.
20th Century-Fox
PRODUCER: Lamar Trotti
DIRECTOR: Harmon Jones
WRITER: Lamar Trotti (story by Paddy Chayevsky)
CINEMATOGRAPHER: Joe McDonald

Love Nest (1951)

William Lundigan, June Haver, Marilyn Monroe (Roberta "Bobbie"
Stevens)
A post–World War II sex comedy, without the sex and short on
comedy, with ex-GI Lundigan and Haver as newlyweds and new
owners of an aged brownstone in New York. Tenant and ex-WAC,

Marilyn's role is described in one review as "an extended cameo," the highlight being a scene in which she emerges from the shower draped only in a towel. 84 minutes.

20th Century-Fox
PRODUCER: Jules Buck
DIRECTOR: Joseph Newman
WRITER: I. A. L. Diamond
CINEMATOGRAPHER: Lloyd Ahern

Let's Make It Legal (1951)

Claudette Colbert, Macdonald Carey, Zachary Scott, Robert Wagner, Marilyn Monroe (Joyce Mannering)

Miriam and Hugh Halsworth (Colbert and Carey), after a twenty-year marriage, are in the throes of a divorce when an old suitor (Zachary Scott) of hers rolls into town. Marilyn's contributions are mostly decorative as she spends much of her screen time in a swimsuit. Of the romantic comedy, one critic wrote, "[It] feels overstretched even at an hour and a quarter." It's hard to believe that this is the best Miss Colbert could manage following her withdrawal only a year earlier for medical reasons as Margo Channing in *All About Eve*, giving Bette Davis the role of a lifetime. 77 minutes.

20th Century-Fox
PRODUCER: F. Hugh Herbert
DIRECTOR: Richard Sale
COWRITERS: I. A. L. Diamond and F. Hugh Herbert
CINEMATOGRAPHER: Lucien Ballard

Clash by Night (1952)

Barbara Stanwyck, Paul Douglas, Robert Ryan, Marilyn Monroe (Peggy)

After a hard-knock life in New York, Mae Doyle (Stanwyck) returns to her hometown, a coastal California village, to live with her fisherman brother. She is courted by a boat owner, Jerry (Douglas), eventually marries him, has a child, and begins an adulterous, reckless affair with the brutal Earl (Robert Ryan), all under the nose of her husband. Monroe is a cannery worker, married to Mae's brother, and they both look great in their beachwear, but add nothing to the goings-on in this noirish melodrama. 105 minutes.

RKO Pictures—(A Wald-Krasna Production)
PRODUCER: Harriet Parsons

DIRECTOR: Fritz Lang
WRITER: Alfred Hayes (based on a Clifford Odets play)
CINEMATOGRAPHER: Nicholas Musuraca

We're Not Married (1952)

Ginger Rogers, Fred Allen, Eve Arden, Paul Douglas, David Wayne, Marilyn Monroe (Annabel Jones Norris)

Five couples are notified that their marriages are invalid because the license of the justice of the peace who performed the ceremonies had not yet kicked in. The couples react to the news in a variety of ways, with Monroe and Wayne's solution easily the most comic: Already a winner of the Mrs. Mississippi contest, Annabel is now free to enter the Miss Mississippi contest, which she also wins. First of two so-called episodic movies featuring Monroe. 85 minutes.
20th Century-Fox
PRODUCER/WRITER: Nunnally Johnson
DIRECTOR: Edmund Goulding
CINEMATOGRAPHER: Leo Tolver

Don't Bother to Knock (1952)

Richard Widmark, Marilyn Monroe (Nell Forbes)

Marilyn moves from featured player to leading lady in this melodramatic, disturbing film noir. She is a suicidal, perhaps homicidal, babysitter whose flirtatious overtures to a war-damaged pilot (Widmark) have unexpected and near-deadly consequences. The film was mounted by studio honchos to assay Monroe's dramatic skills, which proved to be considerable. 76 minutes.
20th Century-Fox
PRODUCER: Julian Blaustein
DIRECTOR: Roy Ward Baker
WRITER: Daniel Taradash
CINEMATOGRAPHER: Lucien Ballard

Monkey Business (1952)

Cary Grant, Ginger Rogers, Charles Coburn, Marilyn Monroe (Miss Lois Laurel)

A lab chimp accidentally dumps a youth elixir into the drinking water, creating a fountain of youth. After ingesting some of it, research professor Grant and wife Rogers revert to their teenage selves with predictable results—screwball or slapstick—though the fun can only go so far before it gets tedious. Marilyn is on hand as Charles Coburn's secretary and holds her own quite well as she fends off his clumsily romantic advances. 97 minutes.

20th Century-Fox
PRODUCER: Sol C. Siegel
DIRECTOR: Howard Hawks
WRITERS: Ben Hecht, Charles Lederer, I. A. L. Diamond
CINEMATOGRAPHER: Milton Krasner

O. Henry's Full House (1952)

Charles Laughton, David Wayne, Marilyn Monroe (as a streetwalker), Farley Granger, Jeanne Crain, Anne Baxter, Richard Widmark

Five classic short stories created by the master of the genre, all with an ironic resolution in their denouement, which O. Henry perfected and which became his signature. Each short film is self-contained with its own writer, director, and cast, and each is introduced by future Nobel winner John Steinbeck. First, in "The Cop and the Anthem," Soapy is an urban hobo (Laughton) who in warm weather sleeps in the park. However, with winter coming, he opts for a nice warm jail cell. But he first must get arrested. A series of petty crimes go for naught: theft of an umbrella, stiffing a restaurant for a meal, vandalizing a window. He tries to offend a lady of the evening (Monroe), to no avail. Finally, he enters a church, has an epiphany, repents, and decides to find a job and go "straight." Alas, his plan is thwarted when a cop arrests him for vagrancy; he is tried and sent to jail for the next ninety days. 19 minutes for segment; 119 minutes for film.

20th Century-Fox
PRODUCER: Andrew Hakim
DIRECTOR: Henry Koster
WRITER: Lamar Trotti
CINEMATOGRAPHERS: Lloyd Ahern, Lucien Ballard, Milton R. Krasner, Joseph MacDonald

Niagara (1953)

Joseph Cotten, Marilyn Monroe (Rose Loomis)

A cuckolded, lovesick husband, suffering from Korean War shell shock, and his gorgeous, adulterous wife are at Niagara Falls—for very different reasons: He wants to repair his beyond-repair marriage; she is meeting with her lover to plot her husband's murder. One can almost feel the presence of Alfred Hitchcock as adultery and murder are played out against the power and grandeur of the unrelenting noise and beauty of Niagara. All does not end well, as Loomis (Cotten) discovers the plot against him and turns the tables on Rose (Monroe) and her lover, dispatching him into the crashing waters. He then goes after Rose, stalking her insistently, finding her in the resort's belltower, and strangling the life out of her. Production values are very high with the breathtaking location filming, lush, saturated Technicolor, and ear-pounding stereo sound. Monroe's first big-budget picture, an assignment she handles to a tee. A big hit with the public. First of three important films for Marilyn released in 1953. 89 minutes.

20th Century-Fox
PRODUCER: Charles Brackett
DIRECTOR: Henry Hathaway
WRITERS: Charles Brackett, Walter Reisch, Richard Breen
CINEMATOGRAPHER: Joseph MacDonald

Gentlemen Prefer Blondes (1953)
Jane Russell, Marilyn Monroe (Lorelei Lee)
Lavishly produced, big-budget film of the hit Broadway musical that starred Carol Channing. In the movie, Jane Russell is first-billed and was paid $400,000 to Marilyn's costar billing and $11,250. Upon being told by someone that Jane and not Marilyn was the star of the film, Monroe responded with perfect logic, "Maybe not, but I'm the blonde." The familiar story: After a few harrowing experiences, including a brush with the gendarmes, a couple of naughty-but-nice, gold-digging chorus girls—"We're Just Two Little Girls from Little Rock"—find notoriety and, eventually, love in the City of Lights. The studio pulled out all the stops in this big-musical treatment— a time-tested Broadway hit, musical score by Jule Styne and Leo Robins, gowns by Travilla, musical numbers staged by Jack Cole with an army of talented singers and dancers, color by Technicolor. Studio boss Darryl Zanuck ordered the big production number at the end of the film, "Diamonds Are a Girl's Best Friend," to be refilmed in CinemaScope and stereophonic sound, the result of which was then used by Fox to demonstrate the studio-perfected process. Other studios were impressed and began to use the widescreen technology as well. 91 minutes.

20th Century-Fox
PRODUCER: Sol C. Siegel
DIRECTOR: Howard Hawks
WRITERS: Charles Lederer, Joseph Fields (based on Anita Loos's play)
CINEMATOGRAPHER: Harry J. Wild

How to Marry a Millionaire (1953)

Betty Grable, Marilyn Monroe (Pola), Lauren Bacall
The studio, since its beginning, has recycled the story of penniless young beauties leaving home to go to the big city in search of bright lights and rich men. These husband hunters acquired the name "gold diggers," and Warner Bros. made a series of very successful musicals in the early thirties using the name and theme. But it was 20th Century-Fox that manipulated and honed the by now familiar story into box-office gold with this movie. It was the first film shot entirely in CinemaScope, but another Fox film, the prestigious religious epic *The Robe*, also filmed in CinemaScope, was released to theaters first, claiming bragging rights as the first film in the new process. To make it clear to audiences that the film was an "event," Alfred Newman, the studio's musical director for twenty years by this time, and the studio's symphony orchestra were arrayed on a soundstage set up to replicate an amphitheater and performed Newman's own composition, "Street Scene." It lasted eight minutes, and after the final note, Newman turned to face the camera and executed a deep bow, which signaled the beginning of the credits as the film's musical score came up on the soundtrack. The three-pronged story line provided each of the stars with an equivalent amount of screen time, all with quite satisfactory conclusions.
96 minutes.
20th Century-Fox
PRODUCER/WRITER: Nunnally Johnson
DIRECTOR: Jean Negulesco
CINEMATOGRAPHER: Joe MacDonald

River of No Return (1954)

Robert Mitchum, Marilyn Monroe (Kay)
Ordained by happenstance or destiny, a beautiful woman, an innocent man newly released from prison, and his son are thrown together in a rough-and-tumble western adventure, photographed in CinemaScope on location in the Canadian Rockies and set in

the era of the California gold rush. Monroe called this beautiful, immensely watchable film her worst film: "Grade Z cowboy stuff." It is very likely that her negative assessment had more to do with shooting the film and problems with the director than what ended up on the screen. Despite the rigors of the location shoot and the requirements of the script, including a swamping of the raft in the river rapids, Marilyn, wringing wet, out of sorts and out of breath, is still a vision. 91 minutes.

20th Century-Fox
PRODUCER: Stanley Rubin
DIRECTOR: Otto Preminger
WRITER: Frank Fenton
CINEMATOGRAPHER: Joseph LaShelle

There's No Business Like Show Business (1954)

Ethel Merman, Dan Dailey, Marilyn Monroe (Victoria Hoffman/ Vicky Parker)

All the stops are pulled out in this big, brassy, over-the-top musical, with the studio creating a role in it especially for Marilyn as insurance against a fizzle at the box office. (She agreed to make the film only if the studio would purchase the film rights to *The Seven Year Itch* for her.) The Irving Berlin songbook is used to tell the story of the Donahue family of vaudevillians, covering the period between the two world wars. The CinemaScope camera captures all seventeen of the dazzling production numbers, including the title song and "Alexander's Ragtime Band," with Marilyn also scoring well in her solo production number, "Heat Wave." Oscar nominations went to Lamar Trotti (original story), Alfred Newman and Lionel Newman (scoring of a musical), and to Charles LeMaire and Travilla for their costumes in a color film. 117 minutes.

20th Century-Fox
PRODUCER: Sol C. Siegel
DIRECTOR: Walter Lang
WRITERS: Henry and Phoebe Ephron; original story, Lamar Trotti
CINEMATOGRAPHER: Leon Shamroy

The Seven Year Itch (1955)

Tom Ewell, Marilyn Monroe (The Girl)

Manhattan book editor Richard Sherman, thirty-eight, dispatches his wife and son to the Maine coast for the summer to escape the sweltering city heat. A gorgeous twenty-two-year-old television spokesperson (Marilyn) subleases the apartment in his building just above his own. She's never referred to by name and the credits list her as The Girl. If this were a device used by George Axelrod, the playwright, to keep an emotional distance between the two, it only works to a point. Although Richard doesn't get to first base with The Girl, he imagines making love to her, leaving him with an overwhelming sense of guilt. Despite this, he continues to set the stage for the great seduction—the smoking jacket, chilled champagne, potato chips, and Rachmaninoff on the record player—all with hilarious results as The Girl successfully avoids the seduction. Marilyn with her skirts a-flying over a subway grate is one of the most famous film images of all time. DeLuxe color and CinemaScope. 105 minutes.

20th Century-Fox
PRODUCER: Charles K. Feldman
DIRECTOR: Billy Wilder
WRITERS: Billy Wilder, George Axelrod
CINEMATOGRAPHER: Milton Krasner

Bus Stop (1956)

Marilyn Monroe (Cherie), Don Murray (Bo)
A macho, twenty-one-year-old rancher from Montana travels to Phoenix to enter several rodeo events and while there finds his "angel" in the person of Cherie, a vocally challenged saloon singer, who's also been known to turn a trick to make the rent money. She is repulsed by Bo's boorish behavior and crude attempts to woo her, only making him more determined. He kidnaps Cherie and forces her to accompany him back to Montana. A snowstorm forces their bus to wait out the bad weather at a bus stop. Cherie is won over by his heartfelt profession of love and accepts his marriage proposal. Marilyn's touching performance earned her some of the best reviews of her career. Murray received a best supporting actor Oscar nomination. 96 minutes.

PRODUCER: Buddy Adler
DIRECTOR: Joshua Logan
WRITER: George Axelrod (based on the William Inge play)
CINEMATOGRAPHER: Milton Krasner

The Prince and the Showgirl (1957)

Laurence Olivier, Marilyn Monroe (Elsie)

The world's greatest actor and the movies' love goddess join forces to bring Terence Rattigan's stage play *The Sleeping Prince* to the screen, with Olivier repeating his stage role and Monroe playing the role essayed by Olivier's then wife, Vivien Leigh. Grandduke Charles of Carpathia (Olivier) is on a mission of state to London to attend the coronation of British king George V on June 22, 1911. On his one evening free from official duties, he visits the Coconut Girl club and invites the voluptuous Elsie Marina to a dinner party at the embassy, only the alleged party is a party of two. The game of seduction begins, the outcome of which is clear from the start, but it is the getting there that makes this sex comedy work as well as it does. Marilyn was never more gorgeous and rarely funnier than in this picture. 117 minutes.

Warner/Marilyn Monroe Productions

Producer/Director: Laurence Oliver

Writer: Terence Rattigan

Cinematographer: Jack Cardiff

Some Like It Hot (1959)

Marilyn Monroe (Sugar Kane), Tony Curtis, Jack Lemmon, Joe E. Brown

Destined to be at or near the top of a number of "best" lists, including best film, best comedy film, and best movie line ("Nobody's perfect"), this picture marks the second working arrangement between Marilyn and director/writer Billy Wilder, the earlier being *The Seven Year Itch*. It was a decision he reached despite the legendary problems she's acknowledged to have caused on that set, or because he knew she was perfect for this role and her appearance in the film would assure its box-office success. (Marilyn would earn $2.4 million during the film's initial run, thanks to a lucrative profit-participation deal with the studio.) The story of two out-of-work jazz-era musicians who, after witnessing the St. Valentine's Day Massacre, go undercover in drag as members of an all-girl band, the premise is established before we even see Marilyn, twenty-four minutes into the film. But what an entrance. For the rest of his life, Billy Wilder would recount the problems Marilyn caused on the set, always forgiving her behavior due to her own insecurities and lack of confidence. And, yes, he would do it all over again. The film received

Oscar nominations in six categories—costumes, writing, directing, cinematography, art direction, and best actor (for Lemmon), winning for Orry-Kelly's costumes. 122 minutes.

United Artists/Mirisch
COPRODUCER/COWRITER/DIRECTOR: Billy Wilder
COWRITER: I. A. L. Diamond
CINEMATOGRAPHER: Charles Lang Jr.

Let's Make Love (1960)

Marilyn Monroe (Amanda Dell), Yves Montand
Marilyn was welcomed back to the studio after a four-year absence, and while the return was not widely applauded among some Fox execs who knew too well the havoc precipitated whenever a Monroe picture was in production, this is a charming musical, vastly underrated at the time, with Marilyn at her comedic best, singing Cole Porter songs and dancing to moves created for her by Jack Cole. As Amanda, she is appearing in an off-Broadway review that targets the foibles of celebrities: Callas, Cliburn, Elvis, and Jean-Marc Clement, a French-born billionaire industrialist living in Manhattan (Montand). Clement impersonates an actor and auditions for the part of Clement himself and wins the role. Inevitably, after a few missteps, Jean-Marc and Amanda fulfill the promise in the film's title. Color by DeLuxe in CinemaScope. Oscar nomination for best scoring of a musical. 118 minutes.

PRODUCER: Jerry Wald
DIRECTOR: George Cukor
WRITER: Norman Krasna
CINEMATOGRAPHER: Daniel L. Fapp

The Misfits (1961)

Clark Gable, Marilyn Monroe (Roslyn Taber), Montgomery Clift
Roslyn, an actress, is in Reno for a divorce when she meets and falls for Gay Langland, an aging, sexily macho ex-cowboy. The stark Nevada desert is the habitat for wild mustangs that are targeted by Gay and two other cowboy roughnecks for capture, an exercise that is as painful to watch as it is to figure out—until we learn the horses are to be sold to slaughterhouses to process as dog food. When Rose learns their fate, she goes ballistic, her passion so intense that she ultimately secures the mustangs' freedom and their return to the wild. Film chronicler Leslie Halliwell wrote: "a solemn, unattractive,

pretentious film, which seldom stops wallowing in self pity."
Considered a failure when released, it has since gained cultlike status
because of the untimely deaths of the three principles. 124 minutes.

United Artists/Seven Arts
PRODUCER: Frank E. Taylor
DIRECTOR: John Huston
WRITER: Arthur Miller
CINEMATOGRAPHER: Russell Metty

Something's Got to Give (1962)
Marilyn Monroe (Ellen), Dean Martin
A remake of the 1940 screwball comedy *My Favorite Wife*, starring
Irene Dunne and Cary Grant, the movie's thirty-seven minutes of
footage, salvaged from eight boxes of raw film in a 20th Century-Fox
warehouse, were included in a documentary about the film that was
shown as a television special in 2001, *Marilyn Monroe: The Final
Days*. Marilyn lost eighteen pounds for this role, which brought to
mind her beauty of ten years earlier when she was in her prime. Film
purists do not consider this movie to be part of the Marilyn Monroe
filmography, since it was incomplete and unreleased to theaters.
But given its importance to the Monroe legacy, and that it perhaps
indirectly contributed to her death, I felt compelled to include it.
The film was finally made in 1963 with Doris Day and James Garner
as *Move Over, Darling*.

20th Century-Fox
PRODUCERS: Gene Allen, Henry T. Weinstein
DIRECTOR: George Cukor
WRITERS: Nunnally Johnson, Walter Bernstein
CINEMATOGRAPHERS: Franz Planer, Leo Tover

INDEX